State and Community Governments in a Dynamic Federal System

State and Community Governments in a Dynamic Federal System

Third Edition

Charles Press
Kenneth VerBurg

Michigan State University

HarperCollins*Publishers*

Sponsoring Editor: Lauren Silverman
Project Editor: Karen Trost
Design and Cover Coordinator: Mary Archondes
Cover Design: 20/20 Services, Inc.
Cover Illustration/Photo: State Flags—left to right beginning at top: Maryland, Ohio, New Mexico, Hawaii, Texas, Michigan, Arizona, California, Colorado, Mississippi, New York
Photo Research: Mira Schachne
Production: Willie Lane/Sunaina Sehwani
Compositor: House of Equations, Inc.
Printer and Binder: R.R. Donnelley & Sons Company
Cover Printer: Phoenix Color Corp.

State and Community Governments in a Dynamic Federal System, Third Edition

Copyright ©1991 by HarperCollins Publishers Inc.

All rights reserved. Printed in the United States of America. No part of this book may be used or reproduced in any manner whatsoever without written permission, except in the case of brief quotations embodied in critical articles and reviews. For information address HarperCollins Publishers Inc., 10 East 53rd Street, New York, NY 10022.

Credits:
Page 1: Conklin, Monkmeyer. *Page 10*: ©Putnam, Picture Cube. *Page 21*: From *State and Community Governments in the Federal System*, 2nd edition, by Charles Press and Kenneth VerBurg. New York: Wiley, 1983. Reprinted by permission. *Page 29*: ©Granitsas, The Image Works. *Page 36*: Collins, Monkmeyer Press. *Page 54*: Holland, Stock, Boston. *Page 60*: ©Delevingne, Stock, Boston. *Page 69*: AP/Wide World. *Page 90*: ©Mark Antman/The Image Works. *Page 121*: ©Rousseau, The Image Works. *Page 140*: Carey, The Image Works. *Page 156*: Conklin, Monkmeyer. *Page 173*: ©Kolvoord, The Image Works. *Page 187*: Conklin, Monkmeyer Press. *Page 206*: AP/Wide World. *Page 216*: Dratch, The Image Works. *Page 233*: ©Sandra Johnson, The Picture Cube. *Page 242*: Courtesy Ben Sargent/Austin American Statesman. *Page 251*: AP/Wide World. *Page 275*: AP/Wide World. *Page 283*: Herwig, Picture Cube. *Page 295*: ©1980, Johnson, Picture Cube. *Page 311*: ©Daemmrich, The Image Works. *Page 319*: ©Daemmrich, The Image Works. *Page 341*: ©1988, Bickerell, Stock, Boston. *Page 351*: ©1989, Vita, Impact Visuals. *Page 354*: ©Spratt, The Image Works. *Page 385*: Falk, Monkmeyer Press. *Page 396*: Grant, Stock, Boston. *Page 415*: Neal Boenzi/NYT Pictures. *Page 437*: Strickler, Picture Cube.

Library of Congress Cataloging-in-Publication Data

Press, Charles.
   State and community governments in a dynamic federal system / Charles Press, Kenneth VerBurg.—3rd ed.
     p.   cm.
   Includes bibliographical references and index.
   ISBN 0-06-045366-4
    1. State governments—United States.   2. Local government—United States.   3. Federal government—United States.   I. VerBurg, Kenneth.   II. Title.
JK2408.P72   1991
353.9—dc20

90-44975
CIP

90 91 92 93 9 8 7 6 5 4 3 2 1

Brief Contents

Detailed Contents vii
Preface xvii

CHAPTER 1 The Study of State and Community Politics 1
POLICY BOX NO. 1 One for the Road   13
POLICY BOX NO. 2 Why Not Regroup the States?   23

CHAPTER 2 The Setting of State Politics 29
POLICY BOX NO. 3 Are Seniors Freeloading on the Rest of Us?   48
POLICY BOX NO. 4 Whither West Virginia?   54

CHAPTER 3 A Changing Federal System 60
POLICY BOX NO. 5 What Is a Commonwealth? What Is Puerto Rico?   66
POLICY BOX NO. 6 Fair Shares in a Federal System   71

CHAPTER 4 State Constitutions 90
POLICY BOX NO. 7 Should Five U.S. Supreme Court Justices Decide Major Policy Questions for the States?   93
POLICY BOX NO. 8 A National Initiative for Constitutional Amendments?   109

CHAPTER 5 Elite and Citizen Participation 121
POLICY BOX NO. 9 The Hispanic Subculture and Full Participation   137
POLICY BOX NO. 10 California's Experiment in Reducing Voter Costs   144

CHAPTER 6 Political Interest Groups 156
POLICY BOX NO. 11 Blacks as a "Cause Group"   161
POLICY BOX NO. 12 Political Conflict in the Schools   166

CHAPTER 7	**Political Parties**	187

POLICY BOX NO. 13   The Party System as a Federal System: Open Primaries Versus National Party Rules   195
POLICY BOX NO. 14   Should the State Pay for Political Campaigns?   208

CHAPTER 8	**State Legislators as Critics**	216

POLICY BOX NO. 15   School Finance Dilemma   219
POLICY BOX NO. 16   The Drug War—Should We Surrender?   239

CHAPTER 9	**Governors as State Leaders**	251

POLICY BOX NO. 17   What to Do with the Office of Lieutenant Governor   271
POLICY BOX NO. 18   Gubernatorial Leadership on the Plains   276

CHAPTER 10	**Administrators as State and Community Managers**	283

POLICY BOX NO. 19   Ethical Behavior for Public Officials   290
POLICY BOX NO. 20   Are Residency Laws Sound Public Policy?   303

CHAPTER 11	**State and Community Judges as Legitimizers**	319

POLICY BOX NO. 21   Judicial Expression and Public Opinion   336
POLICY BOX NO. 22   What Counts in Sentencing? You Be the Judge   345

CHAPTER 12	**Communities in the Federal System**	351

POLICY BOX NO. 23   One Person's Trash . . .   356
POLICY BOX NO. 24   Public Interests and Private Rights in Zoning   379

CHAPTER 13	**Intergovernmental Relations at the Community Level**	385

POLICY BOX NO. 25   Managing Urban Growth   389
POLICY BOX NO. 26   How to Locate LULUs   405

CHAPTER 14	**State and Local Finance in a Dynamic Federal System**	415

POLICY BOX NO. 27   Taxing Catalog Sales   429
POLICY BOX NO. 28   Should Government Promote Gambling?   437

Index   453

Detailed Contents

Preface xvii

CHAPTER 1   The Study of State and Community Politics   1

    The Reformers Grapple with State and Community Governments   3
    The Madisonian System   3
    De Tocqueville and Bryce   3
    Making the System More Efficient   4
    Making the System More Democratic   7
    The Study of State and Community Politics Today   11
    POLICY BOX NO. 1   One for the Road   13
    Intergovernmental Relations in the Federal System   16
    Our Changing Federal System   17
    How State Governments Are Different   19
    State Government Is Less Visible   19
    State Governments Are Vulnerable   20
    POLICY BOX NO. 2   Why Not Regroup the States?   23
    A Final Comment   25
    High Points   26
    Notes   26

CHAPTER 2   The Setting of State Politics   29

    The Lives People Live in Different States   30
    What Mencken Discovered   30
    Explanations for Differences in Quality of Life   31
    Geography, Climate, and Natural Resources   36
    A State's Settlers   38
    A State's History   42
    The Citizens Who Live There Now   44
    POLICY BOX NO. 3   Are Seniors Freeloading on the Rest of Us?   48
    Economic Development—A Major Influence   50
    Politics and Policy Outputs   51

A Final Comment 53
POLICY BOX NO. 4 Whither West Virginia? 54
High Points 56
Notes 56

CHAPTER 3 A Changing Federal System   60

The Legal Structure of Federalism 62
The Weakness of Confederations 62
The Federal Compromise 62
The American Federation 63
Achieving Statehood 63
"Semistate Status" 64
Our Changing Federal System 65
The Period of Dual Federalism (1788–1901) 65
POLICY BOX NO. 5 What Is a Commonwealth? What Is Puerto Rico? 66
The Period of Cooperative Federalism (1902–1963) 68
The Period of Modern Federalism (1964–) 70
POLICY BOX NO. 6 Fair Shares in a Federal System 71
The Division of Functions Today 75
Operating a Complex Federal System 75
Constitutional Clauses 75
Voluntary Cooperation 76
National Coordination 78
The Crossroad Function of the States 82
The Obsolescence of Federalism? 82
A Defense of Federalism 82
How States Avoid National Domination 84
State Political Influence 84
States in the Federal Courts 85
A Final Comment 86
High Points 86
Notes 86

CHAPTER 4 State Constitutions   90

The Legal Theory 91
The Influence of John Locke 92
Why State Constitutions Are So Important 92
POLICY BOX NO. 7 Should Five U.S. Supreme Court Justices Decide Major Policy Questions for the States? 93
State Constitutions Are Political Documents 95
What Do State Constitutions Contain? 96
Our Cluttered State Constitutions 96
What Reformers Want to Change 97

How State Constitutions Got So Long and Complicated 99
The Impact of Social Change 100
Preserving Governmental Legitimacy 100
Democratizing Government 101
The "Special Interests" Add Clauses 102
Our Cluttered Constitutions: An Assessment 104
Keeping Constitutions Current 105
The Federal Government Makes Changes 105
State Constitutional Revision 107
POLICY BOX NO. 8 A National Initiative for Constitutional Amendments? 109
A New Constitution Through Legislative Action 111
A Final Comment 115
High Points 116
Notes 116

CHAPTER 5   Elite and Citizen Participation   121

Political Elites 122
Political Elites and Democratic Decision Making 122
Participation by Nonelite Citizens 127
The Average Citizens 129
Opportunities for Citizen Participation 133
Legal Rules and Citizen Participation 134
POLICY BOX NO. 9 The Hispanic Subculture and Full Participation 137
Other Influences on Political Participation 139
The Costs and Benefits of Participation 139
Information Costs Are Still High 142
POLICY BOX NO. 10 California's Experiment in Reducing Voter Costs 144
The Cynical and the Alienated 148
Political Mobilization Through Social Movements 149
A Final Comment 150
High Points 151
Notes 151

CHAPTER 6   Political Interest Groups   156

The Lobbying Process 158
Who Organizes? 158
Patterns of Organization 158
Which Organizations Are Likely to Lobby? 159
POLICY BOX NO. 11 Blacks as a "Cause Group" 161
What Resources Help Make a Group Effective? 163

Present-Day Interest Groups   165
POLICY BOX NO. 12 Political Conflict in the Schools   166
State Interest Group Systems   167
The Emergence of Second-Level Groups   168
Iron Triangles: How Interest Groups Penetrate   169
The Arenas of Lobbying   171
Democratic Organization   171
Lobbying Practices   172
The Lobbyists   172
Successful Lobbyists and Their Techniques   174
Financing Political Campaigns   177
Controlling Interest Groups   178
Interest Groups Policing Themselves   178
Regulating Lobbyist Behavior   179
Control by Changing the Governmental Process   182
A Final Comment   182
High Points   183
Notes   183

CHAPTER 7   Political Parties   187

Our Distinctive American Parties   188
Responsible or Brokerage Parties?   188
Federalism and Brokerage Parties   189
The Development of American Parties   190
The Birth of Mass Party Organizations   190
The Boss Senators Organize State Parties   190
The Rise of State Machines   191
The Weakening of Political Parties   192
How American Parties Are Organized   193
Who Should Run the State Party Organization?   193
POLICY BOX NO. 13 The Party System as a Federal System: Open Primaries Versus National Party Rules   195
How the Parties Choose Leaders   197
Who Chooses Party Candidates?   198
How Candidates Are Nominated   198
Party Regulars and Nominations   200
Running the Political Campaign   201
Parties Organize Where They Hope to Win   202
Changes in Campaigning   203
The Party in Office   207
How Likely is Responsible Party Government?   207
POLICY BOX NO. 14 Should the State Pay for Political Campaigns?   208
Governors Provide the Party Program   209
The Party in the Legislature   210

A Final Comment   211
High Points   211
Notes   212

CHAPTER 8   State Legislators as Critics   216

What State Legislators Do   217
Lawmaking   217
Constituent Services   218
POLICY BOX NO. 15 School Finance Dilemma   219
Legislative Oversight   221
The Legislative Way of Life   222
Legislative Sessions   222
Lifestyle Demands   223
Legislative Compensation   223
Offices and Secretarial Help   224
Providing Staff Assistance   224
Who Becomes a State Legislator?   225
Who Gets Elected?   225
The Occupations of Legislators   225
Shifts in Legislative Composition   227
How People Become Legislators   227
Why Legislators Quit—Turnover Rates   228
How Legislators Operate: The Politics of Lawmaking   230
Formal Rules of Procedure   230
Legislative Leadership and Committees   234
Informal Rules   236
Legislative Staff Agencies   237
The Politics of Lawmaking   238
POLICY BOX NO. 16 The Drug War—Should We Surrender?   239
Reforming State Legislatures   241
Reapportionment   241
Other Reform Proposals   243
A Final Comment   244
High Points   245
Notes   246

CHAPTER 9   Governors as State Leaders   251

Who Gets to Be Governor?   253
Which Experiences Are Best?   255
Social and Economic Background   257
The Legal Framework for Gubernatorial Leadership   259
The Twentieth Century—
Expanded Legal Powers for Governors   261
Legal Powers in Perspective   262

Exercising Gubernatorial Leadership 262
Governors Set Goals 263
Leadership in Public Opinion 263
Leadership in the Legislature 265
Leadership over State Finances 268
Leadership in the Executive Branch 268
POLICY BOX NO. 17 What to Do with the Office of Lieutenant Governor 271
Leadership in the Party 273
Leadership in Intergovernmental Relations 274
POLICY BOX NO. 18 Gubernatorial Leadership on the Plains 276
A Final Comment 277
High Points 278
Notes 278

CHAPTER 10 Administrators as State and Community Managers   213

Professionalization of the State Public Service 284
The Merit System 284
What Merit Systems Replaced 285
Some Patronage Persists 286
Effects of Merit Systems 287
Sources of Bureaucratic Power—
    Professionalization and Unionization 288
Professionalism in Bureaucracy 289
POLICY BOX NO. 19 Ethical Behavior for Public Officials 290
Unionization of Public Employees 294
Approaches to Controlling the Bureaucrats 300
Administrative Reorganization 301
POLICY BOX NO. 20 Are Residency Laws Sound Public Policy? 303
The Power of Publicity 305
Budget Reforms 305
Management by Objectives (MBO) 309
Legislative Oversight and Control of Bureaucracy 310
Controlling Influences from the Public 314
A Final Comment 315
High Points 315
Notes 316

CHAPTER 11 State and Community Judges as Legitimizers   319

Structure and Jurisdiction of State and Local Courts 320
The Minor Courts 321
Special Courts 323
General Trial Courts 324
State Appeals Courts 325

State Courts in the Federal System:
    The Trend Toward Centralization   326
Development of the Common Law   326
Statutory Law   327
Judicial Lawmaking   327
The Federalization of State Law   328
Diversity Remains   330
The Politics of the Judiciary   331
Why Courts Are Political   331
How State Judges Get Their Jobs   332
The Judicial Bureaucracy—Who Should Manage?   335
POLICY BOX NO. 21 Judicial Expression and Public Opinion   336
Conflicts with Officials of Other Branches   338
Limitations of Judicial Policy-Making   339
Societal Influences as Limitations   339
The Politics of Prosecution   340
Judicial Policy and Public Opinion   343
A Final Comment   344
POLICY BOX NO. 22 What Counts in Sentencing? You Be the Judge   345
High Points   347
Notes   347

CHAPTER 12   Communities in the Federal System   351

Local Governments on Their Own—Almost   352
State Control over Local Powers   353
The Law and Politics of State-Local Relations   355
How Much Authority for Local Units?   355
POLICY BOX NO. 23 One Person's Trash...   356
Lobbying and Local Government Associations   358
The Types of Local Governments   361
The County   361
The Town Meeting   362
The Township   362
The City   363
The Special Case of Schools   366
Other Contemporary Forms   366
How Community Governments Are Organized   366
Five Elements of Reform Organization   367
Basic Organizational Plans   368
Managerial Efficiency Under Attack   373
Choosing the Form of Government   374
Governing Local Communities   375
What Determines Service Levels?   375
The Problem of Service Distribution   376

xiv   DETAILED CONTENTS

        Community-Federal Relationships   377
        POLICY BOX NO. 24   Public Interests and Private Rights in Zoning   379
           A Final Comment   380
           High Points   381
           Notes   381

CHAPTER 13   Intergovernmental Relations at the Community Level   385

        Evolving Patterns of Human Settlement   386
           Life in the Suburbs   387
           What Happened in the Central Cities?   388
        POLICY BOX NO. 25   Managing Urban Growth   389
           The Changed Rural Countryside   392
           An Overview of Metropolitan Areas   393
        The Community As an Intergovernmental Bargaining Unit   394
        Reform Through Centralization and Professionalization   398
        Annexation   398
        City-County Consolidation   399
        Metropolitan Governments   402
        Reform to Achieve Greater Citizen Participation   403
        Neighborhood Control   404
        POLICY BOX NO. 26   How to Locate LULUs   405
        Intergovernmental Relations:
           The Feds and the States in the Communities   407
        Why Federal and State Intervention?   407
        State and Federal Efforts   408
        Coordination from the State Capitals   409
        How States Coordinate   409
        A Final Comment   411
        High Points   411
        Notes   412

CHAPTER 14   State and Local Finance in a Dynamic Federal System   415

        Trends in State and Local Finance   416
        Changes in State and Local Taxes   416
        Factors Affecting State and Local Revenues   417
        Intergovernmental Transfers   418
        Federal Transfer Payments   419
        State Transfers to Local Units   420
        Evaluating State and Local Taxes   423
        General Sales Tax and Other Excise Taxes   425
        Personal Income Taxes   428
        POLICY BOX NO. 27   Taxing Catalog Sales   429
        The Property Tax   432

Business Taxes 434
Other Taxes and Miscellaneous Charges 436
Movement Toward a More Diversified Revenue System 436
POLICY BOX NO. 28 Should Government Promote Gambling? 437
Borrowing and Debt in the States and Localities 439
How Much Our Governments Owe 442
When Should Governments Borrow? 444
State and Local Spending 445
How the States Spend Their Money 445
How Local Governments Spend Their Money 446
Implications for Budget Reductions 448
A Final Comment 450
High Points 450
Notes 451

Index 453

Preface

When we wrote the first edition of this textbook we treated states and communities as part of a federal system—a system we saw then as becoming more centralized when compared to the end of the 1950s and beginning of the 1960s. The role of federal grants had begun to expand dramatically. This pattern, we believe, continued throughout the 1970s. During the 1980s the Reagan administration attempted to reverse the process. It did so with some success, especially with respect to growth in federal grants.

The Bush administration, it seems, is continuing the Reagan policies, if for no other reason than that the accumulated debt and budget deficit rules limit the alternatives. Although we do not wish to be so venturesome as to predict political decision making, with the changes in Eastern Europe and the outlook for falling defense expenditures, it seems possible that the federal role may again expand in time. Hence we have added the word *dynamic* to our title.

During the writing of the first edition and the subsequent revisions, we have found our federal system experiencing both expected and unanticipated developments. Yet we think the states and communities have played an important role in shaping American public policy; in some instances, our strengthened state governments have even been taking a leading role. We suggest that the politics of federalism have thus become vital to the study of state and community governments. Intergovernmental relations—how the national, state, and community governments interact with and influence each other—are key to an understanding of domestic policy choices. We have found this a rewarding approach, one that has enlivened our teaching; we assume other teachers have had similar experiences.

As in previous editions, we introduce policy questions in the form of case studies—we call them policy boxes. As teachers, we agonized over how best to handle topics such as the politics of the environment, or the politics of health and education. Often these topics are found in chapters at the end of government texts where they get brief treatment in the last weeks or days of the course.

We consider that approach unfortunate because these are often the issues that are uppermost in the minds of the students, and indeed of officials as well. These are the issues around which state and local politics revolve.

It was thus a short step, when writing this book, to use policy boxes as a means of relating political structure and form to politics of current issues. We include two in each chapter to give the instructor a choice about how to deal with different aspects of the material. In the 28 policy boxes we cover a variety of subjects by dealing with specific issues. Our expectation is that students will find them both interesting and stimulating as they wrestle with the questions posed. We trust the policy boxes will involve students in classroom discussions as they have in our own classes.

Although we are the authors of this book, many others had a hand in making it a successful product. Lauren Silverman, our editor at HarperCollins, together with Karen Trost and many others at the firm with whom we only met over the telephone, were helpful in so many ways. We thank them for their enthusiastic support and assistance.

We are grateful also to the colleagues who served as our reviewers and critics: Edgar LeDuke, University of Rhode Island; Richard Lehne, Rutgers University; David Lowery, University of North Carolina at Chapel Hill; James Oxendale, West Virginia Institute of Technology; Ken Mladenka, Texas A&M; and Richard Scherr, University of Florida. We also thank those faculty and students who used our book. But there is more—we thank them for taking the time to write or talk to us about it. Their suggestions have helped to make this a better book. We suspect you know that those responsible for the errors that evade the numerous screens are the authors themselves.

Charles Press

Kenneth VerBurg

*State and
Community
Governments
in a Dynamic
Federal System*

Chapter 1

The Study of State and Community Politics

Olga Moore describes how students played politics to get a new library building while she attended the University of Wyoming during the 1930s. The student council chartered a train to get from Laramie to the capital. As the band led them from the Cheyenne station, traffic came to a standstill and people on the sidewalk cheered them on, up the capitol steps and into a joint session of the legislature.

As the last echoes of the Wyoming Cowboy fight song died away, she wrote, "We were greeted with thunderous applause. Handsome Governor Bob Carey greeted us. He announced that win or lose, the legislature would hold a dance for students in the rotunda.... Our Glee Clubs never sang so well, our speakers never conjured up more eloquence. 'Come see us!,' we begged. 'Let us show you the campus we love so much! Eat with us in the Commons, cheer with us on the football field, and sit with us in the old library! *And come soon before it falls down!*'"[1]

Such experiences are great teachers, especially when they are as much fun as this. We learn firsthand how exciting politics can be. Learning from a book is not quite the same. We urge you to get politically involved. In the meantime, though, we hope you will read on and learn some things that will prove useful.

The Study of State Politics We believe the most important fact about our states is that they are part of an ever-changing, dynamic **federal system**. The state and the federal governments both have legal powers that allow them to act directly on citizens. And because neither can abolish the other, we can expect ongoing political bargaining—a pattern of **intergovernmental relations** among the states and between them and the federal government.

The **governmental structure** consists of the public offices and the legal powers of each. The way those who fill these offices and use their legal powers produces **formal and informal "rules of the game"** for political bargaining. **Politics** is the process in which groups and individuals use their **political resources** to shape governmental decisions closer to their liking.

The Wyoming students had few political resources—organization, prestige, or money—with which to bargain. The rules of the game at that time did not even let them vote. But they did have an important resource—their superabundant energy. And they did get their new library!

Other students also have "played politics." In Kansas, students from the six regents' universities and Washburn have their own lobbying group. ASK—Associated Students of Kansas—lobbies the legislature on university appropriations, student aid, and professors' salaries. They called their 1988 campaign HERO—Higher Education Rescue Operation, and concentrated on tuition and faculty salaries.

Others lobby—butchers, bakers, barbers, union leaders, racetrack owners, and bankers, plus mayors and county commissioners, to name a few. All want public policies more to their liking. Some have been a credit to their state or community. You need only look around your own campus or town to see the results. But others have lobbied in less honorable ways and for more questionable purposes. As you read along, you will find examples of both types.

Overview We have four objectives in this chapter. The first is to examine the kind of government the founders of this country designed. Then we note how two reform movements have reshaped that government. We next discuss the problem of uncertainty and then consider the most important aspect of state and community politics and the main theme of this book—that these governments are part of a dynamic American federal system.

THE REFORMERS GRAPPLE WITH STATE AND COMMUNITY GOVERNMENTS

In 1787, the Founders, following ideas best expressed by James Madison, embedded in our Constitution their skepticism about human nature. They designed a government in which no official would be completely trusted; none would have enough power to ride roughshod over everyone else. The states and communities almost immediately copied this system.

The Madisonian System

The Founders built conflict into the system—what we call a **separation of powers**. Each of the major branches—the executive, legislative, and judicial—was given a portion of the total governmental power. To keep one branch from dominating the others, each was given powers to check the others—a system of **checks and balances**.

The rules sound a little like those of a board game. The legislature passes a law, but the executive can veto it. Legislators can override a veto by a two-thirds vote—two checks that equal one balance. The courts can check the other two by declaring a law unconstitutional. But the legislature can check the court using the amendment process. And the executive, with Senate approval, can appoint new judges to vacancies.

Then, by distributing legal powers to both national and state governments, the Founders provided further checking and balancing within our federal system.

Note that even a majority of the citizens can be checked. It takes two-thirds of the members of the U.S. Congress to propose amendments to the federal constitution—a rule that has doomed many proposals. And it takes approval by both houses of three-fourths of the state legislatures to adopt proposals—a rule that made it impossible to pass the Equal Rights Amendment that women's rights groups worked for and which, according to opinion polls, a majority of citizens favored.

The government the Founders designed has not remained the same with respect to either separation of powers or the position of the states within the federal system. Still, the distinctive Madisonian imprint remains.

Criticisms of the Madisonian System Reformers have argued that checks and balances and federalism are inefficient and undemocratic. Let's review how the study of state and community governments and politics is interwoven with these two reformist themes.

De Tocqueville and Bryce

The first persons to study our state and community governments systematically were a French official with an aristocratic background and an English lord who was a professor of civil law at Oxford University. The Frenchman visited in the 1830s, the Englishman in the 1880s.

Alexis de Tocqueville found much to praise in his book *Democracy in America*. He did not share the concern of many later reformers—that checks and balances and federalism would thwart majority rule. Instead, he feared that we would be so concerned about achieving equality that a majority might stamp out individuality and excellence. A government, he thought, could be too democratic.

James Bryce observed that the social and economic makeup of the states, as well as their geography and history, influenced their policy-making and that the checks and balances system was inappropriate for American conditions. He thought that the mass immigrations of people who could not speak English combined with a complicated governmental system led to the boss system in America's cities. Bryce argued that the study of government and politics should be approached in terms of the **political setting**—the mix of social, economic, geographic, historical, and even psychological facts in which they operate.

Making the System More Efficient

Bryce ended his study pleading for changes in government structure that would make it less wasteful and more efficient. Seth Low, a reform mayor of New York, and Frank J. Goodnow, a leading political scientist, agreed. At the turn of the century, they all became part of the **Good Government Reform Movement**. (Machine politicians mocked them as "Goo-Goos.")

The Inefficiency of Bosses and Machines Bryce condemned city bosses and political machines as "the heaviest batteries of Satan." City governments were corrupt, he wrote, because of the **spoils system** (or **patronage system**) that let politicians hand out public jobs, contracts, and other benefits for political reasons. Bryce blamed middle-class citizens. His language seems a little strange today, but he wrote, "The ignorant multitude, largely composed of recent immigrants, untrained in self-government [support the machines] . . . paying no direct taxes and therefore feeling no interest in moderate taxation and economical administration." At the same time, he complained, "Able citizens [are] absorbed in their private businesses [and] cultivated citizens [are] unusually sensitive to the vulgarities of practical politics. . . . Both," he noted, "were unwilling to sacrifice their time and tastes and comfort in the struggle with sordid wire-pullers and noisy demagogues."[2]

The Impact of Scientific Management American political scientists found a beacon of hope—the birth of the **scientific management movement** in American industry. Frederick Taylor and others around the early 1900s invented time and motion studies to analyze manual tasks—from milking a cow to laying bricks. Using stopwatches and later, movies, they analyzed the motions of the fastest workers. They then described the "one best way" to perform specific tasks. Applying these techniques to organizations, they concluded that industries, too, could be organized in one best way—using organizational "principles" of **managerial efficiency** that would maximize profits.

It was a short step for political scientists and reformers to decide that these principles would also produce more economical and efficient government and eliminate corruption. They proclaimed reform of governmental structure as the cure for city and state bossism!

How to Achieve Managerial Efficiency These reformers wanted a government capable of acting. To promote efficiency they proposed **centralization**, concentrating power in a chief executive and loyal agency heads. To promote economy and honesty as well as efficiency they proposed **professionalization** of employees—hiring only thoroughly trained and politically neutral administrators.

They argued that a single executive—governor, mayor, city manager, or department head—would be more efficient than commissions or plural executives at keeping the professional bureaucrats on their toes. Legislators and citizens could then hold the chief executive responsible for the government's successes and failures. So the reformers began detailed studies of government structure—some irreverent critics called them "manhole counters."

Many times throughout this book we meet the principles that "good government" reformers advanced. Diverse groups and individuals—bureaus of governmental research housed at state universities, business and industry groups, taxpayer associations, and organizations such as the League of Women Voters, the National Municipal League, and Ralph Nader's Raiders—still champion them today. The Council of State Governments, the International City Management Association, and other professional groups also advocate them, and so have politicians such as governors aspiring to make a record of achievement.

From these two simple recommendations—centralization and professionalization—flowed a variety of reform proposals.

- Council-manager government to replace the mayor-council system
- Chief administrative officers (CAO) to assist mayors, and directors of management and budget to aid governors
- Restructuring the executive branch into a departmental hierarchy with a chief executive at the top and a director to head each department
- Civil service or merit employment instead of the patronage or spoils system
- Executive budgeting
- The short ballot to replace the long list of elected officials—the executive would appoint those filling essentially administrative offices
- Nonpartisan elections to reduce the influence of partisan politics

Successes of Structural Reform "Good government" reformers were not alone in smashing state and city machines. But they were an important part of the process.[3] They brought businesslike methods to governmental administration and replaced "party hacks" with professionals. Most political scientists also agreed that it made sense to cut down the number of elected positions, especially those with mainly administrative rather than policy-making duties.

Criticisms of "Good Government" Reform Why beginning around 1945 did political scientists criticize so enthusiastically this approach?[4] It was because many began to question whether professional expertise could really solve all problems and make partisan politics unnecessary.

The Problem of Value Conflicts "Good government" reformers assumed a **value consensus**—that all citizens and officials held the same beliefs and had the same wants as they did. Hence, the only problem was to recruit professionals to administer "the one best goal."

But many immigrants in machine-dominated cities did not share the reformers' goals. Managerial efficiency, economy in government, and even honesty of officials seemed unimportant to them. They desperately wanted (as we might in their place) the patronage job for a prospective son-in-law, the political machine's annual summer picnic, the grocery baskets at Christmas—things that made life in the ghettos of their day less dreary. They embraced the machine—even machines clearly corrupt—because it brought some sunshine, brightness, and joy into their lives.

In some communities, most commonly wealthy suburbs, citizens generally agree on goals. That is, they have a **value consensus**. Conflict is unusual because residents agree that good schools, restrictive zoning, and amenities such as a swimming pool or even a golf course are top priorities.

But other communities have **value conflicts**. College students may want rock-and-roll block parties while residents with children in the same neighborhood want peace and quiet. Political bargaining is necessary to hammer out a compromise. The policy that results cannot be described as "right"—participants only agree that it was reached through a process which they accept.[5]

Some critics have accused reformers of trying to solve such value conflicts by designing a government structure that denies representation to some groups, as if their points of view are not worth considering. Others said the reformers had a blind spot about middle-class professionals, thinking that they could represent the varied interests found in most of today's states and communities.

But professional administrators do not always agree on goals among themselves. During the last few years governments have had falling revenues. Which services should be cut? Do the professionals agree? Is a larger state prison system more important than making sure public schools or mental health facilities have enough money? If colleges face financial difficulties should tuition be raised or faculty salaries reduced?

The legislature decides such issues along with the governor who participates in the bargaining. They may compromise with an across-the-board cut. Or they may preserve spending for the institute of arts or symphony orchestra and cut welfare benefits. Reformers, at least in theory, object to political bargaining to make policy when citizens or professionals do not agree. This was a peculiar set of "blinders" for professional political scientists to wear.

The Problem of Administrator Neutrality Critics also pointed out that people, not "neutrally competent" puppets, operate government. The reformers would have been astonished to discover that the professional administrators filling those neat little boxes on organization charts sometimes had policy preferences of their own, occasionally even asserting they knew better than the elected officials, or even the voters, about which policy is best. Moreover, reformers would have been astonished by the strategies the professionals would use to get their way. Politicians of all stripes get into public office with campaigns against "the professional bureaucrat." "Good government" reformers would have been shocked!

Political scientists also believed the reformers were naive about what goes on in bureaucratic organizations. They were so busy perfecting organization charts that they overlooked how employees sometimes subverted the chain of command and how informal relationships become more important sometimes than formal organization. They thought that reformers overestimated the effect of centralization for executives trying to influence the actions of department heads—it did not guarantee that elected officials could hold career administrators accountable.

Citizens also discovered that professional public employees were human enough to be self-serving at times. They might go on strike or sometimes appear more like public masters than public servants. For a common current example, look at the parking arrangements at city hall. For whom are spaces close to the door reserved, citizens or public employees?

Managerial Efficiency and Federalism Although the reformers focused their attacks on the separation of powers, their principles also led them to be skeptical about the value of federalism. They favored centralization and professional uniformity over variety and decentralization. And if this required a more unified government system, many would have perhaps agreed the sacrifice of state independence would be worth what it would achieve.

Making the System More Democratic

The **Progressives** were a second group of reformers around the 1900s. They believed that the American experience was best described as a steady **democratization** of the government the Founders created. The task of every generation, they said, was to make government more responsive to ordinary citizens.

The Attack on the Establishment The idea that America's plutocrats had too much political power has a distinguished lineage. We can trace it back to Tom Paine's attack in his pamphlet *Common Sense* on the mercantilist policies of George III. Andrew Jackson's movement to drop property qualifications for voting, increase the number of elective officials, and destroy Nicholas Biddle's United States Bank also is part of that tradition. In addition, we could include the late-nineteenth-century series of agricultural protest reform groups from the "loco focos" to the "barnburners," the Greenbackers to the Grangers and Populists.

But the Progressives neither wanted nor expected to return to a rural society. They sought procedures that would encourage citizen participation in a society they saw as increasingly urbanized, varied in ethnic background, and whose industrial economy spawned flourishing monopolies. The enemies of democracy, they said, had become too powerful and well organized. They saw political bosses as doing the bidding of the privileged at the expense of the working classes.

Progressives were skeptical about reforms to achieve managerial efficiency. They doubted that such "good government" programs would get at the basic problems. Instead, they wanted social reform—to restructure America's social, economic, and political institutions—to redistribute benefits.[6]

The Contributions of Muckraking Journalists Journalists, who proudly accepted the title **muckrakers**, almost daily dug out shocking examples of corruption. Their exposés told about the so-called respectables, how business capitalists controlled an "invisible government"; how businessmen bribed public officials who closed their eyes to conflicts of interest; how railroad lobbyists "bought" state legislators and rigged elections; how public officials bent rules for the rich and powerful; and how political parties turned into machines to advance the interests of business.

The most important muckrakers were staffers of *McClure's* magazine—Ida Tarbell, who described how John D. Rockefeller cheated and connived to create the Standard Oil "trust"; Ray Stannard Baker, who investigated corrupt labor unions as well as the inhumane ways whites treated blacks; and Lincoln Steffens, who, in *The Shame of the Cities* and *The Struggle for Self Government*, exposed governmental corruption.[7]

Steffens was among the first to discover that he himself preferred the bosses and ward heelers to many "respectable" community leaders. At least the bosses, he said, understood human misery. He quoted Boss Martin Lomasney of Boston, who said that the people wanted "not justice but mercy." In modern terms we might say they wanted programs that would make life in the slums a little more tolerable, rather than an efficiency expert whose concern was whether a person had filled out the forms properly. Academics have pointed out that the political machines often served this welfare function.[8]

The Program of the Progressive Reformers Mostly, Progressives wanted to reduce the influence of wealth and status and redistribute economic, social, and, especially, political power and benefits. Their slogan could well have been that of protestors in the 1960s—"More power to the people!" Their actual battle cry was, "The cure for the evils of democracy is more democracy."[9]

They wanted to alleviate poverty through social welfare programs. They hoped to achieve lower streetcar fares and reduce electric and gas rates for people living in tenements through publicly owned utilities. And they sought to eliminate unfair business practices.

They hoped to "purify" the political process with laws to

- Define and outlaw corrupt practices used to steal elections and bribe public officials
- Regulate campaign spending and lobbying
- Spell out political conflicts of interest
- Establish direct primaries and presidential primaries in place of political party conventions

- Regulate state party organization and activities
- Select judges by nonpartisan elections
- Elect U.S. senators, rather than have state legislatures select them
- Allow citizens to propose legislation and constitutional amendments by initiative petition and to pass on legislative acts in referendum elections
- Recall public officials by petition and vote

The Successes of Progressive Reform Progressives made state and community governments much more democratic, open, and responsive than they were and even more so than the national government is today. Progressive reforms are still being pursued. The direct primary, through which voters themselves select candidates, has largely replaced the convention system, but we continue looking for ways to reduce the influence of money in elections and policy-making. And Progressives of a hundred years ago would applaud those today who push for public financing of election campaigns and curtail lobbying expenditures.

The crusading journalists pushed some political scientists into looking beyond the structure of government to interest group lobbying, political parties, and machines for explanations of what actually occurs in the political process. With all of the faults of sensational reporting, the muckraker journalists were a welcome relief to the clinical stodginess of efficiency and economy studies. The muckrakers were fun to read. They understood that political power was part of the policy-making process. They also reminded us that political theorists as far back as Plato have been concerned about the political influence of the wealthy.

Criticisms of Progressive Reform The muckrakers acted as if mayors and governors were always stooges of a shadowy "they" who made the real decisions. Behind every formal structure they expected to find an organized conspiracy of economic notables pulling the strings.[10] Most political scientists regard this approach as being too simplistic to explain all state and community politics, although many agree it might have merit in certain situations.

The muckraker view leaves too many questions unanswered—for example, if big business is in control, why does it permit policies such as antitrust laws or environmental impact statements? Why did the business magnates allow the welfare services to the poor and middle classes to grow so large?[11] What interest did "they" have in expanding state and local bureaucracies or in regulating business activities? Or why did "they" permit muckrakers to publish exposés of business in the mass circulation newspapers, magazines, and books which the corporations and conglomerates owned?

The "conspiracy theory" of politics tends to warp the way a journalist reports facts. An uncompromising antiestablishment stance inclined the muckrakers to regard politicians as suspect—guilty until proven innocent. Their writing is colorful, but also full of emotional words with a negative, inside-dopester's tone: "boodle," "The Ring," "juice," "graft," and "strike bills." Some crusading reporters were careless with their facts or slanted their stories outrageously in their eagerness to make sensational headlines.

Many political scientists also agree with V. O. Key, Jr., who criticized Progressives for viewing political parties as "the enemy," rather than as a major means of democratic control, superior to the populist institutions Progressives championed.[12] Critics note as well that the Supreme Court, established as an elitist part of the checks and balances system, has often defended basic freedoms more vigorously than have citizens using the initiative, or referendum, especially on issues of school integration, open housing, or criminal rights.

Progressive Reforms and Federalism   The practice of federalism in the early 1900s often conflicted with democratic reform. For example, Progressives were critical when "the special interests" tried to argue for "states rights" to prevent federal regulation. And their followers in the 1920s applauded when the U.S. Supreme Court began protecting civil liberties by striking down state and community laws limiting free speech or discriminating against minorities.

Students protesting investments in South African companies.

THE STUDY OF STATE AND COMMUNITY POLITICS TODAY

A few pre–World War II studies examined government and politics without being either dull or sensational. Belle Zeller, one of the first women political scientists, studied politics in the New York state legislature. Peter Odegard looked at the politics of the Anti-Saloon League, and Harold Gosnell made a dispassionate examination of the Chicago political machine and the place of blacks in it. Harold Stone, Don Price, and Kathryn Stone produced an excellent series of case studies of council-manager successes and failures.[13]

Such studies are still highly regarded because they suggested the direction the discipline might take. They recognized that both government structure and the political process were important in shaping policy.

The Availability of Data Today's scholars now have a major advantage over earlier students who laboriously clipped newspapers to compile data on state and local governments. We have mountains of data, though we must collect some data more systematically.[14] We also have new and quicker ways to analyze the data at hand—computers and more refined statistical techniques. We cite here a few basic sources:

State Governmental Structure: Every two years the Council of State Governments publishes a new edition of *The Book of the States*, Lexington, Ky.

Local Government Structure: The International City Management Association, Chicago, each year issues *The Municipal Year Book*. See also *County News*, the weekly journal of the National Association of Counties, and Herbert S. Duncomb, *County Government in America*, National Association of Counties, Washington, 1978.

State Politics: Sangamon State University publishes *The Comparative State Politics Newsletter*, and every two years Congressional Quarterly Press issues *State Government, CQ's Guide to Current Issues and Activities*. Michael Barone, Grant Ujefusa, and Douglas Matthews, *The Almanac of American Politics*, also published every two years by Gambit, Inc., contains information relevant to state politics.

Election Data: Inter-university Consortium for Political and Social Research, Ann Arbor. Data on governors, and an ongoing project begun in 1987 to collect legislative results beginning in 1968, results of legislative primaries in 16 southern and border states, and information on voter registration. Data are compiled by constituency and county.

Statistical Data: *The Statistical Abstracts*, published by the U.S. Bureau of the Census, Washington. You will find many of these census data reprinted in commercially produced almanacs and encyclopedias. Every five years, the bureau publishes a census of governments. Also see *The State Policy Data Book*, and *State Policy Reports* (issued twice monthly). Also available is a State Policy Data Diskette.

City and State Magazines: Among the best are *Illinois Issues, The California Journal, The New Jersey Reporter, N.C. Insight* (North Carolina), and *The Texas Observer.*

Books on Individual States: University of Nebraska series—to date, volumes on Nebraska and Arkansas.

The Importance of Politics Modern political science is distinguished from many previous studies in that we have come to appreciate the difficulty of professionals designing and carrying out political programs even when everyone is agreed on goals. We are referring to the problem of **political uncertainty**—what one cynic called Howard's Law—"every change may achieve the opposite of what was intended."

The "good government" reformers and the Progressives were certain their proposals would produce the results they desired. Today we know it is not that easy. For example, experts disagree about how to make our nation's inner cities thrive or how to design a welfare system that keeps recipients from becoming dependents.

Side effects—unplanned outcomes of our policies—add to the uncertainty. The reformers who championed managerial efficiency wanted civil service laws to protect government employees from political pressures. These same rules, though, make it very difficult to fire an incompetent employee—an unanticipated side effect. The Progressives imagined that primaries would allow citizens to choose candidates. They do, but they also give a big edge to incumbents and to candidates who spend the most money—today on TV advertising.

Fortunately not everything is uncertain. Before the discovery of the polio vaccine, officials faced a nightmare of uncertainties (just as we do today with AIDS). Should they close swimming pools all summer? Some did. Should schools be closed in hot weather? Some were. At what temperature? Ninety degrees? Should tonsillectomies be stopped? Many were. But once the Salk vaccine was proven effective, establishing a program to rid society of polio was relatively easy.

Now read Policy Box No. 1, "One for the Road." Try your hand at designing a policy with respect to drinking. What kinds of goals will you try to achieve? Do you have value consensus in your dorm? How well can you predict the effect of the regulations you choose?

How Officials Handle Uncertainty Politicians usually do not make sharp breaks with past policies because they cannot predict all the results. They do not want to cause social upheaval, economic convulsions, widespread dissatisfaction, or their own defeat in the next election. So they usually play it safe, a step at a time, to minimize the unanticipated consequences.

They may also try delay, hoping the problem will disappear or that a clear-cut solution will emerge. They make small changes in present policy and wait to see what happens—**incremental decision making**. Or they may compromise, "split the difference" between opposing policies, such as ecologists' demands for clean air regulations without causing factories to close down or move away. The result is a slow, gradual, and sometimes inconsistent process of peaceful change.

Policy Box No. 1

One for the Road

The prohibition movement started to attract followers in the 1870s—much as the antismoking movement has been doing today. Middle- and upper-middle-class people were leaders. Evanston, an upper-class suburb of Chicago, became the headquarters of the WCTU (Women's Christian Temperance Union), which led the crusade for national prohibition. By 1914, 14 states, mostly in the rural South and Midwest plus a few in New England, had prohibition. Twenty-six states had adopted some form of prohibitionist legislation, in 18 states by popular vote.

On January 20, 1919, we adopted the Eighteenth Amendment, for nationwide prohibition. During the 1920s bootlegging and "speakeasies" flourished, openly flaunting the law until, on December 5, 1933, the Twenty-first Amendment repealed nationwide prohibition. Only North Carolina, Mississippi, Kansas, Oklahoma, and South Carolina continued it—at least for a while. Now all states permit sales of alcohol, though some communities are still legally dry.

Americans have opted for temperance rather than abstinence. They also decided that states and local communities should set the policies with respect to alcohol. All states have some regulations, and a few have many regulations. As you read, ask yourself whether the policies described are practical with respect to goals and choice of method. Can we reasonably expect them to achieve what they are supposed to achieve?

One issue is how far, if at all, states should go to discourage consumption. Some states put high taxes on alcohol—"sin taxes" that reformers hope will reduce consumption, especially by the young. In New York State you can buy only wine or distilled spirits at licensed package liquor stores which follow regular business hours. In other states you can buy alcohol over the counter at the grocery store. Other states prohibit Sunday sales. Some go further. Recently at a shopping mall we saw a college student with a T-shirt that said, "Eat, drink, and be merry for tomorrow you may live in Utah." Utah has one of the strictest systems of alcohol regulation. It also has the lowest consumption rate of the 50 states. Utahans in 1968 voted down a referendum that would have allowed liquor to be sold in bars and restaurants by the drink. Resort and restaurant owners complained bitterly. Presently liquor can be purchased across the counter by the bottle until 10 P.M. Patrons at a restaurant must bring their own bottle in a bag, but they may not take it home, since it is against the law to drive with an open bottle in the car. Restaurants may also sell "mini-bottles," but the servers may not pour. The mini-bottles, ironically, are relatively potent since they contain 1.6 to 1.75 oz.; a normal drink is 1 oz. Wherever liquor is sold, sellers must post a sign that says, "The consumption of alcoholic beverages purchased in this establishment may be hazardous to your health and the safety of others." Finally, as in nearly 20 other states, Utah has a monopoly in warehousing alcohol, a revenue advantage but a method of reducing the number of persons who make a profit from promoting alcohol sales.

A related issue is the age at which alcohol may be purchased. In 1933, 45 states and Washington, D.C., set the minimum age for purchasing any alcoholic beverages at 21. Then during the 1960s a number of states dropped the age to 18 or 19.

MINIMUM AGE FOR SPECIFIED ACTIVITIES

State or other jurisdiction	Age of majority	Minimum age for marriage with consent		Minimum age for buying beer or wine	Minimum age for serving on a jury	Minimum age for leaving school
		Male	Female			
Alabama	19	14	14	21	19	16
Alaska	18	16	16	21	18	16
Arizona	18	16	16	21	18	
Arkansas	18	17	16	21	18	15
California	18			21	18	18
Colorado	18	16	16	18	18	16
Connecticut	18	16	16	21	18	16
Delaware	18	18	16	21	18	16
Florida	18	16	16	21	18	16
Georgia	18	16	16	21	18	16
Hawaii	18	16	16	21	18	18
Idaho	18	16	16	21	18	16
Illinois	18	16	16	21	18	16
Indiana	18	17	17	21	18	16
Iowa	18	16	16	21	16	16
Kansas	18			21	16	16
Kentucky	18			21	18	16
Louisiana	18	18	16	21	18	17
Maine	18	16	16	21	18	17
Maryland	18	16	16	21	18	16
Massachusetts	18			21	18	16
Michigan	18	16	16	21	18	16
Minnesota	18	16	16	21	18	16
Mississippi	18	17	15	21	21	
Missouri	18	15	15	21	21	16
Montana	18	18	18	21	18	16
Nebraska	19	17	17	21	19	16
Nevada	18	16	16	21	18	17
New Hampshire	18	14	13	21	18	16
New Jersey	18	16	16	21	18	16
New Mexico	18	16	16	21	18	18
New York		16	14	21	18	17
North Carolina	18	16	16	21	18	16
North Dakota	18	16	16	21	18	16
Ohio	18	18	16	19	18	18

Oklahoma	18	16	16	21	18	16
Oregon	18	17	17	21	18	16
Pennsylvania	21	16	16	21	18	16
Rhode Island	18	18	16	21	18	16
South Carolina	18	18	14	21	18	16
South Dakota	18	16	16	19	18	16
Tennessee	18	16	16	21	18	16
Texas	18	14	14	21	18	17
Utah	18			21	18	18
Vermont	18	16	16	21	18	18
Virginia	18	16	16	21	18	17
Washington	18	17	17	21	18	18
West Virginia	18			21	18	16
Wisconsin	18	16	16	21	18	16
Wyoming	19	16	16	19	19	16
District of Columbia	18	16	16	21	18	

Source: *The Book of the States, 1988–89,* Lexington, Ky. Copyright ©1988 The Council of State Governments. Reprinted with permission from *The Book of the States.*

But in the 1970s some states began shifting back to 21. And during the Reagan years the national government required 21 for all states—by making it a condition for receiving highway funds.

One reason for the change, according to the Michigan Office of Substance Abuse Services, was "a dramatic increase in highway crashes involving young people" after 1972, when the Michigan drinking age was lowered. Among 18- to 20-year-olds the rate was 27 percent higher than for other age groups. And in 1979, after the age was raised back to 21, Michigan statistics showed a 17 percent decline in noninjury road accidents involving 18- to 20-year-olds. A second reason was that school administrators strongly favored the raise, because some 18-year-olds were still in high school.

But others argued that raising the drinking age to 21 did little to curb abuses: Officials are unable to enforce the law because of "phantom purchases." Also, opponents argue, it deprives citizens of constitutional rights when they are otherwise legally considered adults. Finally, they challenge studies that show an increase in consumption when states lowered the drinking age, noting that those states which switched back have not found a decline in per capita consumption.

Finally, the organization MADD, Mothers Against Drunk Driving, has highlighted the issue of drinking and driving. States have responded by increasing penalties and making jail sentences mandatory after a number of convictions. Other states attack the problem by requiring those convicted to attend a series of sessions on the dangers of drunk driving.

> What do you think? Which of these three issues should states consider important? What legislation might they then adopt? Will it accomplish what its sponsors hope? Should states pass and strictly enforce laws against driving if a person has had only one beer or glass of wine, as is the case in Great Britain and Scandinavia? Should establishments be held legally responsible if a patron later has an auto accident? How should liquor be sold? Would college communities be wise to adopt prohibition?

The Problem of Social Justice Such political techniques for coping with uncertainty may be unsettling. Should social tranquility or more certainty about policy outcomes outweigh attempting to right injustices? Should Franklin Roosevelt have desegregated the armed forces during World War II, even though it might disrupt the war effort?

In principle, civil strife, or fear of it, or even the threats by citizens should not be reason to delay. But politicians respond that the rule of law depends on popular support, or at least on popular acquiescence, even in dictatorships. Politicians also argue that in a democracy they should reflect popular sentiment and provide time to adjust as the Supreme Court did in the school desegregation case.

When knowledge is incomplete, uncertainty high, or value conflicts dominant, the democratic process is likely to move slowly. State or community policymakers prefer delay, incremental change, and compromise. Sharp change is likely only when advocates show a groundswell of popular support, when they are able to produce convincing evidence that their proposal will bring about the desired results, or when some calamity, crisis, or disaster cries out for radical change.[15] This is how political policy-making in a federal system usually works. Sometimes you will find it a frustrating and imperfect system.

INTERGOVERNMENTAL RELATIONS IN THE FEDERAL SYSTEM

Our state and community governments are embedded in a dynamic federal system. This point is so important that we have used it in our text's title. Federalism ensures that policy-making does not occur by having the government in Washington issue orders and expecting the states and communities to carry them out loyally as if they were cogs in an administrative machine.

State and local officials sometimes reshape or evade national guidelines to suit the interests of their citizens. We can always expect some conflict and controversy and, occasionally, stalemate. We will find that practice is guided less by theory than by political bargaining and pragmatic responses to problems as they arise.

Interactions among national, state, and community governments will sometimes seem chaotic. For example, officials of Glen Cove, New York, once refused to allow Soviet employees at the United Nations to use its beaches. The U.S. State Department pleaded unsuccessfully with council members to rescind the action.

When they did not, Soviet officials responded by denying similar privileges to the U.S. diplomatic employees in Moscow.

States and communities may thwart each other as well. The Republican governor of Washington blocked construction of the Northern Tier pipeline to transport Alaskan crude oil to the Midwest. He said it would endanger the Puget Sound regional ecology. But the U.S. Energy Secretary, also a Republican, lobbied for the pipeline, for reasons of national security. Governors of most midwestern states favored it also.

Our Changing Federal System

Until the Civil War, state and community governments handled most domestic matters. Since then, and certainly in the twentieth century, national power has gradually increased. But this has not meant that "the Feds" administer all or even most domestic functions. Rather, they use money grants to "encourage" the states and their local governments to give up some independence and help the national government achieve national goals.

In 1916, for example, almost everyone agreed that the nation had to find a way to "pull itself out of the mud." The first federal highway program began with extensive grants to the states. Responding to the misery that the Great Depression caused, President Franklin Roosevelt proposed additional grant programs. The Johnson administration in 1964 concluded that if the nation was to become a "Great Society," the national government must set goals in most domestic policy areas: welfare, civil rights, civil liberties, criminal justice, housing, transportation, health, and education.

But the federal system has become even more complex than this suggests. In very few domestic areas did the federal government set all of the goals. Consider, for example, streets and highways. Most federal funds and goals focus on the interstates. All three levels negotiated their locations, and the states constructed them. But communities with state assistance planned and built the network of streets that you use to get onto the freeways.

In some policy areas, such as civil rights or managing the economy, only islands of state or community control remain. In others, such as fire and police protection or education, states and communities fashion and administer most policies. Theories of federalism did not bring on these conditions. Rather, they result from pragmatic responses to problems that citizens feel need to be solved. The theories to justify them come later.

Expanding State and Community Governments We have had other power shifts as well—from private groups to state and local governments. The states have always regulated trades and professions—but regulations have become more detailed and cover more topics. Federal grants encouraged states to beef up health and safety rules. And communities added a host of new rules—eliminating racial and sexual discrimination, restricting air pollution and noise levels, expanding zoning and building codes.

To take on these new functions, states and communities added employees and sharply increased expenditures. The changes turned these governments into a major growth industry during the 1960s and 1970s. In 1955, for example, their combined revenue was $19 billion, and together they had 1.2 million workers. By 1985 revenues were $658 billion, and 12 million people earned their livelihood working for a state or local government.[16]

With the increase of community decision making, more state activity involves coordinating local government activities and ensuring that they meet minimum state standards. State agencies, for example, review plans for school buildings to make sure the local district installs fire alarms and adequate electrical and plumbing facilities. The state treasurer reviews the financing plan to make sure the school board can pay for the project.

The New Federalism of Ronald Reagan President Reagan came into office in 1981 with a plan to reverse the flow of power from states and communities to the national government. He argued that too much federal centralization and regulation had become the problem. He wanted to turn intergovernmental relations back to what they were in the 1950s, before the centralizing tendencies begun in the Johnson administration.

He began by reducing federal guidelines and cutting back grant funds by 25 percent, and bargaining with the governors over which level would administer and finance certain services. By the end of his term and the beginning of the Bush administration, state reliance on the federal government had decreased, and many states had to raise taxes and cut services to keep their budgets balanced. They also took the lead for many domestic programs. Led by innovative governors, the states emerged stronger than before.[17]

Local Officials Get into the Act As early as the 1930s, the first state, and in a few cases national, associations of officials were formed. These associations provide opportunities for professional contacts—to exchange information at conventions and through association magazines and newsletters. But as power shifted to the national level, especially after the Great Society grant programs, these groups began lobbying for more grant funds with fewer strings attached. This **intergovernmental lobby** attempts to influence the Congress, state legislatures, and each other. They meet with federal agency heads, bring cases to the federal courts, and petition governors. At the same time, they build alliances among themselves for specific projects. Program specialists also organize—from highway engineers, police officials, and social workers to purchasing agents. And all lobby in Washington.

Officials form regional groups as well. The Western Conference of Attorneys General, for example, met in Medora, North Dakota, to discuss federal and state air and water quality laws. Earlier the southern attorneys general meeting at Point Clear, Alabama, considered asking Congress to fund marijuana eradication programs abroad. In Jackson Hole, Wyoming, the western governors met to hear the Secretary of Interior respond to the recommendations they had made earlier. The Coalition of Northeastern Governors persuaded Congress to appropriate $750 million a year to upgrade rail systems in the Boston-to-Washington corridor. Some meetings sound the opening call to arms in a kind of intergovernmental warfare. For example, Michigan's governor proposed to the Midwest Governors

Association a Great Lakes compact to control diversion of fresh Great Lakes water. He hoped "to guarantee a bright economic future for the Great Lakes region.... Without water," he argued, "the Sun Belt growth cannot be sustained."

And in Congress a group of southern and western members formed The Sun Belt Council, a coalition to offset what Representative Charles Wilson of Texas said was "pure nonsense ... the idea that Sun Belt states are wallowing in prosperity while people in the North and East are suffering economic hardship."

HOW STATE GOVERNMENTS ARE DIFFERENT

Two aspects of state government are of special significance in intergovernmental bargaining. They are less visible than the other governments and more vulnerable to interest group pressures than the national government.

State Government Is Less Visible

As early as 1956, V. O. Key, Jr., observed wryly, "The American people are not boiling with concern about the workings of their state governments."[18] Most of us never notice how shy and retiring state governments are. Citizens commonly fail to give them full credit for all that they do, and this limits their bargaining position.[19]

If someone asks what the national government does, you can immediately imagine President Bush sparring over new arms reductions with the Soviets (or with our allies) and announcing more new programs in the Rose Garden or in the White House briefing room. We can tell about Congress debating changes in Medicaid and the Supreme Court justices carving out new positions on the death penalty.

As children, we visited the local fire station and almost daily we see cruising police cars. Our schools, the water we drink, the repaired chuckholes, and the garbage collectors all tell us local officials are on the job.

But what do state governments do? What keeps the governor busy? What is that vast bureaucracy at the state capitol up to?

Most citizens know the state runs university and prison systems. And whether we drive the interstates in Arkansas or Rhode Island, the same neatly dressed state police officers—usually polite to a fault—and their cars with the revolving button lights on the roof are in evidence. We might also associate driver's licenses and automobile licenses with state government. Thinking a little harder we might recall that states run some institutions such as mental hospitals. Almost everything else that state governments do is blurry for the average citizen in most states.

Why States Lack Visibility In the chapter on finance we will see that states give a large portion of their funds to local governments. The states carry out many of their programs with community governments. These governments deliver services where the citizens live and get the lion's share of the credit for programs that the state taxes paid for.

Second, the mass media do not cover state governments in much depth. An old saying sums up the situation: "News depends less on the occurrence of events than on the presence of reporters." Many state capitals are located in smaller cities—those not generally described as "media centers." Newspapers and TV stations can cover local and national stories much more cheaply and more conveniently. The capital news corps tends to be small. Continuous coverage is too expensive for all but the wire services, a newspaper chain, the state's major newspaper or television station, plus those news media located in the capital city.

In addition, as Senator Terry Sanford, a former governor of North Carolina, noted, much reporting about the capital is negative or frivolous.[20] A member of Michigan's highway commission told our students that reporters paid little attention to the large contracts the commission routinely awards. The commission could have stolen 50 miles of Interstate 94 without the journalists noticing, he claimed. But once when the University of Michigan and Ohio State football rivalry was at its peak, as a joke the commission put a fictitious town in Ohio on the official Michigan highway map. They called it "Go—Blu!" "And that," the commissioner said, "got on even the national AP wire."

State government affairs also seem unimportant to the media because until the 1950s and 1960s, rural rather than urban interests dominated state politics. As the state governments changed, particularly after the Supreme Court ordered legislative apportionment, state politics and policies became more relevant to metropolitan citizens. But editors continue to think that the public is not much interested in reading about state government.[21]

State Governments Are Vulnerable

Some liberal critics have argued that state governments are too open to improper influence. Christopher Jencks, for example, argued that the federal government should stop "bailing out the states" with federal grants. They are, he said, "unfit to govern."[22] Michael Kinsley recommended that we allow the states simply to "wither away."[23]

These attacks, we think, are overdrawn, especially now because of the growing professionalization of state legislatures. But one point the critics make is still valid. State governments are much more vulnerable to the influence of organized groups than is the national government, especially to business and industries located within their boundaries.

States and Communities Compete for Industry In 1988 Massachusetts passed a mandatory health insurance law affecting all workers in the state. Its short-term impact was an employer drain for the Bay State. Other state policies such as workers' compensation, collective bargaining rules, product liability regulation as well as the provision of such services as roads, water, and sewerage can also have a dramatic effect on business profits.

Loss of industry can greatly affect the well-being of a state. Laid-off workers put a double whammy on state revenues. The state must pay them unemployment benefits and later, if they are unable to find new jobs, some become welfare clients of the state. Retail sales drop, thus causing a falloff in income and sales tax

The states advertise their wares. (Source: *State and Community Governments in the Federal System*, 2nd edition, by Charles Press and Kenneth VerBurg. Copyright © 1983 by John Wiley & Sons, Inc.)

collections. Further unemployment may result. Thus job losses not only mean loss of state revenues, but increased expenses.

What can states do? Setting up tariffs is not one of their options. Nor can they prevent industries, trained workers, or college graduates from migrating. Officials thus often conclude they must adopt policies attractive to business. They advertise. Governors make statements aimed at neighboring states such as, "I defy anyone to show me anybody in South Dakota who is hungry, or who can't get an education, medical care, or a roof over their head. We don't have people living in parks or in rest rooms."

For the past decade or so, Wisconsin's Department of Development has gathered teams of elected officials, local businesspeople, bankers, and state administrators to go on industry recruiting trips. They visited high technology firms in northeastern states "selling Wisconsin." They tell prospects that "Wisconsin provides property tax exemption for machinery and equipment, has the lowest workers' compensation rates in the Midwest, and has passed legislation to ease Wisconsin's capital gains taxes."[24]

Governors also visit abroad to sell state products or urge foreign industrialists to build plants in their states. Thirty-five states now have offices in Tokyo.[25] In 1988 governors made 87 trade missions abroad. Idaho, with 30,000 Americans of Basque descent, in 1988 signed an agreement with Spain to promote trade and cultural exchange with its Basque region. Former governor Gerald Baliles of Virginia said he sold Virginia chicken feet in Hong Kong, wines in Taipei, lumber in Tokyo, and coal in Seoul. And he routed millions of tons of foreign manufactures into the United States through Virginia's ports.[26]

Some states forgive state taxes on new industry, a technique first used by Mississippi. Some even offer a direct subsidy. Wisconsin made a variety of concessions to American Motors to keep its plant operating in Kenosha. Later Chrysler bought AMC and closed the plant. Chrysler financed a retraining program for laid-off employees, but the community still faced a major economic disaster. This and other similar examples led states to seek stronger commitments from industrialists, but asking for too much in a competitive environment may mean no deal at all.

Influence in Small Republics James Madison, in the tenth essay of *The Federalist Papers*, suggested that a major advantage of a large republic is that it would have many factions and interests with no one of them dominating. The reverse, he noted, is true in a small republic, such as a state, city, or county.

His insight has proven to be the case in some states and many communities. A single producer or a few related interests, or even an important family, has been able to dominate for long periods of time. DuPont dominated Delaware, oil in states as large as Texas and Oklahoma. Corporations such as the Pennsylvania Railroad and U.S. Steel had major influence in Pennsylvania, and one observer wrote with some exaggeration that in Utah, all issues are Mormon or anti-Mormon.

Extractors of natural resources especially desire influence. They are rooted to the state and cannot migrate—coal in eastern Kentucky and West Virginia, lumber in Oregon and California, or iron ore in Minnesota.

In Policy Box No. 2, "Why Not Regroup the States?" we discuss two proposals that would move to regions in place of states. Later we argue that the patterns of dominance described above are gradually changing as industry is dispersing and one-crop economies are less common. North Dakota farmers still grow wheat, but some irrigate to harvest alfalfa, and others produce beef. President Jimmy Carter made his fortune in Georgia planting peanuts instead of cotton. Soybean growers have moved into Arkansas.

Policy Box No. 2

Why Not Regroup the States?

If you look closely at a map, you may conclude that state boundaries are irrational. Look at their shapes. Geographers say governmental units should be compact, with the state capital at the center. They prefer relatively straight boundaries, such as those found in Utah, Wyoming, Colorado, and other western states. Note how West Virginia snakes out, then stems to the north and east like a cantaloupe vine. Why should Florida have all that western coastline that could logically be southern Alabama? Or why should that pipe stem be attached to Idaho?

Others suggest states should be similar in size. Why have area differences as great as those between Rhode Island (1,214 sq. mi.) and Alaska (586,412 sq. mi.)—a variation of 483 to 1? Or instead should we make states relatively equal in wealth? We might try to set up distinctively urban or distinctively rural states. Or we might try for a mix.

Look next at how state boundaries break up natural communities based on similar climate and geography. Since east and west are so different in the Dakotas, should we not have an East and West Dakota, instead of a North and South Dakota? Are not the hill areas of western Virginia, North Carolina, eastern Kentucky, and Tennessee more like each other than they are like the rest of their states?

Geographers say that rivers as boundaries are a hangover from days when a river was a military barrier. Today they say that people who live in the same river valley should be part of the same state—as is the case for the Missouri River along most of its course. But note the exception, they say. The Missouri River flows between Nebraska and Iowa at Omaha and Council Bluffs, adding to governmental problems. Our biggest river, the Mississippi, forms state boundaries along its whole route, except for small portions at each end, in Minnesota and Louisiana.

States, the geographers argue, should be built around a regional center. The *Chicago Tribune* recognizes that it publishes for "Tribuneland," an area they define as southern Wisconsin, southwest Michigan, and northern Illinois and Indiana. Should not Connecticut and northern New Jersey be part of the same state that holds New York City, since so many people living in those states commute daily to the "Big Apple"?

Fifty years ago political scientist Roy V. Peel claimed that America should consist of regional governments, since he argued that political cultures were less distinct than in the past.

The two maps on the next page show how two geographers redrew state boundaries—one reduced the number to 38 states, the other to 16 regional governments. They provided names so that we have clues for why they chose these boundaries.

What do you think? Should state boundaries be redrawn? What benefits might result? What political or social costs? Which groups or individuals might gain and which might lose? Would different boundaries strengthen the states in facing the national government? On what principles would you construct new boundaries? Do you think the effort would be worth the trouble? Why? Or why not?

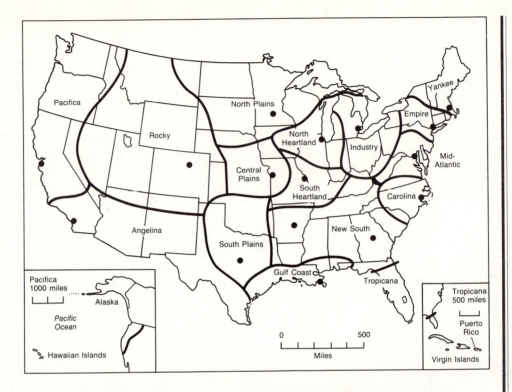
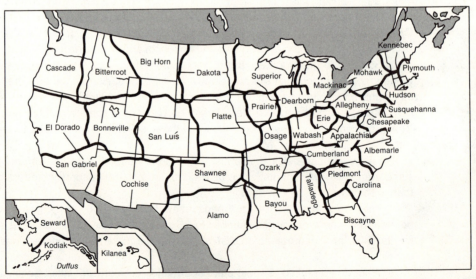

Two geographers' suggestions for realigning state boundaries: (top) The proposed 16 regional states; (bottom) the proposed 38 states of America.

People are also migrating. In "Down East" Maine there are now more people "from away," just as Alaska has more settlers from the "Lower Forty-eight." Each census records changes in representation patterns as the West, South, and Southwest gain at the expense of the Northeast and Midwest. Old families and dominant ethnic groups are thinned out by new settlers.

Vulnerability to Reform Movements It is easy to overlook that state and community governments have been vulnerable also to reform movements—more so than the national government. Social movement activists—environmentalists who oppose nuclear power plants, advocates of low taxes, and supporters and opponents of gay rights—or in the past—abolitionists, prohibitionists, and feminists—achieved state or community victories long before they had similar national influence. And states vary in their policy approaches to the abortion issue.

In part, influence is greater in states and communities that are homogeneous. When the Populist movement among farmers began in the 1890s, "Raise Less Corn and More Hell," the battle cry of one of its leaders, swept Kansas. Almost everyone was a farmer or depended on farming. "Black Power" had the same kind of instant success in urban ghettos. And the call of the Gray Panthers gets an enthusiastic response in parts of Florida and California.

Also, Progressive reformers made it easier to penetrate state and local governments. Most nominate in primaries, rather than in party conventions, and they elect more of their officials than does the federal government. And in every state but Delaware the people must vote approval for new constitutions or amendments. This is usually true for city charter changes as well.

Moreover, in almost half the states voters may propose by petition and adopt constitutional amendments or laws, and again many communities have the same procedure. California's Proposition 13 and Proposition 2½ of Massachusetts, measures that drastically reduced taxes, became law this way. And in about one-fourth of the states the people, through petition followed by election, may remove officials from office as they threatened to do in Arizona in 1988 before its governor was removed through the impeachment process.

This vulnerability to influence affects the pattern of intergovernmental bargaining. State and community officials reflect a different array of interests and constituencies than national bureaucrats, and they are likely to defend their local interests vigorously.

A FINAL COMMENT

Most state and local government texts give little more than token recognition to the importance of federalism and the impact of intergovernmental relations on state and community policy-making. We plan to do more than that—we want to keep federalism as the central focus. At times we may become so involved in describing the structure or politics of states or their community governments that, for the moment, we ignore other levels. But we intend to emphasize and reemphasize intergovernmental relations. Understanding federalism in its changing forms is fundamental to understanding how our state and local governments operate.

HIGH POINTS

We began by looking at (1) the development of the study of state and local politics beginning with de Tocqueville and Bryce, who rooted their analysis in the social and economic environment of politics; the "good government" reformers, who stressed managerial efficiency in governmental organization; the muckraker journalists and Progressive reformers, who stressed the political process and democratization to offset the influence of wealth; and today's political scientists, who are more aware that most state and community policy-making occurs in an atmosphere of uncertainty and compromise—especially so in a federal system. We then stressed (2) an aspect of present-day study of states and communities, the interdependence among national, state, and community governments. We noted that states and communities are embedded in a federal system and that the national government exercises a great deal of influence on state and community policy-making; states and communities have grown in importance as governments now make decisions once made by private groups; state government activities are relatively invisible to the average citizen; and state and community governments have been more vulnerable to influence than has the federal government, whether by interest groups, reformers, or average citizens. Thus they represent a different and wider array of interests than the national government.

In this chapter we defined the following terms in this order: federal system, intergovernmental relations, governmental structure, formal and informal "rules of the game," politics, political resources, separation of powers, checks and balances, political setting, "good government" reform movement, spoils system, patronage system, scientific management movement, managerial efficiency, centralization, professionalization, value consensus, value conflict, Progressives, democratization, muckrakers, political uncertainty, side effects, incremental decision making, and the intergovernmental lobby.

NOTES

1. Olga Moore, *I'll Meet You in the Lobby* (New York: J. B. Lippincott, 1950).
2. James Bryce, *The American Commonwealth* (1888). Book II, Chapter 22.
3. Students also attribute the decline of machines to the end of large-scale immigration after 1924, the welfare policies of the New Deal, the spread of civil service, and the criminal prosecution of some of the major city bosses. See Alexander B. Callow, Jr. (ed.), *The City Boss in America, An Interpretive Reader* (New York: Oxford University Press, 1976), pp. 265–330.

4. Perhaps the most biting criticism of this approach is Lawrence J. R. Herson, "The Lost World of Municipal Government," *The American Political Science Review* 51 (1957): 330–345. We have based much of our comment on Wallace S. Sayre and Nelson W. Polsby, "American Political Science and the Study of Urbanization," in Philip Hauser and Leo F. Schnore (eds.), *The Study of Urbanization* (New York: Wiley, 1965), pp. 115–156.
5. Roland Warren, *The Community in America* (12th ed.) (Chicago: Rand McNally, 1973), pp. 375–402.
6. For a discussion of the difference between structural and social reformers see Melvin G. Holli, *Reform in Detroit, Hazen S. Pingree and Urban Politics* (New York: Oxford, 1969).
7. See also *The Autobiography of Lincoln Steffens* (New York: Harcourt Brace Jovanovich, 1931).
8. Robert K. Merton, *Social Theory and Social Structure* (New York: The Free Press, 1957), pp. 171–182, and Callow, *The City Boss in America*.
9. Melvin G. Holli, *Reform in Detroit* (New York: Oxford University Press, 1969).
10. The classic statement of the "conspiracy" view can be found in C. Wright Mills, *The Power Elite* (New York: Oxford, 1956), and Robert and Helen M. Lynd, *Middletown* (New York: Harcourt Brace Jovanovich, 1927) and *Middletown in Transition* (New York: Harcourt Brace Jovanovich, 1937).
11. However, Francis Fox Piven and Richard A. Cloward argue that welfare programs are designed to control the poor by keeping them at the subsistence level and thus discouraging political activism. *Regulating the Poor, The Functions of Social Welfare* (New York: Vintage Books, 1971).
12. V. O. Key, Jr., *American State Politics, An Introduction* (New York: Knopf, 1956), pp. 133–196.
13. Belle Zeller, *Pressure Politics in New York* (New York: Prentice-Hall, 1937); Peter Odegard, *Pressure Politics, The Story of the Anti-Saloon League* (New York: Columbia University Press, 1928); Harold F. Gosnell, *Negro Politicians, The Rise of Negro Politics in Chicago* (Chicago: University of Chicago Press, 1935), and *Machine Politics: Chicago Model* (Chicago: University of Chicago Press, 1937); and Harold A. Stone, Don K. Price, and Kathryn H. Stone, *City Manager Government in Nine Cities* (Chicago: Public Administration Service, 1940).
14. Malcolm Jewell, "The Neglected World of State Politics," *The Journal of Politics* 44 (1982): 638–657.
15. However, an activist Supreme Court has made sharp policy breaks in pursuit of social justice and with less concern for the immediate political consequences.
16. Tax Foundation, *Facts and Figures on Government Finance, 1988–1989 Edition* (Baltimore: Johns Hopkins University Press, 1988), pp. 5, 22.
17. David Osborne, *Laboratories of Democracy, A New Breed of Governor Creates Models for National Growth* (Boston: Harvard Business School Press, 1988).
18. Key, *American State Politics*, p. 3.
19. Donald Songer, "Government Closest to the People: Constituent Knowledge of State and National Politics," *Polity* 17 (Winter 1984): 387–395.
20. Terry Sanford, *Storm Over the States* (New York: McGraw-Hill, 1967), pp. 48–49.
21. Carl W. Stenberg, "States Under the Spotlight: An Intergovernmental View," *Public Administration Review* (March/April 1985): 319–326.
22. Christopher Jencks, "Why Bail Out the States?" *The New Republic* (December 12, 1964): 8–10. Conservatives, of course, do not necessarily define federal innovation as

"progress." See the essays of Russell Kirk and James J. Kilpatrick, in Robert A. Goldwin (ed.), *A Nation of States, Essays on the American System* (Chicago: Rand McNally, 1953).
23. Michael Kinsley, "The Withering Away of the States," *The New Republic* (March 28, 1981): 17–21.
24. Paul A. Rix, "State Prospectors Head East to Pan for Firms," *Wisconsin State Journal* (September 21, 1981): 15.
25. H. Brinton Milward and Heidi Hosbach Newman, *State Incentive Packages and the Industrial Location Decision* (Lexington, Ky.: Center for Business and Economic Research, University of Kentucky, 1988).
26. Jonathon Kandell, "U.S. Governors Wooing Foreign Investors," *The Wall Street Journal* (December 15, 1988), p. A10.

Chapter 2

The Setting of State Politics

Every state is different. Sometimes we can almost taste the difference.[1] Even the speech is distinctive—sometimes by state and often by region. Those firms that ask us to phone toll-free 800 numbers for merchandise say Nebraskans have "a vanilla voice"—citizens from other states easily understand them. And those who "ride the rods" tell us one state above all others is hostile to hoboes—why Louisiana? And why does Colorado lead in the number of Peace Corps volunteers per capita? Why is the average phone call in Rhode Island three minutes while in

Texas it is five minutes? Why are residents of West Virginia, Wisconsin, and North Dakota most likely to be overweight while those of Arizona, Hawaii, and Utah are likely to be trim?[2]

Are any of these differences of political importance? Political scientists only recently have begun to investigate the way state differences might affect policy.

Overview We begin by looking at setting: the environment in which state government and politics take place. Data reveal that the quality of life varies importantly among states. We then consider factors that may explain why states differ: geography, climate, and natural resources; the original settlers; historical events and personalities; today's population mix; and the level of wealth, education, urbanization, and industrialization. We then look at the independent effect of its political process.

THE LIVES PEOPLE LIVE IN DIFFERENT STATES

During the 1920s and early 1930s an iconoclastic magazine editor and political gadfly, H. L. Mencken, began a series of articles that he called "The Worst American State."[3] He first presented data from the 1930 census and then added whatever reliable data he could locate elsewhere. He ended up with 106 tables comparing the 48 states and the District of Columbia.

That was over 60 years ago. Why should we look at it now? We think you'll be impressed with how, in crude form, the data show a trend in what has been happening in the states since 1930.

Mencken presented his data in four main categories—wealth, education, health, and public order—and ranked the states by some commonsense preferences—that it is better to be rich than poor, educated than ignorant, well than sick, and alive than murdered.

What Mencken Discovered

Oregon, he found, had 1 dentist for every 966 people, but South Carolina had 1 for 4,850—Oregonians with a toothache would have to wait only one-fifth as long to see a dentist. When he looked at deaths of children in the first year of life, the **infant mortality rate**, he found New Mexico's to be 145.5 per 1,000 live births, more than twice the national average and three times that of Washington State, at 49.0 per 1,000. Even the odds of being murdered showed startling differences—murder was about 26 times more frequent in Florida than in Maine, North Dakota, or Vermont.[4]

Would we find that much variation today? Only partly.

The Picture Improves By 1972 a researcher found some remarkable changes.[5] The worst state had one-third more dentists, nearly half as many homicides, and an infant mortality rate of 14.2—about one-tenth of what it was in 1930, and a third of the rate the best state then had.

The best states improved on only one measure—infant mortality. The supply of dentists was lower, and homicide rates were higher.

The gap between worst and best states also was much less, and the gap continues to close. Still, we have a way to go when in the 1980s a baby has almost twice the chance of surviving its first year in Rhode Island than in Delaware. And every year 40,000 babies, who medical experts say might be saved with proper prenatal care, still die.

We should also note that differences within states continue to be great. For example, in 1985 the infant mortality rate in Cleveland was 18.5 compared to 10.3 for all Ohio; in Memphis it was 17.2 compared to Tennessee's rate of 11.4.

Mencken combined his measures and ranked the states. Using similar procedures in 1972 a researcher found that seven of ten top states of 1930 were also in the top-ten category 40 years later. Most of the last ten states still ranked at the bottom. And we found the same to be true using more recent data.

America is not yet a homogenized society. State-based characteristics continue to have an important influence on the lives citizens lead. They tell us something about our chances of being moderately well off, being mugged, owning a home, getting a job, getting health care, or even surviving. They affect both our life-styles and life chances and influence what state and community governments can accomplish.[6]

EXPLANATIONS FOR DIFFERENCES IN QUALITY OF LIFE

Isolating the causes of various factors is not easy. For example, the National Safety Council reports that Wyoming has always been high on auto fatality rates. Why?

For one thing, Wyoming residents have to drive in some severe winter weather. Even Interstate 80 is often hazardous when it snows. And if you have ever traveled up to Yellowstone and Grand Teton national parks, you remember those mountainous roads with the narrow, winding turns and dizzying tilts. Another consideration is that Wyoming is large but not populous. Perhaps it can only afford two-lane highways where wider roads might be safer. Until recently, it was one of four states where the blacktop road mileage was less than the unpaved.

We note that Wyoming citizens own more cars per capita than any other state. Also, it attracts many tourists—perhaps they account for many of the accidents. Its open cattle range also presents driving hazards.

Some people will also surely argue that Wyoming's tradition of individualism, a Wild West prejudice against fencing people in with rules, is important. John Gunther reported in 1946 in *Inside U.S.A.* that Wyoming, along with Louisiana and South Dakota, were the only states that did not require driving licenses. In 1988 Wyoming was the last state to raise its drinking age to 21. (Note: South Dakota also challenged the withholding of federal highway funds for states with an under-21 drinking age and lost in the U.S. Supreme Court.)

No single factor explains Wyoming highway deaths, though some are surely more important than others. Moreover, some of these characteristics are difficult

Table 2.1 SELECTED FACTORS AFFECTING STATE AND LOCAL POLITICS

State	Population[a] Total July 1, 1987 (thousands)	Population[a] Percent urban in 1980	Personal income calendar 1988 (millions of dollars)	Assessed valuation of property 1986[b] (millions of dollars)	Mileage in state and local systems calendar 1987	Public elementary and secondary school enrollment fall 1988 (thousands)	Percent of persons below poverty level[c] April 1980	Recipients of aid to dependent children[d] December 1988
Total	243,400	74%	$ 4,042,110	$ 4,817,779	3,874,026	40,196	12.4%	10,881,514
Alabama	4,083	60	52,019	14,367	88,166	730	18.9	132,467
Alaska	525	64	10,014	46,423	12,082	104	10.7	19,195
Arizona	3,386	84	51,592	17,651	77,723	578	13.2	90,472
Arkansas	2,388	52	29,478	12,251	77,087	456	19.0	67,199
California	27,663	91	531,100	1,059,122	158,932	4,611	11.4	1,708,375
Colorado	3,296	81	54,004	19,216	76,730	560	10.1	94,072
Connecticut	3,211	79	73,772	78,302	19,721	463	8.0	106,689
Delaware	644	71	11,682	12,969	5,341	96	11.9	20,177
Florida	12,023	84	204,792	386,981	100,423	1,729	13.5	307,187
Georgia	6,222	62	95,887	76,380	106,767	1,111	16.6	243,811
Hawaii	1,083	87	18,466	50,517	4,070	167	9.9	41,184
Idaho	998	54	12,644	29,551	71,639	215	12.6	17,501
Illinois	11,582	83	203,305	90,679	135,310	1,788	11.0	681,000
Indiana	5,531	64	82,076	28,833	91,535	964	9.7	150,281
Iowa	2,834	59	41,844	74,386	112,472	477	10.1	103,535
Kansas	2,476	67	39,561	11,090	132,931	426	10.1	67,358
Kentucky	3,727	51	47,603	79,337	69,629	638	17.6	154,636
Louisiana	4,461	69	53,891	15,088	58,272	791	18.6	271,017
Maine	1,187	48	18,065	28,642	21,964	211	13.0	51,818
Maryland	4,535	80	89,692	65,524	27,965	689	9.8	175,832
Massachusetts	5,855	84	121,538	237,511	33,807	826	9.6	233,764
Michigan	9,200	71	152,400	106,244	117,803	1,590	10.4	642,185
Minnesota	4,246	67	72,285	29,446	132,843	724	9.5	161,297
Mississippi	2,625	47	28,875	8,122	72,065	503	23.9	176,246
Missouri	5,103	68	79,605	31,951	119,682	807	12.2	199,986

Montana	809	53	10,186		71,811	152	12.3	28,913
Nebraska	1,594	63	24,305	44,121	92,401	269	10.7	42,720
Nevada	1,007	85	18,479	13,892	44,754	177	8.7	17,067
New Hampshire	1,057	52	20,860	27,760	14,611	166	8.5	10,731
New Jersey	7,672	89	168,923	188,260	34,041	1,081	9.5	320,491
New Mexico	1,500	72	18,842	11,836	53,749	281	17.6	59,952
New York	17,825	85	345,425	163,942	110,321	2,580	13.4	1,018,510
North Carolina	6,413	48	92,199	193,999	93,234	1,081	14.8	171,383
North Dakota	672	49	8,430	986	86,243	118	12.6	14,593
Ohio	10,784	73	168,344	101,702	112,154	1,782	10.3	648,312
Oklahoma	3,272	67	43,292	11,051	111,082	585	13.4	100,651
Oregon	2,724	68	41,068	83,199	93,315	462	10.7	81,005
Pennsylvania	11,936	69	194,459	46,993	115,908	1,655	10.5	538,585
Rhode Island	986	87	16,709	20,989	5,852	134	10.3	41,862
South Carolina	3,425	54	44,586	5,496	63,420	616	16.6	121,688
South Dakota	709	46	8,917	6,906	73,469	127	16.9	18,465
Tennessee	4,855	60	67,183	29,293	83,691	820	16.5	181,061
Texas	16,789	80	245,663	678,953	293,530	3,269	14.7	500,382
Utah	1,680	84	20,315	47,645	49,901	426	10.3	44,366
Vermont	548	34	8,546	169	14,071	96	12.1	20,331
Virginia	5,904	66	105,774	199,104	66,125	988	11.8	144,904
Washington	4,538	74	76,538	159,789	79,509	791	9.8	208,422
West Virginia	1,897	36	21,960	19,709	35,173	336	15.0	110,931
Wisconsin	4,807	64	75,028	110,648	108,925	775	8.7	270,742
Wyoming	490	63	6,455	7,900	40,075	98	7.9	13,100
District of Columbia	622	100	13,431	30,548	1,102	89	18.6	50,244

[a]Estimates, Bureau of the Census; excludes armed forces overseas.

[b]Assessed valuation subject to tax, after deduction of exemptions.

[c]Level based on property index developed by the Social Security Administration in 1964 and subsequently revised by other agencies; nonmoney income is not considered in calculating the poverty threshold.

[d]Total for AFDC includes 184,549 recipients in Guam, Puerto Rico, and the Virgin Islands.

Source: Department of Commerce; Department of Education; Department of Transportation; Department of Health and Human Services.

Table 2.2 HOW STATES VARY: TRENDS IN STATE PRISON POPULATION

State or other jurisdiction	Total population			Population by maximum length of sentence					
				More than one year			One year or less and unsentenced		
	1986	1985	Percent change	1986	1985	Percent change	1986	1985	Percent change
United States	502,251	463,048	8.5	487,391	444,698	8.6	14,860	14,350	3.6
Alabama	11,710	11,015	6.3	11,504	10,749	7.0	206	266	−22.6
Alaska	2,460	2,329	5.6	1,666	1,530	8.9	794	799	−0.6
Arizona	9,434	8,531	10.6	9,038	8,273	9.2	396	258	53.5
Arkansas	4,701	4,611	2.0	4,701	4,611	2.0	0	0	ND[a]
California	59,484	50,111	18.7	57,725	48,279	19.6	1,759	1,832	−4.0
Colorado	3,673	3,369	9.0	3,673	3,369	9.0	0	0	ND
Connecticut	6,905	6,149	12.3	4,043	4,326	−6.5	2,862	1,823	57.0
Delaware	2,828	2,553	10.8	2,026	1,759	15.2	802	794	1.0
Florida	32,228	28,600	12.7	32,219	28,482	13.1	9	118	−92.4
Georgia	17,363	16,014	8.4	16,291	15,115	7.8	1,072	899	19.2
Hawaii	2,180	2,111	3.3	1,521	1,428	6.5	659	683	−3.5
Idaho	1,451	1,294	12.1	1,451	1,294	12.1	0	0	ND
Illinois	19,456	18,634	4.4	19,456	18,634	4.4	0	0	ND
Indiana	10,175	9,904	2.7	9,963	9,615	3.6	212	289	−26.6
Iowa	2,777	2,832	−1.9	2,777	2,832	−1.9	0	0	ND
Kansas	5,425	4,732	14.6	5,425	4,732	14.6	0	0	ND
Kentucky	6,322	5,801	9.0	6,322	5,801	9.0	0	0	ND
Louisiana	14,580	13,890	5.0	14,580	13,890	5.0	0	0	ND
Maine	1,316	1,226	7.3	1,165	967	20.5	151	259	−41.7
Maryland	13,326	13,005	2.5	12,559	12,303	2.1	767	702	9.3
Massachusetts	5,678	5,390	5.3	5,678	5,390	5.3	0	0	ND
Michigan	20,742	17,755	16.8	20,742	17,755	16.8	0	0	ND
Minnesota	2,462	2,343	5.1	2,462	2,343	5.1	0	0	ND

Mississippi	6,747	6,392	5.6	6,565	6,208	5.8	182	184	-1.1
Missouri	10,485	9,915	5.7	10,485	9,915	5.7	0	0	ND
Montana	1,111	1,129	-1.6	1,111	1,129	-1.6	0	0	ND
Nebraska	1,953	1,814	7.7	1,863	1,733	7.5	90	81	11.1
Nevada	4,505	3,771	19.5	4,505	3,771	19.5	0	0	ND
New Hampshire	782	683	14.5	782	683	14.5	0	0	ND
New Jersey	12,020	11,335	6.0	12,020	11,335	6.0	0	0	ND
New Mexico	2,701	2,313	16.8	2,545	2,112	20.5	156	201	-22.4
New York	38,449	34,712	10.8	38,449	34,712	10.8	0	0	ND
North Carolina	17,762	17,344	2.4	16,460	16,007	2.8	1,302	1,337	-2.6
North Dakota	421	422	-0.2	361	375	-3.7	60	47	27.7
Ohio	22,463	20,864	7.7	22,463	20,864	7.7	0	0	ND
Oklahoma	9,596	8,330	15.2	9,596	8,330	15.2	0	0	ND
Oregon	4,737	4,454	6.4	4,737	4,454	6.4	0	0	ND
Pennsylvania	15,201	14,227	6.8	15,165	14,119	7.4	36	108	-66.7
Rhode Island	1,361	1,307	4.1	1,010	964	4.8	351	343	2.3
South Carolina	11,676	10,510	11.1	11,022	9,908	11.2	654	602	8.6
South Dakota	1,045	1,047	-0.2	1,014	1,035	-2.0	31	12	158.3
Tennessee	7,182	7,127	0.8	7,182	7,127	0.8	0	0	ND
Texas	38,534	37,532	2.7	38,534	37,532	2.7	0	0	ND
Utah	1,845	1,633	13.0	1,817	1,623	12.0	28	10	180.0
Vermont	676	677	-0.1	476	443	7.4	200	234	-14.5
Virginia	12,930	12,073	7.1	12,545	11,717	7.1	385	356	8.1
Washington	6,603	6,909	-4.4	6,603	6,909	-4.4	0	0	ND
West Virginia	1,482	1,725	-14.1	1,482	1,725	-14.1	0	0	ND
Wisconsin	5,697	5,442	4.7	5,678	5,412	4.9	19	30	-36.7
Wyoming	865	758	14.1	865	758	14.1	0	0	ND
District of Columbia	6,746	6,404	5.3	4,786	4,604	4.0	1,960	1,800	8.9

[a]ND = not definable.

Source: U.S. Department of Justice, Bureau of Justice Statistics, *Prisoners in 1986*. Copyright ©1988 The Council of State Governments. Reprinted with permission from *The Book of the States, 1988–89*.

Does the rough-and-ready attitude affect driving habits?

to measure—individualism, for example. Still, we have enough hard data to make a beginning in examining differences such as this one.

To disentangle the importance of various factors, political scientists began comparing the states, as Mencken did—but with an important difference—today they use computers and thus handle a good deal more data, and apply sophisticated statistical methods to weigh the influence of different variables.

Geography, Climate, and Natural Resources

Thomas Jefferson began his *Notes on the State of Virginia* by describing his state's geography. Many authors of state studies have done the same. They assume that size, topography, natural resources, and weather set limits on what is possible, and sometimes influence what citizens feel is necessary.

Geography Sets Up Barriers Rivers, lakes, and mountains may encourage a sense of isolation. Idaho has this problem because it is difficult to travel from northern to southern Idaho, except by air.

Swamplands, rivers, or other natural resources also encourage sectionalism—they lead to different crops and cause different industries to flourish. Those who share the same way of making a living, the same geographic hardships (lack of rain, for example), and the same geographic blessings (such as deep fertile soil) tend to view their neighbors as "different." Migrants have sometimes sharpened this sense of difference by settling in areas with conditions similar to the land they left—Finns and Welsh in Michigan's mining areas, Swedes and Norwegians on farmlands in Minnesota and the Dakotas.

Political Effects of Sectionalism Sectionalism sometimes results in half-serious talk about separatism—"setting up the fifty-first state." For example, some citizens want to create a new state to be called "Columbia" or "Lafayette." Its promoters would put together northern Idaho, eastern Washington, and western Montana. Other separatist movements have sprung up in western Nebraska, northern California, Michigan's Upper Peninsula, and on Martha's Vineyard, an island off the Massachusetts coast.

At a minimum, talk of separation gets the attention of capital politicians. They respond by adding people from the disgruntled area to party tickets, having a special "state of the state message" for the area, as Michigan governors have done yearly for the Upper Peninsula, or simply providing special services and benefits.

Often these sectional divisions appear in the state political process as special interest groups, caucuses in the state legislature, or factions in the major parties. V. O. Key, Jr., wove these sectional facts into his political analysis of the South—how, for example, the up-country–low country division of Piedmont and coastal plain in South Carolina is reflected in one or another political campaign. "Pitchfork" Ben Tillman, the enemy of the aristocrats of Charleston and the coastal plain, insisted on placing Clemson University at John Calhoun's home at Fort Hill in the Piedmont. The school was to give the poor of the hill country their "own" university.[7]

Geographic factors cause economic dislocations that find expression in a state's politics. Before World War I the Socialist party of Oklahoma threatened to become a major party. Garin Burbank traced its strength to rural areas with low farm values and marginal wheat and cotton farms—often tilled by tenants—and to the isolated coal mining towns. A falloff in annual rainfall in the early 1900s was associated with agrarian protest votes and third parties.[8]

Other Political Effects Look for a minute at Delaware. It is bigger than Rhode Island, but only 110 miles long and at its widest point only 35 miles across; at its narrowest, just 9 miles. It makes a difference because as one student observed, "Every voter lives within shouting distance of the statehouse."[9]

Not so in Montana, Texas, or Alaska, where many voters live great distances from the state capital. Do these distances contribute to a sense of isolation from government in this jet and television age? Some politicians think so. Alaska relocated its capital from Juneau to a more central and accessible location, 70 miles north of Anchorage.

Evaluating Geographic Influences Geography once had a greater impact on people's lives than it does now. Swamplands brought disease and misery. Distances were more important. So too were geographic barriers.

Technology, medical discoveries, scientific farming, improved transportation and communication systems, and even air conditioning have lessened the impact of brute geographic facts. Ease of travel and migration among states has helped dilute sectional loyalties. But geographic facts are still significant. As yet, though, we have no theory or method of analysis that helps us explain their influence with any precision. We are left with impressionistic observations and occasional voting studies that isolate geographically based political communities. One of the most important geographic facts affecting states is the distinction between the "frost belt" and the "sun belt."

A State's Settlers

Political scientists and historians have speculated about distinctive ways to look at the politics developed by ethnic subgroups and whether they establish distinctive political cultures that persist for generations.

What Is a Political Culture? Political culture is "the set of attitudes, beliefs, behavior, and sentiments that gives order and meaning to a political process." These attitudes, derived from experiences, give people a set of "underlying assumptions and rules that govern individual and group behavior in a political system." They guide political behavior by suggesting what is proper and acceptable.[10]

Our parents, schoolteachers, and clergy, as well as our political leaders, consciously and unconsciously teach us the assumptions of the local political culture—a process called **political socialization**. We learn to accept a set of attitudes and values that guide us in the practice of politics.

Political culture tells us what government should do, how to structure government, the rules of the game to play by, and who should participate. We can trace some of these political cultures to four migration patterns.

American Migration Patterns Northeastern Europeans settled our continent through the 1880s. They were mainly Protestant, along with Irish and some German Catholics. The 1980 census reported roughly 61 million claimed English, Scottish, or Welsh ancestry; 50 million, German; and 40 million, Irish.

Between 1890 and 1920 southeastern Europeans—Italians and Slavs—were the "new migrants." These were mostly Catholic or Jewish. They settled the cities of the Northeast and the Midwest. About 25 million claimed such ancestry in 1980.

Congress closed off massive immigration in 1924, so the third major migration came from within and consisted of African Americans, who beginning during World War I left rural areas in the South for the industrial cities of the North. In 1980 they numbered 21 million. And since World War II the fourth migration consists of Spanish speakers—Mexican Americans, Cubans, and Puerto Ricans—and Asians, totaling roughly 8 million in 1980. The states most affected are New Mexico, Arizona, Texas, California, Colorado, Florida, and New York.[11]

America's First Settlers We still find traces of the first northern European settlers. Note how the New Englanders who first came to Oregon gave its cities such nostalgic New England names as Portland, Salem, Pendleton, Medford, and Newport. But more important is whether their political culture still influences decisions.

Daniel Elazar maintains that three distinct political cultures date back to the northern Europeans who first settled New England, the Middle Atlantic states, and the southern coast. He argues that these persist and the descendants of later migrants have adopted their ways of looking at politics.[12]

The Original New England Settlers The Puritans were moralists who assumed that government should serve the common good; thus Elazar calls their belief system the **moralist political culture.** They believed that politics should be conducted on a high moral plane with each person having a duty to participate.

The moralist political culture, Elazar claims, encouraged reform—those influenced by it were leaders in movements as varied as ecology, abolition, "good government" reform, prohibition, consumer advocacy, feminism, prison reform, and many others. Most of these crusades came thundering out of the Northeast, he says, but he finds that the most moralistic state now is Minnesota.

The Original Middle Atlantic Settlers Those who settled New York, New Jersey, and Delaware came to America to get ahead financially. They wanted government to encourage competition, and do as little else as possible. People, they believed, could best take care of themselves. They could participate in politics as little or as much as they wanted. Elazar calls their belief system the **individualist political culture.**

They were the rugged individuals who settled the Jacksonian frontier, and, later, during "The Gilded Age" of the late 1800s, built the nation's railroads, exploited its mines, forests, and oil wells, and then retired to imitation castles to enjoy their riches. They saw trickery and corruption as an inevitable part of politics. Elazar thinks the state that most purely defines the individualistic ethic today is that haven of get-rich-quick drifters and male and female gold diggers—Nevada.

The Original Southern Settlers The plantation economy of the South inspired a view of politics that valued hierarchy based on birth. Elazar calls it the **traditionalist political culture.** They believed that the aristocracy should rule, but that they were also responsible for the other classes. Family honor and chivalry to women flavored this outlook.

The traditionalist political culture treasured the society portrayed in *Gone With the Wind*—with its loyal blacks, its dashing Ashley Wilkes, and its Scarlett O'Hara, fiercely loyal to her old family homestead, Tara. Which state, according to Elazar, shows the most traditionalist influence? Mississippi.[13]

The Impact of First Settler Political Cultures How would these political cultures guide policy choices today? Consider abortion. The individualist would respond with, "If you have the cash in hand, what you do is your own business." The traditionalist, with notions of family, would oppose easy abortion. As is often the case, we find the moralists a bit tortured. Personally, they might oppose abortion. But they would also conclude that the policy should be "morally right" for society. "Thus under certain conditions..." It comes out that moralists can be either for or against—just so they have a good moral rationalization for whichever course they choose. You can now play this game yourself with such policies as divorce, the Equal Rights Amendment, or campaign financing.

Evaluating the Early Settler Theory A number of scholars have found some relationship between Elazar's political cultures and political participation. Voting and other forms of political participation are highest in "moralist" states, lowest in "traditionalist" states, and in between in "individualist" states. They also found weak but significant relationships with respect to strengthening the bureaucracy and expanding the level of public services. These relationships are even weaker when urbanism and personal income are factored into the analysis, suggesting that these cause part of the relationship. Nevertheless, political cultures have an independent influence.

Ira Sharkansky concludes his examination with reservations about the impressionistic nature of some of Elazar's mappings. He thinks the measures of political culture should be refined by basing them on public opinion surveys.[14] Several students have since made such studies. David Lowery and Lee Sigelman conclude on the basis of survey data, "Elazar's three political cultures are not very distinctive in terms of the characteristic attitudes their publics express concerning the legitimacy of mass political participation." How then, they ask, can one explain the relationship Sharkansky and other students have found? They suggest two hypotheses—that of cultural lag in the operation of key political institutions or that political elites—those who exercise the greatest influence on public policymaking—hold political orientations related to basic cultural values more deeply than average citizens.[15]

As we note later concerning the South, the traditionalist culture benefited the elites. Governmental rules for many years made voting and the expression of black opinion difficult if not impossible. The aristocratic plantation owners at the top of the hierarchy were always more imbued with the traditionalist political culture norms than the poor blacks and poor whites out picking the cotton. The poor seemed to adapt rather easily to individualist, or even moralist, viewpoints when given the opportunity. How else can we explain slave revolts, such as the one Denmark Vesey led in Charleston, South Carolina, as far back as 1822? Why did the South need a national fugitive slave law? Or where did southern populism spring from?

Subsequent events may also reshape those political cultures into new forms. Could Louisiana's "Old South" traditionalism remain unaffected by the onslaught of Huey and Earl Long, whose rough-and-tumble populist approach to politics was to turn traditional ways on their head and shake them? We suggest that a static quality may cling to first settler socialization theories. Follow them rigidly and they lead us to assume that political culture is a kind of "measles" that a society catches in its youth and never recovers from. It thus leads us, perhaps erroneously, to discount many other experiences that people have which may reprogram the outlook gained during childhood. For example, Stephen D. Shaffer, using four statewide public opinion polls, found that "the traditionalistic political culture of Mississippi had been eroded" by 1987. He cites such nationalizing forces as television, federal policies, in-migration, increased urbanization, rising educational levels, and new political generations.[16]

The "New Migrant" Ethnics The Jewish and Catholic migrants who came to America from southern Europe between 1890 and 1920 came to political prominence during Franklin Roosevelt's New Deal of the 1930s. Their first impact was in elections.[17] Politicians played "League of Nations" politics—New York Democrats once balanced the state ticket with a slate of Lefkovitz, Fino, and Gilhooey, a not very subtle appeal to its Jewish, Italian, and Irish voters. The Rhode Island legislature in 1938, as the journalist Samuel Lubell wryly noted, "declared Columbus Day a legal holiday, less in tribute to Columbus's discovery of America than to its discovery that every fifth voter in the state was Italo-American."[18] Even today we find these displays of ethnic pride—for example, the Greek sponge fishing community of Tarpon Springs, Florida, strongly supported Michael Dukakis in the 1988 presidential primary.

In some communities the new migrants did melt into the dominant political culture. Compare the lack of "Irishness" of Ronald Reagan, born in a small Illinois town and moving to California, with that of the Kennedy clan of Massachusetts. Mark Schneider argues that ethnic identifications persist in politics when the migrants are discriminated against. Then the old-country grouping protects individuals in a society that treats them as "outsiders." Note, for example, that in Massachusetts until after the Civil War, Catholic priests could not enter Boston hospitals, even to give last rites.

Evaluating the New Migrant Political Culture Ethnic and religious voting patterns vary. In Pennsylvania, New York, Illinois, and Massachusetts, the new migrant vote in the big cities is still often by nationality. Italians, Poles, and others support their own. In California, where the "new migrants" were accepted on even terms, ethnic and religious identifications tend to fade in politics. The same is true in rural areas where ethnics were few in number.[19]

Just as geographic influences are not as great as they once were, so the importance of ethnic political cultures appears to be waning. Richard Alba, director of the Center for Social and Demographic Analysis of the State University of New York at Albany, found only 27 percent of the American-born descendants of the first settlers and the new migrants married someone completely in their own ethnic grouping.[20]

But even among those integrated into the dominant political culture, some ethnic traits relevant to politics may persist. The Jewish culture is said to place high value on education and the German, Scandinavian, and Dutch heritage to value thrift and hard work. Should we expect to find these qualities reflected in attitudes toward governmental programs? Or are such speculations ethnic stereotypes? More precise studies are just beginning to answer these questions.

To some degree the impact of ethnicity may occur through religious identifications, especially with respect to "social issues," as compared to "economic issues." David Fairbanks compared the strictness of state drinking and gambling laws with the concentrations of Catholics, liberal and conservative Protestants, and fundamentalists. He screened out effects of economic development and found that conservative and fundamentalist religious concentrations were related to strict laws—views on morality "reflect long-standing religious and cultural values which retain considerable influence in industrial as well as in rural environments."[21]

The Black Migration Jesse Jackson's campaign for the presidency in 1988 highlighted two conflicting trends. His support among whites suggests that discrimination against blacks has weakened somewhat. But the persistent question of journalists, "What does Jackson want?" implied no black can seriously run and expect to be elected President—a clear indication that prejudice is still strong, at least among many white voters. Given continued discrimination, we can be relatively certain that a black political culture will persist. And so too will black identification in political battles and preference for distinctive policies.

Hispanics Between 1970 and 1980 the Spanish-speaking population increased by 61 percent to 14.6 million. Persons of Mexican origin made up the largest group. States such as Colorado and California with large concentrations of Hispanics have adopted English as the official language, a move aimed at encouraging integration of the fourth migration. At the same time the federal government requires printing of ballots in Spanish and holding classes in that language where a large group of Spanish speakers exists. Given this kind of ambivalence, we can expect the Spanish political culture also to persist, because its members may feel the dominant culture does not wholly accept them.[22]

The Asian Migration Many Americans become aware of the Asian migration only when Asians win spelling bees or become valedictorians—a suggestion that distinctive traits may exist that are relevant to politics. Presently Asian Americans are less than 2 percent of the population, but they make up the second largest number among the annual 500,000 legal immigrants. Demographers estimate that by 2080, given this rate of migration, Asian Americans will make up 12 percent, a percentage close to that of blacks today.[23]

A State's History

Do past events have any influence on today's politics? Many people think so. In the 1930s Bob Fletcher of the Montana Highway Department put up the first historical marker. We now see such signs in almost every community where states and cities preserve historical sites to attract tourists.[24]

This is another variable that is difficult to put into quantifiable terms. Determining the impact of historical events presents added difficulties as well. We may be tempted to trace every catastrophe or piece of good fortune to some previous event and claim, "That happened because back in 1799 someone did this or that."

To avoid such reasoning, when you look at the history of your own state, look for persons or events that changed the rules of the political game and thus changed the groups and individuals who benefited from government policies. They may have done this by changing governmental structure. Or they may have changed the political process by organizing new groups important even in today's decision making.

The Heritage of Leadership Ralph Waldo Emerson claimed that all institutions are the lengthened shadow of one person. That probably overstates the matter, but the impact of some is still very apparent.

The La Follette family of Wisconsin contributed two governors and U.S. senators to the state's politics between 1901 and 1946. The father, "Fighting Bob," outlined a reform program to break the hold of the railroads and other corporate "trusts." He introduced the direct primary, civil service, and a host of other reforms. His sons carried on this tradition. They left behind a Wisconsin that still strives to meet the reformers' standards of democratization and managerial efficiency.

Those outside Nebraska may not remember George Norris, but he is largely responsible for Nebraska's being the only state with a nonpartisan unicameral state legislature and the only one where public utility districts provide all the state's electricity.

Even private citizens affect a state's politics. The Mayo brothers of Rochester, Minnesota, who established the world famous Mayo Medical Clinic, and William and Karl Menninger of Topeka, Kansas, founders of the Menninger Foundation, the world's largest training center for psychiatrists, have had a direct impact on their respective states—in both cases making them sensitive to health needs.

The Influence of Events Dramatic events have also had a lingering influence on today's government and politics. When the sit-down strikes erupted in the General Motors factories in Flint, Michigan, in 1937, Democratic Governor Frank Murphy refused to call out the state militia against the strikers. The company failed to break the strike, and, as a result, the United Auto Workers (UAW) unionized the first plant in the auto industry. This event began the strong ties of the UAW to the Michigan Democratic party.

In the 1870s Kansas adopted prohibition. William Allen White of the *Emporia Gazette* observed that New Englanders then almost exclusively settled Kansas because Scandinavians and beer-drinking Bohemians looking for farms headed to the Dakotas or Nebraska.

Or look at how federal land policies of the past shape today's politics. The Great Plains were homesteaded, and, as in the eastern states, private individuals own most of the land. But farther west the federal government kept large tracts of land that was unsuitable for settlers. It still owns 87 percent of Nevada and at least one-third of all other western states, including Washington, Oregon, and California.

The Special Influence of the Civil War The losses on battlefields such as Gettysburg and Shiloh, along with General Sherman's march through Georgia, forged political loyalties that persist into the present.

The hill country of western North Carolina and Virginia and eastern Kentucky and Tennessee opposed secession because its citizens had no plantations or slaves. To this day they remain Republican strongholds. Other states have their "Little Dixie" areas that Confederate veterans settled—Audrain County in Missouri or southeastern Oklahoma. Counties in southeastern Minnesota were the first settled in that state and had the heaviest Civil War enlistments and the heaviest casualties. Subsequently these areas also produced lopsided majorities for the Republican party. And at the state capitol in Montgomery, Alabama, the Stars and Bars of the Confederacy flew above the American flag until the mid-1970s. For a century, Alabama and the rest of the South voted solidly Democratic—a memorial to "the lost cause."

But down the street, past the statue of Jefferson Davis on the Montgomery capitol lawn, is the Dexter Avenue Baptist Church. Here the Reverend Martin Luther King, Jr., began his civil rights crusades in the 1960s. A mural depicts events in his life. And his dream of equality appears to have begun the process of dimming Civil War memories—the history he helped write continues to influence governments.

The Influence of the Great Depression   The stock market crash of 1929 led to profound changes. The New Deal of President Franklin Roosevelt, who was elected in 1932, centralized our federal system and increased government intervention in the economy. Most states also had their own "Little New Deals." Political alignments shifted and new political groupings emerged. The increase in local governmental services and expenditures is a major legacy of these experiences.

Evaluating the Effects of History   We can only estimate historical effects by looking at how events and personalities influenced government structure and the political process. We can also be sure that as time passes some of these influences are lessened as new personalities and events crowd onto the stage.

The Citizens Who Live There Now

H. L. Mencken described his home state of Maryland as the most "average" because its population so closely mirrored the nation. He cited rates of illiteracy and murder, salaries of high school teachers, the number of people converted annually at religious revivals, and the percentage of its lawyers sent to prison yearly for felony. Not all states can aspire to such distinction. Their unique mixes of population help set each apart from the others.

The Politics of Population Growth and Decline   Up to the 1960s, the failure to **reapportion** legislative districts, despite constitutional requirements, resulted in state legislatures that overrepresented "outstate" small towns and rural areas that were losing population—and underrepresented the cities and suburbs. In Ohio angry urbanites said "the cornstalk brigade" controlled; New York City fought the upstate "apple-knockers."

But in 1962, in **Baker v. Carr**, the U.S. Supreme Court ordered states to redraw legislative district boundaries so that each legislator represented roughly the same number of citizens. The big winners were suburbanites. New Jersey politicians had dismissed commuters to New York City as "sundowners," with weak ties to their home state, but overnight they became an important political force. In Maryland, politics that pitted Baltimore against the rural areas shifted. Suburbanites of Baltimore and Washington soon outnumbered both.

In some states suburban representatives formed alliances with rural and small town legislators. Bills giving money for a big city problem were amended to finance projects in middle-sized cities and small towns as well. In Illinois, "downstate" versus suburbs conflicts still confront Chicago. In some states, two cities are pitted against each other—San Francisco versus Los Angeles, Kansas City versus St. Louis, Pittsburgh versus Philadelphia.

Some states have had political change as the result of an influx of new residents, as with New Yorkers to Vermont. Frank Bryan wryly notes, "The two decades following World War II were dynamic ones for Vermont. Symbolic of the change was the fact that in the early sixties the human population finally surpassed the cow population."[25] Other states have lost population and have reduced clout in federal bargaining. The way population is distributed throughout a state also affects what kinds of services states and communities can provide at reasonable cost.

The Politics of Race and Language Segregation and racial prejudice have brought about the politics of school integration, busing, and equal opportunity employment programs for minorities; bilingual instruction for Spanish-speaking and a few other ethnic groups; and occupational training for native American Indians.

Political parties field minority candidates. Since 1965 the number of black elected officials, for example, has risen from 70 to 6,793 in 1988. Some 406 were state legislators, 8 were judges of supreme courts plus 641 other judges, 301 were mayors, and in all, blacks held 5,581 city, county, school, and regional offices. It was not until 1990, when Virginia inaugurated Douglas Wilder, that any of the states elected a black governor, although in Virginia and other states as varied as Michigan and California blacks have been major party candidates. Blacks have thus joined the ranks of other groups such as Hispanics and women, who also at one time were excluded from this office.[26]

Despite political gains, blacks still lag far behind whites economically. An average black family started out the 1970s making 61 cents to the white family's dollar. By the end of the decade the figure had dropped to 59 cents. The black underclass remains large. Native Americans and Spanish-speaking Americans experienced similar problems.

The Effects of Poverty and Discrimination Minority racial and ethnic groups have almost always been at the poor end of the state statistics on health, education, and welfare. In Alaska, for example, the average life span of Eskimos until the 1970s was under age 40.

Consider differences in infant mortality among "white" and "other races." The national average in 1985 was 10.6/M (per 1,000)—9.3/M "whites" and almost twice that, 15.8/M, for "other races." Washington, D.C., had a rate of 20.8/M, but close to the national average for "white" (10.8/M) and 22.7/M for "other races." The highest state average was South Carolina, with a 14.2/M—below the national average for "whites" (9.6/M) but 21.4/M for "other races."

However, blacks alone do not swell the "other races" totals. South Dakota, with a large Native American population, in 1977 had a state average of 16.4/M —14.8/M for "whites" and 26.4/M for "other races." Industrialized states repeat the pattern—in Illinois metropolitan areas the "white" rate was 13.2/M and the "other races" rate 26.3/M. In Iowa it was 13.6 per 1,000 to 21.3/M; in New York State, 12.4/M to 22.0/M. Only in relatively rural states such as New Mexico and Mississippi is the rate for "other races" higher in the nonmetropolitan areas.

In some rural areas, minority group members live in traditional ways that can be described most accurately as premodern or preindustrial. Lack of modern medical care accounts for some of the difference. Babies die not from disease but because they lack adequate prenatal care, and consequently the babies are too small and frail to survive.

But the ugly fact of racial or ethnic discrimination and the poverty and poor quality of life in America's urban ghettos and barrios explains much of the difference. The nation reached the surgeon general's goal of bringing infant deaths down to 9.0 in 1990, but failed to reach the target of 12.0 for ethnic and racial subgroups, despite many state and city programs. An intensive effort in South Carolina brought the rate of 18.5 for all 1978 births to 13.2 in 1986, with the nonwhite group rate reduced from 26.0 to 17.9. Other outstanding programs occurred in Alabama, Mississippi, Rhode Island, Cleveland, Boston, and Washington, D.C.[27]

But the wide differences among the states are changing. Look at the rate for "other races" in Mississippi. In 1960 it was 54.3/M; in 1985 it was 13.7/M. Part of this drop is the result of state and federal programs for improving prenatal care. Also Mississippi's economy improved. And, as noted, we have seen a slackening of racial prejudice, especially that which is legally applied, since the 1954 landmark case on school integration—**Brown v. Board of Education**. Nevertheless, race and language are an important part of the state political process.[28]

The Politics of Age Georgia was the first state to allow 18-year-olds to vote. Governor Ellis Arnall sponsored the idea during World War II, in part because of his competition with ex-governor Eugene Talmadge, who had running battles with the state university. Arnall hoped that university students would support the kinds of candidates he favored—a generally correct guess. In 1971 the Twenty-sixth Amendment made 18 the voting age in all states.

Young adults are too widely scattered to have much impact as a group on local elections except in university communities. As noted earlier some college students have lobbied to improve the quality of public colleges and universities. It is also relatively easy for those circulating initiative petitions to collect signatures on campuses, especially on ecology issues such as throwaway bottle bills or licensing nuclear power plants.

Older people, on the other hand, are better organized around their many special concerns—the condition of nursing homes, the quality and cost of medical care, property tax exemptions for the retired, and barrier-free facilities for handicapped seniors. In some cases the federal government has stepped in with programs, but a number of these issues are still decided on and administered by state or local governments.

In southern Florida retirees generally vote for conservative candidates, and their impact is great. In other states their influence has been less clear, in part because the retired are a smaller portion of the total population and also because political participation declines among older people.

In 1988 the states with the highest concentrations of those 65 and over were Florida (17.7 percent), Rhode Island (14.6 percent), Pennsylvania (14.6 percent), Arkansas (14.5 percent), and Iowa (14.5 percent). The national figure was 12.0 percent. See Policy Box No. 3, "Are Seniors Freeloading on the Rest of Us?"

Women in State and Community Politics On September 2, 1870, Louisa Swain became the first woman in America—and perhaps the world—to vote in a general election. She was one of about 1,000 women who voted that day in the Wyoming territory. The bill authorizing their vote also granted women the right to control their property and be jurors, permitted married women to work in trade or business and control their own earnings, made a mortgage not binding on a wife unless she signed it voluntarily, and granted equal pay for equally qualified women schoolteachers.

Legislators feared women jurors would be too harsh in cases of male drunkenness or murder in self-defense. That part of the law was repealed in 1871, except for cases in which a woman was being tried. Other parts of Wyoming's pioneering feminist legislation were often loosely enforced.

The first woman mayor was Susanna Medora Salter who, at age 27, was elected to the office in Argonia, Kansas, in 1887. She was unaware that the local chapter of the Women's Christian Temperance Union had nominated her as their candidate. Still, without campaigning she won two-thirds of the vote and served for a year for a salary of one dollar.[29] By the turn of the century "the liquor interests" began a coordinated campaign opposed to the spread of women suffrage, because feminists and prohibitionists were then closely allied.

Wyoming women also sought elective office. In 1882 Elizabeth W. Smith was elected superintendent of schools for Carbon County. Others followed. Estelle Reel became Wyoming's superintendent of public instruction in 1894 and the first woman elected to state office; Nellie Tayloe Ross became the first woman governor in 1925. Wyoming voters chose her to succeed her husband, who died in office.[30]

Today women are competing for more than "set-aside" female offices—vice chair or secretary. Joan S. Carver, in a study of Florida, found the years 1960 to 1978 to be "years of change," when the "golden cord binding women to tradi-

Policy Box No. 3   **Are Seniors Freeloading on the Rest of Us?**

In 1988 Congress passed, and President Reagan signed, the Medicare Catastrophic Coverage Act. It was to take effect in 1989. The first tax payments would have been due April 15, 1990.

The act provided several benefits for seniors: It limited the amount those on Medicare would have to pay for prescription drugs, it protected the income of seniors whose spouses are in nursing homes, and it greatly expanded Medicare benefits for long-term and acute illness.

Unlike other programs benefiting seniors, with the partial exception of Social Security, those over 65 were expected to finance all of the catastrophic care benefits. Even those who were ineligible for benefits because they had not retired would help pay for the program.

A 15 percent surcharge was to be added to the income tax a senior would owe on 1989 income. Those owing less than $150 in taxes would not have to pay the surcharge. Thus, seniors who in 1989 owed $1,000 in taxes would have paid a surcharge of $150, for a total tax bill of $1,150.

But there were limits to the surcharge; a break for those in upper income brackets ensured that no one would pay more than an additional $800 or $1,600 per couple if both were over 65. For each succeeding year the tax was slated to go up $50 per person or $100 per couple until the tax on the 1993 income would have been $1,050 per person or $2,100 per couple. At that point the surcharge would have stabilized—unless Congress changed the law.

The response from seniors was at first favorable—another government program had been passed for their benefit. Then they found out about the surcharge. The pressure on members of Congress became so intense that the House of Representatives repealed the law in 1989; the Senate soon followed suit. Some legislators kept looking for a formula that would preserve the benefits for poor seniors but pay for them out of general revenue or perhaps from the present Social Security surplus. None has yet been found.

But many in the work force said it was about time that the government set up a program in which well-off seniors paid for the benefits that they and other seniors receive. For the first time all seniors were not getting a free ride; they began to realize what their generous benefits cost. Until the surcharge, younger wage earners, even those earning only the minimum wage, were paying the tab for all seniors through annual increases in their Social Security taxes. There is no guarantee that the money will be there when those presently working are old enough to retire.

Meanwhile, many seniors collect a good deal more than they ever contributed to Social Security. Others, fairly well off on private pensions, still collect Social Security money.

The catastrophic health law, some argue, was fair and should not have been repealed. Why else would the major organization representing senior citizens, AARP, have favored it? Seniors argued that catastrophic illness was wiping out their savings and they wanted something to be done. It was.

What the law did was help those least able to help themselves. They would have received a major benefit by paying a good deal less than the maximum surcharge. And even for those paying the maximum of $800 a year, the catastrophic insurance coverage was a bargain. But Congress, they say, listened to those well able to pay this surcharge who were acting as if they were driven into poverty.

Many seniors argued that the law would have been a serious burden for most seniors because they are living on fixed incomes. Many of those not at the poverty level but still living close to the margin would have seen their standard of living decline with the addition of the surcharge.

Since Social Security was passed in 1935, the amount of money its beneficiaries can earn is limited. Those under 65 on Social Security lose $1 for every $2 they earn over $6,480. Almost a million of those on Social Security have lost some of their benefits. The Social Security Administration estimates that an additional 100,000 do not even bother to file for Social Security because of these limits.

In 1990, those over the age of 70 could continue to earn as much as they wished. And others who receive a maximum Social Security payment of around $750 a month could earn up to $42,500 a year before losing all benefits.

Seniors argue that they have paid Social Security taxes all their working lives and they deserve benefits without being taxed further to pay for them. Employed seniors continue to pay increased Social Security taxes as well as Medicare taxes and get no Medicare benefits. Meanwhile, the government talks out of the other side of its mouth about age discrimination in the workplace as it in effect drives seniors into retirement who want to continue to work.

Critics point out that, despite the added surcharge, the catastrophic care act did not cover all of the costs of long-term care in or out of nursing homes. It only expanded such coverage. As a result those who had invested in catastrophic medical insurance with a private company would end up paying double as a reward for their prudence. Meanwhile those who had no private coverage would not be completely covered. People who have worked all their lives say they should be entitled to a brief period of freedom from rising taxes.

Despite the Reagan claims of "no new taxes," seniors have already received a double whammy. Since 1983 those whose income is more than $32,000 per year have half their Social Security payments taxed. Then in 1988 the Reagan administration added the surcharge. The National Center for Policy Analysis says the taxes on seniors would have been the highest in history. Seniors who work would have had their taxes raised 102 percent, and those who were self-employed, 122 percent. Meanwhile the very rich under the Reagan "tax reform law" have had their rates reduced from 70 percent to 33 percent.

What do you think? Is Congress responding to political pressure from seniors rather than fashioning programs for them that are reasonable? Should the catastrophic Medicare surcharge have been eliminated? Are seniors getting too many benefits without having to pay for them? Should they be allowed to work at all when many blacks and others are unemployed? Should those above a certain income level be eligible for any Social Security payments? Should all their Social Security income be taxed? Or do we owe no more to seniors than they are already receiving? Weren't they told that Social Security was an insurance program and that they would receive back whatever they put in? Would it be wise to set up a program of liberal benefits that those now or about to join the work force would receive when they reach retirement age?

tional roles" was weakened, if not fully broken. Twenty-five of the 30 women legislators elected in Florida through 1978 took office after 1962. The number of women mayors, county commissioners, and city councilors also rose even more sharply. Florida still does not elect many women to statewide office even though women comprise 52.6 percent of Florida's population.[31]

Susan Gluck Mezey found that women enter politics on the average five years older than men, those who did had fewer children than male politicians, and they entered office when their children were younger. Only 65 percent of the women were married when elected as compared to 85 percent of the men.[32]

Fifty-four years after getting the vote, the first woman governor was elected in her own right—Ella Grasso of Connecticut.[33] In 1988 Vermont, Nebraska, and Arizona had women governors; Michigan, Minnesota, Massachusetts, and Iowa had women lieutenant governors; and 38 women were elected to other statewide offices. In 1989 women held 150 appointive state cabinet posts, an increase of 114 percent over 1981. Women legislators numbered 301 in 1969 and 1,260 in 1989; 1,653 served on county governing boards and 107 as mayors of cities over 30,000, 13 in the nation's 100 largest cities. Women in 1989 were mayors of the three largest cities in Texas—Houston, Dallas, and San Antonio, as well as Austin. Almost 15,000 women were city councilors or township board members.[34]

Although more women are being elected, the increase has been a very gradual one. The full impact of women as officeholders is still to be felt.

Economic Development—A Major Influence

A state's wealth is related to **economic development**, also called **modernization**, of its human and natural resources. Four factors are involved: (1) education, (2) industrialization, (3) urbanization, and (4) per capita wealth. Researchers have found this set of variables to be related to expenditure levels for a variety of state and community services—most clearly for health, education, and welfare.[35]

The Mencken data of 1930 pointed to the same conclusion—that if you wanted desirable surroundings you were more likely in 1930 to find them in a state that had gone some distance along the road of economic development.

Economic development is the best predictor of living conditions and government performance that we have found thus far. But economic facts are not so overpowering as to rule out the independent effects of many other variables—including government and politics.

The Impact of Economic Development States with higher economic development spend more per capita on services. This should result in higher-quality services and is usually reflected in lower disease rates, better educational opportunities, and a variety of welfare programs. A healthy economy and a more **democratic political process** also often go together and provide opportunities for average citizens to influence government decisions. Prosperity affects the kind of interest groups, power structure, and political participation a state has.

Economic development also influences the role of states and their communities in the federal system. Traditionally, the more economically developed northeastern states, and more recently California, have led in innovations and in quality of government. The less developed states and communities, especially those of the South, have been followers.

In the 1980s the Sun Belt and the energy-rich states experienced an economic boom while some Frost Belt states faced economic decline and crises. Economic changes have been reflected in gradual changes of political leadership patterns. In the past, presidential candidates frequently were residents of Massachusetts and New York, and the governors and mayors of industrialized states set the national patterns and trends. More recently, California and Texas have each provided us with two presidents.

Higher levels of citizen participation and reforms in governmental structure accompanied the economic development of southern states. Southern states also have increased the quantity and quality of the services they provide.[36]

Evaluating Economic Development Students have found that the four elements of modernization do not always rise together or at the same rate, as was once supposed. Utahans, with relatively low economic development, rank high in educational achievement—presumably because of the Mormon emphasis on schooling. Nonindustrialized Alaska, with north slope oil, has risen close to the top in per capita income.

Researchers find that the influence of economic development varies among policy areas. It has little effect on highway and natural resource expenditures; in water and air pollution control it has a negative effect. Sharkansky writes, "The non-economic explanations of public policy are often stronger than . . . economic explanations." He also observes that many of the economic development variables do not correlate strongly with policy outputs. Many states, he writes, "either surpass or fail to meet the political or policy traits that tend to correspond with their social or economic characteristics."[37]

Politics and Policy Outputs

Economic development variables are more closely related to policy outputs than to political variables we can easily measure, such as party competition or reapportionment. Some political scientists assumed this made politics, and even democratic government itself, unimportant or irrelevant. We find four reasons to challenge this gloomy conclusion.

The Democratic Threshold Effect First, studies of developing nations suggest that economic development seems to affect policy-making most clearly below a minimum "threshold" of development. Lack of economic development has an especially important impact on the quantity and quality of health, education, welfare, and other services available.

Mencken's tabulations also reflected this point. States with higher development move about in the preferred "living condition" rankings while the same dozen less modernized states are trapped at the bottom on most measures. Citizens of such "preindustrial" societies seem to be close to the "state of nature" that political philosopher Thomas Hobbes described as having "no arts, no letters, no society, and, which is worst of all, continual fear and danger of violent death, and the life of man solitary, poor, nasty, brutish and short."

Some social scientists have suspected that at the level of grinding poverty, states, like individuals, have few choices. Politics is thus irrelevant. The funds that are available are spent on basics. But when a state passes the threshold and begins to accumulate disposable wealth, a democratic political process can help choose among policy alternatives.[38]

The Green Mountain and Granite States Second, consider similar states that have strongly contrasting policies. Vermont and New Hampshire seem pretty much alike to most of us. The poet Robert Frost noted that on the map they fit together like two wedges, one thick where the other is thin. They are neighbors similar in size, population, and economic development. We would expect to find them spending similar amounts of money on state services.

Yet Richard Winters found that Vermont ranked fourth in the nation in total state expenditures per capita; New Hampshire was forty-fourth. "In program after program," he discovered, "Vermont spends at a per capita rate of one-and-a-half times that of New Hampshire." And Vermont, he points out, is nationally recognized as a leader in land-use planning, pollution control, welfare rights, and correctional programs. New Hampshire is not.

Winters concluded that although economic factors set limits to what is possible, different political histories explained why the taxing and spending policies in these states differ so sharply.[39]

State-Based Political Cultures Third, liberal/conservative ideologies and partisanship also have an impact on policy outputs. Richard Erikson and colleagues examined state partisanship and ideology by looking at the patterns that remain after the influence of demographic characteristics, including ethnicity, wealth, and so on, is removed. The resulting attitudes do not correspond with Elazar's political cultures.

They found living in ideologically liberal Minnesota and conservative Indiana had as great an effect on political attitudes as having a high or low income. When comparing states by party voting they found the political culture of Georgia the most Democratic and that of Nebraska the most Republican—again differences as great as voting patterns found associated with demographic variables.

The Erikson researchers suggest the need to determine whether the political cultures they discovered are state-based or cross state lines. We may also question whether they are associated with governmental units or populations. Also unanswered is whether the culture found is a sum of substate variations or a reflection of attitudes generally accepted throughout the state.

Earlier, V. O. Key, Jr., and Frank Munger found what they called political communities in county voting patterns of Indiana—patterns not explained by demographic variables. This suggests that political cultures are not always statewide and may well grow out of political experiences in specific governmental units.[40]

The Politics of Redistribution Fourth, states with similar levels of spending on public services may vary widely in who receives the services—states with similar per student spending may vary on how money is distributed among school districts.

V. O. Key, Jr., in his study of southern politics in 1949, found low levels of economic development and a generally stagnant one-party politics in the South. With a few exceptions he found large masses of citizens who benefited little from government programs. Key suggested that perhaps greater citizen participation through more democratic politics would encourage politicians to distribute benefits more widely.[41] However, as noted, students discovered that the level of expenditures was related to the disposable income available.

But other researchers then discovered that a democratic politics encourages what political scientists call **redistributive policies**—taking wealth or some other advantage from those who have them in abundance and redistributing to the "have nots." The level of "average spending" remains the same under widely differing systems of distribution, but benefits can vary dramatically. A state's politics then influences which citizens benefit, which services are expanded and which cut, what changes in spending levels may occur, and how the money is raised.[42]

Evaluating the Influence of Politics Not unexpectedly, we conclude what common sense tells most of us already—that we are more than pawns in the grip of economic forces, that a democratic political process can affect the way state citizens live, once they have managed to rise above the poverty level. And politics, rather than market forces, may determine who gets what, when, and how.

See Policy Box No. 4, "Whither West Virginia?"—a state whose many difficulties have many sources. Along with its problems, West Virginia possesses great mineral wealth. We give you an opportunity to suggest a way out of its difficulties—an exercise that will illustrate vividly the importance of state-based characteristics for public policy-making and the difficulty of changing these patterns.

A FINAL COMMENT

We have reviewed a host of internal influences on the lives citizens live within individual states. The underlying theme of this discussion is that a state's setting is important—but not as important as it once was.

Differences in wealth and modernization are narrowing. Some of the impacts of geography are being lessened by modern technology. Ethnic and religious identification in political life are somewhat less important—at least for the descendants of the earlier migrants. Even the picture with respect to racial minorities is changing slowly and gradually as these groups gain a voice in the political arena. And the events of a state's past such as the Civil War or Great Depression often take on an antiquarian tone as new events elbow them out of their position of importance.

Policy Box No. 4

Whither West Virginia?

Many state characteristics are givens. We can do little about them directly. But through government and the economy we may lessen or even guide the impact of some of the givens. We are asking you to look at West Virginia to figure out what can be done to improve the lot of its citizens.

We begin with the problems. The people of West Virginia are among the nation's poorest—in 1980 West Virginians ranked forty-third in per capita income, 17 percent below the national average. Because of mechanization of its coal mines, strip mining, plus the uncertain demand for coal since 1945, unemployment has generally been high—up to 40 percent in some coal areas. In November 1980 the U.S. Department of Labor figures placed it third nationally. Half the state's counties have had 15 percent or more of their citizens on relief. The federal government's war on poverty was born there when John Kennedy saw living conditions as he campaigned for the presidency.

The citizens of West Virginia are among the most isolated from modern trends. Many live back in the hollows and the hills in isolated communities with poor communication among them and fierce sectional rivalries. Only 40 percent of the women have jobs outside the home, the lowest percentage in the nation. The terrain

encourages isolation—every county is in the Appalachian range. Over 75 percent of the state is wooded. Roads are expensive to build. Flat land for airstrips, agriculture, or industry is scarce. The state's educational system and many of its other public services rank toward the bottom.

West Virginia's history is peppered with violence. The state was torn out of Virginia during the Civil War. We are amused by songs about the blood feuds between the Hatfields and the McCoys, but they were a grim and senseless slaughter that decimated families during the 1880s. Unionization of the coal mines in 1912 brought full-scale warfare, with 40 persons killed in one confrontation. The year 1921 brought further battles. Mine disasters have been frequent and tragic.

The state has been largely one-party Democratic, patronage-oriented, and corrupt. In one election, 33 of 55 counties turned in more votes than they had eligible voters. A former governor went to prison. In 1989 the house impeached the treasurer on charges of mismanaging the state and local consolidated investment fund. The mine owners have always fared well—strip mining was largely unregulated until the federal government acted. Until 1971 no tax was placed on coal—and this severance tax brings in only a fraction of what the state sales tax brings. The mines are absentee-owned. West Virginia miners are heavily unionized, but twice in recent decades union leaders were found guilty of conspiracy with mine owners ("sweetheart contracts").

Only 5 percent of the people are black, and many are leaving. So, too, are many whites. It is one of three states with a massive population loss reported in the 1970 census—by age 24 about 70 percent of its youth had migrated. But between 1970 and 1980 it had an 11.8 percent population gain, close to the national average of 10.9 percent. The largest gains were around Harpers Ferry, a community of commuters to Washington, D.C.

Some positives also exist. The state has vast mineral wealth—it ranks fourth nationally in mineral production and natural gas and first in bituminous coal production, providing 20 percent of the national output. A chemical processing industry has grown up around Charleston, and the state's beauty invites tourism. In 1976 an heir to a fortune, "Jay" Rockefeller, became governor. He first came to the state as an antipoverty worker, won the office of secretary of state, and began to clean up corruption in voting. He now represents West Virginia in the U.S. Senate. Its other senator is the former majority leader. In 1988 Democrat Gaston Caperton was elected governor. He set about streamlining state government—he won legislative approval to consolidate 150 executive agencies and boards into 7 departments. The legislature also approved a constitutional amendment which would eliminate as elective offices the secretary of state, treasurer, and agriculture commissioner. In 1940 West Virginians had rejected the same proposal by a 3 to 1 margin. The governor hopes to save the state $100 million during his four-year term by reducing the size of its bureaucracy.

What do you think? If you were an advisor to the governor, what would you recommend to improve conditions in West Virginia? Would you try to attack the communications, education, or economic problems, make the government more efficient, or try to clean up the state's politics first? Could you improve the life of the citizens without changing the culture and lifestyle of the people who live back in the hollows? Is this kind of cultural imperialism justified? How would you try to encourage

> economic development? Would you encourage reopening of coal mines by keeping taxes low or reducing regulations on mine safety? How about tourism, or developing new industry? Could you attract industrial development by advertising its pool of unemployed workers? Or perhaps the answer is through a federal program. What kind? How much should the federal government intervene? Or will federal intervention just make the state a large welfare reservation? Or do you think nothing can be done?

These trends suggest we are becoming a more united states. In the next chapter we look at a major influence from outside the states that has contributed to this blurring of distinctions—the national government and its role in our federal system.

HIGH POINTS

We found (1) differences in living conditions among the states. We then examined (2) the highway death rate of Wyoming and concluded that there are a number of influences, and they may vary in their importance. We next considered (3) the major explanations for variations in quality and quantity of services: (a) geography, climate, and natural resources, (b) settlement patterns considering the effects of the four major ethnic and racial migrations, (c) what historical events and personalities contribute, (d) the segments of a state's present population mix, and (e) modernization, the set of variables found to have major influence, especially on health, education, and welfare policies. We ended by weighing the influence of (4) governmental structure and politics.

In this chapter we defined the following terms in this order: infant mortality rate, political culture, political socialization, moralist political culture, individualist political culture, traditionalist political culture, reapportion, *Baker v. Carr*, *Brown v. Board of Education*, economic development, modernization, democratic political process, and redistributive policies.

NOTES

1. McDonald's varies the mix of mustard and ketchup from state to state, so perhaps you can literally taste the difference.
2. Center for Disease Control, "Overweight Populations by Selected States," *Lansing State Journal* (May 10, 1988): 15.
3. Charles Angoff and H. L. Mencken, "The Worst American State," *The American Mercury* 24 (1931): 1–16, 177–188, 355–371.
4. Some of the differences Angoff and Mencken found may result from poor reporting procedures. We selected illustrations that were likely to be accurate: deaths, murders, and lists of dentists that professional dental groups compiled, rather than less reliable data such as reported robberies.

5. John Berendt replicated the Mencken-Angoff study using 1970 data in "The Worst American State, A Statistical Reckoning," *Lifestyle* (1972): 6–13.
6. The U.S. infant mortality rate in 1985 was 11, compared to 6 in Finland, Japan, and Sweden. You may be astonished to learn that 18 nations have better records than the United States, including East Germany, Hong Kong, Canada, France, and Singapore.
7. V. O. Key, Jr., *Southern Politics in State and Nation* (New York: Knopf, 1949). The only attempt we are aware of to cover these facts and systematically relate them to politics in a kind of national rundown of the states is found in an excellent brief summary: Edward W. Chester, *Issues and Responses in State Political Experience* (Totowa, N.J.: Littlefield, Adams, 1968), Chapter 2, "Sectional Rivalries and Capital Transfers," pp. 12–27.
8. Garin Burbank, *When Farmers Voted Red: The Gospel of Socialism in the Oklahoma Countryside, 1910–1924* (Westport, Conn.: The Greenwood Press, 1976). A. C. Townley founded The Nonpartisan League in North Dakota after he, like many others, failed as flax farmer, wiped out by lack of rain. He blamed the bankers and grain elevator owners who he claimed should have extended further credit rather than foreclosing.
9. Both quotes are from Charles Hyneman, C. Richard Hofstetter, and Patrick Y. O'Connor, *Voting in Indiana* (Bloomington: Indiana University Press, 1979), p. 16.
10. Lucian Pye, "Political Culture," in *The International Encyclopedia of the Social Sciences* (New York: Macmillan, 1968), Vol. 12, p. 218.
11. "The Great Melting Pot," *U.S. News and World Report* (July 7, 1986): 30–33.
12. Daniel J. Elazar, *American Federalism, A View From the States* (2nd ed.) (New York: Crowell, 1972). See also Daniel J. Elazar and Joseph Zikmund II (eds.), *The Ecology of American Political Culture* (New York: Crowell, 1975).
13. Elazar's categories are reflected in several historical studies. The influence of the moralist or Puritan belief system on western settlement is described in Louis B. Wright, *Culture on the Moving Frontier* (New York: Vintage Books, 1941). Individualists are described in Glyndon G. VanDeusen, *The Jacksonian Era 1828–1848* (New York: Harper & Row, 1959), and Lee Benson, *The Concept of Jacksonian Democracy* (New York: Atheneum, 1961). A standard study of the traditionalist South, but one that discusses other southern belief systems as well, is W. J. Cash, *The Mind of the South* (New York: Vintage Books, 1941).
14. Ira Sharkansky assumed political culture could be scaled on three basic attitudes—encouraging political participation, strengthening the bureaucracy, and gaining high levels of service performance. He rated the traditional as least favorable and the moralist as most favorable, with the individualists in between, and then categorized each state in terms of Elazar's map symbols. He correlated the ranking with 23 measures of the three attitudes and found statistically significant correlations in the expected direction on 15 measures. Ira Sharkansky, "The Utility of Elazar's Political Culture, A Research Note," *Polity* 2 (Fall 1969): 66–83. Also see Charles A. Johnson, "Political Culture in American States, Elazar's Formulation Examined," *American Journal of Political Science* 20 (August 1976): 491–509, and Eric B. Herzik, "The Legal-Formal Structuring of State Politics: A Cultural Explanation," *Western Political Quarterly* 38 (1985): 413–423.
15. David Lowery and Lee Sigelman, "Political Culture and State Public Policy: The Missing Link," *Western Political Quarterly* 35 (1982): 376–384.
16. Stephen D. Shaffer, "A Traditionalistic Political Culture in Transition." Paper presented at the annual meeting of the American Political Science Association, 1987.
17. Duane Lockard, *New England State Politics* (Princeton, N.J.: Princeton University Press, 1959).

18. Samuel Lubell, *The Future of American Politics* (New York: Harper, 1951), pp. 73–74.
19. Mark Schneider, "Migration, Ethnicity, and Politics, A Comparative State Analysis," *Journal of Politics* 38 (1976): 938–962, and "Ethnic Regions of the United States, 1890–1970," *Polity* 12 (1978): 273–290. See also Paul Kleppner, *The Third Political System, 1853–1892, Parties, Voters, and Political Cultures* (Chapel Hill: University of North Carolina Press, 1979).
20. Nina Nirenberg, "Ethnic Boundaries Fall to Marriage in America," Gannett News Service, January 11, 1985.
21. David Fairbanks, "Religious Forces and 'Morality' Policies in the American States," *Western Political Quarterly* 30 (1977): 411–417.
22. Walker Connor (ed.), *Mexican-Americans in Comparative Perspective* (Baltimore: The Urban Institute Press, 1985).
23. "A Non-Anglo America by 2080," *The National Journal* (November 20, 1982): 2006.
24. Jonathan Walters, "History Is Hot! Cities and States Are Cashing In," *Governing* (June 1988): 33–39.
25. Frank M. Bryan, *Yankee Politics in Rural Vermont* (Hanover, N.H.: University Press of New England, 1974), p. 51.
26. Joint Center for Political Studies, *Black Elected Officials, A National Roster* (New York: Uniput, R. R. Bowker, 1989), pp. 8–23.
27. Kathleen Sylvester, "Infant Mortality: It's as American as Apple Pie," *Governing* (July 1988): 49–56.
28. U.S. Bureau of the Census, *Vital Statistics of the United States 1977* (Washington, D.C.: U.S. Government Printing Office, 1985).
29. The Kansas State Historical Society, Topeka, Kans.
30. Shirley W. Belleranti, "Vote of Confidence, Early Wyoming Suffragists Cast in a Pioneering Role," *The Chicago Tribune* (August 30, 1987), Section 6, p. 7.
31. Joan S. Carver, "Women in Florida," *Journal of Politics* 41 (1979): 941–955.
32. Susan Gluck Mezey, "Does Sex Make a Difference?" *Western Political Quarterly* 31:4 (December 1978): 492–501.
33. The first women governors took office as widows of former governors—Nellie Tayloe Ross in Wyoming in 1924—or as stand-ins for husbands ineligible to run—Lurleen Wallace in Alabama in 1966 (an incumbent could not succeed) and Meriam A. "Ma" Ferguson of Texas in 1924 and 1932 (whose husband had been impeached).
34. Fact Sheets issued in 1989 by The Center for the American Woman and Politics (CAWP), National Information Bank on Women in Public Office (NIB), Eagleton

35. Richard Dawson and James Robinson, "Interparty Competition, Economic Variables, and Welfare Politics in the American States," *Journal of Politics* 25 (May 1963): 265–289; Thomas R. Dye, *Politics, Economics and the Public, Policy Outcomes in the American States* (Chicago: Rand McNally, 1966); Richard I. Offerberg and Ira Sharkansky (eds.), *State and Urban Politics, Readings in Comparative Public Policy* (Boston: Little, Brown, 1971); and Thomas R. Dye and Virginia Gray (eds.), *Determinants of Public Policy* (Lexington, Mass.: Lexington Books, 1980).
36. Jack Bass and Walter DeVries, *The Transformation of Southern Politics, Social Change and Political Consequence Since 1945* (New York: Basic Books, 1976).
37. Ira Sharkansky, *The Maligned States, Policy Accomplishments, Problems and Opportunities* (New York: McGraw-Hill, 1972), pp. 38–39. See also Ira Sharkansky, *Regionalism in American Politics* (Indianapolis: Bobbs-Merrill, 1970), Chapter 5.

38. Seymour Martin Lipset suggested this hypothesis in *Political Man* (Garden City, N.Y.: Anchor Books, 1959), pp. 27–63. B. Guy Peters found a drop in socioeconomic influence after the middle levels of development had been reached. "Public Policy, Socio-Economic Conditions and the Political System, A Note on Their Development Relationship," *Polity* 5 (Winter 1972): 277–284.
39. Richard Winters, "Political Choice and Expenditure Change in New Hampshire and Vermont," *Polity* 12 (1979): 598–621. The economist Milton Friedman argued further that Vermont's higher expenditures do not result in services much superior to those of New Hampshire in "Parkinson Revisited," *Newsweek* (July 12, 1976): 58.
40. Robert S. Erikson, John P. McIver, and Gerald C. Wright, Jr., "State Political Culture and Public Opinion," *American Political Science Review* 81 (September 1987): 797–813. See also V. O. Key, Jr., and Frank Munger, "Social Determinism and Electoral Decisions: The Case of Indiana," in Eugene Burdick and Arthur J. Brodbeck (eds.), *American Voting Behavior* (Glencoe, Ill.: The Free Press, 1959), pp. 281–299.
41. V. O. Key, Jr., *Southern Politics in State and Nation* (New York: Knopf, 1949). Key's argument has sometimes been oversimplified as "party competition equals payoffs for have nots." Charles O. Jones points out that Key made a much more politically sophisticated argument, specifying political conditions other than party competition that would affect payoffs and noting that party competition might not in itself be a sufficient condition for such payoffs. Charles O. Jones, "State and Local Public Policy Analysis, A Review of Progress," in *Political Science and State and Local Government* (Washington, D.C.: American Political Science Association, 1972), pp. 33–34. See also Eric M. Uslaner, "Comparative State Policy Formation, Interparty Competition, and Malapportionment, A New Look at V. O. Key's Hypothesis," *Journal of Politics* 40 (1978): 411–432.
42. Brian R. Fry and Richard F. Winters, "The Politics of Redistribution," *American Political Science Review* 64 (June 1970): 508–522, and Yong Hyo Cho and George Frederickson, *Determinants of Public Policy in the American States* (Beverly Hills, Calif.: Sage, 1972), p. 49.

Chapter 3

A Changing Federal System

John Steinbeck, the Pulitzer-prize-winning novelist, set off at age 60 in an RV from his New York apartment for a "side road tour" of America. As a young man during the Great Depression, he had bummed freight trains and hitchhiked across the country. From these experiences he wrote novels such as *The Grapes of Wrath*. This time he drove leisurely across the nation. His novelist's eye noticed that states differed in their road signs. New England issued terse, tight-lipped instructions "without a word or a letter wasted." New York State signs shouted commands every few feet—"Do this! Do that!" Ohio phrased its signs as polite suggestions. And so on across the country.

But he discovered that technology was washing away the differences. Americans got the same fare on radio and television and consumed the same products, from white bread to country music. Twenty years later William Least Heat Moon observed the same drift to homogeneity. In reaction, he sought out the back-country places along the highways printed blue on his maps. Here he found that regional distinctions and a sense of local history still survive.

Steinbeck found something else he had not anticipated—a united American citizenry. He wrote, "This is not patriotic whoop-de-do; it is carefully observed fact. California Chinese, Boston Irish, Wisconsin German, yes and Alabama Blacks now have more in common than they have apart.... Americans from all sections and all racial extractions are more alike than the Welsh are like the English ... or the lowland Scot like the highlander. It is an astonishing fact that this has happened in less than two hundred years and most of it in the last fifty. The American identity is an exact and provable thing."[1]

The Nationalization of America The moving van and the U-Haul are American institutions. The U.S. census studies reveal that half of America changes addresses every five years. The Great Depression, World War II, and the postwar boom accelerated the shift of blacks from the South, migration of families to the West and Southwest—especially during the 1980s, from the Midwest to the South and West—and the continuing movement from farm to city to suburb. As a result, each state becomes more diversified and a little more like every other state.

The national government programs, beginning with the New Deal programs to combat the Great Depression of 1929 to 1939, also help to blur regional differences. We have become more impatient with state-by-state differences that seem to make little sense.

Our federal system also has changed. Students of state government during the Roaring Twenties studied a different system than the one we study today. States and nation no longer act as independently of each other. Our federalism is much more interdependent, nationally integrated, and complex. States and communities, however, still hold significant clout, and during the Reagan administration, state and local influence increased.

Overview In this chapter, we look at the relationships among the national, state, and community governments. Our first concern is the legal structure of state-federal relations; then we study the political needs and pressures that have changed the system the Founders devised. We next examine how the system operates—the methods used to solve political problems at each stage of the system's development. We then discuss the value of states at "the crossroads" of the federal system, and end by looking at how states defend themselves from federal domination.

THE LEGAL STRUCTURE OF FEDERALISM

Governments are of three types. **Unitary governments** concentrate all legal power at the center. They set up local units as they please with whatever legal powers they wish them to have. They may also abolish them. Most nations have unitary governments—France, Denmark, Great Britain, Israel.

Some political scientists would hardly call the second type—**confederation**—a government at all. Subunits set up a central unit, usually for a temporary emergency. But they keep the real power and can secede from or abolish the central unit as they wish. The United Nations is a confederation.

A third type—**federalism**—is a compromise. In a **federation**, both states and central government have significant legal powers. Both act directly on individuals. Neither can abolish the other.

The Weakness of Confederations

Americans twice experimented with confederations, both times as leagues of states to fight a war. Our first attempt at union in 1775—the Continental Congress—was formalized as the Articles of Confederation. The second occurred between 1860 and 1865 when 11 southern states formed the Confederate States of America.

Both ran into difficulties. Member states made decisions on supplies, governmental powers, and even the terms of soldier enlistments. (General George Washington crossed the Delaware River to New Jersey on Christmas Day, 1776, because the enlistments of many state militia serving under him were to expire on January 1, 1777. "His" soldiers would then return home.)[2]

A second difficulty was that with each state exercising a veto, the Continental Congress was often incapable of governing. The legacy of that government is summed up in the phrase "not worth a continental dollar."

Some leaders, such as Alexander Hamilton, hoped to correct defects in the Articles of Confederation by setting up a unitary government. It never had a chance of being adopted. The states were too strong to be abolished.

However, we do have 50 unitary governments in America—the states themselves. As we discuss further in a later chapter, local units have only the legal powers states choose to grant them. And states can create or abolish them as they wish, as they have sometimes done with townships or school districts.

The Federal Compromise

Scholars have found a few federations among the Greeks and in biblical Israel. But the framers of the U.S. Constitution made a sharp break with past practice—they invented the modern form of federalism. Early federations grew out of military necessity and often fell apart when the danger passed. Or one unit of the federation became so strong that it was able to dominate and soon swallow up the others.

Our federation includes features to reassure those who feared that the states would be swallowed up. Initially the states handled most of the governmental functions that affected citizens. The major exception was foreign affairs. And to gain support of the "Anti-Federalists," the Founders agreed to add to the Constitution a **Bill of Rights**—ten amendments to guarantee individual freedoms from national action.

But the American federation, unlike most of those of the past, also contained important "nationalist" clauses that allowed the system to centralize as conditions changed. The Constitution was the supreme law, above all state constitutions or laws. And the **national supremacy clause** further stated that if the nation and state were in conflict when both were acting according to their constitutional powers, the national action would prevail.

Preserving our federation has not always been easy. We had a bloody civil war over the meaning of the Constitution. The U.S. Supreme Court has changed its mind a number of times on the powers granted to states and nation. Because we have adapted our federation to changing social conditions, the federal union has survived.

The Founders were not political theorists who chose federalism after much thought. At the opening of the Constitutional Convention only a few delegates would have made it their first choice. But it would have been the second choice of most delegates. The convention was a gathering of skilled politicians who chose federalism because it seemed a workable compromise.

THE AMERICAN FEDERATION

Only the national and state governments have **sovereign power**—governing power guaranteed in the Constitution. Article 1, Section 8, lists 18 powers that the national government may exercise—these are the **delegated powers**. The last on the list of national powers is the **necessary and proper clause** that says the national government may use any means "necessary and proper" to carry out its functions. Both the states and nation may exercise the same powers—these are called **concurrent powers**. The Constitution and its amendments also list **prohibited powers**—powers that neither level of government may exercise. Powers not listed are **reserved powers**—these the states may exercise as long as they do not conflict with national powers.

The District of Columbia, the territories, and commonwealths can only exercise powers the nation grants them. Cities, villages, counties, school districts, towns, townships, and special districts can only exercise powers that states grant them. Legally none of these units is sovereign.

Achieving Statehood

To become a state, territorial citizens must petition Congress, asking permission to elect delegates to draft a constitution. Then Congress must pass an enabling act giving such permission. If the local voters approve a constitution, the unit may formally apply to be admitted. If Congress accepts and the president signs, the flag makers begin figuring where to add another star.

Can Special Conditions Be Imposed? Can Congress or the president set conditions before they approve? Yes and no; "yes" because becoming a state involves careful politicking, and "no" because the Supreme Court ruled that all states are legally equal and no special conditions can be imposed.

Yet Wyoming was denied admittance for a time because of its women suffrage law. Asked to change it, the territorial legislature wired Congress, "We will remain out of the union a hundred years rather than come in without women suffrage." For them it worked and they were admitted.

But Arizona submitted a constitution in 1912 that President William Howard Taft, in a fit of pique, vetoed. It allowed recall of judges. Arizonans dutifully removed the offending clause and once admitted, promptly put the provision back into their constitution. Earlier, in its first constitution, Nebraska restricted voting to whites. It removed the clause permanently at the demand of President Andrew Johnson.[3]

"Semistate Status"

We Americans are uncomfortable about colonies. We call our nonstates commonwealths, possessions, territories, and trusteeships. Our nation's capital is the "District of Columbia."[4]

Residents of these units, except for the possessions and trusteeships, are U.S. citizens. They elect a delegate to Congress who can vote in the House Interior and Insular Affairs Committee, but not on final actions of the Congress. They are subject to military draft. Yet, except for Washington, D.C., they cannot vote in presidential elections. They have their own constitutions and elect their own legislatures and executives. Possessions and trusteeships, though, have executives whom the president appoints.

Some of these units, such as the Philippines, have become independent nations. Others, Hawaii and Alaska, became states—both in 1959. Others maintain an in-between status.

The District of Columbia In 1988 Washington had a population of 635,233, larger than that of Vermont, Delaware, Wyoming, or Alaska. The Twenty-third Amendment, adopted in 1961, gave its residents the vote in presidential races, with three electoral votes. Residents also elect their own mayor and council and levy local taxes. But Congress may veto its city ordinances. In 1978 Congress submitted a proposed constitutional amendment to the states to give the district representation in Congress similar to that of the states. It failed adoption.

The Commonwealth of Puerto Rico In 1989 President Bush suggested that Puerto Rico should hold a referendum to determine its future. He hoped it would choose statehood rather than become independent. This Caribbean island has a population greater than the combined population of 20 states. Since 1950 Puerto

Ricans have elected their governor and legislators. They have their own court system and their own constitution, flag, anthem, official flower, tree, and bird. But Puerto Rico is not sovereign. Its governmental actions must concur with the U.S. Constitution and the Federal Relations Act of 1950. Only Congress can change the terms of the act. Consider their predicament further in Policy Box No. 5, "What Is a Commonwealth? What is Puerto Rico?" It discusses the choices Puerto Ricans may face one day.

The Territories and Possessions What distinguishes the territories and possessions? They all have populations of less than 100,000, small geographic size, and strategic military value. Most are islands in the western Pacific. The territories include the Virgin Islands (purchased from Denmark in 1917), American Samoa, and Guam (both acquired from Spain as "spoils" of the Spanish-American War). The possessions include the Panama Canal Zone (officially a government reservation until 2000 when it will revert to Panama); Wake; Midway; and the United Nations Trusteeships in the Carolines, Marianas, and Marshall Islands and other small islands in the Pacific and Caribbean.

OUR CHANGING FEDERAL SYSTEM

The U.S. Constitution established a legal pattern of intergovernmental relations between states and nation. If we try to understand federalism with only the logic of constitutional law, we likely will become frustrated, baffled, and even outraged. The same constitutional phrases meant one thing in 1800, another in 1900, and something else in the 1990s. Supreme Court justices interpret its clauses according to the problems and mood of their own times.

As the political scientist Roscoe Martin observed, we can best understand the practice of American government as a pragmatic response to felt needs. The states, Congress, and the president have all contributed to change. While we describe the different periods and types of federal-state relations, remember that change is gradual and the dates approximate.

The Period of Dual Federalism (1788–1901)

It is difficult to read the U.S. Constitution without concluding that the Founders expected the national government to handle a few functions and leave the rest to the states. Legal scholars call this **dual federalism**. The state and national governments carry out their functions without much contact with each other. Morton Grodzins compared this kind of federal system to a "layer cake."[5]

The Founders "delegated" a bare minimum of functions to the national government—foreign relations, including defense and foreign trade, regulating interstate commerce and disputes, and handling a few standard services such as a common currency, a system of weights and measures and copyrights, and a postal service. And the national government controlled the admission of new states and governed the District of Columbia.

Policy Box No. 5

What Is a Commonwealth? What Is Puerto Rico?

For years Fidel Castro has hung the "imperialist" tag on the United States over Puerto Rico; Cuba's UN representatives periodically urge the United States to give that island its freedom. In 1991 Puerto Ricans will vote once more on the question, choosing statehood, independence, or an enhanced commonwealth. The last alternative is similar to their present status with some increased autonomy in economic matters. President Bush favors statehood, giving Puerto Rico two senators and seven representatives in Congress. The university-educated and the urban intelligentsia tend to favor independence more than other citizens. In elections in 1951 and 1967, Puerto Ricans voted 3 to 1 for commonwealth status, principally for economic reasons. Independence was not then an option, and groups favoring independence boycotted the elections.

Puerto Rico is about the size of Connecticut or Delaware. It became a part of the United States as spoils of the Spanish-American War. It provided a major military base. The people speak Spanish; less than 20 percent speak any English. The culture is a mixture of Spanish and American. Burger King advertises "la Casa del Whopper," but most Puerto Ricans refer to Spain as the "mother country." Those opposed to statehood fear that it will destroy the Spanish and Puerto Rican influences—that Congress may require English as the official language in government and the schools. Ajura Gonzalez de Roses, an 80-year-old Puerto Rican, thinks that the battle is already lost. She told a reporter, "Christmas is the only time of the year in which you find genuine Puerto Rican food now. The rest of the time we eat like Americans. The young people are American even in their way of dressing. They go around half naked."

Puerto Rico has the highest per capita income in the Caribbean, aside from the Bahamas and the Virgin Islands. But it is a fragile economy built on tax breaks to U.S. industries that operate there—jobs that would be lost under either statehood or independence. Its income still is only half that of the poorest state. About 60 percent of the population receive food stamps; the unemployment rate runs between 15 and 20 percent.

About 3.5 million people live on the island. Its population density of roughly 900 people per square mile is among the world's highest. (Nearby Cuba has 140 people per square mile.) As a result, an additional 1.5 million Puerto Ricans have migrated to the mainland—70 percent to New York City, and others mainly to the New England states.

Through 1916 Puerto Rico was called a territory. It had its own house of delegates. The president of the United States appointed its governor and the majority of its executive council. The Circuit Court of Boston handled its court cases. Puerto Rico sent a resident commissioner to the U.S. House of Representatives who could speak on issues but had no vote.

In 1917, during World War I, Congress made Puerto Ricans American citizens. This act increased their powers of local government, but also made them subject to the military draft. As citizens they also could migrate freely to the U.S. mainland.

During the 1930s Congress would not consider statehood while the U.S. Navy opposed independence because of the island's strategic importance in protecting the Panama Canal. In 1946 President Truman appointed the first island native as governor. In 1948 Congress permitted the island to elect its governor for the first time. Luis Muñoz Marín, who had been political leader of the legislature for many years and was the son of the island's first resident commissioner, was elected. In 1950 the United States granted Puerto Rico commonwealth status with power to draft its own constitution.

What does commonwealth status mean? It is not the same as statehood. Puerto Ricans pay no federal income tax but do pay Social Security taxes. Industries migrating from the mainland pay few federal taxes. Commonwealth taxes are low. Congress may overrule any act of their legislature. U.S. criminal laws apply. Residents receive federal welfare benefits that other U.S. citizens are entitled to, such as food stamps and aid for dependent children, as well as services of almost every federal department, from the Conservation Service to the Weather Bureau. But Congress has put a cap on the welfare benefits paid. Puerto Rico receives about $5 billion a year in federal aid, though, a little over half of what states receive per capita.

The residents cannot vote for president but hold a presidential primary and send delegates to both national party conventions.

In the 1930s, during the Depression, a small faction of the independence movement turned to violence. Their most dramatic actions were an attempt to assassinate President Truman in 1950 and in 1954 spraying bullets onto the floor of Congress, wounding five representatives. More recently, an underground group called FALN killed two U.S. sailors and wounded ten others and has set off bombs in Chicago and at Pennsylvania Station and Kennedy Airport in New York. When a group of its leaders were captured in April 1980, the FBI found plans to kidnap then-candidate Ronald Reagan's son Ron. Most FALN recruits are college-educated second-generation Puerto Ricans born on the U.S. continent. Leaders of the peaceful independence movement predict violence such as that of Northern Ireland should Puerto Rico become a state. In 1989 an estimated 12,000 Puerto Ricans marched in a Marxist-Socialist-party-sponsored parade with "Yankee Go Home" signs. The occasion was a Senate subcommittee holding hearings on the upcoming plebiscite. Yet polls suggest less than 5 percent favor independence.

What do you think? Should Puerto Rico become the fifty-first state if their citizens desire it? What standards should Congress use in granting admission? Would allowing Puerto Rico to become a state create special problems for Puerto Ricans? For other Americans? Would they be better off independent? Should we grant them aid if they desire independence, at least during the transition period? Can the ambiguous commonwealth compromise remain unchanged indefinitely?

Each state government decided almost all of the governmental questions that affected the average citizen. States decided whether one would be slave or free, defined almost all crimes and spelled out the punishments, including how and when to use the death penalty. The states handled public health, safety, education, welfare, and morals, and regulated the physical environment.

Shared Functions There were a few instances when the two levels collaborated. But until the mammoth intervention over slavery, national impacts on "local" functions were limited. In 1808 the nation began financing over 80 percent of state militia costs—its main role was to protect frontier settlements from Indian raids. Also, the U.S. Corps of Engineers built some state canals and roads—again in part for military reasons. Other national actions that aided the states included exploring the frontier by Lewis and Clark in 1803 and passing the Homestead Act of 1862 to provide free land for settlers.[6]

Only once prior to the Civil War did the national government intrude greatly on state powers, and even this action was only a kind of time bomb that later generations would set off. In 1817, in **McCullough v. Maryland**, Justice John Marshall's Supreme Court reaffirmed the national supremacy clause. Equally important, the court insisted on a broad interpretation of what might be considered "necessary and proper." That decision formed the policy followed in the twentieth century to expand national power. Some now call it the **elastic clause**.

How the Relationship Began to Change The federal government ended slavery after the Civil War, but it was much less successful in using the Fourteenth and Fifteenth amendments to guarantee voting rights to blacks or to end state racial and religious discrimination.

It next intervened in response to the intense cries of farmers for help. Congress passed the Land Grant College Act in 1862 to set up agricultural colleges. In 1887 it established agricultural experiment stations. And between 1887 and 1889, with considerable hesitation, Congress created the Interstate Commerce Commission to regulate rail freight rates and passed the Sherman Silver Purchase Act to inflate the currency to aid those who had mortgaged their homesteads, and the Sherman Antitrust Law to control monopoly "trusts" that farmers and others thought kept prices of manufactured products artificially high. Even members of Congress who voted for these bills thought they were unconstitutional because they invaded state functions.

The End of Dual Federalism Some say the end of dual federalism came as early as the Civil War. Others place the turning point during the presidency of Franklin Roosevelt when the Supreme Court finally rejected dual federalism as a legal theory. And others point out that state governments still handled many functions without federal aid or regulation as late as the 1960s.[7]

We suggest that the presidency of Theodore Roosevelt, beginning in 1901, is probably as good a date as any. It is not just a question of when the national government began to enter more fields that once were reserved for the states. It is that Theodore Roosevelt was the first president to argue consistently and without apology that the states needed federal help to fulfill state goals.

The Period of Cooperative Federalism (1902–1963)

Supporters of **cooperative federalism** argued that state and federal action must intermingle as in a "marble cake." Theodore Roosevelt set about demonstrating

The Great Depression—federal projects such as this resulted in jobs for the unemployed and public improvements for cities and towns throughout the nation.

how the national government could help the states, whether the problems involved regulating business or settling strikes in the coalfields. He called the first conference of governors to see how national and state governments might cooperate on conservation policy. President Woodrow Wilson next questioned whether the states could plan and build a national highway system without federal cooperation.

Ideas about cooperative federalism came to full bloom during the presidency of Franklin Roosevelt. In 1932, at the depths of the Great Depression, state and city governments needed money to handle welfare and unemployment. Governors turned to the national government as their only hope. They welcomed programs for massive public works projects—the Works Progress Administration (WPA), the Tennessee Valley Authority (TVA), and the construction of public housing. Also, the national government assumed responsibility for the depression-created problems of the economy—business, labor, agriculture.

Still largely regarded as "local," though, were most problems involving public safety, health, education, and morals. As late as the 1960s, some members of Congress still said federal aid to education was probably unconstitutional and undesirable.

The Period of Modern Federalism (1964–)

In 1964 President Lyndon Johnson announced a new national goal—the creation of a "Great Society." All problems, he argued, should be viewed as national problems. And the national government would set about solving them—crime, sewage disposal, education, poverty, library services—all of them. Johnson called this **creative federalism**. He intended that the national government would provide funds, leadership, and guidelines to states, communities, and even private groups, and they in turn would carry out the programs.

National leaders stopped talking about cooperating to achieve state purposes. As James L. Sundquist points out, federal laws stated that their purpose was to achieve **national goals**.[8] The pattern of state-federal relations had shifted—the system became more centralized, one of a senior partner with juniors. The frosting moved to the top, something like a pineapple upside-down cake. In Policy Box No. 6, "Fair Shares in a Federal System," we find that sometimes state officials do not share equally as the nation attempts to achieve national goals.

We have had almost three decades of this type of federalism. Students generally have not adopted President Johnson's name for it—perhaps because it was less creative than he had hoped. Critics argue that the federal government tried to achieve too much too quickly and has created an overly complex system. David Walker described it as "an increasingly overburdened and dysfunctional federalism wherein intergovernmental relations have become more pervasive, more expansive, less manageable, less effective, and above all, less accountable"—what some called "fruitcake federalism"—one more addition to the list of cake analogies.[9]

Students have observed several trends, some of which conflict. Here, we disentangle some of the main strands of modern federalism practices.

Fiscal Federalism   In fiscal federalism, the national government has become the banker of the federal system. In 1955 federal aid to the states and communities was 4.7 percent of all federal spending. By 1978 it was 17.0, dropping to 10.9 in 1989. In 1955 this was 10.2 percent of state and local spending; it climbed to 26.5 percent in 1978 and dropped to 17.1 percent in 1989.

In terms of funding, the national government has exclusive responsibility in national defense, the post office, and 90 percent of the interstate highway system. State and local governments assume most of the costs of education, local streets and state roadways, health, and police and fire protection. Welfare costs are shared.

Permissive Federalism   By 1964 the Supreme Court had rejected the doctrine that the Constitution "reserved" any functions exclusively for states. State functions were those that the federal government still permitted states to administer—Michael Reagan called this new legal relationship **permissive federalism**.[10]

Court decisions to abolish racial discrimination swept aside "states' rights." Justices also extended civil liberty guarantees in the Bill of Rights to state actions.

Policy Box No. 6

Fair Shares in a Federal System

In 1987, Virginia, home of the Pentagon, ranked first among the states as the recipient of federal expenditures per person. In terms of the total amount of federal dollars received, California ranked first, but only sixteenth on a per capita basis.

The state receiving the least in federal funds per capita was Michigan. It received $2,543 per capita to California's $3,634 and Virginia's $5,954. New Mexico was second with receipts of $5,752 per capita, followed in this order by Alaska, Maryland, Hawaii, North Dakota, Massachusetts, Connecticut, Missouri, and in tenth place Washington, which received $3,963 per capita.

At the other end of the scale, the bottom ten starting in fiftieth place with Michigan are Indiana, Wisconsin, North Carolina, Illinois, Vermont, Louisiana, Kentucky, Georgia, New Hampshire, and in fortieth place Texas, with $2,949. The figures are from the Bureau of the Census report *Federal Expenditures by State, Fiscal 1988*.

What accounts for some of the differences? In part, military spending. California received 16 percent of the total followed by Virginia, Texas, Florida, and New York. These five states receive 40 percent of the military total. But only Virginia is in the top ten states. California is 16, Texas is 40, Florida is 21, and New York is 26.

A closer look at the figures reveals the Rust Belt states of the Great Lake area in general at the bottom. Such figures add fuel to the controversy in Congress that has been going on since 1976, when the Northeast-Midwest coalition was formed and financed with contributions from northern representatives' office funds. The coalition has a staff of six researchers. Complementing it is the Northeast-Midwest Institute with a set of private offices on Capitol Hill, a staff of 18, and a budget of $1.1 million. It is financed from private contributions.

This prompted the organization of the Sun Belt Caucus in 1981—a group with less staff and financial backing. But it also has a complementary Sun Belt Institute.

Recently the Sun Belt Institute released a study which claims that Congress has discriminated against the South in grant programs. New York, the study said, gets back $1 for every 75 cents it pays in federal taxes. The Northeast-Midwest Coalition immediately counterattacked, noting that the study had omitted from its totals such items as federal payrolls, pensions, Social Security and other payments to individuals, and the salaries of personnel on military bases. The study focused, they said, on grants alone, which are just 37 percent of the federal expenditures; therefore the totals were bound to be misleading.

The issue raises the question of how federal funds should be allocated. The contestants in the struggle often argue as if funds should be distributed equally on a per capita basis. That way each state would have the same federal funds to spend on solving its problems.

Another approach is to argue that a state's residents should receive a dollar back for every dollar they pay in taxes. Thus one of the first studies of the Northeast-Midwest Coalition pointed out that for every dollar of federal taxes they sent to Washington, the Midwest got back 79 cents in grant funds, the Northeast 94 cents, the West $1.05, and the South $1.12. Alaska, which had just given grants to its citizens as a result of its oil wealth, was getting back $1.45.

A contrary view is that federal spending should go where the need is greatest. We did not list the figures for all of the states, but what we did report shows that some of the states not generally considered among the most wealthy were at the bottom of the list. Add West Virginia which is in thirty-fifth place, South Carolina at thirty-fourth, and Alabama at twentieth. At the same time we already noted Alaska was third and Massachusetts and Connecticut seventh and eighth in per capita federal receipts. One study of the early 1980s found that the Reagan cuts of social welfare programs especially disadvantaged the South, where such programs shored up the economy and aided the Northeast, which was then booming with electronics prosperity.

But others argue that wealth of a state should not be the only consideration; money should be targeted where the problems exist. If AIDs became epidemic in wealthy states such as New York and California, that, they say, is where the federal funds should be spent. And some state needs call for a major initial outlay. The Tennessee Valley Authority required such an expenditure but has paid off in major dividends for the region and the nation. If all states had received equal per capita amounts the project never could have been started. The same is true for massive reclamation projects in the West.

Some studies suggest that federal expenditures are a major reason for state economic growth. That being the case, some have argued that federal spending should go where the most returns can be expected. For example, in 1981 President Ronald Reagan's Commission for the National Agenda concluded that the aging industrial cities of the North were beyond help. The commission suggested directing federal activity to the Sun Belt.

Others say the problem would be managed fairly if politics could be removed from the process. Well-financed interest groups skew the federal expenditures for their own benefits. They are aided by senior members of Congress who chair some of its important committees and see to it that the "pork barrel" projects to benefit their districts get into bills and fight tooth and nail to prevent closing of military bases and other federal facilities in their district that are no longer needed.

What do you think? Is the present pattern of federal spending a fair one? How should it be changed? Do the Rust Belt states of the North have a legitimate gripe that they are being shortchanged? Do you feel the growing Southwest should be receiving more aid to handle the new problems caused by population influx? Is it more important to reduce the gap between the top and bottom states than to worry about which state happens in any year to end up on top? Is the real problem the politics that are inevitable in a federal system?

They were especially concerned for groups they saw as inadequately represented in state and community political processes—ethnic, racial, and religious minorities, and those accused or convicted of crimes. Presidents and members of Congress feel pressures from states and communities for greater local autonomy more directly than do Supreme Court justices. But they agreed with the Court's thrust.

Look in a metropolitan area phone book under "United States Government" to get a sense of how deeply the federal administrative agencies have penetrated into our communities. Even the Reagan administration substituted national programs for state and local policy-making with respect to the 21-year-old drinking law and several other functional areas.

Functional Federalism Once Congress passes a grant program, power shifts to administrators. Terry Sanford, when governor of North Carolina, compared the levels of federal administrators to a "picket fence" (hence the term **picket fence federalism**). The crossbars that hold the pickets together he called the national, state, and local governments. Each picket represents a coalition of professional administrators—one for welfare administrators, another for highways, and so forth.

Samuel Beer used the term **functional federalism** to describe the pickets. Agency administrators work with functional area program specialists that universities, business corporations, and private research agencies employ. These program specialists, no matter who employs them, tend to share goals. They may have attended the same or similar professional schools, as happens with forestry or education administrators. Interchange of personnel from one level to another or interaction at national conventions and through professional journals strengthen these professional loyalties. At times the loyalty of program specialists to a professional guild and its values may clearly overshadow the loyalty to the unit of government that employs them.[11]

Grantsmanship Federalism If these were the only trends, we might describe the pattern of intergovernmental relations as "centralized federalism." And we would begin to speculate how long states would continue. But we also have a strong decentralizing trend. One reason is that state and community administrators have become grant experts whose lobbying influences the content and conditions of grants.[12] This process is called **grantsmanship federalism**.

The Johnson administration, by providing grants for almost every public function, opened up a basketful of benefits. Over 30 states and 100 cities now have permanent offices in Washington, D.C. So, too, do organizations representing other local governments and all types of functional specialists. The National Governors' Association has 80 lobbyists and researchers in Washington; the National Conference of State Legislatures has 35; the U.S. Conference of Mayors, 70. These "public interest lobbies" pressure Congress to increase funds and give local administrators more power.[13]

Competing with each other for grant funds makes public administrators less united than "functional federalism" theory suggests. Though still agreeing on professional goals, state administrators want grants for their states and want to handle them through state agencies; county and city administrators want grants coming directly to them.

Many "cause" groups have also been attracted to this expanded system of grants and regulatory policies. Getting their reforms attached to grants as required mandates is easier than lobbying them through 50 state legislatures.

Civil rights groups want affirmative action requirements, ecologists want environmental impact statements, labor unions want contractors to pay the local prevailing wage, and the handicapped want barrier-free access.[14]

Grantsmanship Federalism: An Assessment How successful has public interest lobbying been? In 1981 David B. Walker found over 60 mandated requirements as conditions in a variety of grant programs—these represent victories for the "cause" groups. Other grant provisions require recipients to purchase services from certain types of private agencies or corporations.

But states and communities have also done reasonably well. In many cases the federal government has changed or relaxed its regulations to meet their demands. And, as we note in a moment, the states and communities have pressured Congress to experiment with new types of grants—those that give them increased decision making with less federal regulation. An effort that state officials began ended with congressional-state cooperation to achieve welfare reform in 1988.[15]

The negative side of grantsmanship federalism is the confusion and the lack of coordination among programs and failures to target them to groups the programs are meant to reach. The legislative guidelines for programs are often vague. This postpones the decisions until the program is implemented in states and communities. Congress tries to satisfy as many groups as possible, even when their goals are in conflict. Some members follow "grant politics by printout." They want to see precisely how much each proposed formula will bring to their own constituencies and are reluctant to vote before the computer churns out the information.

George E. Hale and Marian Lief Palley thus suggest that the old model of cooperative federalism no longer applies. The new politics of federalism today is similar to the way government regulates private firms—those being regulated use their influence in Congress or with the president to bargain for special concessions.[16]

A State-focused Federalism Some students argue that the initiative in the 1980s shifted from the national government to the states and localities.[17] This was President Reagan's announced program.

But only a few parts of Reagan's **New Federalism**, such as reducing some federal regulations and cutting back some social grant funds, were adopted. Yet the president achieved his purposes indirectly. The tax cuts and increased defense expenditures resulted in a large federal deficit and curtailed new federal program initiatives and the expansion of established ones. States and localities, losing federal revenue sharing and other federal funds, were forced to cope as best they could. Most states were not able to replace the loss of funds, especially in the environmental area.[18]

But many states passed tax increases, and as the budget crunch lessened they also innovated and seized the momentum, particularly in relation to economic development. David Osborne lists over 70 new state units in this field. The most successful attempts were to develop investment in new products rather than "smokestack chasing"—luring industries from other states.[19]

State and local goals also began to replace national goals—for example, in resegregating some public schools. Ohio regulators of air pollution were more concerned about economic development and employment than were federal regulators.[20] Some observers doubt that Congress will permit this condition to continue despite the federal budget crunch.[21] Robert Nathan argues that the federal system goes through cycles—it becomes more decentralized when conservatives are in control nationally and more centralized when liberals are in control.

The Division of Functions Today

In a few fields in which states once were responsible, the national government now exercises major control. Since the Great Depression it makes major policy for industry, labor, and agriculture. The states supplement these policies, enough so that corporations, unions, and farm organizations do some lobbying also at the state capitals. The same is true of the interstate transportation system. But with respect to social welfare, public housing, affirmative action, the environment, air pollution, gun control, and drug abuse, states and localities have been taking up the slack of lagging federal action and are innovating.

Other functions are still exclusively state controlled, though national grants and court actions affect them in important ways. Among this group are higher education, regulating professions and trades, mental health, marriage, divorce, election procedures, adoption and wills, prisons, and almost all criminal prosecutions and civil cases. The states also still incorporate businesses and regulate many such as insurance companies, public utilities, state-chartered banks, and transportation firms.[22]

And communities still handle many functions, but now with varying degrees of state and federal supervision. These include primary and secondary education, law enforcement, fire protection, land-use control, recreation, and water and sewage services.

OPERATING A COMPLEX FEDERAL SYSTEM

Our government system is now highly complex and one in which national, state, and community governments sometimes cooperate and sometimes frustrate each other. Coordinating the activities of these governments and providing uniform services where we believe it important to do so remains a major problem. How can we bring about order and prevent chaos or stalemate?

Constitutional Clauses

The constitutional devices that the Founders invented to smooth out anticipated intergovernmental problems are still in use. In addition, the states in some areas cooperate voluntarily.

Full Faith and Credit The Constitution provides that each state must recognize as legal in civil matters the acts and court decisions of other states. Wills, marriage licenses, corporation charters, and a host of other legal transactions are covered by the **full faith and credit clause**.

But criminal decisions are a different matter. States need not recognize the criminal decisions of other states. So conduct that Connecticut defines as criminal, for example, is not necessarily illegal in Missouri. Only occasionally do difficulties arise. In divorce, child custody cases, and even wills, for example, states may disagree over the legal residence of the people involved. California, Nevada, Utah, and Texas all claimed the late billionaire Howard Hughes as a resident and the right to tax his estate. The case has traveled through a half dozen state and federal courts.

Interstate Rendition A couple commits a crime in Montana and flees to New Mexico, where police arrest them. If Montana wants to prosecute, its governor must formally request New Mexico's governor to turn the prisoners over to Montana officials[23]—a process called **interstate rendition**.

The Supreme Court has interpreted the Constitution as not absolutely requiring a state to turn over an accused person. A governor may refuse and give no reason. Most of the requests relate to felony cases.

Cases of refusal are rare. Governor Ray Blanton of Tennessee refused Oklahoma's request for a "Grand Old Opry" performer, Faron Young, who was wanted in connection with a New Year's Eve fracas at a performance in Tulsa. In the past, northern state governors occasionally refused to return Afro-Americans to southern states or escapees from chain gangs.

Privileges and Immunities Unreasonable discrimination against out-of-staters is prohibited by the **privileges and immunities clause**. But arguments sometimes arise over what is reasonable. We know that state colleges and universities, for example, may charge significantly higher tuition fees to out-of-state residents. And out-of-staters usually pay more for hunting and fishing licenses. On the other hand, a state may not keep out nonresidents as California tried to do to "Okies" and "Arkies" during the Great Depression. Nor may states prevent nonresidents from starting a business or owning property.

Undoubtedly almost every state discriminates against out-of-staters. They may keep out competing produce or nursery stock, for example, by requiring extensive inspections. Out-of-state lawyers may find it difficult to pass the bar examination. The Supreme Court decides such matters on a case-by-case basis. It has been unwilling to intervene except in extreme cases of discrimination or denial of civil liberties.

Voluntary Cooperation

Part of the reason we have a U.S. Constitution is that New York and New Jersey could not agree on the building of a lighthouse at Sandy Hook. Their representatives hoped to settle the issue at the Annapolis Convention, which set the stage for the Constitutional Convention. In the 1980s boundary disputes were still political issues between Texas and New Mexico, and Kentucky and Illinois.

The advantages of voluntary cooperation generally must be obvious before a state is willing to cooperate. For example, all of us benefited when states agreed to adopt the same type of traffic signals. The states or cities that had already invested heavily in the "wrong" kind of signal, however, were reluctant to scrap their equipment immediately for the common good. Nevertheless, as technology develops, the pressures for voluntary cooperation increase. Then officials are more inclined to join in voluntary programs and ignore sunk costs in existing practices.

Reciprocal and Retaliatory Legislation Perhaps the simplest method of cooperating is mutual regard among states—"We'll honor your law if you honor ours." These arrangements are formalized in **reciprocal legislation**. So you need to obtain an auto license only in one state—the others all recognize it as legal. If some states did not so reciprocate, as is the case with some states with regard to truck licensing, we would expect other states to pass **retaliatory legislation**.

Some reciprocal arrangements involve only a few states. Wisconsin and Minnesota allow each other's residents, under certain conditions, to enroll as state residents in either university system. Other states build retaliatory walls. Florida and California must deal with out-of-state physicians nearing retirement age who wish to practice there. They put up stiff accreditation barriers. Other states have reciprocal arrangements for lawyers, allowing them to practice without demanding they take the state bar examination.

The Uniform Law Movement In 1892 a committee of the American Bar Association proposed that all states adopt a **uniform law** regulating commercial transactions. They formed the National Commission for Uniform Laws, which is now affiliated with the Council of State Governments. Their first success was the Uniform Negotiable Instruments Act. Forty or more states have now adopted a Uniform Narcotics Drug Act, a traffic code, and a consumer credit code. But it is difficult to keep the laws uniform. State supreme courts interpret uniform laws differently. And individual state legislatures from time to time amend the laws to fit local conditions. Thus change creeps in despite good intentions.

Agreements and Compacts States may join with other states in **compacts**—in effect legal agreements to achieve a common purpose—179 are now in operation, most of recent origin. Congress must formally approve but, for some types of compacts, has given advance approval.

At first, states used compacts to develop and control rivers. The seven states of the Colorado River Compact built Hoover Dam. But states now use compacts for a wide variety of purposes—more than 60 are concerned with education. Congress in 1980 required states to join compacts or go it alone to create low-level radioactive waste disposal sites.

The Council of State Governments In 1933 the state governments formed an association to serve as a clearinghouse of information. The **Council of State Governments** publishes the biennial *Book of the States*, a journal called *State*

Government, and a great many specialized reports. It provides technical advice to individual states and is an umbrella organization for many associations of state officials—legislators, chief justices, attorneys general, lieutenant governors, and administrative officials. The governors split off to form their own National Governors' Association.

National Coordination

The framers seemed to believe that little coordination of state activities was necessary. Only rarely would the federal court need to resolve conflict. Their view proved largely correct until the Civil War.

Federal Assumption of Services Very rarely and mainly only in the twentieth century has the national government assumed total responsibility for programs that once were under state jurisdiction. Some exceptions include establishing the Federal Reserve System in 1914, Old Age and Survivors Insurance under the Social Security program in 1935, and the Tennessee Valley Authority in 1935. Each of these actions took over existing programs of some states and merged them with a new national effort. Several required heavy financial investments that were thought to be beyond a state's capability.

Presently some professionals, as well as many of the nation's governors, urge the federal government to take full responsibility for welfare programs—both in financing and in administration. This would include the Medicaid program of health care for those unable to pay.

Change Through Constitutional Amendment Most amendments coming after the first ten have restricted state powers. That is not astonishing because Congress thus far has proposed all the changes. The states, of course, may petition Congress to call a new constitutional convention. By 1990, 31 of the required 34 states adopted such a resolution to enact an amendment requiring a balanced federal budget. It would be a severe check on national powers. In addition, the National Governors' Association has endorsed a proposal to permit states to initiate constitutional amendments.

Several of the adopted amendments have dealt with expanded voting privileges—a matter the framers left to the states. Some states had already liberalized voting, but the amendments significantly changed the political process in other states and communities. Besides these, the major assertions of national authority through amendment were abolishing slavery and allowing the national government to levy an income tax.

Supreme Court Rulings The amendment process is a cumbersome way to bring about change. More changes have come through court interpretations of the Constitution itself. The federal courts act as the referee of the federal system. "States' righters," however, complain that the judges wear the uniforms of the Washington "Nationals" rather than being neutral umpires. The National Association of Attorneys General has a program to improve the effectiveness of state representation before the Court.[24]

Uniform court decisions, though, are necessary concerning many matters today, if chaos is to be avoided. Beginning with Justice John Marshall's early decisions, the Supreme Court has become a force for national uniformity with respect to civil rights; treatment of criminals; free speech, press, and religion; the structure of state governments (one person, one vote); and initially the content of policies on such matters as abortion. John Gates argues that when the court overrules a state law it is generally bringing it into conformity with prevailing political party realignments.[25]

Critics say the Court has moved too fast and too far ahead of public opinion, as for example in the busing and abortion decisions. In matters such as divorce and child custody we might argue that perhaps the Court has dragged its feet too long. It allows a diversity that occasionally leads to unnecessary complications, legal costs, and heartbreak.

In a 1988 decision, *South Carolina v. Baker*, the Court allowed the federal government to tax interest that the owners of state and local bonds receive. If Congress decides to impose the tax, it would raise the interest rates states and local units would have to pay when they borrow.

The Advisory Commission on Intergovernmental Relations In the 1950s President Dwight Eisenhower created a commission to recommend functions that the states could "take back." Though state officials participated, the effort came to little—only two functions, vocational education and design of municipal waste treatment plants, were singled out. To "take these functions back," the states would have to take over financing. Governors listened glumly and declined.[26]

But the commission persuaded Congress to establish a permanent body, the **Advisory Commission on Intergovernmental Relations (ACIR)**, to be made up of state, local, and national officials with a research staff. The ACIR sponsors studies, providing an ongoing assessment of the federal system, and recommends improvements in structure and procedures. Generally it has avoided polemical arguments and, instead, has concentrated on strengthening states and communities and on finding ways for governments to cooperate in pursuit of common goals. Still, it has become sharply critical of some aspects of modern federalism—especially the "overload" features of grantsmanship federalism.

Federal Grant Programs Perhaps the most successful method the national government has used to achieve uniformity and some degree of coordination is the use of grants. Congress has made its own adaptation of the old adage, "You can catch more flies with honey than you can with vinegar." The federal government offers the state or community governments funds for programs—if they agree to follow certain guidelines. As of 1987, the ACIR counted 422 grants, an increase of 30 over the figure three years before.[27]

This practice dates back to before the Union was formed. Under the Articles of Confederation "western" lands were surveyed into townships—6-mile-square areas divided into 36-square-mile sections. Congress required the states to set aside the revenue from the sale of a section in each township, and later two sections, to support public schools. The federal government also used the **land grant** procedure to encourage states to establish agricultural colleges and, of course, to encourage private operators to build railroads. Another type of grant is called **tax offset**. Congress levies a federal tax. Then if a state levies the same tax, the citizen has to pay only the state tax. Congress used tax offset for inheritance taxes, for example.

Most grants today take the form of direct payments. Many require **matching funds** from states or localities, although by 1980 over 90 percent required less than a one-for-one match. Congress also began **bypassing** the states and sending funds directly to communities, so members of Congress would get full political credit for the grant from their constituents. In 1960 only 8 percent bypassed; by 1978 it was 25 percent.[28] More recently, however, states have been more successful with demands that federal grants pass through the state government.

There are several major types of federal grants. Our list begins with those that give the federal granting agency the most control.

Categorical Grants The ACIR estimates that 85.6 percent of federal grant funds in 1987 were in **categorical grant** programs. These are directed at specific, narrowly defined activities. They spell out standards and fund all units that meet them. Most of the funds are distributed by formula. Many of these may also be **open end grants** through which the federal government agrees to pay a fixed percentage of all qualified program costs without regard to an overall limit. Such programs are called **entitlement grants** when individuals who qualify automatically receive benefits.

Some of the largest categorical grant programs are in public assistance and medical care. For example, Medicaid requires states to provide 8 basic services. But they may choose also to offer 17 other programs that the federal government funds at different levels. Washington pays at least half the cost, and a greater share in poorer states. Still, some high-income states provide broader services than do low-income states and consequently draw a disproportionately high share of the federal funds while spending a great deal of their own money too, of course. Thus states have some flexibility. Some say that the feds' payment of much of the bill may encourage "sloppy administration." Medicaid and other such categorical grant programs have been plagued with administrative and cost problems.

James A. Maxwell and J. Richard Aronson observed that categorical open end grants assume that the program services eligible for federal aid can be defined with fair precision and that policy implementation is not difficult. They note that both of these assumptions are seldom correct.[29]

Project Grants **Project grants** are a type of categorical grant, distinguished by the method in which the feds allocate the funds. States or communities compete for these grants. Not all applications are funded. Thus the federal agency administrator can insist that all terms be met—and even force changes. These work well for experimental programs and demonstration projects. They are often used to pioneer in areas of new federal involvement or to improve weak programs. Most authorities recommend that project grants be short-term and that project results be carefully evaluated.

The Johnson administration favored such grants and introduced many of them as part of the Great Society programs. State and community politicians criticize them because it tilts power to the federal officials making the grants and because it gives those units with the best grants personnel most of the money rather than directing it to areas of greatest need.

Block Grants President Richard Nixon proposed to loosen up grant requirements by assigning funds to a general area of activity and allowing local governments to choose projects from a list of approved activities.

In 1987 ACIR estimated that 12 percent of grant funds were in such **block grants**. Congress often allocates block grant funds to all states or localities as a matter of entitlement according to a prearranged formula. The best "grantsmanship players" thus do not gain a lion's share of the funds. But federal funds also may go to units that are not particularly needy.

During Richard Nixon's presidency, Congress tried block grants for housing and community development, crime control, employment and training, and mass transportation. President Reagan supported this approach as well in 1981 and persuaded Congress to combine 57 categorical grant programs into 9 block grants. Although Reagan reduced the amount of money in the programs, he argued that overall efficiency would improve because states would be entangled with less red tape.

General Revenue Sharing In another Nixon program in 1972, Congress passed the State and Local Assistance Act, commonly called **general revenue sharing**. Federal funds were distributed to states and all counties, cities, villages, townships, and Indian reservations. The distribution formula favored poorer states and those with heavier taxes. To the astonishment of many local officials, the program had few federal strings—the most important related to budgetary and audit reports, antidiscrimination requirements, and citizen participation. After renewing the program several times, Congress eliminated revenue sharing altogether in September 1986.[30]

The Future of Federal Grants Michael Reagan identifies the problems associated with federal grants. First is the "distribution problem." Often rich states get richer while the poor states are unable to raise matching funds. Second is an "allocation problem." Local governments skew their budgets to obtain free federal money and underfund other functions. Third is a "problem of neglect." Some functions receive few or no grants. Finally we find a "coordination problem." Grant programs sometimes conflict with each other.[31]

Allen Schick says national leaders in the 1960s blamed all program confusion and failures on inadequacies in local delivery systems. But policy leaders of the 1970s and 1980s saw the problem as too much "intrusion by Washington into the conduct of government by states and localities." They concluded that "meaningful and enduring remedies would not be forthcoming unless the federal government stopped telling local officials how to run their programs." Thus they began experimenting with block grants and revenue sharing.[32]

THE CROSSROAD FUNCTION OF THE STATES

The British political scientist Harold Laski wrote in 1939, "American federalism is obsolescent and should be abandoned."[33] A present-day political commentator, Michael Kinsley, agrees. He writes, "Anyone truly concerned about making America more productive, more democratic, less wasteful, less bureaucratic, would want to hasten the withering away of the states."[34]

The Obsolescence of Federalism?

Some political scientists regard federalism as a transitional or intermediate form of government. Martin Landau suggested we should not struggle to maintain a "specified balance of power and jurisdiction between state and nation." Rather, he says, we should regard federalism as "a problem-solving device that possesses utility only for a specified set of conditions." He argues that "once upon a time this country embarked on a voyage to nationhood." The Founders established a federal system as a way of creating a unified nation. And now "that nation concealed under federalism [has] finally emerged." The need for a federal division of powers has ended. "It is one of those instruments so designed as to outmode itself by its achievements." It has been a "dramatic success" and is now no longer necessary.[35]

A Defense of Federalism

We can defend federalism for America only if the states still fulfill some special role and needed purpose, important enough to outweigh the frustrations and complexities that critics rightfully point out. Supporters say that role is serving as political mediators at the crossroads between the national majority and the majorities that exist in communities. They help in hammering out acceptable political compromises. They help bring about gradual rather than rapid or dramatic changes.

Reducing Value Conflict As a nation we are not yet so united as to wipe out all distinctions among citizens of a state or of different states. For example, states vary widely in their laws on gambling. Nevada and New Jersey have casino gambling. A growing number operate lotteries, while some are relatively straitlaced. If we had a uniform national law, what would the national policy be—wide open gambling in the Nevada style, some nationally regulated gambling, or no legal gambling at all? We may wonder whether having uniformity in this case is that necessary or important and whether variation might not have some benefits.

This boils down, we think, to whether a national consensus exists with respect to an issue and how important that issue is. If most agree on the question, the benefits of diversity among the states are largely imagined—as with traffic markers for example.[36] If we cannot agree, or even if an intense minority disagrees, conflict such as erupted over the Supreme Court's decisions on busing and abortion will likely result. Conflicts tend to be most intense over cultural, moral, and lifestyle issues.

But in some cases we may conclude the issue is too important to allow diversity. We may think conflict to achieve uniformity is a price well worth paying. For example, the decision in **Brown v. Board of Education** declaring segregation in the schools unconstitutional created a great deal of social conflict and still does. But most Americans have now concluded it was a just decision worth the turmoil. Deciding when an issue demands uniformity is a political question in which states can signal the need for change as some did with respect to civil rights.

Administrative Efficiency Vincent Ostrom attacks those he calls "centralists" for assuming that administrative efficiency will result when all direction and decisions come from the center. He argues rather that political power at the state and community levels encourages efficiency. Community feedback must be given attention because these units are more than administrative field offices. It allows selective innovations, which if unsuccessful, are limited to a single unit. If successful, policymakers can make the innovation national in scope.[37]

Political Training Grounds State and community offices have often been a training ground, a place to sort out politicians, an arena from which to select national leaders. Ronald Reagan, Michael Dukakis, Jimmy Carter, and Walter Mondale all first held state offices. State and especially community governments offer ordinary citizens who are nonprofessionals in government work the opportunity to "play" at politics when they are not yet sure they want to make a career of it.

Federalism and Freedom Democracy relies on an effective and critical opposition. The federal system provides important elective offices that the national party out of power may capture. They may be used as a platform to criticize policies of the national administration.

States may also protect the freedom of local majorities to resist national majorities. Some political scientists, though, say that the local majorities states have protected have often been groups that were discriminating against minorities within their boundaries.[38]

Nevertheless, we suspect that many believe that federalism does protect freedom, especially the freedom of citizens to oppose arbitrary national policy—a tendency of national officials who push for uniformity for its own sake. For example, consider the continuing opposition to a single national police force under the FBI.

But opposition does more than fight national initiatives—there are positive aspects. Long before the national government did so, a number of states abolished slavery, repealed the poll tax, extended the vote to blacks, women, and 18-year-olds, provided for direct election of U.S. senators, and established primary elections.

HOW STATES AVOID NATIONAL DOMINATION

Perhaps the framers assumed that the Constitution would preserve the states from national domination. But a centralizing Supreme Court interpreting these clauses has tended to rule against the states. The battle in the administrative arena is something of a standoff. States have defended themselves best in the arena of elective politics.

State Political Influence

The states exercise political influence in many ways. In 1988, for example, 14 U.S. senators and 1 U.S. representative were once governors of their states, an experience that some argue makes them sympathetic to state concerns. Perhaps more important though is the fact that members of Congress as well as the president need local support to be nominated and elected.[39]

Local Congressional Ties The Constitution requires national legislators to live in the state electing them. Custom generally demands that U.S. representatives also live in their districts. Thus, if defeated, the "national" legislator, as a practical matter, can only get back in Congress by being reelected in the home state or home district. So national legislators must cultivate local voters and interest groups.[40]

National legislators also cultivate state and community officials through varied ways. These officials have ready access to the local media. They can give favorable or unfavorable publicity to the national legislator. Our daily newspapers frequently carry small news items that announce formal and informal meetings between these national legislators and governors, members of the state bureaucracy, or state legislators. Members of Congress have their staffs contact state or local officials with specialized knowledge to find out what impact a national proposal may have back home.

At the same time, state legislators and administrators lobby their national representatives. The governor becomes state spokesperson marshaling state forces into temporary coalitions. Such initiatives may also come from state-based interest groups, mayors, professional administrators, and program specialists of private agencies or state legislators. Or the action may begin with a national group prodding local officials "to call or write their representatives in Congress."[41]

Presidential Ties to States and Communities The way presidential candidates get nominated and elected requires cultivation of state and local officials and thus provides another avenue for states to gain national influence. It is "winner take all" with respect to a state's electoral votes. Close elections may be decided by the electoral votes of a few large states. State politicians or interest groups just might be the difference between winning or losing those states.

National Influence on State Officials The reverse is also true. Presidents have no official place in state politics. Still, they can exert informal pressure. They can campaign with state candidates or send members of the cabinet to do so. They can channel funds to state nominees. They can encourage national interest groups, Political Action Committees (PACs), to enter or stay out of a state. They may deny the state patronage jobs or state projects. And they can encourage the justice department or local federal attorneys to prosecute state or community officials when corruption is suspected.

But all of these methods of support or "discipline" hold some risk for the president and also for national party officials. The disciplined state or local politician may get reelected—indeed may gain new popularity by claiming "national interference." And the president may see congressional votes on "must" legislation fade away. Future support in elections may be lukewarm, as it was in some states after the disastrous Republican national convention of 1964, or that of the Democrats in 1972.

State Administrative Resistance State administrators sometimes resist what they regard as unwise or unworkable federal policy. They may get a federal agency to compromise or relax enforcement. Nebraska, Kentucky, Idaho, and Minnesota refused to provide mandatory training and testing for farmers who used toxic chemicals. The national Environmental Protection Agency compromised by requiring farmers to take some training, but agreed they did not have to pass a test to use the materials.

Or administrators may cooperate with other state officials to delay implementing a federal policy. Minnesota became the first state to require a state license from the board of health before a federal atomic energy facility could be built.[42] Federally imposed highway routes for double-trailer trucks were withdrawn in four states where officials challenged the regulations in court. A study of distribution of project grants to cities found local officials to be key decision makers in the process. The number and frequency of grant applications were related to the allocation patterns that emerged.[43]

States in the Federal Courts

States have won a few battles in the courts. The Pennsylvania legislature passed a law allowing it to "reappropriate" all federal grant funds, and the U.S. Supreme Court upheld the state challenge. In 1981 the New York courts ruled that its state legislature had such authority.[44] A number of states joined together to challenge successfully the Reagan administration attempt to add new regulations to the food stamp program.

In **National League of Cities** v. **Usery** (1976), the Court ruled that Congress could not extend the wage and hours provisions of the Fair Labor Standards Act to state and local employees—a decision states hailed as a major victory. But in 1985 in **Garcia v. San Antonio Metropolitan Transit Authority**, Justice Blackmun reversed his vote and overruled *Usery*.

Future results depend on the makeup of the Supreme Court. President Reagan replaced "nationalizing" judges with appointees with a stronger "state" orientation. Prospects for the states depend on who George Bush may appoint.

A FINAL COMMENT

The kind of complex system Americans have created has had many successes. Occasionally it also has been dismaying. Some say it is overloaded and cannot function effectively.

Yet what appears to be among the most complex, conflict-ridden, and frustrating of governing systems may be among the world's strongest because of its flexibility and ability to change gradually. Uniformity occurs when its needs seem clear-cut to many citizens. At the same time, it preserves local power to resist. It survives and is one of the two oldest governmental systems in today's changing world. John Bebout once observed that the national government has been the states' best friend—without its support, states could not otherwise exist as independently as they do.[45]

HIGH POINTS

In this chapter we looked first at (1) the legal powers of states, communities, commonwealths, territories, and possessions. We then examined (2) how power has gradually shifted to the national level. Next we considered (3) how the system operates. We then considered (4) the crossroads function of the states. We ended with (5) how states using their political powers defend themselves from federal domination.

In this chapter we defined the following terms in this order: unitary governments, confederation, federalism, federation, Bill of Rights, national supremacy clause, sovereign power, delegated powers, necessary and proper clause, concurrent powers, prohibited powers, reserved powers, dual federalism, *McCullough v. Maryland*, elastic clause, cooperative federalism, creative federalism, fiscal federalism, permissive federalism, picket fence federalism, functional federalism, grantsmanship federalism, New Federalism, full faith and credit clause, interstate rendition, privileges and immunities clause, reciprocal legislation, retaliatory legislation, uniform law, compact, the Council of State Governments, Advisory Commission on Intergovernmental Relations (ACIR), land grant, tax offset, matching funds, bypassing, categorical grants, open end grants, entitlement grants, project grants, block grants, general revenue sharing, *Brown v. Board of Education*, *National League of Cities v. Usery*, and *Garcia v. San Antonio Metropolitan Transit Authority*.

NOTES

1. John Steinbeck, *Travels with Charley, In Search of America* (New York: Bantam Books, 1962), p. 208, and William Least Heat Moon, *Blue Highways: A Journey into America* (Boston: Little Brown, 1982).

2. Burton J. Hendrick, *Statesmen of the Lost Cause, Jefferson Davis and His Cabinet* (New York: Literary Guild, 1939), pp. 409–432. Hendrick concludes that Davis, president of the Confederacy, was unable to direct the war effort effectively because of the central government's weakness. "It [the Southern Confederacy] was founded on a principle that made impossible the orderly conduct of public affairs" (p. ii).
3. Texans may be aware, though, that their state if it wishes may divide itself into four states—a privilege granted when it left the status of independent nationhood to join the union. So perhaps all states are equal. But in one respect, Texas is four times more equal than other states.
4. Kentucky, Massachusetts, Pennsylvania, and Virginia are called commonwealths. In a legal sense they are "states" nevertheless; the only American commonwealth (legally) is Puerto Rico.
5. Morton Grodzins, *The American System, A New View of Government in the United States* (Chicago: Rand McNally, 1966).
6. Daniel Elazar argues that these interventions indicate that we have from the beginning had a pattern of "cooperative federalism." For Elazar's argument, see *The American Partnership, Intergovernmental Cooperation in the Nineteenth-Century United States* (Chicago: University of Chicago Press, 1962). For a counterargument, see Harry N. Scheiber, *The Condition of American Federalism, An Historian's View* (Washington, D.C.: U.S. Government Printing Office, Committee on Government Operations, October 15, 1966).
7. David B. Walker, *Toward a Functioning Federalism*, (Cambridge, Mass.: Winthrop, 1981), pp. 46–99.
8. James L. Sundquist, "The Problem of Coordination in a Changing Federalism" in *Making Federalism Work* (Washington, D.C.: Brookings Institution, 1969), pp. 1–31.
9. Walker, *Toward a Functioning Federalism*, p. 225.
10. Michael D. Reagan, *The New Federalism* (New York: Oxford University Press, 1972).
11. Terry Sanford, *Storm Over the States* (New York: Oxford University Press, 1967), pp. 80–81; Samuel H. Beer, "The Adoption of General Revenue Sharing, A Case Study in Public Sector Politics," *Public Policy* 24 (Spring 1976): 127–195; and Harold Seidman, *Politics, Position, and Power, The Dynamics of Federal Organization* (New York: Oxford University Press, 1970), pp. 136–163.
12. David Cingranelli, "State Government Lobbies in the National Political Process," *State Government* 56 (1983): 122–127.
13. Donald H. Haider, *When Governments Come to Washington, Governors, Mayors and Inter-Governmental Lobbying* (New York: Free Press, 1974).
14. Walker, *Toward a Functioning Federalism*, pp. 181–184.
15. Julie Rooner, "Welfare Reform: The Issue That Bubbled Up from the States to Capitol Hill, *Governing* (December 1988): 17–21.
16. George E. Hale and Marian Lief Palley, *The Politics of Federal Grants* (Washington, D.C.: CQ Press, 1981), pp. 23–31.
17. Christopher Hamilton and Donald Wells, *Federalism, Power and Political Economy: A New Theory of Federalism's Impact on American Life* (Englewood Cliffs, N.J.: Prentice-Hall, 1989).
18. Charles E. Davis and James P. Lester, "Decentralizing Federal Environmental Policy: A Research Note," *Western Political Quarterly* (1987): 555–565.
19. David Osborne, *Laboratories of Democracy* (Cambridge: Harvard Business School Press, 1988).
20. William T. Gormley, Jr., "Intergovernmental Conflict on Environmental Policy: The Attitudinal Connection, *Western Political Quarterly* (1987): 285–303.

21. John E. Chubb, "Hopes, Fears, and Federalism." Paper given at the Constitutional Bicentennial Conference of the Nelson A. Rockefeller Center, Dartmouth College, October 21, 1986.
22. Walker, *Toward a Functioning Federalism*, pp. 192–203.
23. The process is sometimes called "extradition." But technically that term only applies to transactions between independent nations.
24. Douglas Ross, "Safeguarding Our Federalism: Lessons for the States from the Supreme Court," *Public Administration Review* (November 1985): 723–731.
25. John B. Gates, "Partisan Realignment, Unconstitutional State Policies, and the U.S. Supreme Court, 1837–1964," *American Journal of Political Science* 31 (1987): 259–280.
26. Glenn E. Brooks, *When Governors Convene* (Baltimore: Johns Hopkins Press, 1961), pp. 100–105.
27. ACIR, *A Catalog of Federal Grant-In-Aid Programs to State and Local Government, Grants Funded FY 1987* (Washington, D.C.: U.S. Government Printing Office, August 1987).
28. Chubb, "Hopes, Fears, and Federalism," p. 4.
29. James A. Maxwell and J. Richard Aronson, *Financing State and Local Governments* (3rd ed.) (Washington, D.C.: Brookings Institution, 1977), p. 67.
30. For passage of the act see Richard E. Thompson, *Revenue Sharing, A New Era in Federalism?* (Washington, D.C.: Revenue Sharing Advisory Service, 1973). For evaluations see Committee on Government Operation, U.S. Senate, *Revenue Sharing, A Selection of Recent Research* (Washington, D.C.: U.S. Government Printing Office, 1975), pp. 8–19, and Robert P. Nathan, et al., *Revenue Sharing, The Second Round* (Washington, D.C.: Brookings Institution, 1977).
31. Michael D. Reagan and John G. Sanzone, *The New Federalism* (New York: Oxford University Press, 1981), pp. 81–123.
32. Allen Schick, "Conceptual Perspectives on Policy Management Assistance," *Public Administration Review* (December 1975): 719.
33. Harold J. Laski, "The Obsolescence of Federalism," *The New Republic* (May 3, 1939): 367–369.
34. Michael Kinsley, "The Withering Away of the States," *The New Republic* (March 28, 1981): 17–21. See also Christopher Jencks, "Why Bail Out the States?" *The New Republic* (December 12, 1964): 8–10.
35. Martin Landau, "Baker v. Carr and the Ghost of Federalism," in Glendon Schubert (ed.), *Reapportionment* (New York: Charles Scribner's Sons, 1965), pp. 241–248.
36. Yet we find that Wyoming wants yellow lines on highways rather than white ones—you can see yellow better in the snow.
37. Vincent Ostrom, *The Political Theory of a Compound Republic* (Blacksburg, Va.: Public Choice Publication, 1971).
38. William H. Riker, *Federalism, Origin, Operation, Significance* (Boston: Little, Brown, 1964). See also Franz Neumann, "Federalism and Freedom, A Critique," in Arthur W. Macmahon (ed.), *Federalism, Mature and Emergent* (Garden City, N.Y.: Doubleday, 1955), pp. 44–57.
39. George Rabinowitz and Stuart Elaine MacDonald, "The Power of the States in U.S. Presidential Elections," *American Political Science Review* 80 (March 1986): 65–87.
40. The classic discussion is found in Morton Grodzins, "American Political Parties and the American System," *Western Political Quarterly* 13 (December 1960): 974–988.

41. Martha Derthick, *Uncontrollable Spending for Social Service Grants* (Washington, D.C.: Brookings Institution, 1975).
42. Helen Ingram, "Policy Implementation through Bargaining, The Case of Federal Grants-in-Aid," *Public Policy* 25 (1977): 501–526.
43. Michael J. Rich, "Distributive Politics and the Allocation of Federal Grants," *American Political Science Review* 83 (March 1989): 193–213.
44. Joseph F. Zimmerman, "N.Y. Legislature Given Role in Spending Federal Funds," *Comparative State Politics Newsletter* 2 (August 1981): 26.
45. John E. Bebout, "The States' Best Friend," *National Civic Review* 53 (February 1964): 70–73.

Chapter 4

State Constitutions

Few states have a constitutional heritage equal to that of Connecticut—the "Constitution State." A dramatic incident involving the Charter Oak happened in 1687.[1] The Connecticut colony received an unusually liberal **royal charter** from Charles II in 1662. It did not even provide for a royal governor; it allowed the legislature to choose its own! But his successor, James II, revoked the charter and merged Connecticut into a "Dominion of New England." He appointed Sir

Edmund Andros as governor general. The news that Andros wanted the old charter returned reached Connecticut during Christmas 1686—but the legislative assembly ignored him. Finally, the next October, Andros arrived with a body of soldiers. The "People's Governor," John Treat, spoke all afternoon and into the evening hours against relinquishing the charter. Suddenly the candles went out. When they were relit, the charter was gone.

A Captain Joseph Wadsworth hid it in the hollow of a white oak tree. It lay there for over a year. After the Glorious Revolution of 1688, with William and Mary replacing James II, Connecticut politicians took the document out of the "Charter Oak," dusted it off, and restored it to its old legal position.[2]

Such stirring events remind us of happenings today in the nations of Eastern Europe. But **state constitutions** have fallen on harder times. Most are not held in much reverence anymore. Reformers, as well as academicians, sometimes describe them as outmoded—"horse and buggy" documents. Occasionally we come across an item such as what Diane Blair found in the Arkansas constitution—the highway commission is required to have five members, each from a different congressional district, an impossibility because there are now only four congressional districts.[3] Everyone smiles and nods their heads—"state constitutions are antiques." All the glory that was Connecticut's is forgotten.

A Defense of State Constitutions We are among the defenders of state constitutions. We think that scholars, newspaper reporters, and others should view them with more sympathy and understanding. We suggest that the nineteenth-century politicians who wrote the original drafts of almost two-thirds of our present state constitutions deserve the benefit of the doubt.

Overview We begin with the legal theory of state constitutions and how it gives power to judges. Then we look at why state constitutions are so important—they set rules that distribute long-term costs and benefits. Next we examine how constitutions get cluttered with legislative detail and how this sometimes leads to stalemate. We review recommendations to streamline constitutions. We argue that the detail reformers object to results from citizens attempting to deal with unsettling social change. We then assess the arguments against longer documents. Finally, we note how federal courts and the states themselves bring about change.

THE LEGAL THEORY

The colonists developed a taste for written documents that spelled out governmental structure and their rights as British citizens. The royal charters inspired the first state constitutions—Connecticut and Rhode Island, for example, merely changed the word "king" to "people" and adopted them as their first constitutions.

The Influence of John Locke

The writings of the English political theorist John Locke (1632–1704) guided these early constitution writers. He argued that constitutions are a contract between "the People" and those who govern them. Only the people through special delegates they select should draft these documents—contracts specifying the powers given to officials who run the government. The constitution sets limits on their powers and spells out governmental structure. The people must approve the document before it goes into effect.

Locke argued that these constitutional rules have a higher legal status than ordinary laws. Every official act of governors, legislators, administrators, judges, or local public officials must be in harmony with the constitution, or be declared invalid. These were the conditions that the people set when they agreed to let governments make the day-to-day rules.

Finally, Locke's theory held that the process of making changes in the contract should be more difficult than that used in passing an ordinary law. The people might choose to have a constitutional convention propose a new document. And if a new constitution is proposed or the old one amended, the citizens must approve.[4]

How State and Federal Constitutions Differ The federal constitution is the supreme law of the land. State constitutional clauses that conflict with it are unconstitutional—they have no legal status.

The national government can act only according to the delegated powers granted it. Article 1, Section 8, lists most of these powers. State governments have reserved powers—they can exercise any power they wish, except those specifically forbidden by their own constitutions or by the federal constitution. Listing these "thou shalt nots" makes state constitutions wordy.[5]

Finally, state constitution-making is more democratic. State constitutions allow citizens to vote on the original document and, except in Delaware, on amendments. The national constitution allows neither.

Constitutions Turn Judges into Policymakers Someone has to decide what the phrases in state constitutions mean and whether they conflict with the national constitution. In America, we turn to the judges and call the process **judicial review**. Justices of the Supreme Court thus become major policymakers in our federal system. Policy Box No. 7 asks, "Should Five U.S. Supreme Court Justices Decide Major Policy Questions for the States?"

WHY STATE CONSTITUTIONS ARE SO IMPORTANT

The period before the Civil War was the springtime and summer of our federal system. At that time, citizens saw that the laws hammered out at state capitols often had much more influence on their day-to-day lives than did most of the statutes trickling out from Washington. What went into state constitutions was not

Policy Box No. 7

Should Five U.S. Supreme Court Justices Decide Major Policy Questions for the States?

A major revolution in state government has occurred in the last 50 years or so. Federal courts have read the U.S. Constitution to mean that state and local legislatures, but not the U.S. Senate, must be apportioned on a one person, one vote basis. Their rulings have affected procedures for trying criminals and incarcerating the guilty, abortion, school prayer, and a host of other matters that the states once decided.

Some have criticized the federal courts for reading into the Constitution meanings that aren't there and were never intended to be. But are the meanings of those graceful constitutional clauses so self-evident? Well, not exactly. Take the Eighth Amendment, which reads, "Excessive bail shall not be required nor excessive fines imposed, nor cruel and unusual punishments inflicted." That now applies to state governments.

What is excessive bail? $50? $5,000? $50,000? $500,000? What is an excessive fine? Is the death penalty cruel and unusual punishment, as some people now argue?

Did the federal courts usurp this power? The Constitution is silent on who is to say what its various clauses really mean and how a state law or action is to be declared unconstitutional. Legal scholars have disagreed about the intent of the framers—though in Federalist Paper 78, Alexander Hamilton forecast that judges might undertake the job of judicial review. Nevertheless, the argument has never quite died out. As the legal scholar Alan Westin notes in his introduction to Charles Beard's *The Supreme Court and the Constitution*, "Since the founding of the Court, every political generation in American history has had a major popular debate over the interventionist posture of the Supreme Court."

We list here some of the possibles (other than judges) who might interpret the Constitution. Since we use state legislatures to ratify most constitutional amendments, why not let them be part of the decision making on the constitutionality of major policies? James Madison, the Father of the Constitution, and Thomas Jefferson endorsed such a proposal (called the Kentucky and Virginia resolutions). Or a body of the state chief justices could make such rulings. The state justices themselves made this proposal in the 1950s. Or we could set up a judicial body that contained both state and federal justices, not federal judges alone. Some have even suggested that the state governors could add this function of judicial interpretation to their duties.

Others, such as the historian Henry Steele Commager, have pointed out that in many democracies, including Great Britain, it is the legislative body itself that decides what is constitutional. He argued that this should be the case in a true democracy. The members of Congress and state legislatures are democratically elected, as federal judges are not. Therefore, they can best decide what the citizens desire and what the Constitution means. They, rather than the courts, propose formal constitutional amendments. If the voters don't like their decisions, they can vote them out of office.

The most frequent criticism of letting a five-to-four majority of the Supreme Court make major policy is that this is basically an undemocratic procedure and one unfair to the states. Federal judges are national officials. State views are not represented. And current opinion may also not be represented. Some propose that federal judges should be elected to set terms, as is the case for many state judges.

During the Progressive period, at the turn of the century, it was suggested that Supreme Court decisions should be subject to referenda by the voters, or they should be treated like a presidential veto, with Congress being able to override them with a two-thirds vote. Other reformers proposed that constitutional questions require nine-to-zero votes or at least a six-to-three or seven-to-two majority of the nine judges. Or decisions might be overruled when three-fourths of the state legislatures so decide, as is the case with ratifying constitutional amendments, since what the justices decide is often in effect an "amendment" to the Constitution.

But federal judges as interpreters of the Constitution also have their defenders. No other body, the defenders say, would have time to consider all the policy questions—especially the many laws and practices of the 50 states. In addition, we need some body that has a national rather than a state view of the public interest. Many of the most controversial decisions that the Supreme Court has made have been on behalf of citizens who were not adequately represented in a state's political process—the reapportionment cases, civil rights decisions concerning blacks and other minorities who were discriminated against, and cases that dealt with treatment of those accused of crimes and religious freedom for small and sometimes unpopular sects. Fair play requires that someone from the outside make the decision.

Others maintain that as undemocratic as their selection and tenure are, as a body federal judges do respond in the long run to the best in our democratic traditions. They are sensitive to the public opinion of their day. When they go too far ahead of current opinion or drop too far behind it, a reaction inevitably occurs on the Court itself. Law Professor G. Edward White of the University of Virginia says the justices know that the public will not accept as legitimate a decision that is regarded widely as "immoral" or "unjust."

What do you think? Is it fair to the states to have a body in which they have no representation decide major state issues? Should a democracy allow major policy changes to be made by five elderly jurists—overwhelmingly Protestant, white, and male? Should our elected officials at the state or national level or the people themselves have some say in the process? What kinds of policy changes would result if they did? Which citizens would benefit least from such a change?

just irritating gobbledygook to nineteenth-century Americans—the clauses spelled out the daily rules of how one lived and made a living. And although less influential today, they still affect our daily lives in important ways. For that reason citizens and politicians struggled over constitutional clauses.

State Constitutions Are Political Documents

The Virginia constitutional convention of 1829–1830 was star-studded. Delegates included the governor, ex-governors, and U.S. Senator John Randolph. Former President James Monroe was presiding officer, and when he became ill, Philip Barbour, then Speaker of the U.S. House, replaced him. Ex-president James Madison chaired the committee on the executive department, and U.S. Chief Justice John Marshall headed the judiciary committee. With such talent, the convention should have produced a model document.

Instead, the sessions were acrimonious. Deadlocks were frequent. Delegates talked of splitting into two states! The slaveholding east wanted property qualifications for voting. The high-country west did not.

The Politics of Constitution Writing Chapman Johnson led the westerners. He summarized what the battles were about:

> We are engaged, Mr. Chairman, in a contest for power... Sir, all our metaphysical reasoning and our practical rules, all our scholastic learning and political wisdom, are but the arms employed in the contest, which involves the great and agitating question—whether the scepter shall pass away from Judah.[6]

His language was more biblical than we are used to.[7] Today we would say, "These constitutional debates are not about theory, but whether the rules are to benefit tidewater Virginians at the expense of the rest of us."

Rules are seldom neutral. U.S. Supreme Court Justice Oliver Wendell Holmes (1841–1935) observed that when governments change a statute or a constitutional clause, they take burdens off one group of citizens and place them on the backs of others. Getting those burdens placed in ways that groups or individuals accept is what the politics of constitution writing is all about.

All of us have opinions about how costs and benefits should be distributed. Sometimes we think it only fair that some should pay less and others more. It always comes back to the question of whom the rules benefit. In Virginia the convention delegates fought over whether the new constitution would serve the east's "peculiar institution" of slavery at the expense of the settlers of the western frontier—at least that's how westerners saw it.

How Missouri Allocated Costs A clause from Missouri's constitution, in effect until 1954, provides a striking example of how constitutional clauses distribute political costs and benefits. The content of the first sentence can probably be found in every other state constitution:

> A general diffusion of knowledge and intelligence being essential to the preservation of the rights and liberties of the people, the General Assembly shall establish and maintain free public schools for the gratuitous instruction of all persons in the state within ages not in excess of twenty-one years, as prescribed by law.

Nineteenth-century reformers Horace Mann, Massachusetts superintendent of schools, and William T. Harris, who opened the nation's first permanent kindergarten in St. Louis in 1873, had to fight hard to get state constitutions to guarantee free schooling. Note who receives added burdens.

Free schooling is a **redistributive policy**, one that reallocates costs and benefits. Communities could no longer deprive the children of poor families of an education because their parents could not afford to pay. Girls also had the right to free education. We take this unequal sharing of costs for granted nowadays. We tax all residents to pay to educate children of the poor. Residents who have no children of school age have to pay to educate other people's children! Listen carefully and you will hear this complaint even today. Some groups, for example, suggest that people over age 62 should not have to pay school taxes.

Also in Missouri, boys now had to compete with girls for grades and school prizes. Later, boys may have found the same competition when applying for admission to college or entering the job market, though that took some time coming.[8]

Long-Term Effects Such constitutional clauses have a longer-term impact than ordinary law. Look at the next sentence of this Missouri constitutional clause.

> Separate schools shall be provided for white and colored children, except in cases otherwise provided by law.

This clause was the law, from 1821 when Missouri became a state until the U.S. Supreme Court ruled such clauses unconstitutional in *Brown v. Board of Education*. But in 1903, if the principal of an all-white St. Louis school had decided to admit a dozen or so blacks from the community in which ragtime pianist Scott Joplin then lived, what would have happened? Many unpleasant things. Legally, the sheriff would have had to arrest the principal, unless, of course, the state legislature had specifically authorized school integration. Getting the authorization would have been very, very difficult. And getting that sentence rooted out of the Missouri Constitution in 1903 would have been next to impossible.

WHAT DO STATE CONSTITUTIONS CONTAIN?

To most of us the prospect of curling up in a big easy chair on a rainy Sunday afternoon with a copy of our state constitution is, well, not inviting. Yet many of us have scanned the seven articles that make up our national constitution. Why the difference in our reactions?

Our Cluttered State Constitutions

State constitutions have a growth and weight problem. You can read the 10,000 or so words of the federal constitution in about a half hour. Connecticut, Indiana, Minnesota, New Hampshire, and Vermont have shorter constitutions, and eight others are about as long as the national document. But the average is about three times longer.[9] So you may find your state constitution to be a somewhat bulky document. Moreover, state constitutions keep getting longer. In 1800 they averaged 5,000 words. By 1914 they grew to 19,000. Today the average is 28,254 words. Their growth rate is about 15 percent per decade.[10]

Style Deficiencies   Our national constitution has some class. Its clauses roll out with a fine sweep. Its old-fashioned phrasing breathes an air of quiet dignity. If you dip into your state constitution, you may find your eyes getting tired and restless. You begin skipping and your reading bogs down. Awkward legal constructions and convoluted sentences make for dull reading. Many clauses are likely to deal with minor matters—what critics call **legislative detail** that they say could be better handled in statutes. No one, for example, would want to amend the federal constitution for a matter as insignificant as how to get a dog license or California's guarantee that residents have "the right to fish." Groups, though, have no such inhibitions about state constitutions.

Many of our state constitutions also have shoddy construction. When university researchers looked into Florida's 70-year-old constitution, being the professors they were, they spotted over 200 misspellings and grammatical errors. It is difficult to be properly reverential in the face of such sloppiness.[11]

Detail Invites More Detail   If, as Louisiana once did, we spell out how to choose the members of the Port of New Orleans commission and what they do, we might compose a constitutional article of about half the size of the federal constitution. Moreover, every amendment would require more verbiage. Rolling stones may gather no moss, but not so with state constitutions. As the clauses get more involved, the constitution becomes like a snowball rolling down a hill, picking up whatever rocks, branches, or beer cans are in its way as it rolls along.

Legalese   State constitutions are also likely to strike you as full of "whereas" language—the kind that delights lawyers who revel in litigation over whether beauticians may give shaves and "shags" to male customers.

What Reformers Want to Change

Since the time of Teddy Roosevelt, reformers have criticized state constitutions as being inefficient and undemocratic. In 1921 the **National Municipal League** issued its **Model State Constitution**, a short, streamlined, and businesslike document. Many states have adopted parts of it. From time to time the League puts out revised editions.

Increase Managerial Efficiency   "Good government" reformers, as we discussed in Chapter 1, think the states would become more efficient by centralizing power and professionalizing their personnel. They also suggest getting rid of many constitutional prohibitions. They say states must be able to act promptly and vigorously and want to eliminate what they see as unnecessary checks and balances.

Table 4.1 INFORMATION ABOUT STATE CONSTITUTIONS (As of December 31, 1987)

State or other jurisdiction	Number of constitutions	Effective date of present constitution	Estimated length (number of words)	Number of amendments Submitted to voters	Adopted
Alabama	6	1901	174,000	679	471
Alaska	1	1959	13,000	30	21
Arizona	1	1912	28,876	191	105
Arkansas	5	1874	40,720	160	73
California	2	1879	33,350	768	460
Colorado	1	1876	45,679	231	109
Connecticut	4	1965	9,564	26	25
Delaware	4	1897	19,000		117
Florida	6	1969	25,100	68	44
Georgia	10	1983	25,000	20	18
Hawaii	1	1959	17,453	86	78
Idaho	1	1890	21,500	186	106
Illinois	4	1971	13,200	9	4
Indiana	2	1851	9,377	67	36
Iowa	2	1857	12,500	49	46
Kansas	1	1861	11,865	114	86
Kentucky	4	1891	23,500	56	27
Louisiana	11	1975	51,448	36	22
Maine	1	1820	13,500	184	156
Maryland	4	1867	41,349	231	199
Massachusetts	1	1780	36,690	143	116
Michigan	4	1964	20,000	44	15
Minnesota	1	1858	9,500	203	109
Mississippi	4	1890	24,000	141	70
Missouri	4	1945	42,000	107	68
Montana	2	1973	11,866	21	13
Nebraska	2	1875	20,048	278	184
Nevada	1	1864	20,770	168	103
New Hampshire	2	1784	9,200	272	141
New Jersey	3	1948	17,086	49	36
New Mexico	1	1912	27,200	224	114
New York	4	1895	80,000	272	205
North Carolina	3	1971	11,000	34	27
North Dakota	1	1889	20,564	215	124
Ohio	2	1851	36,900	244	144
Oklahoma	1	1907	68,800	264	124
Oregon	1	1859	26,090	361	183
Pennsylvania	5	1968	21,675	24	19
Rhode Island	2	1843	19,026	98	52
South Carolina	7	1896	22,500	639	455
South Dakota	1	1889	23,300	181	94
Tennessee	3	1870	15,300	55	32
Texas	5	1876	62,000	459	304
Utah	1	1896	11,000	124	75

Table 4.1 Continued

Vermont	3	1793	6,600	208	50
Virginia	6	1971	18,500	23	20
Washington	1	1889	29,400	147	80
West Virginia	2	1872	25,600	102	62
Wisconsin	1	1848	13,500	167	124
Wyoming	1	1890	31,800	96	56
American Samoa	2	1967	6,000	13	7
No. Mariana Is.	1	1977			
Puerto Rico	1	1952	9,281	6	6

Source: Adapted from *The Book of the States, 1988–89,* Lexington, Ky.: Council of State Governments, 1988. Copyright © 1988 The Council of State Governments. Reprinted with permission from *The Book of the States.*

They also suggest taking out details that legislatures can handle, as well as sloppy language and tricky legalisms. Many of these tie the hands of state government and also advantage groups favoring the status quo.

The Oklahoma constitution, for example, stated that the corporation commissioner could regulate "all transportation and transmission companies." Then it went on to list them—"railroads, express companies and [even!] steamship lines." The list did not include airlines, possibly because they had not yet been invented. But in 1947 the Oklahoma supreme court struck down as unconstitutional the corporation commissioner's efforts to regulate commercial airlines because airlines were not on the constitutional list.

These proposed reforms would also shorten constitutions. Reformers recommend that the document need describe only briefly the (1) major state offices and how they are filled, (2) limitations on state powers in a bill of rights, (3) powers and structure of community governments, and (4) methods of amending or calling a constitutional convention. They do not object to worthy ideals in the preamble because the courts do not consider the preamble an official part of the document.

Increase Citizen Participation To democratize state government, another set of reformers wants to curb the power of the business interests, expand opportunities for citizen participation, and make state and community governments more humane. The U.S. Supreme Court justices have also contributed to this democratizing effort. The changes that "good government" and democratizing reformers propose are sometimes in conflict, as we note later.[12]

HOW STATE CONSTITUTIONS GOT SO LONG AND COMPLICATED

A closer look at the content of our cluttered constitutions reveals what moved our ancestors to include so many detailed sections. We might conclude that under certain conditions, extra detail in constitutions may be desirable.

The Impact of Social Change

Constitutions reflect the conditions found in the society that produces them. Texans in the nineteenth century, for example, included a clause that made it a crime to have barbed wire clippers hidden in one's saddlebags. They were dealing with problems of a growing and rapidly changing society—in this case disappearance of open range.

Throughout the nineteenth century the whole nation was changing rapidly. Defeat in war and the end of slavery transformed the southern states. Entrepreneurs were building railroads and sometimes bribed state legislators or community leaders to get rights-of-way or lower taxes on rails and stations. The corruption shocked many respectable citizens. The builders were converting a nation from rural to urban in half a century and spurring it on to full industrialization.

The Bryce Hypothesis What has change to do with state constitutions? James Bryce, in *The American Commonwealth* (1888), observed that changes to state constitutions were more common in states with "fluctuating populations." He found lengthy constitutions in states with "quick and sudden changes" in social and economic conditions, in states whose population and wealth were growing "with unexampled speed," and in the post–Civil War South, where the social and economic conditions of daily life had changed for nearly everyone.

Citizens and legislators, Bryce argued, put detailed clauses into constitutions to "meet new conditions and check new evils." With life less predictable, those upset tried to "cement in" the old ways of doing things. They tried to slow the pace of change and bring what they saw as a runaway situation under control. Others saw new opportunities and wanted faster change. And so constitutions grew longer as groups attempted to stabilize conditions or stake out new positions to their own advantage.

Today, groups also propose constitutional amendments to control or hasten change—low-tax advocates, the consumer and ecology movements, or those who see restoring the death penalty as a way to control heinous crimes.

Preserving Governmental Legitimacy

Constitutions contain "harmless clauses"—phrases and platitudes that seem to have little legal effect. Vermont's constitution still reminds its citizens of the value of piety—"Every sect or denomination of Christians ought to observe the Sabbath or Lord's Day, and keep up some sort of religious worship, which to them seems most agreeable to the revealed will of God."

What political battles lay behind this Sunday worship clause? Puritan New England once required strict observance of the Sabbath. When Vermonters changed this policy, they put in this token clause, perhaps to appease the defeated and probably disgruntled minority who saw the times changing too rapidly. At the same time, it told everyone else that they now had the right to worship or not worship as they pleased.

The result is a piece of nonpolicy that swells the document. Should we criticize Vermonters for using this relatively harmless way of bringing about peaceful change? Perhaps this clause made some of the losers of that political battle feel that all was not lost in a wicked world.

Similar statements are being put into today's constitutions—high-sounding phrases about things we value, or think we should value—racial and sexual equality, ecology, the rights of labor, or of the handicapped. These clauses sometimes have little legal effect. Still, they recognize the importance of certain waning ideals of the past or of ideals whose day has not yet come. Their net effect is to increase **governmental legitimacy**, to encourage citizens to accept state actions as right and justified. A little extra clutter in a state constitution may be a small price to pay if it keeps citizens from becoming disenchanted with their governments.

Democratizing Government

Seventy-nine Virginians from Culpepper County marching to battle in the War of 1812 discovered that only four were eligible to vote. From such discussions the struggle to democratize state and community governments began. It led to spelling out the legal rights of citizens—first to vote and then hold office. Later citizens increased the offices and issues decided by election, and finally, to limit the political power of the privileged. The movement for wider participation slowed for a time, because of prejudice against blacks and fear of laboring classes in the urban centers.[13]

We can thank the Jacksonian pioneers on the frontier in the 1820s for beginning the suffrage battles in earnest. Their solution was election of many state and community officials. In one state, citizens even made the state printer an elected official. They urged local governments to elect such administrative officials as land registrars and drain commissioners. They also argued for short terms in office, one year, two at the most—they proclaimed, "Tyranny begins when annual elections end." Many limited governors and treasurers to one term.[14]

Dorr's Rebellion—Rhode Island Resists Thomas Dorr (1805–1854), a lawyer and Harvard University graduate, agitated to amend Rhode Island's voting provisions that dated back to the original Royal Charter of 1763. Only those owning $134 in land value could vote—a tidy sum in the 1840s.

In 1841 Dorr illegally called a "People's Constitutional Convention." The legislature then called its own convention. Both submitted constitutions to the voters. Dorr's won overwhelmingly. The next year citizens elected Dorr governor under his constitution. But others claimed Samuel King won—under the old constitution. The incumbent governor called out the state militia, which sided with King. Dorr fled, and Dorr's Rebellion was over.

The conservatives then called a second constitutional convention and liberalized voting requirements somewhat. Meanwhile Dorr was caught and put in prison. After a year he was released in poor health, "a broken man." Still, many democratic radicals regarded him as a hero and a martyr.[15] Democratizing state constitutions did not always come easily.

The "Special Interests" Add Clauses

The Jacksonians brought government closer to the people and made it more vulnerable to less idealistic groups as well. State constitutions became especially open to the influence of the organized interest groups that blossomed in America's period of railroad building and rapid industrialization just before and after the Civil War. The interests added clauses that dealt with special formulas for taxing their own property below the usual rate and guaranteed their right to do business or exploit a state's natural resources as they pleased. The cut-over timber areas of northern Michigan and Wisconsin, the strip mine areas of southern Illinois, the disappearance of the buffalo from Nebraska's Great Plain, killed by "Buffalo Bill" to feed the railroad workers, and the virtual elimination of fur-bearing animals in the Far West suggest how free of interference these entrepreneurs became.

Small business groups, such as physicians, lawyers, beauticians, realtors, optometrists, and schoolteachers, added clauses that let them control the boards that were to regulate their activities. At one time the California Constitution established a mining board of five members "representing the mining industry," a board of commissioners for the Oil and Gas Division elected by "oil and gas operators in each of five districts," and a state board of forestry which had "members chosen to represent the pine and redwood industries; forest land, livestock, and agricultural operators; and water users."[16]

Reformers Blame State Legislators Reformers of every stripe during the nineteenth century tried to limit the powers of those they considered the cause of the troubles—untrustworthy legislative officials. They argued the politicians had "sold out" to the interests.

Limiting Legislative Sessions A simple way to cripple "corrupt legislatures" was to keep them from meeting. Lieutenant Governor Richard O. Ristine of Indiana once humorously observed, "Our constitution has the state legislature meet fifty-five days every two years. Some citizens seem to think it should be two days every fifty-five years." He was joking, but it is an attitude that many reformers once held—perhaps with good reason. The clauses also prevented legislators from raising their own salaries by listing the official compensation.

Limiting Financial Powers Another favorite "reform" was to restrict the legislature's power to tax, borrow, or spend. Midwestern states, after the success of New York's Erie Canal in the 1820s, underwrote extensive canal building. But the depression of 1837 and the beginning of railroad building drove the projects into bankruptcy. Still the states had to pay off the bonds. Many thereafter prudently limited the debts a legislature could incur. North Dakota entered the Union in 1889 with "Debts shall never in the aggregate exceed the sum of

$200,000." Others made tax increases subject to voter approval as some states and communities still do today.

Legislation in the Constitution Reformers who distrusted legislators also wrote their own pet bills into constitutions. The Minnesota Constitution at one time described all of the proposed routes of its state highway system, lest some highway engineer persuade the legislators to bypass a county seat.

Reformers of 1890–1914 Add Their Bit The political bosses and those who reformers thought controlled them—America's "Gilded Age" millionaires—inspired new provisions. Wisconsin Governor Robert La Follette, a leading Progressive, tells how an enthusiastic young legislative supporter whom he calls "E," voted against reform when the railroads threatened to ruin his business by giving his competitors rate advantages. With tears in his eyes, "E" told Governor La Follette, "I can't beggar my family. I have a wife and babies."[17]

Progressive Solutions Progressive reforms were thought too important to protect only with legislation—they went into the constitution. We noted in Chapter 1 that these included the rules for primary elections in place of party conventions, direct election of judges and "IRR"—the **initiative** (citizens propose legislation or constitutional amendments), **referendum** (citizens vote on recently passed legislation), and **recall** (citizens remove officials). All of these require petitions with a stated number of valid signatures before an election is held.

The Progressives also tried to stamp out corruption—the South Dakota Constitution required its legislators of the 1890s to swear they had never received a free railroad pass in exchange for a vote on a bill. The Kentucky Constitution declared that any legislator, judge, or other private officer who accepted a free pass would be removed from office automatically.[18]

The Progressives made seats on **regulatory commissions** elective, such as Minnesota's Railroad and Warehouse Commission or the public service commissions in many other states. These commissions regulated public utilities, especially those granted a monopoly such as the gas, electric, and telephone companies. They set rates, checked on how the firm was being run, and listened to citizens' complaints. The Progressives wanted to keep these regulatory bodies "out of politics"—by which they meant free from the influence of "the interests" and the political bosses. They wrote long and carefully detailed clauses into state constitutions.

Reform in California Governor "Holy Hiram" Johnson, who served from 1910 to 1914 and was the son of the Southern Pacific Railroad's chief lobbyist, mounted a massive attack against "the interests." Its impact still lingers. In a fashion that we suppose Freudian psychologists might itch to speculate about, he devoted himself to smashing Southern Pacific's hold on California.

He won the governorship in California's first primary and immediately pushed 23 detailed constitutional amendments through the legislature. The voters approved all but one, and the California Constitution bulged.[19]

The Reformers of Today Since the Vietnam War we have been going through another great period of reform. States have been adding constitutional clauses that the earlier Progressives would have cheered—clauses limiting lobbying activities and campaign expenditures and those dealing with issues such as feminism, ecology, and consumer protection. And we also see clauses added that reformers in favor of managerial efficiency would have deplored—those limiting spending, taxing, and borrowing powers of states and communities, or electing public utility regulators. All of these clauses add bulk—some would argue that today's reformers also want to include "legislative detail."

Our Cluttered Constitutions: An Assessment

It is difficult to exaggerate the importance of the battles between the interests and the Jacksonian and Progressive reformers. State governments, and the national government as well, are now a good deal less oligarchic and aristocratic than they might have been. On balance, having constitutions longer and government more responsive seems a price worth paying.[20]

Special Cases Require Special Treatment Frank P. Grad defends those who wish to introduce more than core materials. He argues that what goes into a constitution is a political decision. How important do citizens consider the issue to be? Do they believe a particular reform requires special protection lest a legislative majority later tries to change it? Is the reform a matter in which a settled rule is necessary? Grad notes that even the Model State Constitution contains a number of "good government" proposals that are "legislative detail," but which reformers consider especially important—"local home rule, intergovernmental cooperation, modern budget and appropriation procedures, the merit system in public employment, and safeguards for public education." Reformers know some of these may require special protection from "meddling" by state legislatures.[21]

As Grad points out, would it not be sensible to give constitutional protection to civil service in a state that had lived with 150 years of spoils politics? Was the Michigan constitutional convention in the early 1960s unwise to include a detailed description of its then controversial Civil Rights Commission, rather than hope that the legislature would not cripple such a body? Were early labor union leaders wrong to insist that workers' compensation clauses or the detailed rights of unions to bargain collectively be given constitutional status?

Grad also points out that states have their own peculiar physical environments and the problems related to them as well as their own political traditions. Reformers generally admire Alaska's constitution. But in it is a long article detailing how the state will develop its natural resources—a burning issue in Alaska. And should outsiders say that in Louisiana matters dealing with the Port of New Orleans do not require a status above that of ordinary legislation? Limitations on debt or balancing of the budget or New Jersey's provision permitting gambling may be so ingrained as part of a state's political culture that if reformers attempt to root them out, citizens will reject the document.

KEEPING CONSTITUTIONS CURRENT

Only 18 states have written new constitutions in this century, although many others have modernized their basic documents through amendment.[22] But states have devised other ways as well to root out "outmoded provisions" or cause them to become inoperative when the current generation finds them a nuisance. Often the perceived need for a reform, such as strengthening the governor's office, has been achieved by legislation or executive order, and only later placed in the constitution.[23]

Sometimes outdated clauses are simply ignored. We trust residents of New Hampshire no longer take seriously their "right to revolution." The Oregon Constitution states that juries must decide both the facts and the law of a case. Iowa limits leases to 20 years. Because these clauses no longer fit contemporary conditions, nobody takes them seriously or pays any attention to them.

States develop "gimmicks" to get around inconvenient clauses. They evade ridiculously low salary limits for legislators by paying an exorbitant mileage or other per diem allowances. Present-day officials persuaded a Kentucky state court to rule that the original constitution writers meant for subsequent generations to take inflation into account. Others argued that present-day standards of living should also be considered. Or to evade the limit on length of legislative sessions, a janitor props up a ladder against the wall and "covers the clock" with a handkerchief. The session then sometimes continues on for several more days, as though bleary-eyed legislators did not notice.[24]

Sometimes reforms have turned out to be stronger than was planned. The Alabama Constitution of 1901 "forbade the state to engage in works of internal improvement, lend money or its credit in aid of such improvements, or become interested in or lend money or its credit to any private individual or corporate enterprise." The clause crippled the fledgling state highway department. Alabamians had to amend the clause seven years later so the state could build and maintain roads and bridges.[25] And, of course, state courts can make some clauses obsolete by ruling them unconstitutional.

The Federal Government Makes Changes

Federal courts have eliminated clauses that deal with the rights of minorities, criminals, people expressing unpopular opinions, and state voting requirements. One landmark decision, **Baker v. Carr** (1962), ordered states to reapportion their legislatures on the basis of one person, one vote. From 1900 to 1962, legislators had blocked the calling of constitutional conventions, fearing such bodies might reapportion. A period of intense constitutional revision has followed this decision. The Court later applied the decision to most community governments as well.

Congress has backed many of these court decisions with legislation such as the Voting Rights Act. Congress and the state legislatures changed voting rights for blacks, women, and 18-year-olds through a series of amendments to the federal constitution.

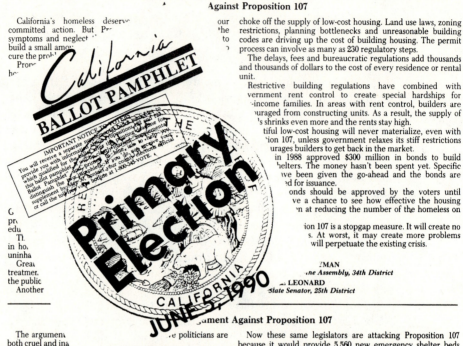

A sampling of the 110-page booklet Californians got explaining the June 1990 ballot issues. Seven were proposed constitutional amendments.

State Constitutional Revision

Elmer Cornwell argues that citizens regard state constitutions as "political documents" subject to frequent amendment while they regard the national constitution to be "above politics."[26] States use several amendment methods.

Legislative Amendment Proposals The majorities required to propose amendments in state legislatures in most states are similar to those of Congress.[27] But Congress has proposed only 30 amendments—and 10 of these, the Bill of Rights, were proposed almost immediately. In contrast, all but a handful of state legislatures have proposed dozens of amendments—Texas, 283 in 110 years. Even Alaska changed its first constitution 20 times during its first 25 years. Hawaii made 77 changes in its first 25 years as a state.[28]

Initiating Proposed Amendments Some states use a second method of proposing amendments. Citizens of Oregon in 1902 adopted a provision that allows citizens to propose constitutional amendments as well as legislation. Seventeen states, mostly western, allow the **constitutional initiative**; 21 allow citizens to initiate ordinary legislation. The most frequent users of the constitutional initiative are California, Oregon, Colorado, and Arkansas. The last decade has shown a rise in its use.[29] In 1988, 67 such proposals were voted on, the largest number in more than 50 years.

To propose by initiative, citizens must circulate petitions of the proposed amendment. After they collect the required number of signatures, the proposal is voted on at the next election, just as is the case for legislative proposals.

The required number of signatures varies. Some states, such as North Dakota, use a specific number—20,000. A more common requirement is 8 to 10 percent of the number of votes cast for governor in the last election. A few states require an absolute percentage of all eligible voters. Some make it a bit more complicated for the petition circulators. For example, Ohio has the kind of requirement you have to read twice to get straight—10 percent of all electors must sign, and the signatures must be so distributed as to include 5 percent of the vote cast for governor in the last election in at least one-half of the counties.

The Content of Constitutional Initiatives Initiatives show what is troubling voters. In the early period Hahn and Kamieniecki found they concentrated on women suffrage, child labor, the eight-hour workday, gambling, prostitution, and prohibition. In the 1930s social welfare was a popular issue. In the 1950s and 1960s interest shifted to civil rights and civil liberties. In the 1970s and 1980s ecology and low taxes were popular issues.[30] California has often set national trends, as with its tax-cutting Proposition 13 in the 1970s and the 20 percent cut in insurance rates ratified in the 1988 election. But Maryland's 1988 referendum upholding the law to ban cheap handguns also received national attention.

Since 1980, a few state courts have declared unconstitutional and banned from the ballot some initiated proposals—in 1984 an attempt to force the Montana legislature to adopt the balanced budget amendment, in Florida a malpractice proposal, and in Arkansas one dealing with abortion.[31]

We cannot amend the federal constitution by initiative, a condition discussed in Policy Box No. 8, "A National Initiative for Constitutional Amendments?"

Ratification of Proposed Amendments The states ratify—that is, approve and thus adopt—proposed amendments in a more democratic way than does the national government—all states except Delaware require an election.[32]

Voter turnout on citizen-initiated proposals is about the same as that on legislative proposals.[33] But David Magleby argues voter turnout for special elections on initiatives often is so low that it makes the legitimacy of the outcome questionable.[34] We found the same was true of legislative-proposed amendments voted on in Michigan at special elections or primaries. One may also question how many California voters in 1988 voted for the 12 initiatives and 17 other measures on the ballot. Voting for the offices at the top of the ballot and ignoring the issues, called falloff, is common.

Magleby also found the voters in ratification elections to be less representative of the electorate as a whole in respect to age, race, education, and income.[35]

Forty states require only majority approval of those voting. A few states make ratification more difficult. Take the so-called brewer's amendment of Minnesota. From 1857 through 1898 Minnesota had one of the easiest constitutions to amend. Then it looked as if there would be a constitutional amendment against the "liquor traffic"—statewide prohibition. The brewers got their own amendment passed first—designed to make it more difficult for voters to adopt statewide prohibition. It required a majority of those participating in the election to vote "yes" in order to pass the proposed amendment. For example, if 100,000 citizens went to the polls but only 50,000 bothered to vote on the proposal and they all voted "yes," the proposal would still fail by one vote. Tennessee and Illinois had similar provisions. As a result Tennessee had no amendments for 83 years. "Good government" reformers in Illinois carefully publicized a "gateway" amendment that would allow adoption if 60 percent voting on the amendment approved.[36]

From 1788 to 1987, the average number of proposed amendments has been 169 per state constitution, with 104 adopted. The legislatures proposed 90 percent of these, 4 percent were proposed by initiative, and the remaining 6 percent by other means. Citizens approved 65 percent of the legislative proposals, but only 34 percent of those proposed by initiative. The number of amendments proposed since 1968 has been in decline, presumably because many state constitutions have been modernized. Sixteen new constitutions were adopted between 1940 and 1985.[37]

We list here the topics for proposed constitutional amendments along with adoption rates since the 1970s in terms beginning with those proposed most often and ending with those proposed least often.

Taxation and finance—66 percent adopted

State functions—73 percent adopted

Legislative matters—54 percent adopted

Policy Box No. 8

A National Initiative for Constitutional Amendments?

In 1977, when President Jimmy Carter was attempting to gain Senate votes for his Panama Canal Treaty, Senator Robert Griffin (R-Michigan) urged Secretary of State Cyrus Vance to suggest an advisory referendum in which all of the citizens could vote their preference. Secretary Vance replied he "would not recommend it."

Yet almost half the states allow voters to participate in lawmaking or to initiate constitutional amendments. And every state except Delaware has elections to ratify constitutional amendments. Great Britain allowed voters to decide whether their nation would stay in the European Economic Community. Quebec voters decided on a proposal for a form of separation from Canada. Switzerland holds referenda frequently. Should American voters be so totally excluded from our national governing process?

Holding such national referenda is not a new idea. Senator Robert La Follette, a Progressive reformer of Wisconsin, proposed the idea in 1917. In 1938 a member of Congress from Indiana suggested that the United States should not declare war without a popular vote—unless we were attacked. The peace groups of the day heavily supported the proposal.

In 1920 Ohio passed legislation that required voters to approve all proposed amendments to the U.S. constitution before they could be considered ratified. After all, the legal doctrine that the U.S. Supreme Court holds is that the people of the states, and not the state governments, established the American system. The U.S. Supreme Court, however, declared the law unconstitutional. The Court said that the national constitution spells out only two ways of ratifying proposed amendments—approval by state legislatures or, if Congress so designates, by specially elected conventions.

We have had a return of Progressive and Populist sentiment. A number of reformers are asking why the national government should not once again accept some of the democratizing procedures that states have used so successfully.

In 1977 Senator James Abourezk (D-South Dakota) and Mark Hatfield (R-Oregon) proposed a constitutional amendment that would accomplish what Senator La Follette had desired some 60 years before. Proposal of amendments to the federal constitution would be by petitions containing signatures equal in number to 3 percent of the voters in the last presidential election—generally that would require about 2.5 million or so valid signatures. Ratification would be by majority vote of the people.

The federal constitution could thus be amended without Congress or the state legislatures being involved, just as is the case in those states having the constitutional initiative.

Senator Abourezk justified his proposal by arguing that "our democracy is based on the notion that the people can govern themselves." He noted that six of the last ten constitutional amendments "have in some way extended voting rights." This proposal, he claimed, would be "a further step in this evolutionary process."

Some feminists, frustrated by the difficulties involved in getting state legislatures to pass the Equal Rights Amendment, may well agree. The public opinion polls have consistently shown that the public approves the proposed ERA by wide margins. And the process makes more logical sense than having to get both houses of three-fourths of the state legislatures to adopt the proposal.

The experiences of some states that use the initiative and use popular votes for ratification give us some guidelines as to what we might expect. For a beginning, it is highly probable that this kind of change would make the federal constitution much easier to amend. For example, one bottleneck has been that Congress has formally proposed very few of the thousands of proposals suggested. Perhaps advocates of low taxes or those who desire a balanced federal budget could then get their proposals considered.

What would be the political effects of easy amendment? To discover what kinds of amendments would be proposed by initiative, we would need to look at which groups might raise the nearly 3 million signatures required and which of them have proposals that the public opinion polls suggest would be adopted. George F. Will, political scientist and newspaper columnist, suggests that "any national initiative would be dominated by an intense, unelected minority using direct mail, television commercials, and other techniques of mass persuasion." He argues that the proposal would strengthen only the "single issue" interest groups with large war chests—and not "the people."

Others argue that a national initiative would allow citizens of the states to influence national decision making—especially those decisions that directly affect what state governments can do.

What do you think? Do you favor extending the initiative to the federal government? Would its use hurt or help the states? How would it affect such groups as blacks, supporters of women's rights, Indians, and civil liberties groups? Would it increase or decrease the powers of Congress, the president, the Supreme Court, or the bureaucracy? Would it help business or labor, liberals or conservatives, Democrats or Republicans? Would it help state governments? Would it reverse the flow of power to Washington? If you oppose the idea, do you think we should also eliminate the initiative from state constitutions? If you favor it, do you think all states should be required to use the initiative? Suggest three amendments you think would be adopted if we had the initiative at the federal level.

Judiciary—80 percent adopted

The Bill of Rights—80 percent adopted

General constitutional revisions—39 percent adopted

State and local debt—49 percent adopted[38]

Of special interest was the high approval rate May discovered for amendments to Bills of Rights. Those dealing with criminal procedures restricted rights; other amendments expanded rights for selected groups such as the handicapped. An extensive Victims' Bill of Rights proposed by initiative and adopted in California in 1982 was an omnibus measure of ten sections of anticrime proposals.[39]

Table 4.2 SUBSTANTIVE CHANGES IN STATE CONSTITUTIONS: PROPOSED AND ADOPTED

Subject matter	Total proposed				Total adopted				Percent adopted			
	1980–1981	1982–1983	1984–1985	1986–1987	1980–1981	1982–1983	1984–1985	1986–1987	1980–1981	1982–1983	1984–1985	1986–1987
proposals of statewide applicability	254	226	228	251	160	149	154	184	63.0	65.9[a]	67.1[a]	72.9[b]
Bill of Rights	13	13	9	12[a]	10	13	7	10[a]	76.9	100.0	77.7	81.8[b]
suffrage and elections	5	5	5	11	5	4	5	10	100.0	80.0	100.0	90.9
legislative branch	43	32	37	49	21	18	19	35	48.8	56.3	51.5	71.4
executive branch	21	19	30	23	10	9	20	19	47.6	47.4	66.7	82.6
judicial branch	23	26	19	18	17	21	16	15	73.9	80.8	78.9[a]	83.3
local government	11	13	16	17	4	9	13	11	36.4	69.2	75.0[a]	64.7
finance and taxation	77	48	67	45	52	28	43	29	67.5	58.3[b]	64.2	64.4
state and local debt	20	26	21	12	13	19	16	8	65.0	73.1	76.2	66.6
state functions	23	31	17	29	16	18	9	22	69.6	58.1	52.9	75.8
amendment and revision	9	2	2	0	7	1	2	0	77.8	50.0	100.0	0
general revision proposals	1	1	0	14	0	1	0	8	0	100.0	0	57.1
miscellaneous proposals	8	10	5	22	5	8	4	17	62.5	80.0	80.0	77.2
local amendments	134	123	10	24[c]	112	107	4	20[a]	83.6	87.0	40.0	79.1[b]

[a] One Delaware proposal was included.

[b] In calculating these percentages the changes adopted in Delaware (where proposals are not submitted to the voters) are excluded.

[c] One Delaware proposal was excluded.

Source: *The Book of the States, 1988–89,* Lexington, Ky.: Council of State Governments, 1988. Copyright ©1988 The Council of State Governments. Reprinted with permission from *The Book of the States*.

A New Constitution Through Legislative Action

Up to this point we have been discussing amendments as a way of dealing with a single problem. But a state can achieve what, in effect, becomes a new constitution by adopting a series of amendments. Legislators prefer this method to a constitutional convention because legislative proposal permits them to keep close control. They also tend to integrate new provisions with existing ones better than citizen-initiated changes. But constitutional revision may bog down when lawmakers have other matters to consider, especially if session length is restricted.

A New Constitution Through Commission Revision   Legislators sometimes lack time to work on details of a package of changes but still want to keep control of the process. A **revision commission** helps them achieve their objectives. Its widespread use began in 1938, peaking in the 1960s. The number of such bodies created is approaching 100.

The revision commission is a small body of prominent citizens and "experts" whom the legislature appoints. They revise the whole document or only certain articles or subjects as the legislature directs.[40] The commission then reports its proposals to the legislature, which may revise or even eliminate parts before submitting the proposals to the voters.[41]

An Alabama study concluded that to be successful a revision commission must establish a satisfactory relationship with the state legislature. At the same time, it needs to obtain the governor's support for the proposals—a tightwire act that some commissions find difficult.[42]

A Phased Revision Commission In the late 1960s the California legislature set up a series of commissions, each with specialists on the constitutional subjects and articles they would review. Over a six-year period, a **phased revision commission** recommended changes annually to the legislature on one article or topic. Indiana, Ohio, and South Carolina have also used this method.

A Constitutional Study Commission A variation is to have the legislature appoint a **constitutional study commission** to determine whether the document needs revision. Arkansas and Montana did this in the 1970s. Both recommended a constitutional convention. The Montana commission prepared an enabling act for the convention, drafted a proposed constitution for the convention to consider, and conducted an information campaign for the election to call the convention. Voters approved calling the convention and later the proposed constitution. The Arkansas convention was less fortunate. Voters rejected the proposed new constitution.[43]

A New Constitution Through Convention Only three-quarters of the state constitutions authorize the calling of a constitutional convention. But the U.S. Supreme Court ruled that all states may set up such bodies.[44]

A **state constitutional convention** consists of a body of citizens and sometimes officeholders. A few may be appointed, but most are elected, usually on a nonpartisan ballot. They generally meet from three to five months. Their proposed new constitution is submitted directly to the voters.[45]

Between 1776 and 1987, the states have held over 230 constitutional conventions. Since 1940, 20 states have held a total of 39 conventions. Seventeen of these proposed constitutions, including those of Alaska and Hawaii and three in Georgia, were ratified. The success rate is thus only 44 percent.

In 1982 Washington, D.C., delegates proposed a Constitution for the State of Columbia. The voters adopted it in 1983, but thus far the U.S. Congress has not acted on admitting Columbia as a state.[46] Since the District is mentioned in the U.S. Constitution, a constitutional amendment would be required.

Legislative Opposition to Conventions State legislators dislike calling conventions because such bodies commonly submit their changes directly to the voters and might upset settled matters by a wholesale revision. Legislators are concerned with the interests of political allies in other branches or with clauses that affect organized groups with whom they are sympathetic.

Legislators also worry that a convention may produce a crop of budding politicians. Such bodies provide a political platform for relative unknowns—George

Romney, for example, who went on to be governor of Michigan. Other delegates of Michigan's "Con-Con" ran successfully for the legislature and Congress.

State legislatures can usually block the calling of a convention by not acting. But 14 state constitutions have a clause that requires the question of holding a convention to be voted on at specified intervals. New York's provision required a vote "at the General Election of 1957, and every twentieth year thereafter." Seven other states use the 20-year interval. The shortest period is Hawaii's—every nine years. The question may also be put on the ballot by initiative petition, as was done in Massachusetts in 1968 and 1970.

Limited Constitutional Conventions Legislatures in the last decades have called conventions that may only consider certain sections of the current constitution—**limited constitutional conventions**. In some states the legislature submits to the voters suggestions that such a convention might consider. In 1968, for example, Tennessee voters agreed to have a convention to consider only one out of the five topics the legislature suggested. Of the 12 constitutional conventions held in the 1970s, state legislators or voters limited 5.

Frequency of Constitutional Conventions Ten states—Alaska, Arizona, Colorado, Idaho, Maine, Minnesota, Oklahoma, Oregon, Utah, and Wyoming—have held only one convention, the one required to gain statehood. But since admission in 1950, Hawaii has had 3; New Hampshire, 16; Georgia, 12; and Vermont and Louisiana, 11 each.

What explains these differences? Edward D. Grant III found that constitutional revision appears to follow crisis. Those that have held constitutional conventions most frequently had "significant increases in population, industrialization, and legislative and general professionalism." Grant found that age of the document had no bearing. Nor did ease of amendment or length of the old constitution seem to make much difference in the frequency of conventions.[47]

Convention Organization Sometimes the current constitution describes how constitutional convention delegates are to be chosen. Most often the legislature sets the rules for the delegates to follow, convention financing, whether delegates will be elected on a partisan or nonpartisan basis, and boundaries of delegate districts. Convention size since 1970 has ranged from 98 in North Dakota to 400 in New Hampshire.

Partisanship of Delegates Some delegates are nonpartisan in approach—sometimes they call themselves independents. They feel they should make decisions objectively, free of the infighting normally found between the political parties. They regard a constitution as a higher law—something special, above partisan politics. Others approach constitution writing as partisans who view their role and the document as distributing power and scarce resources for the future. To them, the convention is an arena in which parties and groups struggle to gain political advantage.

When delegates are elected on a partisan ballot and organize along partisan lines, nonpartisanship becomes more difficult. Nonpartisans prefer a nonpartisan election and to seat delegates alphabetically rather than by party, geographic, or racial groups. They prefer to assign convention offices and committees equally between the parties. Sometimes someone seen as truly nonpartisan, a judge or a university president, is elected presiding officer.

Nonpartisan conventions tend to concentrate on matters of managerial efficiency—centralizing administrative power and professionalizing government. They favor home rule for cities and counties. Conventions organized along partisan lines are more likely to be concerned with social welfare issues and the articles on finance and taxation.

Citizens elected delegates to the Michigan convention on a partisan ballot. Yet political scientists found that a great many delegates described themselves as nonpartisan. On critical roll call votes, party cohesion was almost the same as that found in the state legislature.[48] Even when voters select delegates on a nonpartisan basis they may coalesce into partisan groups. In the 1970 Illinois convention, roll call divisions on partisan lines were frequent.[49] At a New York convention, after some votes followed partisan lines, some nonpartisans changed to partisans. Others remained nonpartisans to the end.[50] Public reaction to the deliberations also affects how delegates behave. In Louisiana some who had political experience in government opposed changes in governmental structure. But they tended to moderate their opposition when they discovered that the public seemed to support such change.[51]

The Election of a Convention Document Despite the effort and cost in holding a convention, voters, as often as not, reject the proposed document. Why? Some are apathetic. The questions posed often are complicated and confusing. The pro and con agitation confuses others. Researchers thought voter apathy was crucial in a Tennessee vote on the series of gateway amendments. The apathy, it seems, increased the influence of officeholders in some counties—most opposed revision.[52]

Conventions can submit their proposed constitution as a series of amendments that can be voted on separately or as a complete document which citizens either accept or reject in total. When citizens vote on proposals separately, some usually are adopted—those states that have taken an all-or-nothing position, as New Mexico, Arkansas, and Maryland did, have seen all of the work of their constitutional conventions go down the drain. Michigan, in 1963, narrowly adopted an all-or-nothing constitution.

The Hard-Core Opponents of Change Officeholders generally oppose change. Some fear being replaced if a new constitution takes effect; others think the proposed changes will lead to unpredictable results. Some, such as justices of the peace who hold offices designed for a rural society and state officials whose jobs might be eliminated, also oppose change. Add to this representatives of interest groups that have a privileged position under the present constitution.

Those who strongly oppose are usually not numerous enough to "kill it." But they do provide the leadership and often funding for the opponents of change. Sometimes they resort to scare tactics. "Why revise the Bible?" was the slogan used in a Missouri campaign.

Elmer Cornwell and his associates concluded that the basic "gut issue" for the more disinterested citizens in seven campaigns was whether they trusted government. Upper-income citizens, usually highly educated, generally accepted the arguments of managerial efficiency. They accepted arguments favoring expertise and thought streamlining state government to be a reasonable goal.

Those favoring the status quo were the less successful—blue-collar workers and less educated citizens. They were skeptical of experts and believed that the less government, the better. They did not understand all of the changes proposed, nor did they particularly want to. In Maryland, suburban Baltimore was in favor, but the rural areas were opposed.[53] In New Mexico the cities favored the change; Spanish-speaking areas voted overwhelmingly against.[54]

In a few campaigns chances for adopting the proposed constitution suffered because it became an issue between political parties. When conventions were organized on a partisan basis from the start, like in New York, voters viewed the proposed constitution as a party campaign document, and they voted along party lines.

Another division that researchers occasionally found was "big city" against the rest of the state. In both New York and Illinois, both in constitutional convention deliberations and in votes against adoption, an outstate versus big-city division emerged.[55]

The Politics of Constitutional Revision   Conventions that propose sweeping revisions face a publicity barrage from a cumulative opposition—groups in opposition that alone may be small, but when banded together can make a great deal of noise in favor of the status quo. Thus compromise in the convention may be necessary to prevent groups such as probate judges, county sheriffs, or other entrenched interest groups from opposing all change.

A FINAL COMMENT

State constitutions should be examined as political documents, rather than as exercises in nonpartisan statesmanship. They are the way a generation attempts to nail down what is important. Later generations should at least attempt to understand.

We suggest that our generation also should introduce changes that will bring state constitutions closer to the needs and desires of present citizens without making our first concern the length or complexity of the documents we produce.

Perhaps one of the more interesting arguments concerns basic rights, particularly those of the accused. Some state judges have attempted to expand the Bill of Rights of state constitutions in reaction to decisions of a more conservative U.S.

Supreme Court. In some cases these decisions have been reversed through constitutional amendment.[56]

HIGH POINTS

In this chapter we began by looking at (1) the legal contract theory of constitution writing, stressing that written constitutions in America are interpreted by federal and state courts. We next asked (2) why constitutions are so important, and concluded it was because they set up rules that confer longtime burdens or benefits on citizens. We then looked at (3) what constitutions contain, and we found them cluttered with legislative detail that sometimes led to governmental stalemate. Authorities, we found, recommend streamlining and shortening. We next looked at (4) the problem of why they were so long, and concluded that it was because they were the target of special interests, reformers, and ordinary citizens in periods of instability and change. We concluded that (5) under certain conditions, adding to the length of constitutions often represented a reasonable attempt to preserve and extend democratic government and give special protection to what is important in the eyes of present-day citizens. We assumed that our generation would do the same without being primarily concerned about length or complexity. We then looked at (6) change coming through the federal and state courts and through constitutional revision. We concluded by looking at (7) the difficulties of constitutional change.

In this chapter we defined the following terms in this order: royal charter, state constitutions, unconstitutional, judicial review, redistributive policy, legislative detail, National Municipal League, Model State Constitution, governmental legitimacy, initiative, referendum, recall, regulatory commissions, *Baker v. Carr*, constitutional initiative, ratify, revision commission, phased revision commission, constitutional study commission, state constitutional convention, and limited constitutional conventions.

NOTES

1. The tree unfortunately blew down in 1856. The state carved it up into souvenirs and used part to make the chair that the lieutenant governor still uses when presiding over the state senate. A monument was put up in Charter Oak Place in Hartford. Historians do not vouch for all details of the story as we have told it. For our source see George Stimpson, *A Book about American History* (New York: Harper & Bros., 1956).
2. Massachusetts has the only constitution that dates back to the Revolutionary War times, about which John Adams coined the phrase "a government of laws and not of men." It was adopted in 1780 and became a model for the federal constitution.
3. Diane D. Blair, *Arkansas Politics and Government: Do the People Rule?* (Lincoln: University of Nebraska Press, 1988).

4. Locke helped draft a royal charter—"The Fundamental Constitution of Carolina" (1691). But despite his theory, it contained no amendment clause, providing that the document "should be and remain the sacred and unalterable force and rule of government of Carolina forever."
5. Frank P. Grad, "The State Constitution, Its Function and Form for Our Time," *Virginia Law Review* 54 (June 1968): 928–973.
6. Quoted in A. E. Dick Howard, "For the Common Benefit, Constitutional History in Virginia as a Casebook for the Modern Constitution-Maker," *Virginia Law Review* 54 (June 1968): 855. Howard reviews Virginia's constitution making: 816–902.
7. Genesis 49:10.
8. Theodore J. Lowi has called our attention to the distributive functions of policymaking in *The End of Liberalism* (New York: Norton, 1969). He distinguishes between "distributive policy" (a settled and accepted division of resources), "redistributive policy" (a new definition of how resources should be distributed), and "regulatory policy" (enforcing the rules that maintain the present distribution of benefits).
9. Albert L. Sturm, "The Development of American State Constitutions," *Publius* 12 (Winter 1982): 57–98.
10. James Quayle Dealey, *Growth of American State Constitutions* (New York: Ginn, 1915), Chapter III.
11. Manning J. Dauer and William C. Havard, *The Florida Constitution of 1885—A Critique* (Gainesville: Public Administration Service, University of Florida, 1955).
12. An early, concise, and often-quoted statement of the "good government" proposals is William B. Munro, "An Ideal State Constitution," *The Annals* 181 (September 1935). See also Robert Dishman, *State Constitutions: The Shape of the Document* (rev. ed.) (New York: National Municipal League, 1968).
13. Fletcher M. Green, *Constitutional Development in the South Atlantic States*, 1778–1860 (Chapel Hill: University of North Carolina Press, 1930), pp. 171–200.
14. Voting requirements in postcolonial times depended on the availability of free or cheap land. In Massachusetts, most white male citizens could meet the land-holding requirements and officials did not always enforce the law here and in other states. Robert E. Brown, *Middle Class Democracy and the Revolution in Massachusetts, 1771–1780* (Ithaca, N.Y.: Cornell University Press, 1955). See also Allan Nevins, *The American States During and After the Revolution, 1775–1789* (New York: Macmillan, 1924, reissued by Augustus M. Kelley, New York, 1969). By 1820, about 75 percent of white adult males in New York were eligible to vote for house members and 40 percent for state senators. In Virginia, at the same point roughly half of white males were eligible; the figure was boosted to 66 percent after the changes of the 1829–1830 state constitutional convention. Merrill D. Peterson (ed.), *Democracy, Liberty and Property, The State Constitutional Conventions of the 1820s* (New York: Bobbs-Merrill, 1966).
15. For a modern study from a "new left" perspective, see Marvin E. Gettleman, *The Dorr Rebellion, A Study in American Radicalism, 1833–1849* (New York: Random House, 1973).
16. Grant McConnell, *Private Power and American Democracy* (New York: Knopf, 1966), p. 186, and California State Department of Finance, *Government: A Guide to Organizations and Functions* (Sacramento: 1951).
17. Robert M. La Follette, *Autobiography* (1911, reissued Madison: University of Wisconsin Press, 1961), pp. 113–114.

18. James Bryce, *The American Commonwealth* (1888), Chapter 38, "Development of Constitutions."
19. Royce D. Delmatier, Clarence F. McIntosh, and Earl G. Waters, *The Rumble of California Politics, 1848–1970* (New York: Wiley, 1970), Chapter 6, "Hiram Johnson and the Progessive Years," pp. 165–191.
20. The first state constitutions are sometimes held up as "models of conciseness and brevity." But they are often incomplete as well, giving evidence of hasty and sloppy draftmanship. We would expect this in times of revolution and its attendant uncertainty. Donald S. Lutz, "The Theory of Consent in the Early State Constitutions," Paper delivered at the national meetings of the American Political Science Association, September 1976.
21. Frank P. Grad, "The State Constitution," p. 949.
22. U.S. Advisory Commission on Intergovernmental Relations, *The Question of State Government Capability* (Washington, D.C.: U.S. Government Printing Office, 1985), pp. 42–44.
23. Charles Press, "Assessing the Policy and Operational Implications of State Constitutional Change," *Publius* 12 (Winter 1982): 99–111.
24. Charles W. Brown, "Guidelines for the Public Finance Article of State Constitutions," *Public Affairs Forum* (Memphis State University) 5 (Spring 1976): 1–8.
25. James D. Thomas, *Government in Alabama* (University: Bureau of Public Administration, University of Alabama, 1969), p. 3.
26. Elmer Cornwell, "The American Constitutional Tradition: Its Impact and Development," in Kermit L. Hall, Harold M. Hyman, and Leon V. Sigal (eds.), *The Constitutional Convention as an Amending Device* (Washington, D.C.: The American Historical Association and the American Political Science Association, 1981), pp. 1–65.
27. Almost half the states use the same method Congress uses—proposal by two-thirds (67 percent) in both the senate and house. In another ten states proposal is almost as difficult—60 percent of both houses. Another half-dozen or so require proposal by a majority, but require that the proposal pass in two successive sessions. Finally we have some that make legislative proposal more complicated and more difficult. Vermont permits amendments to be proposed only once every ten years; the Colorado legislature may not propose amendments to more than six articles at one time; Arkansas, Illinois, Kansas, Kentucky, and Montana limit the number of amendments that can be proposed at one time. In only nine states is the method of legislative proposal clearly easier than at the national level—proposal by a simple majority (51 percent).
28. Council of State Governments, *The Book of the States, 1986–87* (Lexington, Ky.: Council of State Governments, 1986).
29. See latest compilations in the Council of State Governments, *The Book of the States*, and *The National Civic Review*, "State Constitutional Development." Also see David M. Magleby, *Direct Legislation Voting on Ballot Propositions in the United States* (Baltimore: Johns Hopkins University Press, 1984), and David Butler and Austin Ranney, *Referendums, A Comparative Study of Practice and Theory* (Washington, D.C.: American Enterprise Institute, 1978). See especially Chapter 4 by Austin Ranney, on the U.S. experience, and Chapter 5 by Eugene Lee, on California.
30. Harlan Hahn and Sheldon Kamieniecki, *Referendum Voting, Social Status and Policy Preferences* (Westport, Conn.: Greenwood Press, 1987), pp. 2–3.
31. Janice C. May, "Constitutional Amendment and Revision Revisited," *Publius* 17 (Winter 1987): 159.

32. Amendments to the federal constitution are ratified when three-quarters of the state legislatures approve. Ratification may be by three-quarters of specially elected state conventions, as the framers did for adoption of the Constitution and Congress chose for the amendment which in 1933 repealed national prohibition.
33. Rita Harmony and David H. Everson, "Initiatives and Voter Turnout," *Comparative State Politics Newsletter* 1 (May 1980): 1.
34. Magleby, *Direct Legislation*, pp. 183–184.
35. Magleby, *Direct Legislation*, p. 145. See also for the relation of social status to such elections in communities, Hahn and Kamieniecki, *Referendum Voting*.
36. We find two other quirks. In Delaware, if in successive sessions the legislature passes a proposed amendment—each time by two-thirds of the votes—it is adopted. Georgia allowed counties to adopt amendments to the state constitution. But the amendments applied only to the adopting county. Georgia's constitution ballooned to 600,000 words, the longest in the nation. In 1982 a proposed new constitution eliminated this clause. Finally, a few states limit the number of amendments that may be proposed each election or the number of subjects dealt with.
37. The statistical data noted in this section are from Janice C. May, "Constitutional Amendment and Revision Revisited."
38. See May, "Constitutional Amendment": 171–173. Her compilations are based on Council of State Governments, *The Book of the States*, *1982–83*, and *1986–87*. (Lexington, Ky.: Council of State Governments). See also Albert L. Sturm, "The Development of American State Constitutions."
39. May, "Constitutional Amendment": 171–175.
40. Commissions drafted proposed new documents or extensive revisions in Alabama, California, Delaware, Georgia, Idaho, Minnesota, Nebraska, Ohio, and South Dakota. The legislatures of Indiana, Kentucky, New Hampshire, North Dakota, Utah, and Vermont used commissions to propose more limited changes.
41. Florida now allows a revision committee to submit proposals directly to the voters. In 1980 voters rejected all of the first eight proposals submitted.
42. William H. Stewart, Jr., *The Alabama Constitutional Commission, A Pragmatic Approach to Constitutional Reform* (University: University of Alabama Press, 1975).
43. The Virginia Commission issued a study of each article of the old constitution to demonstrate the need for change. The legislative proposals prepared with commission help were adopted by the voters. A. E. Dick Howard, *Commentaries on the Constitution of Virginia*.
44. The basic source on recent constitutional revisions listed state by state is Albert L. Sturm, *A Bibliography on State Constitutions and Constitutional Revision, 1945–75* (Englewood, Colo.: Citizens Conference on State Legislatures, 1975).
45. A Rhode Island convention met between December 8, 1964, and September 11, 1967, to prepare its proposed revision—a modern record.
46. Philip G. Schrag, *Behind the Scenes, The Politics of a Constitutional Convention* (Washington, D.C.: Georgetown University Press, 1985).
47. Edward D. Grant III, "State Constitutional Revision and the Forces That Shape It," *State and Local Government Review* (May 1977): 60–64.
48. Robert S. Friedman and Sybil L. Stokes, "The Role of Constitution-Maker as Representative," *Midwest Journal of Political Science* 9 (May 1965): 148–166.
49. Jack R. VanDerSlik, Samuel J. Pernacciaro, and David Kennedy, "Patterns of Partisanship in a Nonpartisan Representational Setting, The Illinois Constitutional Con-

vention," *American Journal of Political Science* 18 (February 1974): 95–116; and Samuel K. Gove and Thomas R. Kitsos, *Revision Success, The Sixth Illinois Constitutional Convention* (New York: The National Municipal League, 1974), pp. 43–47.

50. John J. Carroll and Arthur English, "Attitudes Toward Constitution Making and the Dynamics of the Convention Process," Paper delivered at the annual meeting of the Midwest Political Science Association, April 1980. The authors report delegates in Maryland and New Mexico continued as less partisan-minded through the deliberations.
51. Richard L. Engstrom and Patrick F. O'Connor, "Restructuring the Regime, Support for Change Within the Louisiana Constitutional Convention," *Polity* 11 (Spring 1979): 440–450.
52. Tip H. Allen, Jr., and Coleman B. Ransone, Jr., *Constitutional Revision in Theory and Practice* (University: University of Alabama Bureau of Public Administration, 1962), p. 153.
53. Elmer E. Cornwell, Jr., Jay S. Goodman, and Wayne R. Swanson, *State Constitutional Conventions, The Politics of Revision in Seven States* (New York: Praeger, 1975).
54. Albert L. Sturm, "State Constitutions and Constitutional Revision, 1967–1969," *The Book of the States, 1970–71* (Lexington, Ky.: Council of State Governments, 1970), pp. 13–14.
55. Cornwell et al., *State Constitutional Conventions*.
56. For citations and a summary of the arguments, see May, "Constitutional Amendment": 164–179.

Chapter 5

Elite and Citizen Participation

When researchers completed the first modern public opinion polls in the 1950s they found some surprising and also, perhaps, some disheartening facts about how citizens participated in politics. Contrary to what they assumed about the needs of democracies, they found that many citizens

1. discussed issues only occasionally during a campaign,
2. often were not very motivated to participate,
3. were poorly informed about candidates and issues,

4. did not seem to vote always on the basis of principle,
5. decided how to vote for illogical reasons such as whether a candidate was handsome or short or tall.

Other researchers studying communities found that a proportionately small number of citizens had major influence on political decisions. The rest seemed relatively powerless.

In both cases, researchers observed that average citizens did not follow all the twists of politics. Rather, they acted like people who had many other things to interest them.[1] The researchers did not conclude that democracy was impossible, but they questioned whether democratic theory, as they had understood it from civics texts, was realistic.

Overview In this chapter we consider how elites and other citizens participate. First we look at the most politically influential citizens—the political elites. We then consider average citizens, some of whom participate only occasionally and some rarely. Next we examine three factors that influence participation: costs, alienation, and social movements. We observe that our state and community governments are more open to citizen influence now than they were in the past.

POLITICAL ELITES

No society has ever distributed wealth, status, and political power equally among its members—at least not for long. Citizens differ in knowledge, talent, skills, and energy. Soon some gain a larger than average share of wealth, social standing, or political power. These are the people we call **elites**.

Native ability is not the only reason for inequalities. Some got a head start by being born into "the right families." They got a larger than average share of wealth, social status, and in fewer cases, political status from their parents.

Holding an important position in an organization also leads to inequalities. Organizations require leaders who will give a sense of direction. This means we must concentrate decision making in the hands of a few people—these have more power than others. Their numbers are especially small in complex, urban, and industrialized societies.[2]

If you look closely at your own state or community, you will find three kinds of elites based on political power, social status, and economic resources. Only a few are members of these elites.

Political Elites and Democratic Decision Making

Who are the **political elite**? In states and communities they include the small group of public officials who have the legal power to make governmental decisions. But we must also include those who have social and economic resources that they are willing to spend on influencing government decisions. These are the **influentials**.[3] Note, though, that having major resources does not necessarily imply possession of great wealth. Being head of a labor union, a church, a social movement—for example, Gloria Steinem or the late Dr. Martin Luther King, Jr.—or other important private organization leads to power.[4]

Influence of Nonelites Does the presence of a political elite mean that "they" make all the decisions and what the rest of us do is little more than window dressing? Some political scientists argue that this is indeed the case. Some even claim many citizens prefer it that way.[5]

We think that governmental decision making is a good deal more complex and subtle. Even those who participate only occasionally exert some influence on politicians. Studies suggest that when a large body of citizens holds an opinion, when some citizens express a view intensely, or when an issue is given major media attention, politicians generally respond.[6] But as V. O. Key, Jr., noted, such popular preferences are filtered through a political elite that may reshape them.[7]

Public officials respond in part because some of them get their jobs by popular election. But even nonelected officials such as police or welfare workers also seek to justify their policies and actions to the public. Americans are taught to believe that the people we call **average citizens**, those who participate only occasionally, have the right to express opinions and grievances and that political elites are obliged to consider them.

Those least likely to influence decisions are those with few resources—the poor and the illiterate. Homeless persons, for example, do little to influence favorable public decisions. For the most part, others plead their case in the public forums. Sometimes, though, even those who generally are **nonparticipants** may suddenly overwhelm the political elite through protest demonstrations, violent confrontations, or peaceably in elections. Blacks, Mexican Americans, women, homosexuals, the Moral Majority, Mothers Against Drunk Driving, low-tax advocates, and groups for and against gun control or abortion have, with little warning, become important political forces. Their leaders become part of the political elite; group activity leads some to run for political office.

The Political Elite of Illinois Students of social science and others occasionally try to identify the most powerful in their states and communities. The Associated Press once listed the ten most powerful people in Illinois. It used the **reputational approach** that Floyd Hunter developed for his study of Atlanta, Georgia. Researchers ask knowledgeable people who they think are the most powerful. The AP experts were 36 active participants of "business, labor, government, education, and other fields."[8]

Only three politicians made the elite list—the governor, Chicago's mayor, and the leader of downstate state legislators. Three others headed major commercial firms—two chaired banks and one a public utility. The list also included the editor of the *Chicago Tribune* and the publisher of the *Chicago Sun-Times*.

The remaining two are more difficult to classify. One was Phyllis Schlafly of Alton, who sparked the national campaign against the Equal Rights Amendment

(ERA), and the other was a former governor who at the time of the survey was a lawyer in Chicago.

Consider the list more closely.

1. Although more than half were in private business, all had important connections to Illinois government and politics.
2. Several were wealthy, but only one, a publisher, reached his position through inherited wealth.
3. Heading a major organization or holding office was more important than having great personal wealth.
4. Heads of state-based firms (the two largest banks and its major utility), rather than heads of larger national firms, represented business, presumably because their type of business was more closely dependent on the decisions of Illinois politicians.
5. Eight were from Chicago, the state's major metropolitan center.
6. Nine were men.
7. The list had no blacks, no one under 50, and no union leaders.
8. Finally, the ten surely would disagree among themselves on many political issues.[9]

Pluralist Power Studies Some students, who call themselves **pluralists**, argue that community power is divided among groups and individuals who do not share the same social and economic characteristics and often seek conflicting goals. Note, though, that pluralists say that only a few groups or individuals hold major power in a community. They argue that democracy results from average citizens having the opportunity to throw support to competing factions within a pluralist political elite.[10]

Robert Dahl asked knowledgeables in New Haven, Connecticut, to identify those involved in making three specific decisions—this is the **decisional approach**. Through interviews his research team attempted to reconstruct each decision to determine each participant's influence. He concluded that except for the mayor and his aides, individual influentials participated only in some—not all—specific policy areas, such as education, political nominations, or urban renewal.[11]

These and other studies highlighted the diversity of opinion within the political elite. The researchers reported that they found "slack" in the system—potential influentials failed to use their influence as much as they might have. Not surprisingly, the researchers emphasized the importance of politicians and elected public officials in the decision-making process.

Power Elite Studies Others argue that in many communities a **power elite** dominates on the basis of economic power. Its members work together harmoniously toward the same goals and control all the important decisions.[12]

An early study expressing this view was of "Middletown"—Muncie, Indiana—that claimed the "X" family, which owned the local industry, made the community's political decisions as well.[13] But it was Hunter's study of Atlanta that inspired many other such studies. Using the reputational approach, he concluded that a business-dominated power elite controlled most aspects of Atlanta, largely in ways unknown to most citizens. Others using this method found similar power elites—usually of bankers, newspaper publishers, and Main Street merchants.[14]

How Influential Is the Elite? A major criticism of the power elite studies was that they left the impression the power elite was a tightly knit group which agreed on policy and met regularly like a community board of directors. As the Illinois study suggests, this is less likely in large cities or states.

But Peter Bachrach and Morton Baratz pointed out that the influence of a power elite may be more subtle. The pluralist approach that examines decisions, they said, does not consider that a power elite may exercise enough informal power to limit government decisions to relatively trivial issues. They asserted that there is a second face of power—**nondecisions**—the items that never get on the community agenda, alternatives that no one proposes. For example, 25 or so years ago state and community officials rarely discussed discrimination in hiring minorities or low pay for jobs that women traditionally have held. A power elite, Bachrach and Baratz argue, can thus exercise power by shaping a community's social and political beliefs—they call it the **mobilization of bias**.[15] Business leaders often have major influence. But that is not the whole story today.

Does Anyone Decide? Norton Long argued that the elites in communities he observed were so loosely knit that no one seemed in control. Community-wide organization, he said, is often weak or nonexistent. "Much of what occurs seems just to happen with trends becoming accidental accumulations over time and producing results intended by nobody."

He described communities as an **ecology of games**. Each of us, he argued, is involved in his or her own career game. We follow goals that we think get us ahead in "the journalist game," "the lawyer game," "the downtown merchant game," or "the student game."[16]

The social results of these choices are accidental—as, for example, the abandonment of central cities when middle-class citizens and industries individually decided to move to the suburbs. It is difficult to imagine a power elite planning this move. In fact, many of the economic dominants in communities fought bitterly to stem this change—to preserve central business district property values.

We probably do not feel comfortable leaving it there. Is what happens in a community wholly the result of one accident piled on another? Most of us likely say "no," if only because we wish it not to be the case—we like to think that, at least collectively, we have more control than that implies. Yet it does appear that some important decisions are undirected—some communities just drift into them.

Variations in Local Elites Perhaps the most persuasive finding which emerges from community studies is that communities have a wide variety of decision-making styles. Political elites—economic leaders or political bosses—in some states or communities, for a time, have exercised control in ways almost totally unresponsive to nonelite citizens.[17] In other communities, at least for short periods, pluralism has verged on anarchy. Nonelites have penetrated deeply into the decision-making process. Sometimes outraged citizens have brushed aside a political elite's leadership and radically restructured the decision-making process, as did the tax revolt movement of 1980 in Massachusetts and California and in many local communities.[18]

The Circulation of Elites   Elites also change and sometimes disintegrate, with new groups taking their place. A study of Greenville, South Carolina, found the traditional southern power elite of business and old family had been replaced with a coalition of fundamentalists associated with Bob Jones University and what the author called "country people."[19]

David Walker examined the impact of federal actions on "Middletown's" former elite. He found that two-thirds of the households now depended to some extent on federal funds. The "X" family no longer can run even its own factories as it pleases—much less the city of Muncie.[20] State governments also are impinging more on community decision making.

The Impact of Protests and Violence   Some argue that disruption-causing protests are the only way to change elite opinion, particularly with respect to those suffering from poverty or racial or sexual discrimination.[21] Some add that protests can properly involve violence. Dr. Martin Luther King, Jr., used the technique of **civil disobedience**, peaceful nonviolent resistance with protesters willing to suffer the legal consequences of their resistance. In this way he dramatized the injustice of the elites.

But violent confrontations also occurred, many sparked by his assassination. Between 1963 and 1968, there were 283 racial incidents in cities of over 25,000. In the previous 50 years, only 76 major protests were recorded. In the 1960s the typical black rioter was a young male, a lifelong resident of the city, unemployed or working in a menial job, politically informed, and better educated than blacks who did not riot.[22]

Although riots over racial incidents reached a high point in the late 1960s, they still occur. In 1989 riots broke out in Miami over the police killing of a young black. It is difficult to deny that these actions do not affect the decision making of community and state elites.

Protest groups take on a wide variety. Antinuclear groups, students, antiabortionists, animal rights activists, environmentalists—all have employed political protest techniques. Community activists have used these methods to reverse the decisions of local business groups and local governments—for example, against developers of shopping centers and apartment complexes. Such protests may concern proposed street widening, intersection changes, or school closings. And some nonviolent protests have been successful because of the possibility of violence.

The tactics, though, have some inherent problems.[23] Members of SDS (Students for a Democratic Society) in the 1960s attempted to change conditions in Newark for poverty area residents and found that they were frustrated even in getting a stoplight installed at a dangerous intersection. The elite stalled until SDS members were worn down and quit. Still, change in elites did come to Newark within the next decade.[24]

The Impact of Judicial Decisions Even if members of a political elite can "arrange things" in city hall or at the state capitol, they may nevertheless find that a single individual armed with a court suit can obstruct elite decisions much more easily now than in the past. One such example concerned a proposal for the city of Detroit to build and lease a new stadium to their professional football team, the Detroit Lions. To sell the bonds the city had to assure bond buyers that if stadium revenues were insufficient, it would levy a tax to pay the bonds and interest. A promise to levy a tax did not require a referendum, but the city was obligated to issue a public notice. An individual filed suit, saying that the notice was misleading. The state supreme court agreed. The project was scuttled and later a nearby city built the stadium for the "Detroit" Lions.

The Impact of Administrators and Reporters Civil service or merit employment systems and the growing use of professionals in government also tend to diffuse power. Sometimes state administrators support the local political elite. At other times they oppose them. City-paid community development workers, for example, may lead neighborhood groups to oppose neighborhood "improvement" projects. Professional administrators may "leak" stories to newspapers to inform the public of misdeeds in city hall or the county courthouse. Investigative reporters also may uncover such "news."

Today's More Splintered Elites Neither a power elite model nor one of pluralism approaching anarchy describes very well the decision pattern in most states or communities today. Private economic groups still exercise considerable influence, with the passive concurrence of nonelite citizens. But government and new emerging groups, as they become part of the changing state and community political elites, often challenge business dominance and encourage a new pluralism. Given such dispersion of power, average citizens can penetrate and influence the political elites of their states and communities more easily than in the past.

PARTICIPATION BY NONELITE CITIZENS

How much participation by average citizens does democratic government require? As few as 25 to 40 percent of eligible voters vote in some state elections; less than 25 percent in local elections. In surveys, 30 percent of eligible voters report they have worked with others to solve community problems. About 20 percent say they have attended school board or other public meetings or contacted public officials.[25] About 10 percent contribute funds to political parties; 5 percent are party activists. Less than 3 percent have ever taken part in a protest demonstration. Less than 1 percent run for office.

Getting citizens to participate has not been as easy as the Jacksonians, the Progressives of the early 1900s, or some modern-day reformers hoped. A study of voting in ten elections found only 4 percent voted in at least nine and 26 percent in at least five. Thirty-eight percent did not vote in any.[26] The English philosopher and reformer Graham Wallis suggested as early as 1908 that most citizens turn to government and politics with an "indifferent and half attentive mind."[27]

Table 5.1 VOTER TURNOUT IN NONPRESIDENTIAL YEARS: 1978, 1982, 1986[a]

State or other jurisdiction	Percent of voting age population					
	1986		1982		1978	
	Registered	Voting	Registered	Voting	Registered	Voting
United States	66.3	35.4	65.2	61.8	66.1	38.5
Alabama[b]	78.5	41.1	80.0	40.1	72.6	27.4
Alaska[b]	75.8	46.9	92.7	67.9	88.5	48.3
Arizona[b]	61.3	33.3	55.4	35.2	54.9	31.2
Arkansas[b]	67.5	39.5	67.6	47.8	66.5	33.3
California[b]	61.4	35.6	63.2	43.0	61.2	43.1
Colorado[b]	73.2	42.6	65.4	43.0	68.1	43.0
Connecticut[b]	67.1	39.9	69.3	45.6	72.1	47.0
Delaware	60.4	32.8	64.5	43.1	65.3	39.0
Florida[b]	58.6	35.7	59.6	32.9	61.5	36.9
Georgia[b]	55.2	26.3	57.3	28.9	59.5	18.1
Hawaii[b]	51.0	40.5	56.6	43.6	60.1	44.5
Idaho[b]	78.5	55.2	81.8	49.5	85.9	48.5
Illinois[b]	70.2	36.8	71.5	44.2	71.4	41.1
Indiana	70.7	38.2	75.2	46.5	74.8	36.8
Iowa[b]	78.4	44.0	73.8	49.6	76.5	40.6
Kansas[b]	64.1	46.0	67.4	43.4	70.3	44.6
Kentucky	72.8	24.7	69.7	26.7	65.9	18.9
Louisiana	68.6	43.1	64.3	[c]	65.9	30.4
Maine[b]	88.5	47.8	92.2	55.4	87.5	47.5
Maryland[b]	61.3	31.9	61.7	35.7	62.6	33.6
Massachusetts[b]	67.6	37.1	68.9	46.7	69.3	48.5
Michigan[b]	85.3	35.3	85.8	46.4	81.6	46.6
Minnesota[b]	82.7	44.8	89.3	60.4	88.9	57.6
Mississippi	88.5	28.1	86.4	37.0	68.8	34.9
Missouri	72.5	38.7	75.5	42.4	73.7	44.2
Montana	75.7	54.3	78.4	56.4	74.8	54.2
Nebraska[b]	72.8	48.3	72.7	47.9	75.1	46.1
Nevada[b]	47.2	33.6	48.7	36.3	51.5	37.5
New Hampshire[b]	67.0	20.7	66.3	40.9	76.6	43.7
New Jersey	63.6	26.1	66.4	39.6	67.6	38.7
New Mexico[b]	57.5	35.9	62.3	43.5	71.1	42.5
New York[b]	59.9	31.9	58.0	39.7	60.4	38.2
North Carolina	62.7	32.4	60.6	29.9	59.4	27.8
North Dakota		59.8		55.4		51.6
Ohio[b]	75.1	39.2	72.8	43.6	68.4	39.5
Oklahoma[b]	83.9	37.8	70.2	38.4	65.6	38.5
Oregon[b]	73.2	51.7	77.6	53.3	81.5	50.4
Pennsylvania[b]	64.5	37.4	64.2	41.5	64.5	43.1
Rhode Island[b]	68.7	42.3	73.6	47.2	75.5	47.0
South Carolina[b]	51.3	29.8	53.6	29.3	52.2	30.1

Table 5.1 *Continued*

South Dakota[b]	84.1	58.2	88.4	57.9	87.7	54.2
Tennessee[b]	66.8	33.1	67.3	37.3	67.3	37.4
Texas[b]	59.4	28.0	63.6	29.6	60.8	25.3
Utah	70.8	40.4	76.0	53.9	77.7	44.9
Vermont[b]	79.6	47.8	83.4	44.6	81.0	35.4
Virginia	57.4	23.0	54.8	34.7	53.4	33.0
Washington	65.3	39.1	66.8	43.4	70.2	36.9
West Virginia	67.7	28.3	67.3	40.1	74.9	36.2
Wisconsin[b]		42.9		45.6	51.5	46.0
Wyoming[b]	67.0	47.0	65.0	47.7	67.9	48.0
District of Columbia	57.7	27.0	74.1	22.7	48.5	20.0

Source: U.S. Bureau of the Census, *Statistical Abstract of the United States* (Washington, D.C.: U.S. Department of Commerce).

[a] Turnout figures used in each case are for the race receiving the highest number of votes in that election.

[b] Has a governorship contest in nonpresidential years.

[c] Special circumstances render data inapplicable.

Modern political scientists have gotten over their shock at voter ignorance or interest. They still believe sufficient linkages between nonelite citizens and officials exist to make democracy a reality. Elections provide the linkage, but scholars disagree over how the linkage occurs. One group argues that people do vote their preferences—if the political elites pose questions in an understandable way.[28] Another group maintains that citizens largely react—they vote for incumbent governors and legislators when they judge "things" to be going as well as can be expected and against them when "things" are going badly. Some Republican governors lost in the 1982 election as a result of the national recession of 1981–1982—an example of what researchers call **retrospective voting**.[29]

Slightly more than one-third of all citizens are regular nonparticipants. They seldom vote or make any other effort to influence officials. At the other extreme of the nonelite are politically active citizens who comprise perhaps 5 to 10 percent of the population—Gabriel Almond aptly called them **attentive publics**—"an informed and interested stratum before whom elite discussion and controversy take place." Attentive publics come and go with changes in issues and political events.[30] Between the nonparticipants and the attentive publics are those we have called "average citizens."

The Average Citizens

Researchers generally use voting as a shorthand measure for other forms of political participation because it is the most basic and widespread form of democratic participation as well as being the most thoroughly studied. Being apathetic about politics and not voting are related to a common set of socioeconomic characteristics.[31] But these may not be relevant for other forms of participation. Elaine Sharp, for example, found that contacting urban public officials was based on

Table 5.2 PERCENTAGE WHO REPORT VOTING IN RECENT NATIONAL ELECTIONS[a]

	1980	1984	1988
Women	58.3	60.8	58.3
Men	56.4	59.0	56.4
White	59.1	61.4	59.1
Black	51.5	55.8	51.5
Hispanic	28.8	32.6	28.8
18–24	36.2	40.8	39.9
25–44	54.0	58.4	58.7
45–64	67.9	69.8	69.3
65+	68.8	67.7	65.1
Northeast	57.4	59.7	
Midwest	62.9	65.4	
South	54.5	56.8	
West	55.6	58.5	
School years completed			
8 or less	36.7	42.9	42.6
9–11	41.3	44.4	45.6
High school grad	54.7	58.7	58.9
1–3 college	64.5	67.5	
College grad	77.6	79.1	
Some college			73.2
Employed	58.4	61.6	61.8
Unemployed	38.6	44.0	41.2
Not in labor force	57.3	58.9	57.0
Own home	70.0	71.8	
Rent	39.8	43.7	
Total	57.4	59.9	59.2

Source: U.S. Department of Commerce, Voting and Registration in the Election of November 1988 (Washington, D.C.: U.S. Bureau of the Census, February 1989, Series P20, #435).

[a] Some survey respondents exaggerate their participation. For example, in 1988 a total of 57.4 say they voted; in fact, only 50 percent of eligible voters cast ballots.

expectations that government would respond. Such expectations are fostered by such procedures as citizen complaint agencies, plus the presence of a perceived need for such action.[32] So too, participation in neighborhood associations may depend on different qualities than voting participation.[33]

Table 5.2 shows socioeconomic characteristics found to be related to many forms of political participation, including voting. The data exaggerate participation in two ways. They are based on self-reporting and on national election participation where participation is highest.

Variation by Status Participation is related to educational level and, secondarily, to position in society, including organizational ties, income, and occupation. Social status is a rough measure of the distance a citizen is from the center of social actions. Every indicator of higher social status appears related to higher political participation. Thus those with the most schooling vote most often; those with just a few years of education are likely to be nonparticipants. The wealthy vote in proportionately greater numbers than do the poor, and the employed vote more than the unemployed. Middle-aged people and seniors vote more than the young (note that seniors were one of the few groups to increase their participation in 1988), long-term residents in a community more than newcomers, property owners more than renters, Protestants more than Catholics, and those with an early migrant background more than those whose ancestors arrived after the Mayflower.

Of course, we can expect to find exceptions in particular elections—for example, Hispanic turnout would likely be higher than usual if one of their number were in a contest for governor. And the status of some groups is changing. Women now vote in slightly greater numbers than men, given the same socioeconomic class, and northern blacks vote at about the same rate as northern whites.

Governmental Level Participation About 50 to 55 percent of potential voters participate in presidential elections compared to an average of 45 percent in governors' races and 25 percent in mayoral elections. Voting in any specific election, of course, varies.

Closeness of the Race Participation rises when voters believe that their vote might make a difference in the outcome. The high-participation states tend to have two-party competition, at least for major office. Those with low participation customarily have been one-party states. Again, there are exceptions.

Participation by State and Region Voting participation tends to be higher in the northern and western states, those that Daniel Elazar described as having a "moralistic" political culture. Lower participation was commonly found in the southern states—those he called "traditional." The gap between the South and the rest of the nation is closing, however. The larger industrialized urban states of the North are at the center of the participation distribution. This regional pattern, though, is a weak one and includes some striking exceptions.[34]

Samuel Patterson and Gregory Caldeira argue that **political mobilizers**, factors that encourage participation, can explain most differences of participation among the states. They studied gubernatorial elections and found the most relevant factors to be party competition, closeness of the race, money spent on campaigns, and whether a U.S. Senate race took place during the same election.[35]

The Importance of Political Ties As we might expect, those who hold public office are political actives. Their relatives and even friends are also likely to vote. An early study of voting in Chicago demonstrated that a voter participation cam-

Table 5.3 PERCENT OF THOSE REGISTERED WHO VOTED IN NONPRESIDENTIAL YEARS: 1978, 1982, 1986

State or other jurisdiction	1978	1982	1986
United States	53.5	61.2	58.2
Alabama[a]	52.3	52.8	37.7
Alaska[a]	68.0	73.3	54.6
Arizona[a]	54.3	63.6	56.9
Arkansas[a]	58.4	70.7	50.0
California[a]	58.0	68.1	70.4
Colorado[a]	58.2	65.7	63.0
Connecticut[a]	59.4	65.8	65.3
Delaware	54.4	66.8	59.7
Florida[a]	60.9	52.6	60.0
Georgia[a]	47.6	50.5	30.4
Hawaii[a]	79.5	77.0	74.1
Idaho[a]	70.4	60.4	56.5
Illinois[a]	52.4	61.8	57.5
Indiana	54.1	61.9	49.3
Iowa[a]	56.1	65.4	53.1
Kansas[a]	71.7	64.3	63.4
Kentucky	33.9	38.3	28.6
Louisiana	62.9		46.1
Maine[a]	54.1	60.0	54.2
Maryland[a]	52.0	57.9	53.6
Massachusetts[a]	56.0	67.7	70.0
Michigan[a]	41.4	54.0	57.0
Minnesota[a]	54.1	67.7	64.7
Mississippi	31.7	42.8	50.8
Missouri	53.3	56.2	59.9
Montana	71.6	72.0	72.4
Nebraska[a]	66.4	65.9	61.3
Nevada[a]	71.2	74.5	72.8
New Hampshire[a]	45.5	63.0	57.0
New Jersey	41.1	59.6	57.2
New Mexico[a]	62.4	69.8	59.7
New York[a]	53.2	68.4	63.2
North Carolina	51.6	49.4	46.7
North Dakota	b	b	b
Ohio[a]	52.1	59.8	57.8
Oklahoma[a]	45.0	54.7	58.6
Oregon[a]	70.6	68.7	61.9
Pennsylvania[a]	57.9	64.6	66.9
Rhode Island[a]	61.5	64.2	62.2
South Carolina[a]	58.0	54.7	57.7
South Dakota[a]	69.1	65.5	61.8
Tennessee[a]	49.5	55.4	55.7

Table 5.3 *Continued*

Texas[a]	47.2	49.7	41.7
Utah	57.0	70.9	57.7
Vermont[a]	60.1	53.5	43.7
Virginia	39.9	63.3	62.2
Washington	60.0	65.0	52.5
West Virginia	41.9	59.6	48.3
Wisconsin[a]	[b]	[b]	89.2
Wyoming[a]	70.2	73.5	70.6
District of Columbia	46.8	30.7	41.2

Source: U.S. Bureau of the Census, *Statistical Abstract of the United States* (Washington, D.C.: U.S. Department of Commerce).

[a] Has a governorship contest in nonpresidential years. Note that it may or may not also have a contest for a United States Senate seat and will always have races for U.S. House seats.

[b] Voter registration not required.

paign increased voter turnout—except in the Irish precincts. There, Irish politicians, who then ran the Chicago machine, had already gotten all the potential Irish voters to the polls.[36]

Participation and Personal Beliefs The earliest voting studies showed that some persons feel it a civic duty to participate. Others have a high sense of **political efficacy**—a belief that their participation will make a difference. Both qualities encourage voting. Generally, communities with higher-level incomes have more persons with such beliefs. The nonparticipation of the very poor and the unemployed in part may be related also to psychological barriers such as a lack of confidence.[37] The belief that their participation may not change things, some scholars argue, is a notion based on reality.[38]

Theodore Macaluso and John Wanat argue that "religiosity" encourages participation. They found holding religious beliefs to be especially important "where the traditional factors of political interest and class status do not support participation." High participation rates in Utah and Idaho may thus be related to their large Mormon populations.[39]

Family Socialization Paul Allen Beck and M. Kent Jennings studied a sample of young Americans drawn from a 1965 to 1973 panel study to determine whether experiences while growing up influenced later participation patterns. They found that the socioeconomic status of parents and adolescent involvement in high school activities were associated with high political participation later in life.[40]

Opportunities for Citizen Participation

Reformers argue that democracy requires that the opportunity to participate must be as great as possible. Still, many issues and decisions never come to the attention of average citizens, even at election time. Political elites compromise issues among themselves, strike bargains that satisfy the interests participating, and that decision becomes state or community policy.

Lest we become paranoid, though, we note that this is the way all governmental systems and most private organizations work. Average citizens delegate decision-making power to the political decision makers and, in effect, to those who have major influence with them—that is, to the political elite with occasional contributions fom attentive publics. It can hardly be otherwise—time usually does not allow for all citizens or members of an organization to be heard and individual wants or needs negotiated on every issue. The average citizen's potential for influence rises when an election is required or when circumstances such as the following bring an issue to public attention.

A Calamity Occurs The assassination of Dr. Martin Luther King, Jr., dramatized for blacks how much had been wrong with racial segregation. Inner-city blacks rioted and as a result entered the political process in larger numbers, demanding changes. Political elites in many states and communities responded positively.

Something less than a catastrophe can also stimulate citizen participation. Many white parents objected, for example, when the courts ordered busing programs for desegregation purposes. In some communities previously casual participants became very active.

A Problem Is Publicized Newspaper stories may focus on a governmental action, whether it be the salary of a new city manager, the administration of a state's Medicaid program, or the condition of county farm-to-market roads. Such news stories bring the decisions of political elites (or their lack of action, which is a nondecision) to the attention of average citizens. Pressure may or may not develop for a review of such decisions.

Political Elites Disagree Publicly E. E. Schattschneider emphasized that widening a conflict beyond the political elite not only involves more average citizens who are amateur participants but also might change the outcome of political disputes.[41] When a state's political elite considers building new quarters for its historical museum, it cannot afford dissension. A decision might be changed if members of the political elite widen the conflict by attacking each other publicly. As more average citizens become involved and hear some expressing doubts, the project might be delayed and even be abandoned.

Legal Rules and Citizen Participation

In the 1890s the newly formed Populist party challenged Democrats in the South. Blacks held the potential balance of power. Old-line Democrats took many of their sharecropper tenants to the polls and instructed them on how to vote. Sensing the potential loss of control, whites then devised laws designed to reduce or eliminate Negro voting. Alabama and Louisiana used the grandfather clause (a person could not register to vote if the grandfather had not voted prior to 1860).

Virginia adopted the **poll tax**, which had to be paid before a person could vote. Others used **literacy tests**. Some tests required explanation of complicated constitutional clauses; others used a "general knowledge" question such as "How many bubbles are in a bar of soap?" These rules excluded blacks as well as many whites from voting. (See Table 5.4.)

Reformers argue that "playing by the rules of the game" still handicaps the powerless. The rules for participating, they say, are part of what is being struggled over. Yet our history shows that often the rules are changed—practices once considered radical are now accepted without comment. For example, women in many states could not vote until 1920, and blacks and other minorities, such as native American Indians and Hispanics, were kept from voting until relatively recently.

Liberalizing Voting Requirements Despite this sorry history, the story of citizen participation is one of steadily eliminating legal barriers. Congress and the federal courts abolished or pressured state and community governments to abolish one legal restriction after another—restrictions based on property ownership, race, religious creed, age, and sex. Discriminatory requirements such as the literacy test, the poll tax, and unusual residence or registration requirements have been eliminated or cut back sharply.

The most striking recent change is an outgrowth of our distinctive pattern of intergovernmental relations. In 1965 the U.S. **Voting Rights Act** required national registrars in counties where more than 50 percent of the potential voters did not vote and where some form of literacy, understanding, or good character requirement was in effect. Threat of federal intervention reduced discriminatory practices that were common just a generation ago.[42] Also the law demands that the Department of Justice approve changes in voting laws before implementing them. Federal rules also require local officials to print ballots in Spanish as well as English where a substantial percentage of Spanish-speaking citizens reside.

As the legal barriers fell, startling rises in voting occurred. In Mississippi, the number of blacks who registered to vote increased from 6.7 percent in 1965 to 55.8 percent in two years. In six other southern states registration rose from 30 to 46 percent. In 1968 citizens in all the states that once made up the Confederacy elected 276 blacks to public office. By 1981 the number was almost ten times as great—2,457.[43]

Table 5.4 BLACK VOTING—EFFECTS OF DISCRIMINATORY LAWS

State	No. of voters/year	No. of voters/year
Alabama[a]	78,311 (1900)	1,081 (1903)
Louisiana	130,344 (1898)	5,230 (1900)
Virginia	147,000 (1900)	21,000 (1902)

Source: Adapted from Jack Bass and Walter DeVries, *The Transformation of Southern Politics* (New York: Basic Books, 1978), pp. 82, 342.

[a] Fourteen black belt counties.

Civil rights advocates argue that subtle discrimination still persists. The crucial section of the Voting Rights Act, they say, is Section 5, which requires local units to submit to the U.S. Justice Department proposed election changes. More than just southern states felt the impact of this section. In 1988 the U.S. Justice Department sued the Los Angeles Board of Supervisors, arguing that although Los Angeles County had the largest community of Spanish Americans in the nation, no Hispanic was elected from its five electoral districts. The Justice Department wanted the county to redraw the district lines.

In Policy Box No. 9, "The Hispanic Subculture and Full Participation," we discuss other federal, state, and community efforts to assist Hispanics in gaining full participation in our society.

Opening the System for Average Citizens Our governments provide many points of **access**, opportunities for a citizen's views to be heard. Federalism and the separation of powers multiplies these access points. For example, a person may write the governor and the mayor or phone a city councilor, state legislator, or administrator. Legislative sessions and many administrative hearings are public. "Sunshine laws" have expanded the list of meetings that members of the press as well as the average citizen may attend. They also require officials to provide many types of documents upon citizen demand. Moreover, many federal grant programs now require citizen hearings. The courts can be used to protest official actions and to enable citizens, as jurors, to participate in decision making.

The separation of the executive, legislative, and judicial branches and regularly scheduled elections encourage a widening of conflicts. Judges review past decisions; councils challenge the actions of mayors and managers; candidates attack decisions made by incumbents. The media, relatively free of governmental controls, report these conflicts. In addition, many officials themselves seek out citizens—governors and mayors have phone-in radio programs. Many units of government have an office to handle complaints or requests for information—many have ombudsmen.

The Challenge of Direct Democracy By **direct democracy**, we mean that citizens rather than their elected representatives make policy. One of the earliest forms was the New England **town meeting**, where the citizens of a community meet once a year to elect officials and prepare the town budget. Such town meetings are not in wide use any longer. All states except Delaware ask voters to make the final decision on proposed constitutional amendments or new constitutions. Forty-two states use the **referendum**, a provision that permits citizens to petition for a vote on statutes or ordinances the legislature has passed and, if they wish, to reject them. Twenty-three states and many communities use the **initiative**. It permits voters to propose statutes or constitutional amendments by petition. If sufficient signatures are collected the proposal is placed on the ballot for a citizen vote. Fifteen states permit voters to **recall** state officials from office. A petition having the necessary signatures is followed by a recall election.

Since 1968 the number of initiatives and referenda voted on has jumped from 10 to over 40 each election year. And we find some dramatic jumps in state and

Policy Box No. 9

The Hispanic Subculture and Full Participation

A few summers ago we taught a group of American students in England. Among the field trips we took was one to the British Foreign Office. We could hardly help but be impressed with the tight security, the long marble halls the guard took us through, and finally the ornate conference room. Here we met the British representative, a young product of the British university system. He was most impressive, dazzling us all with his quiet and urbane erudition as he fielded our questions.

A student asked what he considered America's greatest problem. We expected he would say healing the scars of the Vietnam War, balancing inflation and unemployment, or perhaps eradicating our urban ghettos.

But what he said was, "Integrating into your society the large Spanish-speaking populations in states such as Florida, Texas, and New Mexico." And if Puerto Rico becomes a state, add its citizens to the list.

Some students argued that kind of integration was one of America's strengths. The "melting pot" was the great American success story. Perhaps nothing expressed it so well as one popular concert number called "The Ballad for Americans." When college choirs sang it, a narrator would ask the chorus questions such as "Who are you?" The ringing response came back, "I'm just an Irish, Jewish, Polish, Italian, Swedish, English, etc., etc., Czech and double check American!" Why had this educated English foreign officer said that our greatest problem would be making those of Spanish-American heritage full participants in our society?

Most of us might not be astonished to learn that 50 percent of the children attending public school in San Antonio, Texas, are Spanish Americans. But are we also aware that the same is true in Los Angeles? Or that Hispanic children make up 30 percent of our students in Denver, Hartford, New York City, and Miami?

Hispanics number 16 million today and experts predict that in a few decades they will be the largest ethnic minority in the United States. And, perhaps, the 1990 census will show that Spanish Americans are a majority of the population in many cities and maybe even a few states.

Many speak only Spanish; children entering school know only a smattering of English. How are we to make sure they can participate fully in our democratic system?

The U.S. government has encouraged states to assist Spanish speakers in two ways. Local election officials must have bilingual ballots if the foreign-language-speaking population exceeds certain limits. The ballots give instructions about voting procedures and information about ballot proposals in both English and the non-English language.

The federal government also encourages the states to offer bilingual education programs for Hispanics and other foreign language groups—usually in schools that have 20 or more students who do not speak English. In such schools, teachers teach the basic subjects in the foreign language while students also take English as a second language.

But some citizens question whether bilingual instruction—a reform of the early 1970s—and even bilingual ballots are good ideas. They say that the programs are too costly, and that they will eventually create an America of two cultures.

The financial argument is easiest to understand. The Reagan administration announced that it would cut the bilingual grants by 47 percent, leaving states and school districts to pick up the difference if they wanted to continue the programs. Thus Los Angeles County supervisors, for example, passed a resolution supporting a constitutional amendment that would make English the nation's official language. The supervisors believe the program is too expensive for the results obtained.

But the second argument—encouraging a subculture—is more important. America has always feared cultural divisions such as that of French Quebec in Canada. Benjamin Franklin was the first to propose that ours be an English-only society. And during World War I, Iowa's governor banned speaking any foreign language in schools, churches, public conversation, and even over the phone! By 1919, 15 states had mandated that English be the sole language of instruction in public or private schools.

But Hispanics who favor bilingual instruction claim that only bilingual classes will prevent the creation of a Spanish subculture; they feel that Hispanics will be handicapped if they have to learn in English-only classes, forcing them to become outsiders in our society. Dr. Roberto Cruz argues that bilingual teaching need only be short-term. Studies show, he says, that in two years students learn enough English to fit nicely into their classes.

Besides, the supporters argue, Spanish is the language of our hemisphere—two-thirds of the people in South and North America speak it. In the future America will gain by having many Spanish speakers as diplomats, businesspeople, or teachers. If we stress English only, the language will be forgotten by the third generation, as happened in many other ethnic groups.

Those favoring bilingual programs say that the alternative to these programs is a high rate of school dropouts, and they state that it is already happening. It is the same mistake we made in Puerto Rico where we tried for years to make English the language of instruction. We finally gave up because it didn't work.

But not all Spanish Americans agree with these arguments. Schoolteacher Richard Rodriguez, the son of immigrant Mexicans, in his autobiography *Hunger of Memory*, comes out strongly against bilingual teaching. He says he was forced to learn English in a way that English-as-a-second-language classes never would have taught. He writes, "One day in school I raised my hand to volunteer an answer. I spoke out in a loud voice. And I did not think it remarkable when the entire class understood. That day, I moved very far from the disadvantaged child I had been only days earlier."

Rodriguez writes movingly of the sense of loss he felt as he found himself separated from his parents because he could speak English and they could not. But he argues there was a net gain. He believed it was the only way he could hope to get ahead in American society. Without being at ease with the language of the society, he thinks, one cannot feel a part of that society.

Rodriguez says the bilingual voter's ballot "implies that a person can exercise that most public of rights—the right to vote—while still keeping apart, unassimilated

> from public life." He claims bilingualism "will preserve for the child a separate identity, distancing the child from public culture."
>
> Other critics are more harsh. Journalist Bill Granger says a state and local bureaucracy are the main beneficiaries and defenders of bilingual programs. Bilingualism, he writes, will create a permanent underclass to be treated as welfare children. That is why, he says, the bureaucrats promote it. And, he warns, every bilingual country today is tearing itself apart. He cites Canada and Belgium as examples.
>
> What do you think? How can Spanish-speaking Americans gain full participation in American culture? Will bilingual programs create an underclass of Americans because they will never learn to speak English very well? Has the "melting pot" in fact been a great success? Should states and communities continue to print bilingual ballots? Or will the whole problem take care of itself by "benign neglect"—that is, if the state and community governments do nothing? Is it more likely that Spanish-speaking children will be able to function better in our society if they learn the basic subjects in their native tongue?

community turnouts also—voters rising to the challenge of making important decisions after a hard-fought campaign. But many votes on initiatives range from 10 to 30 percent less than the votes for governor in the same election.[44]

Only 16 state officials have ever had to face a recall election since Oregon adopted the procedure in 1908—13 were recalled. State procedures make such elections difficult by demanding a large number of signatures and allowing a short time to obtain them. A successful recall requires a crisis of confidence in the party which originally elected the official.[45] Local officials are more susceptible to recall, and many have been removed from office in this way.[46]

Reducing Legal Barriers Is Not Enough It would be comforting if we could assume that once all legal barriers were removed, voting would be uniformly high across states and communities. But many citizens still do not participate—voting itself has been declining.

OTHER INFLUENCES ON POLITICAL PARTICIPATION

In the remainder of this chapter, we consider three theories that attempt to explain variations in participation as well as in nonparticipation among average citizens: (1) costs and benefits, (2) citizen alienation, and (3) social movement participation.

The Costs and Benefits of Participation

A moment's reflection suggests that political participation involves some personal cost. **Participation costs** require us to spend our limited amounts of time, energy, and, sometimes, money on politics. When we travel to the polls to vote, attend a

The League of Women Voters recruits new voters.

political meeting, distribute leaflets for a candidate, make a political contribution, or participate in other ways, we are spending resources.

To participate intelligently we also need information—what kind of people the candidates are, and how their stands on issues may benefit or injure us. Such information is not free for most of us. States and communities have been more successful in reducing participation costs than in reducing **information costs.**

Costs Are Lower for High-Status Citizens Stop in a small town around 10 A.M., and you very likely will find the Main Street merchants and some local officials gathered at a café for morning coffee. The conversations include community gossip as well as local politics. At the same hour you would find many of the homemakers and the retired at home, blue-collar workers in factories or on road crews, and the unemployed walking or driving around looking for work or at home working in the yard.

It costs little for these Main Street merchants to keep up with community politics or to participate in community decisions. They, like other higher-status persons, gain political advantage from the positions they hold in society. They are involved at the center rather than at the edges of their social system. They can understand without too much effort how most decisions will affect them. Information costs for them compared to homemakers, the unemployed, or blue-collar workers are lower.

Lower-status persons, especially because of their occupations, experience higher costs in time, energy, and even money to reach decision makers and to participate. They need more than a few clues to get an accurate picture. Unlike you, many of them have not had a course in state and community government. A few are handicapped further by lack of basic reading skills or difficulties with English. Thus for the better educated, higher-status groups, participation and information costs are less—and the benefits of participation also are more obvious.

A cost and benefit calculation turns out to be a good rough indicator of participation differences among average citizens. Any factor that raises the costs—for example, rain on Election Day—inevitably lowers participation. The dropoff is greater among those for whom the costs are highest. All participation costs cannot be eliminated, of course. For the most part, we can probably view most that remain as reasonable burdens of democratic citizenship.[47] An exception, some believe, is voter registration to ensure honest elections.

The Costs of Registration   North Dakota is the only state that does not require **voter registration**, citizens confirming in advance of voting that they meet the residency and other requirements. Some rural parts of other states also do without registration.

Registration is intended to eliminate fraud. Many experts are not sure that it does so. Still, an unpurged roll of those who have moved or died invites fraudulent voting. In Mississippi, for instance, registration is 90 percent, but in over half the counties the number of registrants exceeds the population. Still, Lee Sigelman found a difference in nonvoting patterns over a series of elections between those who reported themselves as registered and not voting and those not registered. The variable best explaining the differences was age—the researcher hypothesized that the young remained nonregistrants until motivated to vote in a specific election; older citizens were more frequently already registered and thus were more likely to vote at least occasionally.[48]

The costs registration places on citizens are often greater than the costs involved in voting. Failure to register is the reason often given by those who do not vote. Citizens must identify themselves as eligible, usually to a city or county clerk and generally some time in advance of the election. The process thus requires a little forethought as well as a special visit to a government office. But in many states if you vote once in four years, you need not reregister.

Registration is also a kind of residence requirement because registration typically closes 30 days before the election. Thus those who have been resident less than a month cannot vote, and other new residents who have lived in the state longer than 30 days may be eligible to register but be unaware of closing dates.

States that require registration every two years add to voting costs. Many citizens, particularly those who vote only occasionally, will not be sure whether they voted two years before. Many stay home and avoid the possible embarrassment of being denied a ballot. Election officials, though, argue that the two-year registration law helps clear the roll of voters who have moved away, keeps election administration expenses down, and reduces the possibility of fraud.

Reducing Registration Costs Maine, Minnesota, Oregon, and Wisconsin now allow voters to register when they appear to vote. In 1978 Ohio voters rejected such a proposal, mainly because many feared fraud might occur. Many states and communities set up registration booths in shopping centers or in student dormitories shortly before registration closes. Others deputize political party workers to go door to door seeking new registrants or deputize school officials to register graduating students.

Among the other experiments to reduce registration costs are the computerized registration system of South Carolina, the postcard registration system used in Maryland and New Jersey, and Michigan's system of registering voters when renewing their driver's licenses. Nineteen states allow registration by mail. Congress, in an effort to reduce registration costs, proposed nationwide requirements for simultaneous driver license and voter registration as well as postcard registration. Adoption of one or both would extend federal penetration in election administration, an area many consider state domain.

Will reduced registration costs increase voter participation? Charles V. Hamilton found that only 52 percent of the new registrants in Harlem voted, as compared with 66 percent of those already registered. Among new registrants, 64 percent of the black middle class in contrast to 46 percent of the black working class subsequently voted. Those who registered in person were more likely to vote than those who registered by mail—66 to 50 percent.[49]

Steven Rosenstone and Raymond Wolfinger estimate that national registration, common in most democracies, would increase voter turnout by more than 9 percent—particularly among low-income citizens. Another study estimates it to be closer to 14 percent.[50] Rosenstone and Wolfinger note, nevertheless, that the greatest voter turnout in recent times was in 1960, when registration and election laws were a good deal more restrictive. Many barriers have been relaxed or removed and the nation's educational level has risen, yet turnout has fallen. They conclude, "Other aspects of the political environment clearly are at work."[51]

Note that unpurged rolls, such as that of Mississippi mentioned earlier, make measures of participation somewhat questionable, since they are usually based on the number of registered voters who actually vote.[52]

Information Costs Are Still High

To vote intelligently, citizens require political information. Woodrow Wilson and Theodore Roosevelt both supported the **Short Ballot Movement** of the early 1900s because they believed it lowers information costs. Faced with a long ballot of candidates they know little about, most voters skip over minor offices or vote blindly. So, the reformers concluded, information costs could be reduced by making the task of voting a reasonable one—ask voters to vote only for major policy-making officials who are visible to the public. Eliminating primary elections or votes on charter or constitutional amendments would also reduce information costs and voter burdens. But it seems unlikely that such suggestions will or should be adopted.

Some states have made the ballot itself more informative by allowing candidates to add slogans or other descriptive material. We review such efforts in Policy Box No. 10, "California's Experiment in Reducing Voter Costs."

The Media Help Reduce Information Costs Can average citizens get all the information they need about state and local governments from newspapers, radio, and television? Many critics argue that such coverage is "spotty"—especially on radio and television. Critics also argue that the media do not offer enough interpretive reporting—filling in background facts or explaining what the issue might mean to voters. Local access cable TV provides information for some.

William Gormley reviewed how 44 jointly owned newspaper and television stations covered state government. He found that newspapers reported more stories, devoted a higher percentage of government reports to state government, and gave these stories more prominence.

The Capitol Press Corps Gormley and others nevertheless questioned whether newspaper coverage was adequate. Of 113 daily papers in Texas, for example, only 13 had full-time reporters at the capitol. The number in Illinois, excluding the Springfield papers, was 8. He cites a study of capitol wire service bureaus that found them "disgracefully understaffed."[53]

David Morgan found that most New York dailies had only one regular reporter in Albany. They sometimes added "session reporters" who came in temporarily. A survey of all state capitol news bureaus found 38 percent had only one reporter during the legislative session; 58 percent were so staffed between sessions.[54] The "regulars," Morgan notes, bitterly criticized session reporters for doing shoddy work—"loose speculation masquerading as think pieces." The result of understaffing, journalists argue, is that they have no time for in-depth research.[55] A veteran reporter told Morgan, "We're more dependent on handouts [politicians' news releases] than ever—there is little help to check releases."[56]

Covering the Legislative Arena Reporters point out that the legislature in part may be responsible for some of the incomplete coverage. An amateur legislature is likely not to have a strict calendar which tells reporters precisely when a bill will be discussed in committee or on the floor. Having many committees and no advance announcement of committee meetings makes the journalist's task more difficult. Some journalists complain of working 16-hour days in such legislatures. Unnecessarily complicated terms and outmoded rules may also cause problems. In Missouri, for example, a rule stated that legislators should not address each other by name. Inexperienced reporters found it difficult to follow the interchanges.[57]

Legislatures vary in the amount of access they allow journalists. Only a few permit computer access to bill files. A 1983 study found 12 of the 99 legislative houses did not allow special floor space to reporters. In a few states journalists had to pay for such facilities. Thirty-one houses did not allow reporters to circulate on the floor during recess, and 86 did not allow them on the floor while the session was in progress. The reason generally given was that the floor would

Policy Box No. 10

California's Experiment in Reducing Voter Costs

Every so often in Oklahoma a candidate named Will Rogers runs for state or local office—he is capitalizing on the name of one of the state's most famous citizens, the cowboy humorist Will Rogers. Periodically in other state and community elections we find ballots in which two candidates with similar or even the same first and last names are running for the same office. Often one of these is a political unknown hoping to get votes intended for a more popular candidate. All such candidates are in effect increasing information costs for the average voter.

California in 1932 attempted to solve that kind of problem by allowing candidates with similar names to identify themselves on the ballot—thus reducing the information costs for voters. In 1945 the state legislature limited nonofficeholder candidates to three words. But they allowed incumbents to use any number of words they wished. A 1963 study by the Assembly Elections Committee and a 1974 study by political scientists Gary C. Byrne and J. Kristian Pueschel confirmed what politicians already knew—well-phrased designations help bring victory. Candidates word these designations carefully. Campaign strategists often carefully pretest them with public opinion surveys.

In 1973, because of uneasiness about changes in districts caused by reapportionment, the legislature extended the law to all elections and eliminated the requirement that it be used only where names were similar. Local election officials were designated to pass on the wordings proposed for minor races, and the secretary of state's office decided for statewide races.

The political scientists who studied races for Republican and Democratic county central committee positions found that certain designations were advantageous—"professor," "incumbent," "engineer," and "lawyer." Some designations neither hurt nor helped much—"scientist," "businessman," "teacher," "skilled labor," and "political officeholder." Some designations hurt—"stockbroker," "doctor," "dentist," "life insurance salesman," "housewife," "salesman," and "real estate broker." Worst of all was no designation. In terms of the ethnicity of candidates' names they found Scandinavian helpful; English, Irish, and Greek having little effect; and Spanish, Jewish, eastern European, and Italian having a negative effect. They also found that candidates with nicknames had a clear advantage.

How have candidates used a designation? An Orange County supervisor running for the state senate listed himself as "Orange County Legislator." A college professor running for Congress became a "National Affairs Analyst." A butcher called himself a "Meat Purveyor" and a candidate for the assembly who first used "Telephone Line Repairman" changed it to "Communications Specialist."

Candidates with little hope of winning may publicize causes, as in "Gay Feminist Activist" or "Socialist Workers' Spokesperson." Highlighting issues one favors presents a more difficult problem. A San Bernardino school board candidate against sex education used "Mandatory Sexology Opponent." Los Angeles had a city council candidate who used "Graft Corruption Fighter."

> Some designations are challenged in court, and such cases may even delay the printing of ballots. A member of Congress who moved to a new district tried "Former California Congressman" and lost in court. A Beverly Hills woman who wanted to use "Jewish Mother" was not permitted to do so.
>
> Some critics concede that in some cases the designations do reduce information costs for voters, but too often they have been used to confuse and even deceive—thus adding to information costs. They suggest instead slogans, such as Oregon permits on the ballot, or allowing each candidate to present a 200-word statement like those mailed with sample ballots in California for some local races. Others argue that the candidate designations at least give voters some information—particularly in nonpartisan races where ethnicity or name familiarity becomes crucial.
>
> What do you think? Should the ballots in all state and local elections give some information about the candidates as is commonly done in mail ballot elections within large private associations? Do you think a three-word limit is unrealistic? Who should decide whether the designation is misleading or false? Do you think the examples given of successfully challenged designations were decided reasonably? Would voters take the time to read the 200-word statements?

become too crowded—senates, perhaps because they have fewer members, were more likely to allow floor access.[58]

Several states now require accreditation to ensure that only certified members of the press corps receive legislative privileges. Some states issue identification cards; 13 states require journalists to wear special badges. Twenty-three states have a dress code.[59] In the North Dakota house a battle erupted when Speaker Tish Kelly sent out a letter asking reporters to voluntarily observe such a code after some representatives objected to a T-shirt that a TV camera operator was wearing. Kelly's code allowed turtleneck sweaters and jeans, but insisted on neatness. In time the press corps decided the request was reasonable.[60]

What Kind of News Is Reported? Morgan and others report that editors believe citizens are not very interested in state government. Thus, he notes, both politicians and reporters aim stories at **target publics.** "Legislators have their constituents, civil servants have their clientele groups, and reporters have their colleagues, editors, and a small group of attentive readers."

For a story to break out of this mold it must have a special twist—reporters describe it as color or human interest. Gormley notes that the media are especially interested in "conflicts between two easily identifiable sides—Republicans against Democrats, haves against have-nots, or wets against drys." These are likely to be "intriguing, but ephemeral controversies" rather than conflicts over basic but complex issues. If two state legislators get divorces and marry each other's former spouses it is "big news." A less dramatic issue, such as how property tax assessments are made, is likely to get less attention.[61]

Media coverage, though, probably has always been of this sort—emphasizing human interest and conflict in order to catch the attention of average citizens.[62]

Journalists believe, probably correctly, that few readers would plow through the less dramatic taxation stories.

Some legislators say journalists are overly critical—a confrontational relationship is most commonly found in the large industrial states of the Northeast and in California, and less so in the Midwest and other western states.[63] The chair of the Organization and Management Committee of the National Conference of State Legislatures argues that the media distort the legislative process and life because of a bias against politicians.[64] He quotes statements from journalism texts that politicians want only to get elected, whereas journalists are interested only in printing the truth (something he appears to doubt).

Manufacturing Government News A great deal of state and community news covers what historian Daniel Boorstin called "pseudoevents." These reduce information costs for the average citizen. The mayor cuts a ribbon to open a new bridge, or the governor drives out to a farm to sign a drought relief bill. Sometimes such pseudoevents are "investigative," as when the governor visits a state prison and eats a meal with inmates or a mayor visits the site of a slum apartment building a day or so after a fire has gutted it. Many such ceremonies are "arranged" to call attention to state or community politicians and activities. "Blue ribbon" study commissions often publicize information already commonly available. However, Richard Cole and David Caputo found that public hearings on general revenue sharing had only a short-term impact on levels of public interest.[65]

The Impact of Media Coverage Most students of media influence conclude that the press "may not be successful much of the time in telling people what to think, but it is stunningly successful in telling its readers what to think about." Newspapers and TV stations, at least the major ones, are involved in **agenda setting**, telling citizens which state or community issues are important.[66]

Coverage of state issues is still haphazard and some important issues never get on their agendas. The newspaper published in the capital city was once the best source of state news and issues. It was likely to be more thorough than the state's large metropolitan dailies. Complete coverage was a matter of pride as well as necessity. The editor of the *Sacramento Bee*, still such a paper, explains that his staff has to cover the "nuts and bolts" of state government because many of the paper's readers are legislators and state employees. But many other capital city papers, many of which have now become part of newspaper chains, have decided citizens are not much interested in state news and have limited their coverage.

The less educated citizens depend on television for what news and public affairs information they do learn about. Television reporting of state news once involved a costly and clumsy technology. But this is changing. TV reporters now have lightweight cameras that do not require special lighting. Stations with mobile transmitters can now send live stories instantly back to the station—generally sound bites for the evening news. Television is also the natural medium for interpretive discussion programs. But few of these programs are presented during prime viewing hours—late night or weekend off-hours seem to be the preferred hours for many station managers. Those that are carried at prime hours commonly are found on public television channels or public access cable channels, and these compete for viewer attention with televised sports or other highly promoted programs. The relationship between low-level participation and dependence on television coverage for public affairs information seems clear. Reliance on 20-second sound bites as the main source of information is not likely to develop much depth of understanding and motivation for participation except with respect to the simplest of issues.

Government Efforts to Reduce Information Costs   Some states, such as North Dakota and Oregon, publish voter information booklets. Candidates and parties buy advertising in a pamphlet that is sent to every voter just before an election. California's booklet also describes the content of each proposition on the ballot.

Oregon publishes a document on campaign expenditures that it distributes to citizens after the election. Governments also commonly use legal advertisements, presumably to inform voters about special elections or other matters. Such "boiler plate" in small boldface type is usually published with the want ads. It often seems to be little more than a handout of public funds to publishers of "the official county newspaper."

Cues from Trusted Sources   Cues are a substitute for fuller information. Political parties serve as important cue givers to uninformed citizens. Nonpartisan elections and candidate-centered media campaigns, though, blur the party message and discourage party identification. Voters turn out in greater numbers in cities with partisan elections than in those with nonpartisan elections.[67]

Some citizens may receive cues from civic associations such as the League of Women Voters or from research organizations such as those sponsored by universities, foundations, businesses, or unions. Others pick up cues from social movements which we discuss later in this chapter, or interest group leaders.

Information Costs and Social Status   David Moore studied the 1978 campaign for the governorship in New Hampshire to determine the effect of a sudden increase in available political information that a campaign produces. He found that the gap in knowledge increased between high-status and low-status voters. He suggests examining whether states with longer campaign periods may reduce this information gap.[68]

The Impact of Experience   Some political scientists believe that the most influential information is that which citizens receive from individual life experiences. Losing your job or being fresh out of school and unable to find work helps remarkably in focusing political opinions and encourages one to seek out information. The same can be said of losing a family member to a drunken driver or drugs. Even much less shattering experiences, such as finding that the water from your faucet is yellow, may have political repercussions.

The Cynical and the Alienated

When Luther Knox decided to run for governor of Louisiana in 1979 he changed his name. He wanted to be listed on the ballot as "None of the Above," He thought that voters were as disgusted with the other eight candidates as he was but had "not had the opportunity to reject all of them." Knox, or "Above," as he came to be called, wanted to give the Pelican State voters that opportunity. He discovered that not all voters were as disgusted as he was.

Can we explain, at least in part, the drop-off in voting by the cynicism about politicians that this story suggests? Some think so.

The Political Cynics Trust in all levels of government has declined since Vietnam and Watergate and later "-gates." And some feel that "political distrust" may be a rational and correct perception.[69] **Political cynicism** is present throughout the population, not only at the ideological extremes. The cynical do not blindly see all politicians as enemies—they have just become more skeptical about government and politics.[70] Public opinion surveys indicate that political cynics participate at about the same rates as do the less cynical.

The Politically Alienated Social scientists define the **politically alienated** as those who almost never participate because they regard the political system as irrelevant. The alienated appear to be beyond trying to calculate costs or benefits. They feel "it's no use trying" to improve conditions through political action. They have a permanent sense of psychological hopelessness and powerlessness. The response of the alienated is usually apathy and nonparticipation. When they do participate, they may act in violently antisocial ways unrelated to possible benefits or damage to themselves. They momentarily strike out at tormenters with vandalism or crime and then, after a time, lapse back into apathy.

Who Are the Alienated? Social scientists are uncertain how many citizens are alienated and which groups should be so designated. Most estimate the alienated to be about 10 percent of the population, well below the estimated 33 percent of nonparticipants. In general, researchers agree that the alienated are concentrated among poverty groups, the uneducated, and those most vulnerable victims of racism. Some blacks in big-city ghettos act in the classic pattern of alienation and frustration. On the one hand are extreme political apathy and such traditional forms of escapism as drugs and gambling; on the other are sporadic outbreaks of rage.

In the barrios of our big cities are alienated Hispanics. Nicholas Lovrich, Jr., and Otwin Marenin concluded that Mexican Americans in Denver were less "assertive" than blacks and more "politically acquiescent." They say that they have not been fully mobilized into the political system and thus they did not fully support Mexican-American candidates for city council. Language and cultural barriers also may contribute to a sense of alienation.[71] The other significant segment of alienated citizens is the very poor uneducated white—especially those who are illiterate. Many of these are concentrated in the mountains of Appalachia.[72]

What Can Reduce Alienation? Michael Baer and Dean Jaros suggest we can reduce alienation by providing jobs. They also suggest that participation itself reduces alienation because those who participate, like many jobholders, have a sense of belonging and being of value to society as well as having a stake in it.[73] No democracy can survive with a significant segment of its population alienated and, as urban politics student Norton Long suggests, walled off on reservations, left to rot in the heart of central cities, or at the bend of the creek in the hollow.[74]

Political Mobilization Through Social Movements

One of the more puzzling phenomena social scientists face is why individuals suddenly sense a common identity and political purpose and, without any previous warning, become part of a **social movement**. The basis of their political action is often a moral sense of outrage. Society may have discriminated against the movement's members for years and even centuries. In the past they seemed indifferent or accepting. Then suddenly they announce that they aren't going to take it anymore. Often they react with an almost religious fervor. Participation in large measure is unselfish—righting a moral wrong is all that seems important.[75]

Such a loosely structured grouping begins to make political demands and often stimulates intense participation among occasional participants and even, sometimes, the previously alienated.

The Social Movement in States and Communities In the next chapter we discuss the rise and decline of such social movements. Here we only list a few. Just mentioning their names shows us how they, perhaps more than any other force, have been important in shaping the way state and community governments operate. All have brought new ideas and new participants into the political system.

Important social movements of present and past include the Jacksonians, Know Nothings, abolitionists, Barnburners and Populists, the Progressive reformers at the turn of the century, women suffragists, prohibitionists, John Birchers, antibusing groups, ecologists, consumer advocates, and other radical right groups. We also include the early labor movement, the Ku Klux Klan, the old age pension movement, civil rights marchers, the Gray Panthers, Right-to-Lifers and Pro-Choice, the student movement, and those opposing higher taxes.

Other active social movements are the Moral Majority, feminists, gay rights groups, and most recently MADD—Mothers Against Drunk Drivers. All have demonstrated at state capitols and city halls. And all have won some policy victories.

Social Movement Participation Many social movements seem to explode into public consciousness. Persons who identify with a movement's goals abruptly begin acting as if the most important thing in life is achieving them. They engage willingly, sometimes at great personal cost, in protest demonstrations. Outsiders sometimes see movement participants as mentally deranged and irrational because they ignore the cost-benefit calculation that characterizes normal civilized behavior. Indeed, movement members sometimes act in clearly illegal ways.

In the 1960s students trashed buildings. Women suffragists chained themselves to state capitol fences or screamed at and physically attacked governors and mayors. Carrie Nation, the Kansas prohibitionist whose specialty was throwing liquor bottles at those large polished mirrors in frontier saloons, announced, "When God tells me to smash, I smash!" The police arrested her often, but she kept on smashing. Antinuclear demonstrators climb the fences of nuclear facilities or lie down before cement mixers to stop construction. One even allowed a train to crush his legs as he lay on the railroad tracks. Pro-lifers have bombed abortion clinics and commonly picket them despite arrests. Animal rights activists have invaded laboratories and set mice free.

As the intensity of a social movement subsides, some of its members drop back to their previous apathy. Some join organized groups that grow out of a movement's activity. The fervor of a social movement is the extra "push" that has moved many Americans from apathy and even alienation, and caused them to enter the mainstream of American participation as average citizens.

A FINAL COMMENT

It is difficult to avoid the conclusion that we Americans still fall short of our own democratic aspirations. We continue the search for ways to reduce participation and information costs. And we need better ways than social movements and protest demonstrations to bring nonparticipants and the alienated into the political mainstream.

Still, we should not expect town meeting democracy in large communities. We should not forget that out of necessity a small minority of citizens—the political elite—shapes most of the decisions made. Some reformers seem to hope that someday the political elite will disappear. But to us it is an unrealistic populist dream—average citizens have matters other than government or politics with which they wish to fill their lives. They desire government by elected representatives because the alternative is usually impractical and, except for very small communities, impossible. Informing and activating the mass of average citizens on issues, except on an occasional basis, is very difficult.

Yet we can also look at our history and note how often states and communities led. There our most important experiments in increasing democratic participation first took place. We can reasonably conclude that our system of governing in the states, imperfect as it is, offers hope for improved participation. From time to time average citizens do influence decisions. And such influence seems to us to be of crucial importance. No political elite is all-wise. And none has yet been discovered that is solely dedicated to the interest of the rest of us average citizens.

HIGH POINTS

In this chapter we argued that (1) our democratic society consists of a political elite that makes decisions and of citizens who are largely part-time or nonparticipants. We reviewed community elite studies and concluded that the political elites of American states and communities are undergoing change. Then we examined (2) explanations for participation and found voting related to a series of socioeconomic characteristics. We next (3) examined three aspects of participation. (a) The costs and benefits of participating and of gaining information vary by status. We concluded that participation costs, except for registration, have been markedly reduced. We argued that information costs are reduced by government action, the mass media, leaders of interest groups, social movements, and political parties, all of which may provide cues to citizens. (b) We noted that some citizens find political participation so lacking in benefits that they become alienated from politics. Finally, we noted (c) how citizens of the states and communities have exercised a great deal of influence through voluntary participation in social movements. We concluded that (4) we should expect only occasional impact on elite decision making by average citizens, but that impact was of crucial importance.

In this chapter we have defined the following terms in this order: elites, political elite, influentials, average citizens, nonparticipants, reputational approach, pluralists, decisional approach, power elite, nondecisions, mobilization of bias, ecology of games, civil disobedience, protest groups, retrospective voting, attentive publics, political mobilizers, political efficacy, poll tax, literacy tests, U.S. Voting Rights Act, access, direct democracy, town meeting, referendum, initiative, recall, participation costs, information costs, voter registration, Short Ballot Movement, target publics, agenda setting, political cynicism, politically alienated, and social movement.

NOTES

1. Bernard Berelson, Paul F. Lazarsfeld, and William N. McPhee, *Voting, A Study of Opinion Formation in a Presidential Campaign* (Chicago: University of Chicago Press, 1954), pp. 305–323. Walter Lippman arrived at the same conclusions intuitively in books written almost 70 years ago: *Public Opinion* (New York: Macmillan, 1922), and *The Phantom Public* (New York: Harcourt, Brace, 1925).
2. The novelist George Orwell succinctly summed up the human condition in his allegory in *Animal Farm* (New York: Harcourt, Brace, 1946). He wrote, "All are equal, but some are more equal than others."
3. We should not assume that members of the political elite are necessarily self-serving. An early study first documented that members of elites were often more liberal and more dedicated to democratic values than other citizens. Samuel A. Stouffer, *Communism, Conformity, and Civil Liberties* (Garden City, N.Y.: Doubleday, 1955).
4. Thomas R. Dye and L. Harmon Zeigler, *The Irony of Democracy* (Belmont, Calif.: Wadsworth, 1970).

5. Joseph LaPalombara, *Politics Within Nations* (Englewood Cliffs, N.J.: Prentice-Hall, 1974), p. 53.
6. Benjamin I. Page and Robert Y. Shapiro, "Effects of Public Opinion on Policy," *American Political Science Review* 77 (1983): 175–190.
7. V. O. Key, Jr., *Public Opinion and American Democracy* (New York: Knopf, 1967), p. 537.
8. Floyd Hunter, *Community Power Structure* (Chapel Hill: University of North Carolina, 1953). We do not distinguish among the concepts of influence, force, and authority here, but use power and influence interchangeably as meaning the ability to achieve one's ends in whole or in part and to limit others in achieving theirs. For a more analytical distinction see Peter Bachrach and Morton Baratz, *Power and Poverty, Theory and Practice* (New York: Oxford University Press, 1970), pp. 19–38.
9. "The Ten Most Powerful People in Illinois," *Chicago Tribune* (July 17, 1977), pp. 23–24.
10. Abstracts of the earlier studies are found in Charles Press, *Main Street Politics* (East Lansing: Institute for Community Development, Michigan State University, 1962).
11. Robert A. Dahl, *Who Governs? Democracy and Power in an American City* (New Haven, Conn.: Yale University Press, 1961).
12. Robert S. and Helen M. Lynd, *Middletown*, and *Middletown in Transition* (New York: Harcourt Brace Jovanovich, 1929 and 1937). Criticisms of the power elite approach can be found in Nelson W. Polsby, "How to Study Community Power, The Pluralist Alternative, *Journal of Politics* 22 (1980): 474–484.
13. Robert S. and Helen M. Lynd, *Middletown*.
14. Hunter, *Community Power Structure*.
15. Bachrach and Baratz, *Power and Poverty*.
16. Norton E. Long, "The Local Community as an Ecology of Games," in Charles Press (ed.), *The Polity* (Chicago: Rand McNally, 1962).
17. Many political scientists believe that the closest an American state has come to a dictatorship was Louisiana between 1928 and 1935 under Governor and then Senator Huey P. Long. For a biography defending Long, see T. Harry Williams, *Huey Long* (New York: Knopf, 1969). For a contrary view see Hartnet Kane, *Louisiana Hayride* (New York: William Morrow, 1941).
18. For a view that masses, indeed, influence too much the decision making of modern societies, see William Kornhauser, *The Politics of Mass Society* (Glencoe, Ill.: Free Press, 1959). For the classic statement of the theory that a military-industrial complex controls all of American society, see C. Wright Mills, *The Power Elite* (New York: Oxford University Press, 1958).
19. Alan Ehrenhalt, "Greenville, South Carolina, Power Shifts in a Southern City as Groups That Took Orders Learn How to Give Them," *Governing* (September 1988): 48–53.
20. David B. Walker, *Toward a Functioning Federalism* (Cambridge, Mass.: Winthrop, 1981), pp. 3–18; 251–261.
21. Richard Cloward and Frances Fox Piven, *Poor People's Movements* (New York: Vintage, 1979), p. 36.
22. National Advisory Commission on Civil Disorders, *Report* (Washington, D.C.: U.S. Government Printing Office, 1968).
23. Michael Lipsky, "Protest as a Political Resource," *American Political Science Review*

82 (1968): 1144–1158. For three reports of protests against developers, see Bernard J. Frieden, "Environmental Politics," *Urban Land* (Urban Land Institute, March 1977).
24. Michael Parenti, "Power and Pluralism: A View from the Bottom," *Journal of Politics* 32 (1970): 501–530.
25. Sidney Verba and Norman H. Nie, *Participation in America: Political Democracy and Social Equality* (New York: Harper & Row, 1972), p. 31.
26. Lee Sigelman, "Voting and Nonvoting: A Multi-Election Perspective," *American Journal of Political Science* 29 (November 1985): 749–765.
27. Grahan Wallis, *Human Nature and Politics* (New York: Appleton-Century-Crofts, 1908), reissued (Lincoln: University of Nebraska Press, 1962), p. 115, and Arthur T. Hadley, *The Empty Voting Booth* (Englewood Cliffs, N.J.: Prentice-Hall, 1978).
28. John C. Pierce and John L. Sullivan, *The Electorate Reconsidered* (Beverly Hills, Calif.: Sage, 1980). See especially "An Overview of the American Electorate," pp. 11–29.
29. Morris P. Fiorina, *Retrospective Voting in American National Elections* (New Haven, Conn.: Yale University Press, 1981).
30. Gabriel Almond, *The American People and Foreign Policy* (New York: Praeger, 1960), p. 139.
31. Stephen Earl Bennett, *Apathy in America, 1960–1984; Causes and Consequences of Citizen Political Indifference* (Ardsley-on-Hudson, N.Y.: Transnational, 1986).
32. Elaine B. Sharp, "Citizen-Demand Making in the Urban Context," *American Journal of Political Science* 25 (1984): 654–670. Lester Milbrath and M. L. Goel suggest that voting may be regarded as a patriotic act of loyalty. They suggest other "modes" of participation have different purposes, such as communicating to officials, protesting, working in parties and campaigns, and political activity in communities. Norman Nie and Sidney Verba define four such modes: voting, campaign activity, citizen-initiated contacts of officials, and cooperative activity through organizations and protests. Most studies, however, have treated participation as a general activity with voting as its central feature, and this is the tradition we follow. Norman H. Nie and Sidney Verba, "Political Participation," in Fred I. Greenstein and Nelson Polsby (eds.), *The Handbook of Political Science* (Vol. 4) (Reading, Mass.: Addison Wesley, 1975), pp. 1–74, and Lester W. Milbrath and M. L. Goel, *Political Participation, How and Why Do People Get Involved in Politics* (2nd ed.) (Chicago: Rand McNally, 1977).
33. John Clayton Thomas, *Between Citizen and City* (Lawrence: University of Kansas Press, 1986).
34. Jae-On Kim, John R. Petrocik, and Stephen N. Enokson, "Voter Turnout in the American States: Systematic and Individual Components," *American Political Science Review* 69 (1975): 359–377.
35. Samuel C. Patterson and Gregory A. Caldeira, "Getting Out to Vote: Participation in Gubernatorial Elections," *American Political Science Review* 77 (September 1983): 675–689.
36. Charles E. Merriam and Harold Gosnell, *Non Voting, Causes and Methods of Control* (Chicago: University of Chicago Press, 1924), p. 41.
37. Hadley, pp. 67–103.
38. Parenti, "Power and Pluralism."
39. Theodore F. Macaluso and John Wanat, "Voting Turnout and Religiosity," *Polity* 12 (1979): 158–169.

40. Paul Allen Beck and M. Kent Jennings, "Pathways to Participation," *American Political Science Review* 76 (1982): 94–108.
41. E. E. Schattschneider, *The Semi-Sovereign People* (New York: Holt, 1960).
42. U.S. Civil Rights Commission, *The Voting Rights Act, Unfulfilled Goals* (Washington, D.C.: U.S. Government Printing Office, 1981).
43. Jack Bass and Walter DeVries, *The Transformation of Southern Politics, Social Change and Political Consequence Since 1945* (New York: Basic Books, 1976).
44. Hugh A. Bone and Robert C. Benedict, "Perspectives on Direct Legislation," *Western Political Quarterly* 28 (1975): 330–351.
45. Charles Press and Larry Sych, "Participation in State Recall Elections," Paper delivered at the Midwest Political Science Association meetings, 1987.
46. Charles M. Price, "Recalls at the Local Level: Dimensions and Implications," *National Civic Review* (April 1983), and Charles Press and Lawrence Sych, "Participation in State Recall Elections."
47. For a list of 15 state requirements that add to or reduce costs for the voter, see Robert R. Blank, "State Electoral Structure," *Journal of Politics* 35 (1973): 989–994.
48. Lee Sigelman, "Voting and Nonvoting: A Multi-Election Perspective," *American Journal of Political Science* 29 (1985): 749–765.
49. Charles V. Hamilton, "Voter Registration Drives and Turnout, A Report on the Harlem Electorate," *Political Science Quarterly* 92 (1977): 43–48. Ronald Terchek argues that such factors as relevance of election issues to blacks, competitiveness of the election, and the symbolic importance of ethnicity also affect turnout of registrants. See Ronald J. Terchek, "Incentives and Voter Participation, A Research Note," *Political Science Quarterly* 94 (1979): 135–139.
50. G. Bingham Powell, Jr., "American Voter Turnout in Comparative Perspective," *American Political Science Review* 80 (March 1986): 17–43.
51. Steven J. Rosenstone and Raymond E. Wolfinger, "The Effect of Registration Laws on Voter Turnout," *American Political Science Review* 72 (1978): 22–45.
52. Richard A. Cloward and Frances Fox Piven, *Why Americans Don't Vote* (New York: Pantheon, 1988).
53. William T. Gormley, Jr., "Coverage of State Government in the Mass Media," *State Government* (Spring 1979). Gormley cites Hoyt Purvis and Rick Gentry, "News Media Coverage of Texas Government," *Public Affairs Comment* (Austin, Tex.: Lyndon B. Johnson School of Public Affairs, 1978): 3; Paul Simon, "Improving Statehouse Coverage," *Columbia Journalism Review* (September-October, 1973): 51; and for wire service coverage, Thomas Littlewood, "What's Wrong with Statehouse Coverage," *Columbia Journalism Review* (March–April 1972): 40. For an argument that the relationship has become more adversarial in the midwest as well, see Robert Gurwitt, "In the Capitol Pressroom. The Old Boys Call it a Day," *Governing* (July 1990): 227–230.
54. Phill Brooks and Bob M. Gassaway, "Improving News Coverage, A National Survey of Statehouse Journalists Indicates What Legislatures Must Do to Gain a Better Media Coverage," *State Legislatures* 11 (March 1985): 29–31.
55. Mary Tier, "First Reading: A Love-Hate Relationship," *State Legislatures* (October 1984).
56. David Morgan, *The Capitol Press Corps, Newsmen and Governing of New York State* (Westport, Conn.: Greenwood Press, 1978), pp. 103–104.
57. Phill Brooks and Bob M. Gassaway, "Improving News Coverage."
58. Sharon Sherman, "State Legislators and the Press: Let the Conversation Begin," *State Legislatures* 9 (May 1983): 7–12.

59. Mary Fairchild, "Reporters and Legislators: Defining the Relationship," *State Legislatures* 9 (May 1983): 9.
60. Sherman, "State Legislators and the Press."
61. Robert W. O'Donnell, "What's Wrong with the Media's Coverage of the Legislature?" *State Legislatures* (October 1985): 29–30.
62. An analysis of early political prints of the 1770s concluded that the artists reached a mass market using scandals of royalty rather than more basic political issues. See Charles Press, "The Georgian Print and Democratic Institutions," *Comparative Studies in Society and History* 19 (April 1977): 210–238, and *The Political Cartoon* (East Brunswick, N.J.: Fairleigh Dickinson University Press, Associated University Presses, 1981).
63. Sherman, "State Legislators and the Press," p. 8.
64. O'Donnell, "What's Wrong with the Media's Coverage of the Legislature?"
65. Richard L. Cole and David Caputo, "The Public Hearing as an Effective Citizen Participation Mechanism: A Case Study of the General Revenue Sharing Program," *American Political Science Review* 78 (1984): 404–416.
66. Bernard Cohen, *The Press and Foreign Policy* (Princeton: Princeton University Press, 1963), p. 13. For empirical evidence that confirms the statement, see also Maxwell McCombs and Donald Shaw, "The Agenda-Setting Function of Mass Media," *Public Opinion Quarterly* (Summer 1971): 170–187. McCombs and Shaw found that a sample of North Carolina residents rated issues roughly the same in importance as did the mass media to which they were exposed during the election of 1988.
67. Everett Carl Ladd, Jr., *Where Have All the Voters Gone? The Fracturing of America's Political Parties* (New York: Norton, 1978).
68. David W. Moore, "Political Campaigns and the Knowledge-Gap Hypothesis," *Public Opinion Quarterly* 51 (1987): 186–200.
69. Vivien Hart, *Distrust and Democracy* (Cambridge, Mass.: Cambridge University Press, 1978).
70. Arthur R. Miller, "Political Issues and Trust in Government," *American Political Science Review* 68 (1974): 951–972, and Jack Citrin, "The Political Relevance of Trust in Government," *American Political Science Review* 68 (1974): 973–988.
71. Nicholas P. Lovrich, Jr., and Otwin Marenin, "A Comparison of Black and Mexican American Voters in Denver, Assertive versus Acquiescent Political Orientations and Voting Behavior in an Urban Electorate," *Western Political Quarterly* 29 (1976): 284–291.
72. Harry M. Caudill, *Night Comes to the Cumberlands, A Biography of a Depressed Area* (Boston: Little, Brown, 1962).
73. Michael A. Baer and Dean Jaros, "Participation as an Instrument of Expression, Some Evidence from the States," *American Journal of Political Science* 18 (May 1974). See also Robert R. Salisbury, *Citizen Participation in the Public Schools* (Lexington, Mass.: Lexington Books, 1980).
74. Norton E. Long, *The Unwalled City* (New York: Basic Books, 1972).
75. Still among the most perceptive analyses of social movements is Neil J. Smelser, *Collective Behavior* (New York: Free Press, 1962).

Chapter 6

Political Interest Groups

Political scientists once wrote about *pressure groups*. The term suggests Jay Fiske twisting arms and bribing his way through the New York state legislature to get special benefits for the Erie Railroad. Mark Twain, reflecting on this period of our history, said, "I think I can say, and say with pride, that we have some legislatures that bring higher prices than any in the world."

David Truman introduced the term **political interest group**: any organized group, governmental or private, that attempts to influence governmental decision making. A **lobbyist** is someone who attempts to influence public policy on behalf of such groups. Truman's term suggests that lobbying is not necessarily a shady operation—indeed, it is encouraged by our basic charter of freedoms, the Bill of Rights.[1]

Recent scholars stress the idea of transaction—contacts and occasionally pressure that goes both ways. Lobbyists seek out public officials, but public officials also seek out interest group representatives for their financial and other support in campaigns as well as for information about the effect of proposed legislation. Because they have specialized information, lobbyists can often reduce uncertainty about a policy's probable impact.[2]

The Interest Group on Trial Bribery today is generally more subtle than stuffing pipes with "green tobacco" ($500 bills) and passing them out as party favors. Corruption in the 1990s is likely to involve only one or a few individuals rather than flourishing throughout state governments—as when Mark Twain wrote in the 1880s. But campaign contributions and lobbyists buying blocks of tickets for legislative "fund-raisers" held at the capital rather than in the district are still common practice.

And lobbying at the state capitol still has its exotic moments. In the 1980s, a Louisiana commissioner of administration went to prison for three years. And in Indiana the Republican senate caucus chair got a six-year jail term for accepting a "legal fee" after repeal of the state's railroad full crew law. The president pro tem of the Mississippi senate was convicted for attempting to get $50,000 in relation to pending legislation. And in Rhode Island the chief justice of the supreme court was suspended for friendship with reputed mobsters. In September 1990, five South Carolina legislators were indicted for vote selling.

David Nice found such corruption occurs least in states with "moralistic" political cultures and where citizens are more educated, but is unrelated to a state's crime rate or degree of urbanization.[3]

Interest Group Penetration Without doing anything illegal, interest groups can penetrate deeply into the decision-making process. Public officials frequently abandon policy-making to boards and commissions staffed with interest group representatives. At the community level, realtors sit on planning boards or are appointed to zoning boards of appeal. At the state level, beauticians, barbers, or hairdressers constitute the board of cosmetology. This type of interest group penetration, some political scientists argue, is of more political significance than is an occasional incident of individual corruption.

Overview We begin by looking at which citizens organize political interest groups, which groups lobby and why, and which resources are important. Then we examine the state patterns of lobbying. We review how government structure encourages lobbying, who become professional lobbyists, and the techniques they use today. Finally, we look at the efforts of reformers to regulate lobbying.

THE LOBBYING PROCESS

State and community governments represent citizens on a geographic basis. Interest groups represent citizens on a functional basis—by activities they participate in.

Who Organizes?

Being a member of some group is, of course, the first step toward getting represented in interest group politics. Alexis de Tocqueville in the 1830s described America as "a nation of joiners," and we like to think of ourselves that way. But if we exclude church or work-oriented groups such as unions or farm organizations, only about a third belong to one group and less than 15 percent to more than one. With churches included, two-thirds of our citizens belong to at least one formal organization.

Joining involves participation costs and, like voting, is related to status.[4] Among the one-third who are nonjoiners we are most likely to find persons of low income, renters, manual laborers, those with less than an eighth grade education, farmers, and those over 60 or under 25.

The political scientist E. E. Schattschneider concluded that a further "flaw in the pluralist [interest group] heaven is that the heavenly chorus sings with a strong upper-class accent." Upper- and middle-class people are also more active in organizations they join. He estimated that roughly 90 percent of Americans were not very well represented in the interest group system.[5]

Patterns of Organization

Interest groups, organized first by function, also structure themselves to fit the political realities of the American federal system.

A "Balkanized" Group System Unitary governmental systems encourage the creation of national organizations. Our federal system encourages state-based groups. Farmers in Oregon and Ohio each have their own state Grange. Churches have their Indiana and Iowa synods, labor unions their Pennsylvania and New Jersey state affiliates, professions their Nebraska and Maine state bars. Organizations of government officials also tend to be state or community based—the Arkansas Education Association, the League of Texas Cities, and community-based labor councils.

To fit their conditions, state branches of national organizations may follow tactics that vary with national policy. William P. Browne and Laurily Keir Epstein examined the senior citizens' organizations and their method of lobbying. They found that in Florida the disorganized state politics led to little forceful lobbying or organization. Rather, despite their voting potential, senior citizens engaged in "low-profile" tactics. But the head of the New Jersey Federation of Senior Citizens had a motto on his desk that said "Robin Hood was right!"

Organization was tighter, and lobbying more confrontational, as are the politics of that state. In Michigan the groups were allowed to penetrate deeply into the state's administrative structure. In Iowa, state legislative activity was limited to mass mailings.[6]

The Choice Between State and Nation James Stever notes that at one time we could assume that interest groups would reinforce the federal structure—that they would be among the major defenders of state powers. But as our federal system has become more centralized, some groups have placed their major effort in national organization.[7] Groups such as the handicapped that wish to standardize a policy across the nation see little reason to lobby every state legislature or city council. One requirement on a federal grant program will apply to all states and communities. Other interest groups shift back and forth between states and nation while some concentrate mainly on states or even on individual communities.

Choice of strategies depends on how a group can most easily achieve its goals within the federal system, as well as where the group's strength lies. The feminist movement was strong enough nationally to get a two-thirds majority in Congress to propose the ERA. Constitutional amendment procedures required feminists to lobby state legislatures. This was not a strategy they would have chosen readily. The movement was unable to get ratification by a sufficient number of state legislatures.

The reverse might be true of representatives of a major state industry, such as oil in Texas, Oklahoma, or Louisiana. They prefer state regulation because they have a strong state base. Other groups, such as labor unions, might shift between states and nation depending on issues and which party controls the national government.

Which Organizations Are Likely to Lobby?

Influencing public officials is a secondary activity for many organized groups. People join organizations to spread a religion, socialize, bargain for wage hikes, sell real estate, hold stock shows, or any number of other reasons.

Members are attracted to groups to achieve selective benefits.[8] Lobbying especially rewards groups in securing economic benefits—what students call **material benefits as a selective incentive**. This is especially true of business groups and public employees.

Consumers also have economic interests but receive less in return for their lobbying efforts because individually they have less at stake. Suppose your telephone company applies to the public service commission to double its pay phone rates. How much would you save in a year if you could stop the raise? Would you save enough to contribute to a lobbying effort? Probably not. Would the costs of lobbying for this increase pay off for the telephone company? Yes! Millions of dollars are at stake.

Or think about a legislative proposal to increase the state sales tax for schools. The tax increase for individual taxpayers will be barely noticed. But for a teacher whose annual raise or even his or her job itself depends on the outcome, contributing to a lobbying effort is well worth the possible return.[9]

Who Lobbies in the States? A study of lobbying in Texas and Iowa found that business groups most often took formal stands on bills. Local governmental organizations, such as the League of Cities, the school board, and county associations, were the second most active lobbyists. The activity of other economic groups tended to concentrate around specific types of bills—unions, for example, on labor legislation.[10]

Who Lobbies in the Communities? Few communities are now dominated by a single interest group. Yet the influence of the traditional economic interest groups remains great—local industry, and local business (including, especially, Main Street merchants). Contractors, realtors, and developers are deeply involved in guiding community change. You are likely to meet their representatives at any city council meeting you attend because, one study suggests, interest groups have more influence through city councils than through executives.[11] Also active are the community government's employees.

The Activation of "Cause" Groups Groups also organize to secure nonmaterial benefits. These are called **purposive groups**.[12]

In communities, new interest groups concerned with other than economic gain, such as gay rights or neighborhood associations, are now active. Or a social movement may inspire formerly inactive individuals to participate in politics. But after a time enthusiasm wanes. Organization becomes a substitute for zeal. The organizations that survive are often **single issue groups**. Only a small portion of the movement, though, end up in these formal organizations. The League of Women Voters emerged out of the women's suffrage movement. Today's feminists formed the National Organization of Women (NOW). The civil rights movement led to Martin Luther King, Jr.'s, Southern Christian Leadership Conference (SCLC) as well as other groups. The consumer and ecology movements spawned a variety of state and community organizations. And perhaps the two most important movements in spreading membership to all levels of society were the religious movement that ended in organized denominations and the labor movement, which organized as the AFL and later the CIO and many unions.

In Policy Box No. 11, "Blacks as a 'Cause Group,'" we examine the problems blacks faced as "the spirit of the 1960s" ebbed.

What Activates Interest Groups? David Truman argued that groups begin lobbying intensely when a disturbance causes citizens to be uncertain about their future. Changes in technology, foreign competition, an industrial takeover, or a recession or inflation result in an inability to predict what may happen next. All that is certain is that change affects individuals and groups unequally—some will gain, others lose.

Harmon Zeigler and Michael Baer found that marked changes in population movement in or out of a state were consistently associated with strong interest

Policy Box No. 11

Blacks as a "Cause Group"

Back in the 1960s, when Dr. Martin Luther King, Jr., was leading marches to integrate American institutions, it appeared to many Americans that the civil rights movement, with its haunting song "We Shall Overcome," was going to change the positions of blacks dramatically. "The Dream" of which Dr. King spoke so eloquently at the great Freedom March on Washington, August 28, 1963, seemed close to realization.

And in the next decade or so blacks did make a great many gains. Politicians competed with each other in claiming credit for helping blacks. Even George Wallace, running once more for governor of Alabama in 1982, highlighted his support of blacks. He was no longer the governor who had "stood in the schoolhouse door" to prevent blacks from enrolling at the University of Alabama. And blacks won important political offices. Some joined the media as newspaper columnists and television personalities and others made visible headway in business and the professions—the "Huxtables" became a national role model.

But many blacks felt a deep frustration—although many blacks had made it to the middle class and beyond, the majority of blacks seemed as bad off as ever. Vernon Jordan, president of the National Urban League, pointed out that the black middle class was less than 10 percent of all black families. In 1954 at the time of *Brown v. Board of Education*, the black unemployment rate was 10 percent; the white rate was half that. Twenty-five years later, despite all of the governmental programs for affirmative action, the black unemployment rate was 11.9 percent and the white rate was 5.2 percent. (The jobless rate for black teenagers was 38.6 percent!)

The same period had a dramatic decline in school dropouts. In 1959 blacks had completed an average of only 8.6 years of schooling; whites had completed 12.1 years. In just a generation, blacks averaged 12.3 years of schooling against the white average of 12.7. But many of the blacks attended schools in the ghetto areas, where the quality of education was poor. Meryl Gordon of the Gannett News Service reported that state education officials freely admitted that many black teenagers still graduated from high school without knowing how to read or write. They then entered a job market where racism (perhaps less overt than previously) was still present. They had to compete with illegal aliens and with the many women also entering the job market in greater numbers. They frequently refused menial jobs ("bus boy," "cleaning lady") that they associated with the days of open discrimination.

Many thus lacked basic skills, previous job experience, or the work habits learned on jobs held while teenagers. Psychologically many were conditioned to fail—and their failure rate was high. And the new jobs that opened up tended to be in suburbs, far from where many blacks lived. Some thus entered the illegal and underground occupations flourishing in ghetto areas—prostitution, pimping, the numbers racket, drugs, robbery, and mugging. Others turned to welfare, collecting their checks as they watched television which allowed them to compare what they had with how well others lived.

This is "the major problem" as defined by the interest groups representing blacks—how to bring the ghetto into the mainstream of working middle-class America.

One proposal is to attack racial discrimination via the courts. But the chief beneficiaries of these actions tend to be well-educated blacks ready to take advantage of the job opportunities that open up at CBS or the FBI. Such middle-class blacks can help other blacks and provide role models for young blacks. But how much does this approach, generally asociated with the NAACP (National Association for the Advancement of Colored People), help the many blacks still in poverty?

A related approach is that of the National Urban League and the Reverend Jesse Jackson. They encourage blacks to educate themselves so they can compete on an equal basis with whites for the jobs available. The Urban Leagues across the country attempt to find jobs for qualified blacks. Jesse Jackson has argued strongly that part of the solution is for blacks to insist on better quality schools—parents, by allowing the schools to deteriorate or be taken over by young "toughs," are sentencing their children to low-income lives. Jackson also takes a more militant stance—threatening black boycotts of products of firms that hire too few blacks or refuse to finance black dealer outlets and arguing for more social welfare programs to help those in poverty. Many groups argue that the government should provide job skills programs for blacks and summer jobs for teenagers. They want government to become the employer of last resort.

Another approach that Jackson and most black interest groups follow is to encourage blacks to participate politically as voters, party workers, and candidates. Most black interest groups lobby, and some voice their criticism of national or local leaders' solutions by giving or withholding endorsements.

Republicans often favor federal programs encouraging black capitalism, attempting to attract new businesses to "free enterprise" zones in ghetto areas by tax write-offs. Federal and state grants contain "set aside" clauses—rules that set aside certain percentages of the money for work to be done by minority contractors. Others want mass transportation lines into the suburbs, and low-income public housing moved into these areas.

What do you think? Assume you are a leader of an interest group representing blacks and have defined the problem as we have: moving the millions of blacks into the mainstream of America's working middle class. What kinds of state or local programs would you fight for? Would you assume that by opening up opportunities for the more talented blacks some of the benefits could be expected to trickle down? Has political involvement been of much help to blacks? Do you recommend drastic action, or do you believe the problem will work itself out as it did for the earlier ethnics? What interest group tactics would you follow to achieve your goals? Would you lobby the state legislature or turn to the state courts? Or do you think the only answer is demonstrations? Can public policy beyond what has been adopted solve the problems of blacks in the states?

---

group activity. The civil rights movement had such an impact on the hierarchical society found in some southern states during the 1960s. Feverish organization and politicking occurred. So too did the movement of industry out of New York and Massachusetts and into Alabama and New Mexico or movement of downtown department stores into suburban shopping centers.[13] J. M. Hansen found that a threat to a group interest is more likely to activate a group than is the promise of improvement.[14]

But Robert Salisbury found that some groups faced with uncertainty still were unable to organize effectively. Other groups sprang up and prospered without a disturbance. A critical factor was the political skill of a group's leaders. He argues that groups often form and become active politically because of a leader who is able to organize and maintain the interest group. He calls them **interest group entrepreneurs**.

To test this theory, Jeffrey Berry studied 83 groups, such as Common Cause, environmental and consumer organizations, and those for or against capital punishment. He found that two-thirds of such groups formed because a skilled entrepreneur started them and found a population group eager to support the cause.[15]

What Resources Help Make a Group Effective?

Interest groups differ in five ways that significantly affect their ability to get what they want: money, members, leadership, organizational cohesion, and legitimacy.

Money and Members Money is a major resource because with it an interest group can buy almost any other political resource—for example, technical expertise and publicity. Members are a major resource because public officials know that they may be translated into votes. Each member is connected to family and friends and thereby influences more votes. Mobilization of group members is generally strongly related to social class. However, one study found that membership in purposive organizations resulted in member activity independent of social class.[16]

The Importance of Leadership Interest group entrepreneurs build on the kind of enthusiasm generated by social movements. This spirit recruits persons willing to support a cause even though material benefits do not result. And the leadership of such groups is often already well known to members —such as Ralph Nader, the Reverend Jesse Jackson, and the Reverend Pat Robertson.

Jack Walker found that leaders who can secure funds from outside the group membership were especially important to certain groups. While groups such as trade associations draw three-quarters of their funds from members, cause groups receive about two-thirds from nonmember contributions.[17]

Purposive group leaders are often in fierce competition with each other for funds and members for their group because interests of purposive groups often overlap. Direct mail is a common form of solicitation. Groups often trade or buy lists from each other, a fact familiar to most homeowners. Leaders may also secure funds from foundations, by getting government grants, playing up to wealthy individuals, selling advertising in group publications, or selling pamphlets, books, or other products.[18]

Organizational Cohesiveness Small interest groups often have the advantage of **group cohesiveness**. Their members are likely to be similar in social background and viewpoint; their representatives can act with little fear of division in the ranks. The National Rifle Association and the Audubon Society have such group solidarity.

Maintaining cohesiveness is sometimes difficult for large-scale organizations. Less active members may not share the commitment of the activists in the group.[19] Associations made up of economic competitors may split over differences between independent and chain outlets. The importance of a labor endorsement is lessened when member unions differ over whom to endorse for mayor or governor. "Umbrella organizations" can be torn apart by all-out warfare among member units.

Legitimacy: What Others Think V. O. Key, Jr., observed that a "group may be accepted, respected, feared, heeded, or regarded as ridiculous, inconsequential, irresponsible, suspect, even contemptible. The spokesperson for one group may be heard with respect, while that of another may have little opportunity to even state its case."[20] **Group legitimacy** is how much respect and acceptance others accord to the group.

Government officials view some groups as having a legitimate claim to participate in policy-making that concerns their activities. Officials will seek out representatives of such groups even when they are not wholly sympathetic to the group's views. Such information may reduce uncertainty about a policy. Few state legislators would consider regulation of auto repairs without listening to the comments of someone representing auto mechanics as well as those lobbying for car manufacturers or the auto insurance industry.

State Research Organizations Some groups earn legitimacy. They provide accurate factual information that legislators, lobbyists, and bureaucrats accept as trustworthy. The Pennsylvania Economy League, Michigan's Citizen's Research Council, Louisiana's Public Affairs Research group, and other similar organizations have such status.

These follow a common pattern. They are financed by large firms—Florida's Citizens Council for Budget Research by Winn Dixie, Publix, and Lykes Brothers. Typically, they are concerned with governmental efficiency. To create legitimacy, they stress fairness and accuracy in their reports. Florida's CCBR, with a staff of five, documented how teachers were underpaid, pinpointed featherbedding in the state's mammoth department of transportation, and criticized the way pension funds were invested in low-yield securities.[21] Michigan's Citizen Research Council was instrumental in getting the legislature to adopt a uniform budgeting act for local governments.

Anticipated Reactions The legitimacy of some groups is never questioned. Legislators and other officials may even anticipate the organization's wants. Such **anticipatory reactions** are common where an industry dominates the economy as agriculture does in the Dakotas or as luxury hotels and other tourist attractions do in Miami. Legislators and administrators may even be ahead of industry in planning ways to attack a developing problem. When important manufacturing industries experience severe problems, state officials may seek out a lobbyist with proposals to help.

The Continuing Advantages of Legitimacy Accepted organizations have a continuing advantage, even when their status begins to slip. Some already may have penetrated deeply into government agencies. Inertia and uncertainty about the effect of policy change make it easier for lobbyists for established organizations to defend their position than it is for lobbyists representing a new group to get policy changes. Feminist groups seeking changes in discriminatory legislation face this handicap, as have all other innovative groups.

Groups Viewed as "Outsiders" Other groups have activities about which citizens and, therefore, officials feel uneasy. They are seen as not quite "legitimate." Advocates of legalized gambling, pornographers, the liquor industry (which prefers the more euphemistic title of the "wine and spirits trade"), and, in some states, the tobacco industry are so viewed. State legislators do not welcome being tagged as "the pal of racetrack operators," although many have no objection to being known as the friend of the Iowa Farm Bureau or the state nursing association. Some groups lack legitimacy because they lack full professional acceptance. Chiropractors and osteopaths, in the past, have had great difficulties largely because the traditional medical groups cast them as outsiders.

Not surprisingly, organizations whose legitimacy is questioned sometimes turn to questionable tactics, perhaps only to get the sympathetic hearing that more legitimate groups get without asking. Racial and ethnic groups, such as blacks, Indians, or Chicanos, have used disruptive tactics, including violence. In part this is a simple way, and perhaps has been the only way, to gain the attention of officials for what they regard as legitimate demands. Other groups, now seemingly accepted, still face reservations. A study of lobbying in Oregon, Utah, Massachusetts, and North Carolina reported that legislators and even other lobbyists considered labor and education lobbyists to "most often exert pressure." But researchers could find little evidence that this was indeed the case.[22] Policy Box No. 12, "Political Conflict in the Schools," suggests some of the reasons for this common belief.

PRESENT-DAY INTEREST GROUPS

The pattern of lobbying in each state depends on its own distinctive mix of economic and social groupings. Some corporations and unions have had more financial resources and employees than their state government. In large and heterogeneous states, however, any single interest will likely be offset by other interests.

Policy Box No. 12

Political Conflict in the Schools

Education is supposed to be free from political interference. That was one of the reasons many states created special districts to govern schools, earmarked revenues for educational purposes, and established elective state boards of education with independence from governors and state legislatures. It was also one of the reasons states passed teacher tenure laws, giving teachers the freedom to teach their subject matter without fear of political reprisals.

But when we examine the position of schoolteachers today we find they are as much involved in state and community politics as any other organized group. And the schoolchildren are caught between warring groups. The intensity with which school politics are now fought is unprecedented.

Traditionally teachers saw themselves as professionals dedicated to teaching. They relied on persuasion rather than threats or force to convince the community to provide adequate support for education. Teachers and school administrators banded together in state education associations, and they worked hand in hand to secure adoption of laws to help teachers do a better job.

And then in the mid-1960s states began revising laws to permit public employees, including teachers, to organize for collective bargaining. State education associations, gingerly at first and then more stridently, took on the task of converting local teacher associations into unions. Already so organized was the American Federation of Teachers, affiliated from the start with the AFL. At first, school administrators could remain members, but later, either forced to or on their own volition, most administrators withdrew. By the 1970s education associations became full-fledged unions.

What do teachers' unions fight for? The most apparent item is teacher salaries and pensions. Without question collective bargaining and legislative lobbying at state and community levels have brought teacher salaries from low-income levels to middle-class ranges. More recently, with falling school enrollments and recession, job security has taken on new importance in the bargaining. Teachers have been holding out for smaller classes. Smaller classes obviously mean that fewer teachers will be let go and, according to the teachers, will improve the quality of education.

The teachers also want a voice in how cutbacks (layoffs of teachers) are to be made. Most state tenure laws do not require a hearing when schools make cutbacks for financial reasons. Union officials argue that administrators and school boards would make the first cuts from among the highest paid and usually older teachers and include those the "superintendent wanted to fire" were it not for the unions and the tenure laws. Teachers' unions want the cutbacks made on the basis of seniority alone. Administrators say that they should have the authority to make cuts on the basis of educational needs.

But the teachers' unions are not limiting their activity to union-management bargaining sessions. They also seek to amass political power. Their basic strategy is to mobilize their membership to support, with volunteer help and money, candidates who will increase the financial support for education. They are especially concerned to find a substitute for the property tax and school millage elections that set local tax rates for education as the major community support of schools. Also they seek to equalize per student expenditures among state districts.

The unions work for candidates at all levels but have become one of the major groups supporting political candidates in state campaigns. In some communities they have been able to "purge" "unsympathetic" school board members at elections. Teachers' unions have especially encouraged their membership to run for the state legislature.

A crucial issue that teacher groups feel they must win is the legal right to strike. Without this, they believe their hand at the bargaining table is weak. Few unions want to experience having strikers fired and new teachers hired in their place—something that could and in some cases has happened where teacher strikes are illegal.

Critics of teachers' unions fear their growing strength. They ask, "If the teachers can tip the balance in the political races, is it possible that they could dominate public policy on education? And is it possible that their influence will be wielded from a narrow special interest perspective, without regard to broader public interest considerations?" They are concerned with the effect of fall teacher strikes on the education children receive and the lessons they learn from the process.

What do you think? Should teachers possess the right to strike? Should laws be passed now to discourage the growing strength of teacher and other public employee groups? What changes, if any, would you suggest? Are teachers any more likely to dominate public policy in education than the state or community Chamber of Commerce dominates public policy over issues in business or the medical association in respect to health? Is the right of interest groups to organize and politick a constitutional right that should not be denied teachers?

State Interest Group Systems

Sarah McCally Morehouse studied recent state literature and classified states on the basis of interest group and party strength.[23]

She found that weak party states have strong interest groups, often one dominant interest or a group of related interests. In strong party states the party dominates the interests, or the major interests are associated with each of the major parties. In moderately strong party states the pattern is mixed. She also observed that where governors had strong legal powers, interest groups were also likely to be weaker. Another study suggested interest groups are strong in more homogeneous states with small urban populations, low per capita income, and a low level of industrialization.[24] Also of importance is lack of professionalism in the legislature and bureaucracy.

Since two-thirds of American cities have nonpartisan elections, we have no continuing political organization to offset interest group influence. Where a single group dominates a community, the group is likely to be a large manufacturer whose interests tend to be in low taxes and matters that directly affect the industry. Otherwise officials of the largest department store, other Main Street merchants, and the daily newspaper may have major influence.

Changing Interest Group Patterns The relationships between parties and interest groups may change over time. California's political parties have been growing stronger because of legislation that repealed antiparty reforms of the earlier Progressive era. At the same time California interest groups may become weaker as the result of the strong lobbying control laws, successfully sponsored by Common Cause and passed by initiative. Anaconda Copper in Montana no longer dominates the economy as it once did. The introduction of an optional primary law has weakened Connecticut's political parties.

What Causes Change? We meet two familiar themes again—the nationalization of the federal system and the growing diversity within states and even communities. State government may no longer be quite as important to a state's major industries. Their lobbying efforts may turn more to Washington, where major decisions affecting their future are made. We can also see that large-scale industries, and even agriculture, are beginning to lose monopolistic status within states. Because of their own geographical decentralization, large corporations such as General Motors and Ford find Michigan less important to them, just as Anheuser Busch, which now brews beer in Newark, New Jersey, as well as in St. Louis, views Missouri policies as less significant. In Hawaii, the Big Five landowners, important since the Great Depression, have been challenged by a growing political force—the Longshoreman's Union and the public employee union AFSCME (American Federation of State, County and Municipal Employees) and sale of hotel properties to foreign nationals.

The Emergence of Second-Level Groups

State-regulated economic groups, contractors, and local government groups, however, fill the vacuum.

Groups the States Regulate State-based professional and service groups are a major element of state lobbying activity. These groups are anchored to the state and its governments. Some even come to state government requesting "regulation," which may be a thinly veiled way of writing into law special advantages for themselves. For example, in 17 states the Milk Producers Association has persuaded the state legislature to set minimum milk prices (to prevent price-cutting competition). Physical therapists want state licensing to differentiate them from those who work in sleazy massage parlors. Thus far the national government touches only marginally the interests of these trades and professions. Also, those who make a living building state highways or the many vendors who sell supplies and services are part of the state lobby.

Public Officials as Lobbyists Other organizations represent elected officials, appointed professionals, unions, or public bodies. Their representatives attend city council and county commission meetings, state legislative hearings, or important sessions in force when an issue affects their working conditions or salaries.

In Alabama the lobbyist for the Alabama Education Association is reputed to decide the fate of important bills by sitting in the gallery and signaling "thumbs up" or "thumbs down." Whether he does so or not, he is regarded as the state's most influential lobbyist.[25] In North Carolina the president of the North Carolina Association of Educators (NCAE) announced to a news conference that the group's legislative scorecard had been a success. The first scorecard issued in 1980 listed 11 legislators as "needing improvement." The second rating showed that all 11 had later voted the NCAE way on most of the targeted education issues. Only one legislator was named by the president for "special negative attention." The NCAE policy was to support proeducation incumbents and "recruit new faces to take the place of incumbents not totally committed to a strong educational system.[26]

State-based Reform Groups As already noted, many reforms in America began piecemeal, state by state, before a national policy evolved. Vermont, Oregon, Michigan, and South Dakota pioneered state bottle deposit laws—a victory for ecologists. Sunset legislation began in Colorado—a victory for Common Cause. New York pioneered civil rights legislation.

Political scientists have traced the patterns of such innovation—many are the result of interest group activities. State and community professionals read about the reforms in professional journals or hear about them at conventions.[27] Or a single-issue interest group keeps local affiliates informed about what is happening in other states. MADD sends out statistics and model laws on drunk driving to its many affiliated groups. Other groups report a victory in an individual state or community, such as antiabortion measures or the gun control law in a small Chicago suburb, and trumpet it to their national audience. The message to them is "Lobby your own state legislature or city council!" Business groups also have such information networks.

Iron Triangles: How Interest Groups Penetrate

Iron triangles, sometimes called "cozy triangles," operate as subgovernment policymakers, usually invisible to the general public. They are the legislators, administrators, and lobbyists most interested in a **policy domain**—policy in a specific subject area. On all but the most major policies, the decisions that are made are a compromise reached among these three sets of actors.

Sometimes all of the interest groups in a domain are part of a single **peak organization**. A domain made up of competing interests, as is often the case, is likely to be characterized by compromise, shifting coalitions, and less doctrinaire fervor.[28] The field of health provides a good example of how iron triangles operate.

The Medical Interest Group Medical groups are well represented among those lobbying state government. Along with the physicians, we find the nursing, dental, and other health care delivery groups, as well as health insurance companies and hospital administrators. They do not agree on all policies, but they form alliances depending on the issue.

The Medical Administrators Robert Salisbury calls administrators who deal with a specific field the "permanent subgovernment." In the health department these are frequently physicians themselves at the top levels or, at middle and lower levels, people who have had some type of medical training. The health administrators thus share many of the goals and assumptions of the private medical profession. They usually see their job as one of cooperating with the physicians who are essential to making many of their own programs successful. Critics who disapprove of this arrangement point out that the regulators are co-opted by the regulated. They single out instances of administrators who leave their jobs and take jobs in industries they formerly regulated—in this case, perhaps, the pharmaceutical industry or medical laboratories.

This kind of cooperation is probably inevitable, given the absence of a competing interest group or publicity. Its root cause is that administrators, and the private groups they regulate, often share many of the same interests, values, and goals. One study suggests that the alliance which sometimes forms between groups and agencies is "a significant, if not the most significant force, in state government."[29]

Public Health Committee Members Public health committee members and their staff write or review most legislation—in this example, the public health committees of the house and senate. At the local level it is the board of health. These legislators also come to know physicians and their problems very well. Some may even have health-related occupations, such as druggist, dentist, or health insurance agent. Physician legislators almost surely are members of this committee.

In some states we find a tendency to "stack legislative committees" with persons from both parties who share the same views or have the same background. Thus the health committee will be pro-physician, the labor committee will have a heavy concentration of union members, and at the same time a committee dealing with private business consists mainly of businesspersons. This makes for harmony in deliberations and increases the degree of cooperation with the other participants in the iron triangles.

The Visibility of Iron Triangles Who really watches how the rules for the practice of morticians are written, the activities of realtors or bankers, or the procedures private adoption agencies follow? In most cases, the process of iron triangle decision making is largely shielded from public view. The working relationships among the legislative committee members, administrators, and the interest group representatives are much quieter and less flamboyant than the wheeler-dealer, high-pressure lobbying that sensationalist journalists describe. At the local level the governmental process is also likely to go unwatched—school boards make major decisions with little citizen knowledge of their activities. It is a rare newspaper that features exposés of the city council.

The Effectiveness of Iron Triangles Members of iron triangles are the people at the state and community levels who generally know and care the most about the problem under consideration. The compromises they hammer out are not always, or perhaps even most of the time, motivated by narrowly selfish goals. Very often, as in the case of health problems, all may work cooperatively to control a disease such as AIDS or to upgrade maternity health services. Still, the result of their negotiations usually is not wholly displeasing to the interest group participants.

THE ARENAS OF LOBBYING

Lobbying organizations are only half the equation. The other half is the conditions found in state or community governments.

Democratic Organization

Few governments of the world are as democratically organized as our state and community governments. Thus interest group representatives often can easily penetrate these governmental structures.[30]

Access Points for Interest Groups It is not only the legislature that provides points of access. Interest groups also find them in the bureaucracy, the governor's office, and even the judiciary.[31]

Governmental structure is never neutral for an interest group. Structural features advantage some groups and disadvantage others. Civil rights groups, for example, have gained major victories through state courts, but have found it more difficult to elect favorable majorities to school boards. Environmentalists have found it easier to get throwaway bottle bans adopted through an initiative than to lobby a bill through the legislature. On the other hand, agricultural and business groups have often found the legislature and community councils and boards easier to convince than the voters. Professionals have often found a sympathetic ear in the state or local bureaucracy. The choice of governmental arena depends on the interest group and the policy involved.

Amateur Politicians Lobbyists are attracted especially to state legislatures because so many lawmakers are political amateurs. The same is true of members of city councils and other local officials.

Legislative pay is often low, the sessions short, and sometimes no office or staff is available. Such conditions are made to order for lobbyists. As newspaper reporter Frank Trippett observed, when state legislators are amateurs, lobbyists appear to be the hosts in the capital city and legislators the guests. Lobbyists who have been around for some time take the legislators in hand. They explain how the system works. They fill in information about the best places to eat, the nearest place to take their cleaning, provide entertainment, supply them with information that they have trouble getting elsewhere, and help them draft bills and key amendments. Full-time legislators with professional political careers ahead are less likely to want or need such help. Still, even they need money for campaigns—a need that lobbyists happily attempt to fill.

Another aspect of amateur status is that the legislator's full-time occupation may be affected rather easily by the lobbyist—either favorably or unfavorably. Lawyers receive retainers, small businesses get new orders, and farmers may wish to buy a truck or tractor at the dealer's discount price.

Officials Are Sometimes Lobbyists We need to remind ourselves that bureaucrats, state legislators, and community councilors, like other human beings, also have prejudices, likes, and dislikes. A state legislator or city councilor who is or was a labor union member may be as interested in legislation affecting labor as any state AFL-CIO lobbyist. The same may be true of realtors, farmers, small merchants, and college professors and other teachers—in fact, of people of all businesses, trades, and professions, and even avocations. They know intimately how a governmental action will affect their respective interests. Such legislators may stir up paid lobbyists to act for bills that they favor, rather than the reverse.[32]

How do the prejudices of officials affect the way the officials treat lobbyists? Knowing that legislators already hold some policy positions should make us less prone to accept the notion that every state or community official is up for sale or will cave to pressure on any issue. We should expect close cooperation with lobbyists where an official already shares a lobbyist's views. Corruption is more likely when officials are somewhat uninformed about the stakes involved or where they are largely indifferent about the outcome of a policy—where it does not appear to affect interests with which they most clearly identify.

LOBBYING PRACTICES

Around most state capitols, somewhere between 100 to perhaps 300 or 400 lobbyists seek to influence at least some legislation. Most of them lobby part time. Many of these, too, are amateurs. Community governments are surrounded by fewer lobbyists—almost all part time in this role. It is sometimes difficult at this level to determine who, in fact, can be called a lobbyist. Many of the elected public officials and appointed members of boards see themselves as "citizens involved in government," though they may serve rather well in representing an interest group's views.

The Lobbyists

Most studies have focused on the small group who make a professional career of influencing public officials. These professionals tend to be slightly better educated than state legislators. About one-half to three-quarters are college graduates. A growing number have law degrees. Two-thirds are in their late forties and fifties. Most are men. Most live in the capital city. Fewer than we would expect, about

Lobbyists at work outside the house chamber.

one-quarter, are ex-legislators or other former officials, but their number is growing. About one-third are from each party and a third independents. About one-third have been lobbyists less than three years, and one-third have lobbied for over ten years. One study reports that a large number drifted into lobbying largely by accident.[33]

As in many other professions, there is an occasional rascal, but these seem to be the exception. The professionals have a reputation and career to protect.

Professional Lobbying Firms Some lobbyists own or work for multiclient lobbying firms. They operate on contract or a retainer, much like a firm of lawyers. They represent several clients on a continuing basis in both state legislatures and administrative agencies. These firms may also contract with clients who are concerned about only one or two issues. When the issue is resolved, the contract ends.

These professional legislative agents are among the most prestigious and wealthy lobbyists. Continuing clients pay a monthly fee; short-term clients pay a fixed fee on a per issue basis. Contract lobbyists' earnings depend on their ability to get results. Many will not take clients for what they regard as hopeless cases or if they already represent competing or conflicting interests. Because they expect to continue in business they seldom are involved in what we might classify as "seedy deals." They refuse to handle clients if they feel that doing so may damage the firm's image.

Washington Middlemen A new type of lobbyist operates out of Washington, D.C., on behalf of national corporations that have concerns in particular states—for example, a ballot issue. The Washington firm has on contract lobbyists in each state who, they assure clients, are the best available there to handle their problem. The state lobbyist provides the Washington firm "a political road map of the legislature and supplies on-site guides." Meanwhile the Washington firm lobbies such Washington-based groups as the National Conference of State Legislatures and the National Governors' Association, hoping that they may include the client's proposal in model legislation that such groups send to their state affiliates.[34]

The Government Relations Specialist Some lobbyists work for large companies, such as Philip Morris, or perhaps the state university or a large school district. Because of frequent contact with the state, the company finds it useful to have an ongoing observer at the legislature, even if only in a watchdog role.

These lobbyists often have other public relations duties within the firm—perhaps publicizing the plant's winning bowling league team, getting stories about the new product line in the mass media, or appearing before city councils, county commissions, or school boards when the need arises.

The Association Director Association executive directors are the most numerous professional lobbyists at the state level. When not lobbying in the legislature, they are doing other organizational chores.

A group such as the state medical association or state AFL-CIO usually has staff assistants aiding the executive director in lobbying. At the other extreme the librarians may have a person whose duties include visiting the capitol as the situation requires. Some, such as labor union representatives, also lobby city councils, school boards, and county commissions.

Amateur Lobbyists We should not idealize the amateurs. Many know little about the legislative process and do not intend to lobby again once the issue that concerns them is settled. Some are thus tempted to use intimidating tactics. A Michigan estimate placed part-time lobbyists at about 85 percent of those at the state level.[35] Almost all community lobbyists are amateurs—many are realtors, merchants, or persons involved in "cause" groups who seek out councilors on their own.

Successful Lobbyists and Their Techniques

One useful way of looking at lobbyists is to look at how and what they try to accomplish. Walter DeVries concluded that the three top qualities of successful lobbyists are personality and sociability, the power and prestige of the organization represented, and experience with legislative procedures.

Casey Stengel once observed that sportswriters somehow found him much more skillful as a baseball manager when he managed the powerful New York Yankees than when he led the then basement-dwelling New York Mets. Lobbying is similar—lobbyists look more skillful when organizations with powerful resources are backing them. As in all games, skill in managing one's advantages always counts. But on lazy sunny afternoons in the fall, underdog college football teams occasionally upset the "favorites." So, too, down at the state capitol, a lobbyist with a knowledge of the legislature and a winning personality may occasionally achieve wonders. It pays to have a skilled coach and an experienced lobbyist, but it still pays off more often to go into the game stronger than one's opponents.

Samuel Patterson, in an Oklahoma study, classified legislative lobbyists as "contacters," "informants," and "watchdogs." We add a fourth—"favor givers."

Building Friendly Contacts Professional lobbyists work closely with legislators who are already sympathetic to their clients. Then they work on legislators who are undecided or neutral. Finally, they may briefly approach those who at the moment are hostile.

One professional lobbyist told our class that his firm keeps a card file on every legislator—including contacts made, his or her interests, names of the spouse and children, and any other information collected. When an issue arises the lobbyist hopes not only to be on a first name basis but to know how to "approach" the legislator effectively.

Pressuring a legislator has costs; pressure tactics can backfire and create lingering ill will. Most lobbyists organize letter writing campaigns or "pack the gallery" only in emergencies. In Michigan, Common Cause appears to have used tactics that some legislators regarded as undue pressure. The legislators reacted by publicizing a minor clerical error that they found in a Common Cause report on how it financed its lobbying activities.

Most lobbyists follow the rule of "Never burn your bridges." When they disagree, they disagree amiably because the opponent of one day may be an ally on the next. Some purposive lobbyists, however, attack individual legislators who they feel will never be won over, feeling they maintain their credibility with members with such tactics.[36] Part of maintaining good relations is being willing to compromise or give in gracefully without hard feelings. Many see finding workable compromises as a main part of their job.

Providing Information A major part of a lobbyist's task may be public relations. If voters back in the district can be influenced or even mobilized to write personal letters to their legislators explaining the problem rather than demanding a particular solution, the job of convincing legislators becomes easier.

But lobbyists out of necessity also seek to preserve their credibility within the legislature. This means answering a legislator's questions honestly, but walking a fine line where damaging information is concerned. Some information will not be mentioned unless it is specifically asked for. In other cases the lobbyist may decide it is best to let the legislator know the worst so that no "nasty surprises" will occur later that sour the legislator on the lobbyist.

But along with credibility the lobbyist must have a message that is factual rather than merely opinion. Because a legislator's time is taken up with many bills, lobbyists often present their facts in written form or as testimony at legislative hearings. Both provide a permanent record. Lobbyists generally also line up expert witnesses for hearings, including officers of their organizations—if they are prestigious. The multiclient firms usually prepare their clients for committee testimony rather than delivering it themselves. If they provide the information themselves, these professional lobbyists usually prefer talking about the bill in pleasant surroundings, such as over a meal, or, at the least, over coffee.

An important aspect of information giving is keeping the organization members informed through legislative alert bulletins or newsletters. Some, like the National Association of Manufacturers, have toll-free 800 numbers that their members can call for specific information. Overloading the system with information about the effect on members of what the legislature is doing is a technique most association lobbyists use to show they are on the job.[37]

Watchdog Lobbying Some interest groups keep a lobbyist at the capitol or even have someone visit community governments occasionally to keep tabs on pending legislation. They do not seek to change so much as they try to preserve the status quo. They assess what any proposed change will mean to them and ask to be consulted before it is adopted.

The watchdog role requires checking all bills and committee actions carefully. Lobbyists with this assignment may spend much of their time away from the capitol and other time just sitting through committee meetings. They may do their work, poring over bills and amendments or a daily legislative report, in a nearby office building.

Granting Favors Perhaps the most difficult problem lobbyists face is dealing adroitly with requests for "favors." Many legislators expect lobbyists to buy drinks or prenumbered tickets to fund-raisers. Some expect lobbyists to pick up the bill even when they are at another table. Or a legislator may ask for a "loan" of $25 to buy lunch. Such loans may never be repaid. Nor does a realistic lobbyist expect them to be.

State universities have been known to offer honorary degrees to legislators. Or they may follow the common practice of providing every legislator with season tickets to athletic events. Is that bribery? Or is the university just allowing legislators to inspect more closely an activity underwritten with state funds? Is it bribery if the state's racetracks provide each legislator with a free season pass?

A Michigan lobbyist makes $100 Christmas contributions in a legislator's name to the Children's Hospital of Michigan. They are tax deductible. A lobbyist may find a legislator's brother-in-law a job with his or her firm. Fewer groups invite legislators on trips to their plants, but the weekend vacation at the group's camp or hunting lodge is common. The list of such favors is endless. Some are highly questionable. Yet all but the poorest and most "squeaky clean" lobbyists are at one time or another forced to be favor givers.

Financing Political Campaigns

Lobbyists are most influential when they can show that their suggested way of voting on a bill will help the legislator get reelected. It follows that they are also influential when their group supports financially the campaigns of candidates who share their views. In running for office, candidates are often pretty much on their own. Each must find a way to finance the campaign. In a few states, such as New York, Ohio, Michigan, and Illinois, the party may channel some funds to targeted candidates for the general election, but rarely is this enough. And in primaries the candidates commonly receive no party help.

Political Action Committees The number of **political action committees (PACs)** in the past decade has increased sharply at both national and state levels. In Louisiana PACs active in state elections increased from 70 to 344 between 1980 and 1983.[38] These groups collect funds and use them to finance campaigns of favored candidates. As long as they remain independent of a candidate or party, their spending is unregulated.

Overwhelmingly, PACs give more funds to incumbents rather than to challengers. This may be true even when the challenger comes closer to reflecting their position. They still want access to the probable winner and may fear retribution if they back a loser. Giving to incumbents is especially prudent at the state level where less than a fifth of incumbents are defeated. Legislative leaders and members of relevant committees also receive more funds than other legislators.

Michael Binford found that Georgia state legislators received less support from ideological liberal, conservative, or labor PACs than they did from the medical, banking, insurance, and corporate PACs. The pattern varies from state to state.[39] In Louisiana candidates reverse the process by contributing to nonconnected PACs. Generally they use the funds to publicize endorsements of such candidates by distributing slate cards or sample ballots. Black and Hispanic groups issue slate endorsements in several other states including California, New York, and Missouri.[40]

A more questionable practice is the **political fund-raiser** that legislators sponsor for themselves to pay "campaign expenses." Tickets to a cocktail party or dinner costing $50 or more are sent unsolicited to lobbyists. The accompanying letter says that the lobbyists may return the tickets if they do not care to attend. One tip-off that lobbyists are being "milked" is that tickets are numbered so contributors can be identified. The other is where the legislator holds the fund-raiser. If it is at the state capital rather than in the district, lobbyists are expected to buy most of the tickets. Routinely their firms buy blocks of tickets and the lobbyists put in an appearance. They know some politicians keep count. In some states legislators may keep these funds when they decide not to run again. Legislators and lobbyists alike deny that their contributions buy votes. Rather, they argue that at best the money buys access—the opportunity to state their case. Others, though, question whether legislators can wholly separate their voting from their contributing supporters.

CONTROLLING INTEREST GROUPS

How can corrupt lobbying be controlled? The first attempt was the result of the Yazoo land scandal in the Georgia legislature of 1795. Citizens of other states sued, challenging the constitutionality of laws that an admittedly corrupt legislature passed. The U.S. Supreme Court ruled against the challenge.[41] Reformers have tried a variety of other methods. Presently most favor publicity and regulations covering political activities.

Interest Groups Policing Themselves

Few believe that self-regulation alone can control undesirable practices. Still, it does little harm and, combined with other methods, may do some good.

A Code of Ethics Following the Watergate scandal most states adopted codes of behavior for legislators and lobbyists. They spell out proper conduct and potential conflicts of interest. But these codes depend on voluntary compliance or, at most, mild social pressure. Still, when breaking the code of ethics brings significant advantages and few disadvantages, it is apt to be bent or broken. Connecticut set up a commission to enforce its code. But it became so wrapped up in procedural issues and court challenges that in its first years it had little time to seek out violations.

Competing Interest Groups A theory of **countervailing groups**, built on ideas from laissez-faire economics, assumes that competing organizations will offset each other. Unions and industry, right-to-life and pro-choice groups will check each other. In South Dakota in 1981, for example, the South Dakota Trucking Association successfully went to court to prevent gas tax money from being used for railroad purposes.

But many groups that lobby do so without having to worry about an effective opposing interest group. Who, for example, is the countervailing interest group to the ambulance firms or locally to realtor and developer groups? Another problem is that the groups involved (and legislators as well) begin to view every issue as having only two groups involved. The general public usually has something at stake as well.

Overlapping and Reaffirming Groups In Minnesota, Lutherans and Catholics supported the Democratic Farmer Labor party. At the same time, many Lutherans and some Catholics also supported the Republicans. The theory of **overlapping memberships** holds that this helps control each group. The religious or political party groups could never get too greedy or the battles too acrimonious because some Lutheran Democrats went to church with some Lutheran Republicans. At the same time, they attended party functions with Catholic Democrats. Overlapping memberships tend to dampen conflict.

Sometimes the theory works, but also, unfortunately, as Robert Salisbury observed, groups sometimes have **reaffirming memberships**. The same people who belong to the Chamber of Commerce are also members of the community church, the country club, and the Republican party. Those in the same community who are members of labor unions often are also members of the Catholic church, an ethnic organization, and the Democratic party. Thus interest group memberships reaffirm conflict and sharpen it rather than blur it. Rather than moderating their stands on issues, interest groups are likely to see those that oppose them as completely in the wrong. We conclude that self-regulation in interest group politics, as in the economy, has some utility. It also has some serious inadequacies.

Regulating Lobbyist Behavior

In the 1800s some states tried to make lobbying illegal—the Supreme Court declared such laws unconstitutional. The First Amendment guarantees us the right to petition our governments for redress of grievances.

Corrupt Practices Laws The earliest **corrupt practices laws** forbade only the crudest practices—across-the-counter bribery, purchase of votes, or fraudulent rigging of elections.

Lobbyist Registration Next an effort was made to find out who was lobbying. Enforcement was poor, and publicity was often nonexistent. And some groups refused to register because they considered themselves "educational associations" rather than lobbies. Others, especially groups representing state or local officials, did not believe they were required to register.

Now, however, the legal definitions are much broader and enforcement is becoming more common. For example, all states now require lobbyists to register. Three-quarters of the states also require PACs to register and allow public examination of the lists.

Spending Regulations Next, states attempted to control spending for lobbying public officials. The limits enacted were generally combined with reporting requirements. Common Cause sponsored an initiative in California in 1974 that limited expenditures to $10 per month to influence any one public official. In California and elsewhere the courts have struck down such laws as depriving citizens of their guaranteed constitutional rights. States thus have had to turn to strategies that depend on the publicity that media and opposing groups give lobbyists' contribution and spending reports. The basic premise is that the publicity will act as a deterrent and possibly as a way of uncovering clearly illegal acts of bribery.

Table 6.1 LOBBYIST REGISTRATION AND REPORTING[a]

State	Frequency	Expenditures itemized (I) or total (T)	Sources of income	Monies or gifts to individual legislators	Legislation support–oppose
Alabama	monthly	T	X	X	X
Alaska	monthly	T	X	X	
Arizona	annually	T		X	
Arkansas	none				
California	quarterly		X	X	X
Colorado	monthly	T	X	X	X
Connecticut	quarterly	T	X	X	
Delaware	quarterly	T		X	
Florida	semi-annually	T	X		
Georgia	none				
Hawaii	semi-annually	T	X	X	X
Idaho	annually	I	X	X	X
Illinois	Jan.–Apr.–July	T		X	
Indiana	semi-annually	I		X	X
Iowa	monthly	I		X	
Kansas	monthly	I		X	
Kentucky	after session	I	X		X
Louisiana	none				
Maine	monthly	T	X	X	X
Maryland	semi-annually	I		X	
Massachusetts	semi-annually	T		X	
Michigan	annually	I		X	
Minnesota	quarterly	I	X	X	
Mississippi	annually	I	X	X	
Missouri	3 times during session	I		X	X
Montana	[b]	I		X	X
Nebraska	monthly	I	X	X	X
Nevada	after session	I			
New Hampshire	Apr.–Aug. & after session	I	X		
New Jersey	quarterly	I	X		
New Mexico	after session	I		X	
New York	[c]	I		X	X
North Carolina	annually	I			
North Dakota	annually			X	
Ohio	semi-annually	T		X	X
Oklahoma	semi-annually				
Oregon	quarterly	I		X	
Pennsylvania	semi-annually	I		X	
Rhode Island	3 times during session		X	X	
South Carolina	annually	I		X	
South Dakota	annually	I		X	
Tennessee	annually			X	
Texas	monthly	I			X

Table 6.1 *Continued*

Utah	none				
Vermont	annually	T			
Virginia	after session	T	X		X
Washington	monthly	I		X	X
West Virginia	after session	T			
Wisconsin	semi-annually	I			X
Wyoming	none				

Source: Council of State Governments, *The Book of the States, 1988–89*, p.143. Copyright 1988 The Council of State Governments. Reprinted with permission from *The Book of the States*.

[a] Indiana and Illinois prosecute noncompliance as a felony. Other states treat noncompliance as a misdemeanor or list fine or jail limits in that range or have no penalty for noncompliance.

[b] Before Feb. 16 when legislature is in session, before 16th day of the calendar month when principal spent $5000 or more the previous month, and 60 days after adjournment.

[c] A lobbyist who receives, spends, or incurs over $2,000 a year files by the 15th day following reporting period in which the cumulative total equaled that amount—Jan. 1–Mar. 31, Apr. 1–May 31, June 1–Aug. 31—and files an annual cumulative report.

Regulating Campaign Contributions The U.S. Supreme Court has ruled that candidates may spend as much of their own funds as they wish. And, as already noted, limits cannot be placed on money spent independently of candidates such as money spent by PACs. Still, the state may require PACs to report contributions and expenditures. Regulation, then, is through the publicity given such reports.

States that help to finance political campaigns do so to reduce a candidate's dependence on lobbyists. Financing is generally limited to the general election and candidates for governor. And when public funds are granted, the states may regulate how much candidates spend, either by absolute dollar amount or by a formula based on the importance of the office and the number of voters in the constituency. They may also regulate contributions accepted.

Regulation by a Lobby Commission Twenty-six states have commissions that require detailed reports of the amount of money spent lobbying public officials and the amount contributed to political campaigns. The advantage of a commission is that someone checks to see that reports are filed and that they are accurate. Newspapers and opposing candidates may publicize the data collected.[42]

Public Interest Watchdog Groups In the late 1960s Ralph Nader began a variety of public interest groups designed to "make government and corporations more responsive to the public welfare." Nader's activities inspired independent offshoots. All argue for more citizen access to the workings of government. They demand information about decisions—how they were made and on what basis. More facts, they argue, should be on the public record.[43]

Most of these groups are specialized. Nader's task forces are concerned with consumer matters, from sports to auto safety. Common Cause has placed major emphasis on regulating lobbying and campaign finance. Other groups have specialized in legislation involving agriculture and food, others in mental health and child care. Often these groups function as the only countervailing groups to lobbies representing business and industry. Some get leverage on public policies by bringing cases to court. Others function mainly as research organizations, hoping to influence public opinion and legislators with factual information. The Pacific Legal Foundation, a conservative public interest group that has battled civil rights groups on affirmative action, had California's nuclear moratorium declared unconstitutional, and fought efforts to protect endangered species.[44]

The larger groups finance themselves by membership contributions; the smaller ones depend on foundation grants. But in 1976 the Ford Foundation announced the end of its support of public interest legal groups. Other such financing has also dried up.[45] The groups then hoped to survive on government grants. Or they argued that defendants who lost in one of their suits should pay full legal fees. The U.S. Supreme Court ruled in 1975 that such awards must be specifically authorized by law. Few states or communities have such laws.

In the past few years many of the smaller public interest watchdog groups have reduced their staffs and activities. Some have disappeared. As we write, the enthusiasm that encouraged the creation of such groups appears to be waning. Thus, despite their effectiveness, they no longer are as great a force in the control of interest group excesses.

Control by Changing the Governmental Process

Marxists argue that the influence of business groups can be reduced only by reorganizing the economy along socialist lines. But other possibilities exist.

Changing Governmental Structure Theodore Lowi suggested the alternative of changing government structure to reduce interest group access.[46] Marcus Ethridge argues, however, that the goal should be to redesign government structure to encourage the access of public interest type watchdog groups.[47]

Strengthening Political Parties Probably the change that would most limit the excesses of interest groups and PACs would be to strengthen the major parties. They offer a counterweight to interest groups and can offer citizens choices on policy that come closer to reflecting a general interest than does the balance of forces that results from interest group lobbying.

A FINAL COMMENT

A *Wall Street Journal* reporter recently examined, at the invitation of a member of Congress, that legislator's association with representatives of PACs. The representative defended his actions, since he made it clear to all groups that although he will listen to those who contribute, they should expect nothing in return. Research backs up the view that PACs may receive only a hearing in return for a contribution. Janet Grenzke found no relationship between PAC contributions and maintaining or changing a legislator's votes.[48]

But the reporter, although sympathetic to the legislator's situation, argued that the legislator was deceiving himself that a form of corruption was not present. He argued that buying access results in a system in which PACs overwhelmingly support incumbents, and this cannot be really in the public interest.

Most of the rest of us are also troubled by the rising influence of PACs, where, as the reporter writes, "America is becoming a special interest nation where money is displacing votes." The problem is not the old one of direct bribery; rather, the author argues that "perverse incentives twist the behavior of ordinary legislators."[49]

HIGH POINTS

In this chapter we began by (1) reporting findings about American groups—that the upper middle class were most likely to be organized, that lobbying paid off most for economic producers and governmental organizations, that groups would lobby actively when facing uncertainty, and that the basic resources for effective lobbying were money and members, lack of internal divisions, and acceptance. We then looked at (2) the patterns of state lobbying and suggested they are changing because of the diversification of business and agriculture and the national government taking over many more important economic decisions. We concluded that the importance of the "big interests" in states was declining. Taking their place are second-level groups—service and professional interest groups that the states regulate, and employees of local government, especially schoolteachers, whose future is affected by state aid formulas. We described a pattern of influence called the iron triangle. Next we looked at (3) the state and community governments as arenas for lobbying, noting especially the decentralization, amateurism, and potential conflict of interest because officials may be strongly associated with a group. We then looked at (4) lobbying techniques emphasizing the giving of information and personal persuasion. Finally, we looked at (5) the methods that reformers have recommended for control of interest group influence—self-regulation, regulation of what lobbyists do, regulatory commissions, publicity, and public interest watchdog organizations.

In this chapter we defined the following terms in this order: political interest group, lobbyist, material benefits as a selective incentive, purposive groups, single issue groups, interest group entrepreneurs, group cohesiveness, group legitimacy, anticipatory reactions, iron triangles, policy domain, peak organization, points of access, political action committees (PACs), political fund-raiser, countervailing groups, overlapping memberships, reaffirming memberships, and corrupt practices laws.

NOTES

1. David Truman, *The Governmental Process* (New York: Knopf, 1953).
2. Robert H. Salisbury, "An Exchange Theory of Interest Groups," *Midwest Journal of Political Science* 13 (February 1989):1–32.

3. David C. Nice, "Political Corruption in the American States," *American Politics Quarterly* 11:4 (October 1983): 507–517.
4. Still valid are findings in Charles R. Wright and Herbert Hyman, "Voluntary Memberships of American Adults, Evidence from National Sample Surveys," *American Sociological Review* 23 (June 1958): 284–293, in Robert Salisbury (ed.), *Interest Group Politics in America* (New York: Harper & Row, 1970), pp. 71–88. See also Lester Milbrath and M. L. Goel, *Political Participation* (2nd ed.) (Chicago: Rand McNally, 1977), and Robert Lane, *Political Life, Why People Get Involved in Politics* (Glencoe, Ill.: Free Press, 1959), pp. 74–79.
5. E. E. Schattschneider, *The Semi-Sovereign People, A Realist View of Democracy in America* (New York: Holt, 1960), p. 35.
6. William P. Browne and Laurily Keir Epstein, "Interest Groups in Political Context, A State-by-State Analysis," Paper presented at the Midwest Political Science Association, April 1980, Chicago.
7. James A. Stever, "Interest Groups and Intergovernmental Relations," *Southeastern Political Review* 9 (Spring 1981): 60–84.
8. Jeffrey M. Berry, *The Interest Group Society* (Boston: Little, Brown, 1984), pp. 67–82.
9. Anthony Downs, *An Economic Theory of Democracy* (New York: Harper & Row, 1957), pp. 353–356.
10. Keith Hamm, Charles Wiggins, and Charles G. Bell, "Interest Group Involvement, Conflict, and Success in State Legislatures," Paper presented at the annual meeting of the American Political Science Association, September 1983, Chicago.
11. Glenn Abney and Thomas P. Lauth, "Interest Group Influence in City Policy-Making: The Views of Administrators," *Western Political Quarterly* (1985): 148–161.
12. Constance Ewing Cook, "Participation in Public Interest Groups," *American Politics Quarterly* 12:4 (October 1984): 409–430.
13. Harmon Zeigler and Michael Baer, *Lobbying Interaction and Influence in American State Legislatures* (Belmont, Calif.: Wadsworth, 1969), p. 30.
14. J. M. Hansen, "The Political Economy of Group Membership," *American Political Science Review* 79 (1985): 79–96.
15. Salisbury, "An Exchange Theory": 1–32, and Jeffrey M. Berry, "On the Origins of Public Interest Groups, A Test of Two Theories," *Polity* 10 (Spring 1978): 379–397. See also William P. Browne, "Benefits and Membership, A Reappraisal of Interest Group Activity," *Western Political Quarterly* 29 (1978): 258–273.
16. Philip H. Pollock III, "Organizations as Agents of Mobilization: How Does Group Activity Affect Political Participation?" *American Journal of Political Science* 26:3 (1982): 485–503.
17. Jack L. Walker, "The Origins and Maintenance of Interest Groups in America," *The American Political Science Review* 77 (1983): 390–406.
18. Jeffrey M. Berry, *The Interest Group Society*, pp. 88–91.
19. James L. Franke and Douglas Dobson, "Interest Groups: The Problem of Representation," *Western Political Quarterly* (1985): 224–237.
20. V. O. Key, Jr., *Politics, Parties, and Pressure Groups* (5th ed.) (New York: Thomas Y. Crowell, 1964), p. 131.
21. Jim Walker, "Research Council Has Big Impact on Government," *Tampa Tribune-Times* (December 28, 1980), p. 12B.
22. Zeigler and Baer, *Lobbying Interaction and Influence in American State Legislatures*, pp. 112–113.

23. Sarah McCally Morehouse, *State Politics, Parties, and Policy* (New York: Holt, 1981), pp. 95–118.
24. Harmon Zeigler and Hendrick van Dalen, "Interest Groups in State Politics," in Herbert Jacob and Kenneth N. Vines (eds.), *Politics in the American States* (3rd ed.) (Boston: Little, Brown, 1976), pp. 94–95.
25. Alan Ehrenhalt, "In Alabama Politics, the Teachers Are Sitting at the Head of the Class," *Governing* (December 1988): 22–27.
26. John Robinson, "NCAE Leader Says Activism Won Votes in Fall Session," *Raleigh N.C. News and Observer* (October 22, 1981), p. 48.
27. Jack L. Walker, "The Diffusion of Innovations among the American States," *American Political Science Review* 63 (September 1969): 880–899; Virginia Gray, "Innovation in the States, A Diffusion Study," *American Political Science Review* 87 (December 1973): 1174–1185; and Susan Welch and Kay Thompson, "The Impact of Federal Incentives on State Policy Innovation," *American Journal of Political Science* 24 (November 1980): 715–729.
28. Robert Salisbury, John P. Heinz, Edward O. Laumann, and Robert L. Nelson, "Who Works With Whom? Interest Group Alliances and Opposition," *American Political Science Review* 81:4 (December 1987): 1217–1234.
29. Glenn Abrey and Thomas Lauth, "Interest Group Influence in the States, A View of Subsystem Politics," Paper presented at the 1986 meetings of the American Political Science Association.
30. Alana Northrop and William H. Dutton, "Municipal Reform and Group Influence," *American Journal of Political Science* 22 (August 1978).
31. Joseph Stewart, Jr., and James F. Sheffield, Jr., "Does Interest Group Litigation Matter? The Case of Black Political Mobilization in Mississippi," *Journal of Politics* 49 (1987): 780–798.
32. Raymond A. Bauer, Ithiel de Sola Pool, and Lewis Anthony Dexter, *American Business and Public Policy* (New York: Atherton Press, 1964).
33. For a detailed discussion of the characteristics of lobbyists in four states, see Zeigler and Baer, *Lobbying Interaction and Influence in American State Legislatures*, Chapter 3, pp. 38–59, and Mark S. Hyde and Richard Alsfeld, "Role Orientations of Lobbyists in a State Setting: A Comparative Analysis," Paper presented at the American Political Science Association meetings, 1985, New Orleans.
34. Tom Watson, "Dale Florio, A Lobbyists' Middleman Who Helps Business Navigate State Capitol Halls," *Governing* (February 1989): 32–38.
35. Walter DeVries, "The Michigan Lobbyist, A Study in the Bases and Perceptions of Effectiveness" (Ph.D. diss., Michigan State University, East Lansing, 1960). See also William P. Browne and Delbert J. Ringquist, "Organized Interests and Their Lobbying," in William P. Browne and Kenneth VerBurg (eds.), *Michigan State Politics* (Lincoln: University of Nebraska Press, forthcoming).
36. Jeffrey M. Berry, *The Interest Group Society*, pp. 120–121.
37. Terry M. Moe, *The Organization of Interests* (Chicago: University of Chicago Press, 1980), pp. 201–218.
38. Charles D. Hadley and Rainer Nick, "The Two Step Flow of State Campaign Funds: PACs as Donors and Receivers in Louisiana," *Western Political Quarterly* (1987): 65–77.
39. Michael B. Binford, "PAC Contributions and the State Legislature, Impact on Legislators and the Legislative Agenda," Paper delivered at the Southern Political Science Association meeting, September 1981, Cincinnati.

40. Hadley and Nick, "The Two Step Flow of State Campaign Funds."
41. *Fletcher v. Peck*, Cranch 87, 123 (1810).
42. Joseph F. Zimmerman, "Lobbying Regulation in New York," *Comparative State Politics Newsletter* 1 (January 1980): 10.
43. Theodore Jacqueney, "Washington Pressures, Public Interest Groups Challenge Government, Industry," *National Journal Reprints, 1975–1980*, "Interest Groups," 20–30, and Jeffrey M. Berry, *Lobbying for the People, The Political Behavior of Public Interest Groups* (Princeton: Princeton University Press, 1977).
44. Margot Hornblower, "Conservative Winds Reshaping Public Interest Law," *Washington Post* (January 14, 1980), p. A3.
45. Jack Willey, "Citizens' Watchdog Group Runs into Money Trouble," *Columbus Dispatch* (September 28, 1981); Timothy S. Clark, "After a Decade of Doing Battle, Public Interest Groups Show Their Age," *The National Journal* (July 12, 1980): 1136–1141; and David Vogel, "The Public Interest Movement and the American Reform Tradition," *Political Science Quarterly* 95 (Winter 1980–1981): 607–627.
46. Theodore Lowi, *The End of Liberalism* (2nd ed.) (New York: Norton 1979).
47. Marcus E. Ethridge, "Collective Action, Public Policy, and Class Conflict," *Western Political Quarterly* (1987): 575–591.
48. Janet M. Grenzke, "PACs and the Congressional Supermarket: The Currency Is Complex," *American Journal of Political Science* 33 (February 1989): 1–24.
49. Brooks Jackson, *Honest Graft: Big Money and the American Political Process* (New York: Knopf, 1989).

Chapter 7

Political Parties

Geoge Washington, in his Farewell Address, warned that political parties "in different ages and countries... [have] perpetuated the most horrid enormities." Many Americans agree, even today. But most of us recognize we need political parties to help us sort out those who run for office.

We are not very well represented in the interest group system. We may influence policy through participation in a social movement—but this tends to be a rare event. So we are back to using our influence through voting.

When we know a great deal about the candidates we may vote without considering party. But at other times we find the party label helps reduce our information costs. Those with less education find the party label particularly helpful.

V. O. Key, Jr., noted that by blindly following the party line we may end up voting against our own interests. But he concluded nevertheless, "We have contrived no other instrument quite so suitable for the translation of democratic theory into working reality."[1]

Overview In this chapter we begin by looking at how distinctive our American parties are. Next we examine how they developed. We then discuss how they function and are organized, how they recruit candidates, how candidates campaign, and how united party candidates are when elected. Finally, we consider how much the state and community parties are now coming under the influence of the national party organizations.

OUR DISTINCTIVE AMERICAN PARTIES

The cowboy humorist Will Rogers once said, "I belong to no organized party. I am a Democrat." What he suggested is true of both parties—they are somewhat decentralized and their units often work at cross-purposes.

Our federal system shapes our parties. Local party units act with some degree of independence, just as the state and community governments do in our changing federal system.[2] On paper the structure of each of our major parties is hierarchical. But in practice their units negotiate with each other rather than blindly follow orders issued from the top.

The separation of powers also inspires splintering. We elect governors and legislators separately and often for different terms. This encourages candidates to strike out on their own, independent of other party candidates.

The reformers, especially those of the early 1900s, weakened parties further. Some tried to democratize the parties; others hating the boss system sought to destroy them.[3] Still, as we note later, the distinguishing feature of our modern parties is a growing professionalism, with full-time paid staffers and state and even local party headquarters.

Responsible or Brokerage Parties?

The Republicans and Democrats are not generally described as **responsible parties**, those that take positions on issues that all of their candidates support. They each appeal to groups with some degree of internal conflict. Yet we can see that they differ—at least in their centers of gravity.

Sectional Voting After the Civil War, the South was the "Solid Democratic South," and those states that provided the soldiers for the Union armies—in the Midwest and Northeast—were almost as equally solidly Republican. Border states with mixtures of northerners and southerners, such as Indiana, Missouri, and Ohio, were competitive.

Sectionalism still influences state elections. Even into the 1980s, Alabama had a senate with no Republicans; in North Dakota only 10 of 50 senators have been Democrats. Yet sectional voting is declining—southern states have elected Republican governors and Republican strongholds of the north such as Vermont have elected Democrats to govern.

Ethnic and Racial Voting Public opinion polls generally show that Democratic candidates receive a larger share of the votes of blacks, Hispanics, and the descendants of the ethnic migrations between 1880 and 1920, most of whom were Jews and Catholics. But increasingly, especially during the Reagan years, the ethnic descendants have occasionally voted for Republicans. And many of the descendants of the first settlers are now voting Democratic.

Socioeconomic Voting Democrats receive more support from those desiring change—labor unions, civil rights groups, lower-educational and lower-income citizens, blue-collar workers, and urban residents. Republicans receive a higher level of support from those groups in the society who tend to favor the status quo—whites, Protestants, white-collar workers, those with higher education and income, older people, suburbanites, and rural and small town residents.

Federalism and Brokerage Parties

The federal system permits the mixture of sectional, ethnic and racial, and socioeconomic factions in each party to find expression. As a result parties often act as **brokerage parties**—their elected officials may support the peculiar interests in their states and communities rather than a national party position. Massachusetts and Alabama Democrats thus seem to be a different breed. So, too, are Georgia and Oregon Republicans.

Candidates reflect the population mix within a state, which sometimes puts them at odds with other state parties and national party policy. South Dakota has relatively small numbers of Catholics, union members, and blacks. James Carlson and Howard Hamilton found that Democrats had to run on personality or stress local issues to win; they hedged on some national party positions.[4]

Yet the Democratic party, in whichever state we choose, seems somewhat more "liberal" on economic and social issues than the state's Republican party. Wisconsin Democrats may think Texas Democrats are generally "conservative," but Texas Republicans are even more so. Georgia Republicans may find Oregon Republicans very "liberal," but Oregon Democrats outdo them. Still, some "nationalization" of the supporters of each party seems to be occurring. Interest groups and voters show the same tendencies—the "have-nots" are more often Democrats, the "haves" more often Republicans. And party leaders are struggling to become more "responsible"—to discipline party officeholders who stray, and to make their organizations more consistent on the issues and the candidates they support. We no longer can expect to see the degree of decentralization in the Democratic party of 1948 when Alabama refused to put Harry S Truman on the ballot as the Democratic party presidential nominee.

We can thus best describe our parties as a compromise between brokerage and responsible parties—a compromise reflecting the degree to which our federal system has become centralized.[5]

THE DEVELOPMENT OF AMERICAN PARTIES

Until the 1820s, holding state office was regarded as an honor for high-status, educated citizens. Party organizations were **cadre parties**—small cliques of like-minded notables—educated and wealthy. Frontiersman Andrew Jackson rode into the presidency to destroy this elitist system.

He fired 2000 government workers and replaced them with his unschooled frontier supporters. Until then only 76 federal employees had ever been fired. Jacksonian methods quickly spread to the states. Critics called it the **spoils system**. Defenders called it the **patronage system**.

The Jacksonians claimed that they were democratizing government by giving its offices back to the common people. They also made it worthwhile for common people to become active in party organizations.

The Birth of Mass Party Organizations

Hand in hand with the spoils system went Jacksonian voting reforms, and party organization changed to appeal to the new mass electorate. The cadre parties had conducted low-key campaigns for a very limited electorate. With the spoils system and the expanded electorate, a new kind of organization arose—the **mass party**. These were brokerage parties. Leaders appealed vigorously for votes, and gave favors and jobs to party activists and supporters.

The pre–Civil War parties were loose patronage-hungry coalitions. The state organizations revolved around the governors, who had trusted lieutenants in every county to pass out patronage. Mayors gave out city jobs and contracts and had party loyalists in every ward. Among the best known of the early organizations was Tammany Hall in New York City.

The Boss Senators Organize State Parties

After the Civil War, President Grant presided over what was perhaps the era of America's most flourishing political corruption. State party leaders needed more systematic organization to secure federal patronage. Those the historian Matthew Josephson called Republican "boss-senators" perfected the system.[6]

The boss-senators built state organizations around such plums as U.S. postmasterships, military commissions, custom house jobs, and Bureau of Internal Revenue positions. From 1865 to 1876 Republican senators also controlled the positions in the Reconstruction officialdom, foisted on the defeated states of the South.

The senators expected officeholders to deliver votes. But they also demanded **kickbacks**—contributions according to the salary of the office they gained. These bosses also traded political favors to Gilded Age capitalists for cash.[7]

It is not entirely true that the builders of the nation's railroads and industries or the extractors of its mineral wealth corrupted state governments. The politicians, from senator to lowly clerk, often were eager to be corrupted. Officeholders sought ingenious ways to extract more from the railroad builders and other industrialists. When a few capitalists fought each other, as when Cornelius Vanderbilt, Jay Gould, and Jim Fiske each tried to take over the Erie Railroad of New York State, legislative bribes and the costs of "staying bought" rose sharply.

The Rise of State Machines

The boss-senator system depended on the ups and downs of its leader in the U.S. Senate and on his political skills. When a leading senator retired or died, the process of building an organization often had to start over.

In the 1880s a more efficient system—what we call a **political machine**—developed in several cities and states. It centralized party organization and corruption.[8] A brief look at how one was organized tells us why reformers of the early 1900s attacked political parties so bitterly.

The Platt Machine of New York State Republican Boss Tom Platt cultivated the image of small town "pious churchgoer and paterfamilias." During the 1870s he worked his way up from state legislator to the U.S. Senate. Then his political ally Senator Roscoe Conkling got into a fight with President James Garfield. In a show of defiance Conkling resigned his Senate seat. He assumed that the state legislature would promptly reelect him. Platt also reluctantly resigned.

But as Platt waited around Albany to be reelected, his enemies dealt him a low political blow. They put a stepladder up to the transom of his hotel room. Then they tiptoed up in stocking feet to peer in. They told reporters that they saw an "unspeakable female" in the arms of the former U.S. senator.

Platt withdrew from the Senate race an embittered man. He had no immediate ambition for, or hope of, attaining elective office again. But he decided to get even with his enemies by reorganizing the state Republican party.[9]

Platt thought the old-style organization was inefficient. Jobholders, who had paid to get their office, paid no attention to party leaders thereafter. Their greed in shaking down bankers and railroad magnates led to scandals and bad publicity. At the same time, Platt thought that the capitalists wasted money because they did not know enough to bribe the right people.

How Platt Organized Platt's goal was to make the party both self-supporting and a centralized organization that would operate without friction. He seems to have personally admired the capitalist entrepreneurs and regarded the job of helping to smooth their way a useful public service. He cut back assessments on officeholders. He turned directly to the capitalists for funds. He sought regular annual payments to be made before the legislature went into session. For example, the Equitable Life Insurance Company gave Platt $10,000 annually for 15 years.[10]

Boss Platt thus acted as a kind of political consultant similar to today's multiclient lobbyists. He was paid a retainer, but unlike today's lobbyists, he could absolutely guarantee that everything would turn out well. He spared capitalists the bother of trying to lobby and bribe every time something came up that affected them. Under the new arrangement they had only to tell their problems to Mr. Platt.

The funds Platt collected from industrialists went into a party war chest. In each house of the legislature he had a half-dozen trusted leaders. Through them, he parceled out funds to their fellow legislators as the need arose.

Platt used patronage to control the party nominating conventions and the state and local election machinery. He also became adept at "balancing the ticket" among varied racial, religious, ethnic, and regional groupings. And on Election Day he hired farmers and their horses to take voters to the polls. He bought other votes by renting, at generous rates, local stores for polling places.

Newspaper editors also shared in the spoils—they got money for "advertising" and were given state jobs with fine salaries and minimal duties. Regularly he sent rural weeklies "boilerplate" news stories about the party organization and its candidates.

Added to all this careful organization was Platt's single-minded concentration on managing the Republican organization—journalist William Allen White called Platt "the Blind Earthworm in Politics." Platt's family life was over. He had few friends. For 20 years he spent all his waking hours in hotel lobbies, endlessly discussing with his lieutenants the details of local races, punishments for party dissidents and reformers, the recruiting of prospective candidates, bills in the legislature, and any other political matter, great or small, that mattered to Republicans or to their capitalist allies.

The Weakening of Political Parties

The turn-of-the-century Progressives faced bosses who were both corrupt and efficient. Reformers set out to smash them. As sometimes happens with social movements, they succeeded rather quickly and perhaps too thoroughly.

How Progressive Reformers Changed the Parties The reformers prescribed a set of simple remedies. We have already noted some of them—hiring and promotions through **civil service** to replace the patronage system and **nonpartisan elections**. About two-thirds of the cities and the Nebraska legislature now hold elections without party labels. The **direct primary** took from party leaders the power to select party candidates at state conventions and gave voters the power to choose them at scheduled elections.[11] The reformers detailed in state law how political parties must organize.

Media Influence on Parties Modern technology has further weakened party influence. The print media—newspapers and magazines—were always a source of political cues for the educated. Political bosses spoke contemptuously of "newspaper wards"—those middle-class and upper-middle-class neighborhoods where newspaper endorsements swayed votes.

Radio and television widened media influence. These media reach all levels of society, from the highly literate to the functionally illiterate. When television became commonplace, candidates began to depend heavily on TV ads and schemed to get on the news reports as a way of reaching voters. Voters responded favorably as **media campaigning** replaced campaigning through party organization.

As a result, parties lost some of their importance as cue givers. More people began telling pollsters they were "independents." **Party identification** dropped. More became **ticket splitters**—voting for candidates of both parties. Some political scientists spoke of the decomposition of political parties—that parties, as they lost their hold on the voters, were falling apart.

But all of these influences have not killed the political party. Candidates in state races who do not win the nomination of a major party seldom get elected. And even when an election is nonpartisan, we often find that a major party may be involved. We need only remind ourselves that Chicago aldermanic elections are nonpartisan.

HOW AMERICAN PARTIES ARE ORGANIZED

The typical textbook party organization pyramidal chart shows the national chair, the national committee, and the national convention in boxes at the top. Lines reach down to connect state organizations with their chairs, committees, and conventions. On the lower levels are boxes for local organizations—the congressional district, county, city, ward, and precinct. The charts hide the variety among these federalized party units.

All state party organizations have a chair, central and executive committees, and periodic conventions. But from that point party units differ as to (1) their names, (2) their size, (3) how they are staffed, (4) the number of party officials, and (5) how local units are organized.

Who Should Run the State Party Organization?

Some say political professionals should control the organization. Others say it should be citizens.

The Case for Professional Control E. E. Schattschneider argued that professional politicians should be responsible for outlining a party program and choosing candidates to implement it. The party would appeal to the voters for support, and citizens would hold party leaders responsible for what the party and its candidates did in office. Parties would then be "responsible," information costs would be reduced, and citizens could vote more intelligently.[12]

The Case for Citizen Control The Progressive reformers argued that parties are public organizations that belong to all citizens—Republicans, Democrats, independents, or whatever—not just to party professionals or party bosses. Hence they should organize democratically so citizens are able to select party officials and candidates.

The theory produces brokerage parties because they must accept as candidates whoever wins their primary, no matter what their political philosophy.

Which Theory Do American Parties Follow? Practice varies from state to state and over time. Most parties are a mixture, with the balance tilted toward citizen control. The long-term trend may be in the opposite direction, but the parties have a long way to go before professional politicians call the shots. Some students argue that more responsible or more centralized parties are neither necessary nor desirable.[13]

We illustrate some of the disharmony in Policy Box No. 13, "The Party System as a Federal System: Open Primaries Versus National Party Rules."

Party Activists The conservative-liberal division between Republican and Democratic parties is sharpest not between opposing party candidates or its citizen supporters, but between those who are party activists.[14] At the state level, these people are found most frequently running the party's two most important units—the state office, which the state chair heads, and the county units.

The State Chair and State Office State chairs have become more closely tied to the national party than in the past, just as local units in many states are becoming more closely tied to their state parties. Since the 1970s each party gives state chairs a seat on its national committee.

The job of state chair, though, is often frustrating, with an average tenure of about three years. The pay is still not exceptional, given the demands of time and effort and the extent of organization that state chairs now direct. State party professionalization is reflected in paid staff, a party headquarters, data archives, and personnel with specialized skills. The state offices are becoming more involved in helping local party units and candidates, offering funds and campaign help, especially in legislative races. Increasingly, state party organizations are recruiting strong legislative candidates and shepherding them through the primaries.[15] In Oregon the state government, presumably as the result of state party lobbying, now provides a subsidy from public funds to these local party units.

The national parties, especially the Republicans, have also begun to aid this state effort.[16] They are aware that in 1992, many state legislatures will redistrict themselves as well as U.S. congressional districts. Some may **gerry**mander, drawing districts to give their party an extra advantage. And so party stakes are high at all levels when the census year approaches and party units recognize their common interest.

Policy Box No. 13

The Party System as a Federal System: Open Primaries Versus National Party Rules

In November of 1979 John C. White, then chair of the Democratic party's National Committee, wrote an open letter to President Jimmy Carter and presidential hopefuls Edward M. (Ted) Kennedy and Edmund G. (Jerry) Brown. He lambasted the leaders of the Democratic party in Wisconsin, accusing them of sabotaging "the entire spirit" of a decade of party reform.

What crime had the Wisconsin Democrats committed? Party leaders there wanted to preserve Wisconsin's presidential primary as an open primary. The national Democratic party since 1974 had favored closed primaries. What compounded Wisconsin's misbehavior, in the eyes of national Democrats, were the subsequent actions of Wisconsin Democratic party leaders. In 1976 the national party excepted Wisconsin along with Idaho, Montana, and Michigan from the closed primary rule. National party leaders assumed that by 1980 these states would change to closed primaries.

But no action had been taken in the Wisconsin legislature or in the legislatures of the other three states. Then early in November of 1979 Wisconsin Democratic party chair Joseph W. Checota asked President Carter and candidates Kennedy and Brown to ignore the rules adopted by the national party and agree "to abide by the results" of Wisconsin's open primary. Supporting his request were the 2 Wisconsin U.S. senators, both Democrats, its 6 Democratic members of Congress, all but 4 of the 81 Democrats in the state legislature, and leaders of organized labor in the state.

Checota told reporters, "If you want to come to Wisconsin and play political stickball, you have to play by our rules." At least one candidate, Jerry Brown of California, said he would follow Wisconsin rules.

Worse, the Wisconsin attorney general sued the national Democratic party in Wisconsin courts. The Wisconsin supreme court ruling favored the state party. The national party appealed to the federal courts.

The other open primary states took varied actions. Montana Democrats sided with Wisconsin, determining to fight the national party. Idaho and Michigan Democrats decided to undercut the primary, though some party leaders in each state favored opposing the national committee. Each state held precinct caucuses before the presidential primary to choose the state's national convention delegates. The presidential primary held later was a popularity contest. Its result would not be binding on the convention delegation, though it is likely the delegates would informally respond to its outcome.

Michigan Democrats went one step further. They asked the major contenders for the Democratic nomination to withdraw their names from the Michigan presidential primary. Both Kennedy and Carter did. In addition, the Democratic party required that all participants in the party precinct caucuses be party members. This meant paying a $10 membership fee (to be waived if one were too poor to pay) and paying that fee two months in advance of the precinct caucus date. (Actually those who did not pay still participated.)

Why does the national Democratic party oppose the open primary? They argue that the open system allows and may even encourage Republicans to vote in the Democratic primary. In Michigan in 1972, Democrats claimed that Republicans had swelled the vote for George Wallace, who won that Michigan presidential primary. The national party also maintains that an open primary encourages persons to regard party loyalty lightly. Party activists and supporters, they say, should be the ones to carry out the function of choosing the presidential nominee. If they are not granted this privilege, why should they be active in the party?

Finally, national party leaders note that opposition to open primaries is part of the charter of the Democratic party, which representatives adopted at a national party convention. National party officers argue that since the rule is a reasonable one and one arrived at through democratic procedures, those on the losing side should honor the decision, rather than try to overturn it in a court case. A closed primary also has the advantage of identifying supporters—the party can more easily prepare phone lists to call on Election Day or call for financial contributions or call to inform about party meetings and other activities.

Opponents of closed primaries emphasize the value of citizen participation. State Senator Jack Faxon, Democrat of Detroit, says, "I think the Democratic party has been helped by public participation, not hindered by it." He believed that the Michigan Republicans who held an open primary gained supporters because they invited people in rather than screening them out of the party process. His argument also supported an accepted truism, that those who vote for a candidate in the primary are likely to vote for that person again in the general election.

Opponents of the national party role also maintain that the closed primary or the precinct caucus gives "independents," who outnumber declared Republicans, no chance to influence the choice of nominees in either major party. The candidates that party activists choose may not appeal to them or address the interests that they represent.

Finally, those who oppose closed primaries argue that the party is a public institution that belongs to more than party regulars. At issue is a basic democratic principle involving more than a "dispute over internal party affairs." They point out that the U.S. Supreme Court did not in the past allow South Carolina to limit its primary participation to whites. The judicial argument was that the political party is not a private organization similar to a private club. Thus when party activists act in ways that are possibly undemocratic, it is proper and even a duty for those opposed to challenge the party leaders in court.

The U.S. Supreme Court ruled that Wisconsin law did not bind the national party. In effect, national party rules took precedence over state law. For 1992 Michigan will return to a presidential primary. Because it will be closed, for the first time in 80 years voters will have to reveal their party preference before they receive a ballot. As early as 1988 objections began to be heard in letters to the editor columns.

What do you think? Who should run the party—citizens or party leaders? State or national officials? Should a national party be able to override primary laws passed by a state legislature? Do you believe that only party activists and known supporters

> should be allowed to choose party nominees? Or would you allow anyone who wishes to vote in either of the primaries to do so? Would you even go so far as to allow citizens to vote, if they wished, in both the Democratic and Republican primaries at the same election? Does closing party primaries increase the suspicions that independents have of party regulars and further weaken rather than strengthen the parties? Or will such rules in time lead to more responsible parties?

The County Unit The skeleton of party organization is its county units. Generally all have a chair known to state headquarters, but as a study in Connecticut and Michigan showed, only in counties that the party has a chance of winning elections will more activists be found.[17] Party volunteers are largely inactive between elections.[18] A steady turnover of precinct and county chairs is common.[19]

Some county chairs take the job as pragmatic professionals; others became involved through issue commitments. But both types seem to conduct their jobs in similar ways.[20] Those most active in campaigns have more of an institutional structure (a complete set of officers, year-round headquarters, a telephone, paid full-time staff, and an annual budget). The state party organization may provide additional resources. But the most important influence on the level of campaign activity is chairs who see their job as building and maintaining the party organization.[21]

How the Parties Choose Leaders

Selection of party officials begins at the precinct level. Some states hold a primary. Other states use a **precinct caucus**, a mass meeting of its party loyalists. One or the other elect a precinct captain and delegates to the county convention. The county convention delegates then meet and select a county chair and delegates to the state convention.

The State Convention This weekend conclave of several hundred every two years or so sets the tone for the state party. Delegates commonly select a governing committee and state chair as well as national party committee members. They also adopt a platform, resolutions, and in some cases endorse candidates in the upcoming primaries. A few still choose some party nominees.

Potential nominees set up tables and campaign for support, as do those favoring issues they want the party to endorse. Old friends greet each other. Party notables rub elbows with unknowns. Factional fights erupt and officeholders make unifying speeches—sometimes to empty seats and yawning delegates and at other times to cheers. And almost everyone has a good time and gets very little sleep.

You will likely find variations in your own state. Oregon, for example, allows voters to elect the members of the national committee in a primary.

WHO CHOOSES PARTY CANDIDATES?

The nomination is the major gift the parties have to offer. When you understand this, all other features of the major parties begin to sort themselves out.

How Candidates Are Nominated

At one time the state political parties nominated their candidates at conventions according to their own rules. Now in all but a few states major parties nominate in a primary election. The state outlines the procedures in state law and pays the costs, state elections officials supervise the process, and community governments conduct the voting.

The Open Primary In nine states, located generally along the Canadian border from Michigan to Oregon, voters select candidates in an **open primary**—voters receive whichever party ballot they ask for or a primary ballot that includes all parties. But they may vote for only one party's candidates. **Raiding** or **crossover voting** can occur—Democrats can vote in the Republican primary and vice versa. Independents can vote in whichever party they choose to. As we have seen, the national Democratic party opposes open primaries.

The Blanket or Jungle Primary Washington and Alaska carry the open primary process one step further. In the **blanket primary**, voters get a ballot that contains the ballots of all parties. They may vote for only one candidate for each office, but may pick and choose among the parties and their candidates as they go from office to office down the ballot.

Thus if only one candidate for governor has filed in the Democratic primary and a hot race is going on in the Republican primary, most citizens, including Democrats and Independents, may vote in the Republican primary. They may then return to vote in the Democratic primary in, say, the state legislative race. The blanket primary tends to produce middle-of-the-road candidates.[22]

The Closed Primary The rest of the states use the **closed primary**, which requires voters to register their party choice in advance of the primary or declare their party membership at the time of voting. The possibility of being challenged is supposed to discourage crossover voting. Voters receive a ballot only for the primary of the party they have declared. Party professionals favor closed over open or blanket primaries.

The Runoff Primary A few southern states, where the Democrats traditionally dominated, hold a **runoff primary** between the top two candidates if no candidate gets a majority of the votes in the first primary.

Louisiana's Nonpartisan Primary Since 1975 candidates for governor in Louisiana's **Nonpartisan Primary** run with or without party designation as each prefers. Then the top two candidates, whether from different parties or the same, face each other in the general election. Democrats hoped by this means to prevent Republicans from electing a governor. But in 1979 voters elected David C. Treen, the first Louisiana Republican governor since Reconstruction. His margin of victory was less than 10,000 votes. Treen received the endorsement of four defeated candidates including some Democrats.

How Communities Choose Nominees Many county and township primaries, and some city primaries, are partisan. Voters select nominees according to the type of primary their state requires.

In nonpartisan elections for city, judicial, and school board elections, candidates file petitions containing voter signatures. All the candidates are listed on the ballot. The two persons for each office who receive the most votes are the candidates in the general election.

Convention Nominations In only a few states do party organizations select some nominees. Minor parties usually select their candidates in conventions—this is also true of the Republican party in several southern states. Michigan party conventions nominate candidates for lieutenant governor, attorney general, and secretary of state as well as for top judicial and educational offices. Virginia party organizations may themselves decide whether to nominate by primary or state convention.

Party Endorsements Other states allow the parties to endorse nominees. This is the case in Colorado, Connecticut, Delaware, Idaho, Massachusetts, New York, New Mexico, North Dakota, and Rhode Island.

One pattern is to place an endorsed candidate on the ballot, with others qualifying if they received a percentage of convention votes (usually 20 percent). Sometimes additional candidates may be nominated by petition. The endorsed candidates may be starred on the primary ballot as a cue for party loyalists. Utah conventions must endorse two candidates; Nebraska allows parties the option of endorsing one or two. Another ten states make such endorsements optional.

Malcolm Jewell found the endorsed candidate for governor won in 78 percent of 85 contested races. The advantages of endorsement included campaign funds, campaign help, ballot position, publicity, and psychological momentum. The effect on voters in general is unclear.[23] Andrew McNitt found that such endorsements made it less likely that another candidate would challenge.[24]

Extralegal Party Organizations Sometimes when state law does not allow party organizations to endorse, or when the party is split, activists may organize **extralegal party organizations**—private groups that hold conventions or executive committee meetings to endorse candidates in their own party's primaries.[25]

The California Republican Assembly first entered Republican primaries in 1933 to endorse liberal Republicans. Between 1940 and 1962 it was able to dominate the party and, through it, state politics. Conservatives later captured this unit. Then other conservatives formed the United Republicans of California in

1964. Meanwhile, liberal Republicans formed the California Republican League. Liberal Democrats organized the California Democratic Council, and moderates, the Democratic Volunteers of California. Similar groups have flourished for a time in Illinois, New Jersey, New York City, North Dakota, Ohio, Pennsylvania, Texas, and Wisconsin. They are also common at the community level, especially where primaries are nonpartisan.

Party Regulars and Nominations

In 1935 Albert B. "Happy" Chandler at 36 served as Kentucky's lieutenant governor. The governor, through patronage, controlled the state nominating convention and favored someone other than Chandler for his successor. But he made the mistake of leaving the state temporarily. As acting governor, "Happy" Chandler at once called the legislators into special session and got them to pass a primary law. Then in a tub-thumping campaign, he won the primary against the governor's candidate and later, the election. The governor's faction could only grit their teeth.[26]

In primaries, dynamic campaigners can occasionally overwhelm a less colorful party-preferred candidate. Media campaigning "against the party bosses" increases the potential for such upsets. But party professionals have discovered that they can generally influence primary outcomes if they are united. They know that usually less than 30 percent of those registered vote in primaries—perhaps less than 15 percent in their own party's primary. Party activists and their families and some of their friends vote in every primary election. A small turnout maximizes this "party bloc" vote.

But the professionals sometimes split into factions, thus providing opportunities for candidates such as Chandler. This occurs especially when an **open seat** exists—the incumbent is not running for reelection. V. O. Key, Jr., described three factional patterns.[27]

Unifactional and Cohesive Parties The most colorful "outsider" had no chance of winning a primary against candidates supported by the **unifactional** political machine that controlled Virginia from the 1920s to the 1950s. The party leader consulted his local chairs and made the choice quietly behind the scenes.[28] Then the organization candidate, whether an incumbent or not, got most of the primary votes with only token opposition.

It rarely happens that a political machine can now dominate a state or city. But such control also once characterized local elections in Chicago and Albany and still does in some small towns where a tightly knit political elite dominates the community. Malcolm Jewell and David Olson thus suggest that we adopt the term **cohesive party** to describe a more common situation. Factions may exist and even be in conflict, but their members are able to compromise their differences and present a unified front in elections.[29]

Bifactionalism In some states Key found **bifactionalism**—two power blocs of party activists competing in every primary. Their differences could not be compromised internally. He used two tests to identify such bifactional competition. In most of the state primaries over a generation (1) the two top candidates would divide most of the votes and (2) neither of them would ever get more than 50 percent of the total vote.

The factions might be geographically based. The Platte River split the Nebraska Republican party into north and south groupings for many years. In Arizona it was urban Maricopa County (Phoenix) against outstate. Jack Bass and Walter DeVries detail how a coalition of blacks, union members, and neopopulists have faced off against older-style conservative Democrats in such states as Mississippi and South Carolina.[30]

The bifactional split might be built around a dominant political personality or may be class or ethnic-based or between business and labor, or during the Reagan years in the Republican party, a division between party regulars and the Moral Majority. Perhaps the most basic division was that found in Kentucky Democratic politics—for many years the only major difference appeared to be between those holding office and those wanting office.[31]

Some community elections are also bifactional. This is especially true in cities dominated by a single political party.

Multifactionalism In Florida primaries, Key found **multifactionalism**—a number of candidates competed but the winner seldom got more than a third of the votes. Candidates had to create their own campaign organizations, and there was little continuity between the winning coalition formed in one election and that in the next primary. Personal ties were important, particularly those Key described as support from "friends and neighbors" in the candidate's home county. Such chaotic multifactionalism is common where one party is dominant and in nonpartisan contests.[32]

The Realities of Party Factionalism We note three facts about party factions. (1) Factionalism is not the exception; it is normal to have conflict within the party. (2) When competition between the major parties becomes intense, factions within each party tend to unite—generally behind moderate candidates. If they do not, a bruising primary makes the nomination worthless. The losers may sulk and refuse to work for the winner, "stay home" on Election Day, or, worse, work for the opposition. (3) Factional alignments seldom last for more than a generation or so.

In looking at your own state you can make some assessment of how cohesive the party organization is by looking at what happens in primaries, especially when an open seat exists.

RUNNING THE POLITICAL CAMPAIGN

A party may be classed as "major" at the national level, but may be "minor" in the state or in some communities because it seldom wins. We begin by noticing how "having a chance" affects community party organization and campaign activity.

Parties Organize Where They Hope to Win

Party leaders sometimes talk as if the party has workers in every county or every city precinct. But in some communities the state organization may not even have the address of someone to whom to mail literature. Some county units may be unable to field a candidate for the state legislative race—few persons enjoy the role of sacrificial lamb in a hopeless cause.

Organization flourishes where major party candidates are in a tight race. Look at your own state or community. In districts where one candidate is a "shoo-in," neither party spends much money campaigning. And party workers are few and do very little.[33]

Party Competitiveness Political scientists have fashioned measures to show how competitive states and communities are. Malcolm Jewell and David M. Olson devised one based solely on state races—votes for governor and the legislature. It covers the period 1865 to 1988.

They find four competitive categories and place the states of the "Deep South," such as Georgia, Alabama, Mississippi, Arkansas, and Louisiana, in a category they call **Democratic party dominant**. Republicans rarely win the governorship and only gain a few legislative seats. Most of the other southern and border states and Hawaii and Rhode Island are classed as **Democratic party majority**. Democrats win more of the governorship races and generally control the legislature. But Republicans win at least 40 percent of the gubernatorial vote and at least a quarter of the legislative seats.

They found that there are no Republican-dominant states, and only New Hampshire and South Dakota could be classed as **Republican party majority**. The other 32 states are **competitive two party**.[34]

But these categories need to be used with some caution when applying them to specific races. Examine the results in your own state or community. Are all races in a single election equally competitive? Generally not. As Joseph Schlesinger demonstrated, competition is only in part between parties; it also varies by candidate. Incumbents usually have an advantage, particularly for offices like secretary of state or attorney general. Other candidates attract votes on the basis of personality or campaigning and do much better than one would expect given their party identification.[35]

Partisan competition also changes over time, sometimes as the result of a sudden, and at other times gradual, realignment of the groups supporting one or the other parties. Students explain changes in terms of urbanization, social diversity, and the strength of party organizations.[36]

Recently we have a growing trend toward independent and split-ticket voting, itself a form of realignment, as well as a move to the Republicans. Some argue the growth is temporary in a candidate-centered era; others that the young are attracted to the Republican party and thus predict change based on generational partisan differences.[37]

But we also experience a partisan lag when a state or community is changing its party allegiances. In the South, for example, Republicans have made gubernatorial races competitive without capturing many state legislative seats. The same is true of Democrats in some western and midwestern states.[38]

Changes in Campaigning

Candidates believe they are most likely to influence voters when they meet them face to face and shake their hand. All other campaign techniques are necessary substitutes because candidates have neither the time nor energy to meet every voter. Today most believe that television, if used carefully, is the best substitute for face-to-face contact.

Old-Style Campaigns At one time, candidates made a few speeches. Party workers did the rest. City precinct captains and county courthouse "rings" in rural areas did favors for voters between elections. At election time, workers buttonholed voters on behalf of the party ticket. Sometimes the organization also gave volunteer workers generous globs of what was euphemistically called "Election Day expenses." In less genteel precincts, organizations bought votes outright.

Such campaigning is rare today. Full-time party workers, who staff precincts between elections, are difficult to recruit. Patronage jobs to reward them with are less plentiful. Reformist laws forbid paying workers to "transport voters to the polls" or to perform other practices that proved very effective in the days of political machines.

Local Party Workers Today Part-time party volunteers can be important in closely contested races. They make telephone calls urging the committed to vote, update computer lists, distribute literature, and do other routine chores. Such recruits most often are those who have free time on their hands—college students and senior citizens. The candidate may attract them; some work because of ideological commitment—low-tax advocates, those pro- or antiabortion, or ecologists. Unions also sometimes urge members to participate.

Such organizational support is spotty in most states and communities. These volunteer efforts fall far short of the efficiency of the old-style precinct organization because today's party workers are vounteers. They decide on their own how much effort to expend, and some prove unreliable.

More helpful to candidates are the party organization professionals who possess skills useful in today's media campaigning. Some act as fund-raisers; others have TV or public relations skills. The party organization may also be able to offer issue research, conduct opinion polls, design direct mail pieces, and provide computerized lists of supporters, precinct census data, and the precinct vote in past elections.

Campaigning with the Media Most candidates, facing strong competition for a major office, are convinced that to win they must spend money on a media campaign—especially on expensive TV time. Challengers without such media coverage usually do not gain **name recognition**. Even in community races, being taken seriously requires a media campaign—newspaper ads, yard signs, or bumper stickers. Incumbents need media coverage to remind voters of their assets and the work they have done for the district or state.[39]

The First Media Campaign During the Depression in 1934 the socialist novelist Upton Sinclair captured the Democratic nomination for governor in California. He campaigned on EPIC—"End Poverty in California." To combat his "radicalism," Republicans hired an advertising agency. In cooperation with movie studios that Sinclair had attacked, they sent camera operators out to the Depression "shantytowns" and "hobo jungles" to prepare "newsreels." As the cameras ground away, an inquiring reporter asked, "Who are you supporting for governor?" Many of the poorly dressed, unshaven drifters answered, "Upton Sinclair!" Obligingly, some kicked aside old beer, wine, or whiskey bottles or scratched themselves in embarrassing places as they pledged their efforts to the Democratic candidate.

Another set of responses was collected from the attractive kind of middle-class citizens we almost always see in Coca-Cola ads. One was of the proverbial "little old lady." When she said she was voting for Sinclair's opponent, the interviewer asked, "Why, Mother?" In a quavering voice she answered, "Because I want to have my little home. It is all I have left in the world." A black Los Angeles minister said he was voting against Sinclair because he liked to preach and play the piano, and he wanted to keep a church to preach in and a piano to play.[40]

The footage then went to editing and cutting. These newsreels when shown in theaters displayed a simple message in documentary form, without advertising or other comment. The "bums" were for Upton Sinclair; the "good people" were for his opponent. Those who saw the films thought them extremely effective—including the losing candidate, Upton Sinclair.

As with so many other things, good and bad, California had introduced the modern media campaign to America. By the early 1970s almost every statewide candidate who had a chance of winning, and many in community races as well, hired **media consultants**.[41]

What Media Consultants Offer Whitaker and Baxter, the California husband and wife team who formed the first campaign consulting firm in the 1930s, argued that the amateurs who staffed the party organization wasted funds and effort. Workers did not show up and many pamphlets never got distributed. Candidates wasted their time at poorly publicized and poorly attended meetings.

The campaign media firm, however, knew how to budget funds and the candidate's time for maximum effect. Their ad agency skills helped them to find the best media outlets per dollar. The media firms also claimed that party regulars often misinterpreted the public mood. Whitaker and Baxter promised to "package" the candidate—that is, create and project a favorable image. Public opinion polling was in its infancy, but they used it to figure out which issues the candidate should stress—what the voters disliked or liked about the candidate.

Style was stressed over content—catchy slogans, a TV personality that exuded sincerity, a winning smile.

Modern Media Campaigning Joseph Parker dates the first use of campaign media firms in Louisiana to the race for mayor of New Orleans in 1946. But the change in statewide campaigning, he says, came during the gubernatorial campaign of 1963–1964. Prior to that, candidates campaigned by making stump speeches around the state beginning July 4. In the north, candidates such as Governor Jimmy Davis who wrote "You Are My Sunshine" brought along a "hillbilly band"; in the south, a "Cajun band." In 1964 the candidates began to use 30- and 60-second promotional spots targeted at specific voters. They turned to professional polling to assess public opinion. By the 1970s not only had stump speaking died out, but the old political divisions between Long and anti-Long factions had also disappeared. Candidates campaigned independently of other party nominees.[42]

DeVries described how his firm helped Republican William Milliken win election as governor in a generally Democratic year. The campaign isolated those precincts in which independent, ticket-splitting voters were found—precincts that had voted for Democratic legislators but had also supported such moderate Republican candidates for governor as George Romney. They found that 80 percent of these voters were concentrated in 19 of Michigan's 83 counties. They spent most of their campaign funds in these 19 counties.

Next the firm analyzed past opinion data and found that ticket splitters were most likely to be people who lived in suburban areas, high school graduates with some college education, more likely to be Catholic than Protestant, between 30 and 50 years old, and watchers of TV news, documentaries, and sports programs. Finally, from phone surveys in the 19 counties, they found that ticket splitters did not like long political discussions and distrusted politicians who made promises.

The firm then developed its final series of TV spots. They showed Governor Milliken briefly mentioning a problem, such as poor housing. He expressed awareness and concern, but made no promises and offered no solutions. To emphasize his competence, the ads were made in his office displaying him at his desk, with flag, paneled walls, and leather chairs. The ads closed with the campaign slogan, "A leader you can trust." The spots ran during and after sports events and TV news.

The average vote for Republican candidates in Michigan that year was 40 percent. Milliken got 50.4 percent and was one of two Republicans elected governor in the Midwest. The media firm could and did take some credit for the victory.[43]

Modern Campaigns Weaken Parties Old-style precinct workers asked voters to support the party ticket. But media consultants encourage candidates to dissociate their campaigns from other party nominees. Candidates who appear independent have broader appeal. When they campaign on personality and style rather than issues, candidates necessarily play down party positions.

Ann Richards, winner of the 1990 race for the Democratic nomination for governor, gives the "Hook'em Horns" sign to a University of Texas audience.

Media Campaigning Is Expensive Running for governor can cost millions. Legislative races run into the thousands. Expenditures vary by size of the state in population and area and closeness of the race. Still, the costs keep rising. As noted in Chapter 6, state efforts to limit what candidates and independent PACs spend in campaigns have often been frustrated by state and Supreme Court rulings. All states but South Carolina and Virginia have limits on campaign contributions. Every state requires candidates to list contributors. But the court has ruled that candidates can spend as much of their own money as they wish.

These rules tend to channel money around party organizations rather than through them. Indeed, we find that contributions to the party often come in a poor third, behind money that candidates raise and monies that PACs spend. Montana, however, in 1983 placed limits on the amount of PAC money a candidate for the legislature may accept—$600 total for House candidates, $1,000 for Senate candidates.

Seven states provide tax money to candidates on a matching basis, and 11 to political parties. Most is for general elections, but Hawaii, Massachusetts, Michigan, and New Jersey also fund primaries. It allows states to limit spending for candidates who accept state funds. Some states give money from income tax checkoffs directly to parties or candidates. Ruth Jones concluded that public finance programs that permit the taxpayer to designate to which party the money goes tend to favor the dominant party in the state, which we have seen generally means the Democratic party.[44]

In Policy Box No. 14, "Should the State Pay for Political Campaigns?" we review some of the ambivalence surrounding taxpayer-funded campaigns.

THE PARTY IN OFFICE

When a party's candidates win state or community office, will they function as a team? Will they act like brokerage or responsible parties—or some combination of the two?

How Likely Is Responsible Party Government?

After the 1988 election, the governor's party had lost control of one or both houses of the legislature in 28 states (56 percent). Republican governors are more often faced with Democratic legislatures than the reverse. Students say that this condition is not the result of poorly apportioned legislative districts but of split-ticket voting.[45]

The likelihood of such splits appears to be increasing. David Everson and Joan Parker report that in Illinois during the 1960s, 3 percent of the Chicago wards, 3 percent of the Cook County suburbs, and 6 percent of the 101 downstate counties had split results. For the 1970s the comparable figures were 23 percent, 12 percent, and 22 percent. In all areas of the state, split-ticket voting was on the increase.[46] The short-term outlook for party government, then, is not hopeful.

Connecticut Once Had Party Government Under the guidance of Democratic party chair John Bailey from 1946 to 1961, Connecticut probably came as close to having responsible party government as any state ever has. Its two parties were closely competitive and tightly organized. Party conventions nominated candidates. Ballot design made ticket splitting difficult. Bailey rode herd daily on Democratic legislators on behalf of the Democratic governor. He used patronage to reward the loyal and punish dissidents.[47]

Citizens knew that a vote for Democrats meant one kind of policy and a vote for Republicans, another. Campaign platforms and promises had meaning. But access to legislators was more difficult—lobbyists had to work through the party hierarchy, rather than through individual legislators. Large-scale organizations—labor for the Democrats and business for the Republicans—dominated these channels. Citizens who did not identify with either party complained they were asked to choose between what they regarded as two extreme positions.

This party system in time crumbled because of the separation of powers structure of American government. Ambitious legislators became more independent of party and governor. Connecticut weakened the rules of convention nomination to accommodate candidates and made split-ticket voting easier. Bailey meanwhile left Connecticut to join Kennedy at the national party level. Connecticut parties became like those of neighboring states—only partially united even when they had the power to govern.

Policy Box No. 14

Should the State Pay for Political Campaigns?

Some states on their income tax forms ask whether you want $2 of your state taxes used to finance political campaigns. If you check "yes" you do not increase your taxes—officials place $2 of state revenues in a special elections fund.

To qualify for funds, a candidate for governor has to raise a certain amount in individual donations, in Michigan $50,000 in donations of $100 or less. There, gubernatorial candidates can expect to receive somewhat more than half a million dollars for the primary and nearly a million dollars for the November election.

With state budgets tight, many argue this is a program that states might well eliminate. Politicians, they suggest, should have to pay their own way, as the rest of us do. All public financing does, they say, is encourage people to run with little financial risk—in 1982 when no incumbent governor was in the race, Michigan had 12 Democrats and 4 Republicans who announced their candidacy. Some legislators were floating trial balloons. Even before the primary elections, some withdrew and ran for their old offices.

The attorney general, Frank Kelley, called the law a "Pandora's box allowing misuse of public funds." He suggested that any candidate who drops out of the race before the election should have to pay back the matching funds. That rule was in the original bill but was eliminated by a conference committee. Others argue that if a state is going to use a check-off system, it should give citizens a wider choice. Some might rather have their money go to the schools or universities or to fix potholes, rather than to help out political candidates. Some might want to put their $2 into improving sport fishing; others might want more money in developing the arts. Without giving you such choices, their argument goes, politicians are milking the treasury and can pretend they are responding to what citizens want done.

But others contend that spending the money this way is far from wasteful. It makes our politics more democratic and opens high office to those who don't have a big bankroll of their own. It gives the "little guy" a chance. In their view, Michigan should be proud of the fact that it had so many candidates from which to choose.

Public funding also allows candidates to run without having to sell out to get the backing of the large corporations or labor unions. And it allows the state to put a ceiling on the amount that candidates can spend in a campaign.

The requirement to pay back the money would keep some experienced officeholders out of the race. The little money the state would save in those cases, critics say, is not worth the loss in candidate quality. And such a provision would very likely be ruled unconstitutional—many feel it would be if attached to an ordinary appropriations bill.

But the best argument, supporters maintain, is the number of citizens who check the box—4 million in Michigan over a four-year period. If taxpayers felt that spending money in this way were unwise, they could easily have checked "No." With less money in the fund, states would have less to distribute.

> What do you think? Should states provide campaign funds for candidates for governor in the primary and general elections? Do you think the money is wasted? Does it free politicians from seeking PAC funds? Does it bring campaign spending under control? How does it affect the political party organizations? Does it encourage independents more than party loyalists? Does it help nonincumbents running against an incumbent? Are minor party candidates helped sufficiently?

Governors Provide the Party Program

Governors, formally or informally, select the chairperson of their state party. Thus they dominate or guide the party organization. They are expected to influence the state party platform and dispense patronage through the party organization. Often they are strong enough to recruit nominees whom the party regulars will back in the primary, and sometimes select their own successors as well.

Legislators expect governors to present a program—even when a different party controls the legislature. The governor's program becomes the party program and the closest thing we have to responsible party government.

The Governor's Program Governors do not take a stand on all of the bills offered during a legislative session. Most select a small number as **must** (or **administration**) **bills**. Aides of the governor pressure legislators of their party to support these bills.

What kinds of bills become must bills? Not all that administrative agencies propose. Even some the governor may approve of are not so classed. Governors may remain neutral or even recommend passage but not insist that party members support their position.

Researchers find that the must actions tend to be of three types: (1) bills involving taxes or expenditures, (2) appointments that the senate or both houses must confirm, and (3) bills on major social and economic issues, especially those involving welfare and labor or business regulation. We also add bills the governor has vetoed, since a vote override is a rebuff to a governor's leadership.[48]

Is the Governor's Program Supported? In states where each major party has a third or more of the legislative seats (enough to sustain vetoes), the governor's must bills tend to divide the legislature along party lines. But some members of each party are likely to cross party lines. Still, the governor's program defines which issues will be acted upon.

For example, a study in Iowa found that the governor had 150 must bills. Support in the senate from legislators of the governor's party was 92 percent and in the house, 86 percent. Opposition-party support in the senate was 48 percent and in the house, 41 percent. The party division is not perfect, but it is still sharply defined. It is likely that many legislators of the governor's party buried their own doubts or preferences "to support the party and not embarrass our governor."

What if a governor's must bills are not typical of their party—if they veer off in what many legislators regard as a radical or reactionary direction? Researchers find some lessening of party support, but also that a substantial number of legislators nevertheless will follow the person they regard as head of their party.

One-Party and Nonpartisan Legislatures   As the governor's party increases its legislative representation above 60 percent, Sarah McCally Morehouse found that gubernatorial influence declined. "Rivalries are generated which the governor cannot control."[49]

Where one party generally dominates, the mood becomes almost nonpartisan. Instead of having a party majority leader to work with in the legislature, the governor has an "administration leader." The Democratic majority Texas legislature, Donald Lutz and Richard Murray found, had little stability in coalitional voting patterns from session to session.[50] Governors in one-party states face a good deal of opposition or indifference from legislators of their own party. Their support coalitions then are not necessarily based on party, but on favors, ideology, or personal friendship.

Sometimes a minority-party governor in a one-party state wins a surprising election victory and faces a legislature composed almost completely of the opposition. In such a case bipartisan alignments are likely. Thus a Republican governor of South Carolina bargained for support for his program and gained the needed majority from a coalition of Republicans and dissident Democrats. But such coalitions are difficult to maintain and often do not endure for the whole of a governor's term.[51]

What Weakens a Governor's Influence?   Morehouse found that those governors who received less than 70 percent of the primary vote when getting renominated lost influence. Legislators concluded that the governor was not fully in control of the party.[52]

The Party in the Legislature

John Carroll and Arthur English found that leaders in the Massachusetts house carefully screened those legislators placed on important committees. Freshmen who were loyal to the party leadership were more likely to become part of the group that ran the legislative business.[53]

In other states the **party caucus**—a meeting of all legislators of the same party—determines the party position on bills. But not much is known about how often party caucuses meet. Caucus votes generally are guiding rather than binding. In New Mexico a cross-party coalition, called Republicrats, caucused and held together long enough to elect the speaker.

Party Voting Party is the best predictor we have of how a state legislator will vote. But often it is not a very good one. Only on votes in which one party gains an advantage over the other, as in organizing the legislature, is party voting likely to be unanimous.

In general, the urban industrialized states of the Midwest and Northeast and those with a history of two-party competition have more party voting. But we find unexplained exceptions. Less party voting occurs when both major parties represent similar types of districts.

A FINAL COMMENT

On balance, the influence of party units at the state and community level is still strong, but not as strong as a generation ago. State governments no longer exclusively write the rules governing party activities and election procedures. The U.S. Supreme Court and state courts have redefined many of these. Both in Congress and at national conventions, independence by state or community party leaders is becoming somewhat more costly to them. More and more the activities of state and community party units are being slowly meshed with those of the national party organization. Many state and local party activists favor this trend.

At the state level we find some tendency toward more responsible parties—though in many states, especially those in which one party dominates, brokerage parties are still typical. Some students doubt that the process of centralization will proceed much further. We are inclined, rather, to believe that just as the balance within the federal system has been tipped to favor national initiatives, so, too, the balance within the political party organizations has shifted somewhat more toward national party leaders. At this point, though, no one can predict that this will continue.

We also suggest that the variety in party organization and their weakness in selecting candidates, campaigning, and governing in office may also be somewhat modified if party organization becomes more centralized.

What we are witnessing, we believe, is a change from old-style independence—what, in practice, was a kind of "dual federalism" organizational form—ill suited to the problems modern parties face. But the "unitary" type of national centralization found in many European political parties seems ill suited to our governmental arrangements. Rather, the major political parties, like the nation itself, appear to be moving to that distinctively American form of organization—the one we have described as cooperative federalism.

HIGH POINTS

In this chapter we began by noting (1) how the federal system and the Progressives' reaction to bosses decentralized American parties. We next looked at how (2) parties were organized, stressing their variety. We then reviewed party functions and noted that (3) the party regulars, because of primaries, had lost control of its most important function—the selection of candidates—and other functions to (4) media firms; and that (5) in office, party candidates do not always work together.

In this chapter we defined the following terms in this order: responsible parties, brokerage parties, cadre parties, spoils system, patronage system, mass party, kickbacks, political machine, civil service, nonpartisan elections, direct primary, media campaigning, party identification, ticket splitters, gerrymander, precinct caucus, open primary, raiding, crossover voting, blanket primary, closed primary, runoff primary, Louisiana's Nonpartisan Primary, extralegal party organizations, open seat, unifactionalism, cohesive party, bifactionalism, multifactionalism, Democratic party dominant, Democratic party majority, Republican party majority, Competitive two party, name recognition, media consultants, must (or administration) bills, and party caucus.

NOTES

1. V. O. Key, Jr., *American State Politics, An Introduction* (New York: Knopf, 1956), p. 11.
2. David B. Truman, "Federalism and the Party System," in Arthur W. Macmahon (ed.), *Federalism Mature and Emergent* (Garden City, N.Y.: Doubleday, 1955), pp. 115–138, and Robert J. Huckshorn and John F. Bibby, "State Parties in an Era of Political Change," in The American Assembly, *The Future of American Political Parties* (Englewood Cliffs, N.J.: Prentice-Hall, 1982), pp. 101–139.
3. Austin Ranney, *Curing the Mischiefs of Faction, Party Reform in America* (Berkeley: University of California Press, 1975).
4. James M. Carlson and Howard Hamilton, "Democratic Electoral Coalition," *Polity* 11 (1979): 290–297.
5. Gary D. Wekkin, "National-State Party Relations: The Democrats' New Federal Structure," *Political Science Quarterly* 99:1 (Spring 1984): 45–70.
6. Matthew Josephson, *The Politicos, 1885–1898* (New York: Harcourt Brace Jovanovich, 1938), and Stewart H. Holbrook, *The Age of the Moguls* (Garden City, N.Y.: Doubleday, 1954). For a perceptive study of the evolution of the Tweed machine in New York City see Martin Shefter, "The Emergence of the Political Machine, An Alternative View," in Willis Hawley et al. (eds.), *Theoretical Perspectives on Urban Politics* (Englewood Cliffs, N.J.: Prentice-Hall, 1978).
7. James Bryce, *The American Commonwealth* (1888), Book II, p. 110. The leading senators included men such as "Zack" Chandler of Michigan, Morton of Indiana, and Conkling of New York.
8. Shefter, "The Emergence of the Political Machine," pp. 14–44.
9. Josephson, *The Politicos*, pp. 314–315.
10. Harold F. Gosnell, *Boss Platt and His New York Machine* (Chicago: University of Chicago Press, 1924), pp. 334–349, and William Allen White, *Masks in a Pageant* (New York: Macmillan, 1928), pp. 30–69.
11. States that hold party conventions for a few offices include Michigan, New York, Rhode Island, and Connecticut.

12. E. E. Schattschneider, *Party Government* (New York: Rinehart, 1942).
13. Everett Carll Ladd, "Party Reform and the Public Interest," *Political Science Quarterly* 102:3 (Fall 1987): 355–369.
14. William V. Moore and Thomas M. Pinckey, Jr., "Grassroots Politics in the Contemporary South, A Comparative Analysis of Party Chairmen in Tennessee and South Carolina," *Southeastern Political Review* 9 (1981): 90–118; Robert J. Huckshorn, *Party Leadership in the States* (Amherst: University of Massachusetts Press, 1976); and Joseph P. Nyitray, "Amateur and Professional Democrats at the 1972 Texas State Convention," *Western Political Quarterly* 28 (1975): 885–899.
15. Richard J. Tobin and Edward Keynes, "Institutional Differences in the Recruitment Process: A Four-State Study," *American Journal of Political Science* 19 (November 1974): 674.
16. James L. Gibson, John P. Frendreis, and Laura L. Vertz, "Party Dynamics in the 1980s: Change in County Organizational Strength, 1980–1984," *Journal of Political Science* 33:1 (February 1989): 67–90.
17. Barbara C. Burrell, "Local Political Party Committees, Task Performance and Organizational Vitality," *Western Political Quarterly* 39 (1986): 48–66.
18. Kay Lawson, Gerald Pomper, and Maureen Moakley, "Local Party Activists and Electoral Linkage," *American Politics Quarterly* 14:4 (October 1986): 345–375.
19. Lawson, Pomper, and Moakley, "Local Party Activists" and Lewis Bowman, William E. Hulbary, and Anne E. Kelley, "Party Organization and Behavior in Florida, Assessing Grassroots Organizational Strength," Paper delivered at the American Political Science Association meetings, September 1987, Chicago.
20. Michael A. Maggiotto and Ronald E. Weber, "The Impact of Organizational Incentives on County Party Chairpersons," *American Politics Quarterly* 14:3 (July 1986): 201–218.
21. Barbara Norrander, "Determinants of Local Party Campaign Activity," *Social Science Quarterly* 67:3 (1986): 561–571.
22. Richard C. Kelley and Sara Jane Weir, "Unwrapping the Blanket Primary," *Washington Public Policy Notes* (Seattle: University of Washington), 9 (September 1981).
23. Malcolm E. Jewell, "The Impact of State Political Parties on the Nominating Process," Paper delivered at the Midwest Political Science Association meetings, April 1983, Chicago.
24. Andrew D. McNitt, "The Effect of Preprimary Endorsement on Competition for Nominations: An Examination of Different Nominating Systems," *Journal of Politics* (February 1980): 257–266.
25. James Q. Wilson, *The Amateur Democrat* (Chicago: University of Chicago Press, 1962); Edmond Costantini and Louis Wechsler, *California Politics and Parties* (New York: Macmillan, 1970); Vicki Granet Semel, *At the Grass Roots in the Garden State, Reform and Regular Democrats in New Jersey* (Cranbury, N.J.: Associated University Presses, 1978); and David L. Protess and Alan R. Gitelson, "Political Stability and Urban Reform Club Activism," *Polity* 10 (1978): 524–541.
26. Jasper B. Shannon, "'Happy' Chandler, A Kentucky Epic," in J. T. Salter (ed.), *The American Politician* (Chapel Hill: University of North Carolina Press, 1938).
27. V. O. Key, Jr., *Southern Politics in State and Nation* (New York: Knopf, 1949), Chapter 14, "Nature and Consequences of the Party Factionalism," pp. 298–311.
28. Larry Sabato, *The Democratic Party Primary in Virginia* (Charlottesville: University of Virginia Press, 1977).

29. Malcolm E. Jewell and David M. Olson, *American State Political Parties and Elections* (rev. ed.) (Homewood, Ill.: Dorsey Press, 1982), p. 67.
30. Jack Bass and Walter DeVries, *The Transformation of Southern Politics* (New York: Basic Books, 1976).
31. Malcolm Jewell and Everett Cunningham, *Kentucky Politics* (Lexington: University of Kentucky Press, 1968), pp. 131–178.
32. Stanley D. Hopper, "Fragmentation of the California Republican Party in the One Party Era, 1898–1932," *Western Political Quarterly* 28 (1977): 372–388, and Bradley C. Canon, "Factionalism in the South, A Test of Theory and a Revisitation of V. O. Key," *American Journal of Political Science* 22 (1978): 833–848.
33. We always find, of course, at least some organization where federal patronage is used to buy support at the national convention and where elected officials appoint aides—for example, the sheriff who appoints deputies or probate judges who appoint the lawyers as administrators of estates. Appointed deputies take no chance of an upset—they work year-round for their boss.
34. Malcolm E. Jewell and David M. Olson, *Political Parties and Elections in American States* (3rd ed.) (Chicago: Dorsey Press, 1988), pp. 24–30.
35. Joseph A. Schlesinger, "The Structure of Competition for Office in the American States," *Behavioral Science* 5:3 (July 1960): 197–210.
36. Samuel C. Patterson and Gregory A. Caldeira, "The Etiology of Partisan Competition," *American Political Science Review* 78 (1984): 691–707, and Charles J. Barrilleaux, "A Dynamic Model of Partisan Competition in the American States," *American Journal of Political Science* 30 (1986): 822–840.
37. Helmut Norpoth, "Under Way and Here to Stay, Party Realignment in the 1980s?" *Public Opinion Quarterly* 51 (1987): 376–391, and Martin P. Wattenberg, "The Hollow Realignment, Partisan Change in a Candidate-Centered Era," *Public Opinion Quarterly* 51 (1987): 58–74. See also Paul R. Abramson, John H. Aldrich, and David W. Rohde, *Change and Continuity in the 1984 Elections* (Washington, D.C.: CQ Press, 1986).
38. Joseph A. Schlesinger, "The Structure of Competition for Office in the American States," *Behavioral Science* 5 (1980): 197–210, and Donald A. Gross, "Changing Patterns of Interparty Competition, Presidential, Senatorial, House and Gubernatorial Elections, 1824–1978," Paper delivered at the Midwest Political Science Association meetings, April 1981, Cincinnati.
39. Charles Press and Kenneth VerBurg, *American Politicians and Journalists* (Glenview, Ill.: Scott, Foresman, 1988), pp. 140–172.
40. Neal Gabler, *An Empire of Their Own* (New York: Crown, 1988), pp. 312–315.
41. Larry J. Sabato, *The Rise of Political Consultants* (New York: Basic Books, 1981).
42. Joseph B. Parker, "Madison Avenue Comes to Dixie, Professional Campaigning in Louisiana and Mississippi," Paper delivered at the Southern Political Science Association annual meetings, November 1981, Gatlinburg, Tenn.
43. Walter DeVries and V. Lance Farrace, *The Ticket Splitters* (Grand Rapids: Wm. B. Erdmans, 1972).
44. Ruth S. Jones, "State Campaign Finance: Implications for Partisan Politics," *American Journal of Political Science* 25 (May 1981): 342–361.
45. Robert Bradley Clark and Charles W. Wiggins, "The Persistence of Divided Party Control of State Governments, A Post Reapportionment Note," *Polity* 8 (1975): 490–495.

46. David H. Everson and Joan A. Parker, "Ticket Splitting, An Ominous Sign of Party Weakness," in *Illinois Elections Issue* (Springfield: Sangamon State University, 1979), pp. 56–59.
47. Joseph I. Lieberman, *The Power Brokers* (Boston: Houghton Mifflin, 1988), and Joyce Gelb and Marian Lief Palley, *Tradition and Change in American Party Politics* (New York: Thomas Y. Crowell, 1975), pp. 189–192.
48. Sarah P. McCally Morehouse, "The Governor and His Legislative Party," *American Political Science Review* 60 (1966): 923–942.
49. Ibid., p. 80.
50. Donald S. Lutz and Richard W. Murray, "Coalition Formation in the Texas Legislature, Issues, Payoffs, and Winning Coalition Size," *Western Political Quarterly* 28 (1975): 298–315.
51. Malcolm E. Jewell and Samuel C. Patterson, *The Legislative Process in the United States* (2nd ed.) (New York: Random House, 1973), p. 457.
52. Morehouse, "The Governor and His Legislative Party," p. 80.
53. John J. Carroll and Arthur English, "Governing the House, Leadership of the State Legislative Party," Paper presented at the Midwest Political Science Association meetings, April 1981, Cincinnati.

Chapter 8

State Legislators as Critics

The public's image of state legislatures is often formed from headlines such as "Legislators Hoot Down Move to Stop Pay Hike" or "Legislative Committee Kills Environmental Protection Bill." Do headline writers dislike legislators? Not necessarily.

It is partly that reporters get a better view of the legislature than of the other branches. They talk to lawmakers on the capital cocktail circuit and see them tense up in the floor debate and committee hearings. All these meetings are open for all to view. Compare that to the governor's private meeting with department heads, or with judges who bargain decisions behind closed doors.

Governors prepare and rehearse their public statements carefully. Judges, too, meticulously labor over their opinions before releasing them to the public. But legislators' statements are often garbled in tense and unrehearsed debate—"We'll have the tail wagging the dog instead of the dog wagging its head" or "We'll have them right where they want us." Thus the public opinion of state legislators is often low.

The Legislative Purpose The central task of legislators is to evaluate policies that others, in the main, propose, advocate, and later administer. Legislators make a **political evaluation**—they seek balance among the many interests that a given bill affects. Nearly every interest group in a state zeros in on the legislature to make sure its point of view is considered. Officials of other branches also evaluate policies for political acceptability, but for legislators, it is the main job. We thus focus on what we call a state legislature's **political efficiency**—how well a legislature processes the variety of opinions on an issue. Legislators typically approach policy problems with an eye to compromising on competing viewpoints. Still, the formal legislative rules tilt the process toward preserving the status quo. They give special advantages to those opposing change and handicap those seeking new directions.[1]

Overview We consider state legislatures under five headings: (1) the legislative task; (2) conditions that contribute to amateurism and professionalism; (3) people who become state legislators; (4) how state legislatures function politically; and (5) attempts to reform state legislatures.

WHAT STATE LEGISLATORS DO

Legislators have three major functions. They pass laws (including appropriations), assist constituents, and oversee the operations of the executive branch. In each function they mainly represent others.

Lawmaking

Each two-year period, the 50 state legislatures consider about 200,000 new bills—mostly to change laws already on the books—and introduce several thousand resolutions—to oppose or support national policies or just to congratulate the state's high school basketball champions. This averages out to 12 or so bills per year for each of the 7,416 state legislators. About 25 percent become law.

Why So Many Bills? Our society rests on a web of sometimes unsettled and complex rules. Groups jockey continually to improve their position. Conditions in urban states tend to be less settled than in rural ones. Thus, during a recent two-year period, New York legislators introduced 73 times more bills than did those of Arkansas.

Legislators introduce bills for many reasons—some with serious intent to pass a law and many others as favors to lobbyists, interest groups, or constituents. Some bills are introduced mostly to get a headline back home. In states with introduction deadlines we find "**skeleton**" **bills**—bills that are virtually meaningless when introduced, but to which content may be added later if the need arises.

Now legislatures are beginning to take steps to cut back on bill introductions. Half the states permit bills to carry over from the first session of a biennium to the second, thereby reducing the need to reintroduce the bills each year. Colorado rations bill introductions—a legislator may introduce no more than ten bills during a biennium. Other states cut down duplication by combining several similar bills into one and setting time limits on introductions.

Where Ideas for Legislation Come From Legislators do not originate the ideas behind most bills. Instead, they are sensitive reactors to problems that others bring to them. The governor and state administrative agencies suggest statutory changes. Some of these will be "innovative"—new policies—but most will make minor amendments to existing statutes. Changes in federal programs or court decisions spur some of the new state laws. Some of these will have a major impact, as Texas legislators discovered when the state supreme court ordered them to revise the state school aid formula, a case we discuss in Policy Box No. 15, "School Finance Dilemma."

Economic interest groups—business, labor, and agriculture—are a major source of legislative proposals. Consumer groups, too, advocate bills on policies they think the state should have. And professional groups, such as social workers, urban planners, psychologists, physicians, and chiropractors, ask for changes mostly to protect or enhance their profession.

Problems back home generate ideas for new laws. Helping a small town build a sidewalk for schoolchildren or permitting a company to drill for oil on state-owned land may be important issues in the district.

And, of course, legislators and their staffs come up with ideas of their own. These remain a distinct minority, but their number is rising as more legislators become full time and as legislative staff increases. In addition, many legislatures have interim committees to study problems and prepare bills when the legislature is not in session.

Constituent Services

Legislators also provide **constituent services**—an important function we sometimes belittle as errand running. Constituents may ask for help in dealing with a state agency. (Again we note that legislators react to problems that others bring to them.) Someone may not have gotten his welfare check or a recent college grad may want help getting a state job—the list is practically endless.

Policy Box No. 15

School Finance Dilemma

The band played "Edgewood All the Way" and the marquee at the high school football stadium read, "Texas Children 9, Kirby 0." October 2, 1989, was a day of great celebration in the Edgewood Independent School District of San Antonio. What brought such joy was a Texas supreme court decision that the state's program for funding public schools was unconstitutional.

After five years of wending its way through the courts of Texas, *Edgewood v. Kirby* (state education commissioner) came to an end and a new beginning. The end of the case came when the Texas supreme court, 9 to 0, banned the school aid system. Per student spending differentials of $17,000 between rich and poor districts, the justices said, was unconstitutional.

The court gave the governor and legislature eight months to make a new beginning in the state school aid program. Somehow it would have to find a politically and legally acceptable way to narrow the per student spending gap, which ranged from $2,112 per student for the lowest and $19,333 for the highest-spending districts.

Texas schools have more than 3.3 million students, second only to California. Whatever action the legislature would adopt, it was bound to have immense implications for state taxes, budgets, and school spending.

The Texas legislature and school districts are not alone in this predicament. Several state courts have ruled state school aid programs unconstitutional. New Jersey was the latest in mid-1990. The reasons in each state differ. In the case of Texas, for example, the state constitution requires an "efficient" school system. Other state programs were found to violate equal protection clauses.

State legislators face the puzzle of crafting an equitable funding program for public schools, because most state constitutions make public education a state responsibility. Most states fund public schools on a combination of state aid and local property taxes.

This combination of circumstances produces a very complex problem politically, legally, and financially. We discuss some alternatives legislators may consider and the difficulties associated with each. We then give you a chance to propose your own plan.

Per student spending could be equalized among a state's school districts very easily by having the state pick up the entire public school bill and by eliminating local school district taxes. State legislatures could set the per student amount and order the state treasurer to send out the money just as soon as a school files its enrollment report. The state could pay the cost through a statewide property tax levy with the state setting the rate and collecting the money. This plan is simple and indisputably results in an equal payment for each student.

What are its problems? In most states, we suspect, many groups would argue that such a plan places too much power in legislators' laps and possibly with the state teachers unions that would then turn up the pressure on state legislators for even more money.

Some school officials would say that the plan is unfair because "We have unequal costs." Officials in small schools in rural areas, for example, might say that their buses must travel hundreds of miles daily to pick up and return students. Districts with high percentages of minority and low-income populations could claim that their students have much greater needs that are not being met with the standard state aid payment. And officials in other districts would insist that although their students have average needs, the cost of living in "our area is so much greater that we cannot hire qualified teachers at this rate."

Another approach the legislature could use, as some have done, is to direct the state aid to the school districts on the basis of their wealth—measured in terms of per student tax base, personal income, or other indicators. This would mean that poor districts might get half their funds from the state while wealthy districts get no state school aid.

Such plans lead to per student spending differences either because middle-class districts approve high taxes or because, in very wealthy districts, even modest tax rates generate high per student revenues. Typically, available state aid is not sufficient to close the gap between high- and low-spending districts.

This combined approach, though, reduces the gap and tends to adjust to tax base changes in school districts. But it also has some undesired side effects. It says that all public school programs in a state are going to be of roughly the same quality—whether poor, mediocre, good, or excellent. But for residents in some school districts it means that they may not have better school programs even if they are willing to tax themselves to pay the added costs. Districts that are held back too much in terms of residents' wants and expectations may begin to lose students to private schools that provide the desired quality of education.

The plan also may cause a falloff in support for public schools as the number of parents with children in private schools increases. Residents and legislators of school districts that are too wealthy to qualify for state aid may have little interest in boosting state school aid. Hence overall quality and support for school taxes may decline.

And, of course, this approach fails to address differing needs among school districts, the students' out-of-school preparation for learning, cost of living, school district environment, and other factors that affect cost and programs.

A third approach is to direct state aid toward students rather than schools. In this plan, each student receives a voucher that he or she can "spend" at a school of choice. The school then exchanges the voucher for money from the state. Minnesota has started a system like this on the theory that it not only equalizes school aid but improves school quality as well. It would force schools to compete for students.

This more radical approach would cause a great deal of uncertainty for school administrators—they would have difficulty in projecting the number of students they could plan on. High-quality schools would likely be overwhelmed with students, and they would have to set admission standards to control their enrollments. Poorer students might not be able to get transportation to the school of their choice. Others fear that competition among schools might produce other unexpected and undesirable results for students, teachers, and school administrators.

State legislators, then, have choices in how to distribute state aid. But all the approaches have costs and benefits associated with them.

> What do you think? What plan would you propose for funding public schools in your state? Does it emphasize uniform per student resources? Does it recognize local initiative and innovation or needs peculiar to particular areas—high cost of living, high transportation costs, underprivileged populations, and so on? Or do you think state and local taxes should be used to support education instead of schools—with each student getting a voucher that he or she can use to pay for education at an area school of choice?

Constituents ask legislators to get schedules for civil service exams, find out when school aid payments will be made, get informational booklets, send copies of bills, or arrange meetings with other, more important legislators. These requests come under the category of constituent services. They come from ordinary citizens as well as from interest group leaders and local officials—city managers, school superintendents, or county officers.

Legislative Oversight

While legislators or their staff chase down this or that request, they may also be exercising another function: **legislative oversight**—keeping tabs on how administrators are managing their agencies.

Oversight is an integral part of lawmaking. A department of natural resources, for example, may propose a change in a law regulating wood cutting in state forests. As a committee considers that bill, a legislator may remember a problem a constituent had a year ago with the department's rules on digging ponds. And so the topic turns from trees to ponds—until the chair interrupts. The legislator, in fact, may have been reminded about the problem by his partisan staffperson whose job demands detailed knowledge of agency policy and spending. Or, it may be that a veteran legislator has simply built up special expertise or interest in a specific area.[2]

Appropriations committees oversee community college and university operations as their presidents explain budget requests. In our experience in budget hearings, rarely did a college president get away without being questioned about some obscure detail such as the percentage of out-of-state or minority students. The purpose may have been unclear and seemed little more than harassment. But it reminded the college president that any disgruntled citizen might complain and be the source of a legislator's question.[3]

Special Committees Special committees to investigate an agency problem or natural disaster are another form of legislative oversight. Often, these have fact-finding duties—Who was at fault? Are changes in laws needed? and so on. Committees have been formed for political reasons as well—perhaps to embarrass the governor or to advance a legislator's career.

The Legislative Veto as Oversight Senates, and in a few states entire legislatures, must approve or reject gubernatorial appointments. And many governors must get legislative approval on executive orders to reorganize agencies or cut budgets. Often these reviews are routine. But they also give legislators leverage to criticize and raise troublesome points. When lawmakers say no, they exercise a **legislative veto**.

The legislative veto is being used increasingly to review **administrative rules**—regulations agencies write up and publish as part of their process of administering the laws. Legislators commonly complain that bureaucrats include provisions the legislature never passed or even rejected. To remedy such "administrative lawmaking," about 30 state legislatures have procedures that involve themselves in the process and allow time to review rules before they take effect.[4]

Other Oversight Activities **Sunset provisions** constitute another opportunity for legislative oversight. These clauses state that an agency or program expires on a specific date. Without positive legislative action before the expiration date, the agency or program dies.[5]

Some legislatures now appoint the **auditor general**—the investigative state office that routinely audits departments and their accounts to determine whether agency actions are legal and efficient and to see if they have spent their appropriations legally. Auditors can almost always find something amiss. Their reports provide legislators with further points for oversight questioning and criticizing.

THE LEGISLATIVE WAY OF LIFE

The political fact that in most states characterizes legislators above all else is that most are amateurs—people engaged in the legislative process on a part-time, short-term basis. In less than a dozen states do most legislators see their positions as professional careers. Length of sessions, lifestyle, salaries, and the staff and facilities available to them all contribute to amateurism—a condition that is frustrating to many legislators as well as to reformers.

Legislative Sessions

State legislatures established a reputation for creating mischief during the 1800s. The people responded with constitutional limits on legislative sessions—in many states regular sessions were limited to 60 or 90 days every two years. Citizens wanted their legislators to be part-time representatives who should get their work done quickly and go home.

These restrictions are being relaxed gradually. At the time of World War II only four legislatures held annual sessions. By 1989, 43 were holding regular annual sessions. Still, three-fourths of the states limit the time their legislatures may meet. A few others have practical limits—pay and expense money stops after a specified time. Some have restrictions but allow extensions by extraordinary majorities—four-fifths in Nebraska, for example.

As a practical matter some issues cannot wait until the next regular session. To handle these situations, states with part-time legislatures permit special sessions. States vary in how special sessions are called—in 20 states only the governor can reconvene the legislature. In the others, legislators may call a special session by petition, or the combined leadership.

Lifestyle Demands

Few legislators would agree that the job is part time. Frank Smallwood, a political scientist at Dartmouth College, was a Vermont legislator. He wrote, "To state it as bluntly as possible, anyone interested in making a major commitment to politics had best be prepared literally to give up all else. There's no way—at least I found no way—to pursue the politics on a casual, leisurely, half-time basis."[6]

The formal schedule alone does not look too difficult. Typically, legislators meet in formal sessions about three days or so per week. Midweek mornings usually involve committee meetings. But add to that the rounds of meetings and nightly circuits of legislative receptions and fund-raisers at the capital city as well as those "back in the district." Legislators' schedules are full and often hectic, at least while the legislature is in session.

Convention Atmosphere State legislators differ from members of Congress and members of city and county governing boards in that state legislators leave their families behind. Members of Congress usually move their families to Washington. And community legislators, of course, have no need to move. But when the legislature is in session, many state legislators are home only on weekends. Thus state legislators are on a kind of four-day convention, especially in states that have limited annual sessions.

Frank Smallwood spoke of his experience with motel life in Montpelier and of his evening routine, which ended with a swim or a sauna. News media reports suggest that not all legislators handle the convention atmosphere quite as well. Some run into problems of alcohol abuse, disrupted family lives, and minor scrapes with the law. The personal disorganization among legislators also provides some insights into the lifestyle imposed by the state legislative role.

Legislative Compensation

Low pay, perhaps more than any other factor, contributes to amateurism. Until the early 1960s legislative salaries were "nominal"—token recognition for public service. (New Hampshire still reflects the extreme, with its "honorarium" of $100 per year.)

In 1964–1965 median compensation, including salary and expense money, was $2,329. But salaries have been rising. In 1989 salaries in eight states were more than $30,000; in five, more than $40,000. New York topped the list with a salary of $57,500.

Compensation, of course, affects the time most individuals can spend on public business. A few states pay enough to maintain a middle-class standard of living. Many also pay additional money for travel and housing at the state capital.

But some legislators must contribute substantial sums to their campaigns. For many legislators, legislative pay is little more than a nice side income.

The Politics of Raising Salaries   The poor public nineteenth-century image of the state legislator still contributes in part to low compensation. Some states such as New Hampshire, Montana, Vermont, Texas, and Alabama set salaries that draw citizen, not professional, legislators.

The method of setting salaries also affects legislators' pay. Nine states set salaries in their constitutions. In these states salaries are at or near the bottom. Other states set salaries by statute. Thus legislators have to take the first steps to raise their own salaries and, because compensation changes ordinarily do not take effect until after the next election, legislators often view a "yes" vote as contributing to their own defeat and benefiting their successors. So getting a majority of legislators to raise their own salaries is usually difficult.

Twenty states now have the governor appoint a board of citizens that meets every two years or so to recommend pay for legislators and other elected state officials. In four states this committee sets the salaries unless the legislature rejects increases. Pay in these states is generally near the top of the scale.

Offices and Secretarial Help

Duane Lockard, once a Connecticut senator, told of a letter asking him to do a small chore. The citizen acknowledged that Lockard was probably busy, but suggested that, perhaps, his "office" could handle it. Lockard's reaction was, "My office! I had no staff and indeed no office except for a corner in my hallway at home, where unsorted and unfiled letters, brochures, notes, and thousands of bills constantly threatened to bury my children under a paper cascade."[7]

Legislators traditionally have made do with minimum physical accommodations. Some have only a desk on the floor of the chamber. This means they meet constituents or lobbyists in capitol corridors, restaurants, hotel rooms, or bars. Committee chairs are usually a little better off because they can take command of the committee room and its secretarial staff. Only about half the states now provide legislators with private or at least shared offices.

Providing Staff Assistance

Most of us could turn out a better-looking term paper if we had a skilled typist to type the final copy. And with some expert research assistance, we might even be able to improve the content. So it is with state legislators—clerical and professional assistance can help make even an incompetent legislator look effective. Securing staff assistants has been high on the agenda of legislative reformers.

We can now report that virtually all states provide both clerical and professional staff to legislative committees, some on a year-round basis. The states have been a little more stingy in providing staff for individual legislators, but nearly all provide some personal staff assistance, sometimes shared, at least during the session. Still, in a few states we wonder if legislators are expected to write their correspondence in longhand or by the hunt-and-peck method on a portable typewriter. About a quarter of the states now provide staff for an office in the district as well. State senators are a little more likely to have personal staff than are representatives.[8]

WHO BECOMES A STATE LEGISLATOR?

The job conditions influence the kinds of citizens who become legislators and how long they remain in the job. They also affect significantly their capacity to be effective political critics of federal, state, and community government programs and agencies.

Who Gets Elected?

Most of us, remembering our democratic training, would say that a state legislature should have a heavy mix of "common people." However democratic this view, state legislatures are anything but microcosms of the general population. State legislators, as a group, are better educated than the general public.[9] They come from family backgrounds of higher than average social standing.[10] In the past, legislators also were likely to have been long-term residents of their districts. But this pattern varies by state and may be changing. In one study of 4,000 legislators in 30 states, more than one-third were "outsiders" of the state they served. Proportions of non-native legislators to their district were likely to be lowest in midwestern and southern states, and highest in the East and West.[11]

Legislators also are overwhelmingly male. Women, who held 17 percent of the state legislative seats in 1986-1987, find their numbers creeping upward little by little each year. State legislatures have a higher percentage of women than Congress.[12] Still, in certain respects, legislators closely reflect their constituencies—especially on such "birthright" characteristics as race, ethnic group, and religion.

The Occupations of Legislators

Legislators also have higher-status private jobs than the general public. Although no comprehensive study of the occupational backgrounds has been made, we can piece together available information and indicate a general pattern. Charles S. Hyneman studied the occupations of legislators in 25 houses (13 lower and 12 upper) between 1925 and 1935. Some 28 percent were lawyers, 22 percent farmers, and 31 percent businesspeople.[13] (See Table 8.1.)

In a more recent study of legislators' occupations comparing 1986 with 1976, the proportion of legislators associated with agriculture has fallen to 9.9 percent. These are concentrated, as we might expect, in the west-north-central region (Iowa, Kansas, Minnesota, Missouri, Nebraska, and the Dakotas). The propor-

Table 8.1 OCCUPATIONS OF STATE LEGISLATORS

	Thirteen lower chambers and twelve senates from 1925 to 1935		All state legislatures 1986	
	Number	Percentage	Number	Percentage
Farmers/agriculture	2,722	21.5	741	9.9
Attorneys	3,555	28.0	1,226	16.4
Teachers (K–12) and school administrators			427	5.7
Other professionals	639	5.0	369	4.8
Union representatives			19	0.3
Journalists & other communications arts	369	2.9	147	2.0
Nonmanagement workers	205	1.6	345	4.6
Government workers			109	1.5
Engineers	184	1.5	73	1.0
Contractors	273	2.2		
Company managers/executives	446	3.5	430	5.8
Insurance or real estate	869	6.8	566	7.6
Bankers/economic consultants	352	2.8	223	3.0
Homemakers			143	1.9
Students			21	0.3
Business owners	1,788	14.1	1,029	13.8
Retirees			498	6.7
Full-time legislators			857	11.5
Not classified	1,287	10.2	238	3.2
Total	12,689	100.0	7,614	100.0

Source: Charles S. Hyneman, op. cit., p. 255, for the 1925–1935 data; Beth Bazar, op. cit., pp. 9–13, for the 1986 data. Some of the authors' classifications have been modified or combined.

tion of lawyer-legislators, though still much larger than the proportion of lawyers in the general population, fell from 22 percent in 1976 to 16.4 percent in 1986.[14]

Lawyer-Legislators Almost half the signers of the Declaration of Independence were lawyers. Ever since, the legal profession has been important to American politics. In 1986, 16 percent of the state legislators were lawyers, but the difference among the states is substantial. For example, in 1986 nearly half of Virginia's legislators were lawyers. About 40 percent of the Texas legislators had outside law careers; in New Jersey almost a third. States below the national average tend to be the western mountain states and rural New England states.[15] States with low numbers of lawyer-legislators include Delaware, which had none in 1986, and New Hampshire and Arizona, with 2 and 3 percent, respectively.

Why is legislative service so popular with lawyers? First, lawyers can accommodate the legislative schedule and the risks of officeholding better than people in many other occupations. Second, whether in private practice or in legislative service, what they do does not differ all that much—representing clients is very much like representing a political constituency.[16] Moreover, service in the legislature may well enhance their future careers—the legal profession has a monopoly on certain public offices—judge, prosecutor, and attorney general.[17]

Is the high proportion of lawyer-legislators undesirable? Some argue that it presents a great potential for conflicts of interest. One apparent conflict is the tendency for lawyers to dominate judiciary committees that oversee legal and judicial affairs. More important, the lawyer-legislator or a law partner may, in fact, be "on retainer" by some of the state's important interest groups, including some the state regulates—utility companies or labor unions. Yet the lawyer-legislator's conflicts of interest may not be substantively different than those of the farmer-legislator or the teacher-legislator.

Shifts in Legislative Composition

The data suggest that the combination of occupations in state legislatures is fairly stable, although the mix changes with shifts in a state's general population. The number of farmers, of course, is down because only a very small proportion of Americans earn their living from farming. But there are other reasons for change as well. The number of teacher-legislators increased during the 1970s.

Higher salaries for legislators and longer sessions account for other changes. Higher legislative pay entices persons—teachers, for example—from previously unrepresented groups to run. But for those in other occupations the pay increases may not be enough to offset the increased demands of the job on legislators' time. So farmers, owners of small businesses, and even lawyers may drop out.

Higher pay has another effect. It increases the number of legislators who identify their careers as "full-time legislator." This designation conceals what outside interests a legislator may have had prior to becoming a lawmaker, but it also indicates the growth in the number of legislators who are not trying to balance a legislative career with another occupation. In fact, the proportions approach one in five if retirees, homemakers, and students are viewed as not having another occupation.

How People Become Legislators

The number of people who seek legislative office is very small. What separates those who do from those who do not?

Self-Recruitment One study of four state legislatures found that legislators commonly developed political career goals early in their adult lives.[18] Many became active first in someone else's political campaign or found a job such as legislative assistant. Others moved into the legislature almost by accident, becoming involved by way of a neighborhood or school issue. Or they may have gotten their start in campus or community political action or in local government.

Others cut their political teeth in union or business leadership positions. Possibilities for a political career begin to emerge. Soon they find themselves reaching for the next rung on the ladder—a seat on the county commission or the state legislature. Such self-recruitment flourishes in most places.

Recruitment by Others Where two political parties are well organized and strongly competitive, local party leaders are likely to recruit legislative candidates. But interest group leaders and community "influentials," who may not be part of the formal party structure, often assist the parties.[19] Party leaders want candidates who appeal to more than the "party faithful," and so may choose a nonparty person, possibly a local hero or a respected community leader.[20] More commonly, though, they play it safe and recruit party activists.

When one party dominates, the majority nomination "becomes a pawn in the adjustment of claims by party groupings and rewards for the party faithful."[21] Being a party person is a prerequisite. Milton Rakove described the "slating" process in Chicago's Democratic party under Mayor Richard "Dick" Daley as follows:

> The primary consideration is, "Can the candidate win?" The second consideration is, "If he can win, can he do us any good? If a candidate cannot win, who needs him? If he can win and can't do the party any good, who needs him? If he can win and can do the party harm, who wants him?" In other words, the interests of the party and the ability of the candidate for public office to serve the interest of the party come first in building the ticket.[22]

In such districts the minority party leaders will have trouble fielding a candidate. In districts where both parties are weak or fragmented, other organizations—farm, business, education, or labor—may recruit candidates.

Why Legislators Quit—Turnover Rates

High turnover contributes to amateurism. Some states still have high turnover, though generally less than in the past.[23]

The 1987 legislative sessions saw 1,120 new legislators come into the lower houses—a 20.5 percent turnover rate. In contrast to 1974, when six states elected a majority of "first termers," none in 1987 had a majority of newcomers. Still, 14 lower houses and 9 upper houses had one-fourth or more newcomers. Turnover in the state senates was lower—15.9 percent in 1987.

What contributes to high turnover? Alan Rosenthal concludes, "No single factor is believed to matter as much as compensation."[24] We agree.

Pay, Ambition, and Frustration But high pay, by itself, does not always ensure low turnover. Legislators' opportunity for advancement also plays a role. Peverill Squire classified 25 lower houses on the basis of pay and advancement opportunity (see Table 8.2). "Career" legislatures—those with high pay and moderate or low advancement opportunity—have high membership stability. Squire calls those that rate low or moderate on both counts the "Dead End" bodies. These have considerably less membership stability. "Springboard" bodies may be either high or low in pay but high in career advancement opportunities. These are likely to have the greatest turnover of members.[25] Career legislatures tend to recruit younger members—in their late thirties. The entry average age of Dead End bodies is higher but varies by state. Legislators in springboard states fall in between—they "need not begin service as young as career legislators because their advancement opportunities can check quickly."

Legislative turnover, in the main, then, results from members who seek other office or voluntarily quit. Election defeats account for very little turnover. Legislators are far more likely to win than lose if they seek reelection.[26] Incumbents in Illinois had an overall win record of 94.4 percent in both primary and general elections from 1972 to 1980.[27]

Table 8.2 LEGISLATIVE TYPOLOGY: MEAN MEMBER YEARS OF SERVICE AND MEAN AGE AT ENTRY

	Advancement prospects								
	High			Moderate			Low		
	State	Mean member service	Mean entry age	State	Mean member service	Mean entry age	State	Mean member service	Mean entry age
High Pay	Calif.	4.1	40.9	Mich.	5.6	38.6	Minn.	4.7	39.3
				Md.	4.4	39.4	Wis.	6.4	37.0
				Ohio	6.3	—	N.Y.	5.0	38.7
							Mo.	6.1	39.9
							Pa.	5.4	40.2
(Overall mean member service)		4.1			5.4			5.5	
(Overall mean entry age)									39.0
Low Pay	Wash.	4.0	42.9	Oreg.	3.7	43.0	S.D.	3.6	47.0
	S.C.	3.7	39.3	N.C.	3.6	45.0	Okla.	5.6	39.0
	N.J.	3.8	41.0	Tex.	4.3	36.9	W.Va.	3.0	41.9
	Alaska	3.1	40.5	Iowa	3.6	41.7	Va.	6.5	41.2
							Conn.	2.8	40.1
							Ga.	4.4	40.2
							R.I.	4.0	39.6
							Vt.	4.3	47.4
(Overall mean member service)		3.8			3.8			4.3	
(Overall mean entry age)			40.9						41.9

Source: Peverill Squire, "Career Opportunities and Membership Stability in Legislatures," Legislative Studies Quarterly 13:1 (1988): 65–81.

Changes in legislative district boundaries to reflect population changes, or **reapportionment** or **redistricting**, also add to turnover. Elections immediately following reapportionments tend to produce more first-time legislators. Finally, some turnover results from the pressures and the frustrations of the process. For example, Rep. Al Riebel of Oregon, in announcing he would not run again said, "You come up here and lose yourself in the capitol. You lull yourself into thinking you are the only one who can make important decisions. Meanwhile, people back home don't even know you're here."[28] Others find the personal sacrifices too high—"family" is an important consideration for those who leave office voluntarily.[29]

Is Turnover a Problem? Whether turnover is a problem depends on the degree and regularity of high turnover, but also on point of view. Having a legislature in which half the legislators are new is like a debating team or theater group that has only a few veterans. The performance will likely not be very professional. High turnover tends to concentrate power in too few hands. Newcomers may be uninformed about governmental issues and procedures, especially if the legislature is part time, and become vulnerable to influence by the governor, administrators, and lobbyists.

On the other hand, some turnover is desirable. Newcomers bring fresh ideas. New legislators may be citizen-legislators, not professionals engrossed in their own ambition and advancement.

HOW LEGISLATORS OPERATE: THE POLITICS OF LAWMAKING

Frank Smallwood described himself as an academic neophyte state legislator. "Little did I realize," he said, "how much I had to learn as I groped to discover some underlying patterns that would provide a coherent understanding of the new world that lay before me."[30] Ultimately he found several reference points to guide him through the procedural maze: formal rules of procedure, legislative leadership and committees, informal rules, and legislative staff.

Formal Rules of Procedure

The route a legislative proposal follows, from initiation to final adoption, is complex and beset with pitfalls. A diagram of the steps that most state legislatures follow is shown in Figure 8.1.

These steps also pose as political hurdles in getting a bill passed. The balance of political parties in a legislature, in part, determines whether a bill becomes law. But the formal set of rules also has political implications. They limit the majority and give strength to minority forces and those advocating the status quo.

Political Strategies and Legislative Rules As we look down on the legislature from the balcony, the floor action usually does not seem to be either orderly or deliberative. Nevertheless, detailed rules govern the behavior we see.

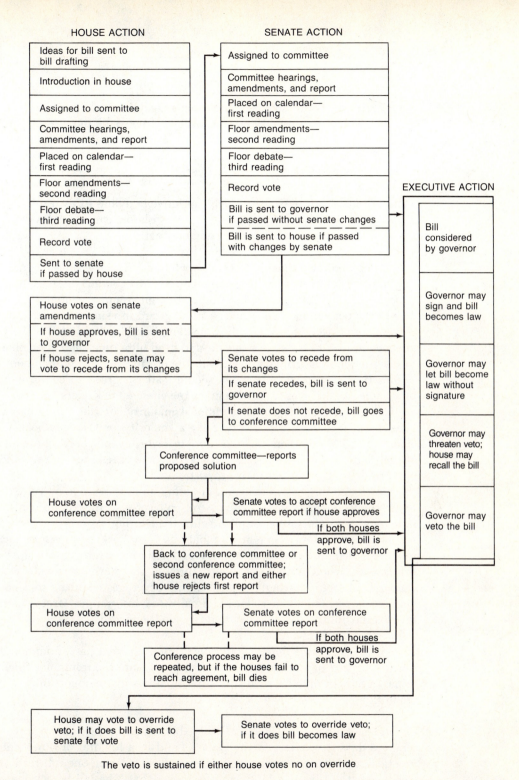

Figure 8.1 The formal law-making process. This diagram shows bills introduced in the house. If the senate originates the bill the interhouse action would be the reverse order.

As in parlor games and sports, the rules restrict, but they also structure the game's strategy. William Keefe and Morris Ogul wrote, "The rules are significant because the methods used to reach decisions often shape the decisions themselves; procedure and policy, in other words, are often interrelated. Never wholly neutral, rules benefit some groups and disadvantage others. They are, commonly, one of the many faces of minority power."[31]

Types of Legislative Rules Each legislative body has its own rules. Some rules set the minimum conditions under which legislators can legislate. Others govern the speed with which a legislative body may act.

Minimum Conditions: Quorum and Vote Requirements A quorum—the minimum number of members present needed to conduct business—usually is a majority of the members. A few states, though, require as many as two-thirds. The larger percentage strengthens a small group in using this rule to bargain for concessions or even to kill the bill. For example, 12 "Killer Bees" of the Texas senate once went into hiding for five days to head off a quick action on changing the Texas presidential primary. Without them, the senate had no quorum. The "Killer Bees" returned only when senate leaders agreed to compromise. When they came back, it was too late to make the change the leaders wanted.[32]

Constitutions specify a **constitutional majority**, or the minimum number of votes needed to pass a bill—typically a majority of the members. Thus in a chamber of 100 members, 51 must vote in favor, even if only 52 are on the floor at the time—a few legislators' votes may become crucial for passage and provide opportunity to bargain for their support.

Few legislators have the luxury of voting on final passage by voice or show of hands—rules in most states require roll call votes so the public can know how individual legislators vote. And in states that do not require a recorded vote, a few members (as few as one in Vermont and New York) can insist on a call of the roll. This demand may also be part of legislative strategy. The first bill that Frank Smallwood tried to shepherd through the Vermont senate would have changed the hours during which alcoholic beverages could be sold on Sunday. Opponents insisted on a roll call. Smallwood lost support from senators who favored the bill but did not wish to do so "on the record."

Speed of Passage Rules State constitutions prevent hasty adoption of legislation with **speed of passage rules**—rules that regulate the minimum time required to pass a bill. In practice such rules give the minority an opportunity to mount its opposition.

The Three-Reading Rule Usually, bills must be read aloud three times on separate days (two times in the Dakotas and in a handful of other states). As a practical matter, of course, time does not allow for even one full reading. As the clerk reads the title of a bill, someone moves that "the bill be considered read," and the presiding officer mechanically intones, "Without objection, it shall be so ordered." As he or she utters the last syllable, the gavel falls. Sometimes the readings may be only for the record even if no one is listening. For example, we noted that after Michigan's 1989 State of the State speech, the house officially remained in session, but reporters were interviewing legislators and other conversations were occurring all over the house floor. Yet up on the rostrum the clerk was methodically reading the titles of bills and reporting the committees to which they were being sent. (The house journal the next day would report what had happened.)

Multiple readings indicate the **status of bills**—the place a bill is in the legislative process—and prevent quick passage. The first reading announces a bill's introduction and committee referral. The second reading tells of a bill's being reported from committee and its readiness for floor action—possibly floor amendments. The third reading precedes the final debate and vote on a bill.

The Layover Rule Another slowdown rule requires a bill passed in one house to lay over in the second house for a specified number of days—typically five. The rule gives legislators and lobbyists time to politick—to marshal forces to support or oppose the bill.

The Effective-Date Rule Normally laws take effect 30 to 90 days after the legislature has adjourned. But extraordinary majorities can give a law "immediate effect." In states where sessions continue year round, immediate effect may be essential to the law's usefulness. It gives minority forces one more chance to trade votes on immediate effect for compromises on the measure itself or on another bill.

Giving testimony to a Massachusetts senate committee.

Legislative Leadership and Committees

First-time legislators follow rather than lead. They have a "Now that I'm here, what do I do, how do I start?" kind of feeling. They puzzle over questions such as "Who makes things happen? Who has the power? How do they use it?"

The Speaker of the House In the lower house the leader is the **Speaker of the House**. The speaker enjoys informal power gained from election by the majority and, through rules and custom, considerable formal power as well. In all but four states the speaker assigns legislators to committees and designates the committee chair. The speaker also usually decides committee bill assignments, presides over the sessions with the power to recognize legislators or ignore "points of order," administers the house budget, and often has hiring and firing power over many of the legislative employees.

Challenges to exercising these powers are rare because of the rich diversity of power tools available to a speaker—the speaker can aid or hinder development of legislative careers. Appointments to important committees, assistance in advancing or "sandbagging" a newcomer's first bill, giving or denying the opportunity for press coverage, or passing out "pork barrel" projects[33]—all are devices speakers have to get votes to support their program. And with the rising cost of election campaigns, possible grants from the speaker's campaign war chest gives them added leverage with the members.

Party control of the governorship, however, affects the speaker's power. When the same political party or faction controls both the governorship and the lower house, the speaker may have to play second fiddle—a potential source of friction. But when the governor is of the opposing party the spotlight is on the speaker. The two must bargain to get bills passed.

Senate Leaders The speakership has no precise counterpart in state senates. In 28 states the constitution specifies that the lieutenant governor presides. Lieutenant governors, though, are "outsiders," not leaders that senators have chosen. Thus in only seven state senates do lieutenant governors make committee appointments.

Majority Leader The senate majority leader or an elected senate president exercises powers approaching those of the house speaker. But majority leaders also share a great deal of the power with others. One Michigan legislator explained the difference between the speaker and senate majority leader—"The 38-member Senate has 38 prima donnas," he said, "while the 110-member House has 109 sheep."[34]

Senate majority leaders or elected presidents look to the party as the source of support. But where the parties are narrowly divided, skills as a legislative strategist and a dose of courage prove helpful. We recall an electrifying session when Republican Governor George Romney of Michigan sought to push an income tax measure through a reluctant Republican-controlled senate. The job fell to Frank Beadle, majority leader. At the Monday evening session in which he decided to take action, he moved that when the evening session adjourned by rule at midnight, it would reconvene at 12:01 A.M. His assistant majority leader led a bloc of conservative senators off the floor to elect a new majority leader. But Beadle managed to hold together a coalition of moderate Republicans and Democrats throughout the night. When we left for home, with the rising sun shining in the rearview mirror, the shaky coalition had hammered out and passed a state income tax.

Committees and Their Chairs Because of the large number of subjects they deal with, legislatures must have a system for dividing the work load and developing specialization. Their answer is **standing committees**.

Specialization Through specialization small groups of legislators become relatively expert in a narrow interest area. But therein lies a dilemma. This creates power centers that may not be very representative of the entire body or of state interests.

Committees use their specialized knowledge in two basic ways: (1) to conduct the oversight function of a corresponding administrative agency—the committee on natural resources over the department of natural resources, for example—and (2) to screen and prepare bills for passage.

Legislators generally prefer having many committees—to afford more opportunities to become a committee chair. But legislative reformers advocate fewer committees. The more committees, the less representative the group that handles the interest area and the narrower its focus. The average number of committees in 1987 was 19.8 in the lower chambers and 15.6 in the upper. Some states still have exceptionally high numbers of committees—North Carolina with 93 and Missouri with 72, for example. On the other hand, six legislatures have fewer than 20.[35]

The Problem of Committee Power Committees and their chairs sometimes kill bills they do not like, hold others hostage as barter, or virtually dictate to executive departments certain policies and practices under threat of budget cutbacks. However, committees and their chairs generally are less important than they once were.[36] Rotating committee assignments from session to session helps to keep individual legislators from developing the expertise and informal relationships on which power rests. Other legislatures require all committees to report out every bill, thus preventing a chair from holding a bill hostage. Most legislatures also require committees to meet in open session. In addition, some make mandatory a record roll call vote to report or "kill" a bill. But committees can still report bills with a "do not pass" recommendation, amend bills so they are unacceptable to the full body, or stall action until other matters become more pressing.[37] A study of the Illinois legislature suggests that the power of committee chairs is often overstated. Committees sometimes get the credit for killing bills that their sponsors want to "let die."[38]

The Need for Power Committees may exercise too much power at times, but widely dispersed power may also cause problems. Legislators may be unable to hammer out needed compromises because no one has sufficient clout to mediate competing claims. And in the absence of a group of powerful committee chairs we may find even smaller numbers of legislators wielding excessive amounts of power. For example, David Roberti, once president pro tem of the California senate, ordered all Republican bills to be sidetracked because he objected to Republican tactics in protesting Democratic reapportionment bills. Omer Rains, chair of the senate judiciary committee, resisted and was told to resign his chair. With his power base in the committee, Rains successfully fought that command as well. Very likely, Roberti found other ways to even the score later.[39]

Conference Committees When the two houses insist on different versions of a bill, a **conference committee** with a few members from each house tries to work out a compromise. Both houses then vote on the compromise. Appropriation bills are common grist for conference committees. The reason is that legislatures usually vote on appropriations at the end of the session when legislators want to get home and thus have little stomach for extended fights. In such cases, conference committees often cut the final deals on budgets. A handful of legislators, then, may make the final decision.

Informal Rules

Smallwood keyed in on the social norms that also guided the behavior of Vermont legislators. Like other groups of people who are thrown into a situation in which they need to work together, legislators develop standards of accepted behavior. Mavericks are tolerated and given their due, but little more.

The Wahlke study of four states cited earlier identified three rules of the game. First, legislators insist on honesty and integrity from each other. Once legislators give their word, the promise must be kept. If they promise their vote on a bill, they are expected to deliver it—"make your word your bond."

Second, legislators are expected to respect each other's rights and obligations. In the words of one legislator, "Don't meddle in others' business—if a bill doesn't affect you, vote for it." Legislators are also expected to respect other legislators' reasons for voting as they did.

Third, avoid personal attacks. Opposition and criticism should be directed against the issue at hand, not against the person sponsoring it. In spite of opening invocations such as "Help us to do what is right for the citizens of our state and *help us do it today*," tempers sometimes get frayed.

The Political Significance of Norms Social norms help create a sense of teamwork and tolerance. They fit the general mood of political compromise. They demand that members take their jobs seriously, defend the body from outside criticism, refrain from using every parliamentary maneuver even when technically permissible, maintain confidences, and avoid "stealing" another legislator's bill. Obviously individuals do not abide by all the norms at all times.

Minor digression is anticipated and expected. But someone who makes a major break risks being labeled an outcast. Such is the case for one representative in the Michigan legislature who votes "no" on virtually every spending measure. In retribution, the speaker refused to assign her an administrative aide.

Legislative Staff Agencies

In college we think very little about a career in the state legislature. But for those like us who attended college near a state capitol, the legislature had good part-time jobs. The legislature met only briefly each year, and while the legislators were away we could hit the books. Legislative employees then were mainly clerks and secretaries—a few patronage appointees handled the mail, the bill room, and other chores.

Expanded Legislative Staff Things have changed since then. State legislatures employed more than 20,000 people year round in 1987, an average of 400 per legislature, and perhaps an additional 9,000 session-only employees.[40]

Why Legislative Staffs Have Increased Some observers attribute the increase in staff to reapportionment of legislatures in the late 1960s. The more representative districts sent "younger, broader based, and probably more competitive, reform-minded leaders to the legislatures."[41]

A more fundamental explanation, we think, is that most legislatures are tired of being "the stepchild of state government" without the resources to compete with the executive and judicial branches. To be independent of the other branches, more information must come from staff whose first loyalty is to the legislature. With their own staff, rather than relying on executive staff, legislators can initiate policy rather than just react to the suggestions of others.[42]

Staff Functions Some legislative staffers perform routine political chores—write letters, help with constituent casework, and manage schedules. Often these decisions affect who gains access to legislators. Other responsibilities are more clearly political, but require more professional expertise.

Bill Drafting In the legislative rush, bill drafters can make foolish mistakes. A Kansas law once required trains approaching each other on the same track to stop on a siding and forbade either from moving until the other had passed. Bill-drafting staffpersons are supposed to prevent such gaffes, as well as craft the legislator's ideas into the bill precisely.

Bill Analysis A **bill analysis** tells legislators how a bill may affect them and their constituents. It answers questions like these: What problem does the bill address? What will the bill do? Who (which interest group) wants the bill? Whom does it affect? Who favors and opposes it? The political importance of such an analysis is obvious. It is equally apparent why legislators want such summaries prepared by their own staff—people who are sensitive to their own political needs.

Policy Analysis and Research Policy analysts have long-term goals for research. They deal with various topics and plan, eventually, to generate or combat proposals on issues relating to economic development, environment, taxation, water supply, waste disposal, and others. From these, legislators may take the initiative on issues or suggest important alternatives to proposals from the governor or interest groups.

Fiscal Analysis and Review Money is the fuel that powers government. Having independent sources of fiscal information is absolutely critical to legislative independence. Hence legislators want their own experts to assess spending proposals, evaluate the governor's revenue projections, and develop independent projections.

Computerized Information If money powers government, computers help keep track of where it is being used. Perhaps more important is the use of computers in making appropriations—staffers can generate numerous scenarios of how funds might be distributed through small formula changes. But computers are also used to research existing statutes for conflicts with pending legislation, to keep track of the progress of bills, and to search laws of other states for new ideas.

Staff Influence on Policy Inevitably, professional staff influence legislative products. When staffers consider projects legislators might work on or when they research policy problems, personal biases and prejudices influence the recommendations. They discard some proposed solutions and embrace others because "the boss just won't buy it any other way." But staff members reject others, or never allow them to surface, because of personal preferences. However, one observer noted that "staff take more cues from the formal policymakers than they give."[43] It is not likely, for example, for a state legislator's staff to be out in front of the boss on a question like the one presented in Policy Box No. 16, "The Drug War—Should We Surrender?"

The Politics of Lawmaking

The legislative process is not neat and orderly. At times it is downright messy. But should we expect it to be otherwise? The legislative arena is a place where competing groups display their differences. It is a place where expression of varying ideas and opinions is encouraged. It is a place where "perfect" answers are seldom sought or reached. "If conflict is inevitable, then accommodation, compromise, and the search for consensus are a necessity, even if each accommodation and each decision is partial, temporary, and mutable."[44]

Policy Box No. 16

The Drug War—Should We Surrender?

During the latter years of the Vietnam War as national leaders were trying to figure how to extricate the United States from the frustrating and deadly quagmire, Sen. Barry Goldwater suggested that "We should declare victory and get out."

A similar solution is now being made about the so-called war on drugs. President Reagan sought for several years to close our borders to illicit drugs by interdicting shipments of cocaine from South American countries. He also introduced the concept of *zero tolerance*. This meant that no matter how small or great the quantity of drugs one might have in his or her possession, punishment would be swift and strong. And any property used in drug trade or that might be the rewards of drug trafficking would be seized and sold. The proceeds would be used to continue the drug war.

When George Bush was sworn into office, he named William Bennett as his drug czar—the person who would devise the new strategy for the war and coordinate the effort until we achieved the equivalent of unconditional surrender. After several months of study and planning, Bennett, who was Secretary of Education in the Reagan administration, announced his plans.

Congress and state officials generally supported the multifront strategy that sought to curb production in Colombia and other countries in the region, and continued interdiction, severe penalties for drug traffickers, and education to reduce the demand for drugs. Members of Congress, governors, and others, however, began to criticize the plan because President Bush, they said, was not putting enough money behind the effort. Governors and mayors were upset because they were being asked to allocate even more resources to the battle.

In Michigan, for example, the governor had committed the state to tripling the capacity of the state prison system to 32,000 beds. His intent had been to make the penalties for all crimes, but especially drug-related crimes, swift and certain. But before the seven-year project was even finished, prison officials warned that upon completion, the system would still be some 16,000 beds short of the need.

Experiences such as this, plus seizures of drugs that weighed in at as much as 25 tons with little impact on the supply or price of street drugs, led some to wonder if the nation should not "declare victory" by legalizing heroin, cocaine, and other pleasure drugs and perhaps then making them available in government-controlled outlets at little or no cost.

One of the arguments offered in support of such a policy is that the criminalization of these drugs creates irresistible financial incentive for drug dealers. James Ostrowski, former chairperson of the New York County Lawyers Association Committee on Law Review, observed,

> Failure [of the war on drugs] is guaranteed because the black market thrives on the war on drugs and benefits from any intensification of it. At best, increased enforcement simply boosts the black market price of drugs, encouraging more drug suppliers to supply more drugs. The publicized conviction of a drug dealer, by instantly creating a vacancy in the lucrative drug

market, had the same effect as hanging up a help-wanted sign saying, "Drug dealer needed—$5,000 a week to start—exciting work."

The argument is that American society should do with respect to drugs what it did regarding alcohol in 1933. In 1920 the nation adopted the prohibition amendment banning the manufacture, sale, and distribution of any alcoholic beverages. After 13 years of trying to wipe out private whiskey stills, close down the speakeasies, and break up alcohol lords such as Al Capone, we repealed this amendment. Some argue that circumstances of the present drug war are similar to those of the alcohol war.

It would be better, they say, to stop wasting public resources on what is inevitably a futile effort. They argue that we should allocate the $10 billion now used in the drug war—for seizing drugs, prosecuting and trying drug dealers and users, and incarcerating those convicted—to programs discouraging the use of drugs and rehabilitating addicts. And they suggest assigning these local, state, and federal resources to programs designed to combat the seedbeds of drug use—entrenched hopelessness and poverty of central cities where addiction is widespread. Some point out that the $25,000 to $30,000 per year it takes to keep one person in prison could go a long way toward eliminating the despair that leads to drug use.

Opponents of legalization, though, argue that most of American society is law abiding and that criminalization of drugs keeps many people from trying them and becoming addicted. Make the stuff legal, they maintain, and its use would increase dramatically just as it did with alcohol when it again became legal. They note that the widespread use of alcohol has had dire consequences—tens of thousands of highway deaths and accidents each year, thousands of deaths annually from cirrhosis of the liver, to say nothing of family disruptions, homelessness, spouse abuse, and lost hours of production in workplaces. Repeal of the prohibition amendment, they say, may have cut down on gangsterism and crime, but it only changed the form of the social costs; it did not eliminate the costs themselves.

Opponents of decriminalization point to Italy, where such recreational drugs are legal, although not distributed by government. Milan, they note, has more than 100,000 heroin addicts and Italy itself has more than 300,000 users infected with AIDS because they share needles. And what of women addicts in our own country who, though pregnant, would continue to use drugs only to give birth to damaged offspring? And even if the government distributed these drugs on a nominal or no cost basis, you would still have a lucrative black market for those occasional users who would not want to register at the government outlet. No, the opponents say, decriminalization of drugs is not the answer. Society must persist in battling this terrible pestilence. By standing strong against it and allocating the resources necessary, decent society will overcome in the end.

What do you think? Would our states and communities be better or worse off if these drugs became legal? Is the hyperprofitability of drug trading the cause of the "drug problem"? Should we renew the war on poverty in place of the war on drugs? Would that reduce drug use? Would you favor decriminalization if drugs were distributed at government outlets? Would you favor a controlled experiment in decriminalization in a state such as Hawaii or Alaska? Should alcohol and cigarettes, both of which cause more deaths per year than "drugs," also be criminalized?

REFORMING STATE LEGISLATURES

One set of proposals for reforming state legislatures seeks to improve their political efficiency—to make them more representative. The other advocates greater administrative efficiency.

Reapportionment

One of the darkest periods in the history of state legislatures occurred between 1920 and 1962, when they refused to reapportion their districts. The underrepresentation of a growing urban population became a national scandal. Before the reapportionment cases arose, an arrogant rural Tennessee legislator said, "I believe in collecting taxes where the money is—in the cities—and spending it where it is needed—in the country."[45] The case that broke the logjam—*Baker v. Carr*—originated in Tennessee.

Legal Arrangements In *Baker v. Carr*,[46] the U.S. Supreme Court ruled that vastly unequal numbers of residents among legislative districts was unconstitutional. In later cases the Supreme Court developed reapportionment standards. In *Reynolds v. Sims*, for example, the Court said that districts should result in "fair and effective representation." Districts should be "compact," "contiguous"—consisting only of connected parts—and avoid dividing political subdivisions if possible.[47]

The Court set two other standards. In *Whitcomb v. Chavis* it ruled that new districts that reduce the political influence of minorities are unconstitutional.[48] And it ruled that equitable representation of political parties can be a reasonable standard for evaluating a districting plan.[49]

The Politics of Reapportionment Politicians evaluate districting plans by different standards—How am I, or how is my party affected by the plan? If the results are favorable, the plan is "fair and equitable." If negative, the plan is "grotesque" or "insidious."

The strength of a political party for a decade is often at stake in a districting plan. But the process is also intensely personal, because people's political careers are on the line or, if not careers, the "safe margin" they have been nurturing so carefully.[50]

Meanwhile party leaders may urge those who draw up district boundaries to narrow the margins of safe districts, to reduce "wasted" party votes, and to make opposition districts more vulnerable—as the chairperson of the Democratic national party did in California.[51] Much is at risk in redistricting, and those directly affected fight with whatever resources they can muster.[52]

Reapportionment Plans In most states the legislature redraws congressional and legislative districts in the same way it passes a law. But increasingly, states are turning to "independent" apportionment commissions—small groups dominated by the majority party. Other states assign the task in the first instance to

the legislature but have a commission in the wings if the legislature fails to reach a compromise.

Motivations and Strategies Reapportionment in states where one party controls the governorship and the legislature might seem to be a nonissue at first glance. But that is not always the case. Liberal and conservative wings of the party might use redistricting to increase their power. Or legislators with an eye on running for Congress might try to shape congressional districts to improve their chances. And minority groups will be attentive to how proposed plans affect their prospects for electing one of their members.

Just because a plan is drawn and adopted does not mean the issue is settled for another ten years. Courts may also become involved. In Texas, for example, the reapportionment board consisted of five elected state officials—all Democrats. Mexican-American groups as well as Republican house and senate groups sued, arguing that the districts underrepresented urban areas, ethnic minorities, and Republicans. In New York, blacks and Puerto Ricans sued, alleging discrimination in plans drawn by a Republican senate and Democratic assembly. In Michigan, the state supreme court ruled the reapportionment process improper and then appointed a retired state elections director as "master" to draw district boundaries following the court's guidelines.

What Is "Fair"? In 1980 Common Cause declared war on **gerrymandering**—drawing district boundaries to give one party or group an undue advantage. Common Cause's goal was to make competitive as many districts as possible—that is, giving each party a good chance of winning each time. But competitive districts do not always ensure that a party's representation in the legislature approximates its voting strength in the population.[53] The majority party has an automatic advantage in states with single-member legislative districts—small increases in voter turnout can produce substantial margins.

Connecticut Republicans discovered this in the 1970s. They were successful in having the court uphold their reapportionment plan in 1972. They called it a "fair plan for representation." Democrats called it a "gigantic gerrymander."[54] In 1972, when George McGovern was the Democratic presidential nominee, Republicans won legislative seats well in excess of their strength among voters. But in following elections, Democrats turned the tables and won both houses by large margins.

Moreover, the U.S. Supreme Court agreed, in a review of an Indiana apportionment plan, that courts may properly consider allegations of gerrymandering. But when it came to establishing legal standards against which to evaluate apportionment plans for gerrymandering, a majority of the Court could not agree.[55]

Effects of Apportionment Reform Students of politics expected substantial changes in the policies of reapportioned state legislatures. Early studies, though, did not reveal many.[56] But others argued that it would take at least two or three sessions for new legislators to gain leadership positions and change the internal mechanisms of state legislatures.[57]

More recent studies, however, argue that this reform has indeed made the state legislature more representative of a state's interests. One concluded that the increase in urban representativeness resulted in policies more responsive to urban areas and, in general, more liberal. And party competition and voting along party lines in the state legislatures increased.[58] Another noted that representational changes were the greatest in states that had severe malapportionment and weak two-party systems.[59] And another found the effects of redistricting to be less in states where the level of spending and the rate of spending increases were already high.[60]

In addition, Democrats generally had a modest gain in seats in the northern states and somewhat larger gains in the states east of the Mississippi River. Republican gains were largely in southern and southwestern states.[61] In general, legislators themselves thought policies had become more liberal, that aid to urban areas increased, that Democratic gains were about twice those of Republicans, but that the reform did not greatly affect tenure.[62]

Other Reform Proposals

Other reforms have sought to make legislatures more professional and administratively efficient.

Unicameralism and Nonpartisanship Jesse Unruh, once speaker of the California Assembly, called **unicameralism**—a one-house legislature—the "wave of the future."[63] But it has made barely a ripple, except in Nebraska and community governments. In 1934, under the leadership of U.S. Senator George W. Norris, Nebraskans established not only a unicameral legislature, but a nonpartisan one as well. A hundred years earlier, Vermont had abandoned its one-house legislature.

How has Nebraska's experiment worked out? Nebraskans are not likely to approve a return to bicameralism; nor do they rate their legislature any higher than do citizens of other states.[64] Competition for legislative seats has steadily declined, but in 1986 its turnover rate was about at the national average.[65] Moreover, nonpartisanship may not be as pure as we might imagine—in 1978 and 1980 the national Republican party began contributing funds to nonpartisan "Republican" candidates, thus breaking a long-standing tradition.[66]

Professionalizing State Legislatures The Citizens Conference on State Legislatures (CCSL) has been the principal advocate for professionalizing state legislatures. Its focus has been on salaries, staff, and office space as well as internal workings.[67] The CCSL recommendations move the legislatures along a path that encourages year-round legislatures and full-time legislators with appointed staff assistants—and administrative efficiency. On the basis of five criteria, it evaluated and ranked all the state legislatures—it said that California's was the best; Alabama's the worst.[68]

Overlooked in the process of administrative reform, perhaps, is that state legislatures may become less efficient politically. As deliberative bodies, a legislature is not necessarily remiss if its decision-making process is slow and careful and it assumes that a varied and broad spectrum of opinions exists on virtually every issue.[69] This view holds that the legislature's job is not to find the one "correct" answer to every problem. The goal is to develop the "best possible" political response, given the particular mix of interests and viewpoints then current in the state. Professional legislators and staff risk emphasizing technical correctness and speed over political acceptability. An administratively efficient legislature may generate laws that reflect the values of the professional staff and that are based on the most advanced technical data. At the same time the citizenry or affected interest groups may find the law unacceptable because, for example, it demands too much change in too short a time, because it makes unreasonable demands on certain parts of the state, or because the framers overlooked a critical point. Legislative reforms thus can and indeed should be administratively efficient but not at the cost of political efficiency.

Political scientists expected that such reformed legislatures would have policy outcomes significantly different from those of the old-style legislatures. Researchers have not been successful in finding measurable differences.[70] Other students, however, argue that reformed legislatures tend to be more capable of making independent budget decisions, of obtaining information about policies and proposing new or alternative policies, and of overseeing their implementation.[71]

A FINAL COMMENT

Many state legislatures have changed substantially since the early 1960s and the upheaval brought on by reapportionment. And many have adopted at least some of the ideas of the "Citizens Conference." Together these reforms and more widespread use of computers have improved the capability of state legisl[atures to] be active players in the federal system and to deal with increasingly [complex] issues such as how to dispose of hazardous wastes, protect environmentally sensitive resources, and compete in world markets. And because of improved capability, we think, legislatures have become better critics and evaluators of the proposals that governors, administrators, and interest groups bring to them.

But legislatures, unlike the other branches, will have continuing difficulty in gaining general public favor and plaudits from journalists. As we noted at the beginning of this chapter, legislative processes are open for all to witness. And because its work products usually are a compromise between competing interests, they will seldom be held up for widespread public praise.

HIGH POINTS

In this chapter we have argued that the main task of state legislators is to evaluate and criticize policies that for the most part others propose, advance, and administer. This evaluation, we have noted, is a political one, seeking a balance that is acceptable to the varied interests within a state.

We have seen that (1) legislatures carry out this function through the lawmaking process, by overseeing the activities of the executive agencies, and by providing services to constituents and representatives of interest groups.

We noted (2) that although conditions are changing gradually, legislators in many states are amateur, rather than professional, a status marked by part-time work, low pay, and inadequate staff and facilities. We discussed (3) how people with occupations in law and business still tend to dominate the state legislator ranks but that other occupational groups are appearing in greater numbers. We found that (4) state legislators are politically ambitious and that this, along with low salaries, keeps legislative turnover fairly high.

We next considered (5) that state legislatures operate by a complex network of formal and informal rules that enable minority coalitions and those opposing change to bargain with a power beyond their numbers. But we also saw (6) that a great deal of the power of these bodies rests with the leaders, including committee chairs.

We discussed (7) the growing use of professional staff in the state legislatures. Finally, we reviewed (8) several reform proposals—reapportionment, which has political efficiency as its main goal, unicameralism, and other reforms that seek a professional and administratively efficient legislature.

In this chapter we defined the following terms in this order: political evaluation, political efficiency, "skeleton" bills, constituent services, legislative oversight, legislative veto, administrative rules, sunset provisions, auditor general, reapportionment, redistricting, quorum, constitutional majority, speed of passage rules, status of bills, speaker of the house, senate majority leader, standing committees, conference committee, bill analysis, gerrymandering, and unicameralism.

NOTES

1. For a brief review of proposed legislative reforms, see Russell L. Smith and William Lyons, "Legislative Reform in the American States, Some Preliminary Observations," *State and Local Government Review* 9 (May 1977): 35–39.
2. Jack R. VanDerslick and Kent D. Redfield, *Lawmaking in Illinois* (Springfield, Ill.: Office of Public Affairs Communication, Sangamon State University, 1986), p. 177.
3. Legislators tend not to give themselves good grades for the oversight work. Alan Rosenthal notes that few legislators specialize in oversight because they get little credit for it. See "Legislative Behavior and Legislative Oversight," *Legislative Studies Quarterly* 6:1 (1981): 115–131.
4. Marcus E. Ethridge, in "Legislative Oversight Mechanisms and Behavior," *Polity* 17 (1984–85): 340–359, suggests legislative committees with oversight functions adopt one of three institutional perspectives as a base for legitimacy and to counter opposition. For a state legislator's perspectives on administrative rule making, see Prescott E. Bloom, "Legislative Oversight: A Response to Citizens' Demands and Needs," *State and Local Government Review* 16:1 (Winter 1984): 34–38. For details on administrative rules procedures see *The Book of the States, 1988–89* (Lexington, Ky.: Council of State Governments, 1988), pp. 132–133.
5. Gary T. Henry and Walter L. Smiley, "Legislative Program Evaluation in the States, The Edge That Cuts," Paper presented at the Midwest Political Science Association meeting, 1981. Also see William Lyons and Larry W. Thomas, *Legislative Oversight, A Three State Study* (Knoxville, Tenn.: Bureau of Public Administration, University of Tennessee, 1978).
6. Frank Smallwood, *Free and Independent* (Brattleboro, Vt.: Stephen Green Press, 1976), p. 223.
7. Duane Lockard, "The Tribulations of a State Senator," in John C. Wahlke and Heinz Eulau (eds.), *Legislative Behavior* (Glencoe, Ill.: Free Press, 1959), p. 296.
8. *The Book of the States, 1988–89* (Lexington, Ky.: Council of State Governments, 1988), pp. 122–123.
9. In the Illinois legislature, for example, 87 percent of the members have a college degree compared to 16.2 percent in Illinois's general population. See Jack R. Van Der Slik and Kent D. Redfield, *Lawmaking in Illinois*, p. 72.
10. John C. Wahlke et al., *The Legislative System, Explorations in Legislative Behavior* (New York: Wiley, 1962). This study of four state legislatures provides an excellent analysis of legislatures and their behavior.
11. Joel A. Thompson and Gary F. Moncrief, "Residential Mobility of American State Legislators," Paper presented at the meeting of the American Political Science Association, 1988.
12. Beth Bazar, *State Legislators' Occupations: A Decade of Change* (Denver, Colo.: National Conference of State Legislatures, 1987), p. 7.
13. Charles S. Hyneman, "Who Makes Our Laws?" in Wahlke and Eulau (eds.), *Legislative Behavior* (Glencoe, Ill.: Free Press, 1959), pp. 254–256.
14. The Bazar study is based on what legislators report about themselves in legislative directories and other documents. Unlike the Hyneman study, Bazar's work includes all the states. And, of course, many occupations such as "agriculture" may be much more inclusive than "farmer" 50 years ago. Legislators now often identify their occupations as "full-time legislator." This, of course, masks the occupations legislators had before becoming a legislator.

15. Frank M. Bryan argues that although the correlation between ruralism and farmer-legislators is strong, the same cannot be said for urbanism and lawyer-legislators. His analysis reveals some connection between the two, but the correlations are not so strong as to suggest that urbanism and lawyer-legislators go hand in hand. See his *Yankee Politics in Rural Vermont* (Hanover, N.H.: University Press of New England, 1974), pp. 36–42.
16. Malcolm E. Jewell and Samuel C. Patterson, *The Legislative Process in the United States* (2nd ed.) (New York: Random House, 1973), p. 76.
17. Paul L. Hain and James E. Piereson, "Lawyers and Politics Revisited," *American Political Science Review* 19 (1975): 41–45.
18. Wahlke et al., *The Legislative System*, *Explorations in Legislative Behavior*, p. 70. This section draws on the research of Wahlke and his colleagues on legislators in California, New Jersey, Ohio, and Tennessee.
19. Samuel C. Patterson and G. R. Boynton, "Legislative Recruitment in a Civic Culture," *Social Science Quarterly* 50 (1969): 243–263.
20. See Lester G. Seligman et al., *Patterns of Recruitment, A State Chooses Its Lawmakers* (Chicago: Rand McNally, 1974).
21. Jewell and Patterson, *The Legislative Process in the United States*, p. 85.
22. Milton Rakove, *Don't Make No Waves—Don't Back No Losers* (Bloomington: Indiana University Press, 1975), p. 96.
23. Duane Lockhard, "The State Legislatures," in Alexander Heard (ed.), *State Legislatures in American Politics* (Englewood Cliffs, N.J.: Prentice-Hall, 1956), p. 103. Mean turnover percentages in state senates and houses by decade are 1931–40, 50.7 and 58.7; 1941–50, 42.6 and 51.3; 1951–60, 40.2 and 44.8; 1961–70, 37.3 and 41.1; 1971–80, 28.8 and 32.2; 1981–85, 24.1 and 28.0. Richard Niemi and Laura R. Winsky, "Membership Turnover in U.S. State Legislatures: Trends and Effects of Districting," *Legislative Studies Quarterly* 12:1 (1987): 115–123.
24. Alan Rosenthal, "Turnover in State Legislatures," *American Political Science Review* 18 (1974): 606–616. Also see Gary L. Crawley, "Turnover in American State Houses" (Ph.D. diss., Michigan State University, East Lansing, Mich., 1982), and Richard G. Niemi and Laura R. Winsky, "Membership Turnover in U.S. State Legislatures: Trends and Effects of Districting," *Legislative Studies Quarterly* 12 (1987): 115–123.
25. Peverill Squire, "Career Opportunities and Membership Stability in Legislatures," *Legislative Studies Quarterly* 13 (1988): 65–81.
26. David Ray, "Voluntary Retirement and Electoral Defeat in Eight State Legislatures," *Journal of Politics* 38 (1976): 426–433. Also see Jewell and Patterson, *The Legislative Process in the United States*, p. 92.
27. *Illinois Issues Special Report* (Springfield, Ill.: Sangamon State University, 1982), p. 31.
28. Salem, Oreg., *Statesman-Journal*, August 1981.
29. Diane Kincaid and Ann R. Henry, "The Family Factor in State Legislative Turnover," *Legislative Studies Quarterly* (1981): 55–68.
30. Smallwood, *Free and Independent*, p. 80.
31. William J. Keefe and Morris S. Ogul, *The American Legislative Process* (5th ed.) (Englewood Cliffs, N.J.: Prentice-Hall, 1981), p. 54.
32. Gary Keith, "The Killer Bees of the Texas Senate," *Comparative State Politics Newsletter* (October 1979): 13–14.
33. Joel A. Thompson in "Bringing Home the Bacon: The Politics of Pork Barrel in the North Carolina Legislature," *Legislative Studies Quarterly* 11:1 (1986): 91–108, states

that legislative leaders use pork to maintain their leadership positions and enhance party discipline.
34. *Detroit Free Press*, September 17, 1976. Eugene Declerq argues that leadership's formal powers generally are greater in houses than in senates. Leadership strength in senates where lieutenant governors do not preside is stronger than where they do preside. "Interhouse Differences in American State Legislatures," *Journal of Politics* 39 (1977): 774–785.
35. Council of State Governments, *The Book of the States, 1988–89*, p. 124.
36. Keefe and Ogul, *The American Legislative Process*, p. 179.
37. William P. Browne and Delbert J. Ringquist note that legislative committees do most of the work in culling bills to be enacted. "Sponsorship and Enactment: State Lawmakers and Aging Legislation, 1956–1978," *American Politics Quarterly* 13:4 (1985): 447–466.
38. Gilbert Y. Steiner and Samuel K. Gove, "The Influence of Standing Committees in the Illinois Legislature," in Irwin W. Gertzog (ed.), *Readings in State and Local Government* (Englewood Cliffs, N.J.: Prentice-Hall, 1970), pp. 164–183.
39. *Sacramento Bee*, August 29, 1981. Also see John J. Carroll and Arthur English, "Governing the House, Leadership of the State Legislative Party," Paper presented at the Midwest Political Science Association meeting, April 1981.
40. William T. Pound, "The State Legislatures," in *The Book of the States, 1988–89*, p. 80. Also see Albert J. Abrams, "The Legislative Administrator," *Public Administration Review* 35 (1975): 497.
41. Abrams, "The Legislative Administrator," p. 497.
42. James J. Heaphey and Alan P. Balutis, *Legislative Staffing, A Comparative Perspective* (New York: Sage Publications, 1975), p. 26.
43. Keefe and Ogul, *The American Legislative Process*, p. 202.
44. Raymond W. Cox and Michael R. King, "American State Legislatures: Models of Organization and Reform," Paper presented at the meeting of the Midwest Political Science Association, April 1985.
45. Gene Graham, *One Man, One Vote* (Boston: Little, Brown, 1972), p. 11.
46. *Baker v. Carr*, 369 U.S. 186 (1962).
47. *Reynolds v. Sims*, 377 U.S. 533 (1964). In *Avery v. Midland County* (Texas), 390 U.S. 474 (1968), the court ordered county boards to reapportion themselves. H. P. Young argues that the compactness rule should be abandoned. If the rule is to be kept, he says, courts should interpret it in dictionary terms, not by mathematical formulas. See his "Measuring the Compactness of Legislative Districts," *Legislative Studies Quarterly* 13 (1988): 105–115.
48. *Whitcomb v. Chavis*, 403 U.S. 124 (1971).
49. *Gaffney v. Cummings*, 412 U.S. 735 (1973).
50. Malcolm Jewell and David Breaux, however, report that redistricting may affect the number of incumbents seeking reelection but not the margin of victory of incumbents who do run. See "The Effect of Incumbency of State Legislators," *Legislative Studies Quarterly* 13:4 (1988): 495–514.
51. *Sacramento Bee*, August 28, 1981.
52. Gilbert Y. Steiner and Samuel K. Gove argue that legislators see reapportionment as threatening (1) their individual preservation (a "safe district"), (2) mutual preservation (the well-being of a fellow incumbent), (3) political party preservation, and (4) bloc preservation (geographic, economic, or ideological—often bipartisan), in that

order. See *Legislature Redistricts Illinois* (Urbana: Institute of Government and Public Affairs, University of Illinois, 1956), p. 7.
53. See Harry Basehart, "The Political Effects of Legislative Redistricting in the Late 1970s," Paper presented at the Midwest Political Science Association meeting, April 1981.
54. See Howard A. Scarrow, "Partisan Gerrymandering—Invidious or Benevolent?" Paper presented at the Midwest Political Science Association meeting, April 1981.
55. The case considered is *Davis v. Bandemer*, 106 S.Ct. 2797 (1986). Also see "The Supreme Court Prohibits Gerrymandering: A Gain or a Loss for the States?" *Publius* 17:3 (Summer 1987): 101–109.
56. See Brett Hawkins, "Consequences of Reapportionment in Georgia," in Richard I. Offerberg and Ira Sharkansky (eds.), *State and Urban Politics* (Boston: Little, Brown, 1971), pp. 273–298; Thomas R. Dye, "Malapportionment and Public Policy in the States," *Journal of Politics* 27 (1965): 586–601; Richard Hofferbert, "The Relations Between Public Policy and Some Structural and Environmental Variables in the American States," *American Political Science Review* 60 (1966): 73–82; and Herbert Jacob, "The Consequences of Malapportionment, A Note of Caution," *Social Forces* 43 (1964): 256–261.
57. Alvin D. Sokolow, "Legislative Pluralism, Committee Assignments, and Internal Norms, The Delayed Impact of Reapportionment in California," *Annals of the New York Academy of Sciences* (November 1973): 291–313.
58. Douglas W. Rae, "Reapportionment and Political Democracy," in Nelson W. Polsby (ed.), *Reapportionment in the 1970s* (Berkeley: University of California Press, 1971).
59. Timothy O'Rourke, *The Impact of Reapportionment* (New Brunswick, N.J.: Transaction Books, 1980), p. 51.
60. Douglas G. Feig, "The Impact of State Legislative Reapportionment, The Effect of Contextual Factors," Paper presented at the Midwest Political Science Association meeting, April 1981.
61. Bruce W. Roebeck, "Legislative Partisanship, Constituency, and Malapportionment, The Case of California," *American Political Science Review* (December 1972): 1254–1255. Also see Samuel C. Patterson, "American State Legislatures and Public Policy," in Herbert Jacob and Kenneth Vines (eds.), *Politics in the American States* (Boston: Little, Brown, 1976), p. 155.
62. David C. Saffell, "Reapportionment and Public Policy, State Legislators' Perspectives," Paper presented at the Midwest Political Science Association meeting, 1980.
63. Jesse Unruh, "Unicameralism—The Wave of the Future," in Donald G. Herzberg and Alan Rosenthal (eds.), *Strengthening the States, Essays on Legislative Reform* (Garden City, N.Y.: Doubleday, 1972), pp. 87–94.
64. John C. Comer, "The Nebraska Nonpartisan Legislature, An Evaluation," *State and Local Government Review* (September 1980). Also see Comer and James B. Johnson, *Nonpartisanship in the Legislative Process, Essays on the Nebraska Legislature* (Washington, D.C.: University Press of America, 1978).
65. Council of State Governments, *The Book of the States, 1988–89* (Lexington, Ky.): p. 103.
66. Robert F. Sittig, "Nebraska," *Comparative State Politics Newsletter* (January 1981): 8–9.
67. Russell Smith and William Lyons, "Legislative Reform in the American States," *State and Local Government Review* (May 1977): 35–39.

68. Citizens Conference on State Legislatures, *The Sometimes Governments* (New York: Bantam, 1971).
69. Raymond W. Cox and Michael R. King, "American State Legislatures: Models of Organization and Reform," Paper presented at the Midwest Political Science Association meeting, 1985.
70. Some of the studies are Leonard G. Ritt, "State Legislative Reform: Does It Matter?" *American Politics Quarterly* 1 (1973): 499–511; Albert K. Karnig and Lee Sigelman, "State Legislative Reform and Public Policy: Another Look," *Western Political Quarterly* 28 (1975): 548–553; Samuel K. Gove, "The Implications of Legislative Reform in Illinois," in Susan Welch and John Peters (eds.), *Legislative Reform and Public Policy* (New York: Praeger Publishers, 1977).
71. Joel A. Thompson, "State Legislative Reform: Another Look, One More Time, Again," *Polity* 19 (1986/87): 27–41.

Chapter 9

Governors as State Leaders

At 7:45 A.M. state troopers usher Governor and Mrs. "Smith" into a shiny black Cadillac. The trip to the capitol is one they have taken many times. This, though, is the last. It is inauguration day!

Smith is leaving office at his own choice, but it is still a rather sad day. He may go on to other successes, perhaps to a job in Washington, a judgeship, or a prestigious law firm. But this is an ending of something very special.

The last few months have been busy. He had many bills to approve and a few to veto. He wrote notes of thanks to officials he had come to know well, and made telephone calls to help assistants find new jobs. Finally, mementos and personal documents had to be sorted, packed, and labeled for shipping—some to the homestead and the rest to the state university library. As the Smiths ride to the capitol, they sense the "perks" will soon be gone.

For "Jones," the incoming governor, the situation is different. It is a beginning, a time of excitement! Winning the election was exhilarating, but now it all begins for real.

Preparing a New Administration   These last weeks have been busy for Jones as well. He attended the National Governors' Association meeting where outgoing governors share their sage and not-so-sage advice with those about to take office.[1] Getting the right staff was more difficult than he had thought. Easily made campaign promises must now be worked into a program during tight financial times.

The handbook for new governors provides a ready checklist of problems to keep tabs on during the transition. But there are rumors and gossip about possible staff as well as speculative stories in the media. These have made matters more confusing.[2]

Inauguration day is a time of celebration. The bright sunshine on the crisp January day looks like a lucky sign.[3] Standing on the platform in front of the capitol with Governor-elect Jones and his family are others for whom it is also inauguration day—the attorney general, the secretary of state, the lieutenant governor, and supreme court justices. The chief justice of the state supreme court administers the oath on the Jones family Bible. As the ceremonies proceed, photographers, professional and amateur, jockey for the best angle.

The Smiths listen politely to the inauguration speech, congratulate each of the new officials, and then quietly slip out the side door. The reality of their new status is almost overwhelming. The state police drivers are not waiting. The ex-governor and his wife smile gamely as they wonder if they should walk or call a cab.[4] That people probably will continue to call him "Governor" for the rest of his life is little consolation.

Is the experience of governors Smith and Jones typical? Yes and no. No doubt most governors leave office with mixed feelings. And most would sense deeply the change in status. But not all, of course, would have transportation problems.[5]

Governorships: The End of a Political Career?   Being governor is memorable. For most, the governorship will be the last political office they hold.[6] A few, such as Jimmy Carter (Ga., 1971–1975) and Ronald Reagan (Calif., 1967–1975), went on to become president. Some were presidential candidates and lost the election. Terry Sanford (N.C., 1961–1965), who also later was elected U.S. senator, became a university president as did Lamar Alexander (Tenn., 1983–1987). Montana's Ted Schwinden (1981–1989), in 1989, became a "distinguished professor in public affairs" at Carroll College in Helena. Others have taken part-time positions as directors of corporate boards of philanthropic foundations.

A few have also ended in tragedy. William Marland, at age 34, was West Virginia's youngest governor (1953–1957). He became an alcoholic and ended up as a Chicago cabbie and skid row bum. Several other governors in the past have

resigned under pressure of impeachment or criminal investigation
removed by state supreme courts. A few have also left the governor's
a jail cell for their misdeeds.

Overview In this chapter we ask first who gets to be governor and consider whether personal characteristics, such as political experience, wealth, occupation, race, or sex, make a difference. Then we discuss how the office developed. Later, we examine the various arenas in which governors exercise leadership.

The Challenge of Being Governor Control of the office is power—power to do something. As most of us would, newly elected governors want to leave a mark, something about which they can later be proud. The challenge they face is one of giving direction, defining what they believe is in the public interest, and building popular support for their ideas.

A bit of apprehension may also creep in. Norton Long noted that in most organizations a new recruit "is taught by superiors and equals." But governors, once on the job, are taught mostly by their own aides, staff of the outgoing governor, or civil servants—"inferiors and those doubtfully loyal."[7]

Some may be challenged, others apprehensive, and a handful may not have been cautious enough and gotten themselves in difficulty early in their term. In 1987, for example, a recall effort began even before Evan Mecham of Arizona took office. Within several months enough signatures were obtained for a referendum. Meanwhile, however, a grand jury indicted him on campaign finance violations. By May of 1988 he had been impeached by the Arizona house and convicted by the state senate. Mecham was the eighteenth governor to be impeached and the eighth one convicted. In 1921 Lynn Frazier of North Dakota became the only governor ever to have been recalled from office.[8]

WHO GETS TO BE GOVERNOR?

Who in your state would you consider a candidate for governor the next time around? You will be impressed, we think, by how small the pool is. Whether your state is large or small, the number of likely candidates will probably not exceed a half-dozen for each party—fewer if the present governor wants to be reelected. In the 1986 Florida and Alaska elections, however, 19 and 13 candidates, respectively, offered their services. However, only a few of these could be considered serious candidates.[9]

Most potential candidates are already in politics. Less than 10 percent of the 995 governors between 1870 and 1950 moved directly from private life into the governor's suite.[10] Only rarely do candidates whom party leaders regard as having little chance catch on—as, for example, Governor Dixy Lee Ray (1977–1980) did in the state of Washington. Why do politicians require gubernatorial candidates to serve an apprenticeship in public office?

Name Recognition Political experience works for would-be governors much as experience does in nongovernmental organizations. At college, for example, a first-year student has virtually no chance of being elected student council president. It is not wholly a question of ability. First-year students simply have not done enough to be well known.

Officeholding helps build **name recognition**, widespread familiarity by citizens with the politician's persona. It is the lifeblood of a political career, and the reason officeholders seldom pass up an opportunity to get their name in the news. Myra McPherson says, "For politicians there is no such thing as indecent exposure. People who hold public office are as dependent on the voter as a heart attack victim is on oxygen."[11]

Political novices begin further behind and have fewer opportunities to break into the news.[12] Even political careerists must do things to get ink and so establish themselves in the public eye. Governor Bob Graham (Fla., 1978–1986), for example, during his campaigns worked at various jobs to show how he identified with "working people." Local television stations thought the visuals were great and gave Graham lots of free exposure.

And although only an occasional speaker may introduce a candidate as "the spouse of . . . ," having a famous wife or husband may help too. We suspect that Phyllis George-Brown, a television personality and former Miss America, helped her husband, John Y. Brown, Jr., who was known as a fried chicken magnate but was a political neophyte, win the Kentucky governorship in 1979. Her fame, however, was not enough to overcome the forces of millionaire Wallace Wilkinson in the 1987 Democratic primary as Brown sought to make a comeback after taking a term off, as Kentucky's constitution mandates.

Candidates may also gain name recognition by being members of a political family. In 1988 Evan Bayh gained the governorship at the age of 32 after having been elected secretary of state in Indiana. His father had served in the U.S. Senate.

Expectations of Others People also speculate that well-known officeholders plan to run for governor. The press corps generates and spreads such rumors, especially on slow news days. It may be all the encouragement a legislative leader needs. Those who wish can easily stifle the talk with a firm denial. Thus the frequent mention of a name usually continues with the would-be candidate's approval. Political novices who announce plans to run face the reverse problem—reporters often fail to take them seriously.

Access to Political Tools Holding office also allows access to the **tools of politics**. Successful politicians learn how to handle hostile questions, relate to complex statewide constituencies, use the media effectively, and develop skills in recruiting and using campaign staffs. In addition, current officeholders usually have a better chance of raising the vast sums of money needed to run a statewide campaign. All candidates in 36 gubernatorial races of 1986 spent more than $254 million; winners spent 41 percent of the total.[13]

Political experience is not the only way to gain political skills. The subtleties are such, though, that the novice is at a marked disadvantage. Through books or videotapes, a person can learn how the basketball jump shot should be made or how to judge a fly ball in the outfield. But political candidates, like most successful athletes, become stars through constant practice and play under game conditions.

Predictability Office experience also helps those on the political scene to judge the way the politician will probably act if elected.[14] Predicting behavior or decisions of the political novice or maverick, such as Governor Mecham, is much more difficult. Insiders, if not others, see them as risky. Who knows who their advisors will be, what policies they may pursue, or whether they will be embarrassing to the party?

Which Experiences Are Best?

During a 100-year period, the 1,300 governors held a variety of public offices before moving into the executive suite. In Table 9.1 we review the major **career paths**, the positions through which a person moves in building a career.

Legislative Experience About half of the governors since 1870 were once state legislators. This should not be surprising—legislators constitute the largest pool of political talent in a state. But legislative office as a stepping-stone has varied over time, as Figure 9.1 shows. Between 1930 and 1960, the governors with legislative experience ranged from 40 to 60 percent. Half of the 1989 governors served in their state's legislature.[15]

Why is legislative experience helpful? Governor Rubin Askew (Fla., 1971–1979) explained it this way: "A person with a legislative background . . . will feel much more confident early on in his administration because he understands the legislative process and knows the key leaders."[16] And, of course, moving from a legislative leadership position to the governorship is even more beneficial, especially if the governor's party controls the legislature.

Statewide Elective Office Lieutenant governorships are the best statewide office to reach the governor's chair. But other statewide elective officers such as secretary of state, attorney general, treasurer, and auditor have made it too.

The 42 lieutenant governors have a big advantage over most others—they automatically become governor when the governorship becomes vacant. Secretaries of state in three states are next in the line of succession and have a similar advantage. Since 1950 about 20 percent of the governors first took office when an incumbent resigned or died. The turnover rate for governors is fairly high because presidents sometimes appoint them to national positions. Also, some governors resign to become U.S. senators, as Wendell Anderson (Minn., 1971–1977) did.[17] Nine of the 1989 governors served as lieutenant governor.

Law Enforcement Positions such as attorney general, district attorney, or judge have been good stepping-stones. Schlesinger speculates that in frontier communities, where maintaining law and order was especially important, law officers often caught the public eye, sometimes as the result of dramatic incidents.

Table 9.1 PATHWAYS TO THE GOVERNORSHIP

Offices	Percentage with this experience		Percentage with this as end office[a]	
	1870–1950	1950–1977	1870–1950	1950–1970
State legislature	52.4	48.9	20.1	24.8
Law enforcement	32.1	25.5	20.1	16.3
Administration	29.3	9.2	13.7	7.4
Local elective	19.8	14.9	7.4	9.6
Statewide elective	18.9	22.3	15.8	19.9
Federal elective	13.9	9.9	11.3	8.2
Other,[b] none	8.8	23.4	15.4	14.9

Offices	Percentage with this as first office		Percentage with this as only office	
	1870–1950	1950–1977	1870–1950	1950–1970
State legislature	31.4	38.7	13.1	20.2
Law enforcement	20.1	19.5	8.5	9.6
Administration	16.8	7.1	5.8	6.0
Local elective	11.9	10.3	3.5	5.7
Statewide elective	2.1	5.7	2.1	3.5
Federal elective	2.6	2.8	2.5	2.1
Other,[b] none	15.1	15.9	8.8	11.7

Source: The 1870–1950 data are from Joseph A. Schlesinger, *How They Became Governor,* (East Lansing: Governmental Research Bureau, Michigan State University, 1957), pp. 51 and 81. Jamie D. Eaker assembled the 1950–1977 data. "Becoming Governor," *Comparative State Politics Newsletter* 3 (Department of Political Science, University of Kentucky, Lexington) (February 1983): 18.

[a] "End office" refers to the last office held before becoming governor.

[b] Includes presidential electors, constitutional convention delegates, governors' councilors, and confederate officials.

More recently, urban constituencies have catapulted prosecutors into the executive office. James R. Thompson (1976–1990), as U.S. Attorney for northern Illinois, successfully prosecuted former Illinois governor Otto W. Kerner (1961–1968) and indicted 350 other public officials. Ten of the 1989 governors had law enforcement experience.

Only occasionally does a judge leave the bench to run for governor. Charles Terry (Del., 1965–1969) did so. Only one of the 1989 governors reported having had judicial experience.

Other Patterns Schlesinger identified a few other categories of career paths of governors, none as important as those already mentioned.

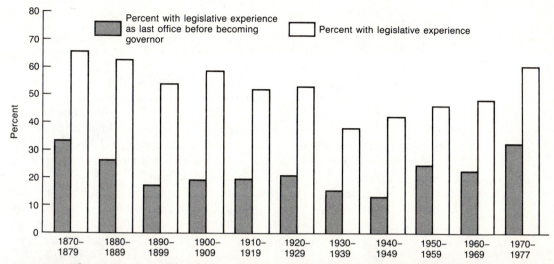

Figure 9.1 The importance of legislative experience in becoming governor, 1870–1977. [*Sources*: J. A. Schlesinger, *How They Became Governor* (East Lansing: Governmental Research Bureau, Michigan State University, 1957), pp. 51 and 81; J. D. Eaker, "Becoming Governor," *Comparative State Politics Newsletter* 3:1 (February 1982): 18.]

Member of Congress The U.S. House of Representatives produced 112 governors from 1870 to 1950. Of the 1989 governors, six served in the House of Representatives and one in the U.S. Senate.

The desire to be a head of government rather than one of 435 representatives may account for some of these moves. Reapportionment of congressional districts may also contribute. In 1982, for example, Michigan representative James Blanchard (1983–) bid for the governorship in a move to ease his party's dilemma when the state lost a congressional seat.

Local Government Experience Local elective office such as city council or school board may be a first stepping-stone, but it is seldom a direct springboard to the governor's chair. However, Governor Neil Goldschmidt (Oreg., 1987–) became the nation's youngest mayor when elected mayor of Portland in 1972. Governor Bob Martinez (Fla., 1987–) made the jump to governor from his position as mayor of Tampa. Jimmy Carter "paid his dues" as a member of the Sumter County school board prior to being elected state senator and, from there, governor of Georgia, and later, of course, president. Eight of the 1989 governors had had some local government experience.

Social and Economic Background

People who run for governor are trying to make one of the big jumps in politics. Campaigns are not something one can manage personally with bumper stickers and the help of a few friends. In most states a candidate faces a complex constituency that she or he can reach only through the media and the help of many strangers.

Can everyone make this jump? In this section we discuss how wealth, social and economic status, as well as race and sex affect the chances of getting into the major leagues.

Wealth   You do not have to be a millionaire to make a good race, although several governors have been. As a practical matter, though, you do not have much chance if you have to worry about whether you will be able to meet next month's rent. Wealth provides the advantage of carrying a candidate through the lean and lonely times before the primary election when money is difficult to raise. Even though several states now provide public campaign funds, candidates must raise money in order to qualify for state campaign dollars.

Money also provides staying power—to come back after defeat. John D. Rockefeller IV came to West Virginia in 1964 as an antipoverty worker. He ran against Governor Arch A. Moore, Jr. (1969–1977, 1985–1989), in the 1972 election and lost. But in 1976 "Jay" Rockefeller could afford to try again. That time he won.

Occupation and Education   If you are choosing a career to help you realize your hopes to become governor, we suggest you go to law school or seek a career in business. Of the governors from 1950 to 1973, 82.5 percent had one of those backgrounds.[18] In 1989 it was not much different—23 were lawyers and 14 had business careers.

And from what the governors of 1989 report about themselves, we also advise you to finish college. All but five said they had attended college—41 had a college degree, 10 had master's degrees, and 2 had doctorates.[19]

Ethnic Origins, Race, and Sex   Ethnic groups are not sufficiently important in most states to require absolutely that a candidate be of the dominant group.[20] Still, having the proper old-world parentage may provide the critical edge, especially in close elections. Scandinavian origin in Minnesota will be no handicap. Nor will Italian in Rhode Island. Martinez, for example, found his Spanish surname helpful in Florida, as have other Hispanics in Arizona and New Mexico. George Ariyoshi (1975–1986) found his Japanese parentage beneficial in Hawaii.

Women and Governorships   For most of our nation's history, parents dreamed that their sons would grow up to be president or governor. Now parents can have this dream for their daughters as well. Not many women have been governor but the number is growing. The first three—Nellie Tayloe Ross of Wyoming, Miriam "Ma" Ferguson of Texas (in the 1920s), and Lurleen Wallace (in the 1960s) succeeded their husbands in office. But Ella Grasso (Conn., 1975–1980) and Dixy Lee Ray (Wash., 1977–1980) won elections outright. Since then other women have been elected governor: Martha Layne Collins (Ky., 1984–1987), Madeleine M. Kunin (Vt., 1987–1990), Kay A. Orr (Nebr., 1987–). Betty Hearns, whose husband had been governor 20 years earlier, lost a race for governor of Missouri. Rose Mofford became governor of Arizona in 1988 after Evan

Mecham was impeached.[21] More women governors can be expected because, like blacks, women now also increasingly occupy stepping-stone offices.

Blacks and Governorships The first black American to be elected governor of a state was Doug Wilder (1990–) of Virginia. Increasingly, blacks are beginning to occupy some of the most politically desirable stepping-stone offices—legislative leadership seats and statewide offices. (Wilder had been lieutenant governor.) Two other blacks, Thomas Bradley, mayor of Los Angeles, and William Lucas, Wayne County (Detroit) executive, were their party's gubernatorial candidates in the 1980s prior to Wilder breaking this barrier. Blacks, like women, still face many more hurdles than white males, but the obstacles are no longer in the "unthinkable" category.

Character or Image Building The qualities we have noted are shorthand symbols that can be used to appeal to the politically conscious sectors of a state. Note how little we have stressed stands on the issues. And even though these positions can contribute to image, we view them as secondary to what the electorate regards as "basic character" and what public relations firms call **image building**. Issues, then, are not irrelevant but at best are a way of projecting "character" traits.

When newspapers and radio were the principal means of reaching the public, candidates depended largely on what the writers and broadcasters said about them. Today candidates with these television and videocassette skills can appeal directly to voters. These place an added emphasis on personal appearance. They are advised that their hair and dress style be fashionable, but not avant-garde. Men should be tall but not awkward, and body weight should be well proportioned. The smile is easy and toothy. Moreover, would-be governors usually project an energetic image, such as Dixy Lee Ray, who prided herself on the kinds of vehicles she piloted—an oil supertanker, sports cars, a hot air balloon, and so forth.

Citizens also often look for a candidate's ability to inspire confidence. This calls for a kind of self-discipline—leaders must be able to control their emotions, showing anger without "blowing up," being sympathetic and sensitive without appearing to "fall apart," and being articulate and decisive without appearing "rash and hasty."

Placed in the hands of public relations specialists, these qualities can be skillfully manipulated to construct a winning political image. We should not become so cynical, though, as to forget that the governors may be projecting what are genuine traits.

THE LEGAL FRAMEWORK FOR GUBERNATORIAL LEADERSHIP

An Indiana humorist once observed, "We've had the same governor for fifty years—only the name and looks change every four years." He implied, of course, that it makes no difference who occupies the executive office. We do not agree. In our system of government, the office becomes the center of political leadership. Some governors seize the opportunity and lead vigorously; others do little. The legal powers of the office also help or hinder what leadership abilities a governor may have.

During the colonial period Americans were suspicious of governors. The king of England appointed most colonial governors and gave them substantial legal power. The king's governors appointed the top administrative and judicial officers who, together, formed the upper house in the colonial legislatures. Governors could convene and dissolve the lower house and refuse to sign bills they passed. The settlers, though, had some bargaining power, in that the governors depended on local taxes for their revenue. But through it all, colonists used them as handy local targets to demonstrate their hostility toward the king.

Early State Governors When the colonists formed state governments, we might have expected them to do away with governors altogether. What saved the executive office was primarily the ineptness of the Continental Congress, a generally ineffective national government which had no executive officer. The colonists agreed on the need for governors, but were determined to keep them under close control—as one student put it, "wholly and irresponsibly subservient to the legislative will."[22]

In Virginia, for example, the legislature elected the governor annually. No person could serve more than three years in a row. The governor could not convene or dissolve the legislature, recommend bills, or veto legislation. In addition, an eight-member council had to approve all administrative actions.

Governors and Jacksonian Democracy The 1820s were years of "discontent, born in depression, shaken by bursts of violence and threats of rebellion."[23] In 1828 a new American hero, Andrew Jackson, became president. A new political truth emerged that changed ideas about the worth of common people—**Jacksonian democracy.** The new philosophy advocated frequent elections of numerous officials and divided power and patronage appointments in the bureaucracy.

The impact of this philosophy on the office of governor was mixed. State after state changed the method for choosing their governors—from election by the legislature to election by the people. Some states even gave their governors the veto power; some made it more difficult for legislatures to impeach their governors.

But Jacksonian ideals also weakened governors by dividing the executive powers among many elected state officials and boards. Leslie Lipson, who studied the American governor in the 1930s, assessed the effect of Jacksonianism this way: "The new maxim of Jacksonian democracy seemed to be, 'Divide your government and it cannot rule you.' In actual fact, the result was to cripple the executive. The chief executive was unable to harm the people, but it was also unable to serve them."[24]

Throughout the nineteenth century the governor's legal powers remained limited. With the growth of cities, each new group demanded protection from and regulation of "the interests." Legislatures responded each time by creating numerous independent executive agencies, thus further weakening the office of governor.

The Twentieth Century—Expanded Legal Powers for Governors

During the 15 years or so before the turn of the century, reformers began arguing that executive officers—governors and mayors—must be strengthened. They proposed new powers for executives so they could clean up what they saw as political corruption and inefficiency.

Corporate business organizations provided the model. Managerial efficiency became the reformers' goal. The Short Ballot and Scientific Management movements advocated removing the shackles on the executives and expanding their **legal powers.**

Administrative Powers The reformers proposed centralizing administrative agencies into a hierarchy controlled at the top by the governor. The number of departments would be of manageable size—say 20 or so, rather than the 100 or more independent agencies then existing.

Many students agree that these changes strengthened the governor's administrative control. But the changes did not produce all the efficiencies that the reformers had hoped for. Reorganization reduced the influence and meddling of the legislature in day-to-day administration, but it did not eliminate it.[25] We discuss the limits of reorganization further in Chapter 10.

Appointment and Removal Powers Short Ballot reformers wanted fewer elected officials and began a process that still continues. But in only two states, Maine and New Jersey, is the governor the only statewide elected official. Most states also elect the lieutenant governor, secretary of state, attorney general, and state treasurer. Legislatures now rarely appoint any administrators, although they or their committees play a role in approving gubernatorial appointees.

But even governors with broad **appointing powers** cannot gain immediate control over all of a state's boards and commissions. They usually must serve a second term before their appointees gain control because many appointees have overlapping terms. And there are limits on a governor's **powers to remove** appointed officials. Some limits are legal, others political. Removal proceedings may produce messy publicity. Forcing the unwanted person to resign can create an undesirable political backlash.

Office Tenure By 1920 most governors had a two-year term. And in 1990 only three (N.H., R.I., and Vt.) did not have four-year terms. Most of the extensions took place after 1960.

Most students agree that **office tenure** or the potential for reelection adds to a governor's power, because legislators, administrators, and others are less likely to defy a governor who serves four years and is eligible for additional terms.[26] Twenty-one states do not restrict the number of terms a person may serve.[27] Most others limit a person to two consecutive terms. Kentucky and Virginia governors are not permitted consecutive terms.

Lawmaking Powers Governors need to persuade legislators to enact their programs. The formal powers of the governor in the legislative process are critical to the overall effectiveness of a governor. Of particular note in influencing the legislative agenda are the governor's **powers to recommend** legislation, veto, call legislatures into session, and develop the executive budget.

Legal Powers in Perspective

The legal powers a governor needs depend on the social, economic, and political milieu in which he or she competes for power and influence. In large urbanized states, such as Texas or California, dominant interest groups have great resources of power. Governors of these states must have them too, if they are to merely hold their own. Governors of less urban states, such as South Dakota, may be able to compete with a lesser arsenal of legal powers. But in most states, gubernatorial powers are increasing.[28]

And although the legal powers are important, they alone cannot account for all the differences between "successful" and "average" governorships. Woodrow Wilson and "Teddy" Roosevelt were effective governors even though they lacked many of the legal advantages of modern governors. What made their governorships stand out? We think their ability to lead goes a long way toward answering this question.

EXERCISING GUBERNATORIAL LEADERSHIP

The job of governor consists mainly in giving direction to a state. Most citizens want one thing above all else from the governor—leadership.

Most of us know people with leadership ability. But we may have difficulty stating exactly why one person is a leader and another is not. A central element of **political leadership** is the ability to define situations and propose policy responses in ways we citizens see as being appropriate.[29] Officeholders with less insight may stick with old solutions that do not work under new conditions or be seen as being so far ahead of popular opinion as to gain a derogatory nickname—"Governor Moonbeam," as Jerry Brown did in California, or "Governor Goofy," as some people called Rudy Perpich of Minnesota (1976–1979, 1983–). Governors must define the serious problems, propose solutions, and then marshal support for their policies. They must also create a belief that their answers represent workable solutions.

Community officials, business leaders, and ordinary citizens look to the governor to harness the political, economic, and social resources of the state and provide a sense of purpose and direction. When they succeed, governors—more than any other state official—encourage a sense of trust in state government and in its legitimacy. When governors fail, the result is often disappointment and cynicism.

Governors Set Goals

Governors can do very little other than lead and give direction. They cannot pass laws, run departments, know all the details of a state budget, or create a healthy economy. They can only intervene periodically to emphasize what they think needs to be done.

Governors know they need to build a record of achievement quickly because the power of the office is transitory.[30] Building a record by having made important differences in a few areas may provide the basis for reelection or future public office, even that of vice president or president.[31]

Achievement depends on the ability to set a tone for the administration, one that responds to what the governor sees as the needs of the day. Al Smith of New York (1919–1921, 1923–1929) is remembered for having insisted that government show concern for the disadvantaged.[32] As governor of California, Ronald Reagan opposed big government spending. Other governors have promised to "attract new industry and create jobs, jobs, jobs."

Leadership in Public Opinion

As the president personifies the national government, so governors symbolize their state governments. As such, governors command the attention of the media and politically conscious individuals in the state. Is it important that the public be convinced? Cannot governors simply make their proposals to the legislature and work quietly in the statehouse, twisting arms to gain votes for their policies? That is needed, but public opinion and support is the fuel that powers the governor's policy-making clout with legislators. Some governors spend one-fourth or more of their time seeking to shape public opinion.[33]

Relating to News Media People Governors are keenly aware that they can reach most citizens only through the media. Governors thus may hold daily news conferences, provide time for in-depth interviews, give photo opportunities, respond to reporters' telephone questions, and appear on interview shows or even popular radio talk shows.

They cultivate relations with the capitol press corps. They entertain reporters and their spouses as a group and make special efforts to know reporters on a first-name basis.[34]

The Governor's Press Secretary The governor's press secretary is one of the most important positions on the governor's staff. This assistant often serves as the governor's alter ego. Governor G. Mennen Williams (Mich., 1948–1960) wrote, "My press secretary was no small part of my brain. . . . He developed my ideas as I would have liked to do if I had had the time."[35] Out of public view, staffers write press releases for every occasion and help to stage many of the public appearances.

Relating Directly to the Public Invitations to speak are numerous. The governor's staff culls through them carefully to choose those that will result in political support for the governor's programs. Such engagements reach only a small part of the state's people at one time. Yet many people get to see the governor in this way. Moreover, the media report such events and keep the governor in the public eye.

Governors also build public goodwill in honoring various groups by declaring special weeks or days—such as Iowa Garden Club Week or Arkansas Rabbit Breeders' Week. Governor Bill Clinton issued more than 400 such proclamations in 1985.[36] Typically, the honor comes at the group's request—often the group itself prepares the proclamation. Such actions may have policy implications, and governors must take care to avoid lending their names to a group that may prove embarrassing.

Governor Rudy Perpich encountered such a problem. An opera society, as part of a fund-raiser, asked to auction off a dinner in the governor's mansion. The governor agreed. Minneapolis's best known "madam" won the bid. For too long, she told reporters, prostitution has been regarded as not quite respectable. Gamely and gracefully, Governor Perpich and his wife, with flashbulbs popping, greeted their guest as she arrived at the promised meal.[37]

Governors tape messages in support of the United Way, fund drives for crippled children, and other charities. They greet touring schoolchildren and send out hundreds of greeting cards to people celebrating birthdays and golden wedding anniversaries.

Governors also get lots of mail of all kinds—a request for a job for a disabled family member, a citizen's complaint about a state car going over the speed limit, the ineptness of a local officeholder, or an appeal for a release from prison. All of the letters are answered.

Why Public Opinion Is Important Why do governors spend so much time on public relations? First, as "governor of all the people," they permit themselves to be seen as "head of government." Much of this activity is nonpartisan and helps build a public sense of trust and confidence—a reservoir of goodwill for political battles with the legislature. Legislators rank the ability to marshal such support next to budget-making as the governor's most important power.[38]

Second, public relations work is educational, or propagandist, depending on your point of view. Governors explain why the state is building new prisons, why the voters should support state lotteries, or why the state cannot increase aid to local governments.

Third, journalists may not only get the governor's messages out, but they reflect citizen opinions to the governor as well. Public opinion surveys are another important source of feedback and give the governor a sense of how citizens are judging him or her.[39]

At the same time, extensive exposure may have a downside. Diane Blair observes that because many people may know the name of the governor but little else about state government, high visibility may cause people to blame the governor for high taxes and other unpopular state programs. In addition, she notes, in the "highly personalized nature of Arkansas politics, the governor cannot possibly give of his personal time to all those who feel entitled to it."[40]

Leadership in the Legislature

Governors make or break their record of achievement in their legislatures. Governors may set policy goals, make promises, and propose ways to solve problems. But if they cannot persuade the legislature to act favorably, the goals go unmet and the promises unfilled. Governors have important legal tools and informal powers to help them get their way in the legislatures.

The Power to Recommend State governments are not much given to ceremony. But each year when the governor presents the State of the State speech, they do engage in a bit of pomp and circumstance. No bands, mind you, but legislators wear carnations or corsages. And legislative leaders make a show of escorting the governor and supreme court justices to the podium in the lower chamber. Usually the galleries are packed with bureaucrats and lobbyists, all waiting to see if the governor will mention their pet project. And reporters, who got advance copies of the speech, occupy themselves by counting the times the governor is interrupted with applause. And now dozens of television cameras send the speech across the state—some stations carry it live, others by tape delay.

The governor's friends tell reporters that the speech was "Great! Creative! Imaginative!" Political opponents invariably say, "It's about what we expected" or, "We'll wait until we see the specifics." The details come later in the form of special messages and bills the governor's allies introduce.

Importance of Recommending Is the recommending power worth anything? Many political scientists think it is worth a great deal. With it governors tell the legislature what they want on the agenda. Second, with good timing and public relations, the governor can strongly influence the legislative schedule. Third, the governor may put the legislature in a defensive position. If legislators do not act, they have to explain why.

Lobbying the Legislature Governors next exercise a great deal of follow-through on their proposals. Legislative lobbying—from friendly contacts to intensive pressure—is now an expected part of the governor's role.

Choosing legislative leaders and committee chairs may be the first matter the governor tries to influence. The governor wants legislative leaders who will cooperate easily and have similar views. But trying to influence these selections is a delicate matter even when the governor and the legislative majority are of the same party. When they are of opposing parties or factions, the governor may have little or no influence.

Typically, governors try to develop friendly relations with the members of both parties. Such friendship is built on a composite of many small actions. The governor may invite sponsors to the "front office" for a bill-signing ceremony (which may get printed in the legislator's hometown newspaper). Or a governor may publicly compliment a legislator, meet with legislators to discuss local problems, check with legislators about nominations for positions, or appoint to state boards or other jobs people a legislator suggests. Governors have perquisites they can share. And they share them purposively.

But legislative lobbying involves more. It is a matter of communicating with legislators on the governor's bills. The governor's **legislative liaison** speaks for the governor, negotiates the difficult problems, offers assistance of the executive departments when required, and may even occasionally threaten if the legislator "doesn't come around" on the big votes. This person is largely responsible for getting the governor's key programs through the legislature.

Do governors engage in such matters personally? Sometimes they attend party caucuses, but rarely do they appear in the legislative chambers. In 1982, though, Governor William Milliken (Mich., 1969–1983) spent virtually an entire night in the house persuading representatives to pass an increase in the state income tax. The governor even went to a nearby hotel to awaken a legislator who had turned in for the night. We also find governors using the time-tested technique of visiting with legislators, one on one, in the executive suite.

Calling Special Sessions In many states, legislative reforms have weakened the power to call **special sessions**—limited purpose meetings of the legislature. They determine the time and at least the priority agenda items. Full-time legislatures with annual sessions eliminate or reduce the opportunities to call special sessions. Many legislatures have the legal power to add matters to the agenda of a special session—a rule that makes such sessions less attractive to governors.

Still, governors exercise their role as chief legislator and call special sessions. Washington's Booth Gardner (1985–), for example, called two one-day special sessions to deal with a state supreme court decision that ruled a business tax unconstitutional and to create a chemical and toxic substances cleanup fund. Governor Michael Hayden (1987–) of Kansas was not so lucky. He called the first special session in 20 years to adopt a road and bridge improvement program and the taxes to pay for it. The governor's special task force, apparently, did not convince legislators and citizens that the program was necessary.[41]

The Veto Governor Otto Kerner of Illinois called the veto the "most direct and important of a governor's legislative powers."[42] It can be a formidable weapon. The **veto** is the governor's authority to reject a bill the legislature passes. Vetoed bills sometimes go back to the legislature for an override vote. The vote fails unless an **extraordinary majority** in both houses—usually two-thirds—favors the override.

Overriding Vetoes Most of the time, the governors' vetoes stand up very well. During the 1986–1987 sessions, for example, legislatures were able to override only 2.2 percent. But the level varies by state. In 1986 Illinois's governor James Thompson vetoed 254 measures but had 29, or 11.4 percent, overridden, and Nebraska's one-house legislature overrode 42.8 percent (6 of 14 vetoes) by Governor Kay Orr.

These are exceptions. Most legislatures must produce a two-thirds vote to override, and few state legislatures are "veto-proof"—most governors have enough legislative allies to deny the required extraordinary majority. Thus a vetoed bill is usually a dead bill. That gives governors bargaining power.

The veto, of course, works mainly to kill unwanted bills. But through skillful politicking, governors also encourage legislators to write a bill the way the governor favors. Governors differ in how they use this power. During 1986–1987, for example, of the 46,253 bills adopted by state legislatures, governors vetoed about 7.7 percent, or 3,582. But more than one-third of the vetoes occurred in five states (California, Illinois, Maryland, New York, and Rhode Island) that had 25 percent of the enacted bills. By contrast, five other urban states (Florida, Michigan, Massachusetts, Pennsylvania, and Wisconsin) passed 5.5 percent of the bills and had only 1.5 percent of the vetoes. What explains these wide variations?

Some governors use a "gun behind the door" approach—they threaten to veto specific bills. These, of course, do not register on the governor's veto score sheet but may be as significant as an actual veto. Tennessee Governor Ned McWhirter, for instance, vetoed only one bill in two years. He follows the strategy of asking the legislature to recall bills to which he objects. If changes are not made the bill is likely to languish and die.[43]

High veto rates tend to show bitter political conflict between the legislature and governor. Usually veto rates are lower in states where one party controls both branches or where the governor and legislature work closely together even though they do not agree on some important issues.[44]

The Item Veto As president, both Ronald Reagan and George Bush frequently urged Congress to give the president of the United States the power "42 governors have —the line **item veto**." This is the authority to veto individual lines in an appropriations bill. Thus, whereas the president and eight governors must take "all or nothing," most governors can cut out objectionable expenditures while letting the rest of the bill become law.

The governors of ten states can also reduce appropriations by item veto. This power may not be very helpful to a governor who thinks the legislature is too tight fisted. But does it make the governor a virtual gatekeeper of state funds as former President Reagan implied?

One study shows use of the item veto varying greatly by state. Several respondents said their legislatures wrote appropriations bills to make them "veto proof"—legislators combine into one line the items the governor likes with those he opposes. The study data also suggest that the item veto tends to discourage legislative discipline because legislators can depend on the governor to veto "district-oriented pork barrel" appropriations.[45] A study of the item veto in Wisconsin also suggests that it has been used as a tool for policy choice and partisan advantage and less so for fiscal restraint.[46]

Executive Amendment Seven states have added another wrinkle to the veto power by giving their governors a kind of partial veto or **executive amendment**. These governors may return a bill to the legislature with an outline of objections. The legislature may change the criticized sections but no others. What the governors suggest is usually adopted. If not, the bill becomes law or dies as the governor decides. Governors in other states sometimes use this procedure on an informal basis.

Leadership over State Finances

The **executive budget**—one of the principal managerial or efficiency reforms—gave governors the responsibility to propose financial plans—revenues and expenditures—for the next fiscal year and the responsibility to administer the budget once the legislature approves it. Many see this as the governor's most important executive tool.[47]

It does not give governors complete control over state revenue and spending plans, of course—the legislature must still approve the budget. But legislatures tend not to stray far from the governor's budget recommendations because in many states, if they appropriate funds in excess of a governor's plan, the governors can use the item veto.[48] And if legislators appropriate much less, the interest groups lobby hard for "at least what the governor recommended."

This picture may be changing. Many legislatures now have their own fiscal staff to develop independent revenue forecasts and set general overall spending limits. This legislative reform has strengthened considerably the legislatures' hand in the budget process while reducing somewhat the governor's budgetary power.[49] In Chapter 10 we discuss the framework for budgeting as a means of controlling administrators.

Leadership in the Executive Branch

The executive branch should be considered home for the governor. With a loyal office staff and at least some supportive department heads, governors should be able to dominate the bureaucracy. But governors can face competition from within as well.

The Governor's Staff The job of governor could prove lonely if governors were not surrounded by a cadre of loyal, dedicated, and mostly anonymous men and women who are the governor's staff. Governors' staffs vary widely in size—from a dozen or so in several states to more than 200 in New York.[50]

The usual qualifications for political appointment—size of political contributions, party loyalty, and place of residence—are not the most important for getting a staff position. The key requirements are a willingness to work long hours, putting the needs of the governor above one's own, working with little or no personal credit outside the governor's office, taking the blame and absorbing the shock for mistakes, and accepting a policy decision once it is made.

You had better be satisfied with less than a well-furnished plush office, too. Unless your state has a new capitol, the chances are your desk will be in a glassed cubicle, a room under a stairwell, or worse, a large closet. It is not that these staffers are not respected. The problem is that when most capitols were built, governors had very few staff—a secretary and, perhaps, one assistant. Modern-day staff must make do.

Who Are the Staff People? "Every politician has to find some persons off whom he can bounce ideas, those who are willing to say 'that's silly or that's crazy or that's great'" said one governor's senior staff person.[51] At least one—the chief of staff—will be an experienced political operative. Several will be lawyers. One, the legal counsel, advises on laws that have been enacted as well as on requests for clemency and interstate rendition. Not least among the group are former journalists. One of these will be the press secretary. Others are likely to be former associates—political operatives if the governor rose through the political ranks, business associates if the governor came from that career line.

What the Staff People Do The staff functions as an extension of the governor. In medium-sized and large states the less experienced staff members oversee one or more policy areas or state agencies. They keep track of the agency's problems, new programs the agency bureaucrats are working on, and new legislation they might be proposing. They also check out citizens' complaints and write letters—over the governor's signature if they can help; over their own, if the answer is "no."

The Office of Management and Budget A step away, in terms of responsiveness, is the **department of management and budget**. This agency typically directs the **staff functions** of state government—central purchasing, personnel, computer services, building management, and construction.

But its most visible responsibility is developing and administering the state budget. Personnel here are largely civil service appointees, but they see themselves as being loyal to the governor's office, if not to the incumbent.

The director is usually a political appointee and close ally of the governor. Few other administrators in state government have the potential for making a success or shambles of a governor's administration. The director controls the information about critical state finances and usually also screens program proposals from other departments. The governor depends on these budget-making skills not only to translate the leadership "tone" into policies, but also to determine where to cut the budget when revenues fall short of expectations.

Other Administrative Departments More distant from the governor's influences are other agencies—some headed by elected officials, others by boards and commissions or appointed administrators. Welfare and mental health and those handling economic development will be fairly responsive. Those headed by an elected official or by a board or commission (even if the governor appoints the members) and those funded by earmarked taxes will be less sensitive to a governor's wishes.

Another hurdle may be a **civil service system** that selects, appoints, promotes, and sets the salaries for state workers. Such a system seeks to create a technically skilled work force without regard to political affiliation. At the same time, though, it may limit a governor's ability to select people who support and are willing to advance his or her programs. Usually, under civil service or merit systems, governors get to choose the department director and one or two other unclassified managers. That is the case in Michigan, but there even the governor's office itself is limited to only eight unclassified staff persons.

Elected State Officials We think it significant that in some state department offices the picture of the secretary of state hangs on the wall while in others we find a framed color photo of the governor. It is a silent reminder of who is in charge in each.

Most states elect four or five statewide officers, but the number ranges from 1 (the governor) in two states to 11 in North Dakota. These people are likely to be responsive to the governor's leadership only if the governor is popular or has a firm grasp on the reins of the political party, and the officers belong to the governor's party. Otherwise, these state officials may be the governor's political enemies. Some may want his job.

The Lieutenant Governor In 42 states, voters choose a lieutenant governor. In other states the secretary of state, president of the senate, or some other state official succeeds to the office of governor in the event of the governor's resignation or death. Twenty-one states elect the governor and lieutenant governor jointly, as is done with the president and vice president.

Typically, lieutenant governors have few constitutional duties and often no substantive assigned duties. Most preside over the state senate and become acting governor when the governor is out of the state. And in a few states, they administer the functions typically associated with the secretary of state. But most of the time they have the job of waiting to take over if something happens to the governor. Some have found the job to be a bore and recommended that it be abolished, a topic discussed in Policy Box No. 17, "What to Do with the Office of Lieutenant Governor."

The Attorney General Attorneys general serve as a state's lawyer and chief crime fighter. They can be important contenders with the governor in the news media and for public attention. Beyond that, the rulings of an attorney general on fine points of law can prove troublesome and embarrassing to a governor. In the seven states where the governor appoints the attorneys general, we might expect relations with the governor to be more friendly.[52]

Secretary of State Secretaries of state probably spell less trouble in policy matters than do attorneys general and the lieutenant governors. They usually have high name recognition because their name is on drivers' licenses, election notices, and many state documents. Some also control many patronage appointments in the branch offices that issue driver licenses and auto plates. Such recognition sometimes encourages occupants to think of running for governor.

Policy Box No. 17

What to Do with the Office of Lieutenant Governor

In joking about the office, John Nance Garner said, "The vice presidency isn't worth a pitcher of warm spit." We're not aware of anyone's using such colorful language about lieutenant governors, but many agree it would apply. For the most part, being lieutenant governor is not an office many politicians aspire to as an end office.

The office of lieutenant governor has been the source of some mischief and problems over the years. Back in the 1960s when straitlaced George Romney was governor of Michigan, T. John Lesinski was his lieutenant governor. Romney was a Republican and Lesinski a Democrat. They had wide personality differences as well.

Romney was never sure when he left the state what Lesinski would do as acting governor. To Romney's chagrin, and Lesinski's—and the media's—great delight, Lesinski always issued a press release taking credit for his accomplishments as acting governor during the time Romney was gone. It got so that Romney was reluctant to travel outside the state.

During more recent times occupants have been stating their frustrations with the office of lieutenant governor in other ways—some have resigned, for example, David O'Neal of Illinois in 1981, who said "Upgrade the office or abolish it." Al Delbello of New York complained that he was powerless working with Governor Mario Cuomo. He also quit.

Others have taken on the governor over policy issues. Doug Wilder (later the first black elected to the governorship) opposed his boss, Virginia Governor Gerald Bailles, over what to do with budget surpluses. Robert B. Jordan III (a Democrat) took on his Republican boss in a race for the North Carolina governorship. Governor Dukakis had similar trouble in the waning months of his last year in office. He had planned a trade mission to Europe only to learn that Lieutenant Governor Evelyn Murphy was planning major cuts in the state budget the minute he left the state. He postponed his trip, and when he did leave, he warned Murphy not to take any drastic action.

What is the problem with this office? The office of lieutenant governor is patterned after that of the vice president of the nation. Its main purpose is to provide a line of succession to the governorship so someone is named in advance to assume the office of governor should a vacancy occur.

Forty-two states have an office of lieutenant governor and wrestle with the problem of making it beneficial to the state. One source of the difficulty is that 20 states do not elect their governor and lieutenant governor as a team as the nation does the president and vice president. Thus the governor and his successor may be of different parties. The state's top two elected officials may be in conflict from the time they are inaugurated.

Of the 22 states that elect the two top leaders as a team, 8 fail to link the two candidates in the nomination process. The winners may be of the same party but still be mortal enemies. Just how deep the feelings may go was shown in the 1986 Democratic party primary when Adlai Stevenson III was nominated for governor and a follower of Lyndon LaRouche got the nod for lieutenant governor. Stevenson resigned as the nominee of the Democratic party and ran as an independent.

One apparent way to make the office less troublesome, it would seem, is to have a party's nominee for governor select his or her own running mate. But that's the way the Cuomo-Delbello ticket was formed. And Lt. Governor Richard Licht of Rhode Island, a Democrat, says, "If you are handpicked by the governor, you have to sit and wait for the governor to give you something to do." His fear, it seems, is that what was said of the vice presidency may also be said of the lieutenant governorship—"He was elected vice president and was never heard from again."

Jo Ann Zimmerman of Iowa sees value in keeping the office independent of the governor. As a Democratic lieutenant governor working with a Democratic legislature and Republican governor, she became a member of the negotiating team. She opposed a proposition to link the two positions in elections unless lieutenant governor duties were spelled out by law.

Some states have tried to assign lieutenant governors meaningful responsibilities—traditionally they preside over the state senate, but usually more challenge is needed. Governor Rudy Perpich of Minnesota, for example, who once held the job himself, gives his lieutenant governor the job of developing the state budget.

But this is a problematic solution as well. Can a lieutenant governor really put the state budget together for a governor? Surely in most situations governors would want to be closely involved in the process. And even in less significant roles, how much independent discretion can a governor give the lieutenant governor? And what about assigning duties by law? Some fear that assigning duties to the lieutenant governor will weaken the governorship itself and that they will be an added source of conflict between the two state officers. Ambitious lieutenant governors may use the responsibilities to win the top spot for themselves.

Perhaps the solution is to have no lieutenant governor at all, as is the case with eight states. Of these, Arizona, Oregon, and Wyoming place the secretary of state first in line of succession. The other five, Maine, New Hampshire, New Jersey, Tennessee, and West Virginia, place the president or speaker of the state senate next in line. They argue that because it is very difficult to make something of the office, it is better to save the money spent on the position and provide a line of succession in other ways. And they insist that this solution eliminates the problem of having a lieutenant governor who has both executive and legislative duties.

But critics of the secretary of state approach maintain that it creates a potential competitor for the governorship in the executive branch, possibly of the opposing party. And other states merge the executive and legislative duties in the person of a legislator who has not been elected statewide or to an executive office. This sets up a situation such as what happened to Governor Bill Clinton of Arkansas, who came back to his state to find that his acting governor-legislator had fired his chief of staff and appointed 20 persons to state boards.

What do you think? Should the office be abolished? How can the states solve the problem of succession without a lieutenant governor? Should they elect the governor and lieutenant governor as a team or is it better to elect them independently? Or, is it better to have the secretary of state be next in line to succeed the

> governor? Is it a good practice to have the president or majority leader of the state senate succeed the governor? Is it necessary to have an acting governor when the governor is absent from the state for a few days or weeks? Could not the states have their legislatures elect a successor as happened nationally when the office of vice president became vacant under President Nixon?

Leadership in the Party

Governors are generally head of their state political parties. The only governor in recent memory who did not have an official political party affiliation was Maine's James Longely, an insurance company executive who won as an independent. Is party leader a significant role? Members of the press and outsiders, at least, appear to view it as an important responsibility.

But in the late 1970s, 15 former governors told two scholars that political parties were not very significant with respect to political ideology or the role of government. Some reported they changed the party's basic positions on some matters; others said they found the party sometimes useful in building support for their own positions. But most said that many of their decisions were nonpartisan—pragmatic rather than ideological responses to state problems.[53]

Party and Policies The governors were even more direct about the relevance of political parties for policy guidance. One governor said, "The political party was almost totally useless as a source of advice, I would say. It just isn't in that line of work."

Regarding patronage appointments, the governors reported that their responsibilities as managers were too important to employ people on the basis of party loyalty if that meant sacrificing competence.

Where Party Is Important Party labels, they said, were most important in the state legislature, although here too they saw many issues as nonpartisan. Most said they found party allegiance would encourage some members of the governor's party to vote with the governor on the "big" issues. However, governors usually are not able to block the nominations of maverick party legislators. These politics are worked out within the local districts, and the governor must make the best of what local party voters send to the statehouse.

A second area of party importance is intergovernmental relations. As we might expect, the governors found the president and other national leaders more responsive and cooperative when they belonged to the same party as the governor.

Finally, most governors acknowledged the party as "gatekeeper" to the gubernatorial nomination. But even here open primaries and campaign funding strategies may render a party impotent to deliver or deny the nomination to a candidate. Once having the nomination in hand the governors believed that they began to drift apart from party leaders. One said, "The party doesn't have much to offer in terms of money, or organizational support and strength." Said another, "It's the individual who gets elected, not the party."

The Governors' Views in Perspective The governors, no doubt, wanted to be candid and frank in these interviews. But we should keep in mind that few would admit that they were party lackeys—doing what party chieftains ordered them to do, making decisions based solely on party ideology, or appointing incompetent party loyalists to important posts. (Think how you might respond if you were a former governor.) Neither we nor the governors should dismiss the parties as being always powerless in these matters.

Governor Michael Dukakis (Mass., 1975–1979, 1983–1991) incurred the wrath of his state party, which made him sit out a term before renominating him again in 1982. Governors run substantial risks when they stray too far from the mainstream of their political parties. Governor Mecham experienced this when he beat the Republican establishment's favored candidate Burton Barr, then the Arizona house majority leader.[54] When he began having difficulties, his party did not rally round. But neither can the governors look to the party as the sole source of political strength. Most must reach out to a broad range of voters.

Leadership in Intergovernmental Relations

Governors deal with other governments on at least three levels in addition to the community level—the national government, governments in other states, and those of other nations.

Relations with the National Government Governors have several avenues for dealing with the federal government. The **National Governors' Association** provides a vehicle for governors to use to influence policies of the federal government. Governor Woodrow Wilson stated that the NGA would be an ". . . instrument, not of legislation, but of opinion, exercising the authority of influence, not of law."[55] The NGA has influenced federal policy decisions, as Wilson predicted it would. For example, in 1982 a number of governors were heavily involved in shaping the Jobs Training Partnership Act (JTPA).[56] And in 1989 and 1990, a cadre of governors worked closely with President Bush to devise national goals for education.

Governors, of course, also often work directly through their congressional delegations to lobby for change in law and policy and to intercede on problems the state has with a federal bureaucracy. Some have permanent staff in Washington to look after their state's interests.[57]

Interstate and International Relations Governors also hold regional meetings, such as the Southern Governors' Conference or the Midwestern Governors' Conference. These focus more on problems within regions than on relationships with Washington.[58] An example of the type of regional problems governors can encounter is described in Policy Box No. 18, "Gubernatorial Leadership on the Plains."

Governors and President Bush respond to reporters after their education conference.

Finally, as we discussed earlier, presidential politics give some governors the opportunity to influence policy. An outstanding example was the role that Governor George Wallace (Ala., 1963–1967, 1971–1979, 1983–1987) played in the 1968 and 1972 presidential elections. His ability to articulate popular feelings toward "big government" and win presidential primaries in northern states influenced the policies of not only the Democratic party, but the Republican party as well. Other former governors since—Ronald Reagan, Michael Dukakis, Jimmy Carter, Bruce Babbitt of Arizona—sought the presidential nomination and had an impact on national discourse.

International relations is the constitutional domain of the national government. But governors often lead state international trade missions to "sell" their states to foreign companies that are considering plant sites in the United States. They now set up their own trade offices in large foreign cities such as Tokyo, London, or Toronto. Governors of states bordering Canada are focusing especially on relations with that country in light of the 1988 agreement to eliminate tariffs on trade between the two nations.

In addition, governors of other border states—California, Texas, Arizona, and Florida, especially—become involved in immigration matters. These are of particular concern in those states that absorb high percentages of international refugees and economic migrants because the states incur substantial costs in providing social, health, and educational services to these populations.[59]

Policy Box No. 18

Gubernatorial Leadership on the Plains

Near the end of 1989 Rand McNally published a new atlas, a book of road maps for each of the states—well, most of the states. It left out maps of North and South Dakota and Oklahoma. No, it wasn't a mistake. Officials at Rand McNally said they didn't have space to include them. Presumably, the atlas without these maps would sell just fine, except perhaps in the Dakotas and Oklahoma.

But the absence of these maps was also symbolic of what has been happening in the states of the Great Plains—roughly the territory between the 98th meridian and the Rocky Mountains. A *Newsweek* article called some of these states "America's Outback."[1]

Deborah Epstein and Frank J. Popper, professors at Rutgers University, explain how the region has suffered its ups and downs. The first major settlement of the Plains came after the Civil War, in part encouraged by technological innovations—construction of railroads, availability of steel plows, barbed wire fence, windmills, and the beginnings of modern irrigation. The early settlers were opportunistic. In the 1870s they experienced good rainfall and several years of bumper crops. And in the 1880s gold, silver, copper, and oil strikes enticed others. But the severe blizzards of the late 1880s and economic panic in the 1890s caused large numbers of settlers to desert.

Pioneers began pouring in again after the turn of the century, but natural and economic disasters were not far behind. Drought and locusts hit the northern Plains in 1919 and economic depression in 1921. Montana, for example, had 214 bank failures by 1925. The dust bowl of the 1930s—the by-product of overly assertive agriculture—darkened the horizons and depopulated much of the region in the 1930s.

Agriculture revived somewhat during World War II, but it supported relatively few jobs because of the widespread use of heavy equipment on large farms. An energy boomlet in the 1970s promised new levels of economic well-being. But the 1980s brought new failures—commodity prices dropped, the 1988 drought revived nightmares of the dust bowl, and the depletion of the Ogallala aquifer in parts of the region forced further abandonment of agriculture.

Meanwhile, the quality of life continues to decline. A tenth of Oklahoma's teachers have lost their jobs, banks have collapsed, farmers and ranchers are quitting their business, houses are being abandoned, and perhaps worst, many young people are leaving the already lightly populated states to seek economic security elsewhere.

Some writers suggest a radical solution. "Three times white civilization has attempted to settle the arid, windy Plains—a land mass that comprises one-fifth of the contiguous United States. Three times the settlement effort has largely failed. The nation and the region should learn from the failures, including the 1988 drought, and help the land revert to a buffalo commons—to the state the land was in before the coming of the whites."[2]

A University of Oklahoma geographer proposed that large portions of the region be returned to prewhite conditions—that is, deprivatize it by having the federal government buy out private rights. He suggests that the government pay farmers the

full value of what they could raise over the next 15 years but requ[...]
land lie fallow. Instead they would reestablish native grasses. At the e[...]
the government would buy out each farmer except for 40 acres for a [...]
Robert Scott of the Institute of the Rockies has proposed that 15,000 square [...]
eastern Montana be turned into the Big Open—a game reserve for buffalo, de[...]
antelope, and elk.

Epstein and Popper believe that the desertion of the great commons is inevitable. But they argue that a controlled and managed exodus is much preferred over "natural" desertion, for the well-being of both the people and the land. But how can that be achieved?

What has been happening to this region, and what should governors of these states try to do about it?

Deprivatizing vast areas, of course, would require leadership of a very special sort. Can governors of these states lead people of their states to leave their homes? Can they collectively persuade the federal government to undertake such a massive game preserve project? Or will local politics render such leadership impossible?

One Montana resident indicated how at least some citizens will respond. He said about the potential for tourism, "What it comes down to is your wife and daughters go to work cooking for tourists and making their beds, and your son is driving a bus around for them or whatever. I'm sure that's fine for some people, but I'd rather stay on the land and starve with the rest of the cowboys."

What do you think? How are state governors likely to respond to such a forecast for large regions of their states? Should they act collectively to form a compact to manage the depopulation of much of the Great Plains? Or is this a problem that the federal government should assume responsibility for? Should the governors approach the problem as they have in the past—hope that conditions will change and renew the future of the Plains as has occurred several times before?

[1] *Newsweek,* October 9, 1989.
[2] Deborah Epstein Popper and Frank J. Popper, *High Country News*, September 28, 1988.

A FINAL COMMENT

When all is said and done, when we have examined all the fine points of the legal arrangements of the governors' offices, when we have analyzed the politics that apply in each state, does it matter who is governor? Does it make a difference? Or are politics and policy outcomes, as some political scientists suggest, mostly determined by the level of economic development in the state? Can a governor make a difference?

In Chapter 2 we suggested that the environment of politics—geography, wealth, and population—sets boundaries on what is possible. Individuals, through politics, process these raw materials into state policy. Governors, we think, do make a difference.

The difference results, in part, from the tone of leadership that a governor establishes. For most public issues there are a number of reasonable policy alternatives. Some get careful consideration and analysis; others are rejected out of hand. The tone and direction a governor sets often determines what kind of people the governor appoints. These in turn influence which ideas get consideration and which do not.

It is too early, as these words are written, to determine whether Charles E. Roemer III, the person who defeated incumbent Edwin Edwards as governor of Louisiana in 1988, in the words of one reporter, can "turn the state on its head." Residents called his plan the "Roemer Revolution"—he proposes to shift the balance of power from the state to the localities and end the heavy dependence of localities on the state and the state penetration into local affairs.[60] Roemer may not be successful in reversing 60 years of governing in the Huey "Kingfish" Long tradition. But as outgoing Governor Edwards said after his defeat, "You're going to miss me. But many of you don't know it now." The office may make the governor, but the governor also makes the office.

HIGH POINTS

In this chapter we examined three main considerations. In the first—Who gets to be governor?—we found that they are people who are (1) political ambitious, (2) experienced in politics, and (3) have gained this experience most often in the legislature. We also found that (4) personal characteristics make a difference for one's chances of becoming governor.

In our discussion of governors as state leaders, we found that (5) during the nineteenth century governors were weak and largely uninfluential and that (6) through various reforms the governors of the twentieth century were gradually able to gain power and direction over their state governments. We closed by noting that (7) governors can be influential in state policy-making, and that who the governor is makes a difference.

In this chapter we defined the following terms in this sequence: name recognition, tools of politics, career paths, image building, Jacksonian democracy, legal powers, appointing powers, powers to remove, office tenure, powers to recommend, political leadership, legislative lobbying, legislative liaison, special session, veto, extraordinary majority, item veto, executive amendment, executive budget, office of management and budget, staff functions, civil service system, and National Governors' Association.

NOTES

1. See Thad L. Beyle and Robert Hueffner, "Quips and Quotes from Old Governors to New," *Public Administration Review* (May/June 1983): 268–270.
2. Norton E. Long, "When the Voting Is Over," *Midwest Journal of Political Science* (May 1962): 183–200. This article is also included in Thad Beyle and J. Oliver Willi-

ams (eds.), *The American Governor in Behavioral Perspective* (New York: Harper & Row, 1972), pp. 76–88.
3. Elections for governor usually occur in November, and the terms typically begin in January except for that of Louisiana, which begins in March.
4. Robert W. Scott, former governor of North Carolina (1969–1973), told of such a transportation problem at the Community Development Society of America in Wilmington, Del.
5. Lester Maddox (Ga., 1967–1971), a restaurateur who passed out ax handles in defiance of integration orders, often bicycled to and from work, occasionally facing backward and sitting on the handlebars. Perhaps he did so the day he left office.
6. Larry Sabato, *Goodbye to Goodtime Charlie* (2nd ed.) (Washington, D.C.: Congressional Quarterly Press, 1983). Sabato covers governors from 1950 to 1975. Joseph A. Schlesinger's study of governors from 1900 to 1950 reports that 53.9 percent did not hold public office after being governor. See "Politics of the Executive," in Herbert Jacob and Kenneth Vines (eds.), *Politics in the American States, A Comparative Analysis* (Boston: Little, Brown, 1971).
7. Long, *When the Voting Is Over*, p. 73.
8. Thad L. Beyle, "The Governors, 1986–87," in *Book of the States, 1988–89* (Lexington, Ky.: Council of State Governments), pp. 24–34. For more on the Mecham saga see Richard R. Johnson, "Recall in Action: The Mecham Recall in Arizona," Paper delivered at the American Political Science Association meeting, 1988, Washington, D.C.
9. A total of 287 candidates in 39 gubernatorial races (an average of 7.4 per race) filed campaign finance reports in 1986–1987. Beyle, "The Governors, 1986–87," p. 26.
10. Joseph A. Schlesinger, in *How They Became Governor*, provides a detailed analysis of gubernatorial career paths (East Lansing, Mich.: Governmental Research Bureau, Michigan State University, 1957).
11. Myra McPherson, *The Power Lovers, An Intimate Look at Politicians and Their Marriages* (New York: Putnam, 1974).
12. See Charles Press and Kenneth VerBurg, *American Politicians and Journalists* (Glenview, Ill.: Scott, Foresman, 1988), p. 1, to see how U.S. Senator Hubert Humphrey broke into the news when he was a political novice.
13. Beyle, "The Governors, 1986–87," p. 25.
14. Lee Sigelman and Roland Smith in their study of 117 post-1950 governors rated as "outstanding" find that youthful ones were likely to be more successful. "Personal, Office, and State Characteristics as Predictors of Gubernatorial Performance," *Journal of Politics* 43 (1981): 169–180.
15. Data reported here for 1988 come from the *Directory of Governors of the American States, Commonwealths, and Territories* (Washington, D.C.: National Governors Association, 1989).
16. Quoted in Sabato, *Goodbye to Goodtime Charlie*, p. 34.
17. The incidence of governors running for the U.S. Senate has been declining, in part because more governors now have a four-year term and no limits on the number of terms. See Frank Codispoti, "The Governorship-Senate Connection: A Step in the Structure of Opportunities Grows Weaker," *Publius* 17:2 (Spring 1987): 41–52.
18. Sabato, *Goodbye to Goodtime Charlie*, p. 23.
19. Mark R. Miller (ed.), *Directory of Governors of the American States, Commonwealths, and Territories* (Washington, D.C.: National Governors Association, 1989).

20. Ethnic origin is a more important factor in gaining the party nomination than it is in the general election. This is especially true when there are several candidates of different ethnic origins seeking the office.
21. Richard R. Johnson, "Recall in Action: The Mecham Recall in Arizona," Paper presented at the American Political Science Association meeting, 1988, Washington, D.C.
22. Rowland Egger, "The Governor of Virginia, 1776 to 1976," *University of Virginia Newsletter* (August 1976).
23. Arthur M. Schlesinger, Jr., *The Age of Jackson* (New York: New American Library, 1957), p. 25.
24. Leslie Lipson, *From Figurehead to Leader* (Chicago: University of Chicago Press, 1939), pp. 23–24.
25. Deil S. Wright, "Executive Leadership in State Administration," in Beyle and Williams (eds.), *The American Governor in Behavioral Perspective*, p. 277. Also see F. Ted Hebert and Deil S. Wright, "The Role of State Department Heads, Politics or Management?" Paper presented at the Southern Political Science Association meetings, 1981, Memphis.
26. Nelson C. Dometrius finds that tenure in office is not the most important indicator of gubernatorial power. He argues that Schlesinger's indices of power—tenure potential, veto, budget, and appointments—correlate more strongly with Beyle's findings if tenure is removed from the computations. See Thad J. Beyle, "The Governor's Formal Powers, A View from the Governor's Chair," *Public Administration Review* 28 (November/December 1968): 540–545. Dometrius's work is "Measuring Gubernatorial Power," *Journal of Politics* 41 (1979): 589–610.
27. Two states (Ky. and Va.) do not permit a person to serve consecutive terms; 5 (Ariz., Del., Mo., N.M., and N.C.) impose absolute limits: two four-year terms; 22 forbid serving more than two terms consecutively.
28. Keith J. Mueller, "Explaining Variation and Change in Gubernatorial Powers, 1960–1982," *Western Political Quarterly* 38 (1985): 424–431. Dometrius, however, argues that there is too little variation across the states and maintains that a new index of gubernatorial powers is required. See Nelson C. Dometrius, "Changing Gubernatorial Power: The Measure vs. Reality," *Western Political Quarterly* 40:2 (1987): 319–327.
29. Robert C. Tucker, "Personality and Political Leadership," *Political Science Quarterly* (Fall 1977): 383–393.
30. Of the governors serving in 1989, 22 had served five or more years. But during the 1980s the percentage of incumbent governors seeking reelections dropped: from 83 percent in the 1980–1983 cycle to 72 percent and 73 percent in the 1984–1987 and 1986–1987 cycles, respectively. Beyle, "The Governors, 1986–1987."
31. Governors and former governors did not fare well in the presidential sweepstakes during the 1950s, 1960s, and in 1972. Adlai Stevenson (Ill.) was the Democratic party candidate in 1952 and 1956. Spiro Agnew (Md.) was the Republican nominee for vice-president during Richard Nixon's election victories. George Wallace ran as the nominee of the American party in 1968. But since then, former governors Jimmy Carter (Ga.) and Ronald Reagan (Calif.) won the presidency and in 1988, Michael Dukakis (Mass.), as Democratic nominee, lost to George Bush who was noted for his long résumé of government jobs, which did not include governor. Also see Louis Harris, "Why the Odds Are Against a Governor's Becoming President," *Public Opinion Quarterly* 23 (Fall 1959): 261–270.
32. Smith showed his concern for the disadvantaged in part by his efforts to reform New

York's penal institutions. Although he was somewhat ahead of his time in this respect, he set the agenda for corrections reforms for decades into the future. See David R. Colburn, "Governor Alfred E. Smith and Penal Reform," *Political Science Quarterly* (Summer 1976): 315–327.

33. Richard D. Michaelson, "An Analysis of the Chief Executive, How a Governor Uses His Time," in William K. Hall (ed.), *Illinois Government and Politics* (Dubuque, Iowa: Kendall/Hunt, 1975), p. 113.
34. See David Morgan, *The Capitol Press Corps, Newsmen and the Governing of New York State* (Westport, Conn.: Greenwood Press, 1978), for a description of how Governor Nelson Rockefeller manipulated journalists covering New York state politics.
35. G. Mennen Williams, *A Governor's Notes* (Ann Arbor: Institute of Public Affairs, University of Michigan, 1961), pp. 16, 60.
36. Diane D. Blair, *Arkansas Politics and Government* (Lincoln: University of Nebraska Press, 1988), p. 153.
37. It is said that reporters asked the madam if meeting such famous persons made her nervous. "No," she replied, "I have already met most of them." Perpich's graceful handling of the situation turned what could have been a minus into a plus.
38. E. Lee Bernick, "Gubernatorial Tools, Formal v. Informal," *Journal of Politics* 41 (May 1979): 656–664.
39. Larry Sabato, "The Governors and Public Opinion," *State Government* 54:3 (1981).
40. Blair, *Arkansas Politics and Government*, p. 154.
41. See *Comparative State Politics Newsletter* 8:6 (December 1987) and 9:1 (February 1988) for Melvin Kahn's report on Kansas and Hugh A. Bone's on Washington, respectively.
42. *The Office of Governor* (Urbana, Ill.: Institute of Government and Public Affairs, University of Illinois, 1963), p. 65. All governors except in North Carolina possess veto power.
43. Steven D. Williams, "1988 Tennessee Legislative Report," *Comparative State Politics Newsletter* 9:3 (1988): 4.
44. Charles W. Wiggins, "Executive Vetoes and Legislative Overrides in the American States," *Journal of Politics* 42 (1980): 1110–1117.
45. Glenn Abney and Thomas P. Lauth, "The Line-Item Veto in the States, An Instrument for Fiscal Restraint or an Instrument for Partisanship?" *Public Administration Review* (May/June 1985): 372–377.
46. James J. Gosling, "Wisconsin Item-Veto Lessons," *Public Administration Review* (July/August 1986): 292–300.
47. In most states the executive budget approach is used—the governor prepares the state budget and the legislature reviews. Eight states require the governor to share this responsibility: Colorado, Kentucky, Louisiana, Mississippi, New Mexico, North Carolina, South Carolina, and Utah.
48. This is not the case in all states, of course. Some governors have weak fiscal powers. For a review of Mississippi, Georgia, and South Carolina see Thomas P. Lauth (ed.), "Executive and Legislative Budgeting in Three States: Who Sets the Agenda?" *State and Local Government Review* 18:2 (Spring 1986): 47–70.
49. Glenn Abney and Thomas P. Lauth, "Perceptions of the Impact of Governors and Legislature in the State Appropriations Process," *Western Political Quarterly* 40:2 (1987): 335–342.
50. Council of State Governments, *Book of the States, 1988–89*, p. 38.

51. *The Detroit News*, January 29, 1989.
52. The states are Alaska, Hawaii, Maine, New Hampshire, New Jersey, Tennessee, and Wyoming. Council of State Governments, *Book of the States, 1988–89*.
53. Lynn Muchmore and Thad L. Beyle, "The Governor as Party Leader," *State Government* 53 (1980): 125–128.
54. Richard R. Johnson, "Recall in Action: The Mecham Recall in Arizona."
55. Quoted in *When Governors Convene* (Baltimore: Johns Hopkins Press, 1961), p. xii.
56. Susan A. MacManus, "Playing a New Game: Governors and the Job Training Partnership Act," *American Politics Quarterly* 14:3 (July 1986): 131–147.
57. Deil S. Wright, "Governors, Grants, and the Intergovernmental System," in Beyle and Williams (eds.), *The American Governor in Behavioral Perspective*, p. 191.
58. For a review of gubernatorial innovations on an interstate basis see Thad Beyle, "The Governor as Innovator in the Federal System," *Publius* 18:3 (Summer 1988): 131–152.
59. See John Kincaid, "The American Governors in International Affairs," *Publius* 14:1 (Fall 1984): 95–114.
60. Rob Gurwitt, "Louisiana's Long Legacy May End with Roemer Revolution," *Governing* (July 1988): 24–30.

Chapter 10

Administrators as State and Community Managers

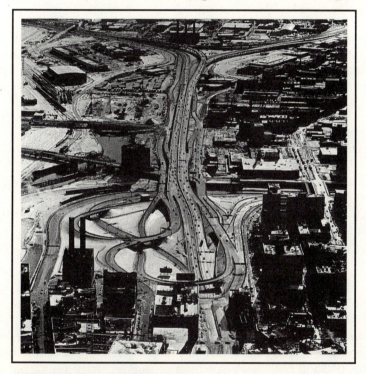

*E*very now and then a candidate campaigns on the slogan "Government should be run like a business." But state and city governments differ fundamentally from business organizations and cannot be operated in the same manner. Yet in some ways their operations and problems are similar.

The Organizational Setting If we were touring a manufacturing plant, we would not understand everything we saw. But we would comprehend the basic flow—raw materials entering, parts being assembled, and finished products coming out and being loaded for transport to be sold to consumers.

We would not see the same thing if we toured a government agency. Its "products" are mostly services and information processing. The state natural resources department, for example, operates parks, tends forests and wildlife, and guards against pollution. The health department works with vital records and monitors contagious diseases.

But the state sometimes also makes products. It builds highways, reservoirs, and other major facilities. Moreover, the forestry and fishery programs plant trees and stock trout streams—tangible products. But seldom does each consumer pay directly for the services he or she uses. The products are efforts to create an environment that makes the lives of residents more enjoyable, healthy, and safe—it produces what economists call **public goods**, products that are indivisible.

Overview In this chapter we consider the people employed by state and community governments—bureaucrats. We begin by reviewing what is perhaps the major reform affecting their jobs—the shift from patronage to merit hiring. We next consider how they have gained power through professionalization and unionization. Then we discuss how some citizens and politicians are attempting to limit or control their power.

PROFESSIONALIZATION OF THE STATE PUBLIC SERVICE

A hundred years have passed since Charles J. Guiteau fatally shot President James A. Garfield in the old Baltimore and Potomac railroad station in Washington, D.C. Historians record that Guiteau was "unbalanced"—angered because he could not get a job in the new administration.

The Merit System

The incident prompted Congress in 1883 to pass the Pendleton Act, which began the process of hiring and promoting federal government workers on the basis of ability rather than according to which party they supported in the last election.[1] Under the plan, the incoming chief executive would appoint only a few people at the top of each agency. These people would direct the affairs of the agencies and make the policy decisions. The permanent workers, who would stay on from one administration to the next, would typify the ideal of **neutral competence**—a phrase Herbert Kaufman coined.[2] They would be "neutral" with respect to partisan politics—to ensure their neutrality, rules forbade their participating in politics, except for voting. The employees would be "competent" because they had met the special job requirements.

The Spread of Merit Systems Civil service systems spread to states and communities slowly. New York and Massachusetts set up partial merit systems in the mid-1880s. Then in 1905, Governor Robert La Follette established the first thorough civil service system as part of his "progressive idea for Wisconsin." By 1934, though, only 17 states and some larger cities had civil service commissions.

The Impact of Intergovernmental Relations Then the dam broke. The Federal Hatch Act of 1939 required that state employees handling federal funds be free of partisan politics. Merit employment got a further boost in 1970 with the federal Intergovernmental Personnel Act that provided grants to improve state civil service systems. Today all states have a civil service or merit employment system, as do most larger communities. Not all states, though, include all employees in the civil service system—a few still extend merit employment only to employees who administer federal grants. The pervasiveness of federal grants, however, makes such dual systems difficult to maintain.

Important Elements of Merit Systems The systems differ in practice but the following conditions of **merit employment** are fundamental:

1. Employees demonstrate their fitness for the job and for promotion by passing a test, by previous work experience, or by completing some type of training.
2. Once past a trial period, employees can be dismissed only if shown to be grossly inefficient or guilty of criminal activity or a moral lapse.
3. Positions across agencies and departments are classified according to duties and responsibilities. Pay is based primarily on the position classification.

What Merit Systems Replaced

Until about 1940 most state and local employees were part of a **patronage system**—they got their jobs through political connections and "paid" for them with "kickbacks" from their salaries. If their party lost the election, the employees lost their jobs.

The Key Criterion: Political Loyalty We can gain a sense of what these patronage systems were like from H. O. Waldby's report of the Oklahoma system of an earlier day.[3]

A prospective employee first had to be endorsed by the local state legislator. Many of these endorsed only those who had supported their own election with time or money or who had the backing of someone who had. Applicants also usually had to get their party's county committee endorsement. These were then turned over to the governor's patronage advisor, who recorded each legislator's voting record and, on that basis, decided how many jobs each legislator "deserved." For instance, Waldby reports, "In 1949 Representative Lonnie Brown of McAlester occasionally had been critical of the administration, while Senator M. O. Counts, also of McAlester, was known as a strong administration man. Counts got to name forty-two employees at the McAlester state prison; Brown sponsored only five."

Employees were expected to work in subsequent political campaigns. In 1932, for example, a colorful governor, William "Alfalfa Bill" Murray, was fighting for voter support for three constitutional amendments. To help out in the final days, he gave all state employees a two-and-a-half-day holiday with orders to spend it working to get out a favorable vote.

Some Patronage Persists

But even today there are evasions of merit systems. In 1980 the city of Chicago employed 25,000 civil service employees but some 14,000 temporary and 900 were exempt workers. These latter two groups were political appointees and were expected to make personal and financial campaign contributions to keep their bosses in power. A stubborn and lengthy legal battle that lawyer Michael Shakman fought finally brought about major cuts in Chicago's patronage system.[4]

It is difficult to imagine how any governor or mayor could operate today under a patronage system. The very large number of positions would take months to fill. And securing competent employees whose careers depend on the candidate's or party's reelection would be next to impossible.

Patronage islands remain in every state and in many communities for several reasons. First, political appointees can be an important source of campaign funds, if not directly, then through their help in raising money. For example, Indiana state legislators repeatedly called for strict federal enforcement of laws against so-called 2% Clubs. But it was not until late 1989 that they were finally abolished. These clubs required some state and local employees to contribute 2 percent of their annual salaries to the dominant political party. As a news item stated, "Both major political parties have used such a system in Indiana for decades."[5] Many of those who worked for state legislators were hired on the basis of partisan loyalties and were relied on to purchase at least a few tickets to legislative fund-raisers. Also, they expected to be dismissed when new leaders took over. The delay in banning the "clubs" is a mark to their persistence. Yet they do succumb to pressure. And more, we suspect, will topple following a 1990 U.S. Supreme Court decision banning political allegiance as a criterion for public employment.

Second, patronage systems make for strong political organizations. As we discuss more fully in Chapter 5, John M. Bailey, onetime Democratic national party chair, built such an organization in Connecticut during the 1950s. Bailey's biographer argued that the skillful handing out of government jobs is as crucial to the politician's art as "the offer of stock options or fringe benefits or high recompense is to the business executive seeking able and loyal co-workers."[6] Governors often still use their powers of appointment to state boards and commissions as a form of patronage. Direct financial rewards for serving in these capacities usually are not significant. However, such appointments are prestigious and often are beneficial in terms of business and other contacts. And they, too, should not be surprised by "invitations" to buy tickets to the governor's fund-raisers.

Third, it is difficult to follow civil service procedures for some jobs—especially those that involve part-time or temporary duties. Thus even in most of the "pure civil service states" we find patronage considerations in hiring summer workers in the highway or parks departments and in appointing lawyers in probate cases and as public defenders.

Assessment of the Modern Patronage System How do state governments that operate largely as patronage systems, such as those of Texas and Missouri, handle its costs? Key to the spoils system in Texas is its unreformed, decentralized executive branch. The spoils system does not operate primarily to serve the interests of political parties. Rather it serves the influentials—legislators, some organized groups, and personal friends of the governor.

Students of Texas say the system is not as deplorable as it might be because (1) most agency heads have a long tenure, which helps to keep worker turnover low; (2) the shortage of qualified personnel lessens the danger of arbitrary dismissals; and (3) those who do fall into political disfavor often can transfer to another of the many state agencies.[7]

Effects of Merit Systems

Today civil servants and the public have a reasonable guarantee that public pay is commensurate with work assignments and responsibilities, and that promotions are reasonably related to performance on the job. Respect for public employees is high enough to attract and retain able and well-trained people to careers in public service.

But All Is Not Well Merit employment systems are not without some faults, however. In fact, some students now criticize certain aspects of merit employment they feel its supporters have carried to excess.

How to Measure "Merit" Some merit employment systems are unable to do what they say they do—select the best applicant on the basis of skills and experience. Applicants are rated on the basis of written examinations. But critics ask whether the tests reliably predict on-the-job performance. Many written tests go unvalidated for relevancy to the actual work the appointees will be doing.

A further problem is that many skills and levels of experience are difficult to evaluate. Whether an applicant gets the job often depends on whether he or she puts down the right buzzwords—the kinds of things the evaluators are looking for. This condition may handicap the timid and those who take too seriously the warning about false information on application forms—some warnings threaten loss of job or even a fine and jail for violations.

Delays and Inefficiencies Critics argue that merit employment systems often lose the best candidates because of delays in the testing and employment process. Public employment agencies often are swamped with applications—Illinois, for example, receives as many as 120,000 each year. Extensive screening and evaluation procedures, then, become counterproductive.[8]

Often central personnel agencies do not have a register of qualified people. Merit employment also tends to break down in selecting candidates for higher-level professional positions. Or the registers may be hopelessly out of date. Civil service then lets agency heads recruit their own candidates and appoint them on a supposedly provisional basis. Later, provisional appointees need only pass a test rather than score at the top to keep the job. This bypasses the principle of competitive examination.

Supervision Is More Difficult Supervisors often find it almost impossible to fire an ineffective employee. They discover that the required hearings are trying—time wasting, filled with personal bitterness, and an emotional drain. If found guilty, the employee may file an appeal—some cases end in the courts. And, of course, the supervisor risks losing the case. If so, the agency is saddled with a now thoroughly alienated employee.

Racial and Sexual Bias Civil service systems have had difficulty dealing effectively with problems of race and sex discrimination. Most states now have affirmative action offices. These have had some successes, but have been unable to root out the more subtle forms of discrimination.

Staff Reductions Cutback procedures also conflict with merit principles. If an agency cuts back through attrition—resignations, deaths, or retirements—managers shuffle people around to fill critical positions, often whether or not they are the best qualified to perform the tasks. If they use seniority, senior employees, who may not be as qualified, bump those with low seniority who may in turn bump someone else.

Civil Service and Control One problem results from the permanent nature of the public employees and the tendency for them to dominate elected officials who are only temporarily on the scene—the governor, mayor, legislators, and city councilors.

Time is usually on the side of the administrators. Some have government careers that span 15 or more years in key positions and total government careers of up to 40 years. Civil service guarantees them long tenure. Elected officials, by contrast, serve set terms and may have changing interests. Thus administrators can sometimes wait out a hostile governor, mayor, or powerful legislator, or wait for better economic times or some other set of favorable conditions. Indeed, in one study, administrators of longer tenure reported lower levels of gubernatorial influence than did others.[9]

Delay tactics, of course, do not guarantee that administrators get their way. But governors or mayors, to be successful against the opposition of professional bureaucrats, may have to invest more effort than they planned. Elected officials, who operate on a much shorter time horizon, are likely to accept compromise rather than battle resisting professionals. The delay strategy also holds some risks—conditions and priorities change, financial and political resources drift away, and new technical and professional values take over.

SOURCES OF BUREAUCRATIC POWER— PROFESSIONALIZATION AND UNIONIZATION

To be sure, most of us would prefer a professional public work force. But such employees may not always be sensitive to the demands of the political system.

Professionalism in Bureaucracy

Professional administration has resulted in notable triumphs. Look around your own state or community. Professionals have designed and built modern highway systems and city parkways that combine beauty with utility. They have turned degrading mental institutions into centers of humane treatment. Wildlife preserves, local parks, and points of natural beauty and historical interest are preserved for future generations. Public libraries have amassed impressive and well-cataloged collections of books and other valuable materials. Most of these are products of **professional values**—qualities that guide professional behavior. Professionals possess a "powerful knowledge" that is highly organized and systematic, and strange to average citizens.[10] The professional feels bound to act as this specialized knowledge requires.

Professionals Require Autonomy A profession regulates itself through such devices as standards of knowledge and moral conduct, peer controls, regulated admissions, as well as legal mechanisms, such as state licenses, which the professions largely control. Professionals seek to keep the door closed to those they judge unqualified.

These characteristics are intimidating and elitist. Fortunately, many professionals readily acknowledge that their special status also imposes on them a service orientation, a high obligation to exercise their power for the welfare of their clients. The *Encyclopedia of the Social Sciences* gives special emphasis to this aspect of professionalism.[11] Professionalism, for example, demands that professionals place the interest of their clients ahead of personal comfort, that they will not sacrifice professional goals to political pressures or for personal gain. Such values and standards of conduct are often drilled into professionals during their training. For most, these internal compasses give direction for appropriate behavior. Written rules, as we discuss in Policy Box No. 19, "Ethical Behavior for Public Officials," are an effort to prescribe proper conduct for the few.

Professionalization Also Causes Political Difficulties Professional values can readily conflict with bureaucratic duties: Social workers dealing with welfare clients may rebel against rules that, in their opinion, do not allow adequate income maintenance. Lawyers on the state's legal department may interpret statutes in ways that clash with those of the elected attorney general.

Professionals, like others with something at stake, seek to influence policymaking. But often they base their demands on values that contrast sharply with those of elected officials. Should the public health professional stand by quietly while state legislators and the governor seek to patch up a faulty nursing home inspection program? And should the city fire chief not resist budget cuts that reduce staffing to an unsafe level?

The Political Resources of Professionals What resources do professionals have to influence state or community policy and resist direction from elected officials?

Policy Box No. 19

Ethical Behavior for Public Officials

Issues of misconduct or unethical behavior among politicians surface in the media every once in a while. The episodes that gain the most notoriety are those that take place in Washington.

Two national-level scandals during the 1980s involving administrators, members of Congress, and groups doing business with the government cost the nation billions of dollars. One was the breakdown of the savings and loan financial institutions that bankrupted the Federal Savings and Loan Insurance Corporation—the agency that guarantees citizens' deposits. The other scandal involved HUD, the Department of Housing and Urban Development.

As we discussed in Chapter 6 on interest groups, such scandals occur in states and communities as well, although on a smaller scale and usually with less media attention. Some scandals involve out-and-out thievery, such as a worker in a welfare office who set up phony child-care centers to which he wrote checks for nonexistent services. Others may be nothing more than dumb actions that, at least in retrospect, turn out to have given some private interest exorbitant gains on a deal they had with the government. The first of these is a violation of the criminal code; the second, probably nothing more than inept administration. Neither behavior is the target of codes of ethics for public officials.

Government codes of ethics attempt to deal with something much more subtle, official conduct that falls in a gray area—otherwise legitimate conduct that involves conflict of interest or the appearance of impropriety. For lawyer-legislators, or sometimes administrators, it may mean representing a client who has business with a state agency. Or it may deal with revolving door practices—public officials leaving government employment for a job with a business they previously regulated. It could also involve a government "risk capital" loan to a private company as part of the state or community economic development program. It could include an unpaid zoning board member who shortly after leaving the board is invited to invest in community projects.

Ethical conduct concerns other questions such as the following:

1. Is it proper for an official to accept a gift from anyone who is or may be doing business with the government?

2. May an official accept modest stipends or honoraria from groups for making a speech or perhaps writing an article in a group's "house organ"? What about accepting travel expenses and lodging at a resort hotel where the group to be addressed is meeting?

3. Should a full-time public official be barred from accepting income from any outside source? Should these officials be required to file an income statement? Should a citizen member of a local planning or zoning commission be required to file such a report?

4. Is it improper for a public official to allow a businessperson to pick up the tab for a lunch or an expensive dinner?

5. Is it proper for a legislator or elected executive to solicit campaign funds from lobbyists or groups seeking to have a bill passed or a permit issued? What about after the bill is passed or the permit issued?
6. Should a governor's or mayor's aide call a state university official and ask the person to announce his or her support for a ballot issue the governor or mayor supports?

Well, you get the idea of ethics issues. Mainly they deal with matters that give rise to suspicions about a conflict of interest that could cause the public official to compromise decisions on public policy or situations where someone pressures a public official to gain a favorable decision. They also involve appearances—webs of relationships and interests that lead others to question if a particular decision was compromised for personal gain or benefit—and the use of knowledge or skills learned on the job for personal gain.

To what sort of standards should public officials be held? Should the codes of ethics apply uniformly to appointed, elected, and merit employees? Should the standards be related to the level of pay or position? Should the standards be higher than what is required from counterparts in private business?

City and State, a periodical for elected and appointed officials, asked readers to volunteer their opinions about ethics in government by completing a 25-question survey. The responses, of course, were not from a scientific sample, but of major concern to the respondents were matters of public perception. Large majorities thought (1) the public generally does not perceive state and city officials as honest; (2) that we are experiencing an erosion of ethical standards; (3) that public officials should be held to higher standards than leaders in the private sector; and (4) that public officials are not now being held to unrealistic ethical standards.*

Solving problems concerning unethical behavior, some say, is fairly easy. As society does with other matters of morals and values, the government can pass a law or adopt a rule defining certain acts by public officials as unacceptable and even illegal, punishable as a misdemeanor, or perhaps administratively. We've done that with respect to theft, burglary, murder, corrupt practices, and other deeds. If we think that public officials' independence or objectivity can be bought off with a gift, lunch, or dinner, their agency should adopt a rule forbidding them to accept such gratuities. We could also require them to file a report on their financial status each year to make sure they're obeying the rules.

And if we are fearful that a bureaucrat or legislator will sell out for a high-paying job in private business, we could impose a waiting period for an official to accept employment in a company that he or she regulated.

But others say it is not quite that easy. First of all, they say, public officials have rights too. They are residents of a community and citizens whose government job should not restrict their right of association. Are we saying that government workers may not do the natural thing of making friends with people they meet in the course of their work? Sometimes those associations permit them to do their government work more effectively.

Second, those who question the need for stricter rules of conduct say we need to recognize that government now has to compete with private business for workers.

> If government develops a code of ethics spelling out a bunch of picayune and unreasonable rules and doesn't pay competitive salaries and benefits, can it expect to get a work force that is little more than dull or lazy? And as soon as someone discovers another practice they do not like, will they add another rule?
>
> Third, this view asks, Who says public sector employees need to set an example or have higher standards than the private sector workers? If ethics has to deal with social morals and values, why should these groups have different standards? Why would we say it's all right for private sector workers to use their knowledge, skills, contacts, and energy to generate extra income and outlaw it for public employees? Should our rules not set a single standard of ethical conduct? A double standard will only weaken the public service.
>
> What do you think? Is the work of government so distinct from that of private workers that different ethical standards should apply? Do we have a problem of inadequate standards, or is it a case of people not following reasonable standards already in place? What are your answers to the questions on ethics included in the policy box? Why?
>
> *Joseph M. Winski, "Ethical Laws Draw Broad Support," *City and State*, June 19, 1982, p. 1.

Full-Time Specialization Administrators not only work full time, they focus their efforts on a narrow range of problems. The activities of the director of the state police or the community police chief do not fluctuate according to public mood—they work steadily, day by day. If mental health or environmental problems become major political concerns, that does not distract the police professionals from their main responsibility—to control crime. Elected officials, however, usually can afford to focus on a narrow issue only briefly.

Financial Independence Sometimes top professional administrators, especially in state government, almost get to be their own bosses, especially if they have virtual control of the spending power of their agencies.

If gasoline tax receipts are earmarked for highway programs, for instance, its administrators determine where the available money will be spent. Elected officials might criticize these priorities, but if questioned, the professionals coldly reply that the earmarked money is being used according to law and widely accepted professional standards.

The Effect of Intergovernmental Relations Federal grants also encourage administrative independence. Commonly administrators have a good deal of discretion on how to spend program funds, including those the state contributes. One study of state agency heads who received at least 25 percent of their funds from federal sources reported that the heads were considerably less responsive to state political controls, were more likely to lobby in the state legislature for more funds than the governor recommended, and felt that they were, in fact, less subject to supervision by the governor or legislature than were other agency directors.[12]

But as federal funding of programs declines and as more of them are consolidated into block grants, previously independent state agencies are likely to come under greater gubernatorial and legislative control. In these instances, state agencies depend more on the governor's budget recommendations and on controls imposed by the state legislature.[13]

Expertise as an Influence on Lawmaking Most governors, mayors, and legislators cannot describe precisely how government programs operate. But professionals know, to the minutest detail, about the program they administer. They are experts. The head of the elections agency knows all the ins and outs of electronic voting machines and can give ten reasons why a particular proposal won't work and what needs to be done to make it work. Legislators may ask tough questions, but they are hesitant to ignore the advice of the professionals.

Professional influence is greatest in areas where the public believes that expertise works—for example, in control of contagious diseases. Professional influence is lower in controversial areas, such as welfare or criminal rehabilitation.[14]

Client Groups Influence Lawmaking Professional administrators usually enlist the support of their client groups. Even large private industries help lobby their programs, when their goals and those of the professionals coincide.

Limits of Professionalism Professionalism has its drawbacks as well as its benefits.

Administering the Laws Art Buchwald, the political satirist, once described what happens when a law to repair potholes gets into the hands of Plotkin, a $20,000-a-year bureaucrat—"The guy who really runs this country." Plotkin examines the legal language and, finding it vague, asks, "What kind of pothole does the law cover? How much should be spent to fill a pothole?" and "What constitutes a pothole in the first place?" The story winds on with Plotkin setting up a study commission. After a time he decides he needs a panel of experts and later, a building to house his growing staff. Finally everyone else forgets about the pothole program.[15]

All administration does not follow this route. But the story also is not entirely fanciful. Professionals, through detailed rules they develop, have leeway in deciding what the law means and how to implement it.

The Single-Mindedness of Professionals Difficulties may arise when the public believes that professional administrators are too dedicated to the values of their clients or profession at the expense of other values. Citizens criticize probation officials who emphasize prisoner rehabilitation over public safety and, for example, grant furloughs to dangerous inmates. (George Bush repeatedly stung his opponent, Governor Michael Dukakis, in the 1988 presidential campaign for precisely such an inmate furlough.) Or farmers accuse highway engineers of planning a new freeway without regard for the farmland they destroy in the process.

And, of course, two sets of professional values may conflict occasionally. For example, experts in solid waste management urge waste incineration to save sanitary landfill space; other professionals want to shut down burn plants because the ash is too toxic. Whenever professionals pursue their own values single-mindedly, as often they must, they run the danger of damaging values equally important to other professionals and to citizens. Such dilemmas and conflicts, of course, open the way for elected officials to generate a political compromise.

Professional Faddism Professionals also get caught up in fads. This, in part, results from the intense competition among professionals to achieve major improvements—innovative "breakthroughs." For example, some forest service personnel follow a policy of not trying to extinguish forest fires ignited by lightning unless human life or property is endangered. In the summer of 1988 foresters slavishly followed this policy while watching thousands of acres of Yellowstone National Park burn to a crisp. Such experiments can be costly and sometimes have tragic consequences for clients and, in this case, animal life.

The other side is that professionalism also encourages a self-criticism that may be self-corrective. In the case of the Yellowstone National Park fires, professionals, with some encouragement from politicians and citizens, realized that human beings may have a duty to intervene and attempt to stop even a *natural* disaster in progress.

Administrative Policy-making in a Democracy A final and major objection to excessive influence by professional administrators in policy-making is that they sometimes quietly oppose or subvert programs that elected officials advance.

Though professional administrators influence and even make policy, the key point is that the public, through its representatives, should have the opportunity to review and even reverse such policies. Democratic values hold that elected representatives, when they follow accepted procedures, have "the right to be wrong." That faith assumes that the majority, in the long run, will adopt policies beneficial to society.

Unionization of Public Employees

Another major source of power for public employees is the **labor union**—organizations through which employees band together to bargain for improved working conditions.

Why Public Sector Unionization Lagged Through the 1950s unionization of public employees was relatively rare. Unionization of workers occurred most commonly among private sector blue-collar workers. Beginning in the middle 1960s, though, the growth of public employee unions advanced rapidly. The American Federation of State, County, and Municipal Employees (**AFSCME**), for example, gained 800,000 members between 1962 and 1978.

The "Public Service" Concept Public employee unions were slow in developing earlier because public workers viewed themselves as public servants,

Public employees on the picket line.

people privileged to work on behalf of the general public. Moreover, such unions were seen as unnecessary—their jobs were secure, the work was clean, retirement benefits generous, and bosses humane.

Also, dedication to a professional outlook conflicted with self-interested behavior. Service to the public in a profession was its own reward. If the pay was low, that came with the territory.

Legal Provisions Most states outlawed strikes as a way to enforce bargaining demands. The underlying premise was that government provides essential public services that cannot be interrupted. And many public employees feared being fired if they did strike.

Other Means of Resolving Disputes Public workers had other means of resolving the kinds of problems unions deal with. The merit system gave them virtually automatic raises based on seniority, promotion based on tests and experience, and elaborate protections against firings and/or demotions.

Why Unionization Progressed Several conditions of the 1970s explain why public unions grew. First, union leaders began targeting private and public white-collar workers as industrial union growth slowed when the American economy began shifting to a service base.

Second, the dramatic expansion of public employment especially as a result of increased federal grants in the 1970s presented labor unions with a major new untapped field for growth. (See Figure 10.1. Also see Table 10.1 for current staffing levels.)

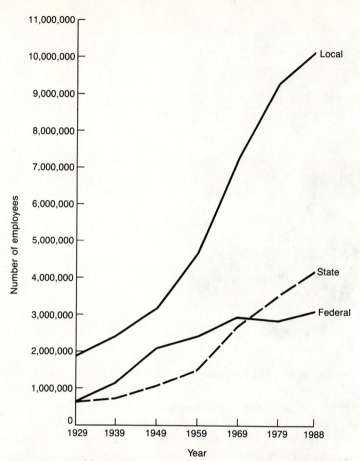

Figure 10.1 Public employment trends, 1929–1988: state and local public employment grows; federal holds steady during the 1970s and 1980s. [*Source: Significant Features of Fiscal Federalism*, Vol. II, 1989. (Washington, D.C.: ACIR), p. 112.]

Third, public attitudes toward public employee unions began to change in part because of the experience with private sector white-collar unions and because the public grew somewhat tolerant of civil disobedience as a legitimate means of protest against the Vietnam War and racial discrimination, making public employee groups using similar tactics seem less objectionable.

Finally, although public employees had secure jobs, their pay lagged behind that for similar private jobs. As some groups began to back wage demands with work stoppages and win wage gains, other groups saw unionization as an effective means to improve their own work arrangements.

The Goals of Unionization The playwright George Bernard Shaw once described trade unionism as "the capitalism of the working class." Union members, like capitalists, he observed, act out of self-interest, although both sometimes provide some desirable social benefits as by-products.

Union goals center on improved **job conditions**—better salaries, fringe benefits, pensions, hours, promotions, grievance procedures, and other matters.[16] Union goals involve a number of procedures, some of which conflict with the merit approach and with professional values.

Unions seek to discourage competition among workers. Thus unions favor seniority and experience over "merit" for raises or promotions. Unions want work tasks and duties defined precisely. They want detailed grievance procedures. And unions want union membership mandatory for all workers in the bargaining group—a **union shop**.

Unions prefer to organize by skill groups across the whole of a state or community government, rather than on a department-by-department basis. Usually, they also want contracts for a specified period—typically two or three years. Because union members judge their union by the improvements obtained, union leaders are involved in a constant search for improved benefits and working conditions.

Unions usually want to enforce their demands with the ultimate weapon—the strike—which makes life less convenient for the public and leads to pressure for resolution.

The Variable Legal Framework Wisconsin, in 1959, was the first state to allow collective bargaining for public employees. But most states do not permit public employees to strike legally, and those that do deny that right to police and fire department employees. Instead, police and fire-fighting units have **binding arbitration** that comes into play after bargaining talks break down, and an independent arbitrator determines the terms of the final agreement. Collective bargaining laws are most advanced in the industrial Northeast and Midwest, where many citizens themselves are union members.

Controlling Employee Strikes Although most states forbid public employee strikes, public employees still strike or organize work stoppages or slowdowns. The first statewide walkout in Massachusetts occurred in 1976. For a time it was chaotic. Drawbridges left open caused traffic snarls. Lifeguards left the beaches. Operations at one of Boston's two sewage treatment facilities stopped, and the superintendent of the Paul Dever School for the Mentally Retarded asked parents to take their children home.

Minnesota, whose law permits many of its employee groups to strike, had 60 percent of its employees on walkout in 1981. The governor reported that "essential services were continuing with minimal disruptions." Supervisory personnel staffed the offices and hired private guards to patrol the capitol grounds.

Both the Massachusetts and Minnesota stories have been repeated whether state laws allow strikes or not. President Reagan's firing of striking air traffic controllers in 1981 perhaps stiffened the resolve of some state and community executives, but most do not have the option of replacing striking employees. The problem with no-strike laws, of course, is that they are nearly impossible to enforce. A judge may order strikers to return to work but cannot put them all in jail if they defy the order. And jailing union officers makes martyrs of them. The main judi-

Table 10.1 STATE AND LOCAL EMPLOYMENT PER 10,000 POPULATION, 1987

State	Total	Rank	State	Rank	Local	Rank
New England						
Connecticut	479	39	181	19	298	42
Maine	489	32	178	21	311	40
Massachusetts	492	30	158	30	334	26
New Hampshire	434	49	149	37	285	45
Rhode Island	448	46	201	9	247	49
Vermont	489	31	215	6	274	47
Mid-Atlantic						
Delaware	537	12	287	3	250	48
Maryland	498	28	176	24	322	37
New Jersey	499	26	129	43	370	9
New York	628	3	154	33	474	2
Pennsylvania	395	50	105	49	290	43
Great Lakes						
Illinois	447	47	112	47	335	25
Indiana	470	40	138	40	332	29
Michigan	485	34	140	39	345	18
Ohio	459	43	116	45	343	20
Wisconsin	487	33	132	41	355	15
Plains						
Iowa	539	10	182	18	357	14
Kansas	554	6	173	26	381	6
Minnesota	481	35	150	36	331	30
Missouri	446	48	130	42	316	39
Nebraska	606	4	186	16	420	3
North Dakota	547	8	227	5	320	38
South Dakota	515	19	186	15	329	31
Southeast						
Alabama	499	25	172	27	327	33
Arkansas	463	41	162	29	301	41
Florida	454	44	105	48	349	16
Georgia	552	7	153	34	399	4
Kentucky	454	45	173	25	281	46
Louisiana	530	14	191	12	339	24
Mississippi	541	9	169	28	372	8
North Carolina	504	22	156	32	348	17
South Carolina	526	15	204	8	322	35
Tennessee	479	38	146	38	333	28

Table 10.1 *Continued*

State	Total	Rank	State	Rank	Local	Rank
Virginia	515	18	176	23	339	23
West Virginia	499	27	177	22	322	36
Southwest						
Arizona	480	36	114	46	366	11
New Mexico	592	5	235	4	357	13
Oklahoma	524	16	197	11	327	34
Texas	500	24	118	44	382	5
Rocky Mountain						
Colorado	536	13	156	31	380	7
Idaho	515	20	182	17	333	27
Montana	538	11	198	10	340	22
Utah	480	37	191	13	289	44
Wyoming	714	2	213	7	501	1
Far West						
Alaska	750	1	382	2	368	10
California	463	42	105	50	358	12
Hawaii	503	23	390	1	113	50
Nevada	497	29	152	35	345	19
Oregon	520	17	180	20	340	21
Washington	514	21	186	14	328	32
U.S. average	496		143		352	

Source: S. D. Gold and J. A. Zelio, *State-Local Fiscal Indicators* (Denver, Colo.: National Conference of State Legislatures, 1990).

cial strategy is to order the two sides to bargain continuously until they reach agreement.

Illegal striking is rather uncommon, especially considering the number of groups that have organized. Strikes are expensive for the unions and members. In addition, strikes generate resentment among the public, which in the long run may be damaging to the union cause. Although union leaders want the right to strike, they do not usually rush to use it. Other strategies such as lobbying, using the media to influence the public, and in general being politically active are more beneficial over the long term.

Criticisms of Public Employee Unionization The negative aspects of unionization stem from what citizens regard as overprotection for the public employee.

Union goals also conflict with professional values. To many professionals, the closing of the Paul Dever School for the Mentally Retarded was inexcusable. The professional will damn with equal impartiality the executive or legislature that permits such happenings, or a union that encourages such an outcome for the private benefit of employees. The professional argues that the client's interests are sacrificed—a practice that cuts the heart out of professionalism.

Other critics maintain that collective bargaining undercuts the merit system.[17] Although unions usually begin with demands for better pay and benefits, they eventually want a voice in job classification, duties, conditions for promotions and advancement, discipline, grievances, and other working conditions. Merit boards tend to end up with only the initial selection of employees.

Political Clout of Public Employee Unions Public employee unions are also criticized because of their partisanship. In 1972 AFSCME leaders played a critical role in the passage of the first federal revenue sharing package.[18] (In the mid-1980s, however, their influence was not enough to preserve the program.) In one year public employee groups in California contributed $1.7 million in campaign funds. In 1981 Vermont employees voted to begin endorsing candidates for public office. Education unions, especially, have increased their effectiveness by encouraging their members to run for the legislature.[19]

Union Influence over Policy-Making Can public employee unions use their political clout to influence policy-making? Let's look at the settlement of the 1976 Massachusetts strike.

The state recognized the right of employees to negotiate working conditions as well as salary. In return, the state would be allowed to set productivity and performance standards for all employees, a power most citizens assumed it already had. And salaries would depend not on the governor and legislature, but on the results of state tax collections—whether the state had a surplus and how much. In effect the legislature gave up its independent power to spend a surplus as it wished.

Perhaps more significant, unionization adds an important new element to the policy-making process. That process has been dominated by legislators, executives, and more recently by professional, high-level administrators. Add to that list the leaders of state and community public employee unions.

APPROACHES TO CONTROLLING THE BUREAUCRATS

In this section we review some of the reforms employed and proposed to redress the balance of powers between bureaucrats and governors and legislators as well as the general public. These programs began around the turn of this century, and focused on gubernatorial control. The modern-day efforts show a growing and continuing concern.[20]

Administrative Reorganization

In 1909 The People's Power League of Oregon, a "radical reform" group, proposed to concentrate executive power in the hands of the governor, checked only by an independent auditor. Reformers around the country immediately endorsed the idea.

The Illinois Reorganization The first state to reorganize for "executive leadership" was Illinois, in 1917. A remarkable new Republican governor, Frank O. Lowden, wanted to "harness more effectively the new economic and social forces born of the industrial age."[21]

Lowden's accomplishments provide a blueprint for **administrative reorganization**. He followed all the tenets of what we now call traditional public administration—and also most of the ideas the "good government" reformers had been talking about. He proposed to

- Place agencies of related functions into one department with no agencies outside the departmental structure.
- Put individual directors rather than commissions or boards in charge of departments.
- Organize lines of authority into a hierarchical scheme with the director at the top.
- Have few enough departments so the department heads can form a governor's "cabinet" of directors.
- Have the governor appoint directors to serve at the governor's pleasure.
- Organize staff functions—personnel, purchasing, printing, and so on—into a department of administration to serve all "line" departments.
- Create a department of finance responsible for money management.
- Appoint an auditor, independent of the governor, to determine whether departments spend funds legally. (Lowden saw this officer as one to be directly elected. Today many are legislative appointees.)

The general pattern today is to shift control of all departments to single executives who are appointed and subject to removal by the governor. Regulatory agencies and education are the major exceptions. Moreover, some states are cutting the number of departments to as few as five.

The Politics of Administrative Reorganization Administrative reorganization has not always come easily. As expected, decentralized agencies independent of the executive have had their dogged last ditch defenders. Mississippi's Legislative Fact Finding Committee, according to York Willbern, reported the following as the typical response of agency heads: "I think this is one of the very best things that has ever been done in the state of Mississippi.... However, my department is of a type, character, and kind that cannot be consolidated with any other agency, as its duties and functions are unique.... Transferring any of this department's duties would prevent citizens from receiving benefits to which they are entitled."[22] Legislators often support administrators' claims and resist reorganization as well, as was the case in Oklahoma and Washington in recent years.

Forces for Independence and Autonomy Agency independence means having a sign on the door that says, "Chief Executive, Department Heads, and Legislators—Keep Out!" An important force for separatism, one Lowden recognized as too difficult to attack, are the elected department heads. Their status is often embedded in the state constitution and city charters.

Interest groups also often oppose reorganization, especially if they have close relations with the agency. Farmers, for example, may not want the urban-oriented governor appointing the director of agriculture.

Reformers, ironically, also want independence for their favored agencies. When new functions—civil service agencies in their time or environmental, consumer protection, or civil rights agencies today—are begun, reformers fear that old-line department heads or executives may undercut the new program. It is better, they argue, to put the new function in an independent agency where administrators support the goals of the new program.

Sometimes the public wants to keep a function free from politics. After a series of scandals, for example, Alabama set up its prison system out of the administrative hierarchy with an independent board of corrections to replace the appointed department head. State university systems often have independent status. The idea is to free them from political meddling.

Professionalism also encourages agency independence. "What do governors, mayors, or legislators know about child abuse?" professional social workers may ask. "Why should politics have anything to do with scientific harvesting of the deer herd?" natural resource professionals may argue. Independence and separation from the governor's administrative hierarchy lessens political interference. And they may ask, What do residency requirements, commonly favored by local politicians, have to do with employee performance?—a question we discuss in Policy Box No. 20, "Are Residency Laws Sound Public Policy?"

The Spread of Administrative Reorganization By 1919 Massachusetts, Nebraska, and Idaho adopted the Illinois model; two years later California, Ohio, and Washington followed suit. Cities and counties also adopted features of the plan. In 1949 another spurt of such reorganization was inspired by the 33 state "Little Hoover" commissions. Today all states and most communities have adopted some of the features of reorganization. During the 1970s Louisiana, Missouri, and Kentucky undertook major reorganization.[23] In the mid-1980s Iowa reduced the number of departments from 21 to 5, and Oklahoma consolidated some 200 agencies into 15 departments.[24]

Is Administrative Reorganization Successful? Even as governors and mayors implement new reorganization plans, critics ask whether reorganization accomplishes all that Governor Lowden in 1917 hoped it would. Executives have gained greater influence in the hierarchy and especially, as Lowden anticipated,

Policy Box No. 20

Are Residency Laws Sound Public Policy?

Washington, D.C., has a degree of home rule, but Congress still has a say over policies the city adopts. One city rule that irritates some members of Congress is the city's residency rule. It makes it illegal for the city to hire nonresidents and requires all employees to reside in the city. Congress has barred the use of federal funds to enforce this provision.

Dozens of cities across the land have similar laws. Some cities, however, hire nonresidents but then give newly hired workers a few weeks to become residents. One of the complaints Congress has about Washington's practice is that city officials are not able to find enough qualified applicants to fill the vacant positions. Mayor Marion Barry denied that was a problem, noting that the city can grant waivers when resident applicants cannot be found.

Usually it is the larger older cities that maintain a residency rule, often over the objection of employee unions. Policymakers argue that the residency rule is important, especially for a city with large minority and low-income populations. People who live in a city and who pay the taxes ought to have the first chance at getting the city job, they say. And if nonresidents are hired, what is so bad about requiring them to become residents in a reasonable time? In the words of Coleman Young, mayor of Detroit, "If the city isn't good enough for a person to live in, it's not good enough for them to work in either. Our city doesn't need outsiders to enforce our laws."

Besides, residency rule advocates maintain, having your workers, especially police and fire fighters, live in the city can make a critical difference in case of an emergency such as the San Francisco earthquake. They can be on the job in a matter of minutes rather than having to commute. Moreover, workers have a greater stake in the city if they live here rather than in the suburbs. If they're members of a union, advocates say, they may temper their demands if they know that they and their neighbors will have to pay part of the tab. Nonresidents not only can hold out for ridiculous demands but also escape the city's income tax and higher property taxes. Whatever state aid comes on a per capita basis goes to the suburbs the nonresidents live in rather than the city, and they spend their paychecks at businesses outside the city. Why should the city, with all its financial problems, subsidize its wealthy neighbors any more than it does?

And they argue that it really does not have a negative impact on the quality of its work force. Employment with a larger city offers many advantages that smaller units do not—usually they have higher wages and better benefit programs, and they offer better opportunities for career advancement without having to change jobs. And, if the city can grant a waiver in filling critical positions, the city has no difficulty in recruiting and maintaining a first-rate work force.

But workers respond with a battery of complaints. One problem they often mention is that they cannot find suitable housing at prices they can afford. Workers in Washington, for example, say that a single-family home in the city costs $170,000, and a police officer's starting salary is only $23,667. And today most families need two breadwinners to make ends meet. What about a family where both the wife and husband have a job? Is it unreasonable for them to want a house halfway between the two jobs? And what are they to do if both spouses work for different cities that have residency rules—maintain two houses?

Workers also complain that the rule is very difficult to enforce. Many workers caught up in the dilemma have a small apartment in the city or a room in a friend's home so they have a city address. They may or may not sleep there a few nights a week. But if the rule is enforced, the city has to hire spies to sneak around to find out what people are doing in the nonworking hours. The city should make better use of its resources than that. And if the city policy permits waivers it soon has a double standard—higher-echelon employees are permitted to live wherever they wish while those who can least afford it have to find a place in the city.

Policymakers may think their residency policy has no effect on the quality of the city work force just because they can find somebody to fill their positions. What they don't know is that many first-rate workers, including new graduates, don't even file an application when they learn about the residency rule. And for many it may have nothing to do with pay, benefits, cost of housing, careers, or whatever. If they have children, they want to make sure their kids are able to go to a quality school and live in a nurturing neighborhood.

Why should a city want to interfere in the personal lives of its employees and make captives of them? they ask. As one Allentown, Pennsylvania, employee wrote, "Many cities get half their money from the state. Local governments should no longer be permitted to discriminate on the basis of residence as a condition of employment in jobs that are funded in any way by nonlocal taxes." All city officials should worry about is whether the workers' performance meets acceptable standards.

What do you think? Should a city tell its workers where they must live? Do you think workers are likely to be more loyal to the city and their jobs if they are residents? Will resident workers perform differently from nonresidents? Do you think a residency rule would affect your interest in a city job? Can you devise a reasonable compromise between the two positions? In the case of Washington, D.C., should outsiders from Virginia, Maryland, and other states dictate a nonresident policy to city officials?

in the budget process. With a tightknit administrative structure under the governor, and fewer elected department heads and independent commissions, the number of access points for citizens and interest group representatives is reduced somewhat. Yet most students would say that reorganization by itself has achieved only partial success.

James Q. Wilson put it this way—"The behavior of persons who lead or speak for an organization can best be understood in terms of their efforts to maintain and enhance the organization and their position in it."[25] Administrators do more than meekly carry out the orders of the governor or mayor or city manager—they are at least as concerned with building up their own agencies and with advancing their own careers. They are neither "conservative" nor "liberal"—self-preservation, or agency preservation, comes first.

Still, numerous governors attempt to make their mark through reorganizations. Although they may have other political objectives they attempt to justify organizational refinements on the basis of improved efficiency largely by reducing or slowing the growth in the number of public employees and public spending. Does reorganization make a difference?

Kenneth J. Meier studied reorganization efforts in 16 states and compared the rates of growth in the state work forces and spending before and after reorganization. He found that short-run growth rates of state employment declined in five states, and five had short-term increases. Long-term results were different—eight states experienced slowing rates (three statistically significant), and eight states (two statistically significant) increased. In terms of state budgets, five experienced statistically insignificant decreases, but 15 of the 16 experienced increases in the growth rate of their budgets.[26] (See Tables 10.2 and 10.3.)

The Power of Publicity

Governors and mayors can focus media attention on an agency. In extreme cases, the executive may publicly join the criticism and suggest that the agency head resign or that agency functions be changed. Or he or she may simply avoid the whole issue and let the department head "twist slowly in the wind." But these executive responses are much less likely if the department head is a gubernatorial appointee rather than a designee of an independent commission.

Administrators prefer anonymity to open warfare with the mayor or governor. Thus the usual pattern is one of at least outward respect and cooperation.

Budget Reforms

During the 1800s legislatures were the principal budget makers. Administrators would tell legislative committees how much money they needed. Legislators responded with "line items"—$450 for postage, $925 for office supplies, $1,100 for printing, and so on. These narrow limits kept administrators in close check.

The Executive Budget In 1913 Ohio became the first state to adopt an **executive budget**—the governor and the budget staff develop the revenue and spending plan for the entire government and then give it to the legislature for approval. Executive budgets provide an overview plan and an indication of the governor's or mayor's program priorities.

Administrators know that legislators seldom raise appropriations much above levels the executive recommends. And in most states, if the legislature approves spending plans too far out of line, the governor will probably use the item veto.

Performance Budgeting In 1947 the Hoover Commission report on U.S. government reorganization recommended that budget items should be related to specific performance goals. In **performance budgets** each budget request is tied to a particular function, activity, and project with specific goals and purposes. Legislators then have a better idea of why the money was requested.

Table 10.2 IMPACT OF EXECUTIVE REORGANIZATION ON STATE EMPLOYMENT

State (year)	Regression coefficients for employment			R^{2d}
	Average yearly increase[a]	Short-term impact[b]	Long-term impact[c]	
California	10,485	−789	−3,209	.993
1968	(28.3)[d]	(0.2)	(4.0)	
Colorado	1,725	3,786	171	.989
1968	(5.2)	(3.0)	(0.8)	
Delaware	357	2,600	−11	.940
1970	(7.0)	(2.9)	(0.1)	
Georgia	3,883	−4,070	1,159	.939
1972	(9.4)	(1.7)	(1.3)	
Idaho	601	1,093	247	.919
1974	(8.4)	(1.6)	(0.7)	
Illinois	6,909	3,149	−4,449	.935
1969	(9.6)	(0.8)	(3.9)	
Kentucky	1,970	6,329	−440	.963
1973	(15.0)	(1.6)	(0.3)	
Louisiana	2,289	2,579	−1,662	.941
1975	(13.4)	(1.3)	(1.0)	
Maine	476	−159	277	.971
1971	(14.4)	(0.2)	(1.7)	
Maryland	2,260	−100	1,789	.975
1970	(9.3)	(0.1)	(3.8)	
Massachusetts	1,573	12,343	−12	.992
1969	(17.1)	(8.7)	(0.1)	
Missouri	2,685	1,164	−931	.924
1974	(10.9)	(0.6)	(0.8)	
South Dakota	530	−839	35	.956
1973	(13.9)	(1.5)	(0.2)	
Virginia	3,865	345	563	.943
1972	(9.6)	(0.3)	(0.2)	
Washington	1,971	10,950	779	.995
1967	(17.3)	(8.2)	(3.8)	
Wisconsin	2,451	10,300	−1,239	.971
	(10.0)	(3.6)	(2.8)	

Source: Kenneth J. Meier, "Executive Reorganization of Government: Impact on Employment and Expenditures," American Journal of Political Science 24:3 (August 1980): 396–412.

[a] Average annual expansion of the bureaucracy before the reorganization—therefore the number of people the bureaucracy would have added per year had the reorganization not occurred.

[b] Number of persons added to or subtracted from the bureaucracy in the year immediately following the reorganization.

[c] The change in the bureaucracy's annual employment over the long run.

[d] t-scores in parentheses.

Table 10.3 IMPACT OF EXECUTIVE REORGANIZATION ON STATE EXPENDITURES

State (year)	Percentage of expenditures			R^{2a}
	Average yearly increase	Short-term impact	Long-term impact	
California	10.7	−0.7	−0.3	.998
1968	(53.5)[a]	(0.2)	(0.6)	
Colorado	9.0	−0.3	4.0	.997
1968	(45.0)	(0.1)	(6.6)	
Delaware	9.6	9.4	1.0	.984
1970	(19.2)	(1.0)	(0.5)	
Georgia	9.8	−0.2	3.1	.987
1972	(19.6)	(0.03)	(1.6)	
Idaho	8.8	6.4	6.3	.988
1974	(22.0)	(0.9)	(2.4)	
Illinois	8.9	20.1	3.9	.990
1969	(17.6)	(2.6)	(2.8)	
Kentucky	10.6	−12.2	4.6	.992
1973	(35.3)	(1.4)	(1.5)	
Louisiana	7.9	−1.2	22.6	.992
1975	(39.5)	(0.2)	(1.8)	
Maine	8.5	26.4	2.4	.981
1971	(17.0)	(2.6)	(1.0)	
Maryland	9.8	23.5	2.7	.996
1970	(32.7)	(4.4)	(2.5)	
Massachusetts	7.5	23.9	4.6	.993
1969	(18.8)	(4.1)	(4.6)	
Missouri	9.0	3.4	1.7	.987
1974	(22.5)	(0.5)	(0.5)	
South Dakota	7.9	0.1	4.9	.996
1973	(39.5)	(0.02)	(2.9)	
Virginia	9.8	2.9	3.6	.990
1972	(24.5)	(0.5)	(2.1)	
Washington	7.6	8.5	3.1	.993
1967	(25.3)	(1.7)	(3.9)	
Wisconsin	10.1	5.9	1.5	.998
1967	(33.7)	(2.0)	(3.8)	

Source: Kenneth J. Meier, "Executive Reorganization of Government: Impact on Employment and Expenditures," American Journal of Political Science 24:3 (August 1980): 396–412.

[a] t-scores in parentheses.

Instead of listing individual expense items, the budget agency lists the money needed for each activity or goal. If, for example, the Conservation Department published a monthly magazine for outdoor enthusiasts, the budget would show "monthly magazine" and the total activity cost rather than showing line items for typesetting, artwork, printing, paper, postage, and so on. Bureaucrats liked the change to performance budgeting because it freed them from legislative control over minor details. Legislators, too, welcomed the idea because it promised them more effective control.

But performance budgeting had weaknesses. Legislators and budget experts could evaluate programs that produced tangible results—new roads built, trees planted, acres of grass mowed, children inoculated. But evaluating activities that had intangible outcomes—public information or administration—was more difficult because the outcomes were not easily measured or tied to program efforts.[27]

Program Planning and Budgeting (PPB) The Rand Corporation, a think tank in California, developed the **program planning and budgeting (PPB)** approach to public budgeting. PPB carried performance budgeting to its logical extreme. The process begins by setting broad state or community objectives, usually ten or less. Budget makers divide these into several levels of categories and subcategories. Each administrative unit then states its five-year goals in relation to these categories, ranks them in importance, spells out alternative methods for achieving them, and analyzes the cost-benefit ratio for each alternative. Administrators project the cost of achieving the goals and tell the governor or mayor how much they need for the next year.

Perhaps the major impact of PPB was that for a year or two it threw bureaucrats off balance and thus strengthened the hand of the executive and the budget officers. It also seems to have encouraged suspicious legislatures to develop their own budget staffs. But critics pointed out that bureaucrats soon learned to work the system to their advantage.

PPB was made to order for professional bureaucrats because spending plans were based on a web of stated and unstated assumptions. Once a governor or legislators accepted the underlying assumptions about goals, they were committed to expensive programs.

PPB advocates assumed that budgeting was fully rational, not subject to the politics of resource allocation. Aaron Wildavsky was more direct in his criticism. He wrote, "PPB does not work because it cannot work. Failure is built into its very nature because it demands abilities to perform cognitive operations which are beyond present human (or machine) capacities."[28]

Robert S. McNamara, then head of the Department of Defense, first used it in budgeting the Vietnam War. In 1965 President Johnson directed all federal agencies to employ the PPB approach. But by 1970 PPB was abandoned quietly by neglect in the federal government, and the same began happening in the states and local units that had been experimenting with it.

Zero-based Budgeting Peter A. Phyrr, a management consultant, was the first to use the zero-based budgeting technique in two divisions of Texas Instruments, Inc., in 1970. Jimmy Carter popularized it when, as the newly elected governor, he installed the system in Georgia in 1971.

The central idea of **zero-based budgeting** is that every agency starts from zero in building up its budget. Just because an agency got so much this year, it has no claim on that amount for next year. It will have to justify all its budget requests.

Managers describe a "decision package" for each activity the agency performs. Administrators develop cost estimates and performance measures for each package and state the consequences of not performing the activity at all, as well as alternative methods for doing it. The manager must then show what would happen if the activity received 85 percent of the current appropriation, then 90 percent, and so on, to a 10 percent increase. The executive then has decision packages from which to assemble the executive budget based on his or her priorities.

Georgia began with 10,000 decision packages, which swamped the budget bureau. It ended up giving about 2,000 to Governor Jimmy Carter.

Critics of zero-based budgeting question especially whether a large bureaucracy isn't wasting a great deal of time and resources to go through the paperwork and trauma of the zero-based budgeting process each year. And they note that it pays little attention to the politics of administration—ways administrators can use the system to their own advantage while scuttling its general goals.[29]

Effectiveness of Budget Reforms One student argues that "agencies still request sizable increases from previous budget levels, governors still pare budget requests, and legislatures still appropriate roughly what the governor recommends."[30] And while governors focus mainly on the big-ticket departments—education, health, welfare, transportation, and law enforcement—state legislatures appear to be taking a more affirmative role in budget expansions. The budget reforms seem not to have diminished greatly the tendency toward incrementalism in budget allocations.

Management by Objectives (MBO)

Another approach is to concentrate on specific tasks, as in **management by objectives (MBO)**. The boss and subordinates agree on a series of short-term goals and the period in which each should be achieved. Within the MBO framework, subordinates in turn develop objectives with their subordinates, and so on down the line. The system is supposed to create a flow of productivity as each employee works to meet personal and agency objectives. The goals have an **efficiency and economy** ring to them—produce more at the same cost or maintain service levels with lower costs.

Some lower-level employees find MBO threatening, often seeing it as a speed-up system to make them work harder. The most difficult problem subordinates face is determining what their objectives should be and what they should report up the line. Another is that the system tends to become clogged as administrators rush to MBO meetings to check on progress and leave the other work undone. On the other hand, MBO probably tightens some organizational slackness—at least in its early applications.

Civil Service Reforms Some observers say the most promising solution is an overhaul of civil service. They recommend that we should turn away from trying to create neutrally competent automatons—what Meg Greenfield, *Newsweek* columnist, describes as "the great holy grail of American political reform... an idealized, unattainable—and frankly, weird state in which there is no discretion, no judgment, no flesh and blood, no better and worse—in short, no human politics."[31] She and others who share her views argue for being less concerned with partisan bias and more concerned with productivity.

Whenever a new administration comes into office, they say, it can make relatively few high-level appointments. These patronage appointees may have ideas about new policies, but they are stuck with civil servants who know governmental procedures but may be unsympathetic to the new policies.

The way to make bureaucracies more responsive is to allow political appointees to choose the top-level civil servants from a pool of senior executives.

Senior Executive Service Twelve states have a **senior executive service** from which incoming politically appointed department heads can select their top-level professional administrators. In most of these states the persons in the SES pool continue to have civil service protections and can retreat to a civil service position, if for any reason and without prejudice the executive is dismissed. Also, under the SES approach, the department head usually has authority to set the pay for the SES personnel. Political appointees thus gain more influence through the ranks of the agencies. The federal government and several states have now adopted this reform.

Ersa Poston of the U.S. Merit Systems Protection Board said that a study of SES in eight agencies found federal employees thinking that the approach would not affect their individual performance. Of those in SES, only 52 percent said that they would stay voluntarily.[32] Over half said that they saw examples of "personal favoritism" where salary increases seemed unrelated to personal or agency performance.

James L. Sundquist believes that as incoming administrations remove the senior executives who served under the prior administration, the process will create not a single talent pool but two, one Democratic and one Republican like the majority and minority staffs in state legislatures.[33] In a study of California's program where several shifts in partisan control took place, only about 5 percent of the SES appointees changed with the change in governors.[34]

Legislative Oversight and Control of Bureaucracy

Perhaps the most frustrated of the participants in policy-making are state and local legislators. They often suspect that administrators willfully misinterpret laws they pass. Sometimes they are correct. But legislators have developed a number of techniques to reassert control.

Bureaucrats help explain the state budget.

Reinvolvement in Budgeting Legislators, of course, were never cut out of the budget process—they always had to approve. But without their own staff, they had to depend heavily on information from the governor, agency heads, and lobbyists. Many legislatures now have their own fiscal staff who analyze revenue projections and spending proposals and develop alternatives to the executive budget. Thus, not only the governor, but the legislative finance committees hold hearings and prepare budget proposals.

In addition, many states have auditors general departments that are as responsive to legislative demands for information as they are to executive office requirements. Reports on postaudits of expenditures inform legislators how state agencies spent their appropriations.

Legislators "Help" Administrators Administer In Chapter 8 we discussed the legislative veto over administrative rules to implement legislation. Legislators sometimes criticize bureaucrats for developing rules that contravene what legislators had in mind.[35]

In 1947 Michigan became the first state to establish a legislative committee to review proposed rules. About 35 state legislatures now have a procedure to review administrative rules.[36] Some legislatures must indicate in the statute itself that it will review the rules; others must file an official complaint to the governor.

Usually, the legislative committee must approve or deny a proposed rule within a specific time after submission, or it goes into effect. Not surprisingly, administrators sometimes present controversial rules when legislators are busiest. To counteract this strategy, a few legislatures now pass laws that require the legislative committee to approve administrative rules, or they do not take effect. Twenty legislatures have authority to suspend or amend proposed rules.[37]

Review of Administrative Plans Legislatures have found another way to use their veto power—they require legislative approval at specific stages.[38] In acts appropriating funds for state building projects, for example, the legislature may require that a legislative committee approve the architect, preliminary and final plans, contracts, and many other administrative details.

Sometimes such rules backfire on the legislature. A recent Michigan law, for example, demanded that administrators provide a cost-benefit analysis of renting versus state ownership of office space. One analysis showed a $40 million savings if the state built its own office building for the social service department. But the legislature approved a rental contract anyway.

Sunset Provisions Colorado, in 1976, was the first state to adopt a **sunset law**. These laws set timetables to review regulations, programs, and agencies and require a decision on extending the life of the law. If it is not renewed, the provision expires. Adopting sunset provisions became somewhat of a fad. A few states now officially have abandoned use of them, and others have done so informally.

Supporters say that legislative review of an agency's appropriations is not enough. During the budget process, the legislature does not have sufficient time for a thorough review. Sunset procedures set up such a review according to a schedule—usually every five years or so. Advocates say that sunset rules thus keep administrators conscious of self-examination and the need for self-evaluation and to improve operations.

Others, though, say that sunset provisions aren't necessary—that the legislature can review an agency any time it wants. The review, they say, becomes a mechanical exercise with legislators and administrators shuffling mountains of paper. Smart administrators, they say, devote much of their time to "image building" and publicity to make the agency or program look good.

Surely, sunset reviews have become a routine and mechanical exercise in some states. And decisions to renew a statutory provision are likely to be based on the same political grounds as when the law was initially passed. But sunset rules do require worthy programs to muster a majority of votes in the legislature to survive. And occasionally, legislatures do not renew provisions that may otherwise have continued. As Robert Behn says, "It is difficult to oppose a program designed to require periodic termination of all spending programs, to improve efficiency and effectiveness, and to terminate the obsolete ones."[39]

Privatization of Programs Reformers of the 1980s came up with a new term—*privatization*. They use it to describe the practice of hiring private companies to provide services and functions commonly provided by government. It is recommended because advocates say it cuts down on the number of government workers and assures the public of quality services at the lowest cost. Its advocates have argued that many government operations—from operating correctional facilities to trash collection and custodial services—can be handled more efficiently this way. The concept also is said to improve bureaucratic performance because it introduces competition.[40]

Privatizing can be implemented through various formats—by contracts, franchises, grants and subsidies, vouchers, volunteers, and self-help.[41] And, of course, the approach is not new. Businesses commonly contract to provide cleaning services. Governments have contracted for numerous services for many years—constructing office buildings and highways or for financial auditing, for example.[42] In a study of eight privatized functions in the Los Angeles area, contracting out was found to be less costly—"the efficiency was found to be accomplished through labor and equipment practices rather than at the expense of effectiveness."[43] This study showed that functions requiring regular replacement of equipment and functions that can benefit from flexible personnel practices such as incentive systems lend themselves to contracting out.

Not all functions are easily contracted out. Some require high capitalization costs that private companies are not likely to provide except on the basis of long-term contracts. Others are concerned that once the government gets out of a particular activity, resuming it may be more difficult and costly. And, in the absence of sufficient competitive bidders for a governmental contract, the service costs, in fact, may not be cheaper, especially where contractors cream off the relatively easy service components and leave the government with the difficult ones.

Other criticisms of privatization are that it erodes hard-fought merit programs, may lead to interruption of services because of work stoppages, or the possibility of bankruptcy, fraud, and corruption—all possibilities in the public sector as well, of course.

Perhaps the most serious charge is that privatization may work against the interests of low-income persons. Some of these services, such as public transportation, are provided on the basis of fees and charges rather than tax subsidies. This practice, for example, may impose a disproportionate burden on the poor.[44]

Although privatizing may not be the solution to all governmental services, its advocates provide a public benefit by causing policymakers to consider it as one of several alternatives. Moreover, it serves to remind many public employees that their operations may not be quite the monopolies they thought them to be.

Quality Circles A relatively new innovation in government settings, **quality circles** consist of small groups of workers, usually 6 to 12, who meet regularly to identify, analyze, and resolve work-process problems. Although the technique was developed in private industry, it is being used on a limited basis in governments such as the city of Dallas and Missouri state agencies. It is a strategy for self-supervision and used to encourage lower-level employees to assume greater responsibility for the work product.[45]

Controlling Influences from the Public

Media Influences The media through their role of providing information to citizens also have an effect on administrators' behavior. It is not difficult to imagine how an agency head might feel reading negative newspaper reports about the agency. An article in the metropolitan newspaper reported that the economically depressed city of Detroit was the only city police department in the nation that had its own jet airplane and told about how the administration circumvented the city council in acquiring the plane, as well as the more expensive operating cost of jets versus propeller planes.[46] The *Indianapolis Star*, a regular critic of the patronage-dominated Indiana licensing bureau, reported that the Davies County branch office was $77,000 short and that auditing of the branches was three years behind.

After a time administrators might become a little callous of criticism and assume a "take what comes" attitude. But they know that people, and especially personal acquaintances, will be talking, and that their families are aware of the criticism if stories continue. Eventually, the governor or a legislative committee—as happened with the jet airplane purchase—will have them on the carpet. Thus, it sometimes forces administrators to respond with detailed explanations in the hope that it will put a stop to the criticism.

Citizen Complaints Anyone who has worked in the office of the governor, mayor, or director of a large state agency knows that these offices regularly receive reports from citizens of how someone was driving a particular state vehicle. "Why can people in a state car, license plate number 876543, drive 75 on Interstate 88 at 2:30 in the afternoon of October 4, 1990, when the speed limit is 65?" they ask. Or "What was that state car doing later at the Woodland shopping center?" When the citizens report the license number of the vehicle the letter gets sent back to the driver's department for an explanation. Such citizen "patrols" tend to restrain administrative conduct.

Citizen Membership on Public Boards Traditionally boards and commissions that oversee various state regulatory and licensing agencies have as members only persons from the professions or trades being regulated. But now many state laws require "citizen" members as well.

We should not be too optimistic about the results of such changes. For the most part the interest group members still widely outnumber citizen members. In addition, citizen members are likely to have a difficult time dealing with the jargon and the other complexities of the professions and the regulations covering them. Still, we occasionally learn of incidents where such citizen members have been influential in policy decisions.

Ombudsman Offices The *ombudsman*, or government complaint officer, is an attempt to make bureaucrats more responsive to the general public. At the same time he or she may keep the executive informed about the service problems of the administration.[47] This is a relatively recent, but not widespread, innovation in the United States; it is more common among community than state governments. Sweden and other Scandinavian countries have had ombudsmen for 100 years or more. Ombudsmen intervene and make recommendations regarding agencies or procedures that repeatedly cause problems for citizens.[48]

Ideally, ombudsmen are independent of all other bureaucratic agencies. In most states and communities they are appointed for set terms. A few states, such as New Mexico, assign the responsibility to the lieutenant governor.

A FINAL COMMENT

It is popular almost anytime to acclaim the virtues of business and decry the inefficiencies of government. We find some critics suggesting that governments should employ more management techniques of business.

These are oversimplifications. Yet it is clear that Americans are going through a period of experimental actions with respect to bureaucracies. We hope you recognized the budget procedures, MBO, SES, sunset, and privatization provisions as responses in part to demands for more government efficiency as well as efforts to increase political control.

Our democratic processes are designed to keep governments operating as we Americans wish. Again, in recent times we as citizens have dealt sternly with our state and local administrators—we have modified basic rules, changed the leaders, cut the revenues, occasionally put some agencies out of business, and adopted new codes of ethics for government workers. These are haphazard, somewhat uncoordinated, and often only partially effective methods of reform. Yet as long as citizens continue to exercise such influence, state and local administrators will likely remain within bounds acceptable to most of us.

HIGH POINTS

In this chapter we began by considering (1) the merit system as the principal means of professionalizing state and community bureaucracies. We also reviewed (2) political patronage and how merit employment replaced it. We noted that (3) merit employment principles cannot always be completely translated into practice.

We next considered two major sources of bureaucratic power, professionalization and unionization. We saw that (4) professionalism in bureaucracy tends to lead to administrative policy-making at the expense of elected officials. We noted that (5) unionization is a relatively recent phenomenon among public employees and that it also adds to the policy-making power of bureaucracy. Finally, we considered a variety of approaches for controlling bureaucratic policy-making. We looked at (6) administrative reorganization, (7) new budget strategies, (8) MBO, (9) civil service reforms, (10) privatization and quality circles, and (11) media and citizen involvement as means for democratic control.

In this chapter we defined the following terms in this order: public goods, neutral competence, merit employment, patronage system, professional values, labor union, AFSCME, job conditions, union shop, binding arbitration, administrative reorganization, executive budget, performance budget, program planning and budget (PPB), zero-based budgeting, management by objectives (MBO), efficiency and economy, senior executive service, sunset law, privatization, quality circle, and ombudsman.

NOTES

1. For sponsoring this "reformist" legislation, the Ohio Democratic party denied George H. Pendleton renomination to the U.S. Senate in 1885. President Grover Cleveland, sympathetic to civil service, took care of Pendleton—he appointed him minister to Germany, a major patronage plum.
2. Herbert Kaufman, "Administrative Decentralization and Political Power," *Public Administration Review* 29:1 (January/February 1969): 3–15. He names the two other themes we deal with—"representativeness of patronage practices" and "executive leadership."
3. H. O. Waldby, *The Patronage System of Oklahoma* (Norman, Okla.: Transcript Co., 1950), and Frank J. Sorauf, "Patronage and Party," *Journal of Political Science* 3 (May 1959): 11–26.
4. Anne Freedman, "Doing Battle With the Patronage Army: Politics, Courts, and Personnel Administration in Chicago," *Public Administration Review* 48:5 (September/October 1988): 847–859.
5. "Rousch Expects '2% Clubs' Ban Enforcement," *Indianapolis Star* (October 5, 1976).
6. Joseph J. Lieberman, *The Power Broker, A Biography of John M. Bailey, Modern Political Boss* (Boston: Houghton Mifflin, 1966), p. 341.
7. Clifton McClesky et al., *The Government and Politics of Texas* (Boston: Little, Brown, 1978), pp. 215–216.
8. For a more detailed review of some of these problems see E. S. Savas and Sigmund G. Ginsburg, "The Civil Service, A Meritless System?" *Public Interest* 32 (Summer 1973): 72–85.
9. F. Ted Hebert, Jeffrey L. Brudney, and Deil S. Wright, "Gubernatorial Influence and State Bureaucracy," *American Politics Quarterly* 11:2 (April 1983): 243–264.
10. Bernard Barber, "Control and Responsibility in the Powerful Professions," *Political Science Quarterly* 93:4 (Winter 1978): 599–615.
11. C. F. Taeusch, "Professional Ethics," *Encyclopedia of Social Sciences* (Vol. 12) (New York: Macmillan, 1934), pp. 472–476.
12. George E. Hale and Marian Lief Palley, "Perceptions of Federal Involvement in Intergovernmental Decisionmaking," Paper presented at the Midwest Political Science Association meeting, 1977.
13. David M. Hedge, "Fiscal Dependency and the State Budget Process," *The Journal of Politics* 45:1 (February 1983): 198–208.
14. Fred W. Grupp, Jr., and Alan R. Richards, "Variations in Elite Perceptions of American States as Referents for Public Policy Making," *American Political Science Review* 69 (September 1975): 850–858.
15. Art Buchwald, "President's Power Pivots on Pleasing Plotkin, the Plodder," *Detroit Free Press* (August 22, 1976).

16. Unions also want state workers to have the same benefits as federal workers. The power of the unions was evidenced in persuading Congress to extend overtime and minimum wage provisions to state and local workers. In 1976 the U.S. Supreme Court ruled the action unconstitutional in *National League of Cities v. Usery*, 426 U.S. 833 (1976). In 1985 the Court reversed *Usery*, holding that the Tenth Amendment did not restrict Congress from using the Commerce clause to relate these issues. *Garcia v. San Antonio Metropolitan Transit Authority*, 105 S.Ct. 1005 (1985). The president of AFSCME said *Garcia* brought an end to nine years of "second class citizenship" of state and local public employees.
17. See, for example, E. S. Savas and Sigmund G. Ginsburg, "The Civil Service, A Meritless System?" p. 165.
18. Richard E. Thompson, *A New Era in Federalism?* (Washington, D.C.: Revenue Sharing Advisory Service, 1973), p. 103.
19. Harmon Zeigler and Michael Baer, *Lobbying, Interaction, and Influence in American State Legislatures* (Belmont, Calif.: Wadsworth, 1969), pp. 32–33.
20. The intellectual roots of administrative reorganization are traceable to Woodrow Wilson in 1887, the Louis Brownlow Commission appointed by President Franklin Roosevelt in 1937, and the Hoover Commission in 1948–1949. See James K. Conant, "In the Shadow of Wilson and Brownlow: Executive Branch Reorganization in the States," *Public Administration Review* 48:5 (September/October, 1988): 892–898.
21. William T. Hutchinson, *Lowden of Illinois, The Life of Governor Frank O. Lowden* (Chicago: University of Chicago Press, 1975), pp. 293–326.
22. This section is based on the perceptive comments of York Willbern, "Administrative State Governments," in the American Assembly, *The Forty-Eight States, Their Tasks as Policy Makers and Administrators* (New York: Columbia University, Graduate School of Business, 1955), pp. 115–119.
23. For a survey from which some of these data are taken, see Neal R. Pierce, "State/Local Report, Structural Reform of Bureaucracy Grows Rapidly," *National Journal* (April 4, 1975): 502–508. For brief summaries see the recent editions of *The Book of the States* (Lexington, Ky.: Council of State Governments).
24. Thad L. Beyle, "The Executive Branch: Organization and Issues, 1986–87," *Book of the States* (Lexington, Ky.: Council of State Governments), pp. 47–50.
25. James Q. Wilson, *Political Organization* (New York: Basic Books, 1973). See especially pp. 3–91.
26. Kenneth J. Meier, "Executive Reorganization of Government: Impact on Employment and Expenditures," *American Journal of Political Science* 24:3 (August 1980): 396–412.
27. Bertram M. Gross, "The New Systems Budgeting," *Public Administration Review* 29:2 (March-April 1969): 113–137.
28. Aaron Wildavsky, *Budgeting, A Comparative Theory of Budgeting Processes* (Boston: Little, Brown, 1976), p. 364.
29. For critical evaluations of zero-based budgeting see Donald Axelrod, "Post Burkhead, The State of the Art or Science of Budgeting," *Public Administration Review* (Nov./Dec. 1973): 576–584. See also John D. LaFever, "Zero-Based Budgeting in New Mexico," *State Government* 47:2 (1974). For more supportive views see Peter A. Phyrr, *Zero-Based Budgeting, A Practical Tool for Evaluating Expenses* (New York: Wiley, 1973), and "The Zero-Based Approach to Government Budgeting," *Public Administration Review* 37:1 (January/February 1977): 1–8.
30. Joel A. Thompson, "Agency Requests, Gubernatorial Support, and Budget Success in State Legislatures Revisited," *The Journal of Politics* 49:3 (August 1987): 756–779.

31. Meg Greenfield, "What Is Merit?" *Newsweek* (March 13, 1978).
32. *Public Administration Times* (Aug. 1, 1981): 12.
33. James L. Sundquist, "Civil Service Reform, Pitfalls, and Opportunities," *Good Government* 95:2 (1979).
34. Frank P. Sherwood, "Two State Executive Personnel Systems: A Comparative Analysis," *State and Local Government Review* 20:1 (Winter 1988): 3–10.
35. See Eugene Bardach, *The Implementation Game: What Happens After a Bill Becomes Law* (Cambridge: MIT Press, 1977).
36. For a comprehensive review of administrative rules procedures, see R. Craig Williamson, "Legislative Review of Administrative Rules and Regulations," Paper presented at the Midwest Political Science Association meeting, April 1981. Also see the recent editions of *The Book of the States* (Lexington, Ky: Council of State Governments).
37. See William Pound, "Legislative Review of Administrative Rule Making," *State Legislatures* (Nov./Dec. 1975): 23.
38. Carol S. Weissert, "The Politics-Administration Dichotomy Revisited, An Intergovernmental Perspective," Paper presented at the Midwest Political Science Association meeting, April 1981.
39. Robert D. Behn, "The False Dawn of Sunset Laws," *Public Interest* 49 (1977–1978): 103–118.
40. E. S. Savas, *Privatization: The Key to Better Government* (Chatham, N.J.: Chatham Publishers, 1987).
41. Harry P. Hatry and Carl F. Valente, "Attentive Service Delivery Approaches Involving Increased Use of the Private Sector" (Washington, D.C.: International City Management Association, 1983), pp. 199–217.
42. The involvement of private auditing firms in government has led to the standardization of governmental auditing practices. See Larry P. Bailey, *Governmental GAAP Guide, 1989* (New York: Harcourt Brace Jovanovich, 1989).
43. Eileen Brettler Berenyi and Barbara J. Stevens, "Does Privatization Work? A Study of the Delivery of Eight Local Services," *State and Local Government Review* 20:1 (Winter 1988): 11–20.
44. David R. Morgan and Robert E. England, "The Two Faces of Privatization," *Public Administration Review* 48:6 (November/December 1988): 979–987.
45. Robert B. Denhardt, James Pyle, and Allen C. Bluedorn, "Implementing Quality Circles in State Government," *Public Administration Review* 47:4 (January/February 1987): 304–309.
46. *The Detroit News* (July 16, 1989), pp. 1A, 12A.
47. See Carolyn Stieber, "Talking Back: States and Ombudsmen," *State Government* 55:2 (1982): 40–42.
48. For an assessment of ombudsmen in a state and community see Robert D. Miewald and John C. Comer, "The Complaint Function of Government and the Ombudsman," *State and Local Government Review* 16:1 (Winter 1984): 22–26, and Lynn W. Bachelor, "Patterns of Citizen Contacts with a Central Complaint Office: The Case of the Detroit Ombudsman," *State and Local Government Review* 16:2 (Spring 1984): 69–74.

Chapter 11

State and Community Judges as Legitimizers

"**P**eople simply don't understand courts and lawyers and their relationship with the people of the state." So said Robert Rose, chief justice of the Wyoming Supreme Court, to a high school journalism convention in Cheyenne. He went on to comment that people "can't make informed decisions about the court and don't know whether it is performing as it should."

However, things are changing somewhat. Television coverage of some trials, reports in newspapers and magazines, and more realistic and popular television shows are helping us to become more aware of the courts than we were just a few years ago. Still, we have a long way to go, in part because the courts wall themselves off to prevent outside interference and also because the media tend to report only the results of the trial and seldom on the process itself.[1]

The symbol for judicial impartiality is a blindfolded woman holding a scale. The judges' black robes, their personal demeanor, and curious courtroom rituals are other symbols of impartiality. Through them, judges seek to appear detached from the issues they decide and to inspire trust in the courts.

Impartiality is essential to their role as "legitimizers"—people who decide when society may deprive us of our liberty (and sometimes of life itself) and who have the authority to resolve the disputes that arise among us. If citizens consider our courts as unworthy of our trust and confidence, the system of rule by law breaks down because the only other recourse to resolve a dispute is brute force and special privilege.

Another aspect of impartiality is the idea that judges only interpret or apply the law to specific cases, but do not make public policy. As we see later, judges are policymakers—on some matters, the *major* policymakers. But, of course, they are policymakers of a special sort and with a style that differs from those of legislative or executive decision makers. They are less subject to direct and overt partisan political pressures than other officials. Still, there are pressures—from the public, interest groups, other public officials, and professional colleagues.

Overview We begin by examining the major patterns the states use in organizing their courts. We next look at the way U.S. Supreme Court decisions have brought the state courts together, giving national structure to many areas of law even though the national court system is separate from those of the states. We then review the politics of the judiciary. Finally we consider the limits—institutional constraints and public opinion—on judicial policy-making.

STRUCTURE AND JURISDICTION OF STATE AND LOCAL COURTS

State and community courts are of two major types—those that have original jurisdiction and courts that review appeals from decisions made in other courts.

Original Jurisdiction The authority to handle and process a case in the first instance is called **original jurisdiction**. States have three main kinds of courts of original jurisdiction.

At the first level are the **minor courts** such as justice of the peace courts and city courts that handle civil cases of low value and criminal charges for which possible fines are small and jail sentences are less than a year. This is the type of court you appear in for speeding (if you dispute the ticket) or for disorderly conduct (if, for example, your dorm party gets out of hand). You could also find yourself in such a court if a merchant sues you for not paying a small bill.

Second are the states' **general trial courts**, which handle the major cases. They are the workhorses of the state court systems. These handle people accused of felonies—robbery, murder, rape, embezzlement, and other major crimes.

Third are courts of special jurisdiction. These are family, probate, and surrogate courts, which handle divorce problems, child custody cases, wills and estates, and crimes by juveniles.

Appellate Jurisdiction All states have an appeals court system as well. Courts with **appellate jurisdiction** mainly review lower court decisions when the losing party believes that the trial judge made a mistake. The **court of last resort** in each state is usually called the state supreme court and is usually the top management center for a state's court system.

A growing number of states also have an **intermediate appeals court**. This court handles virtually all of the decisions that are appealed. A few of the cases this court decides go on to the state's highest court for another appeal and review.

The Federal System It is worth noting that the national or federal court system parallels this basic structure across our land. In each state are one or more federal district courts that in the main are trial courts of original jurisdiction on charges of violating federal law.

Overlying these federal district courts is a group of intermediate appeals courts strategically located around the nation. And then, of course, there is the U.S. Supreme Court, which is the final arbiter of our laws.

The Minor Courts

States use many names for their minor courts—names that do not always tell us the level of the court. Typically, these minor courts are city or municipal and justice of the peace courts. Some states also add small claims courts, common plea courts (although Ohio and Pennsylvania use this term to designate their general trial courts), magistrate courts, police courts, and county courts. The term *district court* may refer to a minor court in some states and to a general trial court in others.

Jurisdiction What distinguishes the minor courts from the others? As a general rule the minor courts deal with the lesser crimes (**misdemeanor offenses**) and sometimes with low-level felonies and violations of municipal ordinances.

Legislatures also define minor courts by the sentences they may impose—in criminal cases usually not more than a year. But minor courts are also involved with major crimes through **arraignment proceedings** in which they assess whether a crime was committed and if the evidence against a person is sufficient to "bind the person over for trial" in the general trial court. The judge conducting the hearing, in most instances, also sets the bail. Judges in these courts often are also involved with police work when investigators request permission—a warrant—to search a residence or building.

These courts also settle minor civil disputes—a repair bill we think we shouldn't have to pay, or a fight with a landlord over a rental deposit we think we should get back. Minor courts may consider civil cases only where the dollar amount in dispute is relatively small—no greater than $500 in some states.

The Quality of Minor Courts Courts of limited jurisdiction sometimes are referred to as "inferior courts." Critics such as H. Ted Rubin suggest they are inferior because judges may be poorly paid laypersons, rather than lawyers, who work in poor physical surroundings.

These minor courts process perhaps 90 percent of the criminal cases of the nation. Most involve more than middle-class Americans pleading guilty to traffic tickets. It is here where "justice" is doled out to the poor—the drunk and disorderly, vagrants, prostitutes, and petty gamblers. This may also be where petty but full-time criminals sidestep the law. Rubin, a former judge, describes a scene in a Cleveland municipal court.[2]

> The Criminal Division is located in the Police Building at 21st and Payne. The courtroom is well worn, crowded, and noisy. Row on row of benches are peopled with defendants out on bail, witnesses, friends and relatives of defendants, attorneys, social service personnel, and others.... The arraignments, hearings, and conferences which occur at the bench are largely inaudible beyond the second or third row of the spectator gallery. Witnesses generally testify from standing positions off to the side of the judge. There is little dignity to the setting. Jailed defendants are brought in and out from a door behind the judge and off to his right. People leaving the courtroom go out a door in the front of the room and off to the judge's left, where outside noise enters the courtroom as the door opens and closes.

In many localities these minor court judges dispense justice, "production-line style," to a continuing stream of people. Proper facilities correctly maintained may appear to change the atmosphere of these courts a little, but the reality of relentless processing of cases is never far removed.

Justice of the Peace Courts Justice of the peace—JP—courts are the counterpart of municipal courts in the outlying areas of many states. In the Jacksonian tradition, JPs are usually elected from districts. Often, they are people with no formal legal training. According to the National Center for State Courts, about one-half of these judges are nonlawyers. What they know about the law may have come only from what they learned on the job. One Harlan, Kentucky, JP readily admitted that his knowledge of the law was vague. "But," he said, "I've got a whole lot of common sense."

The JPs Under Attack About two-thirds of the states now ban nonlawyer judges. Other states limit severely their jurisdiction—California, for example, forbids any nonlawyer judge from handling cases that may involve a jail sentence. Why?

Some argue that nonlawyer judges do not understand the fine points of the legal arguments. Others maintain that holding court on the front porch of a residence, as some do, is demeaning to our system of justice. And in some states the JPs still operate on a fee basis—their pay comes from defendants who plead guilty. This practice led some cynics to say that JP stands for "judgment for the plaintiff," for if a defendant is declared innocent the JP gets no compensation in the case.

Yet the JP system survives in some states because it has a good deal of democratic appeal—that common people rather than the professional elites should judge those charged with breaking the law. And each time a legislature proposes to end the JP system, state associations of JPs draw on their political resources to counter the effort.

The issue also has a financial dimension—how to replace the relatively inexpensive system of dispensing justice in minor cases. Even where JP systems have been eliminated, critics note, the reorganized courts permit magistrates (sometimes nonlawyers) to process traffic tickets, accept guilty pleas for minor offenses, and act in the place of the judge on a variety of matters.

Small Claims Courts Some states have **small claims courts** to handle minor civil disputes. A lawyer-judge or magistrate presides while litigants present their own arguments somewhat like those litigants on the television show "People's Court" where Judge Wapner presides. Proceedings are informal, speedy, and inexpensive.

Consumer groups were among the early advocates of small claims courts. They saw simple procedures and low costs as benefiting individuals in legal battles against business and monied interests. But Robert L. Spurrier found that in Oklahoma the "little person" has become the "little defendant." Merchants, landlords, utilities, and finance companies were much more knowledgeable about small claims courts and used them effectively to their own advantage. Spurrier found that businesses were filing the overwhelming proportion of the cases and that they were also more likely to win than the average citizen.[3]

Special Courts

Special courts also are courts of limited jurisdiction, but their jurisdiction is limited by subject matter or clientele. Some of the more common special courts are juvenile courts and probate courts. One of the newest types is a housing court dealing with landlord-tenant issues. Family courts that handle divorce and child custody cases are another type. Delaware's chancery courts specialize in hearing business cases.

Special Court Procedures Procedures in special courts tend to be somewhat less formal than in other courts. Judges often conduct juvenile proceedings, for example, more as conferences than as trials. Similarly, judges of probate or surrogate courts, who process wills, oversee estate administration, and rule on requests to commit people for mental care, follow procedures that seem as much administrative as judicial.

These courts as well are experiencing the trend toward professionalization. The U.S. Supreme Court now requires court-appointed attorneys serving at public expense in child custody or neglect cases if the parents cannot afford their own lawyer. The involvement of lawyers in such cases will likely eliminate nonlawyer judges in special courts eventually. In a case argued before the Tennessee

Supreme Court, the state attorney general defended the use of lay judges, saying that "in the simple findings of fact . . . no great constitutional or legal issues are likely to arise." But the attorney for two Coffee County teenagers, charged with truancy, maintained that "lay judges are not trained to rule on the complex issues affecting the liberty of juvenile defendants." Both Kentucky and Tennessee grant automatic appeal to a higher court if the juvenile defendant requests it. But many may not be aware of this possibility.

Special Court Administrators Special courts sometimes operate rather large administrative divisions as well. Courts dealing with divorce, for example, may oversee workers who process child support payments and chase down those who skip town. Juvenile courts also may operate community detention centers as well as halfway houses and foster homes that care for persons under court jurisdiction.

Special Courts and Attentive Publics Because special courts deal only with limited types of cases, professionals and other citizens with a stake in decisions of these courts develop a special interest in them. When the Massachusetts legislature considered establishing a business court, for example, one of the supporting arguments was that it "would make Massachusetts a more comfortable state for business."[4] And lawyers who specialize in wills and estates have a direct interest in probate court operations, who the judges are, and their own relationship to the judges. Also, judges who appoint estate administrators may be an important source of business for lawyers. Similarly, social workers who handle child abuse or adoption cases may also develop special links to surrogate or probate court judges.

This activity comes under the heading of **court watching**, by which special interests and citizen interest groups evaluate and influence court actions. Court watching has been on the increase, especially by feminist groups with respect to divorce cases and MADD (Mothers Against Drunk Drivers) with respect to penalties for drunken driving.

General Trial Courts

General trial courts are the cornerstone of a state's judicial system. The Great Lakes states generally call this court the circuit court, as do some states in the South. The Great Plains and Mountain states usually label them district courts; the New England and Far West states call them superior courts. New York's designation of them as supreme courts is confusing, at least for non–New Yorkers.

Jurisdiction General trial courts are courts of varying jurisdiction—it extends to almost any type of case involving a state's law, whether criminal or civil. Their criminal work concerns felonies—serious or major crimes. Their civil cases are those in which the sum of money involved may be high, and other types of cases that state legislatures see as too important for the minor courts. These trial courts deal with misdemeanor cases or minor civil matters only on appeal.

General trial courts are usually organized on a county basis. In large urban areas a court may have 20 or more judges. Where population is scattered, the court territory may consist of several counties in which the judge "rides circuit," holding court in the county seats. (Abraham Lincoln rode such a circuit as a lawyer, following a circuit judge through a group of Illinois counties.)

Professionalization General trial courts in all states are professionalized. The judges are lawyers and are not permitted to have a private law practice, although they occasionally lecture law classes.

Lawyers compete to get these jobs, not only because they are prestigious, but also because they pay well—for the most part between $60,000 and $100,000 per year.[5] State legislatures typically set the salary level, but counties may pay an additional amount. This payment and the county's usual responsibility for facilities and staff tends to foster a local perspective on the judges.

The Trial Judges The judges of these trial courts determine the quality of a state's judicial system. First, they decide the most important state cases. Their decisions are subject to appeal, of course, but most litigants are not successful in overturning the trial court ruling. Second, their ability to manage the court docket is critical to determining whether a person will get a "speedy" trial. Effective docket management means running a tight ship—dealing firmly with lawyers who seek delays, encouraging lawyers and their clients to settle out of court, or discouraging prosecutors and police officers from bringing certain cases into court at all. Third, they determine most of the sentences for perpetrators of serious crimes. Deciding whether a person should be put away for five years or allowed to go free on probation is not yet a science.

State Appeals Courts

Thirty-seven states now have an **intermediate court of appeals**. Many are recent additions. This court rests in the hierarchy between the general trial courts and the state's court of last resort.

All states also have a court of last resort, which in all but five states is called the state supreme court. West Virginians call it the supreme court of appeals. In Maine and Massachusetts it is the supreme judicial court; in New York it is simply the court of appeals.

The Appeals Function Charles Joiner, former law school dean and federal district judge, said that appellate review has two purposes: to prevent miscarriages of justice and to teach "judges, lawyers, and all citizens something about the law."[6]

The work of the appeals court judges thus differs substantially from that of trial judges. Appeals judges generally accept the facts presented in the trial court and do not consider new evidence. Rather, they deal with a review of the process and abstract legal issues that the cases raise. They work with legal briefs and hear only limited oral arguments. Rarely do appeals court judges even see the accused. But occasionally a person such as Marx Cooper, a convicted bank robber, argues his or her own case. While in prison, Cooper became an expert on double jeopardy. He argued and won his own appeal before the Michigan Supreme Court, as the lawyers say, *in propria persona*.

Organizational Patterns The major reason states have an intermediate court of appeals is to broaden the opportunity for review of trial court decisions and even out the quality of justice across a state. At the same time, intermediate appeals courts permit state supreme courts to be more selective and to accept for review cases that have the greatest potential for teaching and instructing. There are three major patterns of organization.[7]

Iowa and a few other states structured their intermediate appeals courts to operate as a central court. Its six judges hold court in a single location and help to reduce the supreme court's workload. But this approach has some drawbacks. When an appeals court sits *en banc* (all together), it operates much like the supreme court itself without expanding greatly the opportunity for appeals.[8]

Some other states divide their intermediate courts of appeals into districts. District judges, usually sitting as small panels, review cases on behalf of the entire intermediate appeals court. Thus they are quite dissimilar from the highest courts in those states. Larger states, such as Illinois, Michigan, and Pennsylvania, employ this approach.

Alabama and Tennessee use a third method—they set up different intermediate appeals courts for civil and criminal matters. In Oklahoma, the court of last resort consists of two divisions—civil and criminal—although it also has an intermediate appeals court that reviews both types of cases.

STATE COURTS IN THE FEDERAL SYSTEM: THE TREND TOWARD CENTRALIZATION

Over time trends have been both toward and away from centralization in law. In our day the diversity within the federal system is being reduced. The U.S. Supreme Court has been centralizing our state and federal courts by unifying the law they apply. It also has been making them more professional by establishing highly technical procedures and by urging state and local courts to raise the standards of acceptable judicial conduct. The effect is to centralize the judicial systems within states.

Development of the Common Law

Historically, nations considered the resolution of private disputes so important that kings themselves did the judging. It was as a wise judge that Solomon, the third king of ancient Israel, gained his reputation.[9] The law was centralized then in one person.

Our national judicial heritage has its roots in judgments and decrees of early English kings as well as in the later codification of these decisions into written law. In time the kings had to appoint magistrates to act for them. At first, magistrates acted only in the king's name and were expected to apply his prior rulings. But these judges also had community ties that pressured them to figure out what local citizens would accept as just.

The rulings of these judges fashioned the **common law**—the body of law derived from custom and tradition, based not on constitutional law or legislated statutes but on what people and institutions accepted as appropriate. Note that the politics of the judiciary from early times involved concern for how the public would respond.

The body of common law became more consistent as magistrates studied each other's decisions or as appeals were made directly to the king. By applying judgments of prior cases, the judges created a body of "judge-made" law. This common law remained relatively constant, but as judges found earlier decisions inappropriate to cases at hand, they would introduce new precedents.

Statutory Law

Current law, in the main, differs because it is based largely on written law—constitutions and statutes.[10] As law takes on statutory form, legislatures rather than courts, at least in theory, bring law into line with citizen beliefs and customs. We say at least in theory because judges continue to produce judge-made law, or case law, as they apply constitutions and statutes to particular situations.

Judicial Lawmaking

Judges, of course, cannot initiate policy changes as legislators or governors can. They may create new policy only as cases come to them. Their decisions and opinions explain their reasoning. Each decision that modifies current policy, then, is based on the particular facts of a genuine case involving real people. Their opinions, in effect, become instructions to lower-court judges and law enforcement officials on how to handle similar cases in the future. The U.S. Supreme Court expresses such policy changes for the nation. State supreme courts do so only for their respective states, although precedents from other states may be influential in some cases.

Few any longer underestimate the importance of these judge-made policies. Often these policy changes upset long-standing state or community practices, some that technology, economics, or even public opinion have made obsolete.

Consider, for example, a court decision on community regulation of manufactured houses. Many communities used zoning ordinances to ban mobile home parks. They relented when some state supreme courts ruled that local boards could not outlaw mobile home parks just because people thought them unsightly. Later, as manufacturers came out with new products that looked the same as site-built houses, courts overturned local laws that said such housing could not be placed on individual lots. The courts, rather than the state legislature or community governments, set these policies.

The Politics of Judicial Appeals Litigants ask our national and state supreme courts to review far more cases than they can possibly consider. These courts thus screen the appeals for the cases they choose to review. Lawyers and interest groups are attuned to the leanings of particular courts and tend to appeal those cases they think have the best chance of getting another hearing and a favorable decision.

When Earl Warren was chief justice of the U.S. Supreme Court, the Court gained a reputation for ruling favorably for civil liberties groups and criminal defendants. As we might expect, prosecutors under these circumstances often regarded appeals to the national court as futile. But the balance in the court changed with appointments by Richard Nixon and Ronald Reagan. In the first six years of the Warren Burger court, for example, 75 percent of the criminal cases accepted for review came from prosecutors.[11] Criminal defendants and civil liberties groups since then have been less optimistic about appealing adverse local decisions.

The Federalization of State Law

State cases, of course, are tried and reviewed in state courts, but they may become federal cases if the appellants can persuade a federal judge that their federal constitutional protections may have been violated.

Often this is done by claiming that the **due process clause** and **equal protection clause** of the Fourteenth Amendment to the U.S. Constitution have been breached. The U.S. Supreme Court has extended the federal Bill of Rights to the states through these clauses—that no state "shall deprive any person of life, liberty, or property, without due process of law; nor deny to any person within its jurisdiction the equal protection of the laws." The overall effect has been to make one system of the national and 50 state court systems.

Extending the Bill of Rights Chief Justice Marshal, writing in 1833, confidently stated that "the Fifth Amendment must be understood as restraining the power of the general government, not as applicable to the states."[12] But at that time the Fourteenth Amendment was not yet part of the Constitution—the states ratified it in 1869.

Gradually, beginning in 1925 with *Gitlow v. New York*,[13] the U.S. Supreme Court extended to the states the liberties and protections of the U.S. Constitution. In *Gitlow* the Court stated that the First Amendment—guaranteeing free speech—protected against state as well as federal intrusion. Later, the Court extended the principle to freedom of the press,[14] religion,[15] and other protections.

Treatment of the Accused Ultimately these decisions began to affect the way state and local law enforcement agencies and the courts handled persons accused of committing a crime. One of the early extensions of liberties concerned the right to have the help of a lawyer, a right guaranteed by the Sixth Amendment. Previously this right pertained mainly to accused persons who could afford an attorney. Others faced prosecution without a lawyer unless the offense was serious, in which case bar associations voluntarily provided legal counsel. In the Scottsboro case (1932) the U.S. Supreme Court held that legal counsel had to be provided without cost if the defendant's case involved the death penalty and the defendant could not afford to hire a lawyer.[16]

In the last two decades the Court extended the right of free legal counsel in felony cases,[17] for accused juveniles,[18] and for criminal misdemeanors where the accused's freedom is in jeopardy.[19] These cases, together with *Mapp v. Ohio*,[20] which prohibited the use of illegally seized evidence, and *Miranda v. Arizona*,[21] which required police to inform suspects of their constitutional rights (including the right to remain silent), have had a significant impact on the law enforcement community.

One effect has been a demand for more professional judicial and law enforcement personnel. More stringent standards set by courts and prosecutors require that the police be better educated and trained than ever before.

A second effect is increased expenditures for law enforcement. Higher expenditures for professional personnel is one aspect. But county governments, which bear most of the costs of prosecuting criminal cases, must now pay the lawyers for the defense as well in many cases. Many of these cases would have been disposed of after perhaps one courtroom appearance, but they now go to trial and are appealed because legal counsel is provided. As a result, the courts demand more judges and staff. In addition, some state attorney general offices and county prosecutors have set up separate divisions to specialize in appeals work.

Offsetting some of this cost increase, and a third effect, is a rise in the use of **plea bargaining**—the accused agrees to plead guilty to a charge lower than the one originally booked in exchange for a lighter sentence.

Finally, the courts and judges have become more openly involved in state and community politics and the issues of crime sentencing, prison facilities, and law enforcement budgets.

Other Effects of Federalization Federalization of the Bill of Rights extends well beyond the way law enforcement officials deal with accused persons. It has changed the way citizens relate to the courts and removed most remaining barriers to federal intervention in state affairs.

Citizens and the Courts Civil rights legislation has also changed the way citizens relate to the courts. The young and old, blacks, Hispanics, women, government agencies, political parties, ecologists, and other groups now generally find the courts willing to review virtually any state or community law or practice that may have a discriminatory impact.

Former U.S. Supreme Court Justice Potter Stewart contends that the courts have replaced the frontier in American consciousness. When the nation was new, he noted, a nonconformist could always go west. "Now," he said, "there is no more space and the courts have been called on to protect the rights of these individuals."[22]

Extension of Federal Involvement In terms of the federal system, the results appear even more significant. The Supreme Court decisions, especially in combination with federal grant programs, created a permissive federalism—no functional areas remain where some federal court or agency may not now intervene. A person does not get involved in a state or local government before running into some rule established by the U.S. Supreme Court or by act of Congress, whether the involvement concerns education, employment, welfare and mental health, corrections, or other fields.[23]

Note that it was not federal grant programs which gave the federal courts the proverbial foot in the door. The changes result from the application of constitutional principles to virtually all aspects of our governmental and social system.[24]

Diversity Remains

Centralization, though, is not all-pervasive. Most issues, by far, involve state law and are brought to state courts. Because state laws and judicial precedents within each state still differ, important diversity remains, as, for example, in divorce, child adoption, and insurance law. In addition, some observers believe that since 1975 the U.S. Supreme Court has been less likely to overturn state actions. Daniel J. Elazar notes that "state prerogatives are being preserved at least half of the time."[25]

Moreover, state courts do not always apply U.S. Supreme Court decisions as closely as the federal courts might wish. Students have found that state courts sometimes have disregarded or misapplied federal decisions such as those involving prayer in the public schools, desegregation and busing, obscenity and pornography, as well as those guaranteeing criminal rights.[26]

State supreme courts sometimes resist complying with U.S. Supreme Court precedent decisions when they think the level of disruption within the state would be high.[27] In fact, U.S. Supreme Court Justice William Brennan, Jr., mused that elected, rather than appointed, state judges may have difficulty resisting popular pressures.[28] As we see later, the record of elected judges in this respect is not much different from that of appointed judges. If state justices find federal rulings too threatening to their own political careers or philosophical leanings, they can lessen the threat by not applying the federal rule without great risk of being overruled—to have a decision overturned, someone must appeal and that costs money, time, and continued uncertainty.

Judges' Personal Bias Personal bias of judges also is reflected in decisions. It is another reason for continuing diversity in our state and local judicial systems. Stuart Nagel found, for example, that Democrats, Catholics, and members of ethnic minorities were more likely to rule for the criminal than for the state. Republicans, Protestants, and Anglo-Saxons were more likely to rule the other way. Ethnic Catholic Democrats also tended to favor bureaucracies over corporations, employees over corporations in injury cases, debtors over creditors, and wives over husbands in divorce actions.

As is the case in any large-scale system, central control over detailed individual decisions is never absolute. Professional values, of course, discourage conduct too far from the mainstream, but personal values do influence judicial decision making. Not the least of these personal values are factors that affect careers, which, for most judges, lie in the milieu of state and community politics.

THE POLITICS OF THE JUDICIARY

As citizens we see judges almost entirely in their professional capacity, dressed in black robes, presiding over courtrooms, scolding a disrespectful lawyer, or agonizing over the future of a young offender being led away to the state penitentiary. People see judges as legitimizers of the law, impartial referees who decide how a law applies in a specific instance. But rarely do we see their political side. Less frequently citizens see judges as members of a professional bureaucracy. Here we pull the curtain aside somewhat and examine the political aspects of the judiciary.

Why Courts Are Political

State courts and judges are unavoidably political because they are important—not only to groups inside the judicial system, but outside as well. The politics center around a continuing battle for control and influence over policy. Internal participants are the judges themselves. Upper-level judges do not always agree with each other or with the judges of the lower courts over how to manage and operate the courts. Also taking part in the internal contests are lower-level actors in court systems—the growing bureaucracy of nonjudicial employees who work in the courts.

Special interest groups also seek control and influence. Among these are industrial and financial groups, labor unions, lawyers, physicians, teachers, state officials, and court watchers—those whom court actions can favorably or adversely affect. State and local legislators who set judges' salaries believe they also should carry some weight with the courts. Governors, as heads of state government and party chiefs, believe they should have special consideration in some issues.

Such influentials, of course, are not interested in every court decision, but mainly only in those that affect them directly. For example, a state manufacturers' association may not care much whether a court upholds a state law that requires motorcyclists to wear crash helmets. But they will be very interested in workers' compensation decisions. One of the important ways to gain influence is through the procedure that states and communities follow to select judges.

How State Judges Get Their Jobs

Those who select the people who become judges, of course, influence the policy outcomes of the courts, if for no other reason than because personal biases of those judges figure heavily in court decisions.

Methods of Selection   The American states do not select judges in a uniform way. During the early years of our nation, governors, and later state legislatures, made the choices. They tended to recruit legislators or other active politicians. Judges who made rulings contrary to the wishes of the governor or the legislature ran the risk of not being reappointed. Thus many regarded the judges as not being sufficiently independent.

With the rise of Jacksonian democracy, states began electing judges on a partisan ballot. This gave party activists power in the selection process because they controlled the party nominating conventions. Judges often became captives of the party bosses.

New York City lawyers formed the first bar association in 1870 in part to promote nonpartisan elections and direct primaries.[29] Today, states select judges in partisan and nonpartisan elections as well as appoint them.[30]

Control Techniques of Judicial Elections   Politicians have found ways to short-circuit election methods. James Herndon studied over 400 elected state supreme court justices and found that 56 percent of them first gained office through gubernatorial appointment to a vacancy.[31] Later, they ran as incumbents. To increase the number of appointment possibilities, judges who belong to the governor's political party and are considering retiring commonly do so before their term ends. The governor can then fill another vacancy. Some states counteract this tactic by declaring interim judges ineligible for election.

To strengthen their influence, lawyers' groups make their own evaluations of candidates and publicize the results to guide voters. Gradually the position of the legal societies has evolved into a new method of selecting judges, one reform groups generally favor. It is the merit system, or the Missouri plan—the state that first gave it prominence in 1940.

The Missouri Plan   Missouri selects its judges for its supreme court, court of appeals, and large city general trial courts through a three-step procedure under the **Missouri plan**. A judicial selection commission screens and nominates three candidates for each judicial vacancy. The governor then chooses one of them. After the judge has served for one year, the voters decide in a **retention election**—"yes" or "no" on whether to elect the appointee to a full term. No other name is on the ballot as opposition.

Effects of the Missouri Plan   Richard Watson and Randal Downing compared the results of the Missouri plan to the previous partisan election outcomes.[32] They found voters tend to be less interested in retention elections and that "plan" judges were likely to be older than elected judges, have lower-court judicial experience, and have attended a Missouri law school.[33]

Not surprisingly, Missouri lawyers strongly believed that the plan resulted in better judges—after all, the plan gave lawyers, as a group, more influence over judge selection than would an elective or other appointive system. Significantly, Watson and Downing conclude,

> the Plan has not eliminated "politics"... that is the maneuvering of individuals and groups to influence who will be chosen as judges.... Nor has the Plan even eliminated partisan politics in judicial selection. What one can say is that the Plan has altered partisan factors in judicial selection so that... local leaders and persons active in electoral politics are no longer the major figures in selecting as they were under the elective system.... Instead, it is now the governor who looms large in such decisions.[34]

The State Patterns of Selection The Missouri plan did not spread rapidly to other states. In fact, not until 1959 did a second state—Alaska—adopt it. By 1989 15 states and Guam were using the Missouri plan or all of its key elements to select at least some of their judges. (See Table 11.1.) In the late 1980s, reform along the lines of the Missouri plan was rejected in both New York and Ohio.[35] One study suggests that adoption of the Missouri plan is related to legislative reapportionment, that legislatures dominated by rural legislators sought to preserve as much power as possible before power shifts occurred as a result of reapportionment.[36]

Parts of the Missouri plan have been adopted in judicial selection procedures of other states. Some states, for example, require gubernatorial appointments

Table 11.1 JUDICIAL SELECTION METHODS AND TERMS FOR SUPREME COURT JUSTICES

Merit plan	Nonpartisan election	Partisan election	Gubernatorial appointment	Legislative appointment
Alaska(10)	Georgia(6)	Alabama(6)	Delaware(12)	Connecticut(8)
Arizona (6)	Idaho(6)	Arkansas(8)	Hawaii(10)	Rhode Island[b]
California(12)	Kentucky(8)	Illinois(10)	Maine(7)	So. Carolina(10)
Colorado(10)	Louisiana(10)	Mississippi(8)	Maryland(10)	Virginia(12)
Florida(6)	Michigan(8)	New Mexico(8)	Massachusetts[b]	
Indiana(10)	Minnesota(6)	New York[b]	New Hampshire[b]	
Iowa(8)	Montana(8)	No. Carolina(8)	New Jersey[b]	
Missouri(12)	Kansas(6)	Pennsylvania(6)	Vermont(6)	
Nebraska(6)	No. Dakota(10)	Tennessee(8)[a]		
Nevada(6)	Ohio(6)	Texas(6)		
Oklahoma(8)	Oregon(6)	West Virginia(6)		
South Dakota(8)	Washington(6)			
Utah(10)	Wisconsin(10)			
Wyoming(8)				

[a] Intermediate judges selected by merit plan.

[b] Denotes lifetime appointment, Mass. and N.H. to age 70; N.Y. and N.J. may be appointed to age 70 after serving 14- and 7-year term, respectively.

Source: *The Book of the States, 1988–89* (Lexington, Ky.: Council of State Governments), pp. 158–165.

from a prepared list, others demand some form of judicial commission approval, and a few states with partisan elections have incumbents run on nonpartisan retention ballots. Proponents of retention elections argue that although nonretention results are very low—only 1.6 percent of the judges in 1,499 such elections were defeated between 1972 and 1978—retention elections serve their intended purposes of providing judges with lengthy tenure and giving the voters a measure of control.[37]

But many states also maintain some partisan connections through gubernatorial or legislative appointments and senate confirmation procedures. In states without a formal screening committee, a state or local bar association usually ranks candidates as "well qualified," "qualified," or "not qualified."[38]

Those who advocate reform of judicial selection methods argue that the appointment method results in more qualified judges. Do the claims hold up? One study compared appointed with elected judges in California and Iowa. It concluded that the changes the reformers promised often did not occur, and in a few instances the characteristics that the reformers noted as being undesirable actually became more pronounced.[39]

As noted earlier, Justice William J. Brennan, Jr., asserted that decisions of appointed judges would comply with U.S. Supreme Court decisions more closely than would those of elected judges. Current studies of this issue produce little evidence to support Brennan's assertion, although exceptions have been found, especially in decisions of a generation ago. State supreme court decisions now have a high percentage of compliance with U.S. Supreme Court decisions.[40]

Tenure, Discipline, and Removal Federal judges are appointed for life; state judges are not, except in Rhode Island.[41] Judges in major trial courts have terms ranging from 4 to 15 years. How can states or citizens rid the courts of judges they consider unfit? The most frequent method, it seems, is to wait for their mandatory retirement or death. But there are other methods.

Elections as a Means of Removal The method that probably accounts for most of the involuntary removal of judges is the election process. But this often falls short of the need—most incumbent judges, especially in nonpartisan elections, have no opposition. Even when they do, they rarely lose, in part because many states make judges secure by starring incumbents or allowing a descriptive line such as "Supreme Court Justice. . . ." And in states using the Missouri plan, of course, judges do not even have opposition from other candidates. As the saying goes, "It's difficult to beat somebody with nobody."

Recall and Impeachment Recall is an even more rarely used method because most citizens seldom know about the quality of judges, and only a few states permit judicial recall. In 1986, however, voters recalled Rose Bird, chief justice of California's supreme court, and two other justices. Governor Jerry Brown appointed her in 1977, and she won her retention election a year later. Immediately after that election, however, reports began circulating that the court had delayed announcing decisions to which conservatives would have objected until after the election. In 1982 Howard Jarvis, the leader of California's Proposition 13, announced a campaign to recall Chief Justice Bird. The remainder of her tenure was stormy, with many of the accusations centering on the court's refusal to uphold any of the 55 death penalties that came to the court on appeal. Voters overwhelmingly voted the three out of office. After her defeat, Bird said such efforts pointed "an invisible gun of fear" at every judge.

This, of course, was a rare event, as was the case of the recall of a local judge that we discuss in Policy Box No. 21, "Judicial Expression and Public Opinion."

Legislatures in most states have the power to impeach judges. Tennessee law, for example, names misfeasance or malfeasance in office as an impeachable offense; Oklahoma specifies "willful neglect of duty, corruption in office, habitual drunkenness, incompetency, or any offense involving moral turpitude." In some states the governor, with the consent of the legislature, may remove judges from office.

The fine language of what offenses constitute grounds for impeachment matters little, as do the provisions that allow governors and legislatures to remove judges. Most are loath to undertake the task, and few do.

Judicial Tenure Commissions The most recent method for disciplining the judicial corps is through **judicial tenure commissions**. Judges generally favor this approach because it lets courts handle their own problems without outside interference. It also permits a range of remedies to discipline a judge—penalties may range from a reprimand, suspension for a period, or removal from the bench.

There are major problems with this approach. The judicial commissions usually conduct their inquiries in private. And there may be special difficulties when charges involve the state supreme court itself. The Justice Bird episode in California is a case in point. The Commission on Judicial Performance found no cause to file formal charges of misconduct. Later, however, it recommended constitutional changes to give the commission greater powers and independence.[42]

In general, the judicial tenure commission approach works reasonably well—better, perhaps, than removal by impeachment or election. The major fault, it seems, is that judges on the commission are sometimes reluctant to deal sternly with their errant colleagues.

The Judicial Bureaucracy—Who Should Manage?

Historically, nearly all state court systems have been decentralized. The route that appeals follow, of course, is established, as are major rules of judicial procedure. Beyond this, though, the general trial courts, special courts, and minor courts have been outposts of fierce judicial independence—judges, especially elected ones, have strongly resisted top-down interference.

Independent courts leave local courts vulnerable to a variety of local influences. Few judges, of course, would tolerate open pressuring of their courts, but judges are people and do live in the community. No doubt, many have other lawyers as friends or acquaintances and they are, at least, fellow members of the

Policy Box No. 21   # Judicial Expression and Public Opinion

In November 1976 three black youths, 14 and 15 years old, sexually assaulted a 16-year-old white girl in a Madison, Wisconsin, high school. It occurred during the middle of the day while the high school band was practicing nearby. The event stirred public concern, for there had been a wave of recent sexual assaults in downtown Madison.

The three youths were apprehended and prosecuted. One of them turned state's witness in the case and was not charged. The judge sentenced the 14-year-old to a year in a Milwaukee group home for his part in the case. Testimony revealed that the third boy was a friend of the victim and attended the same church; he was released to the custody of his parents.

Meryl Manhardt was the assistant prosecutor handling the case. She argued that this boy, of all of them, should have been sent to a group home. It was at this point that Dane County Judge Archie Simonson made some remarks that set off a recall drive against him. It was in response to Manhardt's pleadings for the judge to be responsive to community desires, to let people in Madison know that sexual assaults would not be tolerated, that the judge lit a fuse which was to result in an explosion about him. Judge Simonson said,

> And then you are saying that I should be responsive to the community in what their needs and wishes are. Well, how responsive should I be? Should I adopt a double standard? This community is well known to be sexually permissive; look at the newspapers; look at the sex clubs, the advertisements of sex, the availability of it through your escort services, the prostitutes, they are being picked up daily. Even in open court we have...women appearing without bras...and they think it is smart as they sit here on the witness stand with their dresses up over the cheeks of their butts and we have the same type of thing in the schools. Sex is really wide open and we are supposed to take an impressionable person fifteen or sixteen years of age who can respond to something like that and punish that person severely because they react to it normally.

Assistant Prosecutor Manhardt interceded, "Your Honor, with all due respect, I find your remarks about women's clothing particularly sexist."

"You bet it is," the judge replied.

Shortly thereafter, the Madison chapter of the National Organization of Women, the Women's International League for Peace and Freedom, and the Madison Rape Crisis Committee began circulating recall petitions. Their stated concern was that the judge made sexist remarks and that he seemingly imposed a penalty too light for the crime.

Governor Patrick Lucey said that an apology from the judge was in order, but that recall was not. Judge Simonson offered no apologies.

Early in the recall campaign, both city newspapers supported the petition, but later one backed off—reportedly because of the racial implications in the case. The editor noted that there was a chance the judge might win the recall vote and wondered what message that would convey to the nation.

Some Madison conservatives, too, were upset with the judge's light sentences for the youths. They argued that the courts should "crack down on crime."

Some liberals in the city viewed the issue in the context of civil liberties. They maintained that the judge was entitled to freedom of speech, especially as a judge. They felt that Simonson was an inept judge, but did not believe he should be recalled. He should be removed, they said, in April 1978—when his term expired. One person from this group said, "This is what a witchhunt is like. This is what it was like with McCarthy in the 1950s."

Judge Simonson himself argued that the whole judicial system was at stake in the election. "A judge," he insisted, "must be absolutely free to make decisions. He shouldn't have to reflect public opinion."

In September 1977 Judge Simonson became the first judge to be recalled in the nation in more than 35 years. In his place, the voters put Moria Krueger, a lawyer who had been specializing in juvenile law. After the election she revealed that her older sister had been the victim of a rapist ten years earlier. She said she did not stress feminist issues during the campaign and hoped that men would not fear her when she became judge.

After the votes were counted, Judge Simonson said that he had not campaigned against the others in the election, only against the idea that he should be recalled for what he said.

What do you think? Should Judge Simonson have been recalled? Did the community handle the problem appropriately? Should the governor or the supreme court of Wisconsin have interceded in the case? Should Simonson have apologized? Should Wisconsin change its judicial selection and removal laws? How much freedom of expression should judges have on the bench? Should judges be exempt from recall, or should they be treated like all other politicians?

local bar association. Most judges must stand for reelection periodically, and lawyers are a very likely source of campaign funds. County boards determine and pay a part of the judges' salaries and approve appropriations for court staff, court furnishings, equipment, and other perquisites.

All these can subtly, and sometimes openly, become a medium of barter. Judges who consider themselves adequately provided for might find it more difficult to rule against the county or against community values in a court battle.[43] Southern judges in the 1960s and before found it especially difficult to take tough stands for racial integration, and some who did experienced lessened local popularity.

The vulnerability of judges is not the only criticism of a decentralized system. The legal profession argues for uniform quality of and access to court services throughout a state. Dockets may become overloaded and cases, especially civil ones, delayed up to five years. Former Chief Justice Warren Burger noted, "Delay itself, with the loss of witnesses and the clouding of memories, diminishes the ability of the courts to do justice. It is too serious to be any longer ignored."[44]

Local judges appreciate the supreme court's support when it orders a county board to pay the costs of a court-negotiated contract with court employees. But they are also likely to label as "bureaucratic timidity" a supreme court administrator's order to follow the usual local procedures in buying courtroom furniture. Some prefer to think that they should not be subjected to procedures that regular county employees must follow.

Judges whose dockets are hopelessly backlogged sometimes receive favorably those judges whom the court has temporarily assigned to help them, although they may also regard such assignments as implied criticism. Similarly, judges getting data from a central computer may consider such technology a solid advance unless it shows them in a bad light. When they have to provide caseload and other data for the file, they might wonder why "court bureaucrats at the capital" insist on such "red tape." Judges may greatly appreciate the training programs the court administrator's office puts on for general court employees, but they may be less pleased with the programs that they themselves are required to attend each year. And, as happened in Wayne County (Michigan), judges do not take kindly to criticism from the state's chief justice about the work schedule some judges had been keeping.

Rubin suggests that some state court systems, especially those of Colorado and New Jersey, have become too centralized—local judges may lack the discretion they need to do their job.[45] This criticism is one we might expect about any highly bureaucratic system—lower-level judges may feel they are just cogs on a gear cranking out decision after decision.[46]

Conflicts with Officials of Other Branches

State constitutions establish courts as the third branch of the government—separate from the legislative and executive branches. But disagreements over what separate means in daily operation can cause some first-rate battles.

Conflicts over Court Budgets Is equality among the branches upset when the budget office cuts the court's appropriations requests? What should the governor and the legislature do when the courts ignore budget limits? Such constitutional confrontations do occur.

Patrick Lucey, as governor of Wisconsin, for example, budgeted less for the state supreme court than it requested. Chief Justice Harold Wilkie responded by saying, "The court has inherent power to appoint the number of personnel it deems necessary to perform its constitutional functions." He announced that the court was going to begin an educational program for judges and more personnel would be hired.[47]

Both the Michigan and Pennsylvania supreme courts have made similar rulings. Michigan's top court once ruled that a general trial court judge could require the county board to appropriate funds for as many probation officers as the judge deemed necessary.[48] The judge had threatened the county commissioners with jail if they failed to appropriate what he said he needed. The Pennsylvania court ordered the Philadelphia city council to restore reductions made in the common pleas court budget. The opinion in effect said that if the court in reality is to be "a coequal independent branch of our government," the cuts must be restored.[49]

We personally experienced the emotion such battles can arouse. In one county facing a severe financial crisis the presiding judge told the board of commissioners it would have to eliminate all discretionary programs before the court would accept a budget cut. "If I have to close the old people's home," said the board chair, "I will personally wheel those patients to the judge's courtroom."

Not all courts employ a confrontational strategy, but they are no longer uncommon as state court systems gradually reorganize into a single *state* system of judicial administration.

Centralizing State and Local Court Management Court reformers have sought to reduce interbranch conflict by reorganizing court structure, improving administrative techniques, and developing administrative support staff. Their plan would place all courts into a single state judicial system with the state paying all costs.[50] At the tip of the pyramid of the state system is the chief justice, backed by the rest of the state supreme court.

Overseeing most of the day-to-day operations in the court system is a **court administrator** who administers court policy as expressed in the court rules. Other duties include scheduling cases, collecting data, administering court rules, and arbitrating disputes between local judges and county boards. Lower-level courts, under the plan, also elect a judge to provide administrative leadership, often with the help of a local court administrator.

Attitudes of legislators and governors toward this kind of change are gradually changing, but the major roadblock is finding the money—state legislatures are reluctant to take on the added costs. In Michigan, county boards have filed a class action suit against the state to force payment of all court costs. In this instance, the state supreme court will face an interesting conflict of interest because it, ultimately, will rule on an issue that the court itself has been unable to lobby through the state legislature.

LIMITATIONS ON JUDICIAL POLICY-MAKING

During the 1970s the state courts in many states took gigantic steps to centralize and professionalize their judicial systems. But have the courts gained so much momentum that legislative and executive checks and balances may not be adequate to maintain a balanced democratic system?

Societal Influences as Limitations

Are we in danger of having an "imperial judiciary," as some have suggested?[51] Our state and community courts have not yet become so centralized or professionalized that they are politically immune to citizens' values and actions, as the episode about Chief Justice Rose Bird showed. Besides the influences of electoral and appointive processes, the courts have other linkages that keep them from straying too far.

The Politics of Prosecution

Prosecutors—state attorneys general, district attorneys, and county prosecutors—are political officials who interpret community values concerning law enforcement. They staff the gate between police agencies and courts by deciding when and when not to file charges against violators.

To be sure, legalities are involved in this process, but it is also highly political. Most prosecutors are elected with partisan opposition ready to criticize their performance. Many are also politically ambitious—the office of prosecutor is an important stepping-stone to perhaps a judgeship, a congressional seat, or even the governorship. Few are strangers to television cameras as they discuss, for the evening news, the capture of a suspect in a string of murders, the details of a nighttime raid on a drug house, or a jury verdict.

Prosecutors cannot enforce all laws with equal vigor. Thus they make choices, basically political choices, about where to focus their resources. Most, of course, come down hard on murder, rape, and armed robbery. But whether to crack down on street prostitution and not on prostitution in convention hotels is a political choice—the latter could be bad for the convention business. And what about adult bookstores or gambling at the city club, or on the numbers rackets in the back rooms of the working-class bars, or on shoplifting, fraudulent consumer practices, or "welfare cheats"? All are political choices.

Prosecutors also have a good deal of discretion in individual cases. Usually, they have discretion in how serious they make the charges. Filing charges more serious than perhaps can be sustained in court and then plea bargaining permits prosecutors to screen out many cases before they reach trial. This still affords a prosecutor the opportunity to build an impressive record of convictions unless a political opponent uses the list of plea bargains as evidence for being soft on crime. (As a practical matter, the volume of cases in many jurisdictions requires a pattern of plea bargaining. Available personal and financial resources are seldom adequate to bring all charges to trial.)

The Jury System In only a few ways do citizens participate directly in governmental decision making. The citizen jury is one. Jurors are ordinary people untrained in the law in a world of legal jargon and technicalities.

The Trial Jury The task of a **trial jury**, or **petit jury**, is to decide guilt or innocence and, in some cases, the penalty. Not everyone endorses the system of trial by a jury of one's peers, in spite of its traditional importance. The professionals—lawyers and judges—often attack the juror selection process as cumbersome, expensive, and time consuming. Typically, names of juror candidates come from random selections out of lists of drivers' licenses or registered voters. Administrative cost, then, is a problem.

The jury's decision may depend on the way the witness explains the document.

A second problem is that trial juries are not representative of all of us. First, lawyers trying a case seek jurors biased in favor of their clients or, at least, not prejudiced against them.[52] Second, few of us happily respond to a call for jury duty because we consider it a disruption of our regular routine. And so we offer an excuse we hope the judge will accept.

Jury trials also occasionally result in a **hung jury**—the jurors cannot agree on a verdict. Usually the case then has to be retried with a new jury. The U.S. Supreme Court ruled in 1972 that verdicts by majority vote rather than unanimous agreement are appropriate in some cases.[53] Some states also permit 6-person juries, rather than the traditional 12, as a further way to cut time and dollar costs.

A fourth point of attack involves the process by which a jury actually comes to a decision. Jurors sometimes are sequestered for weeks and are undoubtedly eager to pick up their lives again. They want to decide quickly. How do they decide? What pressures do they impose on a few holdouts? What do they do when the judge orders them to reach a verdict? Critics ask if this is the way modern jurisprudence should be administered.[54] Finally, the critics note that many cases today involve technical complexities that ordinary people cannot understand.

Despite the shortcomings, the trial jury has its defenders, even in civil cases. They counter by saying that judges, trained as they are in the law, may not be any better equipped to understand the complexities of some cases. At a minimum, they say, the citizen jury "imposes fierce discipline" on the lawyers trying the case to organize the mass of information in an understandable form.[55] Also, some jurisdictions, with concurrence of the attorneys, now permit jurors to ask questions directly.

Defenders also suggest that a jury has certain advantages over a judge. Juries can individualize justice without creating precedents to influence future cases. A key duty of a judge is to provide uniformity of justice. A judge's written opinion is likely to affect future cases, and in the effort to make justice uniform it is not individualized to the case at hand.

Defenders also note that citizen juries have important functions other than fact finding. They serve as a check on judicial power by expressing community values. They also maintain public participation in the judicial process, which is essential to continued popular support of judicial decisions. In a 1980 Michigan murder trial, for example, a jury, perhaps influenced by feminist arguments, decided that a woman who admitted killing her husband by setting fire to his bed should be acquitted on the grounds of temporary insanity. A long history of physical abuse was thought to have influenced the jurors. Since then other women have been acquitted in similar cases of spouse abuse. Perhaps the judge deciding such a case would have been reluctant to break precedent.

The Grand Jury The **grand jury**, consisting of 20 or more citizens, has two functions. First, it determines whether a prosecutor has sufficient evidence to bring a suspect to trial. Grand juries have proven costly and cumbersome, and less than half the states now use them. Other states have turned the function over to lower-level courts through arraignment proceedings in which the prosecutor establishes before a judge that a crime indeed has been committed and that the evidence is sufficient to bind the accused over for trial.

A second function of the grand jury is to investigate corruption in public offices or to uncover the intricacies of organized crime and criminal conspiracies. In this capacity jurors operate in secrecy and can compel witnesses to testify. Grants of immunity frequently enable law enforcement officials to gather evidence that could not otherwise be uncovered. In these proceedings prosecutors draw out the evidence for the jurors to hear, and they decide whether charges should be filed.

Various groups attack this use of the grand jury, largely because the proceedings may violate the civil liberties of those being investigated.[56] Investigators may be too aggressive and citizen jurors too easily swayed. States that have become especially sensitive to this danger have discarded the system and replaced it with a professional jurist—a judge or highly respected community lawyer—who supervises the investigation and proceedings.

Corrections Administration The administration of corrections also limits judges in their policy-making. Once a person is convicted and sentenced to the state prison, the convict leaves the judge's control and comes under state corrections department supervision.

The judge may make special efforts to ensure that a dangerous criminal will be in prison a long time with a sentence of "life plus five years." Still, the corrections department and parole board, not the judge, determine how long the person will actually be behind bars. State rules govern eligibility for and conditions of release. But corrections officials may not always release a prisoner on the basis of how much "correcting" has been done. Overcrowding in state prisons and county jails and inadequate funding, as well as the socioeconomic standing of the convict, may often influence their decisions.

Judges face similar limitations when they release to the state's mental health department persons who are guilty, but mentally ill. Such persons may undergo psychiatric treatment, be declared well, and be released from custody after only a few months. This problem received national attention when a federal court jury declared John Hinckley, the man who shot President Reagan, mentally ill. The notoriety of this case plus his own subsequent behavior has made it difficult for federal authorities to release him.

Judicial Policy and Public Opinion

Does public opinion also influence judicial policy-making? The answer, we think, is a clear yes. As we have indicated, judges as legitimizers of the law walk a tightwire between professional perspectives and political sensitivities that most of them have honed as they worked their way to the bench.

Customs and Beliefs of the Public Customs, beliefs, and social actions were the starting point for observing how judges reach decisions. We see them as still important today. State and community judges dealing with pornography, for example, could rule that freedom of speech means exactly that, and that all laws prohibiting pornographic material are unconstitutional. But judges have not so ruled, because a significant portion of society thinks that some limits are necessary on material which appeals solely to prurient interests.

Or take the matter of crime. Judges watch television and see a string of shows in which crime fighters are relentlessly pursuing and bringing criminals to justice. As we saw in the dispute surrounding the California Supreme Court, judges are also aware of the public—they read the newspapers and watch TV anchors—and quickly sense that public opinion favors taking "drug dealers and other criminals out of circulation for a long time," or perhaps "restoring the death penalty," or advocating some other bumper-sticker solution. Pollsters continue to report public opinion favoring "surer punishment of criminals" and building larger prisons and jails to back up a get-tough-on-crime policy.

Legislators have also translated the angry public opinion about crime into mandatory sentences and, in many instances, have eliminated **indeterminate sentences**. These give prisoners the opportunity to earn early release for good behavior. Such rules have come over the protest of corrections professionals who argue that mandatory sentences give prisoners no incentive to improve. Sentencing guidelines are a third measure that many states are employing. These instruct judges as to the sentences they should impose for specific types of crimes.

However, this get-tough-with-criminals approach is beginning to have a backlash effect in some states. In spite of major expansion of the state prison and county jail systems, overcrowding and skyrocketing costs are forcing some states to reconsider their policies about incarceration.

The judiciary objects to such restrictions. District Judge Gene Franchini of Albuquerque, New Mexico, even resigned to protest mandatory sentencing rules. He said that it makes judges like people "dressed in black who walk out on the battlefield after the battle is over and shoot the wounded."[57] In Policy Box No. 22, "What Counts in Sentencing? You Be the Judge," we give you a chance to try your hand at deciding a sentence for a hypothetical crime.

The other side of the public's feelings, though, is that most do not want a police state. They are not happy with "third-degree" methods, roughing up suspects, police bullying citizens, or having accused persons railroaded through the courts to jail.

The political balance that the supreme court justices are striving for is between the rights of the law abiding (that is, protecting the security of the community and the innocent) and protecting the rights of the accused. Guilt of the accused is often established by police methods that may involve invasion of privacy. But social costs resulting from what may be too great a concern for the rights of the accused may also be high—higher than society is or should be willing to pay.

As Andrew Hacker states, "Certainly crime tests the limits of liberalism."[58] Complete safety does not seem appropriate if we achieve it in exchange for our liberties or the liberties of others. Nevertheless, we cannot ignore the fact that preventable crime also deprives its victims of their safety and their liberties. Therein lies the American dilemma over criminal conduct. It is a dilemma that state supreme court justices face regularly. It is also a concern of judges in general trial courts who conduct most of the trials.

Pressures from Politically Aroused Legislators Judges also take into account how public opinion may affect changes in legislated law. Judges may temper their rulings on certain policy questions because of concern for the legislative actions that respond to an aroused public opinion. Legislatures may pass laws that automatically add two years to the prison sentence of a person who commits a felony with a gun.

Such concerns for public opinion and possible changes in statutes or constitutions, of course, do not find their way directly into court decisions. But many judges strive for temperateness so as not to goad the public into taking drastic actions that will limit even more the authority of the courts to judge individual disputes on their merits and according to the law.

A FINAL COMMENT

We stressed two major themes in this chapter. One is that the U.S. Supreme Court has nationalized many of our state laws by extending the federal Bill of

Policy Box No. 22

What Counts in Sentencing? You Be the Judge

Many aspects of decision making in the courtroom and in judges' chambers involve judgment. Still, the act of judging perhaps never becomes quite so significant as when the judge looks at the criminal standing before the bench and decides what punishment to impose. It is a highly personal matter for trial court judges.

In large cities, routine crimes—robbery, breaking and entering, and others—are barely worth a few lines in the metropolitan newspapers. So only a few—the criminal, the criminal's family and friends, the lawyers, the court administrator, and perhaps a few clerks who tabulate the statistics—know the sentences that the judges give.

In this policy box we are giving you details of a hypothetical case. They are the same facts a reporter gave 12 judges of a large city court. The reporter asked the judges how they would sentence the convicted person. You will have a chance to compare the sentence you would give with those of the judges.

Here is the case:

A 23-year-old woman sleeping alone in her home suddenly awoke to see a man standing over her. Swiftly he clamped his hand over her mouth and said, "Shut up and I won't hurt you. I'm just going to take a few things." He lingered momentarily, ran his hands over her body, and then began rummaging through her closet and bureau.

Too frightened to scream, the woman groped for the telephone, only to find it dead. After a few minutes that seemed like hours, the stranger returned to the window, carrying her television, camera, and other items. As he was leaving he again warned her to keep quiet.

Later the police caught the man, a 20-year-old army veteran. On the advice of his lawyer, he pleaded guilty to breaking and entering and second-degree sexual assault.

The presentencing report informed the judge that the man had had one juvenile conviction for breaking and entering. He had also been arrested at age 17 for possession of drugs, but the courts dismissed the charge. He had no record of using drugs.

He'd recently received an honorable discharge from the army and was living with his mother and two sisters. He was due to start working soon in his uncle's landscaping business.

He explained his actions by saying that he'd been having a hard time adjusting to civilian life without an income. He said that he hadn't committed any crimes since his juvenile conviction, and he claimed that he'd knocked on the woman's door and rang the doorbell before breaking in. He said he thought no one was at home.

Now it's time for you to decide. Write out the sentence you would give and the points you think would be influential in your decision. Remember, there are two charges—breaking and entering and second-degree sexual assault. In the state in which these crimes occurred, the maximum sentence for each crime is 15 years. If you sentence the man to prison, he'll probably spend about half the sentence in prison and the rest on probation.

> When you have finished writing, read on to see how your sentence compares to that of the judges. Were you as tough as the judges? Don't read on until you have decided what sentence you would impose.
>
> Ten of the judges said that if this were a real case they would have ordered the man to spend time in a state prison. Most gave sentences ranging from two to five years; four gave sentences of four years. The other two judges ordered that he be placed on probation, with the first six months to be spent in a county jail.
>
> What was their rationale? Some said that this was a crime of terror and that even though there was no physical injury, the woman suffered shock from sexual assault and from having her domicile "violated." Another judge, whose home had been burglarized, said, "You can take your gun cases, your dope cases, and auto theft cases and put them aside. But not these."
>
> Going in favor of the defendant were comments such as, "The man came to burglarize the place and backed off rape. I think he still has some sense of decency about him." But another judge said, "If he came to burglarize the place, he should have gotten the hell out as soon as he saw the woman."
>
> Finally, a judge noted, "I don't fully understand the defendant's intentions. If I don't understand a situation, my policy is to err on the side of leniency. I'll have him on probation for three years. I don't have to jump in right away and be superpunitive."
>
> What do you think? Were the judges more or less severe than you and your classmates? Should they have been more severe? Less severe? Did their reasoning make sense to you? Would your decisions have been different if you had known something about the man's family and his lawyer or if you had personally seen him, his attitude, how he spoke and moved? Is it appropriate for such considerations to influence how a state punishes a person as the judges said they might? Would it be better if the state set a specific sentence for these crimes so that no matter who the judge is, the person gets the same penalty?

Rights. This extension opened the door for federal review of virtually all state policies and practices. It also encouraged both the federal and the state court systems to review many matters once considered "political"—matters to be resolved through the political rather than judicial process.

The other theme is the trend in our court systems toward greater professionalization and administrative centralization of state courts. The gradual shift from elective to appointive selection methods and requirements for in-service training contribute to building a professional judicial corps. Close supervision of lower courts by the state supreme courts contributes to professionalism as well.

We ended by noting that the public's mechanisms to influence the courts tend to be of two strains—one having only a subtle effect on the courts and the other leading to a kind of protest that may not produce altogether desirable results in the short run but that does remind judges to give some heed to public opinion.

HIGH POINTS

In this chapter we began by (1) emphasizing how the federal system encouraged diversity in the organization of state courts. We discerned an underlying pattern similar to that of the national courts, but emphasized how much any state could diverge from it. We next looked at (2) how federal court decisions since have centralized that system by using the Fourteenth Amendment to apply many of the guarantees of the Bill of Rights to the states. We examined (3) the political environment of the judiciary, noting how states select judges and how the courts seek to assert their independence from the other branches of government—in part by professionalizing court management and consolidating administration under the control of the state supreme court. Finally, we considered (4) some of the limitations on judicial policy-making. We noted that prosecutors, citizen juries, corrections departments, and judges themselves influence and limit judicial decisions as well as the matters that reach the judicial agenda. We also discussed how public opinion influences judicial policy-making.

In this chapter we have defined the following terms in this order: original jurisdiction, minor courts, general trial court, appellate jurisdiction, court of last resort, intermediate appeals court, misdemeanor offenses, arraignment proceedings, justice of the peace, small claims court, special courts, court watching, common law, due process clause, equal protection clause, plea bargaining, Missouri plan, retention election, judicial tenure commission, court administrator, prosecutor, trial or petit jury, hung jury, grand jury, and indeterminate sentence.

NOTES

1. David Strom, "Media Coverage of the Courts," *Judicature* 65:1 (June/July 1981): 340–347.
2. H. Ted Rubin, *The Courts, Fulcrum of the Justice System* (Pacific Palisades, Calif.: Goodyear Publishing, 1976), p. 47.
3. Robert L. Spurrier, Jr., "The Trial Court Writ Small, Small Claims Adjudication in Oklahoma," Paper presented at the Midwest Political Science Association meetings, 1981, Tallahassee. Elizabeth Purdum found similar results in "Examining the Claims of a Small Claims Court: A Florida Case Study," *Judicature* 65:1 (June/July 1981): 25–37.
4. Christi Harlan, "Massachusetts Bill Seeks Courts for Business," *The Wall Street Journal* (December 8, 1988).
5. *The Book of the States, 1988-89* (Lexington, Ky.: Council of State Governments, 1989), pp. 174–175.
6. Charles Joiner, "The Function of the Appellate System," in William F. Swindler (ed.), *Justice in the States, Addresses and Papers of the National Conference on the Judiciary* (St. Paul, Minn.: West Publishing, 1971), p. 102.
7. Rubin, *The Courts, Fulcrum of the Justice System*, p. 127.
8. The similarity of the two Iowa courts is reflected in the number of cases each handles. Each processed about the same number per year. Donald E. Boles, *Comparative State Politics Newsletter* (August 1980).

9. See, for example, the account in I Kings 3:16–28.
10. Only in Louisiana, whose tradition is French rather than English and whose law is based on the Napoleonic Code, has any substantial part of the common law prevailed into the second half of the twentieth century.
11. Nathan Lewis, "Avoiding the Supreme Court," *New York Times Magazine* (October 17, 1976).
12. *Barron v. Mayor and City Council of Baltimore*, 7 Peters 243 (1833).
13. *Gitlow v. New York*, 268 U.S. 652 (1925).
14. *Near v. Minnesota*, 283 U.S. 697 (1931).
15. *Zorach v. Clauson*, 343 U.S. 306 (1952).
16. *Powell v. Alabama*, 287 U.S. 4S (1932).
17. *Gideon v. Wainwright*, 373 U.S. 335 (1963). James P. Levine, in a study of how well public defenders serve clients, found the service generally equal to that for paying clients. See his "Impact of Gideon, The Performance of Public and Private Criminal Defense Lawyers," *Polity* 8 (1975): 215–240.
18. In *Re Gault*, 378 U.S. 1 (1967).
19. *Argersinger v. Hamlin*, 407 U.S. 25 (1972).
20. *Mapp v. Ohio*, 367 U.S. 343 (1961).
21. *Miranda v. Arizona*, 384 U.S. 436 (1966).
22. In Richard Reeves, *American Journey* (New York: Simon and Schuster, 1982). The comments were made in an interview with Reeves, who was retracing de Tocqueville's route of 1831.
23. The most definitive of the cases concerning patronage is *Branti v. Finkel*, 62 L.Ed 2d 595. For a review of the implications see Kenneth J. Meier, "Ode to Patronage, A Critical Review of Two Recent Supreme Court Decisions," *Public Administration Review* 41:5 (May 1981): 558–563.
24. The U.S. Supreme Court has not been the only "activist" court. See Peter J. Galie, "The Other Supreme Courts, Judicial Activism among State Supreme Courts," Paper presented at the Midwest Political Science Association meetings, Milwaukee, 1982.
25. Daniel J. Elazar, "Contradictory Trends in Contemporary American Federalism: Court, Congress, and Centralization," *Journal of State Government* 62:1 (January/February, 1989): 46–49.
26. Neil T. Romans, "The Role of State Supreme Courts in Judicial Policymaking, Escobedo, Miranda, and the Use of Judicial Impact Analysis," *Western Political Quarterly* 27 (March 1974): 38–59.
27. G. Alan Tarr, *Judicial Impact and State Supreme Courts* (Lexington, Mass.: D. C. Heath, 1977).
28. William J. Brennan, Jr., "The Bill of Rights and the States: The Revival of State Constitutions as Guardians of Individual Rights," *New York University Law Review* 61: 535–553.
29. Richard A. Watson and Randal G. Downing, *The Politics of the Bench and the Bar, Judicial Selection under the Missouri Non-Partisan Court Plan* (New York: Wiley, 1969), p. 7.
30. Philip J. DuBois argues that voters have about the same interest in judicial elections as they have in elections for other offices when the elections are held under similar conditions. Participation in judicial elections is likely to be highest if elections are partisan, held at the same time as other "high interest" elections, and have ballot formats that discourage voter "falloff." "Voter Turnout in State Judicial Elections," *The Journal of Politics* 41 (1979): 865–887. See also Susan B. Hannah, "Voting in Local Judicial Elections, The Case of the Faithful Electorate," Paper presented at the Midwest Political Science Association meetings, Milwaukee, 1982.

31. James Herndon, "Appointment as a Means of Initial Accession to Elective State Courts of Last Resort," *North Dakota Law Review* 38 (1982): 60–73.
32. Watson and Downing, *The Politics of the Bench and the Bar, Judicial Selection under the Missouri Non-Partisan Court Plan*, p. 343. For examples of how advocates of various election plans idealize their preferred systems, see Elmo B. Hunter, "There's a Better Way to Choose Their Judges," and "Don't Destroy the People's Right to Choose Their Judges," in Robert L. Morlan (ed.), *Capitol, Courthouse, and City Hall*, 5th ed. (Boston: Houghton Mifflin, 1977), pp. 129–134.
33. Larry T. Aspin and William K. Hall, in a study of 783 retention elections in which 15 judges were not retained, found voter falloff to be about one-third; falloff was greater in judges' nonhome counties of multicounty districts. Voters in home counties, however, were not necessarily likely to deliver a higher percentage of yes votes. "The Friends and Neighbors Effect in Judicial Retention Elections," *Western Political Quarterly* 40:4 (December 1987): 701–715.
34. Watson and Downing, *The Politics of the Bench and the Bar, Judicial Selection under the Missouri Non-Partisan Court Plan*, p. 352.
35. Joseph F. Zimmerman, "New York Judicial Report," *Comparative State Politics Newsletter* (August 1988): 33–35. See also Paul Hain, "Changes in the New Mexico Judicial System," *Comparative State Politics Newsletter* (December 1988): 28–29.
36. Marsha Puro, Peter J. Bergerson, and Steven Puro, "An Analysis of Judicial Diffusion: Adoption of the Missouri Plan in the American States," *Publius* 15:4 (Fall 1985): 85–97.
37. Susan B. Corbon, "Judicial Elections: Are They Serving Their Intended Purpose?" *Judicature* 6:4/5 (November 1980): 211–233.
38. See Charles H. Sheldon, "Influencing the Selection of Judges, The Variety and Effectiveness of State Bar Activities," *Western Political Quarterly* 30 (1977): 397–400.
39. Larry L. Berg et al., "The Consequences of Judicial Reform, A Comparative Analysis of the California and Iowa Appellate Systems," *Western Political Quarterly* 28 (1975): 263–280.
40. Craig R. Ducat, Mikel L. Wychoff, and Victor E. Flango, "State Judges and the Protection of Constitutional Rights," Paper presented at the Midwest Political Science Association meetings, Chicago, 1989. For a comparison of state supreme court decisions with federal appeals court decisions regarding libel cases, see John Gruhl, "Patterns of Compliance with U.S. Supreme Court Rulings: Libel," *Publius* 12:3 (Summer 1982): 109–126.
41. Massachusetts and New Hampshire appoint their top judges to serve until age 70; New Jersey does so after the appointee has served a seven-year term. General trial court judges have the same appointments as the supreme court justices in Rhode Island, Massachusetts, and New Hampshire.
42. Irene Testitor, *Comparative State Politics Newsletter* (January 1980).
43. Some current court practices permit judges to retaliate even when the county is not involved in a case. For example, a Pontiac, Michigan, judge, unhappy with the treatment from the city council, assessed only fines. Court costs and fees which would have gone to the city coffers were not assessed.
44. Warren Burger in a Foreword to "Symposium on Judicial Administration," *Public Administration Review* (March/April 1971): 112.
45. Rubin, *The Courts, Fulcrum of the Justice System*, p. 211.
46. G. Alan Tarr argues that court centralization or consolidation meets only partially the goals its advocates claim for it. "Court Unification and Court Performance: A Policy Assessment," *Judicature* 6:4 (March 1981): 356.
47. Wisconsin Legislative Reference Bureau, *The Powers of the Wisconsin Supreme Court*

(Madison: Wisconsin Legislative Research Bureau, 1976), Research Bulletin 76-RB-1.
48. *Wayne Circuit Judges v. Wayne County*, 383 Mich. 10 (1969).
49. *Commonwealth ex rel. Carroll v. Tate*, 442 Penn. 45 (1971).
50. National Advisory Commission on Criminal Justice Standards and Goals, *Courts* (Washington, D.C.: Law Enforcement Assistance Administration, 1973), p. 164.
51. See Nathan Glazer, "Towards an Imperial Judiciary?" *Public Interest* 41 (1975–1976).
52. For another technique see Arthur Lapham, "The Jury Card System of Obtaining Data on Prospective Jurors," *Texas Bar Journal* 24 (1961).
53. *Apodaca v. Oregon*, 406 U.S. 404 (1972), and *Johnson v. Louisiana*, 406 U.S. 356 (1972).
54. See Jerome Frank, "Something's Wrong With Our Jury System," in Robert L. Morlan (ed.), *Capitol, Courthouse, and City Hall* (Boston: Houghton Mifflin, 1977), pp. 138–143.
55. Peter W. Sperlich, "The Case for Preserving Trial by Jury in Complex Civil Litigation," *Judicature* 65:8/9 (March 1982).
56. For criticisms of the grand jury system see Stanley H. Friedelbaum, "The Grand Jury System in New Jersey, Current Proposals for Reform," *Comparative State Politics Newsletter* (February 1982): 21–22.
57. Associated Press dispatch in *Salt Lake Tribune* (October 1, 1981).
58. Andrew Hacker, "Getting Used to Mugging," *New York Review of Books* (April 19, 1973), pp. 9–14.

Chapter 12

Communities in the Federal System

Local governments affect our lives directly. Most of us have been born in their hospitals, ridden their buses, and learned from their teachers. Even so, Americans often are perplexed about how they fit together.

The view is even more confusing from our nation's capital. From Washington, D.C., we would see the 83,000 units—and a great deal of variety as well. What these units do, how they select their officials, what powers they exercise, and how they relate to each other and to their state governments differs among states and often within the same state. These varied arrangements create problems for members of Congress and national administrators who try to decide which local units should qualify for specific programs.

Even their names are sometimes befuddling. In Alaska, for example, boroughs are similar to counties elsewhere. But in Pennsylvania, Connecticut, and New Jersey, boroughs are urban governments, only a step below a city.

Is the number of local governments increasing? The answer depends on how far back we go. In 1952 the nation had almost 117,000 local units. By 1972 it had dropped to 78,000 as the states began consolidating school districts. But since then citizens have been creating more special districts and organizing new city governments. By 1987 the total had climbed to 83,186. (See Table 12.1 for overall totals, Figure 12.1 for state totals).

Overview In this chapter we consider how the states have delegated power to community governments and how local officials use their political resources to loosen such ties. We next review the types of local governments. We then discuss how the reformers of this century have emphasized both managerial efficiency and democratic participation values in local organization. Finally we consider how community and federal officials relate to each other and the problems community officials face in delivering services.

LOCAL GOVERNMENTS ON THEIR OWN—ALMOST

Local governments owe their legal existence to their respective state governments. States, though, are uncertain about how to treat the community governments they have created. Municipal governments possess a broad range of functional powers, but states also direct their officials to carry out these duties in very specific ways. Local officials complain that instructions from the state are too detailed. They ask with some justification, "Are we to be treated as adults or as children?"

Table 12.1 NUMBER OF LOCAL GOVERNMENTS: SELECTED YEARS

Type of local government	1987	1982	1977	1952
Counties	3,042	3,041	3,041	3,052
Municipalities	19,200	19,076	18,862	16,807
Townships	16,691	16,734	16,822	17,202
School districts	14,721	14,851	15,174	67,355
Special districts	29,532	28,078	25,962	12,340
Total	83,186	81,780	79,862	116,756

Source: U.S. Bureau of the Census, *1987 Census of Governments, Government Organization*, Vol. 1, No. 1 (Washington, D.C.: U.S. Department of Commerce, 1988).

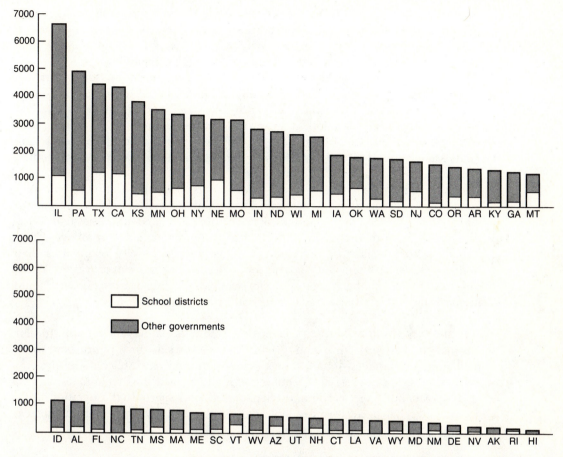

Figure 12.1 The number of local governments by state. [Source: Tax Foundation, *Facts and Figures on Government Finance* (Baltimore: Johns Hopkins University Press, 1990), p. 4.]

State Control over Local Powers

History helps us sort out these intergovernmental conflicts. Many cities, and in some cases counties, were operating before the states themselves were organized. Some, for their time, had extensive service programs. In the beginning, state officers were not greatly concerned with these fledgling communities. They attended to other matters—developing natural resources and attracting new residents.

Often, administrators in the cities, not the state, first developed administrative and functional expertise. City officials thus became leaders and state officials, followers. Just when, where, and how the state should exercise greater influence over its urban centers was later to become a puzzle for state officials.

The Rural-Urban Division of Local Government Systems Early state officials were concerned with finding pragmatic responses to what they saw as needs. They saw a sharp division among the responsibilities of urban and rural governments. Rural governments would have much less to do.

Most states established counties to govern rural areas. In some northern states, townships supplemented the county. Counties were to be mainly branch offices for a few state functions that had to be carried out on a statewide basis—elections, education, taxation, land records, and legal functions associated with criminal and civil law. Rural areas did not need much more government than that. Many states designed counties so a rural resident could travel to the county seat and return home in a day's buggy ride.

State officials recognized that urban units needed additional powers—authority to pass local ordinances and regulations, as well as provide more kinds of services. As a first step, residents of developing urban communities had to ask the state legislature to give the settlement legal standing as a city or village. Cities usually assumed many of the county's duties within the city boundaries, had representatives on the county board, and continued to pay county taxes.[1] When residents living on the fringe of a city wanted municipal services, they could become part of the city by way of a legislative act or an election.

Technology Brings Changes Over time technological advances began to blur distinctions between rural and urban. Transportation—first interurban trains and later, automobiles—enabled people to live in small satellite communities outside the cities. Moreover, new septic systems and well-drilling techniques, as well as the availability of electric and telephone services, permitted amenities in the countryside that once were available only in the city. Eventually, technological

changes drew the rural governments into providing such urban services as public transportation, recreation programs, and land-use zoning. Modern technology has also contributed to society's generation of vast quantities of waste materials and has been less helpful in converting waste products into useful commodities. Policy Box No. 23, "One Person's Trash...," provides a glimpse of the problem for local and state officials.

THE LAW AND POLITICS OF STATE-LOCAL RELATIONS

State constitutions provide legal standing for at least some local governments. Legislative acts, however, define most of their legal powers. As we see, their apparent tenuous legal standing does not seem to cause local officials to adopt an apologetic posture. They challenge the governor or berate legislators.

How Much Authority for Local Units?

Some states give local citizens wide choice over how they organize themselves and what functions they exercise; others allow very little choice. County residents, for example, traditionally have had little direct voice in organizing their governmental structure. City residents in many states may choose from among council-manager, mayor, or commission forms of organization and decide what services to provide.

Dillon's Rule—The Strict Constructionist Approach John F. Dillon, a judge in Iowa, issued the benchmark decision in 1868 on the question of inherent municipal power. **Dillon's Rule** came down so hard on the community governments that we might imagine Dillon to have been a crotchety and vindictive judge. He wrote that a "municipal corporation can exercise the following powers and no others":

1. Those the states grant in express words.
2. Those necessarily implied or necessarily incident to the powers expressly granted.
3. Those absolutely essential to the declared objects and purposes of the (municipality)—"not simply convenient, but indispensable."

He added a fourth—if there is any fair doubt as to whether a power exists, the doubt is to be "resolved by the courts against the local government."[2]

Some state judges disagreed and ruled that local units indeed have inherent powers—powers they can exercise without prior state approval.[3] But in 1903 the U.S. Supreme Court upheld Dillon's view.[4]

This, though, is not the end of the story. Local interests have used their collective political influence to curb state legislative interference—some say meddling—in local affairs and have weakened, if not entirely eliminated, the impact of Dillon's Rule.

Policy Box No. 23

One Person's Trash...

The usual ending to this cliché "is another person's treasure." For local officials, though, trash is no treasure and deciding what to do with it can be a first-class headache. Consider the following accounts.

Dade County, Florida, generates about 6,400 tons of garbage and trash every day. It has two landfills that will last about 20 more years if somehow it can reduce the daily volume. The odds of getting more landfill sites are slim because of the risk of polluting the high groundwater table.

Dade County also has an incinerator, but in 1988 it needed a $50 million overhaul to process its projected 2,574 tons per day. Without the improvements its capacity is only 1,700 tons, a little over a quarter of the daily trash production. The incinerator provides some resource recovery because it produces electricity that is sold to local utilities.

In Jackson County, Michigan, commissioners faced a similar problem—dwindling landfill space. To preserve long-term use of the landfill, the county board had an incinerator built. Finally the time to fire up the new facility came. It worked just fine, and trash haulers began dumping their loads. In fact, the county made arrangements for haulers from other nearby counties to feed the voracious appetite of the fire-breathing apparatus. Things were going swimmingly.

But then state natural resources department officials reported that toxicity levels of the residual ash exceeded permissible standards. Too many batteries were dumped in the trash, thus producing an ash with excessive quantities of lead. The ash could not be disposed of in the county landfill. Special facilities would be required. The county had to cease incinerator operations.

By that time, however, it was time to begin paying off the interest on the funds borrowed to build the incinerator. To raise revenues for the financially strapped

How long it takes for certain products to decay if left by the side of the road.

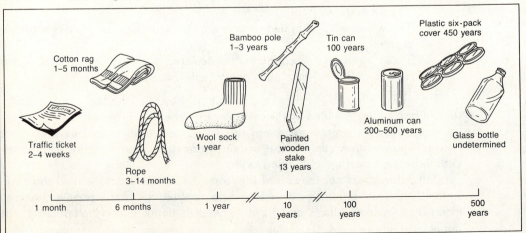

(*Source*: Michigan State University Extension Service.)

county, officials had to encourage trash haulers to dump their collections in the county landfill. For about a year, the landfill capacity was being consumed at an unprecedented rate—precisely the outcome county officials had been seeking to avoid.

Eventually the legislature resolved the immediate problem by changing the environmental standard for disposing of toxic wastes.

Dade County tried a different approach—it paid a firm $8.25 a ton to haul trash to another firm's cement processing plant. There it sorts the trash, especially for aluminum and newspaper. The newspaper will become part of a fuel mixture to produce heat to make cement. Whether the mixture will meet permissible air emission standards is problematical. If not, Dade County officials will have to go back to the drawing board.

Most experts agree that reducing the waste stream is the key to coping with, if not resolving, virtually every American community's waste disposal problem. Widespread participation of households could reduce the waste stream by about 15 percent. Usually this involves recycling—reprocessing discarded materials into new products. The level of recycling varies by commodity.

RECYCLING IN THE UNITED STATES, 1988

Commodity	Quantity	Percentage
Aluminum cans	750,000 tons	54.6
Glass	2.5 million tons	25.0
Wastepaper	25.7 million tons	26.2
Plastics	250,000 tons	0.9
Steel	56 million tons	56.0

Source: *City and State*, August 14, 1989.

In order to be usable, recyclable materials must be sorted. Experts prefer "source separation"—sorting before it gets loaded onto a truck. For homeowners, it means having different containers for clear glass, colored glass, aluminum, newsprint, plastic, yard wastes, and so on. This is possible for people with large garages but difficult for those who live in small apartments.

Voluntary citizen source separation has not come easily in the relatively few communities that have tried it. Prince George's County, Maryland, gave $100 prizes each month to a few households. (Interestingly, Rockford, Illinois, pioneered this tactic in 1986 but abandoned it in 1987 because of lack of interest.) St. Cloud, Minnesota, offered a lottery for participants in which they gave away a trip to the Caribbean. In 1986 Rhode Island charted a new course by mandating curbside pickup of recyclable materials.

Recycling has other problems—converting the materials into desired products at competitive prices is a major one. Reprocessing paper, for example, has some costly aspects because the ink residue from used paper cannot merely be dumped into the nearest stream. And many users do not always appreciate the quality of reprocessed paper, especially when it costs as much as paper made from virgin forest products. Indeed, collectors of wastepaper and metal must pay periodically to have it hauled away rather than sell it.

The situation is similar with reprocessed plastics. One manufacturer processes plastic milk containers into picnic tables, synthetic wood posts, and other products used in parks. But the state department of natural resources in that state could not buy them for the state parks because they were more expensive than similar wood products. That the plastic products are more durable, require no maintenance, were impervious to weathering, and were virtually indestructible seemed not to matter to the price-conscious bureaucrats in the purchasing department. Elsewhere, waste hauling companies and manufacturers are developing other techniques to recycle plastics into tennis balls, sleeping bags, and other products. In some states used tires are being mixed into road asphalt. Generally the product is considered highly acceptable, but some state officials choose not to use it because they fear they will be blamed for deviating from approved standards.

In addition, state legislatures often fail to appreciate the need to reduce wastes or to recycle. Illinois, for example, forbids community governments from requiring source separation. And only a handful of states yet require cash deposits on beverage bottles and cans to encourage their return to vendors rather than disposal in landfills or along roadsides. Beverage processors and merchants typically oppose such legislation because it increases the purchase price of the products and presents a handling problem in stores.

What do you think? Are the community and state governments too timid in dealing with the solid waste and recycling situation? Is it a problem that has reached the crisis stage? How is a community likely to get the best rate of compliance with source separation of household wastes: education and incentive awards, legal penalties and refusal to accept unsorted materials, or cash discounts for sorted materials? Should states impose deposits on all nonbiodegradable packages, refundable upon return, such as some states now do with beverage containers? Should states require public agencies to use only recycled paper? Should states subsidize recycling efforts or let its success rise and fall with market prices for the materials? What should the federal role be in dealing with waste and recycling?

Lobbying and Local Government Associations

Although legally the states have a virtual life and death hold over local governments, they are not able to use these powers fully. Politics softens a state's legal powers.

Almost every local government group has its own state organization. Many also have national affiliation. Together, they form what we have called the intergovernmental lobby, the state and national organizations that provide officials with information when a state or national government is about to act on an issue of interest. The executive director sounds the alarm—"Contact your legislator about this matter soon!" Occasionally the national organizations participate in court cases important to their members.

Cities and Villages The state municipal league usually represents the middle-sized and smaller cities and villages, which of course far outnumber the large cities (see Table 12.2). Larger cities are also members but have somewhat different interests and often have their own lobbyists. They even lobby the state association sometimes.

At the national level, the National League of Cities speaks for both large and small units. Mayors of large and middle-sized cities are also members of the U.S. Conference of Mayors. Some large cities have their own lobbyists in Washington as well.

Counties County commissioners work through a state association of counties. County clerks may have their own state associations—as do sheriffs, health boards, probate judges, dogcatchers, and others. With so many voices, the messages sometimes become garbled and competitive. The National Association of Counties is the main voice for county commissioners in the nation's capital. Many county officer groups have national associations too. Nearly 87 percent of all counties have fewer than 100,000 residents (see Table 12.3).

Schools School boards, school administrators, parent groups, and teachers all have their own state associations. These groups face a situation like that of the counties—the subgroups have competing or conflicting goals. The teacher groups usually want improved economic and working conditions. School board members and administrators, parents along with teacher groups, lobby for bigger budgets and higher performance standards, but the groups part company over whether school boards need more control of teacher unions or easier procedures to fire incompetent teachers. Parent groups lobby for laws dealing with sex education, minimum drinking age, busing, and textbooks.

Table 12.2 NUMBER OF CITIES BY POPULATION SIZE

Population grouping	Number of cities	Percentage
Over 1,000,000	8	0.1
500,000–1,000,000	16	0.2
250,000–499,999	36	0.5
100,000–249,999	125	1.8
50,000–99,999	312	4.4
25,000–49,999	665	9.4
10,000–24,999	1,596	22.5
5,000–9,999	1,785	25.2
2,500–4,999	2,124	29.9
Less than 2,500	428	6.0
Total	7,095	100.0

Source: Adapted from *Municipal Year Book, 1989* (Chicago: International City Management Association).

Table 12.3 NUMBER OF COUNTIES BY POPULATION SIZE

Population grouping	Number of counties	Percentage
Over 1,000,000	22	0.7
500,000–1,000,000	53	1.7
250,000–499,999	92	3.0
100,000–249,999	230	7.6
50,000–99,999	382	12.6
25,000–49,999	628	20.6
10,000–24,999	935	30.7
5,000–9,999	436	14.3
2,500–4,999	169	5.7
Less than 2,500	95	3.1
Total	3,042	100.0

Source: Adapted from *Municipal Year Book, 1989* (Chicago: International City Management Association).

Towns and Townships These units, too, have their state associations, although some are members of the state municipal league. The National Association of Townships and Towns is the newest of the group. It was formed in 1980.

How the Associations Function These organizations, of course, are not part of the formal governing process. Yet they play an influential role in intergovernmental relations and in shaping national policies.

Building the Agenda The intergovernmental lobby does more than just react—members initiate policy proposals. Annually, each association has a major issues meeting to approve lists of policies they want state legislatures or Congress to accept.

With the list in hand, the executive director and the association's professional staff get to work. They draft bills for sympathetic legislators to introduce, gather data to bolster their arguments, and write articles for the association newsletters to inform members as well as legislators and administrators. The executive director refers to the issues in speeches and asks local officials to discuss their concerns with area legislators. With hard work and some luck, the state legislature or Congress will take up an item and change the law as the association wishes.

The Effectiveness of Local Officials' Lobbying Local officials get much of their clout because state legislators are elected from local districts where they must explain their voting records and gain support. Community officials, especially if they are of the same political party, can make it tough for a legislator who is not helpful. Withholding personal and financial backing, encouraging primary opposition, and just "forgetting" to invite the legislator to meetings are a few of the techniques local officials may use to encourage their legislators' support.

Interassociation Conflict When local government interest groups disagree, the most likely result is stalemate. Frequently, fights are internal rather than against a common outside "enemy."

We recall an incident in Michigan when the state teachers' union was pressing for the right to strike. The school board association opposed this change and demanded greater freedom to fire tenured teachers. After months of haggling, the speaker of the house "locked" representatives of the two groups in a nearby motel. He told them to hammer out a compromise. After more than a week of continuous bargaining, they failed to agree. The legislature, as a result, made no changes. It is not unusual for the very difficult disputes to go for ten years or more before being resolved.

THE TYPES OF LOCAL GOVERNMENTS

If the states could revise their systems of local government every other generation or so without worrying about local political pressures, we would find a far different pattern. But what exists is a compromise between what the state officials may desire, what localities residents and officials prefer, and what is—the status quo. Past practices are especially influential; changes are seldom sweeping.

The County

Colonial settlers established counties on the basis of structures they knew in England and adapted them to fit conditions in the new land.

New England Pattern The settlers of New England faced a fierce climate, hilly areas, angry Indians, and difficult traveling. These conditions led them to organize small, compact communities. The religious orientation of the settlers, as well as their fishing and shipping economy, also contributed to a focus on town development—each town with its own government. Under these conditions, county government gained little stature and had few functions.[5]

The Southern County Land grants in the South were made to individuals, not groups as was the case in New England. Moreover, the parcels granted were large. The climate was mild, the rivers wide and navigable, and the Indians hospitable. A plantation economy of widely dispersed settlements developed. For county government the result was large areas, with the landed gentry in control.

Pennsylvania and New York Patterns Pennsylvania and New York developed a blend of the New England and southern types. Pennsylvania had both counties and townships. But the county, with a board of only three directly elected commissioners, became the dominant rural local government unit.

New York, influenced by New England's approach, began by establishing towns. It later set up county commissions similar to Pennsylvania's, but neither system satisfied all. The disagreement led to a compromise—New York would have both townships and counties, but the county board would consist of township supervisors. The two levels would share local powers and duties. Later, New Yorkers transplanted this form to several midwestern states.

Counties in the West Western states established large counties but no form of rural township government—an expected pattern in areas where the population is sparse and settlements scattered. Five member boards of directly elected commissioners head the government.

County Government Today Richard L. Black, a county administrator in South Carolina, wrote, "Even if county government had not previously existed in the American system, the second half of the 20th century would have produced such a form.... Practitioners grappling with urban and rural problems and the need for effective governmental mechanisms below the state and above the municipal level [would have demanded it]."[6]

Black obviously favors county government. Still, there is support for his statement. Many states are now adapting county governments to deal with urban service problems in suburban and rural communities.[7] As we will see later, the counties also are adopting new organizational structures. County leaders and administrators generally seem to be less concerned about the organizational structures and service powers than they are with their fiscal powers. This is especially the case with the decline in federal assistance and what many consider inadequate state aid.[8] County governments continue to function with many organizational vestiges of an earlier day.[9]

The Town Meeting

New England towns followed church parish lines and, for the most part, were "natural communities"—urban settlements surrounded by a rural countryside. Such picturesque towns still exist outside metropolitan areas. Most characteristic of the **town meeting** organization is direct democracy—citizens making public policy themselves rather than through elected officials. Each year, citizens meet to discuss and vote on local issues, listen to reports from citizen committees, elect officers, and adopt the town budget. Larger towns, however, now use a form of representative democracy—they elect a hundred or so citizens to act for the others. Many towns have hired managers or have full-time clerks as administrative officers.

The Township

Townships formed in New York, New Jersey, and Pennsylvania were of an irregular shape. But the Northwest Ordinances of 1785 and 1787 required the western territory to be surveyed into square **townships**, 6 miles to a side. Thomas Jefferson hoped that "pure and elementary republics" would develop in each—governments similar to the town meeting.

In most of the states formed out of the Northwest Territory, townships have not survived. States transferred many of their powers—road management, welfare, property tax administration—to other governments. Where townships still exist as active governments, they often perform functions similar to those of cities.[10] Townships receive their legal powers through general state laws. Commonly within each state their governing bodies are uniform, typically consisting of an elected supervisor, clerk, treasurer, and two "legislators." They generally hold annual meetings of citizens, but these barely resemble those found in the New England town meeting.

The City

Counties, townships, and school districts, for the most part, have gotten their legal authority from legislative statutes that spell out their powers and duties in great detail. State governments commonly have kept them on a short leash in keeping with the philosophy of Dillon's Rule. State officials have argued that they need a high degree of uniformity among these types of local governments.

The states, however, as we saw earlier, have had a somewhat more difficult time agreeing on the powers city governments should exercise. City officials argued that they are different from the other types and from each other, and hence each city needs its own distinctive set of powers. Over time and after working through several stages, city governments in many states have made their case successfully.

Special Act Charters Legislatures first delegated governing powers to cities through **special or local charter acts**—charters that applied to a single city. Such an act would spell out in detail a city's legal powers and organizational structure. And changes in the charter could come only from the state legislature.

Granting powers in this way proved to be an especially bothersome practice because local acts made the cities vulnerable to legislative whim and enabled legislators to manipulate local officials. If a state legislator from a particular city, for example, wanted a particular local bill to pass, other legislators would usually support it out of "legislative courtesy." The city officials, though, may not have wanted the law, and the legislator may have wanted only to punish political enemies or to reward some friends back home.

To curb this practice, local interests supported constitutional amendments to limit local acts or make them more difficult to pass. Massachusetts, for example, now permits a local act only if local citizens or officials petition for it or if the governor proposes it. And the legislature can pass such a bill only by a two-thirds vote in each house. Several states, mostly in New England and the South, continue to employ this approach.

General Law Charters As early as the 1850s, Indiana and Ohio delegated authority to cities by **general law charters** which spell out powers and duties for cities of differing sizes. But this approach also has problems. A change affects all the units within a class. Local officials who want a specific change—having the auditor appointed rather than elected, for example—may not be able to convince officials in other cities of that class to support the change. Without agreement from the cities involved, legislators would likely leave the law unchanged.

To solve that problem, more classes of cities were established. But that subjected cities to **bracketing**—targeting one city by creating classes of cities that would define only one city in the class. Of course, this technique opened the way for state interference and political meddling in local affairs. Some states convey powers and distribute state aid to local units using this approach. Often legislators make a special case out of a state's largest city or county—Illinois, for example, with Chicago and Cook County. To limit legislative abuses, some state constitutions require a class of local government to include at least two municipalities.

Optional Forms A variation in the general law approach offers cities a kind of catalog of charters or **optional forms** from which to choose. Option A may allow for a strong elected executive form; Option B an appointed manager, and so on. New Jersey offers its cities 14 different options. Other states using this approach have a much smaller product line.[11]

Home Rule Charters Some states use another approach—constitutionally based **home rule**. The state constitution grants cities and in a few states, counties, broad powers beyond the reach of the state legislature. The National Municipal League used the Latin phrase *imperium in imperio*—state within a state—to describe home rule. The League suggested that the state constitutions should list the powers that the home rule units could exercise.

The difficulty has been that as new problems arise, local officials may find that a needed power is not on the list. The courts then tend to take a Dillon-like approach and decide on the basis of the **exclusionary rule**—if the power is not listed, it is excluded.

The Importance of Home Rule Home rule does not allow local officials to do whatever they please, but it does give local units a good deal of **discretionary authority**—citizens decide issues regarding organizational structure, functions and services, some financial decisions, and methods of managing and employing municipal personnel. It provides a psychological backing for independent action.

The process works this way. Voters elect a charter commission to draft a **city charter**—a kind of local "constitution" spelling out the organizational structure and governmental powers—that the citizens then vote on. Later the voters may amend the charter by referendum or initiative. The charter must conform to state laws and the state constitution. Iowa, in 1851, was the first state to grant home rule by statute. But in 1875 Missouri pioneered home rule by constitution. The home rule movement for cities and villages reached its peak in the early 1900s. Home rule had a brief resurgence in the 1950s with adoptions in two southern states (Georgia and Louisiana) and two border states (Maryland and Tennessee). New England and most southern states do not use it.[12]

The Benefits of Local Home Rule   Under home rule, residents of a community, rather than state legislators or other officials, can choose the form of government and general pattern of representation—whether to have at-large or ward and partisan or nonpartisan elections, how many officials to have, and which of them to elect. Home rule allows local citizens to decide to what degree they base their government on the values of managerial efficiency, how much democratic participation to allow, and any limits on taxes they wish to impose.

Home rule also permits communities to respond to changing conditions. As population grows more diverse, for example, the people may begin to feel that the council-manager form of government does not meet their needs for political leadership. They may then change the charter to have a full-time mayor or to elect the council from wards.

Citizens in home rule states have been more successful in establishing forms of organization that emphasize managerial efficiency—destruction of "machine" politics, introduction of nonpartisan elections, appointing rather than electing administrative officers, and greater citizen participation in the affairs of local governments.

What Home Rule Does Not Provide   But at best, home rule is limited self-government. Some states limit home rule to municipalities that meet specific population or tax-base standards. More importantly, home rule does not put local government beyond the reach of state legislatures. General state laws, such as those that require freedom of information, open meetings, collective bargaining, or uniform accounting, and election procedures, affirmative action, barrier free access, and other conditions usually still apply. The fine print in the law usually says "local charter provisions to the contrary notwithstanding" and thus restricts what local units can do.

The "Devolution of Powers" Approach   Another strategy to home rule reverses the approach. The **devolution of powers** proposes that state constitutions grant municipalities *all* the powers capable of being delegated. But it also gives legislatures the authority to withdraw any powers essential to state goals. In other words, if a state constitution or a state statute has not withdrawn a specific power, the municipal governments have it. Jefferson B. Fordham advanced this proposal in a model state constitution in 1953.[13] He argued that this approach would make state legislatures, rather than courts, the principal architects of local powers. As a practical matter today, however, the courts become involved when a state legislature withdraws a specific power. Some states employ this approach fully, others only partially.[14]

At the same time this approach, perhaps, gives state officials an adequate degree of control. In 1988, for example, the city of Detroit had a rent control initiative on the ballot. Thinking that the rent provision would worsen housing conditions in the city, the Michigan legislature was persuaded to pass a law denying local units the authority to adopt rent control ordinances.

The Special Case of Schools

Most states have treated education as a function that required its own special organization—the local school district. In a day when foot power—horse or human—was the only way to get around, the distance that small children could walk became the primary consideration in setting school district boundaries. A large number were created—67,355 in 1952. But school buses made school consolidation and large districts possible; they were able to provide courses and facilities that smaller districts could not afford. By 1988 the number of districts nationwide was fewer than 15,000.

Most Americans believe that education should be free of politics. Thus only a few states organize education as a major department of a city or county even though at the state and national levels there are such departments. Establishing independent school districts, of course, has not freed them of politics. Schools rely heavily on state grants to balance their operating budgets. This, together with the unionization of teachers, teacher certification, teacher competency tests, sex education controversies, busing, and other issues draws public education foursquare into the tuggings and pullings of state and local politics—and, to a lesser degree, into federal politics as well.

School systems deal with a host of state regulations. But schools that are independent units have locally elected governing boards—they hire the school superintendent and teachers (usually certified by the state) and levy taxes.

Other Contemporary Forms

Recent contributions to local governmental structure have been mainly attempts to create units that cover larger areas. Some are advisory, some are single-function units, some carry out several related functions, and a few are special purpose governments.

The Special District The most important mechanism for handling problems that overlap local government boundaries is the **special district**. Several local governments together create a separate unit to handle one or two functions—trash incineration, for example. Officials sometimes also establish special districts to get around state or charter tax restrictions. And citizens sometimes encourage formation of a special district for only part of a governmental unit so that the special district can provide a service such as a public water system, mosquito control, health care or sanitary sewer systems, and parks, and only those who benefit pay the cost. Financing comes from property tax levies and charges for services. The number of special districts is increasing rapidly—more than 3,500 were formed between 1977 and 1987.

HOW COMMUNITY GOVERNMENTS ARE ORGANIZED

Alexander Pope dismissed the debate over governmental structure with the couplet,

> For forms of government let fools contest. Whate'er is best administered is best.

The difficulty is that citizens and students conclude that the form of government chosen is related to how well a system will be administered.

As we discussed in Chapter 1, reformers became dissatisfied with the separation of powers system, especially as it was adapted to urban government. They became uneasy over deadlocks between a mayor and the council. Some reformers wanted more efficiency, others more democracy.

What brought the issue to a head, we think, was the boss system. The reformers considered political machines to be both inefficient and undemocratic because they were corrupt and graft-ridden. They saw separation of powers as encouraging bossism because it sometimes resulted in stalemate. Although some residents—the immigrants, the poor, widows, and unemployed—wanted a government with a heart and one that dealt with the basics of human survival, the "good government" reformers had the last word with respect to structure. They put their indelible stamp on city governments and other local units.

Five Elements of Reform Organization

The most difficult problem the reformers faced was in centralizing power and finding a way to control such centralized power democratically.

They used five structural elements. And organizers of local governments since have produced a variety of governmental forms by the way they mix these elements—usually in search of a balance between managerial efficiency and democratic participation.

The Executive Power The reformers wanted a strong executive—a leader who would hire and fire, prepare budgets, and supervise the administrative branch. Thus they favored a short ballot rather than the election of competing administrative officials.

Whether to organize the executive function for political or policy leadership is perhaps the most important question reformers faced. Should the structure concentrate executive power in a democratically elected official such as the mayor who is a political leader elected by citizens? Or should a professional administrator selected by the legislative body, such as a city manager or school superintendent, head up the governmental unit? Their answer is perhaps the most important consideration in the balance of managerial efficiency and democratic participation values.

Term of Office How long should the terms of office be? The longer the term, the more independent officials will be of citizen groups. But long terms also provide opportunity to gain expertise and carry out programs. Should the terms of all elected officials including legislators expire at the same time?

If all are elected at one time rather than having staggered terms, citizens will find it less difficult to change majority control and policies. They can throw all the rascals out in one election—a more democratic solution. But staggered terms offer a degree of continuity and stability.

Partisan Versus Nonpartisan Elections Should elections be partisan or nonpartisan? Again we see some possible tradeoffs, especially in large communities. Citizens of lower social and economic status will have less influence in nonpartisan elections. Partisan elections, on the other hand, may mean that control rests with a small party clique. Gaining access to power may then be difficult. But except in one-party areas, citizens generally will be able to hold a group accountable for existing policies.

Basis for Representation Should city councilors be elected from **council districts** (or wards) or by **at-large elections**, where voters from the entire city select the whole city council? Should the council be structured to bring together people who represent the various minority, ethnic, and economic groups, as ward elections tend to do? Councilors chosen at large tend to reflect a broader majority viewpoint. Or should cities use a combination of at-large and district elections, perhaps nominating candidates by ward and conduct the elections at large or electing some from wards and some at large?[15]

Size of Legislative Body Two considerations are involved. First, small councils or legislative bodies tend to broaden the interests of the council members—they tend to be generalists concerned with overall operations. Members of large councils will probably have a narrower range of concerns and possibly tight control over these matters. Large councils and ward elections often go together.

The second consideration is access of citizens to public officials. Opportunities for people to know city officials personally tend to be less for low-income and minority populations if the governing body is small rather than large. Smaller councils thus are likely to lessen opportunity for broad democratic participation.

Basic Organizational Plans

We next consider four basic forms of municipal organization—weak mayor, strong mayor, commission, and council manager. Reformers focus mainly on arrangements for the executive power and rely less on the other four elements. As we discuss these four plans of organization, note how each deals with the issues of managerial efficiency and democratic participation.

Weak Mayor-Council Plan Jacksonian Democrats were the architects of the **weak mayor-council plan**. Its key values are that executives should not be politically powerful and citizens should have a strong voice in government.

Jacksonians wanted their chief executive and many other community officials—administrators such as the treasurer, clerk, assessor, and members of administrative boards—to be elected. They intended these officers to be independent of the mayor and responsible directly to the voters.

The result was a weak executive—one with little direct authority over the administrative units. Consequently, unless the mayor was able to gain political power, as through a party machine, administrative units would not necessarily follow the mayor's directives.

The Jacksonians provided access to the city government through a large city council—as many as 50 councilors in some cities. And some even had a **bicameral** city council, with both an upper and a lower house. Now all city councils have but one body—they are **unicameral**. The councilors ran in a partisan election, terms were short—a year or two—and seldom were staggered.

Jacksonians gave only minimal attention to managerial efficiency. Although mayors usually had a veto power, the council had the responsibility of developing the budget. Mayors thus could check reckless councils, but they did not have many administrative tools with which to lead (see Figure 12.2).

The Weak Mayor-Council Plan Today Smaller cities are the primary users of this plan. But most have made some changes, nearly always to increase managerial efficiency. Councils now are usually small, elections mostly nonpartisan, and the mayor usually presents and directs the budget.

Professional administrators and municipal experts generally view the plan as being ill-suited to large modern cities. But Chicago, referred to as "the city that works" under Mayor Richard Daley, is a weak mayor-council form. Daley overcame its inadequacies by chairing the Cook County Democratic party and thus controlled Democratic party politics. But his successors have had less political power and less success. Mayor Harold Washington seemed to be assembling political power comparable to Daley's, but he died shortly after beginning his second term. Chicagoans now wonder if Mayor "Dick" Daley, who won election in 1989, will amass the kind of power his father had.

Counties and townships in some states employ some of this plan's features, especially with respect to the number of independent elected officials and the use of administrative boards and commissions. But many counties do not have a chief executive. Instead they have councils or boards that use a committee system to run things. These combine the executive and legislative functions. They thus violate one of the principles of the weak mayor-council form—separation of powers.

The Strong Mayor-Council Plan The reform movement that began during the 1880s saw the **strong mayor-council plan** as the answer to the problems of the large industrialized cities. These reformers concentrated primarily on strengthening mayors' powers. They gave the mayor power over policy development and administration. They made most other positions appointive. Under the ideal plan the mayor has the authority to appoint and fire all department heads. The mayor

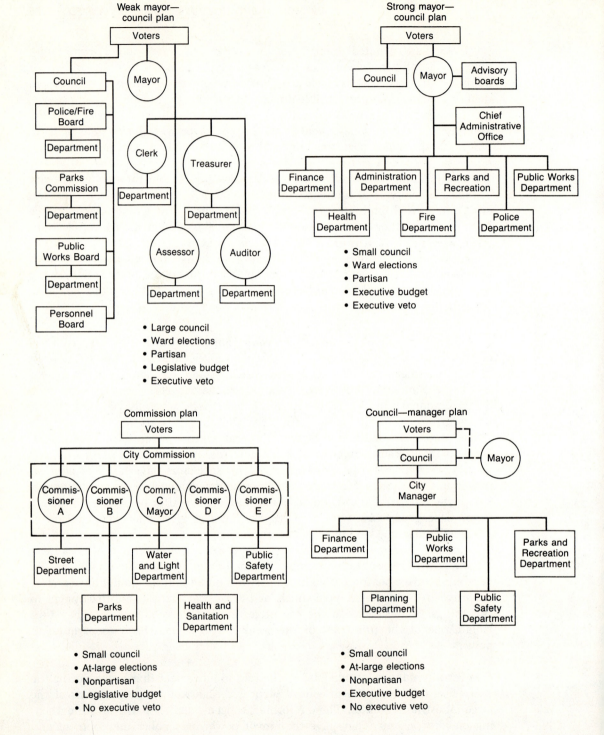

Figure 12.2 Basic forms of local government structure.

also has a veto power and is responsible for developing and administering the budget.

Councils, under this plan, are small—usually from seven to nine persons, often elected from wards on a partisan basis. They generally serve part time, except in a few large cities, and have no administrative duties.

The CAO Modification Some cities expect that their citizens will not always elect a skilled administrator as mayor. They also provide a position for a **chief administrative officer (CAO)** who serves at the mayor's pleasure. CAO duties differ from city to city but usually include responsibility for the budget and other functions of day-to-day administration of the government.

This arrangement allows the mayor to concentrate on providing political leadership, fashioning and seeking support for his or her policies. The mayor may lobby the council and bargain with the important power centers at community, state, and national levels, as well as meet with citizens. Overall, about 3,550 of the communities (58 percent) with populations over 2,500 have mayor-council governments. But sources generally do not distinguish them by type because of the many variations that community governments employ. What we do find, though, is that the larger such communities are, the more likely it is that they will have a strong mayor form and some type of CAO as well. Parallels to the strong mayor-council form in other types of local government are generally rare, although a few states permit an elected county executive.

The Commission Plan Galveston, Texas, suffered a devastating hurricane in 1900. Its government came to a virtual standstill and the state legislature temporarily put in its place a special commission to oversee rebuilding the city. It appointed five business leaders and gave each responsibility for a separate city department.

The rebuilding effort went so well that after the crisis Galveston adopted a new charter and made the **commission plan** permanent. The 1903 charter provided for the election of five commissioners.

The central idea of the plan is the election of three to five nonpartisan officials. This city commission legislates, but each commissioner also manages a city department or two. One also serves as the ceremonial mayor. Usually there are no other elected officials.

Although the plan began accidentally, other cities soon adopted it. It offered a businesslike efficiency as well as a nonpartisan and short ballot, which reformers were then beginning to tout.

But, as we might anticipate, troubles began to develop—topflight executives could not always be recruited as was true during the Galveston crisis; the government lacked a central administrator to coordinate activities and set priorities. The politics of being commissioner required **log-rolling** or back scratching—"You vote for my department and I'll vote for yours." Departments of noncooperating commissioners soon began to suffer. Individual commissioners came into conflict over their respective powers.

The Commission Plan Today Commission plan adoptions peaked rapidly. By 1917 the number began a gradual decline that has continued.

We find the highest use in the Dakotas—half of North Dakota's cities have a commission plan, and 9 of South Dakota's 23 cities use the plan. Galveston abandoned commission government. The largest city in Texas still using the commission plan is Texas City (population 39,000). Only a few large cities such as Tulsa (population 332,000) and Kansas City, Kansas (population 170,000), use the commission plan. Many of these, though, now have a city administrator and thus overcome what is probably the plan's major weakness—managerial inefficiency because the plan lacks a single executive.

The central feature of the commission plan—at-large election of a small board with mixed legislative-administrative powers—is most common today in county governments. County boards of commissioners in all but 11 states have nine or fewer members. Many have only three or five.

The Council-Manager Plan

Perhaps the commission plan would have been used more had not reformers devised the **council-manager plan**. It follows the business model even more closely. It emphasizes both centralization of executive authority and professionalism.

Origin and Growth Staunton, Virginia, claims to be the first council-manager city. In 1908 its council hired an engineer as its manager. But Sumter, South Carolina, argues that it was the first to become a genuine council-manager city. In 1912 it adopted a new charter implementing the plan of Richard S. Childs, once president of the Short Ballot Organization, and later, guiding light of the National Municipal League.

By 1920 more than 150 adopted the plan. By 1990 about half the cities with 2,500 population were council-manager.[16] Cities with populations between 25,000 and 250,000 are most likely to have city managers; few having more than 1 million use this plan.

The Basic Provisions The council-manager plan answered very well the reformers' criticisms of mayor-council governments—it coincided with the desires of the Short Ballot Organization, it copied very closely the structures of business corporations (voters are the "stockholders," the city council is the "board of directors," and the manager is the "chief administrative officer"), and it eliminated partisan politics, which reformers asserted to be the bane of the cities, and favored at-large elections to represent broad policies on the council.

The council-manager plan assigned administrative leadership to a professional manager or administrator, whom the council hires and fires. The ideal plan centralizes administrative power, giving the city manager complete administrative responsibility. The manager appoints and removes department heads, is responsible for developing and administering the budget, and recommends solutions for city problems to the council.

Councils under this organizational form are small, from five to nine members. Citizens elect them for staggered terms from the city at large on a nonpartisan basis. They have no administrative duties; in fact, many city charters prohibit councilors from even dealing directly with a department head. Complaints and problems are to be channeled through the manager. The task of the councilors is to react to proposals of the manager and establish broad policies. But because the council hires and fires the manager, it, too, must share responsibility when things go wrong. The mayor's duties under the plan are mostly ceremonial. Purists argue that the council should elect one of its own members rather than have the mayor directly elected.

Modifications in the Plan Most cities adapt this "pure" form to meet local preferences. One study of 309 council-manager cities, for example, noted that more than 80 percent had nonpartisan elections or elected their councilors at large. But only 67 percent had both features.[17] Some go even further and include a full-time mayor, a potential source of friction between the mayor and manager.

Managerial Efficiency Versus Democratic Participation Childs, describing himself as the "minister" for the council-manager plan, praised the "neutral competence" he said the professionals would bring to city hall.[18] Since then Norton Long and others have argued that city managers are not neutral administrators. Rather, Long argued, they are politicians, though not openly partisan.[19]

City managers once denied in their code of ethics that they had a policymaking and political role. (And even by 1990 their association did not have an official lobbyist in Washington.[20]) Their only role outside of administration, they said, was supplying alternative solutions for city councilors. Now, although readily acknowledging active participation in shaping policy, they deny using "political" means to influence council decisions. Most prefer the "expert advisor" role.[21]

But since the early 1970s these professional public managers have experienced a new dilemma—they do not always have the resources necessary to play a political role successfully. As long as municipal problems were primarily technical—building sewers and water lines or laying out subdivision streets—they felt confident in making recommendations. Many residents were pleased to have professional experts solve such technical problems. But as community governments began dealing with problems of social disorganization such as inadequate housing, crime, poverty, rapid urban development—and in school systems, desegregation, busing, sex education, vandalism, and drugs—the best solutions were not readily apparent. These issues involve uncertainty and thus require political leadership.

Managerial Efficiency Under Attack

Citizen groups have challenged the professional recommendations. Added to these challenges were questions of democratic representation, neighborhood participation, equal employment opportunity, and employee participation in management (primarily through unions). These further complicated the politics of community decision making.

From the data in Table 12.4 we see that municipal administrators were not united in how to deal with this dilemma. Yet they basically opposed structural

Table 12.4 ATTITUDES OF MANAGERS AND CITY ADMINISTRATIVE OFFICERS REGARDING ELECTION AND STATUS OF MAYOR AND CITY COUNCILORS

Election and status of mayor and councilors	Percentage in favor	Percentage neutral	Percentage opposed
Full-time paid mayor	5.7	22.4	72.3
Direct election of mayor	47.6	29.9	22.5
Councilors elected by district	17.9	25.6	56.5
Councilors elected at large but residing in district	44.4	32.8	22.8
Mixed councilors: some at large, some by district	24.4	38.3	37.3
Full-time paid council	3.7	14.7	81.6
Full-time staff for mayor	8.7	20.1	71.3

Source: Adapted from *Municipal Year Book, 1975* (Washington, D.C.: International City Management Association), p. 151.

arrangements that would give more importance to nonprofessionals. City administrators preferred part-time mayors and councilors. They opposed full-time staff for mayors or councilors chosen from districts.

Council-Manager Cities and Democratic Participation Is the council-manager plan, with its professional emphasis, failing? Probably not, but it is undergoing change. Arthur J. Holland, longtime mayor of Trenton, New Jersey, observed that structures of city government change in times of economic and social unrest—he was thinking of the Great Depression, the civil rights issues of the 1960s, and ongoing demands for minority representation in the 1980s.[22] Hence adaptations to the model form are being made, especially in the larger cities. A Dallas newspaper publisher noted, for example, that after 12 years of experience with district, rather than at-large elections, "Individual council members have a hold in those districts now, and the manager has less power." Based on our discussions with city managers who face conflicting political demands, we find these administrators consciously offering alternative solutions rather than a single "best" solution. They seem more inclined to have elected officials and residents choose solutions to social problems.

Are these professional public managers, then, becoming more the neutral competents that Childs described? Not entirely. The alternatives they propose to city councilors may still be a stacked deck favoring actions that professionals prefer. During periods of uncertainty, when solutions to public problems are not so apparent, professionals can expect to find their political role reduced and that of democratic participation increased.[23]

Other Uses of Professional Managers A variety of local governments employ adaptations of the manager plan. Special districts depend heavily on professional managers—superintendents in school districts, hospital district administrators, airport district managers, and physicians in mental and public health districts are but a few examples. In addition, a growing number of counties and towns rely on professional managers.

Choosing the Form of Government

Why do some communities adopt a mayor-council form while others use the council-manager plan? Political scientists have theorized that certain community-based variables influence such decisions.[24] Managerial efficiency is emphasized in communities where citizens have a general consensus over community goals. Democratic participation is of greater importance in communities which experience a diversity of values and goals. Thomas P. Ryan, mayor of Rochester, New York, makes the point this way: "A council-manager form works just fine if you have a cohesive majority on the council, they know what to do and can generally agree. But a manager can't work well for nine different people with differing ideas."[25]

On the basis of data from 243 central cities, Thomas Dye and Susan MacManus found that ethnicity is a factor in choosing the form of government. Cities with a high percentage of foreign-born residents were more likely to have the mayor-council form and ward elections; council-manager forms were more likely in communities with low percentages of foreign-born residents. Carol Cassel in a survey of 4,659 cities with over 2,500 population notes that only 32 percent of the cities in the Northeast are nonpartisan, half that of cities in the West. She attributes the differences to historical reasons—cities already settled by the time of the Progressive movement were less influenced by it.[26]

Other students suggest that reformed city structures—council-manager forms mainly—have a middle-class bias. These "reformed" governments tend to be more open to community groups, especially those that are politically attentive and active—usually individuals of some social and economic status.[27] Cassel's study supports this thesis and indicates that the bias is strongest on city councils that have both nonpartisan and at-large elections.[28] The studies of Susan Welch and Timothy Bledsoe support this finding but argue that nonpartisanship has little effect in district or ward elections.[29]

GOVERNING LOCAL COMMUNITIES

What is the job of community governments? Most would agree that it is to provide a complement of public services and regulations that keeps the community safe and healthy, and one that offers residents a range of opportunities for development and fulfillment.

Creating such communities demands a wide-ranging array of services that differs from community to community and state to state. In broad terms, the municipal services bundle that these governments provide probably includes public works and transportation, public utilities, public safety, parks and recreation, health and human services, educational, cultural, and arts programs, and a variety of administrative support activities. Moreover, they offer them in a variety of ways—directly through their own employees, by contract with other units of government, perhaps by licensing private companies to provide the service, or by an areawide level of government.

What Determines Service Levels?

Home rule governments can select the services they may wish to provide from a thick catalog. General law units such as counties and townships may have a somewhat more limited range of choices. School districts and special districts are usually more restricted, but within the area of educational services they have a variety of choices. Who decides and why?

State governments usually take a first cut at the choices, again especially for the general law units including schools—the laws that create them typically spell out the required and prohibited functions. School districts in your state, perhaps, do not assess property, collect taxes, or conduct elections because the state law assigns those functions to other units. Similarly, other units may have little or no say in the public education programs.

Beyond that, numerous considerations come into play. The density of development affects service levels—places such as New York City demand a higher public service level than lightly developed suburbs or rural areas. In densely settled urban environments, people can do little individually. Collectively, they call on community and other governments to provide for them. In addition, the degree of interdependent relationships among people and institutions is high, and government is called on more to regulate those relationships. Natural conditions influence public service demands—residents of the Snow Belt expect the city and county to keep the roads clear; those in arid climates expect an ample supply of fresh water at the turn of the spigot.

The composition of the population is influential. Wealthy communities probably insist on top-rate educational and cultural programs and back-door rather than curbside trash pickup. The poor may be more interested in housing programs and rent control. Communities dominated by young families want school crossing guards, neighborhood parks, sidewalks, and child-care programs. Where seniors dominate, the emphasis may be more on programs for the elderly and perhaps low taxes. The unemployed may push public officials for economic development and job creation.

Finally, we note the obvious: Financial resources affect community services. The community governments rely heavily on the property tax to finance local services, but taxable property is not evenly distributed among communities. Some units are richly endowed with industries and businesses that impose relatively minor costs on the government while making substantial payments in property taxes. Others may have a small property tax base and residents with low personal incomes. State and federal grants-in-aid offset some of these disparities of resources and needs, but seldom does it eliminate them.[30]

The Problem of Service Distribution

But even within communities, there are problems of distributing services on the basis of need. Various students have hypothesized that the level of urban services is directly related to the average income in a neighborhood—the lower the residents' income, the lower the level of municipal services. Robert Lineberry posed what he called the "underclass hypothesis"—the idea that the poor, black, and powerless regularly benefit less than others.[31]

Later, other students concluded that urban services usually vary from one neighborhood to another but that the variation seems to have no clear, consistent pattern—for some services in some cities poorer neighborhoods receive a higher level of service than do other neighborhoods; for other services in other cities, the poor and minority populations receive less. But as Bryan D. Jones and his colleagues concluded, "The question of whether the governmental effort is 'enough' or 'equitable' is not answered by this research; all we can say is that the lower classes do not consistently receive the lowest level of services."[32]

COMMUNITY-FEDERAL RELATIONSHIPS

We began this chapter by mentioning how officials in our nation's capital are sometimes confused by the maze of local governments. This might not be important if the federal administrators had not needed to make a variety of direct program contacts with many of these governments, especially the nation's large urban centers. Even though cities and counties are not mentioned in the U.S. Constitution, these relationships have been important in shaping our federal system.

Such contact is a trump card that local officials and administrators occasionally can play in the game of state and local relations as well. Federal grants have enriched local treasuries. Also, federal pressures on state legislatures and governors have helped change practices that community officials found restrictive. Here we review briefly the relationships of the community governments to officials in Washington, D.C.

Direct Local-Federal Relations In the 1930s the federal government began dealing on a relatively regular basis with community governments. Among the first such programs were grants for public housing projects, and under the Works Progress Administration (WPA) many communities also received federal grants and loans to build public water, sewer, and other facilities. The contacts expanded sharply in the 1960s, with programs intended to solve the problems found in America's great cities—poverty, racism, crime, and other forms of social disorganization. To a lesser extent, federal programs also reached rural communities, especially those with poverty problems. Others dealt with water, air pollution, sewage plants, airports, mass transportation, expressways, and, in rural areas, agricultural production—programs dating back to the 1930s.

Local-federal programs continued to expand during the 1970s. Then in 1972 under general revenue sharing, Congress granted virtually unrestricted funds to every community in the nation, and for the first time the federal government had direct contact with every general-purpose local government on a regular basis. As we have noted, Congress eliminated general revenue sharing in 1986.

Other federal programs reached into the community governments as well. The Housing and Community Development Act of 1974 consolidated seven categorical grants programs. Larger cities (those over 50,000) participated in **entitlement grants**—funds are assured and not subject to bureaucratic scrutiny. Smaller ones had to compete for project grants.

Expanded State Involvement The states were not included in these and many other programs. At least part of the reason was that many federal officials regarded state governments as inefficient, undemocratic, and unsympathetic to urban problems. But as we saw in Chapter 1, this picture has changed. The National Governors' Association and the Conference of State Legislatures argued that earlier criticisms were no longer valid. They point to the reapportioned state legislatures, the strengthened governorships, professional state bureaucracies, and open democratic procedures. They began lobbying for a coordinating role.

During the Reagan administration, Congress converted many federal programs to block grants on a **state pass-through** basis. Some federal grant programs (1) made state approval necessary for community participation and (2) required grant funds to be subject to state controls. The Small Cities Community Development Block Grant (CDBG) program illustrates the type of transfers that were beginning to be made. In 1980 the Department of Housing and Urban Development (HUD) picked Kentucky and Wisconsin as experimental sites for state management of the funds for the under-50,000 cities. By 1987 all but two states had exercised the option of administering these funds. The states have been better able to direct funds to towns under 10,000 than HUD. Moreover, the states were able to employ the funds for economic development, public facilities, as well as housing—HUD had tended to direct all of the funds toward housing, which is not always a problem in smaller communities.[33]

The Impact of Federal Courts One set of local-federal relations the states have been less successful in curtailing is that of the federal courts to the community governments. All of us have become familiar with the concern of the courts over community efforts to achieve racial desegregation of schools through busing. But a great many other types of community concerns, from the regulation of pornography to elections administration, crime control, housing, and prayer in public schools, have come to the federal courts for decisions and policy-making. It is a rare city mayor, county commissioner, or school superintendent who today is not sensitive to the actions of this arm of the federal government. More recently they have had to keep an eye on the Supreme Court's developing view of the use of zoning powers and the possibility of liability for money damages when the community government oversteps its bounds. This conflict is reviewed in Policy Box No. 24, "Public Interests and Private Rights in Zoning."

| Policy Box No. 24 | Public Interests and Private Rights in Zoning |

One of the most common, and perhaps important, regulatory powers that American communities exercise deals with how individuals use their land. They exercise this power by adopting zoning ordinances.

A typical zoning ordinance outlines several districts or zones in which the government allows only certain types of land use. In one district, for example, an owner may build only single-family houses. The zoning ordinance also may require that lots in this zone must be at least 100 feet wide, distances between the lot line and the house at least 15 feet, or that the house be at least 30 feet from the street. Other zones may permit only apartments, stores, or factories. Other zones may be designated for farming. Zoning ordinances contain very detailed rules.

A board of zoning commissioners oversees the administration of the ordinance. Its main task is to decide whether to change the ordinance in response to requests to use the land for something different than the zoning ordinance allows. After notifying adjacent property owners and holding a public hearing, the zoning commission decides what to do.

If the request requires a change in the zoning class, the ordinance itself must be amended. But if the local council approves the change, and the residents do not approve, they can demand a vote of the citizens on the matter. When that happens, it has the effect of making zoning commissioners of all those who decide to vote.

Community zoning ordinances are based on the general principle of public health, safety, and welfare. It recognizes that the residents of the whole community have a collective public interest, and perhaps private interest, in how the land in the community develops. To permit someone to put a factory with the possibility of smoke, noise, and truck traffic next to a residential neighborhood would likely diminish the value of the houses as well as require the local government to widen roads, build new water and sewer lines, and so forth, to meet the new needs of the factory.

The problem, however, is that the Fifth Amendment to the U.S. Constitution says, "...nor shall private property be taken for public use without just compensation." The U.S. Supreme Court has said that property may be regulated to a certain extent, but if the regulation goes too far it will be recognized as a "temporary taking" requiring compensation. That is, excessive regulation may mean the community must pay money damages to the owner who is denied use of the property.

The legal principles involved were set out in *First English Evangelical Lutheran Church v. County of Los Angeles*. This case began when the church bought some land in a canyon in Angeles National Forest where it built Camp Lutherglen for handicapped children alongside Mill Creek. After a flood destroyed the camp, Los Angeles County adopted an ordinance prohibiting reconstruction of any buildings on the Mill Creek flatlands. The county's objective was to protect the public health and safety from flood hazards.

The church sued the county and asked for monetary damages for the regulatory taking because, the church argued, the county had denied any possible use of the land. California's supreme court ruled against the church, saying that improper takings should be corrected by reversing the regulation, not paying money damages. But the U.S. Supreme Court disagreed and said that money damages could be appropriate if overregulating amounts to a temporary taking.

The Supreme Court returned the case to California to work out a settlement. But the principles of the case were picked up quickly elsewhere. Landowners who did not get their way in rezoning cases sued for monetary damages for temporary takings. Grand Blanc Township (Michigan) was ordered to pay a mobile home park developer $82,000 even though the board had approved the rezoning request. The problem was that residents petitioned for a referendum on the ordinance change and reversed their board of trustees. In the end, the developer not only got approval to build the mobile home park but the money as well.

The implication for the zoning function was severe. The impact on permitting referenda on zoning changes was even more pronounced. Some began to think the cases chilled community control of its land use. Others thought that the matter had become too complex (and potentially costly) to let citizens continue with their role.

Others suggested that such responses were overreactions. The new rules only mean that local zoning boards need to be more objective in making zoning decisions; they should apply the zoning ordinance rules and make their judgments without regard to the emotional and political pressures residents display or threaten. They also suggest that denying citizens the right of referendum on zoning changes is a worse cure than the illness. Citizens can now be told of the financial risks associated with rezoning elections if the voters' decision is proven unconstitutional. They should be permitted to run the risk of money damages if they want.

What do you think? Did the Supreme Court in *First English* undermine local zoning? Will many local zoning boards be intimidated by developers who threaten to sue for money damages for temporary takings? Should ordinary citizens be allowed to vote on administrative matters like zoning? Is it likely that voters will understand the concept of and risk involved in temporary takings? Should communities back away and give landowners a relatively free hand in how they use their land?

Local as well as state officials during the last half of the 1980s were most concerned over the extent to which the Tenth Amendment could hold off Congress's forays under the commerce clause into areas once thought out of bounds. The Court overturned the application of minimum wage and hour provisions to the state and local governments in 1976 and later reversed it. However, since then, in several cases, the Supreme Court has indicated that local and state officials should seek relief from the Congress and not the Court. Application of federal labor laws to municipal and state operations as well as further federal limits on the use of tax exempt bonds are just two areas where local and state worries have been heightened.[34]

A FINAL COMMENT

The 1980s was a decade of difficult financial adjustment for co… ments. Coming off a period of unprecedented inflation and progran… the late 1970s, communities suffered from the national recession in 1980s. Accompanying this was severe economic dislocation in some communities, especially those in the northern midwestern states. Many saw industrial plants being closed and abandoned. Farm states experienced plummeting land prices and economic distress in the rural communities. To make matters worse, the federal government reduced or eliminated key assistance programs.

But adjust they did, with a combination of strategies. Some reexamined program priorities and cut back on the less important ones and reduced their work forces. Some combined such cuts with increases in taxes and service fees. Some looked to new ways to provide public services through intergovernmental contracting and privatizing public service programs. And some sought to build new futures through aggressive economic development efforts.

Many communities, of course, still face difficult circumstances. But most community governments have recovered from the stress of the 1980s and are beginning to emerge with a leaner administrative structure and stronger sense of governmental mission and priorities. Some officials still occasionally look to Washington for financial assistance, but most base their planning on their own resources and aid they can expect from their state capital.

HIGH POINTS

The states created local governments on the assumption that (1) two basic sets of local government were needed—one for rural areas and one for urban areas. We saw that (2) the states were reluctant to extend broad grants of power to local units; instead, state legislatures have kept local officials and citizens on a rather short leash. But we also saw (3) how the community governments employed political resources to free themselves, at least in part, from tight state control.

We reviewed (4) the various types of local governments and saw that in many respects they were pragmatic responses to the needs and problems of the time. We then discussed (5) the ways local governments are organized. We noted especially the tendency of community governments to adopt the reforms reflecting the values of managerial efficiency and to lessen democratic participation.

We next considered (6) the services the local units provide and the several considerations that affect the type and quality of service that is provided. We also considered whether community governments distribute their municipal services fairly, especially with respect to the poor. Finally, we considered (7) the relationships of the community governments with officials in our nation's capital. We noted that for most local units now, intergovernmental contacts are with state rather than federal officials.

In this chapter we defined the following terms in this order: Dillon's Rule, town meeting, townships, special or local charter acts, general law charters, bracketing, optional forms, home rule, exclusionary rule, discretionary authority, city charter, devolution of powers, special district, council districts, at-large elections, weak mayor-council plan, bicameral, unicameral, strong mayor-council plan, chief administrative officer (CAO), commission plan, log-rolling, council-manager plan, entitlement grant, and state pass-through.

NOTES

1. Almost everywhere cities are part of a county, and their residents pay both city and county taxes. But Virginia's cities and a few large cities such as St. Louis and Denver are separate from counties. New York City as we know it today is comprised of five counties or boroughs.
2. *Merriam v. Moody's Executors*, 25 Iowa 163 (1868).
3. *People v. Hurlburt*, 24 Michigan 44 (1871).
4. *Atkins v. Kansas*, 191 U.S. 207 (1903). The court reaffirmed the decisions in *City of Trenton v. New Jersey*, 262 U.S. 182 (1923).
5. This analysis of the development of county government in America was first articulated by James Bryce in *The American Commonwealth* (New York: Macmillan, 1888).
6. Richard L. Black, "Full Partnership for Counties," *Public Management* (December 1981): 2.
7. Louisiana calls its counties parishes and Alaska calls them boroughs. Rhode Island never established a county system; Connecticut abandoned its system in the 1960s.
8. See William L. Waugh, Jr., and Ronald Hohn Hy, "The Administrative, Fiscal, and Policymaking Capacities of County Governments," *State and Local Government Review* 20:1 (Winter 1988): 28–31, and John P. Thomas, "A Perspective on County Government Services and Financing," *State and Local Government Review*, 19:3 (Fall 1987): 119–121.
9. County government has variously been called the "headless wonder" and the "dark continent of American government." In part this is because most counties have no executive officer to attract attention and because very few books deal with county government on a national basis. The basic ones are Paul W. Wager (ed.), *County Government Across the Nation* (Chapel Hill: University of North Carolina Press, 1950); Herbert S. Duncombe, *County Government in America* (Washington, D.C.: National Association of Counties, 1978); and John C. Bollens et al., *American County Government* (Beverly Hills, Calif.: Sage, 1969). For a description of county government in Michigan, see Kenneth VerBurg, *Guide to Michigan County Government* (East Lansing: Michigan State University, 1987).
10. The U.S. Bureau of the Census identifies Michigan, New Jersey, New York, Pennsylvania, and Wisconsin as being "strong township" states. Illinois permits townships on a county option basis. For a comparative study, see John W. Beutler, *Townships, Towns, and Their State Associations* (Kalamazoo: Western Michigan University, 1980). Also see Kenneth VerBurg, *Managing the Modern Michigan Township* (2nd ed.) (East Lansing: Michigan State University, 1990).
11. More rarely, states allow counties such options. Utah permits three options. Pennsylvania, New York, Michigan, and Wisconsin also permit counties to choose from among alternative forms of organizations.

12. Home rule for counties has been longer in coming. Even now only a few states permit it. California and Maryland adopted county home rule over 60 years ago. But other states such as Illinois and Pennsylvania have permitted it only since the early 1970s.
13. Jefferson B. Fordham, *Model Constitutional Provisions for Municipal Home Rule* (Chicago: American Municipal Association, 1953).
14. Advisory Commission on Intergovernmental Relations, *Measuring Local Discretionary Authority* (Washington, D.C.: Advisory Commission on Intergovernmental Relations), p. 20.
15. Of course, electing members of governing bodies from wards or districts requires a periodic redrawing or reapportionment of the districts. For a review of this process in cities, see W. E. Lyons and Malcolm E. Jewell, "Redrawing Council Districts in American Cities," *State and Local Government Review* 18:2 (Spring 1986): 71–81.
16. International City Management Association, *The Municipal Yearbook, 1988* (Washington, D.C.: International City Management Association).
17. Raymond E. Wolfinger and John O. Field, "Political Ethos and the Structure of City Government," *American Political Science Review* (June 1966): 306–326.
18. Childs argued that mobilization of support required condensation of the idea to a "catch phrase, even if false in many of its material applications." See Richard J. Stillman, "The City Manager, Professional Helping Hand or Political Hired Hand?" *Public Administration Review* 37 (November/December 1977): 659–670.
19. Norton Long, "Politicians for Hire," *Public Administration Review* 25 (June 1965): 119. Also see Karl A. Bosworth, "The City Manager Is a Politician," *Public Administration Review* 18 (Summer 1958): 216–222.
20. Kathleen Sylvester, "City Managers Consider a Political Role," *Governing* (February 1978): 45.
21. William R. Fannin and Don Hellriegel, "Policy Roles of City Managers: A Contingency Typology and Empirical Test," *American Politics Quarterly* 13:2 (April 1985): 212–226. Also see James H. Svara, "Dichotomy and Duality, Reconceptualizing the Relationship Between Policy and Administration in Council-Manager Cities," *Public Administration Review* (January/February 1985): 221–232.
22. Jane Mobley, "Politician or Professional? The Debate Over Who Should Run Our Cities Continues," *Governing* (February 1988): 42–48.
23. For more on the condition of the council-manager plan, see "Symposium on the American City Manager," in Keith F. Mulroney (ed.), *Public Administration Review* 31 (January/February 1971): 6–46.
24. Among them are James Q. Wilson and Edward C. Banfield, "Public Regardingness as a Value Premise in Voting Behavior," *American Political Science Review* (December 1964): 876–887; Robert Alford and Harry Scoble, "The Political and Socioeconomic Characteristics of American Cities," *The Municipal Year Book*, 1965 (Chicago: International City Management Association), pp. 82–97; and Raymond C. Wolfinger and John Osgood Field, "Political Ethos and the Structure of City Government," *American Political Science Review* (June 1966): 306–325.
25. Quoted in Jane Mobley, "Politician or Professional? The Debate Over Who Should Run Our Cities Continues," p. 46.
26. Carol A. Cassel, "Social Background Characteristics of Nonpartisan City Council Members: A Research Note," *Western Political Quarterly* (September 1985): 495–501.
27. Alana Northrup and William H. Dutton, "Municipal Reform and Group Influence," *American Journal of Political Science* (August 1978): 691–711.
28. Cassell, "Social Background Characteristics of Nonpartisan City Council Members: A Research Note," p. 499.

29. Susan Welch and Timothy Bledsoe, "The Partisan Consequences of Nonpartisan Elections and the Changing Nature of Urban Politics," *American Journal of Political Science* 30 (February 1986): 128–139.
30. Robert M. Stein and Keith E. Hamm, "A Comparative Analysis of the Targeting Capacity of State and Federal Intergovernmental Aid Allocations: 1977, 1982," *Social Science Quarterly* 68:3 (1987): 447–465.
31. Robert L. Lineberry, "Equality, Public Policy and Public Services, The Underclass Hypothesis and the Limits to Equality," *Politics and Policy* 4 (December 1975): 67–84.
32. Bryan D. Jones et al., "Service Delivery Rules and the Distribution of Local Government Services," *Journal of Politics* 40 (1978): 338–339.
33. Dale A. Krane, "Administering the Small Cities CDBG Program: A Federal-State Experiment," *Intergovernmental Perspective* 14:3 (Summer 1988): 7–11. Also see David R. Morgan and Robert E. England, "The Small Cities Block Grant Program: An Assessment of Programmatic Change Under State Control," *Public Administration Review* (November/December 1984): 477–482, and John P. Pelissero and James S. Granato, "Local Officials' Evaluations of State-Administered Community Development Programs," *State and Local Government Review* 21:1 (Winter 1989): 31–37.
34. See A. E. Dick Howard, "Garcia: Of Federalism and Constitutional Values," *Publius* 16:3 (Summer 1986): 17–31. Key cases in addition to *National League of Cities v. Usery*, 426 U.S. 833 (1976), are *Garcia v. San Antonio Metropolitan Transit Authority*, 105 S.Ct. 1005 (1985), and *South Carolina v. Baker* (1988).

Chapter 13

Intergovernmental Relations at the Community Level

More than 75 percent of us live in areas that the U.S. Bureau of the Census calls Standard Metropolitan Statistical Areas (SMSA).[1] They contain a complicated maze of cities, villages, towns, townships, counties, and special districts linked together with ribbons of concrete and blacktop, tubes, tunnels, and wires, as well as social and economic interaction.

Some of the units, mostly new suburbs, are growing and flourishing. Some are central cities and older suburban cities that are decaying and losing population. A few communities are rural, some stable and others struggling to survive.

But all are encountering problems in dealing with waste disposal and coping with air pollution and deteriorating **infrastructure**—roadways, bridges, public transit systems, and water and sewer facilities. Many have inadequate educational systems. Some fear energy shortages and train or truck accidents involving hazardous toxic materials. In some are abandoned industrial waste sites so contaminated the land cannot be given away. Thus not all communities within an SMSA experience the same set of difficulties.

Overview How should government deal with the economic, social, and technological interdependence of metropolitan population? That is the key question we deal with in this chapter. We begin by considering the forces that contribute to the development of metropolitan areas and by looking at the local setting for intergovernmental relationships. We then discuss the problems and benefits associated with these patterns and review various strategies that depend on voluntary cooperation. We next review how familiar strains of reforms—the attempt to centralize and professionalize governmental administration, achieve greater efficiency, and enhance democratic participation—have been employed in an effort to deal with the metropolitan areas. We note how efforts to centralize are resisted by advocates of democratization. Finally, we consider how the states, in order to coordinate community activities, use reforms championed by both sets of reformers.

EVOLVING PATTERNS OF HUMAN SETTLEMENT

The cities of the 1800s were centers of commerce and industry. They attracted masses immigrating from Europe to American shores. Today, they attract immigrants largely from Latin American countries and the Pacific Rim. But they also have been targeted by internal migrations—from the farm to city, the South to North, Snow Belt to Sun Belt, and from central city to suburb. Most of these migrants were in search of economic opportunity. As Lewis Mumford noted, cities were built not to please residents but as economic enterprises. "The law of urban growth," he wrote, "meant the inexorable wiping out of all the natural features that delight and fortify the human soul."[2] Many settlers have been willing to forgo, at least temporarily, the natural delights in exchange for a job or other economic opportunities. Paul E. Peterson makes the point that economic circumstances and objectives determine most of the city's political agenda and that the most important issues have to do with maintaining or improving the economic base.[3]

The means of transport—foot, horse, trolley, and waterfront—largely defined the boundaries of these early cities. Workers, then as now, could live no greater a distance from the job than the transportation system would permit.

Wealth and Technology Encourage Urban Sprawl Transportation changes were the keys to outward movement. With light rail lines toward the end of the nineteenth century, some people found they could live farther from their places of work. They could escape the smoky, grimy, and crowded parts of the city. Some could even avoid the city's social problems—crime, poverty, disease, and other hazards.

At first, small suburban communities began to develop along interurban lines—Philadelphia's Main Line suburbs, for example. Later on, after World War I, America began to produce reliable automobiles in volume. Opportunities for suburban living broadened.

It was not transportation alone, however, that made the difference. Other technological advances contributed. Extending electricity to outlying areas provided amenities customarily associated only with cities—for example, it meant that outlying houses could now have inside running water.

Suburbanization slowed during the years of the Great Depression and World War II. People coping with gasoline rationing and seeking jobs in war industries crowded back into the cities. Construction of new housing came to a standstill.

The Postwar Suburban Movement The war created an immense backlog in housing. The shortage worsened as returning veterans and the millions of new families they created sought a place to live. The market for housing outstripped financial and technological capacities—but not for long.

The federal government, through the Federal Housing Administration (FHA) and the Veterans Administration (VA), guaranteed mortgage loans to "qualified" home buyers. These policies solved the financial logjam.

Abraham Levitt and his sons led the way in the technological breakthrough. Originally, they had planned to construct on Long Island, New York, a housing project of 2,000 homes for "veterans only." They began building in the summer of 1947. Before finishing the project four-and-a-half years later, they had built 17,447 houses—a place that became known as Levittown.[4] Similar developments sprang up around every other large and middle-sized city.

Central City-Suburban Competition Telephone, electric, and natural gas companies happily extended their services to these new markets. Schools, water and sewer services, and municipal functions in most areas were different. Older cities often made **annexation**—merger with the city—the price for these services. Some suburbanites, caught with polluted water wells or failing septic fields, annexed. For others, annexation was too high a price. Mortgaged to the hilt, they voted new taxes for improvements of all kinds, including schools.

Life in the Suburbs

In the new suburbs the percentage of poor, unemployed, aged, and ill was negligible. Moreover the percentage of citizens with a substantial disposable income was relatively high. But in the 1950s some older, industrialized suburbs eventually began experiencing problems similar to those that had plagued the central cities. Residential areas became blighted, factories obsolete, and municipal revenues began tailing off.

Such suburbs also began to find their populations leaving for greener pastures farther out. Some citizens took advantage of the newly built interstates to move to small towns completely outside the metropolitan areas. Others conditioned themselves to twice daily train rides of an hour or more. And companies experimented with factories in small towns located near a convenient interstate. Residents in some such communities, both small and large, beset with growth that outstrips the infrastructure capacity, have pushed for local zoning and other policies to slow the pace of development and expansion. We explore strategies for managing urban growth in Policy Box No. 25, "Managing Urban Growth."

In the words of one suburban city mayor, "We are now into throwaway cities." He made the remark when he learned that a major hospital in his community was closing to relocate in a suburban community farther out. His comment might well have been made by many mayors of central cities who experienced the same throwaway mentality—of housing, factories, stores, railway depots, and other facilities.

What Happened in the Central Cities?

Many of the nation's central cities have been the victims of modern transportation systems and technologies that contribute to throwaway neighborhoods, commercial centers, and industrial complexes. City officials were inadvertent contributors as they planned and helped build freeways in the hope of luring suburbanites to their central business districts. "Shoppers could again get downtown with ease," advocates claimed. Others cooperated in urging "beltways" to relieve in-town traffic congestion, only to find businesses leaving the high-cost confining areas of the central city for the now accessible beltway developments.

As the middle class left for the suburbs, central cities became the repositories for the low-income, aged, unemployed, and underemployed groups. Blacks and other minorities became the dominant groups. Suburbanites organized separate cities. Their citizens became less and less concerned with what they had left behind—poverty, the victims of racial discrimination, and a variety of problems of social disorganization.

The Urban Condition For a time during the 1960s and 1970s, writers, the media, and politicians referred to these changes as the **urban crisis**. As Alan Campbell and Donna Shalala noted, this term is not well defined because the urban crisis affects people in different ways.[5] For black or Hispanic ghetto youths the crisis may be the poorly staffed school that fails to help them learn. For the welfare mother, it may be the continuing struggle to get money enough for food and housing to last until the end of the month.

For the old woman living next to a drug house and walking daily to the grocery store, it may be the fear of having her purse snatched or even of being raped or murdered. For the commuter to the downtown office building, it may be congested freeways. For the small merchant frustrated by holdups, break-ins,

Policy Box No. 25

Managing Urban Growth

Many governors and mayors have made economic development and job creation the cornerstone of their campaign platforms. Governor Neil Goldschmidt, for example, programmed half the state lottery receipts to reverse Oregon's image of "You're welcome to visit, but please don't stay." He wants to encourage tourism, lure light manufacturing, maintain agriculture, and nurture a growing high-tech industry.

In many places, though, that is going out of style. Citizens and officials in hot growth spots are crying, "Enough. We don't want more development because it will destroy the community we have come to love."

One might expect this in the Amish community of Lancaster County, Pennsylvania, which numbers about 10,000. They have carried on an old-world lifestyle in the region for the last 250 years. Their communities attract from 3 to 5 million tourists annually.

In 1988 highway planners proposed building a new road across the Amish country to handle the traffic. About 1,500 Amish attended a public hearing and silently protested. In January 1989 Governor Robert Casey banished the superhighway plan, saying that the traditions of the Amish should not be "destroyed, dislocated, or interrupted." Lancaster County is not unique. Yogi Berra, once the catcher and manager of the New York Yankees, put his finger on the dilemma in his inimitable way. Berra said, "That place is so busy, nobody goes there anymore."

Public officials and citizens in the growth areas are devising ways to slow down, some say manage, development. Efforts are being waged on both community and state levels.

Residents who are settled in a community protest that more projects only congest the streets, parks, and commercial centers and further pressure the infrastructure. Critics say their mindset is to close the community gates so no one else can move in.

San Francisco and Seattle restrict the number of square feet of office space that may be added downtown each year. They establish a competition among developers to fill the quota—a panel of experts that evaluates proposals for particular projects. The criteria include overall design, location, employment opportunities, and conformity to the community master plan.

San Diego and Riverside counties (California) impose absolute limits on the number of residential units that may be built. They want to slow the population growth—79,000 persons moved to San Diego County in 1987. They argue that the county cannot accommodate more "hypergrowth" because of "polluted air, dwindling space for landfills, increased crime, jail overcrowding, raw sewage spills, and related problems."

In some states, however, growth management is becoming a state function. Maine, Vermont, Rhode Island, and Delaware, for example, have passed statewide land-use planning laws. Others have passed similar rules but only for critical regional areas such as the Chesapeake Bay area in Maryland or California's coastal areas.

Other states permit community governments to develop their plans but then require them to get state approval. Florida state officials, for example, reject local plans if they do not also include ways to pay for infrastructure improvements. Texas officials tell their local units that they may impose impact fees—charges on developers for infrastructure improvements—but only if the community governments have adopted plans.

These "solutions," however, represent dramatic changes from the way urban development has occurred in the past. Before, economic market conditions dictated what would be constructed and what would not. People with money to invest would decide what was needed and where. Now politicians, administrators, and residents interfere with market demands. In doing so, they do not take all interests into account.

Developers claim that they have a right to develop their land and make a profit. They answer critics who accuse them of building only for the wealthy that they do so because community governments make such high improvement requirements—for example, water, sewer, roadways, street lighting, parkland, schools, and others. They say it is impossible to build housing for people of average means. And many insist that development impact fees are discriminatory because everyone paid for and benefits from previous improvements. Newcomers should not have to pay twice.

Others argue that their opportunities are being limited. They say they should not be denied the chance to live in some of the most desirable areas of the country just because they came later. Our country, they argue, is based on the principle that people could live anyplace they want to pursue their dreams. Now artificial barriers are being set up.

But environmentalists argue that uncontrolled development ravages the natural environment. Community governments, they say, first have an obligation to their own residents, not to the crowds who stampede an area and ruin it for everyone. Besides, they say, controlling growth in some areas gives communities that otherwise would not grow a chance to share in economic expansion.

In their view, our technologies lag behind our living patterns in many areas. Cars and power plants that despoil the air, demands for water that exceed the supply, and impossible waste flows threaten the quality of life for all. Officials and citizens have no choice but to restrict and manage the growth of some places.

A growing number of state officials and administrators, though, are arguing that community planning is not enough. Many land-use and urban service problems skip far beyond the boundaries of a city or county area. At a minimum, they say, we need to have regional agencies, especially to protect environmentally sensitive areas.

And maybe, according to them, state planning is the only way to manage growth. Local and regional people may succumb to local political pressures. And only at the state level will anybody be able to deal with LULUs—local unwanted land uses. But LULUs like landfills, incinerators, power plants, prisons, and other essential facilities should be planned. Communities can only stumble through these problems.

What do you think? Do new methods of controlling urban growth unfairly discriminate against would-be newcomers? Can politicians and residents regulate development more effectively than economic market conditions? Who should pay the costs of infrastructure expansion—just the new development projects or the entire community? Are these developing practices likely to discriminate against the poor and limit their opportunity for advancement? Should we expect communities to volunteer for LULUs?

and soaring insurance costs, the urban crisis may have come in the form of an offer to torch the building for a share of the insurance payoff.

For the police officer on the beat, the urban crisis may be drug dealing, prostitution, and the related armed robberies, murders, and witnesses afraid to testify. For the mayor it may be bankrupt city coffers, the result of a shrinking tax base, rising wages of city personnel, and program failures.

But few any longer describe central city problems as the *urban crisis*. It is not that conditions have improved. To the contrary, they have worsened and spread to many middle-size communities. Edward C. Banfield argued that the urban crisis is essentially the result of a large and concentrated culture of poverty for which there is no known cure. Other "crises," he said, are exaggerations about the inconveniences inherent in city living.[6] Perhaps society has accepted Banfield's explanation.

Indeed, some have suggested that we should give up trying to restore the very large, older cities.[7] William C. Baer wrote that urban death—at least the death of urban neighborhoods—is a reality that needs to be recognized. He suggested it may be "hindered by expertise, detoured by cajolery, impeded by charismatic leadership, and delayed by simple faith, but it will come."[8]

The Economics of Central-City Decay Why have so many of the nation's larger cities reached this point? At root are the economics of development in central-city neighborhoods, though racism and social disorganization contribute to the economic downward spiral.

Lewis Mumford, as we have seen, argued that city builders have been speculators concerned only with short-term economic returns. When a given property investment becomes unprofitable, the normal course is for the owner to sell, usually to someone less financially able. Typically, the property deteriorates, and after a succession of ownerships the building is eventually abandoned and left to city hall to demolish. Unless this process of disinvestment is somehow interrupted, it is likely to spread. The residents and businesses who can, seek other locations. The exodus often means loss of jobs, and with jobs personal income and tax base. In this kind of tailspin the ability of a community government to cope with an increasingly poorer population declines steadily.

The Long Road Back for Central Cities Central cities may never return to what they once were. Some of the outlines of what they may become are now more apparent. And city officials make new efforts to spur economic development projects, especially in the central business districts—cities' mayors compete vigorously for projects to build new office buildings, convention centers, and hotels to stimulate business and create jobs.

Changing State Policies States, albeit somewhat reluctantly, are assuming greater responsibility for their central cities—developing more broadly based tax programs; assuming a greater share of welfare, health, and primary education costs; and underwriting the costs of cultural facilities such as universities, zoos, museums, art galleries, and symphonies. And increasingly they outlaw redlining by banks and insurance companies.

Moreover, New Jersey, Massachusetts, Michigan, California, and other states are adopting policies on taxes, roads, parks, and government job locations to redirect the outward flow of jobs and people. New Jersey, for example, has adopted a statewide growth plan that is intended to curb urban sprawl. Local community compliance is voluntary and some appear unhappy with it. But local officials are expected to cooperate in developing the plan if not in complying with it in every respect.[9] And Frank Keefe, Massachusetts State Planning Director, notes, "It is unproductive for us to spend money extending a sewer line or highway to your development out in the middle of nowhere."[10]

Gentrification of Blighted Areas Young professional couples are finding that some of the older houses in the big cities can be made over into new and attractive homes—a process called **gentrification**. They are restoring whole neighborhoods and creating new expensive shopping areas—German Village in Columbus, Queen's Village in Philadelphia, Larimer Square in Denver, and others. In addition, central-city buildings, rather than being torn down, are now being remodeled for professional office suites and residential condominiums, many with the help of federal grants and local tax breaks. More restoration may occur as costs of commuting and new construction point up the economic advantages of central-city locations.[11]

But not everyone finds the welcome mat out. The poor who had rented such structures often resent these "gentry." They claim that the new middle-class residents are pushing them out and that there are no other places they can afford.

The Changed Rural Countryside

The National Association of Towns and Townships makes a great effort to inform anyone who will listen that 85 percent of the local governments in the United States serve fewer than 10,000 people. Many of these, of course, are included in the nation's metropolitan areas. But the others are home for about 27 percent of the nation's rural population. This population is declining as economic opportunity in the rural areas falls. Some of this drop results from the gradual shrinking of persons engaged directly in agriculture. The percentage of this group fell from 8.7 percent (15.6 million) in 1960 to about 2 percent in 1989.[12]

But large portions of the nation's countryside are used for nonagricultural purposes. We see new restaurants, gasoline stations, and motels clustered around crowded freeway interchanges. Mobile home parks and even factories are plunked seemingly in the middle of nowhere. And there are subdivisions that offer peace and quiet and the aroma of the nearby hog or chicken "factories"—highly intensive hog or chicken raising complexes. Some urban workers move into rural areas and drive long distances to work. Others set up vacation homes. Places for retirement are common. And tucked away off the main roads we see an affluent society's "get-away-from-it-all" facilities—racetracks, athletic stadiums, amusement parks, lodges for skiers and hunters, and KOA campgrounds.

The Changing Rural Governments The intrusions of such land uses have drawn the rural governments into fashioning new policies and programs to cope with the changes.

How does the rural county sheriff patrol traffic heading for the racetrack or stadium? Or how does the county deal with the polluted wells and inadequate drain fields in lakefront cottage developments, many of which are occupied year-round? How does it provide emergency medical care to senior citizens now living in a mobile home park? How does a small town maintain a hospital when Medicare funding is insufficient and when physicians argue that malpractice suits require them to have access to the technical equipment common only in large and modern hospitals? And as the small hospitals close, rural residents worry about getting access to health care at all. How do they manage a zoning code, subdivision regulations, or a building ordinance? Or solve multiple-family murders, or pay the ballooning costs of murder trials?

Moreover, rural governments have become involved in environmental quality concerns—controlling agricultural runoff from animal feedlots, soil erosion from nonfarm excavations, groundwater contamination from landfills, and growing toxicity of lakes and streams. And they deal with the effects of rural poverty, health care, slum housing, and unemployment. Many rural officials, like their big city cousins, must gather data for grant applications and reports and adopt new accounting and budgeting practices, administer equal employment opportunity programs, and engage in collective bargaining.

Growing Dependence on Professionals City governments have long depended on professionals. Now rural governments are being transformed. They too have become dependent on experts—professionals who somehow seem not to fit the folkways and values of the old county politics. The close-knit family feeling of the county courthouse is gradually disappearing.

Nor are rural governments isolated from the governments around them. Especially on the fringes of metropolitan areas we find a gradual merging of interests—not in the sense that rural citizens always want the same things the urbanites want, but because each has a stake in the policies of the other.

An Overview of Metropolitan Areas

Metropolitan areas summon up a set of images about what they are like. But several observations about them should be noted. First, most are not border-to-border concrete office buildings, factories, and houses. In fact, most of them have large areas of open land, much of it for farming.

Second, the boundaries and number of SMSAs change as population and employment data change. By 1980 the number had increased to 323, including 5 in Puerto Rico. All states had at least one such area.

Third, many SMSAs are contiguous and together may include large portions of a state—such as in Massachusetts, New York, Florida, California, and other states. Recognizing this fact, the Bureau of the Census began to report data on what they called Standard Consolidated Statistical Areas—a grouping of contiguous SMSAs.

One such megalopolis extends from Boston to Washington, D.C. It covers an area 450 miles long and 150 miles wide and is home for 50 million Americans. Experts foresee others developing—from New York to Chicago; along the California coast; and someday, perhaps, from Florida and Atlanta to New Orleans, Houston, or Dallas.

Perspective on Metropolitan Areas A review of the nation's metropolitan areas enables us to gain some insight into the characteristics of these complexes.

Population Trends What happens in the metropolitan areas is of crucial national importance because it is where most of us live—about 73 percent of us in 1989, compared with 56 percent in 1950. The major movement of population is toward metropolitan areas again after a period in the 1970s when the growth in rural communities exceeded that in metropolitan areas.

Governmental Fragmentation One feature of metropolitan areas is their **governmental fragmentation**—many local governments providing different services to the same citizens. A metropolitan resident may live in the jurisdiction of several local governmental units—for example, a city government, a school district, a county, an intermediate school district, a community college district, and, perhaps, several special districts that operate the airport, provide water and sewer services, community hospitals, recreation programs, special education, and mental and public health services.

Growing Interdependency Governments in metropolitan areas are increasingly interdependent. Disputes among them often are based on the assumption that each unit is independent of the other. Such, of course, is not the case. They sometimes cooperate with each other for clean water and air, for sanitary and storm drain systems, for waste disposal, health care facilities, economic well-being, and many other functions.

Specialization of Metropolitan Units But within the networks of interdependence there is a substantial degree of unit specialization. Some suburbs serve only the single-family homeowner and are often dominated by specific ethnic or income level groups. Other suburbs may specialize in high-rise apartments. Others develop the reputation for having the "proper address" for corporate headquarters or the location for retail shopping centers far out of proportion to what their own population can support. And a few end up being the place where the industries of the area tend to concentrate.

Specialization means that these units depend greatly on each other. Specialists cannot trade exclusively in their own wares.

THE COMMUNITY AS AN INTERGOVERNMENTAL BARGAINING UNIT

A kind of special bargaining, or what reformers describe as voluntary cooperation, also occurs between and among neighboring communities and attempts to bring about a degree of metropolitan coordination. The three major forms of voluntary cooperation are special districts, intergovernmental contracts, and councils of government. Voluntary cooperation among communities does not threaten local unit identity. Consequently, officials and residents commonly respond favorably even though these approaches also may reallocate power in an urban area.

Special Districts We noted in Chapter 12 that special districts are the most rapidly growing form of local government. As a general rule they are obscure because local governments create them; their tax rates are usually modest, their charges are related to service consumption, and ordinarily their officials are appointed rather than elected.

Robert C. Wood's observation of 30 years ago—"special districts become the principal means by which the suburban governments meet the new needs that arise in the transition from rural to urban"—is valid today.[13] But they also have become vehicles by which central cities involve suburbs in paying for services—mass transit or airport services, for example.

State-created Special Districts Community governments establish most of the special districts. But occasionally state officials use this mechanism to deal with particular issues in a metropolitan area. These state-established units operate much as other special districts and generally replace, rather than supplement, local efforts with respect to the function. Usually, they are single function agencies. Funding comes from state funds, property taxes, and users' fees.

But they differ in major ways from other special districts in that they are state established and the governor, usually with legislative consent, appoints the members of their governing boards.

Massachusetts, for example, as early as 1889 set up a Metropolitan Sewage Commission for the Boston area and followed it with a Metropolitan Parks Commission in 1893 and a Metropolitan Water Commission in 1895. These were merged in 1919 as the Metropolitan District Commission.

States continue such authorities for a variety of functions, especially with respect to areawide problems such as air pollution control, public transportation, and water and sewage. But we also find some with unusual missions—New York set up a commission for urban development, and Maryland set up one to handle environmental concerns.[14]

Assessment of the Special District Mechanism The most serious problem special districts produce is their tendency to become independent of the governments that create them and the residents they serve. Those financed by their own revenues may become important power centers that decide where to locate important public facilities, who gets construction contracts, and how many employees to hire. Moreover, they often set their own service rates—an important consideration when the district has a monopoly and the customers have no possibility to withdraw or the local governments cannot disenfranchise the special district.

Special districts also focus only on the service they provide. They cannot balance their program against other community needs as a general government might. For example, a community may badly need new buses, but it gets a new airport because the special district's authority concerns airports, not bus service.

Finally, many reformers frown on the special district as a solution to community problems because the districts fragment local government. Special districts add complexity to the maze of intergovernmental relationships and often become "functional fiefdoms" beyond citizen control.

Intergovernmental Contracts More common than special districts are **intergovernmental contracts** for services. Most commonly these agreements deal with potential "peak-load" problems, such as in police and fire services—**mutual assistance pacts** to help a neighboring community with extraordinary situations. But contracts go beyond mutual assistance. They may involve the buying and selling of services—police, fire, ambulance, water, library, and others. These arrangements reduce the duplication of facilities and provide economy of scale that smaller units could not attain.

Residents of Laguna Niguel, California, assessing the prospect of cityhood.

The Lakewood Plan Perhaps the most extensive intergovernmental contract network takes place in Los Angeles County. Here suburban cities buy dozens of services from the county and are said to be cities by contract because some provide few services on their own.[15]

The arrangements began evolving in 1954 when Lakewood became a city to ward off annexation to Long Beach. It began buying services from other cities and the county. This **Lakewood Plan** spread rapidly to other California counties as well. Some argue that expansion of this approach produces a consolidation of governmental functions in the county. Individual suburban units can provide a kind of marketplace of communities offering a range of services from which people can choose the mix they prefer.[16] Gary Miller, however, argues that the approach does not produce efficiency, but winners and losers—an economically segregated metropolis.[17]

Assessment of Intergovernmental Contracts The approach has other difficulties. Pricing public services also offers problems. Most communities cannot get competitive bids. Contract services may be cheaper than providing them on their own but still be very expensive. And once a contract service is established, changing the arrangement may be cost prohibitive.

Also, if the contracts do not establish criteria to determine later cost changes, one community customer may incur excessive costs (or enjoy unfairly low prices). Officials in older cities suspect they may be subsidizing newer ones; new ones think the county may be overcharging them. Some states now supervise rate setting for municipalities as they do for private utility companies.

Substate Regional Councils Councils of governments (COGs) provide a forum for officials in a metropolitan area to work on solutions to common problems. They grew out of a five-county committee formed in southeast Michigan during the middle 1950s. In 1957 the Michigan legislature gave the committee legal status and ten years later it was expanded to include seven area counties and organized as the Southeast Michigan Council of Governments (SEMCOG).

Later all of the states, with federal government encouragement, began dividing each state into **substate regions**. These regional councils were not governments. They levy no taxes, elect no officials, and participation is voluntary.

Federal agencies, looking for more ways to deal with both urban and rural development, gave the regional councils a boost by making them eligible for Section 701 regional land-use planning grants, and by 1980, 39 other federal programs with a multijurisdictional impact.[18] An additional critical tool was OMB (U.S. Office of Management and Budget) Circular A-95. It required regional council review and comment on most community applications federal grants.

Assessment of COGs Substate regionalism fell on hard times in the Reagan era. The movement to block grants, administered at the state level with state legislative control and oversight, led to elimination of the A-95 review process. In addition, reduced funding for planning and other research grants made regional councils almost entirely dependent on local and state funds. Of those that continue, most do so with few professional staff. They do little in the way of taking on the larger issues within the regions and instead focus on providing specific services such as planning to individual communities on a fee basis. Some also serve as a source for data and other information about the region.

Some advocates of substate regional councils saw them as the first step in building a system of regional governments and in focusing attention on the metropolitan areas as well as rural development.[19] Others argued that regional councils were merely bargaining units to cut up whatever federal largesse came their way. As Henry J. Schmandt notes, regional councils provided little incentive for politicians to invest the energy and resources in regional council activities—they saw little political payoff in it.[20] The outlook for their recovery in the future is not bright, especially now that governors and state legislators coordinate most federal grant programs.

REFORM THROUGH CENTRALIZATION AND PROFESSIONALIZATION

Students of metropolitan areas typically have criticized governmental fragmentation on the grounds that many units are too small and weak to meet important urban needs or that they do so only at excessive cost. Some students have also maintained that divided government permits some communities to benefit at the expense of others. Smaller units, they point out, do not equip their fire or police departments adequately and depend on the larger ones for specialized equipment. Moreover, the critics argue that the areawide problems, the problems that no single unit is responsible for, such as air or water pollution, go untended.

At the same time, they note that suburbanites avoid responsibility for problems of central-city residents—problems that the flight to the suburbs made worse. What is needed, some experts argue, is a linkage between a greater city's major problems and the area's resources. Those resources, they say, include not only a tax base, but also the stability and leadership that a middle-class citizenry provides.

Thus such critics of governmental fragmentation often recommend joining together the separate units into some larger body—ideally, they say, one government that would cover the whole of a metropolitan area. The states have several legal mechanisms for accomplishing this.

Annexation

Most states have laws that permit annexation (adding unincorporated areas to cities) and merger (consolidation of two or more units). Had either of these procedures been completely effective, governmental fragmentation in metropolitan areas would be less pronounced than it is.

Until the 1920s the larger cities routinely annexed most of the outlying settled areas. It was the only way many residents could get urban services. Annexation activity slackened off until after World War II, when the pace again quickened. Central cities of 50,000 nearly doubled their territory between 1950 and 1970. Between 1970 and 1978 all cities added about 3.3 million people and 9,800 miles of territory.[21]

The Importance of State Policies Easy incorporation permits small cities to form around central cities and effectively close off future expansion. Some states permit areas with populations as low as 100 people to incorporate or form a city government. **Consolidation**—the merging of two or more units into one—rarely occurs.

Some states also make it difficult for cities to annex unincorporated areas. New Jersey law, for example, recognizes all units—cities, towns, boroughs, and villages—as incorporated units, thus permitting no annexation at all.[22] For annexation in other states, the crucial element is whether state law requires approval of the residents in the area to be annexed. Where annexation occurs by order of a state boundary commission (in California and some other western states) or by judicial decree (as in Virginia), annexation is easier and more likely.

But large-scale annexation has been most likely in Texas and Oklahoma, where cities have extraordinary power to annex territory. By city council action alone, a Texas city can annex unincorporated areas. In addition, a city council can make preemptive strikes by declaring its future intentions to annex areas. This protects annexation rights without having to provide services in the area to be annexed in the future. Still, Houston and its small neighbors have had classic battles over the issue—in some instances, two cities annexing the same territory. In one such battle, mayor of Houston Fred Hofheinz said, "We get them when they're ripe." David Riley, a Clear Lake City official, responded by saying, "If they could grab everything up to the Canadian border, they'd do it."[23] Houston's territory covers more than 550 square miles—equal to the combined area of New York, Philadelphia, and Chicago.[24]

Annexation has limited use in states that permit easy city formation, where central cities are already ringed, or where the central city-suburb social status differences are great.

City-County Consolidation

Over the years counties have been involved in various reorganizations of local governing systems. In 1854 Philadelphia extended its boundaries to include all of Philadelphia County. The county and city operated as separate governments until 1952, when a new charter consolidated them.

In 1876 St. Louis more than tripled its territory and then was separated from the county in which it was located. Later, this would mean that the city would become hemmed in by suburbs in adjacent counties.[25]

New York City was formed in 1898 when five counties were consolidated—Queens, New York (Manhattan), Richmond (Staten Island), Kings (Brooklyn), and the Bronx. The five counties became boroughs of the new city.

Recent City-County Consolidations A high percentage of the nation's metropolitan areas lie completely or predominantly within single counties. Metropolitan government reform advocates argue that significant gains in efficiency and economy would occur if cities transferred some urban powers, such as utilities, water treatment plants, police, public health, public transportation, and others, to their county governments. Such **city-county consolidation**—a merger of city and county governments—has been accomplished in about two dozen metropolitan areas since World War II. But none occurred during the 1980s.

In 1947 Baton Rouge and East Baton Rouge Parish, Louisiana, formed a new government in which both maintained their identity and provided some services. The merger had aspects of a federation. It revived interest elsewhere in city-county reorganization.

The next major reorganization involved Miami and Dade County, Florida, in 1957. Here both units also maintained their identities and formed a two-tier metrogovernment. Others that followed were Nashville-Davidson County, Tennessee, in 1962; Jacksonville-Duval County, Florida, in 1967; and Indianapolis-Marion County, Indiana, in 1970. City-county consolidations receiving less public notice were Juneau–Greater Juneau Borough, Alaska; Lexington-Fayette County, Kentucky; and Columbus-Muscogee County, Georgia.

The Politics of City-County Consolidation Students find some common threads in these reorganizations. Most, if not all, had similar sponsoring groups—business, professional groups, and the League of Women Voters. Managerial efficiency appears to be the principal motivator. Opponents generally stressed the values of democratic participation in smaller units.

We review here some of the problems encountered, problems characteristic of those faced by reformers who wish to centralize metropolitan governments.

State Legislative Involvement State legislatures were significantly involved in all of the consolidation deliberations. Consolidations occurred primarily in states where legislatures still adopt local charters and where home rule traditions are weak.

State constitutions usually require election of certain officials in all counties. Dealing with such provisions requires creative legislating. Such restrictive constitutional provisions were critical in the design of government for Miami-Dade County in 1957. In contrast to the other city-county consolidations, the Miami-Dade County reorganization plan provided a two-level government. The county serves as the areawide government; the municipalities provide the local level. (The unincorporated county areas, though, have a one-layer government, that provided by the county.) Dade County received broad authority to provide areawide services.

The political influence of local elected officials makes constitutional and statutory changes difficult. This was so in Indianapolis. Marion County continues to exist as a legal entity—the council sits as both a county board and a city council. In both Baton Rouge and Miami the local legislative delegation negotiated the law that permitted the areas to adopt local home rule charters. The Florida legislature created the Jacksonville charter commission, named the membership, and later approved an amended version of the charter and submitted it to the electorate. The Indiana legislature established "Unigov" for Indianapolis and Marion County at a time when Republicans controlled state, county, and city governments.[26] Involvement of state legislators provided the framework for cutting the deals to weaken or neutralize opposition.

Influence of Local Officials Influence of local politicians can be pivotal to the final charter compromises reached. In 1975, for example, the Nevada legislature passed a law merging Las Vegas and Clark County. City and county officials at first supported but then later opposed it. They fought the legislation in court, where it was declared unconstitutional.[27]

Tax Policies How to assess local taxes is an important political question officials need to resolve. Outlying areas are likely to receive little direct service, no matter what the form of government. Thus their officials will likely oppose consolidation if they do not receive tax concessions.

The usual solution is to establish two or more taxing districts—areas receiving few services pay only a general tax; high service areas pay an additional urban-service tax.

Representation Blacks, who may constitute a majority of the central city, typically demand power in the new government. In Jacksonville they accounted for more than 40 percent of the city's population—support of their local representatives was essential. Midstream, during the charter campaign, the council districts were changed to avoid pitting two black councilwomen against each other for a seat in the new government.

Popular Voting Most major city-county consolidations included voter referenda—overall, 16 came about by referenda and 8 by legislative enactment alone. Typically, adoption required concurrent majorities in both the central city and in the unincorporated parts of the county.

The Small Cities Suburban units within the county typically have the right to decide independently whether they will be part of the consolidation. Most often they vote to remain separate. In Nashville-Davidson County six cities did so. And even in Indianapolis, where the legislature created the new structure, a number of municipalities, towns, and special districts were continued as before.

Under the city-county reorganizations the independent suburban cities relate to the county functions of the government as they had previously. But they also frequently contract with the consolidated government for specific services. Usually, they cannot expand their boundaries, and no new suburban cities may be organized.

An Assessment of City-County Consolidation City-county consolidations generally have occurred in middle-size cities with rapidly growing suburbs—suburbs that rely on the county for urban services. Inadequate service in the suburbs, it appears, has encouraged suburban interest in alternative arrangements.

For reasons that are less clear, many consolidations have involved state capitals—perhaps because of the politics of locating state office buildings and because of heavy state involvement needed for such plans to succeed.

But we also note that other circumstances may play a part in consolidations. The favorable vote in Jacksonville, for example, followed formal charges of grand larceny, bribery, and perjury against eight city officials. Suburbanites in Nashville had an added incentive to support consolidation when the city required a "green sticker" tax of $10 on all cars used on city streets more than 30 days per year.[28]

Determining the effect of consolidation in terms of a cost-benefit ratio is difficult at best. The consolidations do not resolve the urban ghetto problems, but neither do they leave a decaying central city ringed with blossoming suburbs as is likely where consolidation does not occur. At least the "old city" enjoys some benefits from a broader and more competitive tax base. But it is also true that boundaries of the consolidated city-county are seldom coterminous with the metropolitan area. As in times past, burgeoning new developments occur without consideration of municipal boundaries, no matter what the scope of the reorganization.

Metropolitan Governments

The most comprehensive metropolitan governments in North America have been created by the Canadian provinces. The Ontario parliament formed the model by reestablishing the Toronto government as a metropolitan federation. None has been created in the United States, but Minnesota (for the Minneapolis–St. Paul area) and Oregon (for the Portland area) have established regional agencies that handle a variety of public services.

The Twin Cities Metropolitan Experiment The Minnesota legislature established the Twin Cities Metropolitan Council in 1967. The governor appoints the 14 council members from districts that cut across municipal boundaries. The council has a modest taxing power. It makes policy on some matters of regional concern and recommends plans and programs in several policy areas that include airports, transportation, sewage disposal, regional parks, and housing. In 1976 the legislature required all units within the region to develop land use plans to be consistent with the Metropolitan Council's regionwide policies.[29]

These decisions are advisory for state agencies such as the state highways and health departments. But for local agencies, such as the sewer board, the transportation board, and the counties, the policies are binding. The Metropolitan Council may veto plans of agencies such as the airports commission, but may be overridden by the state legislature.

The council's second major function is to make funding recommendations for the various regional programs in the area. Special districts carry out some of the regional programs, but local governments, especially the seven-member counties of the region, also jointly undertake other areawide projects.

A second Minnesota innovation, begun in 1972, was a metropolitan tax-base-sharing plan. Forty percent of the increase in industrial and commercial property tax receipts in the Twin Cities area goes to the Twin Cities Metropolitan Council. They are then distributed to the local units of the region according to a state formula. The remaining 60 percent of the industrial and commercial tax revenues are retained by the local jurisdiction in which the increase takes place. This program was intended to reduce intra-area competition for industrial and commercial development and permit all area units to share in the region's development.

The metropolitan council lost some of its luster during the 1980s. Politics and inadequate leadership have diminished the council's role.[30] Changes in legislative control of federal grant funds may be key. Federal grants bypassed state legislatures in the early days of the metropolitan council. Later, as the Minnesota legislature and the governor gained control of federal grant funds, they were less than willing to share control and decision making with the Metropolitan Council. Both the legislature and the governor bypassed the council in several siting decisions, and the council was the object of critical reviews from the state planning agency, the legislature, and the legislative auditor.

Council leadership also was criticized. The Citizens League—a prestigious business and civic leaders association that was instrumental in the council's formation—became very critical of directional drift. Moreover, council leaders found dealing with quality of life issues to be more difficult than physical infrastructure kinds of decisions.

The Twin Cities Metropolitan Council will likely continue to play a role in the area. But it appears that it will have to share the limelight with state and other local officials.

The Portland Metropolitan Approach In 1978 the Oregon legislature set up a general governing body for the Portland area. The effort was the result of a process that began with special districts created by local units. Then followed a voluntary areawide COG organization, and in 1970 the legislature set up an authority for zoos and solid waste planning.

In 1978 the legislature merged some of these units into the Portland Metropolitan Service District. It has responsibility for zoos, solid waste planning, regional land-use planning, sewers, flood control, and transportation planning and operation.

In 1979 voters began electing members to the governing board from 12 districts that overlie the existing communities. Also elected was a chief executive.

Initially, financing was limited and most of the activities concerned planning rather than implementing policy. Nevertheless, the new unit had a base of several services—generally those that cut across community boundaries and were handled by special districts, or the specialized functions that few communities handled, such as the zoo.[31]

REFORM TO ACHIEVE GREATER CITIZEN PARTICIPATION

Some students argue that centralized management increases the problems of community residents. They say that those who argue for larger and larger community governments give little thought to how citizens might gain access to decision makers and bureaucracy.

Advocates of larger units also fail to recognize that citizens of different communities may prefer different services and service levels. In such a situation, large-scale bureaucracies, even when professionalized, may be unable to establish a satisfactory set of priorities.

Some studies have shown that larger is not necessarily more efficient or more economical. In a study of metropolitan policing, for example, Elinor Ostrom found that larger departments respond less quickly to calls, are viewed less favorably by residents, and are more likely to have a higher proportion of their personnel in administrative positions than small departments.[32] Other studies indicate that overall revenues and expenditures of consolidated governments tend to rise rather than fall, although some of the increase may be the result of improved services.[33]

Still others note that consolidation of small units dilutes the power of significant minorities. Blacks or Hispanics, for instance, who now control many large city governments, see their votes and influence being threatened by or submerged in central city–suburban mergers.

Thus what these reformers propose is units that are small enough in scale to allow ordinary citizens to make their influence felt. In addition they see these units as bargaining with other units to attain goals that their citizens especially desire.[34]

Neighborhood Control

Some have argued that large-scale governments have contributed to the deterioration of neighborhoods. People move to suburbia, they insist, not only to escape the social problems of central cities but to gain some influence over what happens in neighborhoods where they live. Some Great Society programs within large cities stressed grass roots citizen participation to give blacks and the poor involvement in shaping their own destiny—mainly through community action projects.

Similar developments have occurred in rural areas. Since the New Deal days, the Department of Agriculture has set up committees of local farmers to control policies that affect them. Among the most widespread of such organizations are the Soil Conservation Committees. However, even those who favor neighborhood or community control recognize the difficulty it presents when it comes to siting LULUs—locally unwanted land uses. We discuss one such dilemma in Policy Box No. 26, "How to Locate LULUs."

Forms of Local Control The move to revitalize central-city neighborhoods has taken many forms. In some cases central cities established mini-police stations and district offices of other city departments. Kansas City's neighborhood ombudsmen guided local residents to city officials to expedite the handling of complaints.

Policy Box No. 26

How to Locate LULUs

Technological society depends on many types of facilities, which most people agree are necessary because they are better off because of them. Many of these, though, are LULUs—locally unwanted land uses. They are electric power plants, landfills, or waste-to-energy incinerators. They might be prisons, halfway houses, sewage treatment plants, or a technology park that may release unknown and perhaps uncontrollable biological organisms.

Most of us would also choose to receive and use the benefits of radioactive processes. Not all, of course, want nuclear reactors to generate our electrical power, but few would want to depend on medical care without the use of the X-ray machine or the tests that depend on radioactive trackers. Nor, if you are majoring in one of the physical sciences, would you get very far without using radioactive materials to measure the results of your experiments.

The problem, though, is that these processes produce radioactive wastes. These are not wastes that can be dumped in a nearby landfill. For many years, the nation has been depositing such low-level radioactive wastes in three sites located in South Carolina, Washington, and Nevada. The waste materials, for the most part, consist of clothing, equipment, and tools used in university and industrial research laboratories, hospitals, and power plants.

As long as these states were willing to accept these materials from around the country, no one seemed very concerned about the problem. But in 1980 these states decided that it was time to share the responsibility of radioactive waste disposal. Congress passed a law stating that each state, beginning in 1993, would become responsible for its own low-level radioactive wastes.

The most efficient way to meet the new standards, Congress said, would be for groups of states to form compacts. The compacts would then decide how best to dispose of the wastes generated in its member states. Most of the compacts represent states from a geographical region. A few compacts, though, have noncontiguous member states.

The Midwest Interstate Low-Level Radioactive Waste Compact has seven members—Iowa, Ohio, Michigan, Missouri, Minnesota, Wisconsin, and Indiana. The Midwest compact, after some deliberation, decided that the first dump site should be located in the state that generated the most waste. That turned out to be Michigan, after Illinois left to join another compact.

The radioactive waste dump to be built needed to be large enough to last for 20 years. After that, the compact would build another site in another state. The actual storage site would be 20 to 30 acres, but this area would be buffered by 1,200 acres. The materials were to be stored in concrete-encased tubes that require monitoring for 500 years. A fence to keep out intruders for 100 years also was needed to surround the site.

For a time, Michigan officials were playing the NIMBY role—not in my backyard. Governor James Blanchard was chagrined over the compact's decision to use Michigan for the compact's first project. In fact, he threatened to withdraw his state from the compact. Upon the threat of immediate cutoff of the use of the South Carolina facility and resolution of technical details about joint responsibility for the site, Blanchard relented, and the compact proceeded with steps to locate the site.

But a radioactive waste facility is a LULU. No community volunteers to accept such a facility. In fact, community comprehensive master plans seldom, if ever, include sites for LULUs. So the issue becomes one of determining how the site for this LULU should be selected. What process should be used? Who should decide: the legislature, a state agency, the electorate?

Most would agree that if such a facility is going to be built in a state, expert scientists should describe the geographical conditions required for the facility. Once that is determined, the sites meeting these criteria can be identified and put on a list of prospective sites. These sites can be checked out more closely and perhaps a few will be scratched.

But now comes the difficult part. Who should decide? What should be the process for selecting the one site from among several qualified locations?

It is likely that residents from the qualifying sites will take up the NIMBY role. In fact some began an organization called "Don't Waste Michigan." The first strategy was to enlist the support of other Michiganians and attempt to keep the facility out of the state. They argue that all citizens should be concerned because it is too dangerous. No one, they say, can be sure that a fail-safe facility can in fact be built. They point out that the 500-year life of the dump is a long time—from the time Columbus sailed his three little ships to America until now. No one even knows if the concrete will last that long, they say.

And what happens if a leak does develop and drinking water becomes contaminated? How could anyone compensate us or our children or their children if they develop cancer because of a faulty site? Already, they point out, we have three radioactive waste sites in the United States that have been closed because of leaks. "If Michigan is going to have this kind of dump where radioactive junk from all over the Midwest will be brought, at least the local people should be able to decide whether to accept it. That's what a democracy is all about."

Others say that they appreciate these concerns but that they are to be expected. After all, this is a LULU, which by definition nobody wants. Thus this is not the kind of project people step forward for. Such a project cannot be located by election, referendum, or other democratic process. Local residents, they say, are too easily controlled by their fears and cannot be expected to view the project with any degree of objectivity. Once we have selected the site, say the experts, the best we can do is keep the people informed about all safety precautions being taken. "We'll let them know how safe we're building the facility and how closely it will be monitored to prevent accidents."

What do you think? How should a state deal with this siting problem? Should the legislature pass a law giving local communities a veto of the siting decision? Should the legislature be involved in the siting process? Why or why not? Should a state legislature develop general policy guidelines for LULUs? Should communities or neighborhoods be compensated for accepting LULUs? What form of compensation would you suggest? What protections against accident can the neighborhood or community reasonably demand?

Others experimented with voluntary block clubs. Most dealt with specific problems—crime control or managing neighborhood facilities such as playgrounds.[35] Some wanted also to decentralize political decision making by permitting neighborhood councils to veto or approve city hall decisions. New York and other communities experimented with decentralizing the school systems.[36]

More recently, the emphasis, especially in New York City, has been on *community integration* with central-city government. Key to community integration is officially recognizing community organizations and giving them access to the political agenda. Robert Pecorella notes that this generates an accommodationist strategy as opposed to confrontational tactics.[37] Similarly, in Birmingham, Alabama, where city officials established 93 neighborhood associations covering the entire city, the program has opened avenues of communication between neighborhood leaders and city officials. Poorer neighborhoods and those with greater internal cohesion benefit from the program more than do middle- and upper-class neighborhoods. The latter are able to use the traditional avenues of contact.[38]

An Assessment of Neighborhood Control Experiments with neighborhood decision making have generally faded—in part because they increased government costs, but mainly because neighborhood actions frustrated citywide policies. Neighborhood volunteer experiments that continue serve mainly as a means for citizens to express complaints and make suggestions, although in 1989 Chicago schools were turned over to locally elected boards with authority to hire and fire the school principal. Former Secretary of Education William Bennett once called Chicago's schools the worst in the nation, and some observers noted that neighborhood control was probably worth trying because the schools had little place to go but up. Amid claims and counterclaims of racism, local boards fired 14 school principals.

A modern adaptation of neighborhood influence, if not control, is high tech—a few cities now promise expedited response to persons who file their questions and complaints on a city computer network. Voluntary neighborhood councils and block clubs continue to form but usually fade away when the problems they were formed to resolve become less important.[39]

INTERGOVERNMENTAL RELATIONS: THE FEDS AND THE STATES IN THE COMMUNITIES

Some students argue that too much effort is wasted on trying to reform local governmental structure. Rather, they say, we should accept structures already in place and seek reform through grant programs and state and federal regulation.

Why Federal and State Intervention?

Federal and state governments became extensively involved with community problems as an outgrowth of programs established during the Great Depression. These programs moved many concerns of life (safety, shelter, economic security, and health) from being wholly private concerns to making them matters of public policy.

Federal and state officials were motivated by more than simple altruism. In the words of Robert Wood, "Public programs are authorized for purposes other than the satisfaction of the material wants of all the residents or even of a majority. They are devices whereby political organizations survive. Taxes and public expenditures represent not just 'costs' and 'products,' but 'votes' and 'influence.'"[40]

At first the federal government was concerned only with the serious problems in America's great central cities. But by the 1970s both state and federal governments realized that poverty, social disorganization, and even racial discrimination were not confined to cities—nor were the votes, because about one-third of the U.S. population lives in small communities. What had been urban programs became programs for all local governments.[41] Federal mandates regarding clean lakes and streams, groundwater protection, solid waste disposal, and floodplains development restrictions are but a few that apply to small and large local units. And during the 1980s efforts to curb the sale and use of drugs joined this list.

State and Federal Efforts

Involvement of state and federal governments has encouraged professionalization in community governments. As we noted in previous chapters, the federal courts have spelled out community police procedures and the relations of local governments to their citizens with respect to many other matters.

The courts have also encouraged centralization while sometimes leaving local structures unchanged. They now regulate many matters once left exclusively to community control. In some services, such as welfare, federal regulations dominate. Other regulations have affected the way restaurants operate, the recreation time county prisoners must have, and a multitude of other matters over which communities once had complete control. And in a few instances states have encouraged restructuring of local governments, most notably with respect to schools.

The Special Role of the States A local editor said, "As I look back over ten years it seems to me that many of society's attempts to deal with its problems evoke a state rather than a federal response... *because the states turn out to be just about the most manageable unit of government* [emphasis added]."[42]

The national government likely will continue to define national goals, sometimes through grant programs but also in the form of legislative and judicial mandates. However, it increasingly depends on the states to coordinate the programs among the localities because the states stand at the crossroads of the three major levels of government. Thus we focus our attention on state relations with local communities—how they have attempted to realize both state and federal goals through guiding and coordinating the activities of their own community governments.[43]

Coordination from the State Capitals

We noted in Chapter 12 the states' original ambivalence over their role as coordinators of local governmental affairs. We saw that this attitude, in part, resulted from the early state concern with economic development—settling the hinterlands and harvesting the natural resources.

State officials continue to be very much concerned with economic development, but for most this means they focus on attracting industry to the urban economic base while not ignoring natural-resource-based segments of their economies. The effectiveness of the community governments relates directly to economic development—a fact that raises the level of state interest in local affairs. But other state bureaucracies have expanded state concerns to almost every local function as well.

How States Coordinate

State officials employ primarily five methods to carry out their coordination role.

Direct Participation in Service Functions Many state agencies now have the administrative capacity to carry out services directly. State police, for example, patrol the state freeways, stake out drug houses, and have command posts throughout each state. State police thus are readily available to assist local communities in both specialized and general police work. The "Matt Dillons" of the counties and cities in most of the states no longer stand alone to face the forces of lawlessness—state police troopers generally are not far off.

State highway or transportation departments played an important role in locating urban and rural expressways. State departments of public and mental health now develop and oversee detailed program activities for local agencies. And welfare services are now largely a state responsibility.

A number of states have become directly involved in zoning for "critical state areas" and supervising the use of environmental resources such as rivers and streams and adjoining wetlands. States operate major public recreation areas. Some states have their own housing authorities to finance and build low-cost housing around the state.

What we find, then, is that states administer directly many services once considered local responsibilities. State actions do not entirely close out local involvement, although the overall pattern is one of increased state participation.

State Mandates State mandates take various forms. A state law, for example, may require all units to enforce a uniform state building ordinance that increases state influence on the quality of construction in every community in the state. The state may require local tax assessors to pass state tests before being permitted to value property. Local police officers may need specific training before pinning on their badges. And state elections officials may set the standards for a statewide computer network of registered voters.

States often require local officials to follow a state open meeting law; local candidates to disclose personal finance information and campaign receipts and spending; local governments to follow uniform budgeting and accounting procedures; state approval of bond issues; and state review of school curricula, school building plans, annexation proposals, and land subdivision plots.

State Redistributive Taxation Providing financial assistance for selected functions is another way states coordinate local efforts. State aid for basic local mental or public health programs or for patrol of local roads are examples. The states are also achieving a modest amount of redistribution of resources through state taxation, as we see in Chapter 14. Such shared revenues give the states added coordinating power.

Another redistributive tax policy is the property tax "circuit breaker"—by which the states assume the costs of property tax breaks for senior citizens, veterans, the handicapped, and those who pay high property taxes in proportion to their income. Such a policy, although applied statewide, tends to benefit central-city residents most—especially if renters can claim a deduction.

Another provides special financial assistance to localities for certain public facilities that produce statewide benefits. Typically these are cultural attractions that the great cities were once noted for—art centers, symphonic halls, museums, city universities, libraries, zoological parks, and others.

The Politics of Redistributive Assistance The states enact redistributive policies only after much bargaining and compromising in the state legislature. They also require firm gubernatorial support and a formula ensuring that most communities share at least some of the subsidy. Such bargaining, of course, reduces the redistributive effects, but also causes all local units, not just those in dire straits, to become more dependent on state aid.

Assessment of State Coordination Strategies These state strategies for coordination are often a mixed bag of motivations, at least in terms of how they are initiated. A governor may be seeking added vote-getting power in a portion of the state, and hence sponsor an initiative. Or a program to save a critical natural resource may be the dream of an environmentalist group, perhaps of the professionals in a state agency, or more likely, the two groups collaboratively. Or it may be the product of an interest group such as the state's county sheriffs' association, the organization of mental health workers, or a public health nurses' group that seeks additional state funding for their services and enhanced economic well-being for their members. They lobby the legislature and bureaucracy for the program, often in concert with local officials, and with the funding comes a variety of conditions that gives the state leverage at the community levels.

The difficulty with this strategy is that some functions which could benefit from state coordination do not have an interest group to bring the issue to the attention of state officials or the political clout to gain support in the legislature. Or, a relevant interest group forms or gains strength only long after a particular problem has become severe—transportation of hazardous and toxic materials, for example. The flip side of this problem is that the interest group's concern may not coincide entirely with the broad public interest or perhaps would be of a lower priority were it not for the political pressure applied. Thus, because of the political nature of state coordination, the states may focus some of their efforts on matters of lower priority or too much of their resources on a few matters while ignoring others.

A FINAL COMMENT

Our national government now touches a great many aspects of daily living. We are a society that depends on many others for the necessities, as well as the amenities, of life. These interdependent relationships do not stop at the city limits, the county line, or even the state boundaries. Some extend even beyond the national shorelines. They are complex and interwoven.

In perhaps no other area do the values of managerial efficiency and democratic participation come into such stark conflict. Conditions that become intolerable, such as lack of water and sewer facilities, crowded streets and roads, and health problems, force us in the direction of centralization.

Yet as the stiff resistance by suburbs to any form of consolidation suggests— indeed as suburban flight itself suggests—citizens want to feel their governments are not so large and complicated as to be beyond their influence. We have reviewed the various forms of compromise between these two desirable values. But in the United States, as we noted, one has never been tried.

Someday, perhaps, we should give federalism a chance at the community level. It worked to solve national-state conflict of the same order.

HIGH POINTS

We began this chapter by observing that (1) many of the problems we classify as "urban" are not only faced by central cities—they are evident in suburbs and rural areas as well. Thus we saw (2) the network of intergovernmental relations as linking both rural and urban governments together with state and federal governments. We next considered (3) various voluntary approaches to the conduct of intergovernmental relations, including neighborhood control, intergovernmental contracts, and special districts. We then reviewed (4) annexation and consolidation as methods for unifying local government systems and methods favored by those who believe that centralization will result in more efficiency and more professionalism. Finally, we discussed (5) methods used by the states, utilizing both reform approaches, to coordinate community governing to achieve broad state purposes.

In this chapter we defined the following terms in this order: infrastructure, annexation, urban crisis, gentrification, governmental fragmentation, intergovernmental contracts, mutual assistance pacts, Lakewood Plan, substate regions, consolidation, city-county consolidation, and LULUs.

NOTES

1. Officially, these SMSAs include a central city of at least 50,000 and the county or counties with which that city is associated economically and socially.
2. Lewis Mumford, *The City in History* (New York: Harcourt Brace Jovanovich, 1961), p. 425. See also Robert D. Thomas's essay "Cities as Partners in the Federal System," *Political Science Quarterly* 101:1 (Winter 1986): 49–64.
3. Paul E. Peterson, *City Limits* (Chicago: University of Chicago Press, 1981).
4. For a favorable analysis of Levittown, see Harold L. Wattel, "Levittown, A Suburban Community," in William M. Dobriner (ed.), *The Suburban Community* (New York: Putnam, 1958).
5. Alan K. Campbell and Donna E. Shalala, "Problems Unsolved, Solutions Untried, The Urban Crisis," in A. K. Campbell (ed.), *The States and the Urban Crisis* (Englewood Cliffs, N.J.: The American Assembly, Prentice-Hall, 1970).
6. Edward C. Banfield, *The Unheavenly City, The Nature and Future of Our Urban Crisis* (Boston: Little, Brown, 1968).
7. See, for example, George S. Steinbeck, "Are Cities Worth Saving?" in Robert K. Yin (ed.), *The Cities in the Seventies* (Itasco, Ill.: Peacock, 1971).
8. William C. Baer, "On the Death of Cities," *Public Interest* 45 (Fall 1976): 3–19.
9. Anthony DePalma, "In New Jersey, the State Tries to Rein in Local Sprawl," *The New York Times* (January 1, 1989).
10. Neal R. Peirce, "States Take Big Steps to Save Large Cities," *Detroit Free Press* (October 2, 1977).
11. "Recycling Houses: Making New from Old," *U.S. News and World Report* (December 21, 1981): 56–57.
12. U.S. Bureau of the Census, Department of Commerce, "Farm Populations of the United States," 1975 Series Census-ERS, no. 47 (Washington, D.C.: U.S. Government Printing Office, 1976), p. 27.
13. Robert C. Wood, *1400 Governments* (Cambridge: Harvard University Press, 1961), p. 74. Also see Annmarie H. Walsh, *The Public's Business* (Cambridge: MIT Press, 1978).
14. See Joseph F. Zimmerman, *The State Response to Local Problems* (Syracuse: Maxwell Graduate School of Citizenship and Public Affairs, Syracuse University, 1981).
15. Gary J. Miller, *Cities by Contract: The Politics of Municipal Incorporation* (Cambridge: MIT Press, 1981).
16. Charles Tiebout, "A Pure Theory of Local Expenditures," *Journal of Political Economy* 64 (October 1956): 416–424.
17. Gary J. Miller, *Cities by Contract: The Politics of Municipal Incorporation* (Cambridge: MIT Press, 1981).
18. Lewis G. Bender, William P. Browne, and Thaddeus C. Zolty, "The New Federalism and Substate Regionalism: Changing Perceptions of Rural Officials," *Publius* 17:4 (Fall 1987): 161–174.
19. U.S. Advisory Commission on Intergovernmental Relations, *Regional Decision Making: New Strategies for Substate Districts*, Vol. 1 (Washington, D.C.: U.S. Government Printing Office, 1973).
20. Henry J. Schmandt, "Intergovernmental Volunteerism, Pro and Con," in Kent Mathewson (ed.), *The Regionalist Papers* (Detroit: The Metropolitan Fund, 1974), pp. 149–158.
21. Joel C. Miller, Frances Barnett, and Richard L. Forstall, "Annexations and Corporate Changes, 1970–1978," *The Municipal Yearbook, 1980* (Washington, D.C.: Interna-

tional City Management Association), pp. 64–67. In this source, city-county consolidations are treated as annexations.
22. David A. Mattek, "Spotlight on the New Jersey County and Municipal Government Study Commission," *Intergovernmental Perspective* 14:3 (Summer 1988): 5–6.
23. "The Octopus," *Newsweek* (June 13, 1977): 7. Jacksonville, Florida, a consolidated city-county, is largest with 827 sq. mi. Oklahoma City, which has also enjoyed liberal annexation policies, is second with 650 sq. mi.
24. For a detailed review of Houston's annexations see Robert D. Thomas, "Metropolitan Structural Development: The Territorial Imperative," *Publius* 14:2 (Spring 1984): 83–115.
25. More recently, reorganization of local government in the St. Louis area has been the subject of three studies. For review and comment on these efforts see Roger B. Parks and Ronald J. Oakerson, "St. Louis, The ACIR Study"; Donald Phares, "Reorganizing the St. Louis Area: The Freeholders' Plan"; Donald Elliott, "Perspectives on the St. Louis Metropolitan Area"; and James M. Brasfield, "Reconciling Perspectives on the St. Louis Metropolitan Area," all in *Intergovernmental Perspective* 15:1 (Winter 1989): 9–27.
26. C. James Owen and York Willbern, *Governing Metropolitan Indianapolis: The Politics of Unigov* (Berkeley: University of California Press, 1985). Also see York Willbern, "Unigov, Local Government Reorganization in Indianapolis," in *Regional Governance, Promise and Performance—Case Studies* (Washington, D.C.: Advisory Commission on Intergovernmental Relations, Report A-41, 1973), pp. 48–73.
27. Andrew D. Grosse, "Las Vegas–Clark County Consolidation, A Unique Event in Search of a Theory," *Nevada Public Affairs Report* (Las Vegas: Bureau of Governmental Research, University of Nevada, May 1976).
28. David A. Booth, *Metropolitics, The Nashville Consolidation* (East Lansing, Mich.: Institute for Community Development, Michigan State University, 1963). Also see Robert E. McArthur, "The Metropolitan Government of Nashville and Davidson County, in *Regional Governance, Promise and Performance—Case Studies* (Washington, D.C.: Advisory Commission on Intergovernmental Relations, Report A-41, 1973), pp. 26–35.
29. Ted Kolderie, "Regionalism in the Twin Cities of Minnesota," in Kent Mathewson (ed.), *The Regionalist Papers*, pp. 99–121. For a more detailed account of the approach, see John J. Harrigan and William C. Johnson, *Governing the Twin Cities Region, the Metropolitan Council in Perspective* (Minneapolis: University of Minnesota Press, 1978).
30. William C. Johnson and John J. Harrigan, "Political Stress and Metropolitan Governance: The Twin Cities Experience," *State and Local Government Review* 19:3 (Fall 1987): 108–113.
31. For a discussion of the role of states in urbanized areas, including consideration of the Twin Cities and Portland experiments, see Charles Press, "State Government in Urban Areas, Petty Tyrants, Meddlers, or Something Else?" *The Urban Interest, A Journal of Policy and Administration* 2 (Fall 1980): 12–21.
32. Elinor Ostrom, Roger B. Parks, and Gordon P. Whitaker, *Policing Metropolitan America* (Washington, D.C.: National Science Foundation, Superintendent of Documents, 1977). Also see Elinor Ostrom, "Metropolitan Reform: Propositions Derived from Two Traditions," *Social Science Quarterly* 53 (December 1972): 474–493.
33. See, for example, J. Edwin Benton and Darwin Gamble, "City-County Consolidation and Economies of Scale: Evidence from a Time-Series Analysis in Jacksonville, Florida," *Social Science Quarterly* 65:1 (March 1984): 191–198, and Richard D.

Gusely, "The Allocation and Distributional Impacts of Governmental Consolidation," *Urban Affairs Quarterly* 12 (March 1977): 349–364.
34. For a spirited defense of an intergovernmental system comprised of many local units bargaining with each other and with state and federal officials, see Aaron Wildavsky, "A Bias Toward Federalism, Confronting the Conventional Wisdom on the Delivery of Governmental Services," *Publius* 6:2 (Spring 1976): 95–120.
35. Dick Simpson, "Empowering America's Neighborhoods," *Citizen Participation* (November-December 1981): 6–7.
36. Marilyn Gittell et al., *Demonstrations for Social Change, An Experiment in Local Control* (New York: Institute for Community Studies, Queens College, 1971).
37. Robert F. Pecorella, "Community Empowerment Revisited: Two Decades of Integrative Reform," *State and Local Government Review* 20:2 (Spring 1988): 72–78. Pecorella notes elsewhere that New York City's program retrenchment of the 1970s opened the way to greater participation by "attentive nonelites" by placing neighborhood issues on the political agenda. See his "Coping with Crises: The Politics of Urban Retrenchment," *Polity* 17:2 (Winter 1984): 298–316.
38. Steven H. Haeberle, "Good Neighbors and Good Neighborhoods: Comparing Demographic and Environmental Influences on Neighborhood Activism," *State and Local Government Review* 18:3 (Fall 1986): 109–116.
39. See Joseph F. Zimmerman, *The Federated City, Community Control in Large Cities* (New York: St. Martin's Press, 1972). Also see David Caputo and Richard Cole, *Urban Politics and Decentralization* (Lexington, Mass.: Heath, 1974), and Howard W. Hallman, *Neighborhood Government in a Metropolitan Setting* (Beverly Hills, Calif.: Sage, 1974).
40. Wood, *1400 Governments*, p. 18.
41. Neal R. Peirce, "Small Cities, Rural Areas Reflect the Problems Plaguing Major Cities," *Detroit News* (January 22, 1978).
42. Joe H. Stroud, "Power of the States Still Irreplaceable," *Detroit Free Press* (September 1978).
43. In 1980 the U.S. Department of Housing and Urban Development published a series of studies on the urban strategies of several states. For an overall analysis of the findings, see Charles R. Warren, *The States and Urban Strategies, A Comparative Analysis* (Washington, D.C.: Office of Policy Development and Research, U.S. Department of Housing and Urban Development, and National Academy of Public Administration, Washington, D.C., 1980).

Chapter 14

State and Local Finance in a Dynamic Federal System

Few of us recall when we first paid a tax, but we can safely wager that it was a state sales tax. We did not pay much attention—the tax was only a few pennies. We awakened more fully to reality when we got our first paycheck from McDonald's or Burger King or another employer.

The check stub told the astonishing story. Not only did "they" withhold for Social Security, but for federal, state, and perhaps city income taxes as well. It was shocking that "they" would take so much!

In 1987, the nation's total tax bill was $944.5 billion. The federal government collected 57.1 percent of this, the states 26.1 percent, and the community governments 16.8 percent. The states, communities, counties, schools, and others collected about $405.1 billion in taxes. (They collected an additional estimated $166 billion in service charges, fees, permits, and other miscellaneous revenues.)

Figure 14.1 shows the major revenue and expenditure categories for state and community governments. You will find the chart a useful reference as you read along.

Overview In this chapter we review how state and community governments obtain revenue and how they spend it. We first examine major financial trends, comparing revenues collected to national economic activity and the rate of inflation. We then consider how the governments transfer funds. Next we discuss the kinds of taxes that state and local governments levy. We evaluate each in terms of four standards. Governmental borrowing and debt are our next topic. Finally, we review how these governments spend the dollars taken in.

TRENDS IN STATE AND LOCAL FINANCE

As taxpayers we are concerned with how much we have to pay. But we are almost as interested in whether taxes are going up or down. And we like to have an idea of how our taxes compare with those of others.

Changes in State and Local Taxes

Our collective tax bills from state and community governments both rose and fell during the 1980s depending on what basis we use to compare.

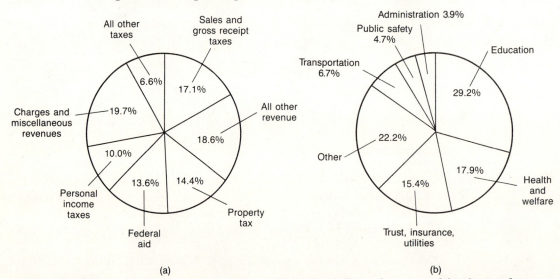

Figure 14.1 (a) State and local revenues—1987, total $842.6 billion; (b) state and local expenditures—1987, total $775.3 billion (the other category includes interest, transfers, and miscellaneous). [*Source:* Tax Foundation, *Facts and Figures on Governmental Finance*, 1990. (Baltimore: John Hopkins University Press), p. 179.]

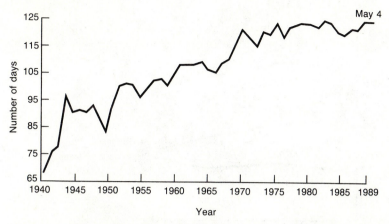

Figure 14.2 Tax Freedom Day, 1940–1989. [*Source*: Tax Foundation, *Tax Features* 33:3 (April 1989).]

Per Capita Amounts The taxes we pay to our state and local governments (including schools) in actual dollars went up dramatically in the 1980s. The average per capita tax in 1980 was $1,041. In 1987 that figure was $1,743—an increase of 67.4 percent. The good news, though, is that Tax Freedom Day—the day on which the average person would finish paying these tax obligations—did not change very much. May 1 was Freedom Day in 1980 and May 4 in 1989. By two other measures we find that these taxes have leveled off or even fallen a little.

Taxes as a Percentage of GNP Gross National Product (GNP) is the value of all the goods and services that the nation produces each year. State and local taxes as a percentage of the GNP peaked at 9.9 percent in 1972. The percentage dropped each year until 1983 and since then has risen a little. We can see from Figure 14.3 that the amount is now 8.95 percent—approximately the late 1960s level.

Taxes as a Percentage of Personal Income How do these tax receipts relate to people's income? By this measure we find that since 1978, the peak year nationally for this figure, the combined state and local tax bill has been falling in all but four states.

To be sure, many reductions have been small, but in Massachusetts and California, states that experienced so-called tax rebellions, the reductions exceed 3 percent. Even in states where only minor reductions occurred, they reflect a turnaround from earlier regular increases. Figure 14.4 shows the state ranks and percentages for 1987 and how these rankings changed since 1980.

Factors Affecting State and Local Revenues

What accounts for these changes? Three factors explain most of them: political actions, general economic activity, and inflation.

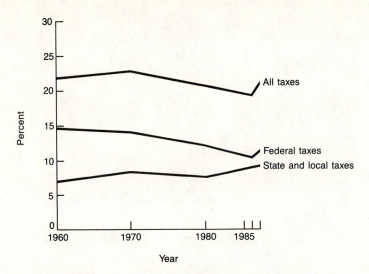

Figure 14.3 Taxes as a percentage of Gross National Product, 1950–1987. [*Source*: adapted from *Significant Features of Fiscal Federalism*, Volume II, 1989. (Washington, D.C.: ACII), p. 31.]

Political Actions Decisions of state legislatures, local councils and commissions, and even in some cases, of citizens, helped change the amount of tax revenues collected.

Until the mid-1970s governmental bodies were generally raising tax rates or adding new taxes. But the late 1970s was a time of tax revolt. In some states citizens used the initiative to order tax cuts or slow the rate of tax growth. In other states the legislatures found it popular to cut taxes. By 1979 the results began to show. The Advisory Committee on Intergovernmental Relations (ACIR) calculates that overall in 1979 and 1980 political actions accounted for a drop of $2.3 billion, or 1.3 percent, in state and local tax revenues.

Economic Activity A generally growing national economy during the 1980s offset some of these tax revenues losses. This enabled state and community governments to take in more funds while adjusting to lower tax rates.

Inflation If you were a budget director in a state or city, you would find some satisfaction in greater revenues. But you would also want to know how much of the gain was offset by inflation. The late 1970s and early 1980s was a period of high inflation—the Consumer Price Index rose 11.9 percent per year—and one when state or municipal finance managers found their revenues growing but their purchasing power declining. Annual inflation of 3 to 4 percent during the late 1980s meant that prices of goods and services to government rose less steeply.

INTERGOVERNMENTAL TRANSFERS

States and communities do not depend entirely on their own tax collections and fees to survive. As we saw in Chapter 3, the federal government, through grant programs, transfers a great deal of money to them. And local governments, espe-

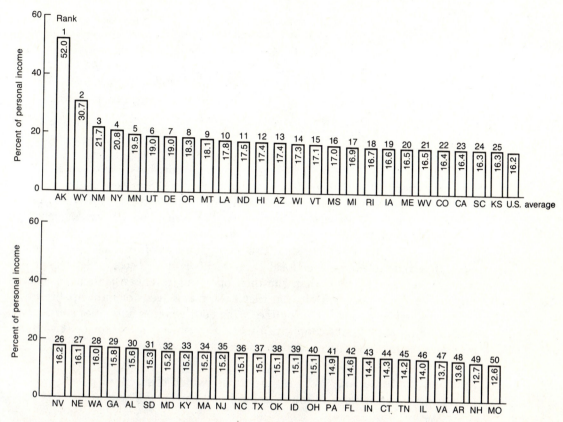

Figure 14.4 State and local 1987 general revenues as a percentage of state personal income. State and local revenues are "own source" revenues. [*Source*: adapted from *Significant Features of Fiscal Federalism*, Volume II, 1989. (Washington, D.C.: ACIR), p. 137.]

cially school districts, receive substantial amounts from their respective state capitals.

Federal Transfer Payments

In the late 1960s, the amounts the federal government transferred to states and local units increased markedly. In 1955 federal aid was about $3 billion, only 10 percent of what the states and communities spent. By 1969 federal aid totaled $20 billion, about 18 percent of their expenditures. Federal aid, as a percentage of state-local expenditures, peaked at 26.5 percent in 1978. During the Reagan administration the dollar amount rose steadily and in 1990 was estimated to reach $123 billion. But as a percentage of state and local expenditures, federal aid fell to about 18 percent—nearly the level it had been 20 years earlier.[1] As a result of the Reagan policies, then, state and local units depended less on federal assistance than they had earlier.

Between 1969 and 1986 the federal government also shifted its functional emphases. In 1969, 25.5 percent of the federal aid went for education; in 1986 education got only 15.6 percent of the total. Money for highways dropped from

22.2 to 12.4 percent; welfare increased from 32.7 to 38.5 percent, housing and urban renewal rose from 4.7 to 9.7 percent. All other transfers rose from 14.7 to 23.7 percent.[2] Hidden in the figures is the beginning and then the demise of federal revenue sharing—the miscellaneous category accounted for 43.1 percent of all federal gains in 1979. As can be seen from Table 14.1, however, not all states end up on the plus side after taxes paid from that state are considered.

State Transfers to Local Units

Amounts the states have been paying their local units have increased steadily. They rose from $9 billion in 1960 to $139 billion in 1987. Most of this money, 63.5 percent, goes for public education. About 11 percent pays for welfare services, and 5 percent for road maintenance. The remaining 10 percent goes for public health, public safety, courts, and other functions.[3]

How important are these state transfers? State aid to schools now exceeds what they themselves raise in local taxes—schools have become dependent on state governments for more than half their operating revenues. State aid to counties accounts for about half of what they raise themselves; for municipalities the range is about 30 percent. During the 1970s both counties and cities were more dependent on state grants. But with the states now responsible for most welfare programs, county and city dependency state aid is lower.

Reasons for State Aid Why do the states, which often plead poverty to the federal government, give so much to local governments? There are several reasons.

Table 14.1 FEDERAL GRANTS-IN-AID TO STATE AND LOCAL GOVERNMENTS AND ESTIMATED FEDERAL TAX BURDEN FOR GRANTS (Fiscal Year 1986)

State	Grants[a] (millions of dollars)	Percent of total tax burden	Estimated tax burden for grants[b] (millions of dollars)	Tax burden per dollar of aid Amount	Rank
Total	$108,724.7	100.00%	$108,724.7	$1.00	
Alabama	1,667.9	1.22	1,324.7	0.79	33
Alaska	579.8	0.26	278.9	0.48	50
Arizona	1,160.7	1.24	1,347.9	1.16	13
Arkansas	1,004.5	0.66	719.4	0.72	37
California	11,583.8	12.80	13,917.3	1.20	10
Colorado	1,199.6	1.31	1,421.7	1.19	12
Connecticut	1,542.1	2.03	2,210.4	1.43	5
Delaware	318.5	0.32	342.8	1.08	16

Table 14.1 *Continued*

Florida	3,415.2	5.17	5,616.8	1.64	1
Georgia	2,959.3	2.29	2,494.0	0.84	30
Hawaii	477.2	0.42	461.6	0.97	21
Idaho	458.1	0.29	310.0	0.68	40
Illinois	4,669.4	5.23	5,684.5	1.22	8
Indiana	1,959.8	1.99	2,168.0	1.11	14
Iowa	1,199.2	0.97	1,058.9	0.88	26
Kansas	873.3	0.95	1,035.7	1.19	11
Kentucky	1,750.7	1.10	1,199.3	0.69	38
Louisiana	2,131.9	1.27	1,381.9	0.65	43
Maine	664.7	0.42	455.1	0.68	39
Maryland	2,004.2	2.24	2,435.5	1.22	9
Massachusetts	3,327.6	3.10	3,368.8	1.01	18
Michigan	4,240.6	3.86	4,198.0	0.99	19
Minnesota	2,117.4	1.78	1,936.4	0.91	24
Mississippi	1,304.6	0.63	680.1	0.52	46
Missouri	1,938.1	1.96	2,130.9	1.10	15
Montana	504.5	0.24	262.9	0.52	47
Nebraska	711.5	0.56	611.3	0.86	28
Nevada	322.8	0.45	490.2	1.52	2
New Hampshire	397.3	0.53	576.8	1.45	4
New Jersey	3,327.5	4.58	4,979.9	1.50	3
New Mexico	726.1	0.44	479.9	0.66	42
New York	12,494.2	8.80	9,571.3	0.77	34
North Carolina	2,296.2	2.19	2,383.8	1.04	17
North Dakota	451.3	0.22	235.0	0.52	48
Ohio	4,693.1	4.20	4,570.2	0.97	20
Oklahoma	1,402.2	1.04	1,133.3	0.81	32
Oregon	1,110.9	0.98	1,064.5	0.96	22
Pennsylvania	5,790.4	4.85	5,273.6	0.91	25
Rhode Island	643.5	0.43	469.4	0.73	36
South Carolina	1,351.3	1.03	1,123.8	0.83	31
South Dakota	439.5	0.21	225.8	0.51	49
Tennessee	2,084.4	1.64	1,779.6	0.85	29
Texas	5,162.2	6.20	6,742.9	1.31	7
Utah	683.7	0.46	503.4	0.74	35
Vermont	323.5	0.20	218.2	0.67	41
Virginia	1,958.8	2.54	2,757.3	1.41	6
Washington	2,131.4	1.86	2,020.0	0.95	23
West Virginia	1,054.7	0.51	556.1	0.53	45
Wisconsin	2,226.9	1.80	1,961.7	0.88	27
Wyoming	273.8	0.16	174.5	0.64	44
District of Columbia	1,615.1	0.35	380.8	0.24	51

[a] Excludes shared revenues and payments in lieu of taxes; includes trust fund aid.

[b] The tax burden for grants is assumed to equal grant payments.

Source: Tax Foundation, *Tax Features* (April 1989).

State Responsibilities   Some traditionally local functions have come to be recognized as state responsibilities as well. Many state constitutions, for example, make education a state responsibility. As local school districts found local property tax revenues less and less adequate to finance public schools, the states felt obliged to raise their aid for education.

State legislatures also use grants to even out educational opportunities across the state. Property taxes do not produce equal funds per student across districts. Wealthy districts have as much as 150 percent more per student than the poorest ones and thus can provide broader educational services. Some citizens argued unsuccessfully that the discrepancy violates the Fourteenth Amendment of the U.S. Constitution. But some state supreme courts, including those of California, Texas, and New Jersey, ordered state legislatures to even out school funding anyway.[4]

Federal Aid Requirements   Another reason states distribute aid is that Congress requires them to distribute some of the funds to localities according to formula. These state pass-through funds are included in the state aid data we have been using.

Tax Collection Efficiencies   As a general rule, larger units are more efficient in collecting taxes. They can better afford the sophisticated equipment and trained personnel to make sure that everyone pays what is owed. It is also more difficult to avoid state taxes. Most people can avoid a city sales or income tax by shopping or living elsewhere. This is also true of state taxes, of course, but usually it is much less easy to do.

So states, in effect, collect taxes for local units—sometimes distributing the receipts to the localities where they were collected, sometimes according to a population or tax-effort formula. Such **state collected, locally shared revenues** account for a substantial portion of state aid.

Special Interest Influence   Special interest groups lobby the state to impose taxes and then allocate the money to communities for specific services. Better Roads Associations, for example, find it much easier to lobby the legislature for more road taxes than to lobby a state's many counties or cities individually.

Program Direction   States also use grants to stimulate specific programs. For example, they may offer financial incentives to merge school districts, or to reimburse local units that give senior citizens or farmers property tax relief. They may use state aid to encourage local officials to consolidate local courts or transfer health programs from small cities to counties. States usually have the authority to force such changes, but financial incentives make it much easier to get such laws passed in the legislature.

Local Pressures   State aid may also reflect the political clout of community governments. For example, consider a governor who wants to help solve the financial problems of a large city. Other cities, and perhaps counties, will not fight to stop the aid, but they will scrap to get a share of the handouts.

Also, more frequently than in the past, localities gang up on the legislature to press for financial aid for **state-mandated programs**—those the state orders communities to provide. Some state constitutions and statutes now require the state to pay the costs of such directives. The provision, of course, makes legislators stop and think before they order local units to take on another duty. But sometimes there is no other way to carry out the function, and the legislature agrees to pay locals for the service. These payments, along with all the others, show up in reports as state aid to local governments.

EVALUATING STATE AND LOCAL TAXES

Most of us agree that taxes are necessary. But we may prefer one tax over another. Our preferences may depend on our personal philosophy or on how a specific tax affects us. Both figure in legislative politics when changes in the tax laws are proposed. (Figure 14.5 shows the growth in major state and local taxes.)

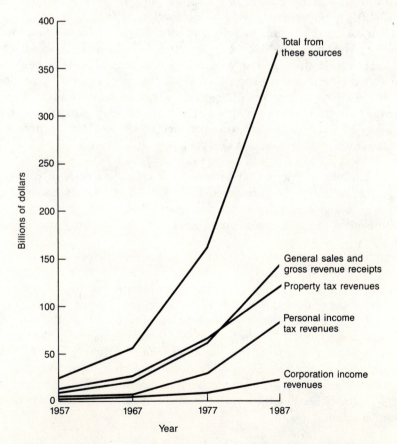

Figure 14.5 How major state and local taxes grew in 30 years. [*Source*: The Tax Foundation, *Facts and Figures on Government Finance*, 1990. (Baltimore: John Hopkins University Press).]

Students of public finance employ several criteria to evaluate particular taxes and overall tax programs. As we discuss these criteria, keep in mind that one of the most important standards for legislators is that a tax must generate revenues. It is why the states and communities continue some tax programs even though they don't always fit the other criteria very well. As we discussed in Chapter 2, tax programs, like spending programs, tend to be fairer or more progressive in states with large manufacturing sectors and competitive party systems.[5]

Equity or Fairness Public finance specialists deal with the concept of equity in two ways. **Horizontal equity** is concerned with whether a tax treats people of equal means alike. **Vertical equity** deals with whether a tax is **progressive**—people or businesses with higher income paying a greater proportion of their income than those with lower incomes. Economists consider as **regressive**, or inequitable, a tax that takes the same or a larger proportion from those with a low income—for example, a flat-rate income tax that requires everyone to pay 1 percent, whether income is $3,000 or $30,000. The economists' assumption is that people with lower incomes should pay a lower percentage of it in taxes because they have little left over after paying for necessities of life.

In evaluating the major state and local taxes, we focus primarily on vertical equity. Moreover, we discuss equity and fairness as measured largely against income, rather than against wealth a person may already possess. At the same time, we note that some specialists argue that people should pay for public services according to the benefits received. These specialists advocate a **user fee** or **charge** to consumers of many public services—parking garages, water supply, and others—just as though these were products or services sold by private companies. This ensures, they argue, that everyone pays at least some tax.

Administration Taxes that involve high collection costs in proportion to the amounts collected are considered inefficient. Tax officials ask whether a tax is easy to evade and whether it will encourage bootlegging and lead to high enforcement costs. They also prefer a tax that citizens easily understand and pay.

Elasticity Tax experts prefer taxes that have **elasticity**—that is, taxes that produce revenues at a rate equal to or greater than the rate of increase in personal income or GNP. An elastic tax, such as an income tax, produces revenue growth at a rate faster than the growth of the economy. (Taxes with high elasticity, of course, also fall in revenue production more rapidly than the rate of decline in economic activity.) A tax that produces the same amount—a fixed vehicle tax, for example—no matter what the level of economic activity is inelastic. Inelastic and low-elasticity taxes require more frequent rate changes to keep pace with rising costs because of inflation or higher service standards. Politicians prefer taxes with high elasticity because these tax programs contribute revenue growth without legislative action.

Competitive Position States are especially concerned that their taxes be generally in line with those of neighboring states, lest they discourage economic activity. Communities face somewhat the same problem, but usually to a lesser degree. How do these criteria or standards apply to state and community taxes?

General Sales Tax and Other Excise Levies

When the clerk at the local hardware store tells you that your purchases come to $1.90 plus "ten cents for the governor," you might ignore the tribute exacted because it doesn't amount to very much. Yet that clerk and all the others around the country collected $136 billion for state and community governments in 1986.[6]

General sales taxes are the single largest revenue generator for the states—$87 billion, about 33 percent of total state revenues in 1988. State **excise taxes**—sales taxes included in the price of such items as gasoline and tobacco—swelled the 1988 total to $130 billion.

Falling property tax collections during the Great Depression brought on the general sales tax. Mississippi in 1932 was the first state to adopt it, but 13 more states followed within a year. By 1940 nearly half had state sales taxes. In 1989 only five states did not—Alaska, Delaware, Montana, New Hampshire, and Oregon. The sales tax on a dollar purchase varied from 3 cents in four states to 8 cents in Connecticut. The median rate for all states is 5 percent. Although most sales tax rates have been rising, two states, North Dakota and West Virginia, cut their rates in 1989. Thirty states also permit their local units to levy sales taxes. These taxes netted about $24 billion in 1987.

Oregon pioneered modern excise taxes with a gasoline tax in 1919. Within ten years, all of the states were using this means to fill state coffers. In 1989, the median fuel tax rate was 16 cents per gallon although the range was from 4 cents in Florida (not including county gasoline levies) to 22.3 cents in Nebraska (see Table 14.2).

Iowa first taxed cigarettes in 1921. By 1961 all the states, even the tobacco-producing states, had such a tax. The rates vary widely—from 2 cents per pack in North Carolina to 40 cents in Connecticut. The national median tax is 20.5 cents. The states have been raising this tax rapidly—California's jumped from 10 to 35 cents. Originally viewed as a sin tax along with taxes on alcohol and gambling, states are now raising the tax to discourage smoking and, in some states, to finance health care.

Excise taxes on liquor are handled in two basic ways—32 states use a license system and assess a gallonage tax. The other 18 are "control" states that monopolize liquor sales. They receive their liquor revenues in the form of taxes and markups on sales. There is no easy way to summarize the various tax rates except to say that the rates vary according to type of beverage—beer, wine, and spirits. Most of the states began taxing these products in the 1930s following the repeal of the prohibition amendment.

Evaluating Sales Taxes The sales tax scores rather well in the ACIR's annual public opinion survey on the worst tax. The sales tax typically ranks as the third worst behind the federal income tax and the property tax.[7] One reason is that everyone pays it, including a state's visitors—an important factor for states that attract tourists.

Table 14.2 MAJOR STATE TAXES AND RATES AS OF JULY 1, 1989

State	Income taxes Corporate (%)	Income taxes Individual (%)	General sales and use tax (%)	Gasoline tax (per gallon) (cents)	Cigarette tax (per pack of 20) (cents)
Alabama	5[a]	2–5[a]	4[b]	11	16.5
Arizona	2.5–10.5[a]	2–8[a]	5[b]	17	15
Arkansas	1–6	1–7	4[b]	13.5	21
California	9.3[c]	1–9.3[c]	4.75[b]	9	35
Colorado	5–5.4[d]	5[c]	3[b]	12	20
Connecticut	11.5[e,f]	1–14[g]	8	20[h]	40
Georgia	6	1–6	4[b]	7.5 + 3% of retail	12
Hawaii	4.4–6	2–10	4	16–22.5	40% wholesale
Idaho	8	2–8.2	5	18	18
Illinois	4[j]	2.5	5[b,h]	13	20
Indiana	3.4[j]	3.4	5	15	15.5
Iowa	6–12[a,c,k]	0.4–9.98[a,c]	4[b]	20	31
Kansas	4.5[f]	3.65–8.75[a,l]	4.25[b]	15[h]	24
Kentucky	3–7.25	2–6[a]	5[b]	15[m]	3.001
Louisiana	4–8[a]	2–6[a]	4[b]	16	16
Maine	3.5–8.93[c]	2–8	5	17	28
Maryland	7	2–5	5	18.5	13
Massachusetts	n	5[o]	5	11[m]	26
Michigan	2.35	4.6	4	15	25
Minnesota	9.5[c]	6–8.5[c,p]	6[b]	20	38
Mississippi	3–5	3–5	6	18[d]	18
Missouri	5[a,e]	1.5–6[a]	4.225[b,d]	11	13
Nebraska	4.75–6.65	3.1–4.8[c]	4[b]	22.3[m]	27
New Jersey	9[f]	2–3.5	6	10.5	27
New Mexico	4.8–7.6	1.8–8.5	4.75[b]	16.2	15
New York	9[c,d]	4–7.875[d,q]	4[b]	8	33
North Carolina	7	3–7	3[b]	15.7[m]	2
North Dakota	3–10.5[a,c]	3.24–14.57[a,k,r]	6	20	30[d]
Ohio	5.1–8.9[e]	0.743–6.9	5[b]	15.1[m]	18
Oklahoma	5	0.5–10[a,l]	4[b]	16	23
Pennsylvania	8.5	2.1	6	12	18
Rhode Island	9	22.96% of federal income tax	6	20[m]	35

426

State							
South Carolina	5		2.75-7		5	16	7
Tennessee	6		6^g		5.5^b	20	13
Utah	5		2.6-7.35^{a,k}		5.094^{b,d}	19	23
Vermont	5.5-8.25		25% of federal income tax		4	16^d	17
Virginia	6^e		2-5.75		3.5^b	17.5	2.5
West Virginia	9.45^d		3-6.5^c		6	15.5	17
Wisconsin	7.9		4.9-6.93^c		5^b	20.8^m	30
Florida	5.5^c		s		6^b	4	24
Nevada	t		s		5.75^b	16.25	15
South Dakota	t		s		4^b	18	23
Texas	t		s		6^b	15	26
Washington	t		s		6.5^b	18	34^d
Wyoming	t		s		3^b	9	12
Alaska	1-9.4^c		s		u	8	16^h
Delaware	8.7		3.2-7.7		u	16	14
Montana	6.75^{f,v}		2-11^a		u	20	16^h
New Hampshire	8		5^d		u	14	21
Oregon	6.6		5-9^{a,k}		u	16^h	27

^{a}Allows federal income tax as a deduction.
^{b}Local taxes are additional.
^{c}Alternative minimum tax is imposed.
^{d}Future reduction scheduled under current law.
^{e}Alternative methods of calculation may be required.
^{f}Corporate surtax is imposed: Connecticut, 20%; Kansas, 2.25%; Montana, 4%; New Jersey's rate is 0.375% beginning July 31, 1989.
^{g}In Connecticut, New Hampshire, and Tennessee, rates apply to income from interest and dividends only. Capital gains are taxed at 7% in Connecticut.
^{h}Future increases are scheduled under current law.
^{i}Additional 2.5% personal property replacement tax.
^{j}A supplemental net income tax is imposed at 4.5%.
^{k}Deductions limited.
^{l}In Kansas and Oklahoma the higher rates apply to taxpayers deducting federal income tax.
^{m}Tax rate is periodically adjusted administratively.
^{n}Excise tax is imposed equal to the greater of $400 or the sum of the tax on net worth or the value of tangible property not taxed locally, plus 9.5% of net income.
^{o}Tax of 10% on income derived from intangibles, and 5% on all other income.
^{p}Additional tax is imposed on income over specified levels, varying with filing status.
^{q}Qualified taxpayers may elect to pay alternative taxes at varying rates.
^{r}Optional tax of 17% of taxpayer's adjusted federal income tax liability.
^{s}No individual income tax.
^{t}No corporate income tax.
^{u}No general sales tax.
^{v}7% rate for corporations using water's edge apportionment.

Source: Adapted from Tax Foundation, *Tax Features* 33:3 (1989).

Equity or Fairness Poor people spend larger shares of their incomes on the necessities of life and therefore spend a larger proportion on sales taxes than the wealthy. The sales tax thus tends to be regressive. Everyone, however, pays the tax. Labor unions, often with the support of other liberal groups, have lobbied to make it less regressive by eliminating the tax on food (28 states), medicine (45 states), other necessities such as electricity and home fuels (29 states), and clothing (6 states).

Administration The sales tax has major administrative advantages: (1) we pay the tax in largely unnoticeable amounts, except when we make a large purchase; (2) as consumers we always have the tax paid up; (3) someone always figures the tax for us; and (4) merchants collect these taxes for the states.[8] The main administrative problems are to make sure that (1) all retailers (especially temporary merchants) register with the state and collect the taxes and (2) the retailers turn over all the receipts. Periodic audits of merchants and computer monitoring of patterns help identify most scofflaws. Another administrative problem concerns collecting taxes due on items purchased from out-of-state catalog order firms, an issue we discuss in Policy Box No. 27, "Taxing Catalog Sales."

Elasticity Economists usually think of the sales tax as an inelastic tax— sales tax revenues do not keep pace with personal income because people, theoretically, save more as their income rises rather than spend it all on taxable items. But that assumes a modest rate of inflation. High inflation rates tend to increase sales tax receipts. During periods of recession, sales tax revenues are stabilized somewhat by those who spend from unemployment compensation, welfare payments, or savings.

Competitive Position Most state officials can set sales tax and excise tax rates without concern about interstate competition. Tax rate differences ordinarily cause only a minor flow of business to lower tax areas, except in a few border towns. But if the tax gap between adjacent states is substantial, such as is the case between Washington, which has a 6.5 percent sales tax, and Oregon, which has none, residents may purchase large items in the low-tax state. (Washington's law may require payment of substitute "use" tax anyway, but the law is difficult to enforce.)

Personal Income Taxes

Wisconsin first levied a personal income tax in 1911, two years before the national government did so. By 1930, 15 states, in addition to the territory of Hawaii (whose income tax began in 1901), had their own. And by 1937, as the states searched frantically for new revenue, the number grew to 29. Not until the 1970s, however, did it climb to the present 43. (Three of these levy an individual income tax only on interest and dividends.)

The individual income tax brings in big money, second only to the general sales tax. The $80 billion it raised in 1988 accounted for 30.3 percent of total state

Policy Box No. 27

Taxing Catalog Sales

Catalog, telephone, and cable TV sales have become big business. Count the catalogs you get in the mail. Or look at how TV commercials hustle goods from out of state. Think how often you see the UPS truck in the neighborhood dropping off packages.

The products being sold, of course, are not just low-cost junk. Cameras, computers, other electronic equipment, and clothing commonly are purchased via the mails or telephone.

Is there anything wrong with this activity? Home state merchants think so. They are unhappy about how the discount and low-overhead operations pick off sales that they might otherwise get. But they're even more unhappy about the "uneven playing field" they perceive the out-of-state operations as having. For the most part, the mail-order establishments do not charge a sales tax on their products. So local merchants see the mail-order companies as having a 4 to 7 percent advantage.

State treasurers also are unhappy with the arrangement. They estimate their losses to be $3 billion or more per year—California $390 million, New York $334 million, Texas $330 million. For the most part, though, state treasurers and their legislators are helpless; the U.S. Supreme Court in *National Bellas Hess v. Illinois Department of Revenue* (1967) ruled that a state cannot impose a tax on sales occurring outside their boundaries.

The states have done about everything they can do to solve the problem themselves. Some, for example, require catalog sales companies to collect sales taxes on mail orders in states where they have stores or employees. This rule catches large national chains such as Sears, Montgomery Ward, or Penney's, which have large catalog operations and stores in many states. But companies such as L. L. Bean (Maine), West 57th St. Photo (New York), and Lands End (Wisconsin) legally get away without charging sales taxes to most of their customers. (A state can require a mail-order company to collect taxes only on sales to local residents of the state in which the company is located.)

The states also try another approach—taxpayer honesty. Michigan, for example, includes a form in the back of its state income tax booklet that citizens must use to report and pay sales taxes on their mail-order purchases during the year. Few taxpayers probably are even aware of the rule. And state officials usually have no basis for knowing who owes this tax and, for the most part, it goes uncollected.

So state officials as well as some local ones want Congress to stop this "revenue leak." Rep. Jack Brooks (D-Texas) and Sen. Thad Cochran (R-Mississippi) in 1989 both introduced bills to require all companies with $12.5 million in annual sales or $500,000 in sales per year in a particular state to collect the sales taxes.

The arguments in favor of such a law seem persuasive. Home state businesses that must collect sales tax should not be discriminated against, say its supporters. The laws should make the same demands on all merchants doing business in a state.

Most mail-order houses cannot claim that they do business only in their own state. To refute this claim, all one needs to do is look at where they advertise. Advocates of the law say that of course most of them meet all the tests for conducting business in a state except that they ship their products from a remote location. Why shouldn't they be treated like every other business?

Other supporters of this legislation say that current practice favors the middle class and wealthy. Look at the products being offered, the prices charged, and the need to have credit, and you know that the poor can't buy much of what they need by mail order. The only effective way to resolve this problem is for Congress to pass a law that overturns *Bellas Hess*.

Moreover, say the bill's advocates, the proposed bills would make it as easy as possible for the mail-order people. It would not require a customer or the mail-order company to keep a sales tax chart for every state and locality within a state. Local sales taxes would be collected only in states where local tax rates are uniform from community to community—currently only North Carolina and Virginia. So much of what the mail-order industry is saying about making things too complex is only a smoke screen. They know the tax rules give them a big advantage, and they'll fight to keep it.

Businesses with large volumes of out-of-state mail-order sales complain that the legislation will create a tax nightmare and put many of them out of business. Not only states but cities and counties levy sales taxes. Catalog sales and discount companies operate on a low margin, say critics of the bills. Every company will spend thousands of dollars on equipment and extra help to figure out how much tax to charge customers and then distribute the money to the various states.

Customers, they say, don't always know the details of their own state's sales tax laws. If they put down the wrong amount on the order form and the check, we have to call or write them. This delays shipping and produces unhappy customers. Across the country there are 6,700 state and local tax rate combinations with no consistency on what is taxable and what isn't. With such complexity, mistakes are unavoidable. And you can be sure, they say, that tax auditors from all the large states will want to see the books to make sure their states are getting what's due.

Bob Kasten (R-Wisconsin) says that the proposed legislation "would be an entirely unwarranted restriction on interstate commerce." Besides, he says, it would be harmful to consumers, particularly the elderly, handicappeds, and rural families who depend on mail-order houses to purchase important goods. Kasten introduced a nonbinding resolution in the U.S. Senate to reject such legislation.

Representatives of the Direct Marketing Association say that even if the bill passes, there won't be the big bonanza of green some state tax collectors expect—the estimates of lost revenues, they say, are way too high. Congress won't pass such a bill, say lobbying experts, until state interests and local interests devise a compromise on how to cut up the pie. (Progress on the law broke down when city and county representatives demanded that the legislation allocate one-sixth of mail-order tax collections to localities.) If the bill eventually passes, say the critics, the states and localities won't have much more money than they have now, many mail-order businesses will have closed, and people who had good jobs will be unemployed. And local businesses will jack up prices.

What do you think? Do current tax policies discriminate against in-state merchants? Do mail-order businesses have an unfair advantage? Is the mail-order interest group claim that the proposed legislation would cause too much complexity a

> legitimate argument? Would states be better off trying to make agreements that would require mail-order houses to collect taxes on a reciprocal basis? Is the dispute between state and local interests appropriate or just a case of two public interest groups (PIGs) going after something rightfully theirs? Is this "tax leak" likely to become more or less significant? Why should Congress be so reluctant to pass one of these bills?

taxes. It is gradually edging up on the sales tax. For a number of states—even those with a sales tax—it has become number one.

Varied Patterns All but four states have **graduated rates**—rates that increase as the level of taxable income increases—but the number of steps and percentages vary widely. New Jersey, for example, has three rate steps: 2 percent for the first $20,000 of taxable income, 2.5 percent on the next $30,000, and 3.5 percent for the balance. Montana, by contrast, has ten steps with rates ranging from 2 percent to 11 percent on income over $50,000.

A handful of states tie their personal income tax plans directly to the federal income tax. Vermont, for example, says its state income tax will be 25 percent of the federal tax—one form of "piggybacking." Most other states also use the major elements of federal definitions of income. This provides simplicity for taxpayers and administrators. However, it also complicates matters when Congress changes the tax rules and rates, as it did in 1986. Many states had to adjust their formulas.

Evaluating Personal Income Taxes How does the personal income tax stack up in terms of the four criteria we use to evaluate taxes?

Equity or Fairness The personal income tax is usually considered as progressive. As we just saw, however, a few states (mostly in the Midwest) tax at a flat rate. Most states have few steps and narrow ranges in the rates, thus tending to limit the progressivity. Many of these, though, have made their income tax moderately progressive through use of exemptions and credits. Iowa, for example, has an "effective" rate of 6.0 percent on incomes of $7,162 and a rate of 13 percent for those $76,725 or more.[9]

Administration States administer personal income taxes rather economically, the cost being less than 1 percent of collections. Costs are low, in part, because income tax evasion is difficult for most of us. Two factors account for strong compliance.

First, the states require payroll withholding. Second, the U.S. Internal Revenue Service cooperates by sharing federal income tax return information with the states. By matching computer tapes, tax administrators can easily identify discrepancies between federal and state tax returns. In addition, federal reporting standards now cover more types of income. Still, the "underground cash society" handles great sums of money that are not taxed.

Elasticity The personal income tax is responsive to changes in personal income. But elasticity depends on whether the state has flat or graduated rates. One source estimated that in three states studied, for each percentage point increase in the GNP, the personal income tax yield increased by 1.75 percent. If the state has a graduated tax, not only is more income taxable as incomes rise, but persons move up to higher tax brackets and then are taxed at higher rates. Legislatures have curbed elasticity somewhat by **indexing**—adjusting personal exemptions and tax rates to the rate of inflation.

The personal income tax is sensitive to economic downturns as well. In times of widespread unemployment, income tax receipts may drop sharply. That is one reason industrial states especially do not put all their revenue eggs in the personal income tax basket.

Competitive Position State officials are concerned about how tax programs affect jobs. Personal income taxes do not greatly influence a state's competitive position—at least in terms of worker movement to various states for jobs. But for employers, it may be different. A state's competitive position is foremost in the mind of economic development oriented legislators and other officials. This may be the reason that Pennsylvania, Indiana, Illinois, and Michigan all have flat-rate personal income taxes. Ohio, which also competes for jobs with these states, has only a moderately graduated income tax at upper-income levels.

At the community level, the effect may be stronger. People do make residential decisions partly on the basis of which local governments have a personal income tax. Local income taxes on individuals are uncommon. They occur in only 11 states and altogether are levied in 3,517 community governments, 79 percent of which are in Pennsylvania. Counties in Indiana, Maryland, and Kentucky levy income taxes; school districts in Iowa and Ohio; and some cities in the other local income tax states.[10]

The Property Tax

During the 1920s the property tax was the most important tax for both state and local governments. In 1927 it accounted for more than 25 percent of state revenues. But the Great Depression ended this dependence. By 1942 state property tax receipts had dropped to less than 7 percent.

The property tax is now mainly a local tax. It pays for a large part of school and community college costs as well as local government operations. Even for local units it is not as important as it once was but mostly because of other new taxes and increases in federal and state aid. During the 1920s it produced about 75 percent of the local revenue; in 1987, about 25 percent. *Yet it is still the most productive local tax.* Property tax revenues nearly double nationwide each decade and in 1987 totaled $116.6 billion.

Computing what people in different states pay in property taxes is difficult. But a study by the Advisory Commission on Intergovernmental Relations based on an index of FHA-insured mortgages determined that, on the average, for a house with a market value of $100,000, the owner would pay $1,150, an index of

1.15. On this basis, New Jersey had the highest property taxes with an index of 2.38; Louisiana, the lowest, had an index of 0.22. Generally, by this measure, the Southeast states had the lowest property taxes.[11]

Evaluating the Property Tax An early authority, Edwin R. A. Seligman, once remarked that the property tax was a good tax, except that it is wrong in theory and does not work in practice.[12]

Equity or Fairness The property tax is a tax on a portion of a person's wealth rather than income. And it is regressive. Many states have made it less regressive by exempting senior citizens, the sight-impaired, and the disabled. In addition, several states have a "circuit breaker" that gives citizens a credit against their state income tax if the property tax on their home exceeds a set percentage of income. In effect, these states subsidize high local property taxes.

The federal government also subsidizes local property taxes by allowing them as income tax deductions. But even when these tax breaks are taken into account, an ACIR analysis indicates that a family of "average" means paid 3.2 percent of its income for property taxes while a family with an income four times greater paid only 1.9 percent.[13]

Administration The property tax is costly to administer. To ensure that each property owner pays a fair share, properties must be valued or assessed fairly within and among local assessing units. Schools, airports, community colleges, and other taxing units often overlap several assessing units. If assessment practices are not uniform, the bill of some taxpayers will be unfairly high while others are unfairly low.

Moreover, the political incentives encourage assessors to set property assessments below market value. Assessors are elected in many states, and citizens are not inclined to reelect them if property assessments rise sharply. In addition, low assessments mean that property owners in small jurisdictions will pay less of the taxes to support larger units of which they are also a part, such as counties or large school districts. At the same time, underassessed units receive disproportionately large state aid payments based on "need."

What are the remedies for such political chicanery? Property tax reformers suggest appointing professional assessors who are sheltered from political pressures. Others would also have larger units—states or counties—do the assessing. And they approve having larger agencies supervise local assessors through spot checks and through **equalization**—a process of comparing property values with assessments across units to ensure equality of assessments.

Elasticity Historically, property values have increased at about the same rate as economic growth or personal income. But in the late 1970s and early 1980s, housing costs rose faster than the general consumer price index. As a result, property taxes rose substantially, even with reductions in tax rates and other limitations in effect—perhaps the main reason for Proposition 13 and other tax revolts.

The property tax provides an element of stability when economic conditions are poor. Because community governments can assume ownership and sell property for taxes due if an owner fails to pay, owners pay their property taxes if at all possible.

Property owners, especially homeowners and farmers, dislike the tax for these same reasons. Unless local officials lower tax rates, owners pay higher taxes just because property values and assessments rise. Farmers may have to pay higher taxes even though the farming operations lost money—a factor in widespread farm foreclosure in the 1980s. And people on fixed incomes may have to pay more while inflation cuts into their purchasing power. Some states have adjusted for these problems—some assess agricultural land on the basis of its productive value. Other states give farmers, seniors, and disabled persons special credits.

Competitive Position States and localities compete by attempting to keep property taxes low. Some give long-term tax exemptions to businesses that locate or expand in their area. The property tax is especially vulnerable to political manipulation and granting of exemptions. Many a group has persuaded its legislature to exempt properties—tools, equipment, and land improvements. Such exemptions erode a community's property tax base, in some instances by as much as one-third.[14] A newspaper analysis of tax exempt properties reported that one-fifth of the total value in Detroit was exempt. Federal and state buildings as well as school, church, cemetery, and city-owned properties accounted for the more than 40,000 exempt parcels. And businesses in the city benefited from more than $500 million in exemptions.[15]

Business Taxes

The most important business tax, the corporate income tax, brought in just under $22 billion in 1988. But just ten states collected almost two-thirds of the total revenues—over $14 billion. Nevada, South Dakota, Texas, Washington, and Wyoming do not impose a corporate income tax.

The corporate license tax is a fee for the privilege of conducting business in a state. Of course, it is also a way for corporations to pay for public services they and the public receive. This tax provided the states with about $3.2 billion in 1988. Seven states accounted for more than three-fourths of the total collected. Texas, which has no corporte income tax, collected 30.2 percent of the total of this tax. Communities collected additional amounts in a few states.

The unemployment compensation tax is also a major business tax—generating nearly $17.5 billion in 1987. This is mostly a payroll tax on employers, although a few states also levy a tax on employees. The average employer contribution is 1.3 percent of wage earnings.

Oil and mining companies as well as lumber and fishing businesses pay **severance taxes**—per barrel, ton, or other measure—to extract a natural resource. Until 1970, just two states—Texas and Louisiana—accounted for more than 75 percent of state severance tax revenues, because of their oil extraction industry. Now other states have discovered it as a way to "export" taxes—Alaska for oil,

Montana, Wyoming, and Kentucky for coal, and New Mexico for uranium. These revenues increased by about 600 percent during the 1970s—from $685 million to $4.2 billion in 1980. By 1988 this tax generated $4.3 billion, about half of it now from Alaska and Texas.

Taxes on gross insurance premiums and on gross receipts from utility companies also add tidy sums to state treasuries—$13.1 billion in 1988.

Evaluating Business Taxes Let us look at business taxes in terms of the criteria we have been using.

Equity or Fairness Are business taxes equitable and fair? The answer, of course, varies by state and with the specific tax or combination of taxes. We might think that a state which imposes a corporate income tax as its main business tax would achieve vertical equity in its business taxes. Most corporate tax rates, though, are either flat or narrowly graduated. Thus the corporate income tax tends to be regressive.

Business taxes may be even less fair in terms of horizontal equity, because of both the diversity of business enterprises and the way a combination of state and local taxes affects particular industries. One firm may be labor-intensive—dependent on labor—and operate on a high profit margin. Another may be capital-intensive and operate on a low margin of profitability. Ensuring across-the-board equity is difficult. In addition, if we consider the differences in lobbying and political power that various business groups have within a state, we begin to see just how difficult it is to gain across-the-board equity. Powerful groups get favorable treatment; others may not.

But what proportion of the total state tax should businesses pay? Some suggest that businesses should not pay taxes because they only result in higher consumer prices. "Business doesn't pay taxes," they say. "It just collects them." But others say high business taxes are necessary to allocate and distribute "true" costs to those who benefit. High severance taxes on coal and oil, for example, cause consumers, wherever they are, to pay the costs of drawing on these resources. High taxes on businesses that export products across state lines may mean higher prices to state residents, but they also mean that consumers outside the state who buy the products pay their share of the true costs. The high-tax-on-industry theory works well, though, only where the state has a nearly exclusive control over a natural resource or manufacturing process.

Administration Some business taxes, such as the franchise tax or the severance tax, are relatively easy to administer because the base of the tax is clear. Most states use the federal income definition for corporations, but determining just how much a multistate or multinational company owes a particular state is complex, and states do not have enough auditors to do much more than an occasional audit.

Competitive Position The struggle to keep a good "business climate" works to keep business taxes down. Should state and local officials be concerned? Most studies find that many factors—nearness to markets and raw materials, availability of trained workers, and natural resources such as water and energy as well as regulatory policies—influence business location decisions. The local tax bill and availability of local services are other factors. One study, however, noted that the important question is how a state treats a company relative to its competitors in other states. Corporate tax managers watch carefully the principal firms in their industry and seek to keep tax costs, like other costs, in line with those of their competitors.[16]

But when a company closes a plant or announces that it is leaving the state, such conclusions often do not quiet criticisms from business, industry, and others. Business climate includes taxes as well as other costs such as workers' compensation insurance, policies toward unions, and environmental standards.[17] Thus even though tax considerations may be marginal in industry locational decisions, governors and other politicians who have made economic development a major goal are seen as having failed when a company moves away. Thus politicians stay aware of tax policies in competitor states or communities.

It is not mere coincidence, for example, that Virginia, Tennessee, South Carolina, and North Carolina all have flat-rate corporate income taxes in the 6 to 7 percent range. Nor is it a happenstance that New York's state corporate income tax rate is just a little lower than Connecticut's, whereas New Jersey and other New England corporate income tax rates are below New York's.

Other Taxes and Miscellaneous Charges

We have now reviewed the major forms of taxes that state and community governments impose. But legislators have come up with many other ideas to keep money flowing in. And although we group other taxes and miscellaneous charges here, they are by no means incidental. Among these other 1988 revenues were the following: motor vehicle and operator license fees ($9.6 billion), taxes on inheritances and gifts ($3.2 billion), and tobacco taxes ($4.8 billion). In addition, state lotteries produced about $5 billion for 23 states in 1988. In Policy Box No. 28, "Should Government Promote Gambling?" we discuss whether states sanction gambling in the efforts to increase lottery revenues.

State legislatures authorize local units to set and collect many of these fees, but the local legislative body decides how much to charge. Local officials pass by very few such opportunities. They require licenses for businesses, going-out-of-business sales, and dogs; fees for inspecting new construction, remodeling, rental properties, and even permit fees for the electronic game machines at shopping malls or the local student tavern. (Table 14.3 summarizes the comparisons we have just made.)

Movement Toward a More Diversified Revenue System

State and local tax revenues have become more diversified than they were in the 1950s or 1960s. A review of all state and local general revenue shows that the revenues were much more balanced in 1987. Property taxes and federal aid

Policy Box No. 28

Should Government Promote Gambling?

It started as a trickle in 1964 when New Hampshire became the first state in modern times to establish a state lottery. By 1990 a total of 28 states and Washington, D.C., had organized their own lotteries. In addition, communities in Nebraska can conduct them, although the state itself does not have a lottery.

Lotteries are the major state-owned gambling operations. But states are involved in many other ways as well—bingo is big in nearly all the states; horse-race wagering in more than 60 percent, dog racing in about 30 percent. A few states allow jai alai, offtrack, and sports betting. Nevada and New Jersey, of course, permit casino gambling, and Iowa in 1989 began licensing riverboat casinos on the Mississippi; Illinois, and perhaps other states along major rivers, will do the same soon. In 1989 Oregon began operating a program allowing citizens to wager on professional football games.

State officials and residents want lotteries for the same reason that the 13 colonies had them—to raise money for state programs. Politicians, caught in the cross pressures of providing public services, cutting taxes, and adjusting to reduced federal aid, find the lottery and other gambling revenues an easy way to reduce some of the pressure.

Indeed, state-approved and -promoted gambling, especially the lotteries, has become big business. Collectively, state lotteries generate some $20 billion in sales annually. Of that about half is paid to winners, and $3 billion goes for administration and advertising. The remaining $7 billion goes into the state treasuries, mostly into budgets for public schools. For some states, lottery revenue has become the fourth or fifth most important source of revenue.

And that may be the heart of the problem. Lottery revenues have become so important that governors and legislators pressure the bureaucrats who run the lottery to increase their contributions over prior years. They conduct investigations or hire consultants to figure out how the state can sell more lottery tickets.

And so states do not only facilitate this form of gambling, they encourage and promote it. They advertise it on television and in newspapers. They make it accessible and convenient by placing outlets in high-traffic commercial centers, convenience stores, and bars. Moreover, they pressure their independent vendors to push sales by threatening to remove the license of those businesses that do not meet monthly and yearly quotas.

Most recently, lottery executives have discovered that sales increase as the size of the jackpots rise. Lottery "rollovers" from one week to another when there are no winners cause the payoffs and players' interest to skyrocket. Having learned this, more and more executives are raising the odds—from 10 to 12 million to 1 to make winning more difficult. They require winners to pick six or seven numbers out of 47 or 50 instead of 42 or 44.

Predictably, rollovers occur week after week until the jackpots reach $50 million or more. (The record jackpot, as we write, is $133 million in Pennsylvania in 1990.) The media add to this frenzy as they report on the vast sum that "may be yours for just one dollar."

Advocates argue that lotteries will bring in money for a worthy cause, a tactic that lodges and churches have used for years. For example, profits from Oregon's licensed professional football wagers underwrite college athletics and scholarships. Many other states use proceeds to support education and economic development.

Another common argument is that people spend a certain amount of their money on bets, numbers, and games of chance anyway—illegally if legal opportunities are not available. So the state, they insist, might just as well generate some public revenue from this activity.

But critics of publicly sanctioned gambling say that the states have gone far beyond providing opportunities for legal gambling. The states, they maintain, promote gambling! And the ads are aimed at the most vulnerable segments of our society, those who can least afford to waste thousands of dollars betting against 10-million-to-1 odds. (see table).

PER CAPITA LOTTERY SALES

Top Ten States in 1988	
Massachusetts	$226
District of Columbia	197
Maryland	177
Connecticut	156
New Jersey	153
Ohio	126
Pennsylvania	121
Illinois	114
Michigan	112
New York	88

> Our governments should not exploit our citizens by appealing to their base dreams of getting something for nothing. And the critics say public promotion of gambling cannot be justified on the basis of its support for worthy public programs. State-promoted gambling is a most regressive tax, unworthy of the states that push it on its weakest citizens.
>
> What do you think? Is it okay for the states to use mass media advertising to encourage people to gamble on lotteries and other public games of chance? Would you favor a rule that forbids media ads and promotions? Should the ads carry tag lines that inform viewers of the odds or the risk of addiction and dangers of compulsive gambling? Or should the lotteries be required to spend, say, at least 10 percent of the ad budget on contra-ads such as some beer manufacturers do about irresponsible use of beer? Do you think that public promotion of playing the lottery and other games of chance is not a problem?

accounted for about 17.5 percent each; sales and gross receipt taxes, 14 percent; personal and corporate income taxes, 14.7 percent; miscellaneous taxes, 11.7 percent; user charges, 12.5 percent; and other miscellaneous receipts, 11.7 percent. (See Table 14.4 for state tax ratios.)

These ratios, of course, vary by state, but most states now generate significant portions of their revenues from several taxes rather than just one or two. No other state, for example, relies on any tax as heavily as New Hampshire does on the property tax—about 35 percent. For that matter, in only a very few instances does any state depend on one revenue source for more than one-quarter of its revenue. Most seek an even distribution across the categories we just listed.

BORROWING AND DEBT IN THE STATES AND LOCALITIES

Historically, the record of state and local debit is spotty—individuals and institutions who loan money to public agencies by buying bonds, notes, or other instruments have not always received payment on time and, in a few instances, not at all. During the 1930s approximately 10 percent of municipal bonds were in default. The record was much better during the 25 years following World War II, but during the late 1970s the situation again became somewhat more risky for investors.

The most publicized fiscal crisis occurred in 1976, when New York City found itself unable to repay some of its short-term debt. Bankers and public officials viewed the problem as being severe and ultimately persuaded the federal government to provide loan guarantees.[18] With that assistance and with an order from Congress to the state and city to get New York City's financial house in order, financial stability in New York City has again been achieved.

Meanwhile, other states have assumed "superintending control" over finances of the few municipalities that have bordered on bankruptcy. In some instances state officials pressured local units to cut back programs and workers' pay. In other cases, state officials insisted that local voters approve tax increases and made them reorganize their government as a condition of state loans. In 1988,

Table 14.3 HOW THE STATE AND LOCAL TAXES MEASURE UP

Tax	Equity or fairness	Administration	Elasticity	Competitive position
General sales and excise taxes	Regressive, but less so with exemptions or tax credits	Low cost for states and communities as well as for individuals; merchants handle the collections, but some enforcement is necessary	Inelastic	Not significant for states except in border areas; can be important for units with local sales taxes
Personal income tax	Mildly progressive, but rates are not steeply graduated; some are flat	Low cost for states and localities, largely because of payroll deductions; citizens have forms to complete	Elastic if rates are graduated, less so if flat	Not significant at state level; may influence residential location at local level
Property tax	Regressive, but less so with "circuit breaker"	High cost; difficult to achieve uniformity in assessments	Inelastic	May be influential in residential or business location; exemptions reduce problem for business location
Business taxes	Generally regressive in combination	Low cost for government; businesses bear major cost of reporting	Generally inelastic	Important for business location; states stay in line with neighbors
Miscellaneous taxes and charges	Highly regressive	Fairly high cost; most involve personal attention	Inelastic	Usually not significant

with at least two cities experiencing extreme fiscal stress because of industrial relocation, Michigan formalized its process for bringing community governments into "receivership." Among other steps, the process permits the appointment of a special fiscal manager with broad powers including the levy of taxes without voter approval.

Table 14.4 BALANCE OF STATE TAX REVENUE, 1987

State	Personal income tax (%)	Rank	Corporate income tax (%)	Rank	Sales tax (%)	Rank	Other taxes (%)	Rank
New England								
Connecticut	10.7	41	15.6	2	41.8	12	31.9	22
Maine	32.8	18	5.3	35	34.1	22	27.7	31
Massachusetts	47.0	3	14.2	3	22.1	42	16.7	49
New Hampshire	1.5	43	27.0	1			71.5	3
Rhode Island	34.2	15	8.3	12	33.4	24	24.1	41
Vermont	30.1	26	7.1	18	20.3	44	42.4	12
Mid-Atlantic								
Delaware	38.1	12	12.8	6			49.1	7
Maryland	41.9	5	5.2	37	25.0	38	27.9	28
New Jersey	27.4	31	11.5	7	30.7	30	30.4	23
New York	50.6	2	8.7	10	20.7	43	20.1	44
Pennsylvania	24.2	35	8.9	9	31.4	28	35.5	18
Great Lakes								
Illinois	29.7	28	8.3	15	32.7	26	29.4	25
Indiana	30.5	24	4.9	39	47.2	8	17.4	48
Michigan	32.5	19			28.7	33	38.8	16
Ohio	33.1	16	4.9	40	34.8	20	27.2	33
Wisconsin	39.2	10	8.3	13	29.1	32	23.4	42
Plains								
Iowa	35.9	14	5.6	33	31.0	29	27.5	32
Kansas	30.4	25	6.6	19	34.9	19	28.2	27
Minnesota	41.7	6	7.6	16	26.5	36	24.2	40
Missouri	31.6	23	6.0	25	41.2	13	21.2	43
Nebraska	29.9	27	5.6	32	32.5	27	32.0	21
North Dakota	14.0	39	5.8	29	33.8	23	46.4	10
South Dakota			5.8	28	49.3	5	44.8	11
Southeast								
Alabama	27.6	30	5.0	38	27.4	35	40.0	15
Arkansas	28.3	29	6.1	21	37.9	16	27.7	30
Florida			6.1	23	55.6	2	38.3	17
Georgia	40.4	9	8.4	11	32.7	25	18.5	46
Kentucky	26.2	33	7.6	17	25.3	37	40.9	14
Louisiana	12.7	40	5.5	34	34.5	21	47.2	9
Mississippi	16.2	37	5.3	36	52.2	4	26.2	37
North Carolina	41.2	7	9.1	8	23.4	40	26.4	35
South Carolina	31.9	22	6.0	24	37.2	17	24.8	39
Tennessee	1.9	42	8.3	14	55.3	3	34.5	19
Virginia	44.3	4	5.8	27	20.0	45	30.0	24
West Virginia	26.3	32	4.9	41	43.2	11	25.6	38

Table 14.4 Continued

State	Personal income tax (%)	Rank	Corporate income tax (%)	Rank	Sales tax (%)	Rank	Other taxes (%)	Rank
Southwest								
Arizona	22.0	36	5.7	30	44.6	9	27.7	29
New Mexico	15.4	38	6.3	20	44.4	10	33.9	20
Oklahoma	25.4	34	3.1	45	23.0	41	48.4	8
Texas					41.0	14	59.0	5
Rocky Mountain								
Colorado	40.4	8	4.8	42	28.1	34	26.7	34
Idaho	32.0	21	5.7	31	35.9	18	26.4	36
Montana	32.9	17	5.8	26			61.2	4
Utah	37.0	13	4.2	44	38.9	15	19.9	45
Wyoming					23.9	39	76.1	2
Far West								
Alaska			13.3	5			86.7	1
California	38.8	11	13.3	4	30.6	31	17.4	47
Hawaii	32.0	20	4.5	43	48.2	7	15.3	50
Nevada					48.9	6	51.1	6
Oregon	65.4	1	6.1	22			28.5	26
Washington					58.2	1	41.8	13
U.S. average	30.8%		7.7%		31.1%		29.3%	

Source: S. D. Gold and J. A. Zelio, *State-Local Fiscal Indicators* (Denver, Colo.: National Conference of State Legislatures, 1990).

How Much Our Governments Owe

Most of what our governments owe consists of federal debt—about 76 percent of the total in 1987. The states, which traditionally rely less on borrowed money, owe about 9 percent of the total debt. The localities' share is about 15 percent.

By most measures, federal debt declined from 1949 to 1969. At the same time state and local debt increased. But during the 1970s and especially the 1980s government debt at all levels increased dramatically, by far the largest portion of it arising from deficits in federal budgets. (See Figure 14.6.) When measured against the GNP, state and community debt rose only modestly. At the end of the 1980s state debt hovered around the 6 percent mark; local debt, around 10 percent of GNP. Federal debt, on the other hand, went from 33 percent of GNP to more than 53 percent.[19]

Balanced Budget Requirements State laws generally require the states and communities to have balanced budgets at the end of each fiscal year. Although

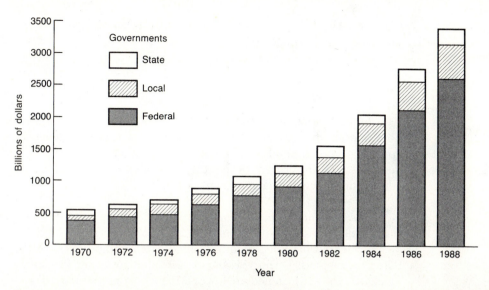

Figure 14.6 How government debt has grown since 1970—state, local, and federal governments. [*Source*: Tax Foundation, *Facts and Figures on Government Finance*, 1990. (Baltimore: John Hopkins University Press), p. 20.]

some laws are vague in defining a balanced budget, the general standard is that these governments should not spend more than they take in together with what might have been left from the previous year. The result has been that the general fund or general operating budgets usually show a surplus at the end of the year. This experience led President Reagan and others to support an amendment to the U.S. Constitution for a mandatory balanced budget for the federal government.[20]

Mandatory budget balancing cuts down on the extent to which the governments borrow for annual operating purposes. But having a surplus at year's end is not necessarily a sign of sound fiscal health. A sharp-penciled budget director's balanced budget might conceal more than it reveals. How much of the prior-year carryover was used? What is the five-year trend for revenue and expenditures? Are essential expenditures being deferred? Did the government benefit from exceptional revenues this fiscal year that will not be available next year? These are some of the questions that might give new insights about a state's financial condition.[21] In addition, governments employ strategies to hide out-of-balance budgets. For example, they may issue special purpose bonds to improve parks or clean up toxic waste sites that arguably should be recognized as annual operating costs. Or they may adjust accounting systems or change fiscal years as Michigan did in 1982 to cover what was then a growing budget deficit. And officials may adopt programs that are **off-budget expenditures**—for example, guaranteeing college tuition rates into the future. These will not show up as expenses in a current year but be obligations—"chickens that may possibly come home to roost"—in a future year for a future administration. And, of course, unlike the federal government, state and communities have **capital budgets**—budgets for buildings or other long-term-benefit projects that may be financed with borrowed funds and that may impose significant obligations in a future budget. The states and communities are not likely to abandon balanced budget requirements. But neither should citizens rest comfortably just because the state or county had a year-end surplus. It may not be the whole story.

Improvements in Debt Management Most state and community constitutions and charters restrict the power to borrow. State agencies also review and approve proposed bond issues before allowing them to be offered in the financial markets. And improved accounting practices and independent audits have advanced municipal financial management.

The Role of Private Financiers National firms such as Standard & Poor, Inc., publish ratings on the financial condition of state and community governments. Such ratings affect significantly the ability to borrow and the interest rates that must be paid. During Michigan's 1982 budget crisis, for example, New York finance houses threatened to lower Michigan's credit rating. In response, the governor proposed a temporary increase in the income tax. To help persuade the senate to approve the measure, representatives of three of the firms conducted a seminar on the senate floor. Said the financiers, "You must have a balanced budget. Either cut services or increase taxes to persuade us that you can get your financial house in order."

When Should Governments Borrow?

As we know from our personal lives, borrowing is not necessarily bad unless you are unable to make the principal and interest payments.

Paying as you go for capital projects appeals to conservatives. Nebraska "paid cash" for its state capitol as did Virginia its highways under the Byrd organization (1925 to 1950). But this approach also means that a community may deny itself use of facilities while it gathers the funds. And it may mean that people whose taxes are being gathered never benefit from the improvement.

A pay as you use policy tends to make those who use and benefit from the new facilities responsible for payment. This policy usually avoids inflationary cost increases, although interest charges may offset these savings.

Borrowing for Capital Improvements Experts generally agree that borrowing for capital improvements is proper. They base their advice on the assumption that a community will grow and that inflation will continue. If so, more taxpayers will be around later to pay for a project, and with inflation, the community will pay the debt with "cheaper" dollars. It often works out that way.

But there are no guarantees. When a large steel or automotive manufacturer decides to close a plant, the local government depending on its tax payments may find itself in financial difficulty. Not only does the government lose the tax revenue from the factory, but other property values in the town may also decline.

And workers may not pay as much income tax. Making principal and interest payments on debt under such economic stress may be very difficult.

Borrowing for Current Operations Experts view borrowing to meet current operating expenses as a sign of financial weakness. Governments that spend more than they take in for very long will soon be devoting a good deal of their revenue to making interest payments. Such was the predicament of the federal government in the 1980s when it expanded its debt significantly.

Financial experts recommend short-term borrowing only to meet cash flow problems during a fiscal year. And in the event of a year-end deficit they may approve borrowing but also insist on spending cuts or tax increases to pay off the borrowed funds and to avoid repetition of a deficit a year later.

STATE AND LOCAL SPENDING

In 1960 total public expenditures were about $150 billion. By 1988 they had risen to more than $1.9 trillion. Government spending relative to the GNP also increased. In 1960 public expenditures were 26.6 percent of the GNP and by 1989, 34.2 percent, close to the highest point since World War II.

The Changing Ratio The ratio of federal to state and local expenditures provides one perspective on how centralized the federal system has become. In 1929 federal expenditures accounted for about 26 percent of total government spending.[22] The Great Depression caused a change—by 1939 the division was 51.1 national, 48.9 state and local. In 1988 the national share was 62 percent, the lowest point since 1975.

A similar shift has been occurring within the states. In 1929 local governments accounted for 73 percent of the state-local expenditures. By 1988 state expenditures accounted for 54 percent of the state-local total. But if we look at expenditures after intergovernmental transfers have been made, community governments still spend about 60 percent of the total.

How the States Spend Their Money

Figuring out what happens to the money our state governments take in can be a little perplexing. We avoid some of the confusion by not distinguishing between money from their own sources and funds they get from the federal government.

State Direct Expenditures Back in Chapter 1 we noted that the states lack visibility—citizens are not quite sure what the states do. If you attend a state university, your student newspaper, more than likely, has reminded you that your tuition is related to state appropriations for higher education. The student newspaper editors probably quote warnings from your college or university president about tuition increases if state appropriations are not larger. As a student, then, you are aware of how one group, through its clients, encourages the state legislature to increase spending.

Many other groups also zero in on "their" appropriations—social workers and welfare clients, public health and mental health workers. Contractors and construction workers take a special interest in appropriations for highways and for new state buildings. Interest groups for corrections, parks and recreation, and others all keep close watch on what state spending levels will be.

Studying expenditures individually becomes very complex. But a broad view makes it simpler—a few major functions account for the lion's share of state spending.

The Broad Picture Overall the states spent nearly $455 billion in 1987. Of this they paid almost $141.4 billion to the local units. Another $92 billion was "restricted," for unemployment compensation, retirement payments, alcohol purchases, and other trust purposes. That left about $221.6 billion for the states to spend directly on their own programs.

The Four Major Functions The states traditionally make about two-thirds of the direct expenditures to support four functions—education (for state colleges and universities and public schools), welfare, highways, and health programs. Natural resources and financial administration (tax collection, accounting, purchasing, etc.) get about 7.5 percent together. The states finance all their other programs—state police, courts, the state legislatures, prisons, public transportation, state promotions, and others—from the remaining 25 percent.

These percentages, of course, vary from state to state. But if you were to examine in detail the spending of your own state, you would likely find that it corresponds closely to this overall pattern. Figure 14.7 shows how these patterns have changed over time.

Some shift in the state-local divisions of these functions has been occurring since 1975. The state share of public school financing has been rising and is now about 50 percent. State spending on welfare has risen and is now about 95 percent. For highways the state share has declined to about 63 percent of the state-local total. For hospitals and health the state share has remained rather steady at about 50 percent.

How Local Governments Spend Their Money

In 1987 the community governments, having received state and federal aid, had more to spend directly than their state governments—about $391.1 billion in all. Their overall pattern of general purpose spending is not altogether different from the state picture. The same four major functions absorb about three-fifths of local funds. Spending for local schools and community colleges, as we might expect, is the major item. It took almost half the total in 1970, but since then has declined to about 42 percent in part because of declining enrollments.

Figure 14.8 indicates that the proportion spent for streets and highways has dropped steadily, as has the share for welfare. (Welfare administration has become largely a state function.) Expenditures for police and fire protection, as a

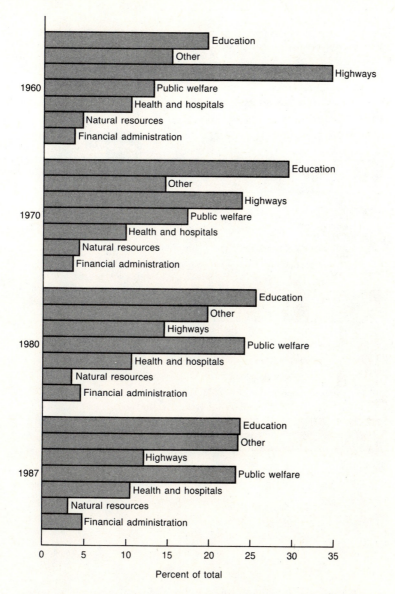

Figure 14.7 State spending changes over time: direct expenditures for own functions as percentage of total, 1960–1987. [*Source*: Tax Foundation, *Facts and Figures on Government Finance*, 1990. (Baltimore: John Hopkins University Press), p. 225.]

percentage of the total, until recently have been less than they were in 1950. After decades of decline, though, local units have been increasing the proportion being spent on public safety functions.

Local increased spending in the "other" category, including such functions as housing, parks, recreation, jails, courts, public buildings, refuse pickup and disposal, and other services, accounts for the balance.

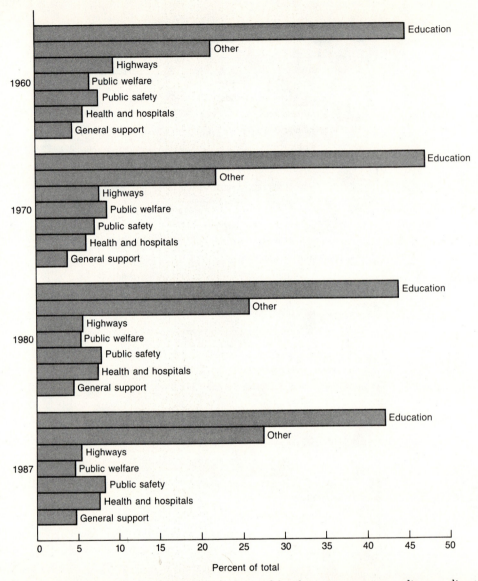

Figure 14.8 Education claims the major share of local government expenditures: direct expenditures by function, 1960–1987. [*Source*: Tax Foundation, *Facts and Figures on Government Finance*, 1990. (Baltimore: John Hopkins University Press), p. 292.]

Implications for Budget Reductions

Many states encountered severe financial crises in 1982. At the end of 1980, the states, on the average, had budget surpluses equal to about 9 percent of their expenditures. This healthy **budget carryover** helped to bring the states through the next three lean years when surpluses dropped to an average of 1.5 percent.

After a rise in year-end surpluses the percentage of unexpended funds again tapered off to about 3.5 percent of expenditures in 1990. State budget officials argue that any amount below 5 percent makes a state especially vulnerable to heavy cutbacks in the event of a recession.[23] (See Figure 14.9.)

How do states deal with budget shortages? At first governors draw on reserves and then make minor cuts—close some state parks or have fewer attendants. They may also raise minor taxes and fees. If the crisis persists, they may try for greater tax increases, and then education, welfare, and public and mental health become targets for budget cuts. Spending for highways usually comes from earmarked monies and so is unaffected by general fund shortages and surpluses.

At the community level, financial control usually is spread among several units. Education may initiate program cutbacks or tax millage increases when property values lag and state aid does not rise. Meanwhile the city or county may be having only a minor problem. For the mayor or city manager the largest expenditure is usually public safety—police and fire. The city may make its first cuts in parks and recreation programs or street cleaning and add fees for garbage pickup. If the city needs to make large cuts, it must look at police and fire services. City officials, too, will find departments with restricted or earmarked funding—especially those financed with service charges—where reductions will not help a general fund budget problem.

Personnel Reductions When states face a budget crunch critics say that the governor should cut the "bloated bureaucracy." During 1981 and 1982 some states did exactly that. Governors ordered department heads not to fill vacant positions. Some ordered layoffs or, as Arizona, Idaho, and Michigan did, workers were ordered to take holidays without pay. But states use only about 40 percent of their general funds for payroll. By far the larger portion goes out in the form of

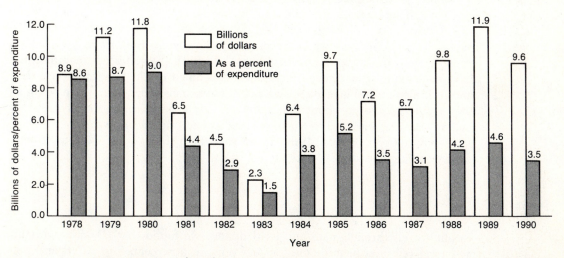

Figure 14.9 Size of total year-end balances, fiscal 1978 to 1990. [*Source*: M. A. Howard, *Fiscal Survey of the States*, 1989. (National Governor's Association, National Association of State Budget Officers).]

transfer payments—to welfare clients, state colleges, or local governments. So personnel cutbacks are only a partial solution.

At the community level, governments are much more labor intensive. Aside from making the preliminary reductions, local officials usually have little choice but to reduce their work force. Some in 1982 followed the pattern of industry and negotiated "contract concessions" with employee unions.

And politics also affects who will be cut. Expenditure patterns differ from one partisan era to the next.[24] Interest groups usually suggest cutting somebody else's budget. In the face of severe financial difficulty, though, executives and legislators alike must make both across-the-board and targeted cuts. Peeling a little here and a little there usually does not do the job in hard times.

A FINAL COMMENT

Our federal system has become financially as well as politically interdependent. Also, the federal system has been one of change with respect to its finances. Much of the change was not planned even though the governors met with Reagan administration agents on numerous occasions over decentralizing programs and services. They discussed basic horse trades—we'll pay for this if you pay for that. It was not the first time that a president had such discussions with the governors. Neither was it the first time they found it difficult to agree.

Yet the Reagan years were years of a declining federal role, at least financially. The reductions resulted from cuts in federal appropriations brought on in part by federal tax cuts and large increases in defense spending. The large accumulated federal debt, large annual budget deficits, and President George Bush's reluctance to increase federal taxes has limited the federal government's ability to maintain the role it played during the 1960s and 1970s.

The impact on state and community governments has been significant. Many raised taxes and service charges and cut back on services and other benefits. While these changes were developing, however, the states were also strengthening their own capacities to govern. Both the states and communities have emerged as leaner governments, less dependent on the federal government, and in firmer control over their own priority decisions. Few, if any, are doing all they would like to do about the problems they experience. Yet most probably believe they are dealing with the important issues in significant ways.

Many students of federalism suggest that these changes in federal-state relations were long overdue. We are among them.

HIGH POINTS

In our travels through state and local finance we found that (1) although state and local revenues have increased each year, as a percentage of GNP and personal income they have been falling. We saw also that inflation and tax limitations adopted during the 1970s curbed the expansion of these governments.

We observed that (2) intergovernmental transfers are an essential part of the financial system. The federal government and the states redistribute centrally collected funds to lower-level units in part to encourage these units to carry out selected programs.

We saw next that (3) the states and communities collect about 35 percent of the total public revenues, but mainly through tax and charge systems that are somewhat regressive and not highly responsive to the level of economic activity. We considered (4) the main state and local taxes according to several criteria. We also noted that (5) they are gradually building more diversified systems.

Because of a number of changes in the administration of state and local debt, we saw that (6) the state and local governments are able to borrow to finance their capital improvement projects. We also discussed the problems such governments may encounter if they take on too much debt or if they must borrow repeatedly to finance current operations.

We noted that (7) expenditures for education, welfare, highways, and health services have dominated spending at the state level. At the community level spending for education comes first, with public safety, health, welfare, and highways next in order of importance. Finally we observed that (8) in times of extended fiscal stress the states and communities must turn to their areas of major spending to achieve substantial reductions.

In this chapter we defined the following terms in this order: Gross National Product (GNP), state collected–locally shared revenues, state-mandated programs, horizontal equity, vertical equity, progressive tax, regressive tax, user fee or charge, elasticity, excise tax, graduated rates, indexing, equalization, severance taxes, off-budget expenditures, capital budget, and budget carryover.

NOTES

1. *Significant Features of Fiscal Federalism* (Washington, D.C.: Advisory Commission on Intergovernmental Relations, Vol. I, 1989), p. 21.
2. *Significant Features of Fiscal Federalism* (Washington, D.C.: Advisory Commission on Intergovernmental Relations, Vol. II, 1988), p. 82.
3. *Significant Features of Fiscal Federalism*, Vol. II, p. 81.
4. The case in California, perhaps, had the greatest impact. *Serrano v. Priest*, 938254, Los Angeles, S.Ct., 29820 (1971).
5. David Lowery, "The Distribution of Tax Burdens in the American States: The Determinants of Fiscal Incidence," *Western Political Quarterly* (1987): 137–158.
6. Data for this section are drawn from various issues of The Tax Foundation, *Facts and Figures on Government Finance*, 1988–89 ed. (Baltimore: Johns Hopkins University Press, 1988), and *Significant Features of Fiscal Federalism* (Washington, D.C.: Advisory Commission on Intergovernmental Relations).
7. *Changing Public Attitudes on Governments and Taxes* (Washington, D.C.: Advisory Commission on Intergovernmental Relations, 1988), p. 3.
8. James A. Maxwell and J. Richard Aronson, *Financing State and Local Government* (3rd ed.) (Washington, D.C.: Brookings Institution, 1977), p. 106.
9. *Significant Features of Fiscal Federalism* (1987), p. 70.
10. *Significant Features of Fiscal Federalism*, p. 83.

11. *Significant Features of Fiscal Federalism* (Washington, D.C.: Advisory Commission on Intergovernmental Relations, Vol. I, 1989), pp. 72–73.
12. Edwin R. A. Seligman, *Essays in Taxation* (New York: Macmillan, 1895).
13. *Significant Features of Fiscal Federalism* (Washington, D.C.: Advisory Commission on Intergovernmental Relations, 1980–1981), p. 49. Henry J. Aaron, in *Who Pays the Property Tax? A New View* (Washington, D.C.: Brookings Institution), argues that the important consideration is whether the combined taxes a person pays are regressive, not whether a single tax is regressive. The ACIR analysis indicates that the combination of federal, state, and local taxes in 1980 was indeed progressive. But combined state and local taxes were regressive.
14. Debra R. Sanderson Stinson, *Tax Exemptions in Central Cities and Suburbs: A Comparison Across States* (New Haven: Institution for Social and Policy Studies, Yale University, 1975). This study of tax-exempt properties covered 20 states where data were available. Because tax exempt properties are not assessed, the actual total value of exempt properties is difficult to obtain.
15. *The Detroit News*, (December 18, 1988).
16. *State and Local Taxation and Industrial Location* (Washington, D.C.: Advisory Commission on Intergovernmental Relations, Report A-30, 1967), p. 62.
17. Strictly speaking, companies pay premiums rather than taxes to meet the costs of workers' compensation for job-related injuries or deaths. But because it is a closely regulated state program and state administered, workers' compensation policies are important business considerations.
18. See Martin Shefter, "New York City's Fiscal Crisis: The Politics of Inflation and Retrenchment," in Charles H. Levine (ed.), *Managing Fiscal Stress* (Chatham, N.J.: Chatham House Publishers, 1980), pp. 71–94.
19. *Significant Features of Fiscal Federalism* (Washington, D.C.: Advisory Commission on Intergovernmental Relations, Vol. I, 1989), p. 14.
20. David C. Nice, "State Support for Balanced Budget Requirements," *Journal of Politics* 48 (1986): 134–139.
21. Robert Albritton and Ellen M. Dran, "Balanced Budgets and State Surpluses: The Politics of Budgeting in Illinois," *Public Administration Review* (March/April 1987): 143–152.
22. These data reflect preintergovernmental transfer expenditures in which federal aid to state governments is counted as a federal expenditure. The national government role is less pronounced when intergovernmental transfers are counted as expenditures by the receiving level.
23. "The Surplus Shortage," *Governing* (December 1988): 56.
24. James C. Garand, "Partisan Change and Shifting Expenditure Priorities in the American States, 1945–1978," *American Politics Quarterly* 13:4 (1985): 355–391.

Index

Aaron, Henry J., 452n
Abney, Glenn, 184n, 185n, 281n
Abourezk, James, 109
Abrams, Albert J., 248n
Abramson, Paul R., 214n
Access, defined, 136
Administration bills, defined, 209
Administrative reorganization, 301
Administrative rules, defined, 222
Administrators
   administrative reorganization, 301–305
   budgets, 268, 305–309
   control of, 300–315
   executive departments, 266–273
   legislative oversight, 221–222, 293, 310–312
   media influence on, 314
   merit system, 284–288
   ombudsmen, 314–315
   patronage systems, 4, 190, 285–287
   privatization, 312–313
   professionalism, 289–294
   sunset laws, 169, 222, 312
   unionization of, 294–300
Advisory Commission on Intergovernmental Relations, (ACIR), defined, 79
AFL-CIO, 160, 172, 174
African Americans. *See* Blacks
AFSCME (American Federation of State, County, and Municipal Agenda Employees), 168, 294, 300
Agnew, Spiro, 280n
Alabama, 18, 23, 46, 58n, 61, 72, 105, 112, 119n, 134, 161, 162, 169, 189, 190, 202, 224, 244, 258, 275, 302, 326, 348n, 407
Alaska, 23, 25, 37, 45, 51, 64, 71, 72, 112, 104, 107, 113, 198, 253, 282n, 333, 352, 382n, 400, 425, 434, 435
Alba, Richard, 41

Albany, New York, 200
Albritton, Robert, 452n
Albuquerque, New Mexico, 344
Aldrich, John H., 214n
Alford, Robert, 383n
Allen, Tip H., Jr., 120n
Allentown, Pennsylvania, 304
Almond, Gabriel, 129, 153n
Alsfeld, Richard, 185n
American Bar Association, 77
American Federation of Teachers, 166
American Samoa, 65
Amish, 389
Annapolis Convention, 76
Anderson, Wendell, 255
Angoff, Charles, 30–31, 44, 56n
Animal rights groups, 150
Annexation, 398–399
   defined, 387
Anticipatory reactions, defined, 164
Anti-nuclear demonstrators, 150
Apodaca v. *Oregon*, 350n
Appellate jurisdiction, defined, 321
Appointing powers, defined, 261
Argersinger v. *Hamlin*, 348n
Ariyoshi, George, 258
Arizona, 25, 30, 38, 50, 64, 113, 201, 226, 253, 258, 259, 272, 274, 275, 279n, 280n, 282n, 348n, 449
Arkansas, 22, 47, 76, 107, 108, 112, 114, 116n, 118n, 158, 202, 217, 264, 265, 272, 281n
Arnall, Ellis, 46
Aronson, J. Richard, 80, 88n, 451n
Arraignment proceedings, defined, 321
Articles of Confederation, 62, 79
Asian Americans, 42
Askew, Rubin, 255
Aspin, Larry T., 349n

453

Associated Students of Kansas (ASK), 2
Atkins v. *Kansas*, 382*n*
Atlanta, Georgia, 124, 394
At-large elections, defined, 368
Attentive publics, defined, 129
Attorney General's office, 270
Auditor general, defined, 222
Audubon Society, 164
Austin, Texas, 50
Average citizens, defined, 123
Axelrod, Donald, 317*n*

Babbitt, Bruce, 275
Bachelor, Lynn W., 318*n*
Bachrach, Peter, 125, 152*n*
Baer, Michael, 149, 155*n*, 160, 184*n*, 185*n*, 317*n*
Baer, William C., 391, 412*n*
Bailey, Larry P., 318*n*
Bailey, John, 207, 286, 316*n*
Bailles, Gerald, 271
Baker, Ray Stannard, 8
Baker v. *Carr*, 45, 105, 241
Baltimore, Maryland, 115, 348*n*
Balutis, Alan P., 248*n*
Banfield, Edward C., 383*n*, 391, 412*n*
Baratz, Morton, 125, 152*n*
Barber, Bernard, 316*n*
Barbour, Philip, 95
Bardach, Eugene, 318*n*
Barnett, Frances, 412*n*
Barone, Michael, 11
Barr, Burton, 274
Barrilleaux, Charles J., 214*n*
Barron v. *Mayor and City Council of Baltimore*, 348*n*
Basehart, Harry, 294*n*
Bass, Jack, 58*n*, 154*n*, 214*n*
Baton Rouge, Louisiana, 400
Bauer, Raymond A., 185*n*
Bazar, Beth, 246*n*
Beadle, Frank, 234
Beard, Charles, 93
Bebout, John, 86, 89*n*
Beck, Paul Allen, 131, 154*n*
Beer, Samuel H., 73, 87*n*
Behn, Robert D., 312, 318*n*
Bell, Charles G., 184*n*
Belleranti, Shirley W., 58*n*
Bender, Lewis G., 412*n*

Benedict, Robert C., 154*n*
Bennett, Stephen Earl, 153*n*
Bennett, William, 407
Benson, Lee, 57*n*
Benton, J. Edwin, 413*n*
Berelson, Bernard, 151*n*
Berendt, John, 57*n*
Berenyi, Eileen Brettler, 318*n*
Berg, Larry L., 349*n*
Bergerson, Peter J., 349*n*
Bernick, E. Lee, 281*n*
Berra, Yogi, 389
Berry, Jeffrey, 163, 184*n*, 185*n*, 186*n*
Beutler, John W., 382*n*
Beyle, Thad L., 278*n*, 279*n*, 280*n*, 282*n*, 317*n*
Bibby, John F., 212*n*
Bicameral, defined, 369
Bifactionalism, defined, 200
Bill analysis, defined, 237
Bill of Rights, 70, 110, 115, 179, 344–346, 348*n*
    defined, 63
Binding arbitration, defined, 297
Binford, Michael B., 177, 185*n*
Bird, Rose, 334, 335, 340
Birmingham, Alabama, 407
Black, Richard L., 361, 382*n*
Blacks
    alienation, 148
    and consolidation, 401
    demonstrations, 126
    discrimination, 45–46, 58*n*, 76, 96, 134–136, 285, 388
    and initiatives, 110
    as interest group, 160, 161–162, 165, 177
    and metro, 404
    migration of, 38, 42
    officeholding, 45, 58*n*, 259
    party faction, 201
    political participation, 68, 134–136, 142, 148, 189
    and reapportionment, 242
    voting rights act, 105, 135–136
Blackmun, Harry, 85
Blair, Diane D., 116*n*, 265, 281*n*
Blanchard, James, 257, 405–406
Blank, Robert R., 154*n*
Blanket primary, defined, 198
Blanton, Ray, 76
Bledsoe, Timothy, 375, 383*n*

Block grants, defined, 81
Bloom, Prescott E., 246n
Bluedorn, Allen C., 318n
Boles, Donald E., 347n
Bollens, John C., 382n
Bone, Hugh A., 154n, 281n
Boorstin, Daniel, 146
Booth, David A., 413n
Boston, Massachusetts, 18, 46, 61, 393, 395
Bosworth, Karl A., 383n
Bowman, Lewis, 213n
Boynton, G. R., 247n
Bracketing, defined, 364
Bradley, Thomas, 259
Branti v. *Finkel*, 348n
Brasfield, James M., 413n
Breaux, David, 248n
Brennan, William J., Jr., 330, 334, 348n
Brodbeck, Arthur J., 59n
Brokerage parties, defined, 189
Brooks, Glenn E., 88n
Brooks, Jack, 429
Brooks, Phill, 154n
Brown, Charles W., 118n
Brown, Edmund (Jerry), 195, 262, 334
Brown, John Y., Jr., 254
Brown, Robert E., 117n
Browne, William P., 158, 184n, 185n, 248n, 412n
Brownlow, Louis, 317n
Brown v. *Board of Education*, 46, 83, 96, 161
Brudney, Jeffrey L., 316n
Bryan, Frank M., 45, 58n, 246n
Bryce, James, 3–4, 26n, 100, 118n, 212n, 382n
Buchwald, Art, 293, 316n
Budget carryover, defined, 448
Budgets, 268, 305–309
Burbank, Garin, 37, 57n
Burdick, Eugene, 59n
Burger, Warren, 328, 337, 349n
Burrell, Barbara C., 213n
Bush, George, 64, 66, 86, 239, 267, 280n, 293, 450
Butler, David, 118n
Bypassing, defined, 80
Byrne, Gary C., 144

Cadre parties, defined, 190
Caldeira, Gregory A., 131, 153n, 214n

Calhoun, John, 37
California, 22, 25, 37, 38, 41, 42, 43, 45, 50, 51, 61, 71, 72, 76, 77, 97, 102, 103, 107, 108, 110, 119n, 126, 144–145, 146, 168, 177, 179, 199, 200, 204, 213n, 236, 241, 243, 244, 249n, 252, 259, 262, 263, 267, 275, 300, 301, 310, 334, 343, 349n, 380, 382n, 389, 392, 393, 396, 399, 417, 422, 425, 429, 451n
Callow, Alexander B., Jr., 26n
Campaigns, 202–207
  media influence in, 204–207
  state financed, 208–209
Campbell, Alan, 388, 412n
Canon, Bradley C., 214n
Caperton, Gasper, 55
Capital budgets, defined, 444
Capone, Al, 240
Caputo, David, 146, 155n, 414n
Career paths, defined, 255
Carlson, James M., 189, 212n
Caroline Islands, 65
Carroll, John J., 120n, 210, 215n, 248n
Carter, Jimmy, 22, 83, 109, 195, 252, 257, 275, 280n, 308, 309
Carver, Joan S., 47, 58n
Casey, Robert, 389
Cash, W. J., 57n
Cassel, Carol A., 375, 383n
Categorical grants, defined, 80
Caudill, Harry M., 155n
Center for the American Woman and Politics (CAWP), 58n
Centers for Disease Control, 56n
Centralization, defined, 5
Chandler, Albert B. (Happy), 200, 213n
Charleston, South Carolina, 37, 40
Checks and balances, defined, 3
Checota, Joseph W., 195
Chicago, 131, 193, 200, 228, 252, 286, 364, 369, 393, 399, 407
Chief administrative officer (CAO), defined, 369
Childs, Richard S., 372, 373, 374, 383n
Cho, Yong Hyo, 59n
Chubb, John E., 88n
Cingranelli, David, 87n
Circuit breaker tax credit, 433
Citizen participation
  costs and benefits of, 139–147
  through demonstrations, 126

Citizen participation (*Continued*)
  direct democracy, 107–111, 136–139
  by elites, 122–126
  lack of, 121–122
  legal rules, 134–139
  media and information costs, 142–147
  by nonelites, 133
  opportunities for, 139
  registration 141–142
  through social movements, 149–150
Citizens Conference on State Legislatures, 244, 249n
Citrin, Jack, 155n
City charter, defined, 364
City-county consolidation, 399–402
City of Trenton v. *New Jersey*, 382n
Civil service system, defined, 192, 270
Civil disobedience, defined, 126
Civil war, political impact, 43–44
Clark, Robert Bradley, 214n
Clark, Timothy S., 186n
Clear Lake City, Texas, 399
Cleveland, Ohio, 31, 46
Clinton, Bill, 264, 272
Closed primary, defined, 198
Cloward, Richard A., 27n, 152n, 154n
Cochran, Thad, 429
Codispoti, Frank, 279n
Cohen, Bernard, 155n
Cohesive party, defined, 200
Colburn, David R., 281n
Cole, Richard, 146, 155n, 414n
Collins, Martha Layne, 258
Colorado, 23, 29, 38, 42, 107, 113, 118n, 169, 199, 218, 281n, 312, 338, 392
Columbus, Ohio, 392
Columbus-Muscogee County, Georgia, 400
Comer, John C., 249n, 318n
Commager, Henry Steele, 93
Commission plan, defined, 371
Common law, defined, 327
Common Cause, 168, 169, 175, 179, 181, 242
Commonwealth ex rel. Carroll v. *Tate*, 350n
Community governments
  annexation, 398–399
  central city decay, 388–392
  city charters, 363–365
  city-county consolidation, 399–402
  city organization, 367–368
  commission plan, 371–372
  council-manager plan, 372–375
  councils of government, 397–398
  county, 361–362
  federal relationships, 377–380
  growth of suburbs, 386–390
  intergovernmental contracts, 396–397
  intergovernmental lobby, 18, 358–361
  intergovernmental relations, 385–411
  metropolitan governments, 402–403
  neighborhood control, 403–407
  rural countryside, 392–393
  schools, 166–167, 219–221, 366
  services, 375–376
  SMSAs, 393–394
  special districts, 395–396
  state control, 353–355, 363–365, 391–392, 407–411
  strong mayor-council plan, 369–371
  towns and townships, 362–363
  weak mayor-council plan, 368–369
Compact, defined, 77
Competitive party majority, defined, 202
Conant, James K., 317n
Concurrent powers, defined, 63
Confederation, defined, 62
Conference committee, defined, 236
Conference of State Legislatures, 378
Conkling, Roscoe, 191
Connecticut, 50, 66, 71, 72, 76, 90, 91, 96, 124, 178, 197, 199, 207, 209, 212n, 224, 243, 258, 286, 352, 382n, 425, 436
Connor, Walker, 58n
Consolidation, defined, 399
Constituent services, defined, 218
Constitutional initiative, defined, 107
Constitutional study commission, defined, 112
Constitutional majority, defined, 232
Constitutions, state
  amendment of, 107–112
  constitutional conventions, 112–115
  importance, 92–96
  legal elements, 91–92
  length of, 98–104
  model state constitution, 104
  politics of, 95–96
  reform of, 97–99, 101–103, 105–115
Consumer Price Index, 417
Cook, Constance Ewing, 184n

Cooper, Marx, 326
Cooperative federalism, defined, 68
Corbon, Susan B., 349*n*
Cornwell, Elmer E., 107, 115, 118*n*, 120*n*
Corrupt practice laws, defined, 179
Costantini, Edmond, 213*n*
Council of State Governments, 5
  defined, 77
Council districts, defined, 368
Council-manager plan, 372–375
Councils of governments (COGs), 397
Countervailing groups, defined, 178
Court system
  appeals courts, 325–326
  common law, 326–327
  court management, 338–339
  federalization of, 78–79, 85–86, 93–94, 105,
    127, 211, 241–242, 321, 326–331, 378–380
  general trial courts, 324–325
  judicial bureaucracy, 335–338
  judicial lawmaking, 327–328
  juries, 340–342
  jurisdiction, 320–321
  limitations on judges, 335–336, 339–346
  minor courts, 321–323
  politics of, 331–339
  prosecutors, 340
  recruitment and removal of judges, 332–335
  sentencing, 345–346
  special courts, 323–324
  structure, 320–326
  symbols of impartiality, 320
Court administrator, defined, 335–338
Court of last resort, defined, 321
Court watching, defined, 324
Cox, Raymond W., 248*n*, 250*n*
Creative federalism, defined, 70
Crossover voting, defined, 198
Cruz, Roberto, 137
Cunningham, Everett, 214*n*
Cuomo, Mario, 271, 272

Dade County, Florida, 356, 400
Dahl, Robert, 124, 152*n*
Daley, Richard, 228, 369
Daley, Richard (Dick), Jr., 369
Dallas, Texas, 50, 313, 374
Dauer, Manning J., 117*n*
Davis v. *Bandemer*, 249*n*

Davis, Charles E., 87*n*
Davis, Jefferson, 44, 87*n*
Davis, Jimmy, 205
Dawson, Richard, 58*n*
Dealey, James Quayle, 117*n*
Decisional approach, defined, 124
Declerq, Eugene, 247*n*
Delaware, 22, 25, 31, 37, 64, 66, 92, 108, 109,
  111*n*, 119*n*, 136, 199, 226, 256, 280*n*, 323,
  389, 425
Del Bello, Al, 271, 272
Delegated powers, defined, 63
Delmatier, Royce D., 118*n*
Democratic party majority, defined, 202
Democratic party dominant, defined, 202
Democratic political process, defined, 52
Democratization, defined, 8
Denhardt, Robert B., 318*n*
Denver, Colorado, 137, 381*n*, 392
DePalma, Anthony, 412*n*
Department of Management and Budget,
  defined, 269
Depression, political impact, 44
Derthick, Martha, 88*n*
de Sola Pool, Ithiel, 185*n*
Detroit, 127, 196, 259, 365, 434
Devolution of powers, defined, 365
DeVries, Walter, 58*n*, 154*n*, 174, 185*n*, 201, 205,
  214*n*
Dexter, Lewis Anthony, 185*n*
Dillon's rule, 363
  defined, 355
Direct democracy, 107–111, 136–139
  defined, 136
Direct primary, defined, 192
Discretionary authority, defined, 364
Dishman, Robert, 117*n*
Dobriner, William M., 412*n*
Dobson, Douglas, 184*n*
Dometrius, Nelson C., 280*n*
Dorr, Thomas, 101
Downing, Randal, 332, 348*n*, 349*n*
Downs, Anthony, 184*n*
Dran, Ellen, 452*n*
Drug war, 239–240
Dual federalism, defined, 65
DuBois, Philip J., 348*n*
Ducat, Craig R., 349*n*
Due process clause, defined, 328

Dukakis, Michael 41, 83, 273, 275, 280n, 293
Duncomb, Herbert S., 11, 382n
Dutton, William H., 185n, 383n
Dye, Thomas, 58n, 151n, 375

Eaker, Jamie D., 256n
Ecology of games, defined, 125
Economic development, defined, 50
Edgewood v. *Kirby*, 219
Edwards, Edwin, 278
Efficiency and economy, defined, 309
Egger, Roland, 280n
Ehrenhalt, Alan, 152n, 185n
Eisenhower, Dwight, 79
Elasticity, defined, 424
Elastic (necessary and proper) clause, defined, 63
Elazar, Daniel, 38–41, 52, 57n, 87n, 131, 330, 348n
Elite participation, 122–126
Elliott, Donald, 413n
England, Robert E., 318n, 384n
English, Arthur, 120n, 210, 215n, 248n
Engstrom, Richard L., 120n
Enokson, Stephen N., 153n
Entitlement grants, defined, 377
Epstein, Deborah, 276–277
Epstein, Laurily Keir, 158, 184n
Equal protection clause, defined, 328
Equalization, defined, 433
Equal Rights Amendment (ERA), 123, 159
Erikson, Robert, 52, 59n
Eskimos, 45
Ethridge, Marcus E., 182, 186n, 246n
Eulau, Heinz, 246n
Everson, David H., 119n, 207, 215n
Excise tax, defined, 425
Exclusionary rule, defined, 364
Executive amendment, defined, 268
Executive budget, defined, 268, 305
Extralegal party organizations, defined, 199
Extraordinary majority, defined, 266

Fairbanks, David, 41, 58n
Fairchild, Mary, 154n
FALN (Puerto Rico), 67
Fannin, William R., 383n
Farrace, V. Lance, 214n
Faxon, Jack, 196

Federalism
 administrator independence, 292–293
 and brokerage parties, 189–190, 195–197
 and community governments, 377–378, 385–411
 cooperation among states, 76–78
 cooperative federalism, 68–69
 defense of, 25–26, 82–85
 dual federalism, 65–68
 dynamic, xvii–xviii, 16–19, 65–75
 fair shares, 71–72
 federal transfer payments, 419–420
 financial interdependence, 450
 fiscal federalism, 70
 functional federalism, 73
 and Good Government reform, 7
 governors' actions, 274–275
 grantsmanship federalism, 73–74, 79–81
 interest group lobbying, 159
 intergovernmental lobby, 18, 358–361
 legal elements, 62–65, 75–76, 78–79
 naionalization, 60–61, 65–76
 and party organization, 188
 permissive federalism, 70–73
 and Progressive reform, 10
 state focused, 74–75
 and Supreme Court, 78–79, 85–86, 93–94, 105, 127, 211, 241–242, 321, 326–331, 378–380
Federal Reserve System, 78
Federation, defined, 62
Feig, Douglas G., 249n
Feminist movement. *See* Women in politics
Ferguson, Meriam A. "Ma," 58n, 258
Field, John O., 383n
Finances, state and local
 borrowing, 439–445
 business taxes, 434–436
 diversification, 436–439
 evaluating tax options, 423–424
 fiscal federalism, 70
 general sales tax, 425–428
 intergovernmental transfers, 418–423
 miscellaneous charges, 436
 personal income taxes, 428–432
 property taxes, 432–434
 spending patterns, 445–450
 trends, 416–418
Fiorina, Morris P., 153n
First Evangelical Lutheran Church v. *County of Los Angeles*, 379

Fiscal federalism, defined, 70
Fiske, Jim, 191
Flango, Victor E., 349n
Fletcher v. *Peck*, 186n
Flint, Michigan, 43
Florida, 23, 30, 38, 41, 47, 50, 71, 77, 97, 108, 119n, 137, 158, 164, 201, 253, 254, 255, 257, 267, 275, 347n, 356, 389, 393, 400, 413n, 425
Ford Foundation, 182
Fordham, Jefferson B., 365, 382n
Forstall, Richard L., 412n
Franchini, Gene, 344
Frank, Jerome, 350n
Franke, James L., 184n
Franklin, Benjamin, 138
Frazier, Lynn, 253
Frederickson, George, 59n
Freedman, Anne, 316n
Frendreis, John P., 213n
Friedelbaum, Stanley H., 350n
Friedman, Milton, 59n
Friedman, Robert S., 119n
Frost, Robert, 52
Frost Belt (Rust Belt or Snow Belt), 19, 51, 71, 72, 376, 386
Fry, Brian R., 59n
Full Faith and Credit Clause, defined, 75
Functional federalism, defined, 73

Gabler, Neal, 214n
Gaffney v. *Cummings*, 248n
Galie, Peter J., 348n
Galveston, Texas, 371
Gamble, Darwin, 413n
Garand, James C., 452n
Garcia v. *San Antonio Metropolitan Transit Authority*, 85, 317n, 384n
Gardner, Booth, 266
Garfield, James A., 191, 284
Garner, John Nance, 271
Gassaway, Bob M., 154n
Gates, John B., 79, 88n
Gay Rights movement, 149
Gelb, Joyce, 215n
General law charters, 363
General revenue sharing, defined, 81
General trial courts, defined, 320
Gentrificaion, 392
Gentry, Rick, 154n

George-Brown, Phyllis, 254
Georgia, 22, 43, 46, 52, 71, 113, 119n, 178, 189, 202, 252, 254, 257, 275, 279n, 280n, 281n, 308, 309, 364, 394
Gerrymander, defined, 194, 242
Gettleman, Marvin E., 117n
Gibson, James L., 213n
Gideon v. *Wainwright*, 348n
Ginsburg, Sigmund G., 316n, 317n
Gitelson, Alan R., 213n
Gitlow v. *New York*, 328, 348n
Gittell, Marilyn, 414n
Glazer, Nathan, 350n
Goel, M. L., 153n, 184n
Gold, S. D., 299n
Goldschmidt, Neil, 257, 389
Goldwater, Barry, 239
Goldwin, Robert A., 27n, 28n
Good government reform movement
  administrative reorganization, 302
  and civil service, 284
  and constitutions, 97–99, 104
  council-manager plan, 372–375
  criticisms of, 6–7
  defined, 4
  efficiency and economy in administration, 289–294, 301–305, 309
  executive budget, 268
  and governors, 261–262, 268–269
  and legislatures, 243–245
  managerial efficiency, 5
  model state constitution, 104
  National Municipal League, 5, 364, 372; defined, 97
  and parties, 192
  and political machines, 4–5
Goodman, Jay S., 120n
Goodnow, Frank J., 4
Gordon, Meryl, 161
Gormley, William T., 87n, 143, 145, 154n
Gosling, James J., 281n
Gosnell, Harold, 11, 27n, 153n, 212n
Gould, Jay, 191
Gove, Samuel K., 120n, 248n, 250n
Governmental fragmentation, defined, 394
Governmental legitimacy, defined, 101
Governmental structure, defined, 2
Governors
  appointment of judges, 332–334

Governors (*Continued*)
    background, 253–259
    colonial governors, 260–261
    executive budgeting, 268, 305–309
    executive departments, 266–273
    intergovernmental relations, 274–275
    Jacksonian influence, 260–261
    leadership functions, 253, 262–278
    legal powers, 260–262
    and party, 209–210, 273–274
    program in legislature, 209–210, 265–268
    public opinion, 263–265
    staff, 268–269
    veto power, 266–268
Grad, Frank P., 104, 117n, 118n
Graduated tax rates, defined, 431
Graham, Bob, 254
Graham, Gene, 248n
Granbato, James S., 384n
Grand jury, defined, 342
Granger, Bill, 138
Grant, Edward D., III, 113, 119n
Grant, Ulysses S., 190
Grantsmanship federalism, defined, 74
Grasso, Ella, 50, 258
Gray, Virginia, 58n, 185n
Gray Panthers, 149
Green, Fletcher M., 117n
Greenfield, Meg, 310, 318n
Greenstein, Fred I., 153n
Greenville, South Carolina, 126
Grenzke, Janet M., 182, 186n
Griffin, Robert, 109
Grodzins, Morton, 87n, 88n
Gross, Bertram, 317n
Gross, Donald A., 214n
Gross national product (GNP), defined, 417
Grosse, Andrew D., 413n
Group cohesiveness, defined, 164
Group legitimacy, defined, 164
Gruhl, John, 349n
Grupp, Fred W., Jr., 316n
Guam, 65, 333
Guiteau, Charles J., 284
Gun control, 169
Gurwitt, Rob, 282n
Gusteley, Richard D., 414n

Hacker, Andrew, 344, 359n

Hadley, Arthur T., 153n
Hadley, Charles D., 185n, 186n
Haeberle, Steven H., 414n
Hahn, Harlan, 107, 118n, 119n
Haider, Donbald H., 87n
Hain, Paul L., 247n, 349n
Hale, George E., 74, 87n, 316n
Hall, William K., 281n, 349n
Hallman, Howard W., 414n
Hamilton, Alexander, 62, 93
Hamilton, Charles V., 142, 154n
Hamilton, Christopher, 87n
Hamilton, Howard, 189, 212n
Hamm, Keith E., 184n, 383n
Hannah, Susan B., 348n
Hansen, J. M., 163, 184n
Harlan, Christi, 347n
Harlan, Kentucky, 322
Harmony, Rita, 119n
Harrigan, John J., 413n
Harris, Louis, 280n
Harris, William T., 95
Hart, Vivien, 155n
Hartford, Connecticut, 137
Hatch Acts, 285
Hatfield, Mark, 109
Hatry, Harry P., 318n
Havard, William C., 117n
Hawaii, 30, 64, 71, 107, 112, 113, 168, 202, 206, 258, 282n, 428
Hawkins, Brett, 249n
Hayden, Michael, 266
Heaphey, James J., 248n
Hearns, Betty, 258
Hebert, F. Ted, 280n, 316n
Hedge, David M., 316n
Heinze, John P., 185n
Hellriegel, Don, 383n
Hendrick, Burton J., 87n
Henry, Ann R., 247n
Henry, Gary T., 246n
Herndon, James, 332, 349n
Herson, Lawrence W., 27n
Herzberg, Donald G., 249n
Herzik, Eric, 57n
Hobbes, Thomas, 51–52
Hofheinz, Fred, 399
Hofstetter, C. Richard, 57n
Holbrook, Stewart H., 212n

Holland, Arthur J., 373
Holli, Melvin G., 27n
Holmes, Oliver Wendell, 95
Home rule, defined, 364
Hoover Commission, 305, 317n
Hopper, Stanley D., 214n
Horizontal equity, defined, 424
Hornblower, Margot, 186n
Houston, Texas, 50, 394, 399, 413n
Howard, A. E. Dick, 117n, 119n, 384n
Huckshorn, Robert J., 212n, 213n
Hueffner, Robert, 278n
Hughes, Howard, 76
Hulbary, William, E., 213n
Humphrey, Hubert, 279n
Hung jury, defined, 341
Hunter, Floyd, 124, 152n
Hutchinson, William T., 317n
Hy, Ronald Hohn, 382n
Hude, Mark S., 185n
Hyman, Herbert, 184n
Hyneman, Charles S., 57n, 225, 246n

Idaho, 23, 37, 85, 113, 119n, 195, 199, 302, 449
Illinois, 41, 46, 71, 76, 108, 114, 115, 118n, 119n, 120n, 123, 143, 200, 207, 229, 235, 247n, 250n, 256, 266, 267, 271, 280n, 281n, 287, 301, 326, 364, 369, 382n, 393, 399, 407, 429, 432
Image building, defined, 259
Incremental decision making, defined, 12
Indeterminate sentences, defined, 343
Indexing, defined, 432
Indiana, 52, 96, 102, 109, 112, 119n, 124, 259, 286, 363, 400, 405, 413n, 432
Indianapolis, Marion County, Indiana (Unigov), 400, 401, 413n
Individualist political culture, defined, 39
Infant mortality rate, 45-46, 57n, 58n
 defined, 30
Influentials, defined, 122
Information costs, defined, 140
Infrastructure, defined, 386
Ingram, Helen, 89n
Initiative, 118n, 119n
 defined, 103, 136
 Proposition 2 1/2, 25
 Proposition 13, 25, 433
In Re Gault, 348n

Interest groups
 access points, 171-172
 cohesiveness, 164
 control of, 178-182
 financial campaigns, 177-178, 181, 182-183
 iron triangles, 169-171
 leadership, 163
 legitimacy of, 164-165
 lobbying techniques, 174-177
 lobbyists, 172-174
 on trial, 157
 patterns, 158-159, 167-169
 penetration, 157, 169-171
 who lobbies, 159-163
Interest group entrepreneurs, defined, 163
Intergovernmenteal contracts, defined, 396
Intergovernmental lobby, 358
Intergovernmental relations, defined, 2
Intermediate appeals court, defined, 321
International City Management Association, 5
Interstate rendition, defined, 76
Iowa, 23, 46, 47, 50, 159, 160, 209, 225, 272, 302, 326, 347n, 349n, 355, 364, 405, 425, 431
Iron triangles, defined, 169
Item veto, defined, 267

Jackson, Brooks, 186n
Jackson, Jesse, 42, 162, 163
Jacksonian democracy
 and administration, 285-287
 and attack on establishment, 7, 57n, 104, 190
 and constitutions, 101-102
 defined, 260
 election of judges, 332
 extending franchise, 101
 on governors, 260-262, 280n
 individualism, 39
 justice of peace courts, 322-323
 and legislatures, 244
 as a social movement, 149
 weak mayor-council plan, 368-369
Jacksonville-Duval County, Florida, 400, 402, 413n
Jacob, Herbert, 185n, 249n, 279n
Jacqueney, Theodore, 186n
Jaros, Dean, 149, 155n
Jarvis, Howard, 335
Jefferson, Thomas, 361

Jencks, Christopher, 20, 27n
Jennings, M. Kent, 131, 154n
Jewell, Malcolm, 27n, 199, 200, 202, 213n, 214n, 215n, 247n, 248n, 382n
Job conditions, defined, 297
Johnson, Andrew, 64
Johnson, Chapman, 95
Johnson, Charles A., 57n
Johnson, Hiram, 103
Johnson, Lyndon, 70, 73, 81, 308
Johnson, Richard R., 279n, 280n, 282n
Johnson, William C., 413n
Joiner, Charles, 325, 347n
Joint Center for Political Studies, 58n
Jones, Bryan D., 377, 383n
Jones, Charles O., 59n
Jones, Ruth S., 206, 214n
Jordan, Robert B., 271
Jordan, Vernon, 161
Josephson, Matthew, 190, 212n
Judges. *See* Court system
Judicial review, defined, 92
Judicial tenure commissions, defined, 335
Juneau-Greater Juneau Borough, Alaska, 400
Justice of the peace courts (JP), defined, 322

Kahn, Melvin, 281n
Kamieniecki, Sheldon, 107, 118n, 119n
Kandell, Jonathon, 28n
Kane, Hartnet, 152n
Kansas, 2, 13, 43, 47, 58n, 118n, 150, 225, 266, 281n, 382n
Kansas City, Kansas, 371
Kansas City, Missouri, 45, 404
Karnig, Albert K., 250n
Kasten, Bob, 430
Kaufman, Herbert, 284, 316n
Keefe, Frank, 392
Keefe, William, 232, 247n, 248n
Keith, Gary, 247n
Kelley, Anne E., 213n
Kelley, Frank, 208
Kelley, Richard C., 213n
Kelly, Tish, 145
Kennedy, David, 119n
Kennedy, Edward M., 195
Kennedy, John F., 41, 54, 209
Kentucky, 22, 23, 44, 71, 76, 85, 87n, 93, 105, 119n, 258, 262, 280n, 281n, 302, 322, 324, 378, 432, 435
Kerner, Otto, 266
Key, V. O., Jr., 19, 27n, 37, 52, 53, 57n, 59n, 123, 152n, 164, 184n, 188, 200, 201, 212n, 213n, 214n
Keynes, Edward, 213n
Kickbacks, defined, 191
Kilpatrick, James J., 27n
Kim, Jae-On, 153n
Kincaid, Diane, 247n
Kincaid, John, 282n
King, Martin Luther, Jr., 44, 123, 126, 134, 160, 161
King, Michael R., 248n, 250n
Kinsley, Michael, 20, 28n, 82, 88n
Kirk, Russell, 27n
Kitsos, Thomas R., 120n
Kleppner, Paul, 58n
Knox, Luther (None of the Above), 148
Kolderie, Ted, 413n
Kornhauser, William, 152n
Krane, Dale A., 383n
Krueger, Moria, 337
Kunin, Madeleine M., 258

Labor union, defined, 294
Ladd, Everett Carll, Jr., 155n, 213n
LaFever, John D., 317n
La Follette, Robert M., 43, 109, 117n, 284
Lakewood (California) plan, defined, 396
Lamar, Alexander, 252
Land grant, defined, 49
Land Grant Act, 68
Landau, Martin, 82, 88n
Lane, Robert, 184n
LaPalombara, Joseph, 152n
Lapham, Arthur, 350n
LaRouche, Lyndon, 271
Laski, Harold, 82, 88n
Las Vegas, Nevada, 401, 413n
Laumann, Edward O., 185n
Lauth, Thomas, 184n, 185n, 281n
Lawson, Kay, 213n
Lawyer legislators, 226
Lazarsfeld, Paul F., 151n
League of Women Voters, 5, 140, 147, 160, 400
Least Heat Moon, William, 61, 86n

LeDuke, Edgar, xviii
Legal powers, defined, 261
Legislative detail, defined, 97
Legislative liaison, defined, 266
Legislative lobbying, defined, 265
Legislative oversight, 221–222, 293, 310–312
Legislative veto, defined, 222
Legislators
　committees, 235–236
　compensation, 223–224, 228–230
　and employee unionization, 300
　functions, 217–222
　gerrymandering, 242–243
　governor's veto power, 266–268
　informal rules, 236–237
　legislative oversight, 221–222, 293, 310–312
　legislative rules, 230–234
　legislative process, 231, 238
　life-style, 223
　lobbying, 265
　nonpartisanship, 243–244
　occupations, 225–227
　officers, 234–235
　party voting, 210–211
　political evaluations of, 217
　professionalization, 245
　reapportionment, 241–243
　recruitment, 227–228
　reform, 241–245
　sessions, 222–223
　speaker, 234
　staff, 224–225, 237–238
　turnover, 228–230
　unicameralism, 243–244
Lehne, Richard, xviii
Lesinski, T. John, 271
Lester, James P., 87n
Levine, Charles H., 452n
Levine, James P., 348n
Levitt, Abraham, 387
　and Levittown, 387, 412n
Lewis, Nathan, 348n
Lexington-Fayette County, Kentucky, 400
Licht, Richard, 272
Lieberman, Joseph I., 215n, 316n
Lieutenant governors, 234, 255, 259, 270, 271–273
Limited constitutional conventions, defined, 113

Lincoln, Abraham, 325
Lineberry, Robert, 376, 383n
Lippmann, Walter, 151n
Lipset, Seymour Martin, 59n
Lipsky, Michael, 152n
Lipson, Leslie, 260, 280n
Literacy tests, defined, 135
Little Hoover Commissions, 302
Littlewood, Thomas, 154n
Lobbyist, defined, 157
Local governments. *See* Community governments
Lockard, Duane, 57n, 224, 246n, 247n
Locke, John, 92, 117n
Log-rolling, defined, 371
Long, Earl, 40, 205, 278, 282n
Long, Huey, 40, 205, 278, 282n
Long, Norton E., 125, 149, 152n, 155n, 253, 278n, 279n, 373, 383n
Longely, James, 273
Long Island, New York, 387
Los Angeles, 45, 137, 138, 204, 259, 313, 396
Lotteries, state, 436–439
Louis Brownlow Commission, 317n
Louisiana, 23, 29, 31, 71, 97, 104, 113, 114, 120n, 134, 157, 159, 164, 177, 202, 205, 214n, 278, 278n, 281n, 302, 348n, 364, 382n, 394, 400, 433, 434
Louisiana's nonpartison primary, defined, 198
Lovrich, Nicholas, Jr., 148, 155n
Low, Seth, 4
Lowden, Frank O., 301–302, 317n
Lowery, David, xviii, 40, 57n, 451n
Lowi, Theodore, 117n, 182, 186n
Lubell, Samuel, 41, 58n
Lucas, William, 259
Lucey, Patrick, 338
LULUs, 390
　defined, 404
Lutz, Donald S., 118n, 210, 215n
Lynd, Helen M., 27n, 152n
Lynd, Robert, 27n, 152n
Lyons, William, 246n, 249n
Lyons, W. E., 382n

Macaluso, Theodore, 131, 153n
McArthur, Robert E., 413n
McClesky, Clifton, 316n
McCombs, Maxwell, 155n

464 INDEX

McConnell, Grant, 117n
McCullough v. *Maryland*, 68
MacDonald, Stuart Elaine, 88n
McDonald's, 56n
McGovern, George, 243
McIntosh, Clarence F., 118n
McIver, John P., 59n
Macmahon, Arthur W., 88n
MacManus, Susan, 282n, 375
McNamara, Robert S., 308
McNitt, Andrew, 199, 213n
McPhee, William N., 151n
McPherson, Myra, 254, 279n
McWhirter, Ned, 267
MADD (Mothers Against Drunk Driving), 15, 123, 149, 169, 324
Maddox, Lester, 279n
Madison, James, 22, 93, 95
Madison, Wisconsin, 336–337
Madisonian system, defined, 3
Maggiotto, Michael A., 213n
Magleby, David M., 108, 118n, 119n
Maine, 25, 30, 113, 142, 261, 272, 273, 282n, 325, 389, 429
Management by Objectives (MBO), defined, 309
Managerial efficiency, defined, 5. *See also* Good government reformers
Manhardt, Meryl, 336
Mann, Horace, 95
Mapp v. *Ohio*, 329, 348n
Marenin, Otwin, 148, 155n
Marianas Islands, 65
Marshall, John, 68, 79, 95, 328
Marshall Islands, 65
Martin, Roscoe, 65
Martinez, Bob, 257, 258
Maryland, 44, 45, 71, 107, 114, 115, 142, 267, 280n, 304, 357, 348n, 364, 382n, 389, 432
Massachusetts, 20, 37, 41, 50, 51, 71, 72, 87n, 116n, 125, 162, 165, 189, 199, 206, 267, 274, 275, 280n, 284, 293, 297, 300, 302, 325, 347n, 349n, 392, 393, 395, 417
Mass party, defined, 190
Matching funds, defined, 80
Material benefits as a selective incentive, defined, 159
Mattek, David A., 413n
Matthews, Douglas, 11
Matthewson, 412n, 413n

Maxwell, James A., 80, 88n, 451n
May, Janice, 118n, 199n, 120n
Mayo brothers, 43
Mecham, Evan, 253, 258–259, 274, 279n, 282n
Media influence
    on administrators, 314
    in campaigns, 193, 204–207
    on the courts, 343
    on participation, 142–147
    on parties, 193
    and progressive reform, 9–10
Media consultants, defined, 204
Medical groups, 169–170
Meier, Kenneth J., 305, 306n, 307n, 317n, 348n
Memphis, Tennessee, 31
Mencken, H. L., 30–31, 44, 51, 56n
Menninger, Karl, 43
Menninger, William, 43
Merit employment, defined, 285
Merriam, Charles E., 153n
Merriam v. *Moody's Executors*, 382n
Merton, Robert K., 27n
Mezey, Susan Gluck, 50, 58
Miami, Florida, 126, 137, 165, 400
Michaelson, Richard D., 281n
Michigan, 15, 18, 20, 23, 37, 43, 45, 50, 71, 102, 104, 113, 114, 142, 159, 164, 168, 169, 175, 176, 185n, 195, 196, 197, 198, 199, 205, 206, 208, 212n, 233, 234, 239, 242, 257, 259, 263, 266, 267, 271, 311, 326, 338, 339, 342, 359n, 356, 365, 380, 382n, 392, 405–406, 432, 434, 440, 443, 444, 449
Midway Islands, 65
Miewald, Robert D., 318n
Milbrath, Lester, 153n, 184n
Miller, Arthur R., 155n
Miller, Gary J., 412n
Miller, Joel C., 412n
Miller, Mark R., 279n
Milliken, William, 205, 266
Mills, C. Wright, 27n, 152n
Milward, H. Brinton, 28n
Minneapolis, Minnesota, 264, 482
Minnesota, 22, 23, 36, 39, 50, 52, 77, 103, 108, 113, 119n, 142, 178, 225, 255, 262, 272, 297, 348n, 402, 403, 405, 413n
Minor courts, defined, 320
Miranda v. *Arizona*, 329, 348n
Misdemeanor offenses, defined, 321

Misssissippi, 13, 39, 40, 46, 141, 142, 157, 201, 202, 214n, 281n, 301, 425, 429
Missouri, 44, 71, 76, 95–92, 115, 143, 168, 177, 225, 235, 258, 280n, 287, 302, 313, 332, 349n, 364, 399, 404, 405
Missouri plan, defined, 332
Mladenka, Ken, xviii
Moakley, Maureen, 213n
Mobilization of bias, defined, 125
Mobley, Jane, 383n
Model state constitution, defined, 97
Modernization, defined, 50
Moe, Terry M., 185n
Mofford, Rose, 258
Moncrief, Gary F., 246n
Mondale, Walter, 83
Monroe, James, 95
Montana, 37, 42, 107–108, 112, 118n, 168, 195, 206, 224, 252, 276, 425, 431, 435
Moore, Arch A., Jr., 258
Moore, David W., 147, 155n
Moore, Olga, 1, 26n
Moore, William V., 213n
Moralist political culture, defined, 39
Moral Majority, 123, 149
Morehouse, Sally McCally, 167, 185n, 210, 215n
Morgan, David, 143, 154n, 281n
Morgan, David R., 318n, 384n
Morlan, Robert L., 350n
Muchmore, Lynn, 282n
Muckrakers, defined, 8
Mueller, Keith J., 280n
Mulroney, Keith F., 383n
Multifactionalism, defined, 201
Mumford, Lewis, 386, 391, 412n
Muncie, Indiana (Middletown), 124, 126
Munger, Frank, 52, 59n
Munro, William B., 117n
Murphy, Frank, 43
Murray, Richard W., 210, 215n
Murry, William (Alfalfa Bill), 285
Must bills, defined, 209
Mutual assistance pacts, defined, 396

NAACP (National Association for the Advancement of Colored People), 162
Nader, Ralph, 5, 163, 181
Name recognition, defined, 204, 254
Nashville-Davidson County, Tennessee, 400, 401, 402, 413n
Nathan, Robert P., 75, 88n
Nation, Carrie, 150
National Advisory Commission on Civil Disorders, 152n
National Advisory Commission on Criminal Justice Standards and Goals, 350n
National Association of Attorneys General, 78
National Association of Counties, 358
National Association of Manufacturers, 176
National Association of Townships and Towns, 360, 392
National Bellas Hess v. *Illinois Department of Revenue*, 429
National Center for Policy Analysis, 49
National Center for State Courts, 322
National Conference of State Legislatures, 73, 146, 174
National Governors Association, 73, 174, 252, 274, 378
  defined, 78
National League of Cities, 358
National League of Cities v. *Usery*, 85, 317n, 384n
National Municipal League, 5, 97, 364, 372. See also Good government reformers
National Organization of Women (NOW), 160, 336–337
National Rifle Association, 164
National Safety Council, 31
National Supremacy Clause, defined, 63
Native American Indians, effects of discrimination, 45–46, 110, 165
Near v. *Minnesota*, 348n
Nebraska, 23, 29, 37, 43, 50, 52, 64, 85, 102, 119n, 192, 199, 201, 222, 225, 243, 244, 249n, 258, 267, 302, 425, 444
Necessary and Proper Clause, defined, 63
Neighborhood control, 403–407
Nelson, Robert L., 185n
Neumann, Franz, 88n
Neutral competence, defined, 284
Nevada, 39, 76, 82, 401, 405, 413n, 434, 437
Nevins, Allan, 117n
Newark, New Jersey, 168
New federalism, defined, 74
New Hampshire, 52, 59n, 71, 96, 105, 113, 119n, 147, 202, 223, 224, 226, 261, 272, 282n, 349n, 425, 437, 439

New Haven, Connecticut, 124
New Jersey, 23, 45, 76, 82, 104, 142, 158, 168, 200, 206, 226, 261, 272, 282n, 338, 350n, 352, 361, 382n, 392, 399, 431, 432, 436, 437
Newman, Heidi Hosbach, 28n
New Mexico, 30, 38, 46, 71, 76, 114, 115, 137, 162, 199, 210, 258, 280n, 281n, 344, 349n, 435
New Orleans, Louisiana, 394
New York, 13, 38, 41, 46, 51, 71, 72, 76, 85, 102, 113, 115, 117n, 162, 177, 199, 212n, 223, 239, 242, 263, 267, 268, 271, 272, 280n, 281n, 284, 324, 325, 332, 333, 348n, 361, 376, 381n, 382n, 387, 393, 399, 407, 414n, 429, 436, 439, 444, 452n
New York City, 44–45, 66, 137, 143, 200, 332, 376, 381n, 393, 399, 407, 414n, 439, 452n
Nice, David C., 157, 184n, 452n
Nick, Rainer, 185n, 186n
Nie, Norman H., 153n
Niemi, Richard, 247n
NIMBY (not in my back yard), 405–406
Nirenberg, Nina, 58n
Nixon, Richard, 81, 280n, 328
Nondecisions, defined, 125
None of the Above. *See* Knox, Luther
Nonpartisan elections, 167, 368
  defined, 192
Norpoth, Helmut, 214n
Norrander, Barbara, 213n
Norris, George, 43, 243
North Carolina, 13, 20, 23, 44, 71, 117n, 165, 169, 235, 247n, 252, 271, 279n, 280n, 281n, 425, 430, 436
North Dakota, 18, 22, 23, 30, 36, 43, 57n, 71, 102, 107, 113, 119n, 145, 147, 165, 199, 200, 225, 232, 253, 276, 371, 425
Northrop, Alana, 185n, 383n
Northwest Ordinances, 79, 361
Nyitray, Joseph P., 213n

Oakerson, Ronald J., 413n
O'Connor, Patrick F., 57n, 120n
Odegard, Peter, 11, 27n
O'Donnell, Robert W., 155n
Off-budget expenditures, defined, 443
Offerberg, Richard I., 58n, 249n
Office tenure, defined, 261
Ogul, Morris, 232, 247n, 248n

Ohio, 31, 44, 74, 107, 109, 112, 119n, 200, 302, 305, 321, 326n, 333, 348n, 363, 392, 405, 432
Oklahoma, 13, 22, 37, 44, 76, 99, 113, 159, 276, 285, 302, 316n, 326, 335, 347n, 399
Oklahoma City, Oklahoma, 413n
Olson, David, 200, 202, 214n
Ombudsman, defined, 314
O'Neal, David, 271
Open end grants, defined, 80
Open primary, defined, 198
Open seat, defined, 200
Optional forms, defined, 364
Oregon, 22, 30, 43, 105, 107, 113, 142, 147, 165, 169, 189, 197, 198, 230, 257, 272, 301, 389, 402, 425, 428, 438
Original jurisdiction, defined, 320
O'Rourke, Timothy, 249n
Orr, Kay A., 258, 267
Orwell, George, 151n
Osborne, David, 27n, 74, 87n
Ostrom, Elinor, 404, 413n
Ostrom, Vincent, 83, 88n
Overlapping memberships, defined, 178
Owen, C. James, 413n
Oxendale, James, xviii

Pacific Legal Foundation, 182
Page, Benjamin I., 152n
Paine, Thomas, 7
Palley, Marian Lief, 74, 87n, 215n, 316n
Panama Canal Zone, 65, 109
Parenti, Michael, 153n
Parker, Joan, 207, 215n
Parker, Joseph, 205, 214n
Parks, Roger B., 413n
Participation costs, defined, 138
Party caucus, defined, 210
Party identification, defined, 193
Patronage system, 190, 285–287. *See also* Spoils system
  defined, 4
Patterson, Samuel C., 131, 153n, 175, 214n, 215n, 247n, 249n
Peak organization, defined, 169
Pecorella, Robert, 407, 414n
Peel, Roy V., 23
Peirce, Neal R., 412n, 414n
Pelissero, John P., 384n

Pendleton, George H., 316*n*
Pennsylvania, 23, 41, 47, 85, 87*n*, 164, 200, 267, 321, 326, 338, 352, 361, 382*n*, 389, 392, 399, 432, 438
People v. *Hurlbert*, 382*n*
Performance budgets, defined, 305
Permissive federalism, defined, 70
Pernacciaro, Samuel J., 119*n*
Perpich, Rudy, 262, 264, 272, 281*n*
Peters, Guy, 59*n*
Peters, John, 250*n*
Peterson, Merill D., 117*n*
Peterson, Paul E., 386, 412*n*
Petit jury, defined, 340
Petrocik, John R., 153*n*
Phares, Donald, 413*n*
Phased revision commission, defined, 112
Philadelphia, 45, 339, 392, 399
Philippines, 64
Phoenix, Arizona, 201
Phyrr, Peter A., 308, 317*n*
Picket fence federalism, defined, 73
Pierce, John C., 153*n*
Piereson, James E., 247*n*
Pinckey, Thomas M., Jr., 213*n*
Pingree, Hazxen S., 27*n*
Pittsburgh, 45
Piven, Frances Fox, 27*n*, 152*n*, 154*n*
Platt, Thomas, 191–192
Plea bargaining, defined, 329
Points of access, defined, 171
Policy domain, defined, 169
Political Action Committees (PACs), 179, 181, 182–183, 206
  defined, 177
Political culture, defined, 38
Political cynicism, 148
Political efficacy, defined, 131
Political efficiency, defined, 217
Political elite, defined, 122
Political evaluation, defined, 217
Political fund raiser, defined, 177
Political interest group, defined, 156
Political leadership, defined, 262
Politically alienated, defined, 148
Political machine, 4
  defined, 191
Political mobilizatins, defined, 131
Political parties
  brokerage parties, 188–190
  candidate endorsements, 199
  citizen control of, 193–194
  competitiveness, 202–203
  development of, 190–193
  factionalism, 200–201
  governor's programs, 209–210
  need for, 187–188
  organization of, 193–197
  party legislative voting, 210–211
  political campaigns, 202–207
  and political machines, 4, 190–192, 285–287
  primaries, 198–200
  professional control of, 193–194
  responsible parties, 188–190, 207–211
  state conventions, 197
  state financed campaigns, 208–209
  unpopularity of, 187
  weakening of, 192–193, 205–206
Political resources, defined, 2
Political setting, defined, 38
Political socialization, defined, 38
Politics, defined, 2
Pollock, Philip H., III, 184*n*
Poll tax, defined, 135
Polsby, Nelson, 27*n*, 153*n*, 249*n*
Pomper, Gerald, 213*n*
Pontiac, Michigan, 349*n*
Popper, Frank J., 276–277
Portland, Oregon, 257, 402–403
Possessions and territories, 65
Poston, Ersa, 310
Pound, William T., 248*n*, 318*n*
Powell, G. Bingham, Jr., 154*n*
Powell v. *Alabama*, 348*n*
Power elite, defined, 124
Powers to recommend, defined, 262
Powers to remove, defined, 261
Precinct caucus, defined, 197
Press, Charles, 118*n*, 152*n*, 154*n*, 155*n*, 214*n*, 279*n*, 413*n*
Price, Charles M., 154*n*
Price, Don, 11, 27*n*
Primaries, 198–200
Prince George's County, Maryland, 357
Privileges and Immunities Clause, defined, 76
Privitization, defined, 312
Pro Choice, 149, 178
Professionalization, defined, 5

468 INDEX

Professional values, defined, 289
Program, Planning, and Budgeting (PPB), defined, 308
Progressive reformers, defined, 7–10, 12
    and community government, 375, 403–407
    and constitutions, 99, 102–104
    control of lobbying, 178–182
    criticisms of, 9–10
    for IRR, 9, 94, 109
    journalist contribution to, 9–10
    as lobbyists, 25
    and parties, 188, 192–193
    as a social movement, 149
Progressive tax, defined, 424
Prohibited powers, defined, 63
Project grants, defined, 80
Prosecutors, defined, 340
Protess, David L., 213n
Protest groups, defined, 126
Public goods, defined, 284
Puerto Rico, 38, 64–67, 87n, 137, 242
Pueschel, J. Kristian, 144
Purdum, Elizabeth, 347n
Puro, Marsha, 349n
Puro, Steven, 349n
Purposive groups, defined, 160
Purvis, Hoyt, 154n
Pye, Lucian, 57n
Pyle, James, 318n

Quality circles, defined, 313
Quorum, defined, 232

Rabinowitz, George, 88n
Raiding, defined, 198
Rains, Omer, 236
Rakove, Milton, 228
Randolph, John, 95
Ranney, Austin, 118n, 212n
Ransone, Coleman B., 120n
Ratify, defined, 108
Ray, David, 247n
Ray, Dixy Lee, 253, 258, 259
Reaffirming memberships, defined, 179
Reagan, Michael D., 70, 81, 87n, 88n
Reagan, Ronald, 18, 41, 48, 49, 61, 67, 72, 74, 83, 85, 86, 189, 201, 239, 252, 263, 267, 275, 280n, 297, 328, 343, 443, 450
Reapportioning, 241–243
    defined, 44, 230

Recall, 136, 253, 258–259, 274, 279n, 282n
    defined, 103
Recall of judges, 64, 336–337
Reciprocal and retaliatory legislation, defined, 77
Redfield, Kent D., 246n
Redistributive policy, defined, 53, 96
Redistricting, defined, 230
Redlining, 391
Reeves, Richard, 348n
Referendum, defined, 103, 136
Registration to vote, 141–142
Regressive tax, defined, 424
Regulatory commissions, defined, 103
Republican party dominant, 202
Republican party majority, defined, 202
Reserved powers, defined, 63
Responsible parties, defined, 188
Retention election, defined, 332
Retrospective voting, defined, 129
Revision commission, defined, 111
Reynolds v. *Sims*, 241, 248n
Rhode Island, 23, 29, 31, 37, 46, 47, 91, 101, 119n, 157, 199, 202, 212n, 258, 261, 267, 272, 334, 382n, 389
Rich, Michael J., 89n
Richards, Alan R., 316n
Richards, Ann, 206
Riebel, Al, 230
Right-to-Life, 149–150, 178
Riker, William, 88n
Riley, David, 399
Ringquist, Delbert J., 185n, 248n
Ristine, Richard O., 102
Ritt, Leonard G., 250n
Riverside, California, 389
Rix, Paul A., 28n
Roberti, David, 236
Robertson, Pat, 163
Robinson, James, 58n
Robinson, John, 185n
Rochester, New York, 375
Rockefeller, John D., 8
Rockeffeller, John D. (Jay), IV, 55, 258
Rockefeller, Nelson, 281n
Rodriquez, Richard, 137
Roebeck, Bruce W., 249n
Roemer, Charles E., III, 278, 282n
Rogers, Will, 188
Rohde, David W., 214n
Romans, Neil T., 348n

Romney, George, 112–113, 205, 235, 271
Rooner, Julie, 37n
Roosevelt, Franklin D., 16, 17, 41, 44, 68–69, 317n
Roosevelt, Theodore, 68, 97, 142, 262
Rose Robert, 319
Rosenstone, Steven, 142, 154n
Rosenthal, Alan, 228, 246n, 249n
Ross, Douglas, 88n
Ross, Nellie Tayloe, 47, 58n, 258
Royal Charter, defined, 90
Rubin, H. Ted, 322, 347n
Rules of the game, formal and informal, defined, 2
Runoff primary, 198
Rust Belt. *See* Frost Belt
Ryan, Thomas P., 375

Sabato, Larry, 213n, 214n, 279n, 281n
Sacramento, California, 146
Saffell, David C., 249n
St. Louis, Missouri, 45, 168, 381n, 399, 413n
St. Paul, Minnesota, 402
Salisbury, Robert, 163, 170, 183n, 184n, 185n
Salter, Susanna Medora, 47
San Antonio, Texas, 50, 137
San Diego, California, 389
San Francisco, California, 45, 303, 389
Sanford, Terry, 20, 27n, 73, 87n, 252
Sanzone, John G., 88n
Savas, E. S., 316n, 317n, 318n
Sayre, Wallace, 27n
Scarrow, Howard A., 249n
Schattschneider, E. E., 134, 154n, 158, 184n, 193, 213n
Scheiber, Harry N., 87n
Scherr, Richard, xviii
Schick, Allen, 81, 88n
Schlafly, Phyllis, 123
Schlesinger, Arthur M., Jr., 280n
Schlesinger, Joseph, 202, 214n, 255, 256n, 279n
Schmandt, Henry J., 398, 412n
Schneider, Mark, 41, 58n
Schools
  conflict in, 166–167
  finance, 219–221
  organization, 366
Schrag, Philip, 119n
Schwinden, Ted, 252
Scientific Management Movement, 4, 261

Scoble, Harry, 383n
Scott, Robert W., 279n
Seattle, Washington, 389
Secretary of State, 270
Sectional voting, 188–189
Seligman, Edwin R. A., 433, 452n
Seligman, Lester G., 247n
Semel, Vicki Granet, 213n
Senate majority leader, defined, 234
Senior citizens, 46–47, 158–159
Senior executive service, defined, 310
Separation of powers, defined, 3
Serrano v. *Priest*, 451n
Setting, defined, 146
Severance taxes, defined, 434
Shaffer, Stephen D., 40, 57n
Shakman, Michael, 286
Shalala, Donna, 388, 412n
Shannon, Jasper B., 213n
Shapiro, Robert Y., 152n
Sharkansky, Ira, 40, 51, 57n, 58n, 249n
Sharp, Elaine, 129, 153n
Shaw, Donald, 155n
Shaw, George Bernard, 296
Sheffield, James F., Jr., 185n
Shefter, Martin, 212n, 452n
Sheldon, Charles H., 349n
Sherman, Sharon, 154n, 155n
Sherwood, Frank P., 318n
Short Ballot Movement, 261, 372
  defined, 142
Side effects, defined, 12
Sigelman, Lee, 40, 57n, 141, 153n, 154n, 250n, 279n
Silverman, Lauren, xviii
Simon, Paul, 154n
Simonson, Archie, 336–337
Simpson, Dick, 414n
Sinclair, Upton, 204
Single issue groups, defined, 160
Sittig, Robert F., 249n
Skeleton bills, defined, 218
Small cities community development block grant (CDBG), 378
Small claims courts, defined, 323
Smallwood, Frank, 223, 230, 246n, 247n
Smelser, Neil J., 155n
Smiley, Walter L., 246n
Smith, Al, 263, 280n
Smith, Elizabeth W., 47

Smith, Roland, 279n
Smith, Russell, 246n, 249n
Snow Belt. *See* Frost Belt
Social movement, 25, 149–150, 160
  defined, 149
Sokolow, Alvin D., 249n
Songer, Donald, 27n
South Carolina, 30, 40, 46, 72, 112, 117n, 126, 142, 157, 201, 206, 210, 213n, 281n, 361, 372, 384n, 405, 436
South Carolina v. *Baker*, 79, 384n
South Dakota, 21, 23, 31, 36, 43, 46, 103, 109, 119n, 165, 169, 178, 189, 202, 225, 232, 262, 276, 371, 434
Southern Christian Leadership Conference, 160
Sovereign power, defined, 63
Spanish Americans
  alienation of, 148–149
  bilingualism, 45, 137–139
  and community consolidation, 404
  and constitutional change, 115
  discrimination, 45–46, 58n, 285, 388
  as interest group, 165, 177
  migration of, 38, 42, 45
  officeholding, 258
  participation, 131, 135–136, 189
  reapportionment, 242
  and voting rights act, 105, 135–136
Speaker of the House, defined, 234
Special courts, defined, 323
Special district, defined, 366
Special or local charter acts, defined, 363
Special sessions, defined, 266
Speed of passage rules, defined, 232
Sperlich, Peter W., 350n
Spoils system, 285–287
  defined, 4, 190
Springfield, Illinois, 143
Spurrier, Robert L., 323, 347n
Squire, Peverill, 229, 247n
Staff functions, defined, 268
Standard Consolidated Statistical Areas, 393
Standard Metropolitan Statistical Areas (SMSAs), 385, 393, 412n
Standing committees, defined, 234
State collected, locally shared revenues, defined, 422
State constitutional convention, defined, 112
Statehood
  achieving, 63–64
  Puerto Rico, 64–67
  territories and possessions, 65
  Washington D.C., 64
State mandated programs, defined, 423
State pass-through, defined, 378
States and their governments
  economic development, 50–51
  geography, 36–38
  history, 42–44
  political cultures, 38–42
  politics and policy outputs, 51–53
  racial and ethnic composition, 45–46
  senior citizens in, 46–47, 158–159
  variability, 29–36
  visibility, 19–20
  vulnerability, 20–25
  women candidates in, 47–50
Status of bills, defined, 232
Staunton, Virginia, 372
Steffens, Lincoln, 8, 27n
Stein, Robert M., 383n
Steinbeck, George S., 412n
Steinbeck, John, 60–66, 86n
Steinem, Gloria, 123
Steiner, Gilbert Y., 248n
Stenberg, Carl W., 27n
Stevens, Barbara J., 318n
Stevenson, Adlai, III, 271, 280n
Stever, James, 159, 184n
Stewart, Joseph, Jr., 185n
Stewart, Potter, 329
Stewart, William H., Jr., 119n
Stieber, Carolyn, 318n
Stillman, Richard J., 383n
Stimpson, George, 116n
Stinson, Debra R. Sanderson, 452n
Stokes, Sybil L., 119n
Stone, Harold, 11, 27n
Stone, Kathryn, 11, 27n
Storm, David, 347n
Stouffer, Samuel, 151n
Strong mayor-council plan, defined, 369
Stroud, Joe H., 414n
Students for a Democratic Society (SDS), 126
Sturm, Albert L., 117n, 119n, 120n
Substate regions, defined, 397
Sullivan, John L., 153n
Sumter, South Carolina, 372
Sun Belt, 19, 51, 71, 72, 386
Sundquist, James L., 70, 86n, 310, 318n

Sunset law, 169
  defined, 222, 312
Sunshine laws, 136
Svara, James H., 383n
Swain, Louisa, 47
Swanson, Wayne R., 120n
Sych, Larry, 154n
Sylvester, Kathleen, 58n, 383n

Taeusch, C. F., 316n
Taft, William Howard, 64
Tallahassee, Florida, 347n
Talmadge, Eugene, 46
Target publics, defined, 145
Tarr, G. Alan, 348n, 349n
Tax freedom day, 417
Tax offset, defined, 80
Tax revolt movement, 13, 25, 126, 149, 433
Taylor, Frederick, 4
Tennessee, 23, 31, 44, 76, 108, 113, 114, 213n, 241, 267, 272, 281n, 282n, 323, 324, 326, 364, 400, 413n, 436
Tennessee Valley Authority, 69, 72, 78
Terchek, Ronald, 154n
Territories and possessions, 65
Terry, Charles, 256
Testitor, Irene, 349n
Texas, 19, 22, 30, 37, 38, 51, 58n, 71, 76, 87n, 107, 137, 143, 154n, 158, 159, 160, 189, 200, 206, 210, 219, 224, 232, 242, 262, 275, 287, 371, 394, 399, 429, 434, 435
Texas City, Texas, 371
Thomas, James D., 118n
Thomas, John Clayton, 153n
Thomas, John P., 382n
Thomas, Larry W., 246n
Thomas, Robert D., 413n
Thompson, James R., 256, 267
Thompson, Joel A., 246n, 247n, 250n, 317n
Thompson, Kay, 185n
Thompson, Richard E., 88n, 317n
Ticket splitters, defined, 193
Tiebout, Charles, 412n
Tier, Mary, 154n
Tillman, (Pitchfork) Ben, 37
Tobin, Richard J., 213n
Tocqueville, Alexis de, 3–4, 158, 348n
Tools of politics, defined, 254
Topeka, Kansas, 43
Toronto, Canada, 402

Townley, A. C., 57n
Town meeting, defined, 136, 361
Township, 79
  defined, 362
Traditional political culture, defined, 39
Treen, David, 199
Trenton, New Jersey, 373
Trial jury, defined, 340
Trippett, Frank, 171
Trost, Karen, xviii
Truman, David, 156, 160, 183n, 212n
Truman, Harry, 67, 190
Tucker, Robert C., 280n
Tulsa, Oklahoma, 371
Twain, Mark, 156, 157
Twin Cities Metropolitan Council, 402, 413n

Ujefusa, Grant, 11
Uncertainty, 12
Unconstitutional, defined, 92
Unicameral, 243–244
  defined, 243, 369
Unifactionalism, defined, 200
Uniform law, defined, 77
Union shop, defined, 297
Unitary governments, defined, 62
United Auto Workers (UAW), 43
U.S. Conference of Mayors, 73, 358
U.S. Voting Rights Act, 105, 136
  defined, 135
Unruh, Jesse, 243
Urban crisis, defined, 388
Urban League, 162
User fee or charge, defined, 424
Uslaner, Eric M., 59n
Utah, 13, 22, 23, 30, 51, 76, 113, 116, 119n, 199, 281n, 382n

Valente, Carl F., 318n
Value Conflict and Consensus, defined, 6
van Dalen, Hendrick, 185n
Vanderbilt, Cornelius, 191
VanDerslick, Jack R., 119n, 246n
Van Deusen, Glyndon G., 57n
Verba, Sidney, 153n
VerBurg, Kenneth, 214n, 279n, 382n
Vermont, 30, 45, 50, 52, 58n, 59n, 64, 71, 96, 100, 113, 118n, 119n, 169, 223n, 224, 243, 247n, 258, 261, 300, 389, 431
Vertical equity, defined, 424

Vertz, Laura L., 213n
Vesey, Denmark, 40
Veto, defined, 266
Vines, Kenneth N., 185n, 249n, 279n
Virgin Islands, 65, 66
Virginia, 23, 36, 44, 45, 71, 87n, 93, 95, 117n, 119n, 200, 206, 226, 259, 260, 271, 280n, 304, 372, 381n, 399, 430, 436, 444
Vogel, David, 186n
Voter registration, defined, 141
Voting Rights Act, 105, 136
    defined, 135

Wager, Paul W., 382n
Wahlke, John, 236, 246n, 247n
Wake Island, 65
Waldby, H. O., 285, 316n
Walker, David B., 70, 74, 87n, 88n, 126, 152n
Walker, Jack L., 163, 184n, 185n
Walker, Jim, 184n
Wallace, George, 161, 196, 275, 280n
Wallace, Lurleen, 58n, 258
Wallis, Graham, 127, 153n
Walters, Jonathan, 58n
Wanat, John, 131, 153n
Warren, Charles R., 414n
Warren, Earl, 328
Warren, Roland, 27n
Washington, 30, 37, 43, 71, 112, 198, 253, 258, 259, 266, 281n, 302, 389, 405, 428, 434
Washington, D.C., 13, 18, 30, 46, 55, 63, 64, 65, 303–304, 393
Washington, George, 62, 137
Washington, Harold, 369
Waters, Earl G., 118n
Watson, Richard, 332, 348n, 349n
Watson, Tom, 185n
Wattel, Harold L., 412n
Waugh, William L., Jr., 382n
Wayne Circuit Judges v. *Wayne County*, 349n
Weak mayor-council plan, defined, 368
Weber, Ronald E., 213n
Wechsler, Louis, 213n
Weir, Sara Jane, 213n
Weissert, Carol S., 318n
Wekkin, Gary D., 212n
Welch, Susan, 185n, 250n, 375, 383n

Wells, Donald, 87n
West Virginia, 22, 23, 30, 53–56, 72, 252, 258, 272, 325, 425
Whitaker, Gordon P., 213n
Whitaker and Baxter, 204
Whitcomb v. *Chavis*, 241, 248n
White, G. Edward, 94
White, John C., 195
White, William Allen, 43, 192, 212n
Wiggins, Charles, 184n, 214n, 281n
Wildavsky, Aaron, 308, 317n, 414n
Wilder, Douglas, 45, 259, 271
Wilkie, Harold, 338
Wilkinson, Wallace, 254
Willbern, York, 301, 317n, 413n
Willey, Jack, 186n
Williams, G. Mennen, 263, 281n
Williams, J. Oliver, 278n, 280n, 282n
Williams, Steven D., 281n
Williams, T. Harry, 152n
Williamson, R. Craig, 318n
Wilson, Charles, 19
Wilson, James Q., 213n, 304, 317n, 383n
Wilson, Woodrow, 69, 142, 262, 274, 317n
Winski, Joseph M., 292n
Winsky, Laura R., 247n
Winters, Richard, 52, 59n
Wisconsin, 23, 30, 61, 71, 77, 102, 109, 142, 189, 195, 196, 200, 267, 284, 297, 336–337, 338, 349n, 378, 382n, 405, 428, 429, 430
Wolfinger, Raymond, 142, 154n, 383n
Women in politics
    ERA, 109–110, 123, 159, 258–259
    feminist movement, 149–150, 342
    lobbying, 165
    NOW, 160, 336–337
    officeholding, 47–50, 58n
    recall of a judge, 336–337
Women's Christian Temperance Union, 13, 47
Women's International League for Peace and Freedom, 336–337
Wood, Robert C., 395, 408, 412n, 414n
Wright, Charles R., 184n
Wright, Deil S., 280n, 282n, 316n
Wright, Gerald C., Jr., 59n
Wright, Louis B., 57n
Wychoff, Mikel L., 349n

Wyoming, 1, 18, 23, 31, 47, 58*n*, 64, 88*n*, 113, 272, 282*n*, 319, 434, 435

Yin, Robert K., 412*n*
Young, H. P., 248*n*

Zeigler, L. Harmon, 151*n*, 160, 184*n*, 185*n*, 317*n*
Zelio, J. A., 299*n*
Zeller, Belle, 11, 27*n*
Zero based budgeting, defined, 308
Zikmund, Joseph, II, 57*n*
Zimmerman, Jo Ann, 272
Zimmerman, Joseph F., 89*n*, 186*n*, 349*n*, 412*n*, 414*n*
Zolty, Thaddeus C., 412*n*
Zorach v. *Clausen*, 348*n*
  voting rights act, 105, 135–136